Language acquisition

the state of the art

Edited by
ERIC WANNER and LILA R. GLEITMAN

CAMBRIDGE UNIVERSITY PRESS

Cambridge
London   New York   New Rochelle
Melbourne   Sydney

Published by the Press Syndicate of the University of Cambridge
The Pitt Building, Trumpington Street, Cambridge CB2 1RP
32 East 57th Street, New York, NY 10022, USA
296 Beaconsfield Parade, Middle Park, Melbourne 3206, Australia

First published 1982

Printed in the United States of America

Library of Congress Cataloging in Publication Data
Main entry under title:
Language acquisition.
1. Language acquisition – Addresses, essays,
lectures. I. Wanner, Eric. II. Gleitman,
Lila R.
P118.L255   401'.9   82-4407
ISBN 0 521 23817 X hard covers   AACR2
ISBN 0 521 28238 1 paperback

Contents

Contributors

Elizabeth Bates
University of California at
San Diego
La Jolla, California

T. G. Bever
Columbia University
New York, New York

Melissa Bowerman
University of Kansas
Lawrence, Kansas

Martin D. S. Braine
New York University
New York, New York

Susan Carey
Massachusetts Institute of
Technology
Cambridge, Massachusetts

Eve V. Clark
Stanford University
Stanford, California

Lila R. Gleitman
University of Pennsylvania
Philadelphia, Pennsylvania

Susan Goldin-Meadow
University of Chicago
Chicago, Illinois

Judith A. Hardy
New York University
New York, New York

Brian MacWhinney
Carnegie-Mellon University
Pittsburgh, Pennsylvania

Michael Maratsos
University of Minnesota
Minneapolis, Minnesota

Elissa L. Newport
University of Illinois
Champaign, Illinois

Charles Read
University of Wisconsin
Madison, Wisconsin

Thomas Roeper
University of Massachusetts
Amherst, Massachusetts

Peter Schreiber
University of Wisconsin
Madison, Wisconsin

Marilyn Shatz
University of Michigan
Ann Arbor, Michigan

Dan I. Slobin
University of California at
Berkeley
Berkeley, California

Eric Wanner
Harvard University Press
Cambridge, Massachusetts

Kenneth Wexler
University of California at Irvine
Irvine, California

Preface

The construction of this book began with a conference held at the University of Pennsylvania, in the spring of 1978. At that time, the Alfred P. Sloan Foundation was in the early stages of its now well-known attempt at midwifery for the emerging field of cognitive science. The foundation funded this conference with the aim of further understanding how the topic of language acquisition fits into the perspective of a computational theory of mind. Just at the moment of this prefatory writing, probably coincidentally, cognitive science has made it into the *New York Times Magazine*, demonstrating its existence beyond further nay or doubt. Still, as the essays in this book will also demonstrate, there is today no single, universally accepted position on the topic of language learning. Nonetheless, these essays represent the most serious attempts to date to state the conditions under which language is learned, what it is that is learned when language is learned, and the mechanisms that underlie such learning. What is more, they attempt to explain why these questions matter, and in what sense the topic of first language acquisition is fundamental to cognitive and developmental psychology. We believe that, owing to the fact that many of the most eminent, interesting, and active investigators in this field have here each contributed their most general theoretical statement, this book provides the best current guide to the state of the art in language-learning studies. As the editors, we began traditionally by trying to construct a commentary on the various essays that would serve to pull them together. However, and no doubt mercifully, the rambunctiousness of the contributions to this book stubbornly resisted our best efforts at unification. Therefore, violating tradition to some extent, we ended by presenting, as well, our own state-of-the-art views of how language is learned, imposing (or at least exposing) our own notions of how best to make a stay against the confusion of available data.

This book is not the proceedings of a conference in the usual sense. As the date of the conference compared to the date of its publication reveals, the book was not constructed by collecting papers read at the meetings, correcting the typos, and sending them off to an acquiescent publisher. On the contrary, we believe it fair to say that authors, editors, and publishers have asked of themselves, and delivered, more than this. With the benefit of hearing all the talks and the conference discussion, and in consultation with the editors (often, of course, in disagreement with the editors' comments and views), each author contributed a second, and sometimes a third and a fourth, version of his or her paper. For some the task was done within a few weeks following the conference. These authors we thank for their gritty patience with those authors (including ourselves) who required many months or even a very few years to construct a final version. And we thank the Alfred P. Sloan Foundation and the Cambridge University Press both for their support of this undertaking and for their very plucky wait-and-see stances as time wore on. As for us, many adages and homilies have come from the experience of administrative oversight of this byzantine venture, of which we mention only "Neither an editor nor a contributor be."

A number of individuals are to be thanked for making this book possible. First, we thank Marian Gilbert, former administrative assistant to Lila Gleitman, for organizing the conference itself; and Janet Krueger, Sharon Armstrong, and many other then graduate students at Penn for being willing to contribute any kind of help we wanted or asked for during it – conceptual, bureaucratic, even menial. Coming out the other end of the tunnel, we thank Annette Luzon and Elyse Topalian, current administrative assistants to Lila Gleitman and Eric Wanner, respectively, again for help that required them to be at once editors, postal clerks, librarians, and therapists. Finally, we thank Susan Milmoe of the Cambridge University Press for administrative and editorial support, and perhaps most particularly Janis Bolster, who stoically performed the most difficult task of all: copyediting the manuscripts of avowed grammarians.

Eric Wanner
Cambridge, Massachusetts

Lila Gleitman
Philadelphia, Pennsylvania

February 1982

Part I

THE LOGIC OF LANGUAGE ACQUISITION

1. Language acquisition: the state of the state of the art

Lila R. Gleitman and Eric Wanner

Language is learned, in the normal course of events, by children bright and dull, pampered or neglected, exposed to Tlingit or to English. In Leonard Bloomfield's words, "This is doubtless the greatest intellectual feat any one of us is ever required to perform" (1933, p. 29). Appreciation of the enormity of this human capacity, given the intricacy and variety of languages of the world, has motivated an intense exploration of language learning by linguists and psychologists alike. Both in topic and in theoretical orientation, these approaches vary marvelously. If there is an anchoring point for the disparate efforts, it is Chomsky's break with the Bloomfieldian tradition of language study and, as a particular consequence, his analysis of the logic of language learning. In this essay, we first review this paradigmatic change in the theory of language learning. Thereafter, we organize current findings in this field (with special emphasis on the chapters in this volume) as they bear on these two opposing theoretical positions, and offer our own state-of-the-art views on how language is learned.

1.1. Bloomfield and Chomsky on language learning

Leonard Bloomfield and Noam Chomsky, in succession, utterly dominated the field of linguistics for periods extending over three decades. Within these time periods, it is small overstatement that investigating language was a matter of agreeing or disagreeing, in detail, with the programs developed by these thinkers. Such a history is commonplace in science; for example, the study of learning in American psychology, for five decades, is a series of responses pro and con to a general problem as framed by Thorndike. For language, it is of some interest that Bloomfield and Chomsky appear to have been in close agreement on the essential nature of the problem. Both their most influential works (Bloomfield, 1933/1961; Chomsky, 1965) open with an analysis of language acquisition, supposing that the problem of learning a first language and the problem of language description are at bottom one and the same. According to both these accounts, the mystery of the learning feat derives from two crucial facts about the human use of language: It is rule governed, and it is creative. Bloomfield wrote:

> It is obvious that most speech forms are regular, in the sense that the speaker who knows the constituents and the grammatical patterns can utter them without having heard them; moreover, the observer cannot hope to list them since the possibilities of combination are practically infinite. For instance, the classes of nominative expressions in English are so large that many possible actor-action forms – say, *a red-headed plumber bought six oranges* – may never have been uttered. [P. 275]

Bloomfield's learner came into the world scantily endowed. He could hear; and he had a single principle of data manipulation that allowed him to classify together materials that occurred in the same positions within utterances. Bloomfield's learning device could also draw inductive generalizations from the distributional properties of the grammatical classes so formed: "A grammatical pattern (sentence type, construction, or substitution) is often called *an analogy*. A regular analogy permits the speaker to utter speech-forms which he has not heard; we say that he utters them *on the analogy* of similar forms which he has heard'." (p. 275).

For Bloomfield, then, a grammar is a description of the analogies that hold for a language, and learning is the set of discovery procedures (the data manipulations) by which the child forms these analogies. The learner first discovers that the continuously varying sound wave can be analyzed into discrete segments (the phones) which appear in discoverable recurrent patterns (the words) which appear in yet larger recurrent patterns (the phrases and sentences), all discovered by extracting generalizations about their relative distribution in the corpus presented to the ear (see Z. Harris, 1951, for detailed proposals about discovery procedures at each of these linguistic levels). The child learns to use each sentence appropriately by connecting the learned situation of its use (the stimulus) with its form (the response).[1]

In all fairness to history, Bloomfield was not so explicit as Chomsky in identifying linguistic theory with the problem of language learning, but his position ("The only useful generalizations about language are inductive generalizations" [p. 29]) derives coherently from the assumption that child and linguist are in the same position, required to identify from scratch a linguistic system that potentially might be anything at all: "Features which we think ought to be universal may be absent from the very next language that becomes accessible" (p. 20). If there are no constraints on the form of a natural language, then each child must be endowed with a set of discovery procedures of an entirely unbiased sort, to guarantee learning.

Chomsky's analysis of the learner's problem begins in much the same way, with the joint assumptions that the input data are heard sentences (in context) and that the learning procedure must be some sort of inductive generalization from such a corpus. But Chomsky asserted that these assumptions answer the questions only by begging them. After all, how does the child manage to generalize (learn by analogy) always and only from old grammatical sentences to new grammatical sentences? How is the learner to avoid wrong analogies and seize on the right ones? Chomsky reasoned that the natural languages could not vary arbitrarily from each other, else Bloomfield's claims must hold and then language learning would be impossible. Rather, the natural languages share universal properties, and human infants are biologically predisposed to consider only languages embodying these properties. In sum, the problem now becomes one of clothing Bloomfield's learner with a variety of presuppositions about the system to which it is being exposed, narrowing the hypothesis space on which inductions are performed. At the same time, these predispositions must be cast in some very abstract form so as to accommodate the detailed distinctions among the real languages: "The real problem is that of developing a hypothesis about initial structure that is sufficiently rich to account for the acquisition of language, yet not so rich as to be inconsistent with the known diversity of language" (1965, p. 58). The focal supposition here is that an unbiased problem-solving device, guessing inductively at a grammar from a finite corpus of instances, cannot arrive at the correct solution. For instance, how is the learner to know whether the sample of sentences it has heard come from the language consisting of exactly those sentences, or from some larger corpus? How could it know from a sample of English sentences that the correct grammar was not the union of English grammar and Bantu grammar only, so far, no Bantu sentences were in the corpus (for discussion, see J. A. Fodor, Bever, & Garrett, 1974, Chap. 8). To the retort "Such hypotheses are mad!" comes the counter-retort "But that is the point." The problem of explaining language learning is essentially the problem of stating which hypotheses are mad or sane for a human learner.

It is worth observing that this problem cannot be ducked by weakening the definition of what it means to learn a language. There are, for instance, reasonable grounds for supposing that the child does something less than fully justified induction when he learns a language. It may be good enough just to learn a grammar that works, not one that is guaranteed to be right. Gold (1967) explored this possibility formally by examining the conditions under which any general induction procedure might successfully identify a grammar "in the limit." Gold's result is achieved by bringing to imaginary life a general induction procedure for grammars – a procedure that works a bit like the British Museum algorithm. In Gold's proof, this algorithm is applied to an abstract class of languages which have the common property that their grammars can be enumerated and that there is a decision procedure for determining whether or not any string is in the language. This class of languages, the so-called primitive recursive languages, is extremely broad, including the class of natural languages in addition to many decidedly unnatural languages. Gold's algorithm exploits the properties of primitive recursive languages by enumerating candidate grammars one by one. For each candidate grammar, it tries to determine whether all the input sentences it has seen so far can be derived from the grammar. If so, it waits for a new sentence and tries the grammar again. If not, it moves to a new grammar and repeats the process.

Although such a device cannot be guaranteed to discover the correct grammar of the target language from a finite corpus of sample sentences (such a guarantee would violate the known limits of any inductive process), nevertheless it can legitimately aspire to identify the target grammar "in the limit" if it manages to find a grammar that continuously passes tests against new input sentences and hence need not be abandoned. However, Gold discovered that even these more limited aspirations are difficult to achieve. Details to one side, what he showed was that so long as a general induction machine receives only positive examples – sentences that are properly included in the target language – it can never be guaranteed to converge upon the target grammar in the limit in a finite amount of time. Unless negative information is made available to the device so that it has some way of determining which sentences are ungrammatical, it cannot learn language in the limit. Moreover, this result holds for any inductive algorithm, not only the enumerative algorithm used for illustration here (for further discussion, see Pinker, 1979; and Wexler & Culicover, 1980). Gold's proof poses a puzzle to inductive descriptions of language learning, for caretakers do not seem to provide the negative information said to be required. Mothers do not respond to their children's rudimentary attempts (say, "Me wuvs yer, Mom") with negative feedback ("String not in the language, Johnnie").

It is, of course, possible to object to this analogy between the conditions of Gold's proof and the conditions the child faces in acquiring language. Though adults rarely correct their fledglings' syntax (Brown & Hanlon, 1970) and though even when they do, children rarely pay attention (McNeill, 1966a), still one could object that negative information might be available to the child in subtle form. A blatantly ungrammatical utterance by the child will probably fail to elicit the desired response from an adult, and this mismatch between childish expectation and adult reaction may be enough to signal the child that something is amiss (although just how he knows that his grammar is the problem is a bit tricky). But true as it may be that negative information of this subtle sort could be available to the child, the objection largely misses the point that children hardly ever *require* correction of either direct or subtle varieties. Of the myriad grammatical generalizations that children might draw from their limited experience with language, somehow they seem to draw the right ones, or very nearly the right ones. Unlike Gold's general-purpose induction machine, which gives all grammatical hypotheses equal benefit of the doubt and therefore needs negative information to be rescued from absurdities, the child requires no such first aid. That this is so is evident even from examples that are sometimes marshaled to argue just the reverse.

For instance, Ervin (1964) showed that children are good, all too good, at forming inductive generalizations. Children who at 2 and 3 years of age spontaneously and appropriately produce both weak (*talked, pushed*) and strong (*brought, sang*) past-tense endings for English verbs frequently at around age 4 produce weak endings almost exclusively; that is, they now say "*bringed*" and "*singed*" in systematic violation of the input corpus. For the stock of most frequent English verbs (the ones children are likely to hear), the weak tense ending occurs far less than half the time on types and still less on tokens. (For further discussion of this phenomenon, see Bowerman, Chapter 11; and Clark, Chapter 13.) This is no formal proof, but it is a clear suggestion that young children are inclined to draw grand inductive generalizations even over noisy data. The corpus violates the generalization the majority of the time; still, the learner evidently prefers a bad generalization to none at all. But the question now must be just how many false generalizations are true of English sentences 30 or 40 percent of the time. For example, it has been noticed that substantives preceding *-hood* are very predominantly kinship terms (*childhood, motherhood, neighborhood*), and yet no child supposes that *robin* is a kinship term.

To approach these issues, Chomsky (1965) designed a hypothetical language learner who would be spared these never-ending inductive pitfalls. In some ways, Chomsky's model is an odd candidate for the attention it has received in developmental psycholinguistics, since it was never offered as a serious empirical account of how the child acquires a language. In fact, Chomsky's model is really no more (or less!) than a description of the problem of language acquisition, and it is a description framed from a particular point of view – namely, that in acquiring language the child must master the rules of a generative grammar. However, Chomsky was able to develop a number of very strong claims about acquisition simply by stating the problem in this way, and much of the empirical work in the field can be seen as an effort to develop these claims, to test them, or to reject them outright.

Chomsky's analysis begins with the impeccable claim that children receive little or no formal instruction about the rules that presumably underlie adult performance. Rather, or so it would seem, the child is exposed only to some finite sample of utterances, different for each child, in the presence of certain events and circumstances in the world. Sometimes, though surely not always, these utterances will be appropriate to the circumstances in some way. For instance, a lucky learner may hear "A rabbit is running by" as a rabbit runs by. From such exposure to utterance/situation pairs, the learner must induce a finite representation of the language that projects an infinite set of sound–meaning pairs.[2]

According to Chomsky's idealization, the child has the internal wherewithal to assign a "partial and tentative" structural description to the input utterance, aided by its context (Chomsky, 1965, p. 32). The child is also armed with an innate linguistic theory that includes all the logical apparatus necessary to construct candidate transformational grammars. An innate learning theory tests these grammars against the input, by matching the structural descriptions generated by the candidate grammar with those given in the primary linguistic data. In case more than one grammar survives this test, Chomsky endows his hypothetical child with an evaluation measure which provides a way of ranking all the empirically successful grammars. If correct, such a ranking would favor just the grammar that the real child actually emerges with from his encounter with the primary linguistic data.

According to Chomsky's idealization, this process of grammar acquisition takes place instantaneously; that is, grammar construction occurs in the presence of a large body of primary linguistic data, and then the evaluation procedure will choose the most highly valued grammar appropriate to these data. Although this is clearly counterfactual, it has never been the source of much controversy because Chomsky was more interested in demonstrating the logical prerequisites to language learning than in making claims about the details of the process. In general, those who have accepted Chomsky's instantaneous model have assumed that it could be "slowed down" without changing any of its essential properties (see e.g., Roeper, Chapter 9). Those who have rejected this model have objected on other grounds.

We organize our discussion of language learning, and review the essays in this volume, against the backdrop of Bloomfield's and Chomsky's formulations of the task. Such an organization leaks, in part, for some work in this field verges on issues outside these idealizations. Granting this, we adopt a historical method that is unblushingly Thucydidean, interpreting the varying research efforts in a way that maximizes their joint coherence. This coherence resides, we believe, in their relation to the logic expressed by these two great linguists, even though some authors will deny, quite correctly, that they were explicitly influenced by them.

1.2. The form and content of the primary linguistic data

As Bloomfield and Chomsky would agree, the nature of learning crucially depends on how the learner naturally organizes what he hears, how he represents the input to himself. On Bloomfield's story, the organizing principles must be very general and subject to revision all along the line, for what is to be learned varies arbitrarily. On Chomsky's story, the languages "out there" are of an antecedently well-defined type, so innate knowledge about them is useful; in fact, to the extent that the forms and categories of language are distinct from the forms and categories of cognition in general, innate knowledge of the language principles is the requirement for learning. In detail, the specification of a learning procedure requires the answer to two prior questions having to do with the state of the organism as learning begins: (a) How does the child make a relevant semantic analysis of the situation while listening to adults talk about it; and (b) how does the child analyze the sound wave that results from the adult talk? We address these two issues below. Afterward, in the presence of a tentative specification of the initial state, we address the learning problem: How does the child project a system that maps between the sounds and the meanings?

Extracting meaning from the situation

On Chomsky's formulation, the child is assumed to hear utterances in situations from which he can recover partial and tentative structural descriptions, including, of course, some characterization of meaning. No matter the theoretical stance, the same assumption seems to be made by all investigators. For Bloomfield, each situation was that extralinguistic event (stimulus) connected by temporal contiguity to a particular linguistic event (response). In Braine and Hardy's terms (Chapter 7), the child hears sentences in circumstances that yield a unique interpretation in terms of an innately given stock of relational–semantic categories. Wexler (Chapter 10) starts with this supposition as a necessary principle: According to his model, learnability can be shown if the input consists of form/meaning pairs, but cannot be shown if the input consists of the forms alone. Since language is learned (in fact), it follows for Wexler that the prerequisite ability to interpret the real world in a linguistically relevant way exists *ab initio*.

It is sometimes assumed that these claims for a learner are quite innocent, that language learning is easy to explain because the child can "rely on meaning." However, it is hard to conceive how such claims could be brought to ground at all. Part of the problem is to constrain the (lexical and propositional) hypothesis space the child might consider. Another is to understand how the real-world situations in which speech is heard give rise to particular hypotheses about its meaning. The difficulty is that neither words nor sentences, nor even propositions, are in any direct way encodings of scenes or situations in the world.

As a simplest instance of problems here, consider the fact that a child observing a cow is observing, *a fortiori,* the nose and ear of the cow at the same time. Should someone now say "cow," this is presumably the situational context from which the child is to learn that "cow" means *cow.* But what is to prevent the child from assuming that the meaning is *nose-ear-complex-of-a-cow* instead? If a (currently unknown) representational theory of mind automatically excludes this as a possible human concept, it is still the case that the child must learn *nose* and *ear,* as well as *cow,* under these frightful circumstances (Quine, 1960).

These problems re-arise at every level of the linguistic hierarchy, reaching their ultimate exacerbation for the case of the sentence unit. A child who observes a cat sitting on a mat also observes, *a fortiori,* a mat supporting a cat, a mat under a cat, a floor supporting a mat and a cat, and so on. If the adult now says "The cat is on the mat," even while pointing to the cat on the mat, how is the child to choose among these interpretations of the situation? Especially as the less probable (whatever this means) choices are sometimes made: The adult sometimes does say, "What a good bed that mat makes for the cat." Such problems are materially worsened by the fact that the adult may speak of one thing while the child attends to another. The adult may say, "Time for your nap" as the child regards the cat on the mat. Worst of all, certain structures in the language, among those most frequently used to children, are specifically reserved for mismatches with the world: the felicitous occasion for positive imperatives, such as "Eat your peas!" or "Go next door to Granny and borrow an egg!" is the absence of pea eating, Grannies, and eggs.

In sum, there is no innocence to the claim that the child learns language by relying on "meaning" or "the world." Nevertheless, it seems impossible to avoid the posit that the child will, in some crucially exploited cases, feel justified in assuming that a sound wave that enters his ear refers in some particular way, from some particular point of view, to a situation he is currently observing, as, for example, cat-on-mat rather than mat-under-cat. Three kinds of evidence bear on (though they do not explain) ways children solve this puzzle: As learning begins, children naturally represent concepts (1) lexically and (2) propositionally; and (3) caretaker and child conspire to converse in ways that map as transparently as possible from these initial lexical and propositional representations.

The word is the natural domain of simple concepts. Generalizing from facts about language learning in many linguistic communities, Slobin (1973) conjectured that children are biased to suppose each concept has its own separate wordlike representation, marked by an "acoustically salient" surface expression. This claim is not easy to pin down because no theory is now available that will define the separable concepts. Nevertheless, a variety of descriptive facts about language learning cohere on the view that the child conceives the word as the natural domain of simple concepts.

In this volume, Carey (Chapter 12) presents a series of experiments designed to ask how the child learns the meanings of words, concluding that lexical items may be acquired holistically. She takes such findings to count against the classical position on word meaning (for discussion of the issues here, see also J. A. Fodor, 1975; J. A. Fodor, Garrett, Walker, & Parkes, 1980; and for the opposing view, J. Katz, 1972). In the classical analysis, words are semantically represented by their definitions. That is, the words are decomposable into a set of necessary and sufficient semantic meaning atoms, or features. Comprehension takes place on this featural vocabulary, not on words. According to such a view, it would be reasonable to suppose that the child's innate equipment consists of the underlying features. Moreover, learning word meanings would consist of learning feature by feature. Indeed, such a position makes sense of a variety of overgeneralizations in the young child's speech, for example, use of the word *ball* to refer to all round things (for extensive discussion and experimental review of this position, see E. Clark, 1973b). Carey questions this view on empirical grounds: It has been hard to identify the supposed semantic features or to describe word meaning in terms of them, and not for want of some hundreds of years of trying. Moreover, insofar as we are able to guess at a featural description of words, the predictions for a learning sequence are not reassuring. For example, children learn verbs with many features (if they have features) as easily as verbs with few (if they have features). *Walk* and *run* are no harder to learn than *move*, and there is no obvious stage of learning at which *run* means only *move*.

As Carey discusses, the situational context for learning radically underdetermines the scope and character of the lexical concept to be acquired. Yet she has evidence that a single exposure to a new word invites the child to form a unitary meaning. The learners' success enforces the belief that they have a representational theory that narrowly constrains the choice of word meaning, triggered by a situation of appropriate use – namely, just that theory which will account for learning under these impoverished circumstances. As Carey notes, no semantic theory is currently available from psychology, linguistics, or philosophy that would explain this feat.

Carey's findings and discussion suggest further that semantic inquiry might be informed by an understanding of just what concepts a child will find natural to encode lexically. Such an inventory will not, of course, answer the question of what can be a word for mature users of language. For example, the Athenians had a word meaning *rich enough to be able to send a four-horse chariot to the Olympics*, and it is to be hoped that this was not a simple concept, even in Athens. One would despair of understanding semantics if, by definition, each word had to be considered evidence for a nondecomposable concept (see J. A. Fodor, 1975, for an approximation of this position, and appropriate despair). Rather, a likely supposition is that there is a lexical syntax that generates complex items, but youngest learners do not exploit this linguistic resource. For them, the word maps onto a single concept.

Morphological analysis is not only late; it is variable in the linguistic population. L. Gleitman and H. Gleitman (1970) showed that the bulk of mature speakers have difficulty analyzing the internal morphology of English compound nouns. Freyd and Baron (in press) have shown that vocabulary size for academically average eighth graders and for precocious fifth graders is about the same for morphologically simple items, but the talented fifth-grade youngsters have a massive advantage for morphologically complex items. Two chapters in this volume (Bowerman, Chapter 11; Clark, Chapter 12) describe the emergence of productive lexical analysis in children. We take up their findings in later discussion. Here it is sufficient to note that Bowerman tenders the same interpretations of her findings as do we: Each early word is an unopened package; only much later does productive lexical analysis begin to appear.

We have so far interpreted the literature to suggest that single words are first identified with single concepts. We believe that early speech is also consistent with the further notion that the child takes a very strict view of the way words function as components of propositions, namely, that *each word must code exactly one of the arguments of a predicate, the predicate itself, or a logical word* (such as *and* or *not*). Let us term this the Three Bears description of the roles words play in earliest sentences: To the extent a received word codes more than one of the countenanced functions, it is too big; less than one, it is too small; exactly one, and it is just right. Because this equation of propositional functions with single words is false of the adult language, the child's interpretation of the scope of a word will often differ from the adult's.

One line of evidence comes from the acquisition of American Sign Language (ASL) by deaf children of deaf ASL users. Newport and Ashbrook (1977) have shown an early tendency to map each relational element of this system as a separate lexical (sign) item. Certain ASL predicates morphologically incorporate some of their arguments; for example, the actor of *give* is uniformly expressed in the mature language as a modulation of the *give* sign, not as an independent sign. These incorporations are preserved in maternal signing to learners. But the children, systematically violating these input data, express the agent of *give* as a separate sign. The generalization is to the effect that each argument and the predicate ought to be carried by a wordlike item. No single word can be both predicate and argument, so *give* is interpreted as carrying only one of these functions.

Even more common is the young learner's indifference to further meanings and functions (other than predicate, argument, logical vocabulary) coded inside the word unit, for example, tense or number. Evidence suggests that complex words such as *knew* (*know* + *ed*) and *don't* (*do* + *not*) are treated as unanalyzed wholes by youngest learners, and only much later unpacked (errors such as *knowed* developmentally succeed instances of *knew*, as we mentioned earlier; and see Klima & Bellugi, 1966, for this treatment of first negative words). In her essay here on ASL acquisition (Chapter 15), Newport demonstrates for a range of lexical items that young ASL users acquire holistic "frozen signs," only later analyzing these into a root form with associated derivational and inflectional modulations (see also Newport, 1981). The appropriate generalization seems to be that semantic information within the word (e.g., tense) that is neither argument, predicate, nor logical word simply goes unanalyzed at earliest stages as our Three Bears description predicts.

This formulation allows us to reapproach a famous incident recorded by David McNeill (1966b) and to interpret it further. McNeill's 2-year-old subject remarks, "Nobody don't like me." His mother corrects him: "No, say 'Nobody likes me.'" The child mulishly repeats himself. The mother stubbornly recorrects. This interchange repeats itself seven times. On the eighth correction, the child says, "Oh: Nobody don't likes me." McNeill takes this as a very strong indication that overt corrections do not very much affect language learning, and we concur. But perhaps we can say more about what the child is willing to revise (adding the *s*) and what he is not (omitting the negative). He is indifferent to the *s* on grounds we have just stated; so he can take it as well as leave it. But he cannot apparently conceive that the logical notion *negative* does not have its own separable lexical reflex. He cannot accept that, in a cranky rule of English, the negative can be incorporated into the subject nominal (and, what is more, still have the verb phrase in its semantic scope).

Summarizing, children appear to approach language learning equipped with conceptual interpretive abilities for categorizing the world. As Slobin proposed, learners are biased to map each semantic idea onto the linguistic unit *word*. We have interpreted Carey's findings of holistic word learning as one explication of this proposal: Internal analysis of the word unit is a late and variable step in cognitive-linguistic development. We also have just examined the word as a functional unit in the sentence, concluding that the lexical items are at first stages the linguistic expressions of predicates, their arguments, and logical items.

The sentence is the natural domain of propositions. A fascinating line of research, beginning with Bloom's (1970) groundbreaking work on the child's spontaneous speech, provides evidence about how children meaningfully interpret the world. From the earliest two-word utterances, the ordering of the component words interpreted against their context of use suggests that they are conceived as playing certain thematic roles, such as *agent, instrument,* and the like, within a predicate-argument (propositional) structure (Bloom, Lightbown, & Hood, 1975; Bowerman, 1973b; Brown, 1973; Braine, 1976). Greenfield and Smith (1976) have maintained that even isolated first words betray, by their relation to events, rudiments of this propositional conception. Feldman, Goldin-Meadow, and Gleitman (1978) showed that a similar componential analysis describes a manual system of communication developing in isolated deaf children who received no specifically linguistic input, who neither heard speech nor saw formal signing (for discussion, see Goldin-Meadow, Chapter 2). To be sure, as Braine (1976) pointed out, it is by no means clear precisely what the first categories are, whether terms such as *agent* are appropriate in scope and content to describe them. In their chapter in this volume, Braine and Hardy (Chapter 7) begin to develop techniques for isolating and documenting such hypothesized categories as "subject of attribution."

Whatever the initial categories, there seems to be little doubt that the child approaches language learning equipped with a propositional interpretation of the scenes and events in the world around him. This is not particularly surprising. After a modest number of observations, David Premack's chimpanzee, Sarah, can learn to put a sticky star on the agent and a sticky circle on the patient as shown in brief video movies (Premack, forthcoming). If Sarah, why not human children?

The question remains how much this tells about learning a language. This depends on whether the categories and forms of natural languages are simple with respect to the preexisting compositional meaning structures. From varying perspectives, both Braine and Hardy (Chapter 7) and Bates and MacWhinney (Chapter 6) assume that linguistic categories and forms map transparently from the meaning structures, and hence that the bulk of explanatory apparatus – for child learner and for developmental psycholinguist – exists when these categories are isolated and described. In opposition, Slobin (Chapter 5) argues that explanation of language learning from the cognitive–interpretive basis is strictly limited by the variation among the natural languages. Partly different aspects of meaning are coded in the syntax of different languages. As one of many examples, the child will have to discover whether his language codes tense or aspect, or both, in the syntax. Moreover, even within a single language, it is obvious that there are many ways to say the same thing. So in this sense, too, it is massively overexhuberant to hope that knowing meaning is tantamount to knowing language. As Bowerman (Chapter 11) argues, the learner must eventually transcend his initial semantic-categorial organization of language to acquire certain grammatical categories and functions.

Motherese: saying the obvious. It is possible to suppose that caretakers' speech to young children has properties that respond to the problems we have been discussing, properties that enhance the probability that learner and teacher will be referring to the same matters from the same perspectives (for the clearest statement of this hypothesis, see Bruner, 1974/75). In detail, to the youngest learners mothers use language that is propositionally simple, limited in vocabulary, slowly and carefully enunciated, repetitive, deictic, and usually referring to the here and now (Broen, 1972; Cross, 1977; Newport, 1977; Phillips, 1970; Remick, 1971; Snow, 1972). These same properties of speech to young children have been reported in various language communities (Blount, 1970; Schieffelin, 1979a; Williamson, 1979) and social classes (Snow, Arlman-Rupp, Hassing, Jobse, Joosten, & Vorster, 1976) and among various caretaker types, even including 4-year-old playmates of 2-year-old learners (Sachs & Devin, 1976; Shatz & Gelman, 1973). Although the syntactic forms vary considerably both within and across caretakers, topics to the youngest listeners are interestingly narrow in range; they are mostly a matter of focusing the listener's attention on a present scene or thing and getting him to act upon, or at least gaze upon, that thing: *action directives* (Newport, H. Gleitman, & L. Gleitman, 1977; Schatz, 1978).

These descriptive facts about maternal speech cohere on the view that it is a matter of getting together with the young listener on what is being meant (for discussion, see Pinker, in press). The motivation for the caretakers is not far to find, nor need it be explicitly linguistic-tutorial. We need only suppose that the mother wishes to be understood and obeyed, and these properties will fall out.[3]

But one's enthusiasm for the explanatory potential of these findings requires a good deal of tempering: They suggest only *that* mother and child endeavor to represent the ongoing scene "in the same way," but do not suggest *how* they manage to do so. The explanation rests on the (unknown) cognitive system that learner and teacher share, such that in some critically exploited cases they will interpret the same scene in the same way. Contributors to the literature on maternal speech assert – both innocuously and probably truly – that mothers say "what is obvious" or "what is salient" to children, but this terminological fiat does not seem to resolve anything. As an instance of the underlying problems here, it is instructive that children blind from birth learn the same lexical items and semantic–syntactic relations in about the same order as do sighted children (Landau, in press; Landau & L. Gleitman, forthcoming), though clearly what is "here" or "now" must differ for blind and slighted listener. A blind 3-year-old knows, for example, that she is to perform different acts if told to *show* an object or to *give* it to a sighted listener. It is not at all obvious how the mothers of blind children differentially model the here and now so as to secure these surprising competencies.[4] Such findings of course do not vitiate the claim that children learn language by "relying on meaning in the world." Rather, they suggest that – because language clearly *is* learned by relying on meaning in the world – explaining language learning is more mysterious than ever.

Extracting form from the sound wave

Though the child may have his own devices for extracting meaning from situations, he will need other kinds of devices for extracting linguistically functioning units from the sound wave. We ask here what kinds of evidence are available, to a listener with the right capacities and inclinations, to determine the forms of particular languages.

The unit "phone." Recall that Bloomfield's learner (and hence classical phonemics) approached the gloriously confusing, continuously varying sound wave in a spirit of complete open-mindedness. This learner, like any objective physicist, would have no excuse to chop the complex and continuous wave form into discrete, linguistically functioning, phonetic units, and even less excuse to classify these units. Chao (1934/1958) demonstrated in a brilliant analysis that no unified discovery procedure for a classificational scheme was likely to be. discovered, because criteria sufficient to isolate the phones could not be simultaneously met (i.e., they were mutually contradictory). Classical phonemics nevertheless continued for some twenty years more to try, apparently on the plausible assumption that, if babies can do it, why not linguists? But babies could not. Therefore, language learners all over the world must be grateful to the Haskins Laboratory group of researchers who have saved them the bother: The children need never learn to segment the acoustic wave, just because they perceive such a segmentation "automatically" (see particularly Liberman, 1970; Liberman, Cooper, Shankweiler, & Studdert-Kennedy, 1967; and for studies of infant phonetic perception, Eimas, Siqueland, Jusczyk, & Vigorito, 1971; and Jusczyk, 1980).

There is much controversy about the size and specific nature of the phonetic segments (for a summary discussion, see Foss & Hakes, 1978; about whether they are the unique property of human organisms or belong to chinchillas and macaques as well (Kuhl & Miller, 1975); and about whether they derive from properties of speech perception in particular or auditory perception in general, an issue taken up by Newport (Chapter 15; see also Cutting, Rosner, & Foard, 1976; Liberman & Pisoni, 1977). But these problems do not mitigate the case for rejoicing among the aspiring language learners. For them, it is enough to note that no learning apparatus is required for an initial segmentation of the acoustic wave into discrete phones. The segmentation has been provided in the nervous system.

At this level, then, an objective, highly instrumented sequence of empirical investigations shows that the language learner has relevant information in advance about the inventory of possible phonetic elements (see Jakobson, 1941, for a seminal discussion in this context). It is interesting that in light of these findings from the acoustics laboratory, American psychology has felt entirely comfortable in adjusting to the fact of innate prespecification at this level. The curiosity is that findings of this sort seem not at all to suggest to many psychologists that higher-level language units may be prespecified in the same or a related sense. However, further findings from language learning suggest that the child has more in his bag of tricks than the phones, as learning begins.

The unit "word." The learner must recover words, word classes, and phrases from their encoding in the wave form. Distributional properties of the phonetic sequences seem to be inadequate bases for these further discoveries, for the phonetic sequences woefully underdetermine the identification of words (is it *an adult* or *a nuhdult?*), word classes (is *yellow* a noun, verb, or adjective?), and phrase boundaries (e.g., *I saw a man eating fish*). Our question, then, is whether there are units, above and beyond the phonetic distinctive features, physically manifest in the wave form and operative in the child's induction of language structure. Slobin (1973) has conjectured that learners are predisposed to identify the conceptual unit *word* (see "The word is the natural domain of simple concepts," earlier in this chapter) with particular physical aspects of the wave form: The child is prepared to believe that each wordlike conceptual unit has an "acoustically salient" and "isolable" surface expression. We agree, but we ask: What is this acoustic property? We now present an argument that the acoustically salient property is an abstract characterization of the sound wave whose surface manifestation in English (and other stress–accent languages) is *stressed syllable*.[5]

The most striking fact about the English speaker's first utterances is that the little "functor" words and affixes are approximately absent; hence the speech sounds "telegraphic" (Brown & Bellugi, 1964). To this extent, the child's early linguistic behavior again deviates systematically from the environmental model; children have their own ideas about the forms, just as they have their own ideas about the meanings. Particularly interesting is that youngsters learning Russian omit the inflectional affixes that are the main device for marking the thematic (semantic–relational) roles in that language, adopting instead a word-order strategy that has poor support in the input data (speech of their Russian mothers; see Slobin, 1966a). In light of this finding, it is impossible to suppose that the functors are omitted on the grounds that they are not semantically important. Surely it is important to distinguish between the do-er and the done-to, and as just stated, the youngest Russian learners do make this distinction, but by means of word orders, not inflections. Given such findings, it is not surprising that some investigators have supposed that word order is easy, inflection is hard, for youngest speakers. That is to say, they have described these findings as facts about earliest *syntax* (see, e.g., Feldman et al., 1978). Notice, however, that it is not easy to bring this syntactic claim to bear on all the little words that are missing from earliest speech. The personal pronouns, the prepositions, the specifiers, are approximately as absent as the inflectionally functioning auxiliaries (e.g., *will*) and affixes (e.g., *-ed*). A bias toward word ordering rather than inflection does not describe these facts very satisfactorily. But if we claim instead that the *unstressed items* are what are missing, we approximate the real facts about early speech very well (see Kean, 1977, for a related hypothesis, and the claim that it is relevant to describing aphasic language).

An immediate objection to this proposed generalization is that, if the child learner is differentially sensitive to stress in the speech signal, he should not be able to tell – for a language like English – the difference between an unstressed morpheme and the unstressed syllables of monomorphemic words. But there is good evidence, widely known but rarely mentioned, that children cannot make this distinction very well. For example, it is striking that words are often first pronounced as their stressed syllables, for example, "raff" for *giraffe,* and "e-fant" for *elephant.* Moreover, even when the unstressed syllables begin to be uttered, it is often in undifferentiated form (as the syllable schwa, /ə/, for all instances), for example, "əportcard" for *report card,* "tape-ə-cordə" for *tape recorder.*[6] Particularly interesting at this stage is the frequent misanalysis of clitic pronouns as the unstressed syllables of preceding words, for example, "read-it" and "have-it," yielding such utterances as "Read-it ə book, Mommie?" and "Have-it ə cookie." Such properties of earliest speech suggest that the child analyzes stressed syllables reasonably well, but is less successful in rendering the unstressed syllables and in segmenting the wave form into words on the basis of these.

Later stages of speech development lend weight to the same generalization. Bellugi (1967) demonstrated that when the elements of the English verbal auxiliary make their first appearance in child speech, the items are in their full, rather than contracted, form – for example, "I will go" rather than "I'll go" – for some developmental time. This is in contradistinction to the input corpus (mothers' speech), in which, as Bellugi showed, these items were contracted in the overwhelming majority of instances. Evidently, the contracted version of a word fails to be the acoustically salient element the child requires, if we take "stressed syllable" to be the appropriate specification of "salience."

Further evidence comes from investigations of input effects on learning. Newport et al. (1977) provided correlational evidence that the rate of learning of English verbal auxiliary elements was accelerated for children whose mothers used them proportionally most often in the noncontractable, stressed, sentence-initial position (by asking many yes/no questions, such as "Will you pick up the blocks?"). Such results are very reliable. The correlations are in the range of .80 even after partialling to correct for baseline differences among the children studied (see Furrow, Nelson, & Benedict, 1979, for a replication of this effect). It is reasonable to hypothesize either that initial position favors learning (a prediction that would follow from any theory of learning in which memory was a factor) or that the noncontracted, stressed form favors learning. We consider it likely that both these properties are relevant to the observed learning effects.

Intriguing new evidence for the same generalization comes from Slobin's findings (Chapter 5) on emerging comprehension among learners of various languages.[7] Slobin's learners of Turkish comprehend Turkish inflectional cues to the relational roles earlier in life than learners of Serbo-Croatian comprehend Serbo-Croatian inflectional cues to the relational roles (see Figure 5.1a). This is exactly the prediction we would have to make on the supposition that stressed items are available earlier in development than are unstressed items: As Slobin states in his chapter, the relevant inflectional items in Turkish are a full syllable long, are stressed, do not deform the surrounding words phonetically, and do not contract or cliticize. In Kean's (1977) terms, these items are phonologically *open class*. The late-comprehended Serbo-Croatian inflectional items are sub-syllabic, stressless, and phonetically deformed by adjacent material (*closed class*). Summarizing, the two languages differ according to whether the inflectional cues to the relational roles are encoded onto isolable stressed syllables, or not. This distinction predicts the differences in learning rate.[8]

In the other two languages Slobin investigates, English and Italian, the relational roles are cued primarily by word order, not inflection. Thus, like Turkish, they do not require the young learner to notice stressless grammatical items in order to recover the relational roles. Accordingly, there seems to be no main-effect difference between Turkish and these other two languages. Only Serbo-Croatian stands apart, showing a clear delay at each point in development.

Slobin argues differently than we have just done, based on a further interpretation of the same findings (Figure 5.1a). This is because he is interested in interpreting possible interaction effects (e.g., at least to the naked eye, it looks as if comprehension of English starts more slowly then catches up to that of the other languages). If these interactions are stable, another explanatory principle may be required. Slobin asserts that this new principle will be a syntactic-typological distinction, namely, word-order language versus inflectional language: Inflection is the easier because it is string-local, while word order is global clue and thus perhaps harder for learners with limited information-handling capacity.

We believe that there are a number of reasons to reject, or at least table, this further learning principle. One is the relative paucity of data (no main effect of this factor in Slobin's results). Another is the fact that speech development seems to proceed on the opposing principle (word order before inflection) to the one Slobin defends here for comprehension (inflection before word order). We will return to that issue in the following section. But notice here that this new principle requires Slobin to explain away, in part, the main effect he has obtained, namely, that one of the inflected languages – Serbo-Croatian – is the latest of all in the comprehension task. Slobin tries to do so by adoption of yet a third principle.

The third principle Slobin considers is that languages with double cueing systems (both sequence and inflection) will make more trouble for learners than those with single cueing systems. Serbo-Croatian requires sensitivity to both word order and inflection to recover the relational roles. But this new confusion or interference principle does not seem to explain the findings any better. The relevant Turkish inflectional items appear in an invariant sequence in the morphological string, but this does not lead to late learning. English is a single cueing system in the relevant domain (excepting the pronouns, it is word-order only) but certainly has no advantage over Turkish.

Our position is that a single principle, the advantage of stressed materials over unstressed materials, accounts for Slobin's main finding: The one language among the four investigated that requires attention to stressless materials for recovering relational roles is the one for which comprehension is delayed. Inflection itself poses no severe problem for the learner when it is encoded on stressed materials, as in Turkish, nor does sequence pose a severe problem under the same circumstances.[9]

The generalizations we have been considering are perforce limited to the stress–accent languages. As Chomsky has pointed out (see Section 1.1), the trick is not to make the learning of some languages easy to describe, if the cost is rendering the learning of others forever mysterious. That is, something more abstract than the notion *stress* in the sound wave may be required to account for this aspect of learning, given the real diversity among the natural languages (see n. 5 to this chapter). The only well-studied case we know of is rather far afield: studies from Newport and her colleagues (Newport, Chapter 15; Newport & Ashbrook, 1977; Newport, 1981) of the acquisition of ASL. We have noted that learners of ASL first treat each sequentially produced sign as an unanalyzed whole; the extraction of derivational and inflectional substructures within these signs appears only in later developmental steps (see also Klima, Bellugi, et al., 1979). The question is how to describe the physical, visually observable, manifestation called a separable *sign*. The linguistic analyses

by this group seem to us to suggest physically based distinctions between the frozen-form morphological means of ASL (e.g., handshapes) and the inflectionally and derivationally functioning morphology (e.g., certain movement types that modulate form and meaning). The latter, specially formed and specially functioning properties of manual language, are the later acquired. That is to say, there seems to be evidence here for "visually salient," "isolable" properties of the visible sign that are analogous to the "acoustically salient," "isolable" properties of the speech signal. Whether this is more than a metaphor remains, of course, a matter for further investigation.

Whatever the ultimate description will turn out to be – broad enough to encompass the real languages, narrow enough to tame induction so that language can be learned – it seems likely that the child does not approach the speech wave or the visible stream of sign like an objective physicist or structural linguist. To the extent that he must learn language by discovering the distributional properties of the input corpus (as Bloomfield stipulates), the inductive machinery appears to be constrained by the way the organism represents the materials on which induction operates (as Chomsky stipulates). In addition to discrete, featural descriptions at the phonetic level, we argue that the child has at its disposal another analysis of the input. For certain well-studied spoken languages, a physical distinction between stress and nonstress is an interim characterization. For ASL, there seems to be a related physical distinction. Appropriate characterization of the unit awaits investigation of the acquisition of nonstress–accent languages.

Sequence. We have so far determined that the child is sensitive, from earliest developmental moments, to (1) phonetic distinctive features and (2) stressed syllables. There is clear evidence, again from early points in language learning, that the child is sensitive to ordering, both of the distinctive features and of the stressed syllables. For the phonetic features, it is enough to say that children seem to know *tap* from *pat*. Errors characterizable as phone-order confusions are rare. There is also very good evidence that sensitivity to the order of words in sentences emerges early.

During the period when the unstressed syllables are mostly missing and ill analyzed, the child starts talking more than one word at a time. The evidence is massive that at this point the words are sequenced in the sentence. To be sure, there is controversy about the nature of the units so sequenced; that is, they might be grammatical units such as *subject*, relational units such as *agent*, discourse units such as *topic* or *old information*.[10] Whatever their correct description, these units are sequenced rather reliably from the first two-word utterances (for analyses of English see, e.g., Bloom, 1970; Bowerman, 1972a; Brown, 1973). As we have seen, sequencing is common even where the data base provides little support for it, as in the Russian cases reported by Slobin. Most remarkably, sequencing of signs according to their semantic–relational roles arises without any input support among the deaf isolates studied by Goldin-Meadow (Chapter 2).

Given these strong and stable findings, it is surprising that Slobin (Chapter 5) seeks to discount sequential ordering in child speech as theoretically uninteresting. He does so because of his reading of the cross-linguistic comprehension findings, namely, that competence with inflection precedes competence with word order in the comprehension tasks (Turkish is understood at an earlier moment in development than English). But as he also acknowledges, attention to word order is clear from earliest moments of speech – an inconvenient fact for the developmental generalization "inflection first, word order second." We have argued that the facts about which comes first, inflection or word order, are artifacts of phonological properties of the particular languages studied: Unstressed material is hardest, and hence, if the inflectional resources of a language are unstressed, they will appear relatively late in the child's speech; if they are stressed, they appear earlier. If we are correct, there seems little reason to take comprehension performances more seriously than speech performances – or the reverse – as indicants of the child's language organization. Findings in both domains are adequately handled by acknowledging that the child is first sensitive to stressed syllables, interpreted as words, and to orderings of these.[11]

It is important to notice, nevertheless, that a characterization of the child's word order is not really simple with respect to the adult's word order (the real utterances the learner hears from his caretakers). Only a small proportion of the sentences a child hears, in English, are subject first, because well over half the input sentences are questions and imperatives (Newport, 1977). Moreover, there is suggestive evidence that the child does not reproduce the subject-first property of the heard language, but rather produces something of his own, perhaps agent first (Bowerman, 1972a). We have already noted that noncanonical position of the verbal auxiliary (stressed initial position, as in "Could you jump to the moon?") favors *learning* of these auxiliaries. Still, the child first *utters* auxiliaries in declarative sentences, where they appear medially ("I could jump to the moon"). The learner, then, seems biased toward a notion of canonical word order, a notion that can arise only very abstractly from properties of the input. This is most striking for instances in which the input language *demands* noncanonical order for certain functions: Young English speakers express questions by intonation ("I could jump to the moon?") but do not invert the order of subject and auxiliary, though this inversion appears in just about every yes/no question they hear.

Summarizing, we must believe the child learner is sensitive to sequence, for he orders the words in his utterances from the time there are two words to order, and the orderings he chooses in general conform to canonical or preferred orderings in the language to which he is being exposed. But learners preserve the canonical ordering even if it is not present in the input speech (as in yes/no questions of English), or if the ordering of the input speech is only a nonsyntactic statistical preference (as in Russian), or if there is no input at all (as in the home sign of the deaf isolates). Hence, though sequence is a property of the wave form that the learner clearly notes and exploits, this property does not explain the character of what is learned.

The unstressed subcomponent of the lexicon. As we will see in discussing inductive processes in language learning, the distinction between open and closed class may play a role in the child's discovery of linguistic structure. This is because, though this distinction may be discovered through a physical property (i.e., stress), it is well correlated with syntactic analyses the child will have to recognize to recover the structure of sentences. We have seen that the closed class is acquired late. The pattern of development, within this class, is also distinctive. For example, Brown (1973) has shown that the closed class is learned in an item-by-item fashion over a lengthy developmental period, and in a very regular sequence (for instance, *-ing* is almost always learned before *-ed*). Moreover, learning rate is dependent on properties of the input corpus much more clearly for closed class than for open class (Newport et al., 1977). In certain cases of linguistic isolation, the closed class may not emerge (Feldman et al., 1978). In Goldin-Meadow's terminology (Chapter 2), the closed class is "fragile."

Slobin (1975) has conjectured, citing evidence from language learning, language change, and creolization processes, that the closed class arises through the fluent user's need to be quick and efficient in language use. In homely terms, the phonological squeezing of closed-class items (e.g., in English, the fact that *will* becomes *'ll*) may be an inevitable concomitant of rapid, fluent communication among linguistic experts. There is good evidence in favor of this hypothesis: The phonologically short, stressless forms of closed-class items make their appearance at late stages of acquisition, in the presence of increasing fluency. An independently interesting fact is that (to use Newport's wording from Chapter 15) these distinctive properties of the closed class are fully achieved only as they are filtered through the learning process, by children who are native speakers. Learning later in life, even in the presence of adequate fluency and habitual use, does not yield these same properties.

In detail, Sankoff and her colleagues (e.g., Sankoff & Laberge, 1973) have made extensive studies of Tok Pisin, an English-based pidgin developed and acquired by linguistically heterogeneous adults in Papua New Guinea. Sankoff showed that, in its historically earliest forms, this language had only impoverished inflectional resources. Notions like *future* were expressed by optional, sentence-initial adverbs (such as *baimbai*, from English *by and by*). In a second stage of evolution – a stage at which the learners were still adults, acquiring Tok Pisin as a second language – this item moved into the verb phrase and became syntactically obligatory as the marker of future. This seems to show that adults are quite capable of expanding the syntactic resources of their language, as it comes into broad use as the ordinary means of communication. But at this point the new inflectionally functioning item is still a word with regular stress.

Recently, the use of Tok Pisin has become so general that children are acquiring it as their native language. These learners, approximately in the period from 5 to 8 years of age, make a further move: *Baimbai* is shortened and destressed to /bə/, becoming an obligatory verb prefix. This is an intriguing suggestion that, at a late stage of the learning process, the closed class makes its appearance even though it is absent from the input language. This is symmetrical with findings we have just reviewed about early stages of learning, in which the closed-class words are absent from speech even though they are present in the input language.

Newport (Chapter 15) provides related evidence from the acquisition of ASL. Very often ASL is learned as a second language, either because it is not used by the deaf child's hearing parents or because deafness is acquired later in life. Newport demonstrates that learners first exposed to ASL after the age of about 7 fail to acquire the inflectionally and derivationally functioning substructure of the signs (the signed equivalents of the closed class). Again, the product of late learning is much like the utterances of native learners at first stages.

In sum, young learners are biased to notice phonetic features, stressed syllables, and sequences in which these are ordered. Learning late in life seems to show sensitivity to these same properties of the wave form. But unlike adults, children become sensitive to the unstressed subcomponent of the language during later phases of language acquisition. At the limit (i.e., in the absence of such features in the speech heard), children can add to the stock of language resources by inventing the closed class.

The unit "phrase." If we are right, the stressed syllable stands out from the rest of the wave form approximately as figure stands out from ground in the child's (innate) visual analysis of space (cf. Spelke, 1982). Although the stressed syllable is by no means equivalent to the mature word form, the evidence strongly suggests that it is available to the child as a bootstrap into the morphological scheme of the language. Recent evidence from speech synthesis and perception studies shows that potential bootstraps exist in the wave form for other linguistic units. For example, speech timing is affected by major syntactic boundaries, by deletion sites, and by lexical category assignment (Sorensen, Cooper, & Paccia, 1978). Whether learners exploit these additional acoustic cues to structure remains an open question, but Read and Schreiber (Chapter 3) provide ingenious, if somewhat indirect, evidence that they may.

Read and Schreiber taught 7-year-olds to play a game in which the children must listen to a sentence and then repeat back some portion of it corresponding to one of its major constituents. Children are remarkably successful at this task, learning to pick out such constituents as surface subject noun phrase with impressive accuracy. However, they show one curious weakness: If the subject noun phrase is only a single word (e.g., a pronoun or a generic nominal), children are regularly unable to disentangle it from the rest of the sentence. In an admirable series of experiments, Read and Schreiber track this clue to its source, showing that, of all the many properties of single-word noun phrases, it seems to be their intonational contour (or lack of one) that accounts for the difficulty that children experience. Unlike longer noun phrases, single-word phrases are not rendered with falling fundamental frequency and lengthened final vowel at the close of the phrase. It is this phonological merging that throws the children for a loop. Apparently phrase boundaries are largely a matter of intonation for these 7-year-olds. They do not appear to be able to locate boundaries by syntax alone.

It would be perilous to reason in a straight line from 7-year-olds to 1-year-olds. Just because a second-grader shows heavy reliance upon the intonational correlates of phrases, it does not follow necessarily that he began learning phrases as an infant by means of their intonational correlates. Bever (1970), for one, has argued that the mastery of an abstract syntactic rule can precede the development of heuristic perceptual strategies that come to replace the rule in practice because they are easier to apply during the rapid-fire business of understanding or producing speech. It is not impossible that phrase-structure learning conforms to Bever's pattern. Read and Schreiber's 7-year-olds may have learned the syntactic structure of phrases first and only then have come to appreciate the intonational correlates of phrases. (It is, after all, undeniable that the well-formed utterances of 7-year-olds reveal an impressive knowledge of the syntactic structure of phrases.) It is also possible that this (judgmental) task captures metalinguistic knowledge that is partly at variance with linguistic knowledge (H. Gleitman & L. Gleitman, 1979). But it is also possible, we think probable, that the 7-year-old's heavy reliance on intonation is a remnant of a dependency formed at the earliest stages of acquisition. If this is the case, it would have important consequences for the way we think about the acquisition of syntax. For, as we will argue later, an infant who is innately biased to treat intonationally circumscribed utterance segments as potential syntactic constituents would be at considerable advantage in learning the syntactic rules of his language.

Whether this particular advantage is one that human infants actually do exploit remains to be seen. However, Newport and Morgan (forthcoming; Morgan & Newport, 1981) have explicitly proposed this hypothesis and have supported it (again indirectly) by showing in an artificial language-learning task that different physical cues to phrase grouping, such as intonation contour (when sentences are presented orally) or physical closeness of within-phrase items (when sentences are presented visually) are sufficient for the adult subject to induce the grammar. When sentences are presented without such phrasal cues (and without alternative semantic cues to the phrases), adults generally fail to learn the language. It is difficult to tell whether infants are as dependent on physical grouping as Newport and Morgan's adults. But their result gives reasonable ground for entertaining this possibility.

1.3. The projection problem: pairing the meanings and the forms

In the preceding discussion, we summarized the information available about the state of the child requisite to language learning; namely, some means for representing input speech signals and some means for representing the real-world context that co-occurs with the signals. We asserted that the input signals are interpreted as ordered phonetic strings bracketed by stress into words and bracketed by intonation into phrases. Acknowledging that some input may be physically too imperfect or indistinct to allow these analyses, we took the findings from the maternal speech literature to suggest that this problem is not greatly damaging to the position; that is, by and large the mother's speech is slow, intonationally exaggerated, and almost always grammatical. As for the meaning representations, we stated that information about these is currently orders of magnitude more fragmentary. The literature does suggest that the child assumes words represent concepts and function as the markers of predicates and thematic roles in a propositional structure, carried by the sentence. What the concepts are and just how the sentence heard relates to a particular proposition (the cat-on-mat vs. mat-under-cat problem) is unknown, but we interpreted the maternal speech literature to suggest a caretaker–child conspiracy designed to respond to these problems. Just as for the speech signals, we assume that the child will have to filter out, as unusable data, the utterances whose interpretation is ambiguous or murky. Granting, then, that much is unresolved here, all parties seem to agree that the preconditions for learning are that the child be able to interpret and represent the sound wave to himself in linguistically relevant ways, and also interpret and represent real-world events to himself in linguistically relevant ways. Having granted these prerequisites, we now raise the question: How does a child learn a language? That is, how does the child project from these data a general system that pairs each possible meaning with each possible form?

The directions for an answer proposed by contributors to this volume differ radically. Not only do the authors disagree. Their essays do not even seem to be on the same topics. Braine and Hardy (Chapter 7) seek to explain how the child connects semantic–relational roles to positions in surface strings. Maratsos (Chapter 8) asks how the child discovers such syntactic categories as noun and verb. Wexler (Chapter 10) asks how an abstract learning device might acquire transformational rules. We believe the disparity of topics arises from a much deeper disagreement among these authors about the complexity of the mapping between form and meaning. Believing that the mapping is essentially simple, Braine and Hardy propose that it can be learned as a direct projection from se-mantic–relational roles to the surface string. Maratsos sees the relation between form and meaning as more complex, but still believes that it can be learned by a direct projection, albeit in quite the opposite direction: from form to meaning. Wexler, in contrast, holds that no such direct projection is possible. For Wexler, the relation between form and meaning is so complex that it must be learned through the mediation of another level of representation.

In sum, investigators' descriptions of the task for learners vary in large part owing to their differing beliefs about what is to be learned: a case grammar (Braine & Hardy), a constituent structure grammar (Maratsos), or a transformational grammar (Wexler). We now take up these hy-potheses in turn. In each case, the authors are asking about the discovery of sentence structure – the main battleground of linguistic and psychol-inguistic theorizing over the last two decades.

Learning a case grammar

In 1966b, McNeill put forward the claim that children essentially "talk deep structure" at earliest developmental moments. That is, the ordering of words looks much like the left-to-right sequence of terminal nodes in deep-structure descriptions of the 1965 variety. This claim was met by an awful howl. Very largely, this was because McNeill's formulation assumed that the categories and functions that figure in early speech are the same as those that figure in adult grammars – *noun phrase, subject of the sentence*, and the like. The retort from developmental psycholin-guists has been that the child's categories are semantic–relational ones of a much simpler sort (see, e.g., Bowerman, 1972a; Braine & Hardy,

Chapter 7; Schlesinger, 1971). We accept tentatively, as a state-of-the-art generalization, the view that the child's initial categories are semantic–relational ones at some preliminary stage of learning.[12]

It is our impression that many investigators believed they are making the problem of language learning easier by pointing – probably correctly – to these functional semantic categories as the ones that operate in early child speech, and by supposing – again, probably correctly – that these categories map onto the child's word orderings or inflectional markings in a simple way. But to the extent the child really makes these suppositions, these can only complicate the problem of learning a language. The reason is that the supposition is false of any adult language.

One problem is that the position of semantically definable propositional components varies with the predicate. John's role, but not his sentential position, differs in *John is easy to please* and *John is eager to please*, and in *John sold a book to Mary* (where he is source) and *John bought a book from Mary* (where he is goal). John's sentential position, but not his role, differs in *John received a tie from Mary* and *Mary gave a tie to John*; in *John collided with Bill* and *Bill collided with John*; and in *Bill resembles John, John resembles Bill,* and *Bill and John resemble each other.* These old saws are no less problematical for being old saws. Moreover, the phenomenon of constructional ambiguity is understandable only if we acknowledge the complexity of relations between surface and logical forms (e.g., *These missionaries are ready to eat* allows two interpretations of the relational role of the missionaries, at least if the listeners are cannibals).

A further problem is that, past the puerile sayings of the first three years of life, it is difficult indeed to describe sentences as syntactically organized by the semantic functions. To understand the descriptive problems here, consider the following first sentence from a recent letter to the editor of *TV Guide*: "How Ann Salisbury can suggest that Pam Lauder's anger at not receiving her fair share of acclaim for *Mork and Mindy*'s success derives from a fragile ego escapes me." This writer, whatever his odd preoccupations, displays some formidable syntactic skills. It is hard to state that the first twenty-seven words of his sentence represent some semantic role. What role would that be? Still, the twenty-seven words function together as a linguistic unit, namely, the unit that determines that word twenty-eight is to end with an *s*. Mature language knowledge involves such semantically incoherent categories as noun phrase, subject of the clause, and so forth, as the domains of these categorial contingencies. Moreover, if there is anything like an agent or do-er in the sentence above, it would have to be *me*. For its predicate (*escape*), this do-er is the second noun phrase. But for predicates of quite similar meaning, the do-er is the first noun phrase. That is, the sentence could be recast: "I fail to understand how Ann Salisbury can suggest that Pam

. . ." The point, an old point, is that the grammatical notion *subject* (the noun phrase immediately dominated by S, the noun phrase that agrees in number with the verb) is only complexly related to semantic notions such as agent or experiencer. Thus, if we claim the child is preprogrammed to construct a semantic representation to match each sentence that he hears, we have arrived only at the beginning of the language-learning problem. The rest of the problem involves acquiring the system of rules that relates surface forms to their underlying meanings. Recapitulating, we do not deny the relations between form and meaning (for learner or user). We only deny these relations are simple and direct.

Developmental psycholinguists usually reject the standard arguments we have just given. They have assumed, to the contrary, that a case grammar (roughly of the sort envisaged by Fillmore, 1968a) is the appropriate "psychologically real" descriptive mechanism. In Fillmore's proposal, the underlying categories are semantic–relational. The surface configurations of sentences arise by rule from these semantic categorial (deep case) representations, and hence no separate interpretive device would be required for the semantic interpretation of the grammatical configurations. It has sometimes gone unnoticed that Fillmore postulated a mediating system of rules operating on the initial case representations to account for the complex relations between surface orderings and semantic roles: To our knowledge, Fillmore never argued that these relations would be simple, that is, immediate. Moreover, a number of questions have been raised about the descriptive adequacy of this approach. For instance, Chomsky (1972) has pointed out that the same case description would apply to *pinch* and *pull*, accounting for the surface manifestations *John pulled Mary's nose* and *John pinched Mary's nose*. But then it is hard to explain why *John pinched Mary on the nose* is acceptable, but *John pulled Mary on the nose* is anomalous, on the relevant reading. Chomsky's approach has been to state the syntactic–categorial facts, and separately an interpretive system that carries the grammatical structures to the logical structures. Another approach is to list the case relations for each predicate, and surface specifications for that predicate, as lexical information (Bresnan, 1978). Thus, though linguists disagree on *how* to state the relations between semantic roles and grammatical dependencies, none (to our knowledge) assert that these relations will turn out to be simple.

Braine and Hardy's discussion of these matters is to the effect that a sane creator who had the language-learning problem in mind would write a case grammar that mapped semantic–relational roles onto surface structures in simple ways. Braine and Hardy present five principles of simplicity and efficiency in Chapter 7. We do not disagree with these directions to a good God, but we have just argued that the real deity has not been so benevolent (probably this is only one of many grounds for questioning the goodness of God). That is, the evidence of natural language design fails to suggest a transparent mapping between meanings and sentence forms. Rather, successful descriptions have had to postulate transformational rules, or lexical rules of a complexity just as great, or rules of like complexity that generate phrase-structure rules recursively, and so on. Though the complexity can be moved, then, from component to component of a grammar, it evidently cannot be *re*moved.

The controversy between linguistic theories and most developmental psycholinguistic theories that we know of really arises on one question: Is it valuable to postulate a system that describes the earliest stages of learning (i.e., the speech of a 2-year-old, as the simplest case systems do, passing well) even if this simple system fails to describe the learner who manages to survive to age 3 or 4? If learning is taken to be continuous – that is, if the earliest learned properties are a proper part of the full learning to follow – the semantics-based syntax is a false step.

Summarizing our position thus far, empirical and commonsense evidence is not inconsistent with the view that the first version of a grammar is one that maps simply (one-to-one) from underlying semantic to surface structures. But this claim for an initial "conceptual language" commits one to a discontinuous claim about language learning, just because the final knowledge state partly dissociates semantic and grammatical categories.

In this volume, Bowerman (Chapter 11) goes beyond the logical arguments we have just made, developing evidence about child speech that empirically establishes a good case for reorganization. Her main method is to look at "errors" over developmental time. With a variety of contents and structures, she shows that the child errorlessly uses certain accepted language forms at early stages. Presumably what is going on here is item-by-item adoption of the heard forms. At a later stage, the errors suddenly make their appearance. As Bowerman argues, through internal analysis of these late-appearing error types, the novel usages imply that the learner has seen through to a new organization that relates the items learned separately and allows the child to project beyond the heard instances in various ways (some of them wrong).

The question arises: What causes the child to reorganize his grammar – especially to reorganize it in a way that increases the abstractness of the relations between forms and meanings? Bowerman takes no stand on this matter. But it is possible to imagine that reorganization is motivated by a data-driven process, an aversion to "clutter" in the original data organization. Bowerman remarks that individuals, both children and adults, might differ in the extent to which they are inclined to tolerate first organizations, or to carry out these deep reanalyses.

There is another possible interpretation of the basis for reorganization, however. It could be that there are relevant neurological changes in the learner that cause him to reinterpret linguistic evidence. Putting the same thing another way, it could be that there are a succession of learners, each of whom organizes the linguistic data as befits his mental state. This is a kind of metamorphosis, or tadpole-to-frog, hypothesis. To the extent it is correct, perhaps it is quite reasonable to do as many developmental psycholinguists have done: write a grammar for the 2-year-old, and assume no responsibility for that description as a basis for describing the 3-year-old (for discussion of the metamorphosis position, see L. Gleitman, 1981).

Whatever the causes of change, both discontinuous theories of language development assert that the surface-meaning mappings of an earlier semantics-based system are dropped, and learning begins anew with fairly trivial residue (including, perhaps, the lexical items and the guess about canonical order). The two theories differ, though, to the extent that the data-driven reorganizational hypothesis might claim there is a necessary movement through stages, while the metamorphosis theory says there is not. Opposing predictions arise in many places, for example, in second-language learning by young children. A 4- or 5-year-old Hungarian (presumably, neurologically already "a frog") transplanted to an English-speaking community would have to traverse the semantic transparency stage according to the data-driven, but not the neurological, hypothesis. Notice that the second hypothesis may offer a ready explanation for the known speed of second-language learning by youngsters.

For the sake of the current discussion, the important thing to notice is that for the most plausible (continuous) view of language acquisition, Braine and Hardy's semantic transparency hypothesis about the form–function relation does only harm. The child has to reshuffle his agents and recipients so as to get the subjects, objects, and so on that also figure in adult language representations. On the discontinuous hypothesis, a semantic transparency stage does no harm – for one does not get from stage to stage by learning, using the units of prior stages. So we have a mismatch of plausibilities here. Obviously, that children's units are semantic and that language learning is learning (i.e., that it builds continuously from present knowledge) are the commonsensical hypotheses. But you can't have them both at once. If children's initial units are semantic, learning must be discontinuous (getting from stage to stage by a process distinct from learning), because adults have some semantically incoherent units (e.g., subject of the sentence). If language is learned in a continuous process, the initial units must be the grammatical ones.

Learning a Bloomfieldian grammar

The case grammar approach to language learning takes as certain the child's mastery of a small set of semantic distinctions (agent–patient, possessor–possessed, etc.) and attempts to build the rest of syntax acquisition on this base. We have argued that such a building will never get past the ground floor. In contrast, the neo-Bloomfieldian position, to the extent that one exists, builds in an altogether different direction and begins with an entirely contrary certainty, namely, the unarguable fact that adults control some syntactic categories that have little if any direct correlation with matters semantic. More than anyone else, Maratsos and his colleagues (Maratsos, 1979; Maratsos & Chalkley, 1980; Maratsos, Kuczaj, Fox, & Chalkley, 1979) have been identified with the renovation of Bloomfieldian ideas. Chief among their labors has been the simple but essential reminder that adult grammatical categories, such as *noun, verb,* and *adjective,* cannot summarily be reduced to the semantic definitions of grade school. It follows that such categories must be acquired on some basis that is at least partly independent of semantics, a fact that is something of a conundrum for any theory of acquisition run exclusively on semantic machinery.

In Chapter 8 of this volume, Maratsos makes a new and interesting pass at this argument. He begins with the fact that there are some syntactic distinctions, such as the German gender distinction, which are notorious for their failure to show any semantic correlation. For such categories, there is no alternative but to learn category members word by word on the basis of the syntactic contexts in which they appear. For example, upon hearing "das machen," one can unequivocally assign *machen* to the neuter gender (semantics be damned) and predict that *machen* will pronominalize via *es,* take *dem* in the accusative, and so forth. It is this correlated set of syntactic effects which, according to Maratsos, makes up the German neuter gender. To learn the neuter gender is to learn that these syntactic phenomena predict each other, and nothing more.

From here, the argument moves to interesting ground. In effect, Maratsos argues that, if *some* syntactic categories must be learned as clusters of distributional facts, then why not *all* syntactic categories, including among them the major grammatical categories, such as noun and verb, as well as the major constituent categories, such as noun phrase and verb phrase? Why postulate more than one sort of language acquisition unless forced to it? A very good question, one worth some pursuit.

Maratsos's learning device is basically an inductive scheme capable, in principle, of classifying words together on the basis of shared contexts. We have argued from the beginning for the failure of unbiased induction to account for the fact of language learning. Nonetheless, learning must ultimately be by inductive generalization. This follows from the fact that languages differ from one another and hence must be learned, in the classical sense of the term *learning* (just Bloomfield's point, as we stated in our introductory remarks).

The problem is to isolate units on which induction takes place, given the capacities and inclinations of a human language learner. Maratsos's explicit proposal seems to be for a general distributional analyzer that recognizes associations among (any) morphemes. We believe, however, that to the extent this proposal seems plausible, it is because it really (albeit implicitly) builds upon a quite narrow and interesting hypothesis about the nature of these units, specifically, the distributional analyzer Maratsos sketches seems to be particularly sensitive to the open-class–closed-class distinction we have described earlier. The bulk of Maratsos's *co-predictors* (correlations exploited to determine word-class membership) turn out to be associations between a closed-class item and an open-class position. For instance, "takes plural -s" predicts noun status for a stress-bearing word; "takes -*ed* and *will*" predicts verb status for other such words. Notice that a blind inductive device might focus on quite different, and ultimately useless, potential correlations, such as the correlation of a word like *black* with *ink, cat, crow,* and *coal* (but not *chalk, polar-bear, swan,* and *milk*); no syntactically functioning units are picked out by these latter correlations. To the extent that Maratsos's distributional analyzer is plausible, then, it is because it has eyes for something like an open-class–closed-class distinction. These eyes rescue Maratsos's analyzer from contemplating the limitless false analogies that it might otherwise be forced to consider as potential bases for grammatical categories. But this rescue raises problems of its own.

First, there is serious empirical question whether the closed-class items are generally available to children to support the initial construction of grammatical categories. The evidence we have presented thus far suggests that the closed class and relevant distinctions among the closed-class items are beyond the grasp of the youngest learners. If this is so, these items would not be available to the inductive device at the stage – a very early stage, as the literature tells us – when the initial distinction between noun and verb is acquired (as evidenced by ordering).

Moreover, nouns and verbs apparently emerge without difficulty at early stages of Turkish, which has few closed-class resources, according to Slobin's analysis, and in Tok Pisin in its historically early version which, according to Sankoff, has virtually no inflectional resources. Hence, whatever the facts for normally circumstanced English-speaking learners, it cannot be maintained that the distinction between noun and verb, in general, arises from a distributional analysis of open-class–closed-class relations.

In Chapter 8, Maratsos tries to resolve these problems, but succeeds only by weakening the pure Bloomfieldian strain of his proposal. Following Braine (1976), Maratsos acknowledges that at the initial stages of language acquisition, grammatical categories (perhaps they should be called pregrammatical categories) are probably formed on semantic grounds. Subsequently, when the closed-class distinctions have been mastered (at about the age of 3), the child is in a position to renovate his categories on the basis of distributional properties. Such a renovation is necessary to account for the fact that children make so few category errors based on semantic uniformities. Thus the verb *like* and the adjective *fond (of)* mean much the same thing. Yet children are not heard to invent *John was fonded of by Mary* on analogy with *John was liked by Mary*; at least this is uncommon. Presumably, it is the child's growing appreciation of the ways in which nouns and adjectives covary with closed-class items that prevents overgeneralizations of this sort.

All this seems plausible enough, but it leaves rather mysterious the acquisition of the closed class itself. Notice that this is not simply a problem of picking out phonetic segments that seem to have low initial salience in the wave form. The child must also learn the grammatical significance of these phonetic segments. It is not, for instance, the location of a word just prior to the appropriate sounds for an *-ed* ending that predicts verb status. Consider, as evidence, that there are no verbs *to lightheart, to lighthead*, or *to lightfinger* corresponding to the adjectives *lighthearted, lightheaded*, and *lightfingered*. Evidently it is not the *-ed* ending per se, but only *-ed*-used-to-signify-past-tense, which signals verb status. It follows that if the child learns the verb category in part by learning about its deployment with respect to *-ed* as a marker of past tense, then she must first have learned that *-ed* marks past tense. This much Maratsos acknowledges explicitly in his essay. But the unanswered question is just how the child manages to accomplish this crucial prior feat. Put generally, the child's move from categories based on semantic properties to categories based on the syntactic distribution of grammatical morphemes is not just a matter of changing the basis of induction. The child's new syntactic base *presupposes* the analysis of grammatical morphemes, and this analysis requires an explanation of its own.

One traditional way in which the syntactic values of grammatical morphemes have been determined in linguistics is by means of their relative position in the phrase structure of the sentences in which they appear. The advantage of the phrase-structure representation is that it permits global description of the sentence so that the values for grammatical morphemes can be assigned in a way that is consistent with the entire sentence. For example, if the child possesses the mental equivalent of grammatical rules that allow her to construct a parse tree like this,

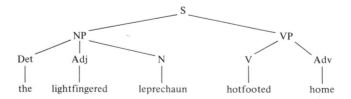

then there could be little if any uncertainty about the appropriate syntactic categorization of *lightfingered* and *hotfooted* and the correct assignment of the morphemic value *past* in the second case but not the first. The reasons are straightforward: *Lightfingered* appears before a noun and after a determiner, hence in a position appropriate to an adjective, in which *-ed* cannot signal simple past. *Hotfooted* appears just after a noun phrase, a context in which verbs are permissible, and hence *past* is a possible analysis of *-ed*.

If we accept the moral of this story, then the child must learn to parse (though tacitly and unconsciously), and she must acquire syntactic rules on which parsing depends. As we have argued throughout, neither un-abetted semantic learning nor induction over surface regularities escapes this conclusion. The residual question is just how syntactic rules, which embody these parsings, are learned.

Learning a transformation grammar

The question how syntactic rules are acquired returns us to the first principles of the debate between Chomsky and Bloomfield. Now, how-ever, we can restate the issues in terms of the territory since covered:

1.   Given that the child is innately enable to "hear" the wave form of parental speech as an ordered string of words, intonationally brack-eted into major phrases (unlabeled, of course); and
2.   given that the child can, by dint of his own conceptual abilities and by parental efforts to direct his attention, achieve an accurate in-terpretation for some of the sentences he encounters – even in advance of achieving a full grasp of the language he is learning – and
3.   given that the mapping between the semantic interpretation and the surface string is not sufficiently simple to be learned either as a direct projection from semantic representation to the surface string (Braine & Hardy) or vice versa (Bloomfield); it follows that
4.   we must provide some independent account of how the rules that map between the semantic interpretation and the surface string are acquired.

This task is severely complicated by the fact that there is no single gram-matical system now known to be the psychologically valid statement of these mapping rules. Among the best studied of the alternative gram-matical systems are transformational grammar in its several incarnations (Chomsky, 1965, 1980; Fiengo, 1980), lexical functional grammar (Bres-nan, 1982), arc pair grammar (Johnson & Postal, 1980), and relational grammar (Perlmutter, 1980). Given the uncertain choice among these (and other) alternative descriptions of the adult system, it is difficult to achieve definite results about the process of acquisition. However, it is possible to study some of the boundary conditions under which such acquisition could conceivably take place. It is noteworthy that the study of such conditions can place constraints on the choice among possible grammatical systems, because whatever else is true of the adult grammar, it must be learnable by the child. Kenneth Wexler and several colleagues have carried out an extended study of such constraints, and Chapter 10 provides an important overview of this work, which may be unfamiliar – both in style and substance – to many developmental psycholinguists.

Put very simply, Wexler's work is an examination of the compatibility of holding two assumptions: (1) that children learn a mapping between form and meaning (equivalent to our assumption [4] in the preceding list) and (2) that the mapping they learn is, at least in part, a transformational grammar of the so-called "standard theory" vintage.

Wexler examines the consistency of these two claims by designing a hypothetical learning device for transformational grammars and determining under what conditions it will converge "in the limit" (in Gold's sense; see Section 1.1) on the correct transformational grammar for a given language. His earliest result (Wexler & Hamburger, 1973) showed that no such convergence is possible so long as the learner has access only to positive examples of sentences in the target language. This is a significant extension of Gold's similar finding for primitive recursive languages because it shows that positive examples alone are insufficient to permit the acquisition of a class of languages (those generable by a transformational grammar) presumably very close to the class of natural languages.

This negative result motivated Wexler and his colleagues to examine an altered scenario in which the child is considered able to derive the meaning of adult utterances from extralinguistic circumstances (our assumption [2] in the preceding list) and able to derive the deep structures of a transformational grammar from such meanings. On these assumptions, the child is confronted with data consisting of a word string paired with a deep structure for every sentence he can interpret in this fashion. Wexler's learning device is extremely simple. Whenever a string/deep-structure pair arrives, it attempts to find a set of transformations in its current grammar that will map from the deep structure to the string. If it is successful, it makes no change in its grammar. If it is unsuccessful, it either deletes one of its current rules at random or attempts to formulate a new transformation (given only its knowledge of elementary transformational operations) that will permit a successful mapping of the current input pair. If such a new rule can be found, it is added to the current grammar.

Hamburger and Wexler (1975) were able to prove that, with this kind of input, a learning device of this simple type can successfully converge in the limit on the target transformational grammar, but only if the grammar includes certain constraints on the operation of transformational rules.

Such constraints (the details of which Wexler provides in Chapter 10) are needed in order to insure that if the learner makes an error (infers an incorrect transformation), it will not require a sample sentence of un-bounded complexity to reveal that error. A learner requiring examples of unbounded complexity might have to wait an unbounded amount of time to stumble onto even one such example. Hence convergence in the limit could not be guaranteed.

One of the chief thrusts of Wexler's work is linguistic. With Culicover, he has tried to show that the constraints required to guarantee learnability have independent linguistic motivation (Wexler & Culicover, 1980). To the extent that the learnable grammar is also the most successful descrip-tion of the adult language, it becomes possible to offer learnability as an explanation of descriptive success: The language is as it is just because it must be learned.

No one, including Wexler, would propose that his learning device is a full model of how children acquire syntax. It may be that Wexler's current scenario assumes both too much and too little about the input to the child: Too much because it is unknown how the child gets from meaning to deep structure without additional learning to supply this map-ping (a problem Wexler & Culicover, 1980, address specifically); too little because, as we have suggested in connection with the work of Read and Schreiber, the child may have intonational access to major phrase bound-aries, while Wexler has worked from the assumption that the learner recognizes only the linear string of words. That access to surface phrase structure can render certain erroneous grammatical hypotheses detectable by the learner is evident from Wexler's illustration of an undetectable error on p. 301. With availability of the phrase structure, this particular error in Wexler's illustration would not remain undetectable. At any rate, whether the availability of phrase bracketing might have a sufficiently general effect on detectability to render unnecessary any of Wexler and Culicover's transformational constraints is another question, but one that may be worth attention.

Wexler's study of learnability is an important move in developmental psycholinguistics. Where much work in the field seems to have aimed at description for its own sake, Wexler's program serves to refocus attention on explanatory goals. Moreover, it sets exacting standards for the ac-ceptability of explanatory proposals that are a model for future work. How many current notions about how language is learned can offer hard proof that language is, even in principle, learnable in the proposed way? Many arguments in developmental psycholinguistics rest upon unexam-ined assumptions about learnability that prove to be false once their consequences are examined by Wexler's techniques. An example of just this sort, and further discussion of Wexler's formal results, will concern us in the following section, describing the "Motherese hypothesis."

Although the Wexler group's work is surely the most extensive effort to examine the conditions under which a transformational grammar might be acquired, it is by no means the only way to conceive of such a process. In fact, as transformational grammar has evolved away from the so-called standard theory, and as the complexity and variety of the transformational rules has steadily diminished, it has become increasingly clear that the learning of transformations is only a small part of the task of learning a transformational grammar. Moreover, the very difficulty of establishing rapid convergence for a learning system that proceeds by enumerating and testing grammars has led Chomsky (1980) and others to consider a more restrictive framework in which the child's innate knowledge of universal grammar hypothetically goes well beyond the elementary transformational operations countenanced by Wexler, and instead includes rich knowledge of universal rule schemata. In theory, such schemata contain empty slots that the child needs only to fill in to learn his own language. Under this idealization, which is often called "parameter setting" to distinguish it from the hypothesis-testing framework, the child might come pre-armed with schema for core grammar rules informing him that (say) a noun phrase is composed of a head noun plus specifier, but leaving open the problems of determining which order these elements appear in, how specification is marked in this language, and so on.

In Chapter 9, Roeper provides an interesting illustration of this approach. Roeper's experiments suggest that very young children may have remarkably subtle knowledge of the differences in grammatical relationships conveyed by noun phrase gerunds and verb phrase gerunds. According to Roeper, this knowledge is innately given and needs only to be triggered by the child's acquisition of the (language-particular) English system for marking noun phrases and verb phrases.

Although Roeper's tests are demonstrational and do not examine the postulated triggering function in any detail, he provides a skeletal framework for conceptualizing parameter setting as a realistic psychological process in which knowledge of universal grammar interacts with other mental faculties in the course of language acquisition. Unlike the Wexler group, Roeper has attempted to explore the consequences of dropping the idealization of instantaneous grammar acquisition. Thus he holds his model potentially accountable for intermediate stages of knowledge in ways in which Wexler does not. Whether this accountability improves the prospects of the model depends ultimately upon the transparency and tractability of the data used to characterize the stages of acquisition. Although developmental psycholinguists often assume that empirical coverage of the course of acquisition is a desirable end in and of itself, it remains to be seen whether the underlying explanation will be revealed by attempting to account for these data. (See L. Gleitman, 1981.) On this issue, Wexler implicitly votes no; Roeper yes.

Caretakers' role in the learning process

As we mentioned earlier, a number of investigators have suggested that properties of caretaker speech may, in addition to easing the utterance–meaning inductions, contribute causally to solution of the projection problem: relating the language forms to the meanings, that is, acquisition of grammar. The general idea behind this approach is that the caretaker could order the presentation of syntactic types, so as to narrow the candidate generalizations the child would be in a position to entertain, consistent with his data. Certain properties of speech to youngest children give some support to such a claim. Earliest utterances to children are short and propositionally simple; hence they are uniclausal. Possibly, mothers say easiest sentences first to littlest ears, successively adding the complications as learning proceeds, and so being responsive at all times to the requirements of an environmentally dependent learning device. This has been called the "fine-tuning" hypothesis. See Cross (1977) and Newport (1977) for arguments pro and con.

There are a number of problems in making good this claim. First, if it is intended to remove requirements for endowments supporting language learning, it could succeed only by transferring this claim from learner to tutor, that is, by placing apparatus in the mother so that she could effectively determine (a) the syntactic simplicity of her potential utterances and (b) the current grammar of the child, in order to carry out her tutorial aims. It is not obvious why "endowment with linguistic-tutorial skills" should be any more palatable than "endowment with linguistic-learning skills."

Apart from this problem, the evidence of maternal speech does not support the view that it would aid the acquisition of syntax. For example, the earliest utterances to children are by and large not canonical sentences of the language, and a sizable percentage more are fragments (e.g., isolated noun phrases) and interjections. The majority of the full sentences are imperatives and questions. If a transformational grammar is the envisioned end point of learning, it is clear that the child is not selectively receiving simple syntactic structures (i.e., the straightforward, least transformationally deformed outputs of base rules and the obligatory transformations). More generally, it would seem that *any* syntactic theory would have to regard the active, declarative sentences as simplest, but these are not the forms favored by caretakers in their speech to the youngest learners. Moreover, as the child grows older, the percentage of canonical declaratives said to him increases rather than decreases, while the noncanonical forms decrease in proportion. Reliable predictions of the child's growth rate from properties of the maternal speech style that vary among mothers are also limited. In fact, they are limited to acquisition of the closed-class morphology. Many correlations of other kinds, between child's linguistic stage and mother's current usage, disappear once these are corrected for baseline differences among the child learners. These empirical outcomes limit the extent to which the child's learning of syntax can be assigned to the effects of "intelligent text presentation" by the mother (for discussion, see Newport et al., 1977; Wexler & Culicover, 1980).

Other problems with this hypothesis are logical. Chomsky (1975) and Wexler (Chapter 10) have pointed out that narrowing the learner's data base, although it might do no harm, certainly cannot do good if the outcome of learning is to be a grammar covering the full range of the language. The narrower the range of data, the more hypotheses can describe them. In fact, the difficulty of proving the learnability of language would be reduced considerably if it were plausible to suppose that the learner received and could analyze complex input data. This is because the transclausal relations within sentences (the transformations, on one formulation) are revealed only in complex sentences, quite obviously.

The major result achieved by the Wexler group thus far has been to devise a set of constraints on transformational operations such that learning is demonstrable from "degree 2 input" (sentences that are constituted, at maximum, of a clause within a clause within a clause). If the child were assumed able to deal with yet more complex input than this, fewer constraints. (i.e., *less* innate apparatus) would be required, as Wexler and Culicover have shown in detail. Summarizing their position, the formal description of learning is materially *complicated* by the plausible assumption that mothers speak *simply* to their young offspring. Constraints on transformations are required just so that learning can take place, even though the real data are simple (of no more than degree 2 complexity). Why this point has been so hard for developmental psycholinguists to grasp is itself hard to grasp. It seems reasonably obvious that learning should be more difficult from limited and biased ("degenerate," in Chomsky's wording) data than from rich and unbiased data. The degree 2 result and the constraints on transformations required to make it work provide a formal demonstration that would seem to render unassailable the logical point that partial ("simplified") input does not ease the problem of acquiring complex systems (see Chapter 10 for Wexler's description of degree 2 learnability).

Despite the logical and empirical difficulties just described, the Motherese hypothesis continues to be pursued in the developmental psycholinguistic literature (see, for example, the collection of essays in Snow & Ferguson, 1977). This is usually done by claiming that maternal speech aids the young learner in some other and more subtle ways: Perhaps it is the gestures that accompany maternal speech that secure learning; perhaps the mother limits herself, in using a certain form, to a single (semantic) function for that form. Shatz (Chapter 4) delivers the coup de grace to many of these fallback positions by submitting them to a series of observational and experimental tests. She finds that the form–function relations are not materially simplified to young learners, and that children are quite insensitive to whatever gestural supports to comprehension these parents might be giving. Most important, she provides a review and discussion of the "omniscient-mother" hypothesis and its experimental investigation that brings the burgeoning literature in this area into a unified, but pessimistic, perspective. Her discussion secures that we will have to look primarily at children, not at their mothers, to understand language learning. It should go almost without saying that Goldin-Meadow's (Chapter 2) demonstrations of the survival of syntax in the absence of linguistic input similarly diminish hope that the environment of the learner determines the character of what he learns.

There is a counterattack, however, that Shatz does not consider. This is the point that general social-interactive properties of the mother–child discourse will causally determine the actual form–meaning pairings the child learns. This position is explicated by Bates and MacWhinney (Chapter 6). Their discussion is important, for it recognizes the essentially social nature of language, and tries to bring this to bear on the problem of acquisition. Understandably, this *functionalist* approach to language and its learning is in its infancy, and to this extent the discussion by Bates and MacWhinney is programmatic. It is hard to say, at the present state of the art, whether social properties of conversations will account for the fact that English babies put the verb in the middle while German babies put it at the end; that English babies learn to say "I won't put up with that" but not "I won't tolerate with that," and "I painted the wall blue" but not "I painted the wall beautiful"; that they can interpret the *he* in "When he sang, John entranced the audience" anaphorically, but not the one in "He sang, when John entranced the audience"; and all the myriad other facts about how to interpret English sentences meaningfully. On functional grounds, so far as we can see, these issues threaten to require independent explanations, yielding an infinite variety of things that must, and therefore cannot, be learned. Perhaps a functionalist grammar can be written for adults and for children that will bring this approach under control. At present, we believe that the Bates and MacWhinney discussion is a useful corrective to those who think about language as sentences, without regard to the fact that language use takes place, ordinarily, in interchanges between at least two people. However, the descriptive apparatus does not now exist on which to support or falsify the various detailed suggestions these authors have offered.

A much more restricted, and therefore more tractable, look at language structures whose appropriate use is dependent on conversational competence and cooperation is taken by Clark (Chapter 13). She discusses the learning of so-called denominative verbs in various languages (e.g.,

"Litter-basket your empties!" an admonition printed on beer-can cartons). As Clark points out, there seem to be almost no limits on such innovations: Notice, for example, that almost any body part you can name has by this stage in the development of English a fairly well entrenched denominal meaning or meanings. Beginning even before the end of the third year of life, children creatively use denominal verbs (e.g., "I monstered that towel," "That truck is cementing"). Some of the child's usages seem quite odd, but it is a very subtle matter, as Clark discusses, to ask just what is wrong with them, that is, what the adult constraints might be on formation of novel denominative verbs (see also Aronoff, 1980; E. Clark & H. Clark, 1979). Though certain of the constraints she proposes are of the kind common in linguistic descriptions of both syntax and morphology, it appears that these are not enough. Rather, both the invention and the interpretation of novel denominals seem to be partly governed by conversational conventions – conventions of language use. As one example, Clark asserts that a speaker must predetermine what his listener knows and could infer from context as a condition of creating the denominal, for in principle, "there is no limit on the number of senses" these expressions can potentially convey. Her discussion concerns the processes and strategies by which the learner might acquire such conventions.

1.4. Final thoughts

At the very bottom of any scientific paradigm lies a set of beliefs that are usually called metaphysical. It is sometimes claimed that these deep beliefs about the nature of theories and the things they describe cannot be confirmed or disconfirmed by empirical means. It is, however, quite possible to compare different metaphysical beliefs according to the degree of success of the scientific programs they support. Moreover, substantive arguments for one set of metaphysical assumptions over others can be constructed on this basis.

At its deepest level, Chomsky's break with Bloomfield is just this sort of argument. If a grammar can be construed, not as a physical description of linguistic behavior à la Bloomfield, but instead as a description of the linguistic knowledge represented in the human mind, then – so Chomsky argued – it will be possible to construct a more successful and interesting theory of language. Chomsky's familiar commitment to linguistic competence as an object of study is at once a metaphysical decision about what sort of thing a theory of language is about and a very practical decision about what sorts of data the theory will be responsible for and what sorts of constraints on the theory will prove most fruitful. If a grammar describes the speaker's linguistic knowledge, then it is only indirectly revealed in linguistic behavior, and it is not to be held accountable for the physical facts about linguistic behavior for which Bloomfield's grammar must take responsibility. However, if a grammar is to be interpreted as a psychological description of human knowledge, then it necessarily raises questions about how such knowledge is acquired. Much of our discussion has attempted to summarize just how well these questions have been answered.

Recently, however, Jerrold Katz (1981) has mounted an argument against Chomsky's psychologistic interpretation of grammar, one that formally parallels Chomsky's argument against Bloomfield's physicalistic interpretation of grammar. In effect, Katz argues that it is possible to achieve a better theory of language if we drop both the idea that grammar describes human knowledge and the attendant responsibility for showing how such grammatical knowledge is learnable. This can be achieved in Katz's view, only if we adopt a Platonic (or realistic) interpretation of the grammar in which grammatical principles are supposed to describe an abstract reality entirely independent of human knowledge of it, much as the reality of a mathematical relationship (e.g., the Pythagorean Theorem) is sometimes held to be true independent of human appreciation of that truth. According to Katz, this metaphysical interpretation is to be preferred because it permits a full-blooded account of necessary linguistic truths (such as lexical entailments of the "vixen is a fox" variety), which would otherwise have to be held contingent on the nature of the human mind. Moreover, Katz holds that Platonist metaphysics permits simpler solutions to certain thorny problems of grammatical description once the grammar is freed of the requirement that it be rendered in a form learnable by human beings. It may be worth noting that this is exactly the opposite of the views advanced by Wexler (Chapter 10) and Newport (Chapter 15), who take the position that the requirement of learnability and its incorporation into grammatical theory explain otherwise mysterious grammatical facts.

In Chapter 14, Bever explores the possible consequences of the Platonist challenge to the Chomskian paradigm for our theories of language acquisition. First among these consequences is the unhooking of linguistic theory and acquisition theory. Linguistic theory describes the set of possible natural languages, and acquisition theory describes the set of languages learnable by humans. According to Platonist assumptions, there is no theoretical reason to expect these two sets to be identical. Thus, Bever argues, the Platonist paradigm remains unembarrassed when it turns out that certain cognitive operations never show up in language, just as certain linguistic operations never appear elsewhere in cognition. The Chomskian paradigm can handle such facts by postulating the mental segregation of the linguistic faculty: Language is as it is because of the structure of the human mind, but language is unlike the rest of mind in some respects because the mental organ devoted to language is unlike the rest of mind (in just those respects necessary to explain the difference). Bever claims that there is circularity in this formulation: "It is not a literal contradiction to maintain . . . that the essence of language is caused by an organ of the mind. But it does present a picture of language as resulting from a capacity that is mentally isolated in sporadic ways. That is, many aspects of cognition as a whole are reflected in language use and structure; why are the specific exclusions the way they are?" (p. 436). By this route, Bever rejects what he takes to be Chomsky's claim that the essence of language is necessarily caused by the structure of the mind: If there is no independent evidence (independent, that is, of the evidence provided by language itself) for the shape of the mental organ devoted to language, then the claim that the essential structure of language is caused by that mental organ is just a hypothesis, no more certain, although certainly more testable, than the Platonist claim that language is independent of mind.

But once Chomsky's claim has been shown to be hypothetical, one must ask whether Bever's revelation really changes the empirical problem of explaining language acquisition. Bever argues that one consequence of Platonist assumptions is that it becomes *unnecessary* to hold that language is acquired by a mental organ specifically designed for the task. Fair enough. But it does not follow from this that language acquisition can have a *sufficient* explanation in terms of general learning mechanisms. Even if *language* is caused by the exigencies of some abstract, Platonic reality, as Bever suggests, human beings' *knowledge of language* must be psychologically caused. Children must come to know their native tongue. And, as we have been at pains to argue, this knowledge cannot be acquired by unconstrained induction. Exactly what these constraints are and just how they relate to linguistic theory and to general cognition are, we take it, open empirical questions. Indeed, they are perhaps the central questions that motivate the chapters that follow and shape the state of the art.

Notes

1 Bloomfield (1933/1961) emphasized that the pairing between speech and event must be complex: "Even if we know a great deal about a speaker and about the immediate stimuli which are acting upon him, we usually cannot predict whether he will speak or what he will say." He put this problem down to "the fact that the human body is a very complex system . . . so that a very slight difference in the state of the body may result in a great difference in its response . . . [we could predict] whether a certain stimulus will lead [someone] to speak and, if so, the exact words he will utter . . . if we knew the exact structure of his body at the moment or, what comes to the same thing, if we knew the exact makeup of his organism at some early stage – say, at birth or before – and then had a record of every change in that organism including

every stimulus that had ever affected the organism" (p. 33). Thus Bloomfield had the courage of his materialist convictions. Probably no avowed mentalist would disagree with this global claim that speech events are ultimately "caused" by a combination of internal structures and states and the external events they confront. But a large disagreement is whether the description of such (speech-to-event) relations would constitute an appropriate theory of language knowledge or performance; the problem is that only certain states, events, etc., are relevant to language organization. That is, the relations between sentences and events are mediated by the relations between sentences and their meanings. Presumably, the latter relations constitute a theory of language.

2 Notice that though the environment could pair only utterances to situations, the character of learning must be more general than this: To a remarkable degree, adults can assign a compositional meaning to sentences on request, in the absence of external context. And they can comprehend books about ancient history. The theoretical task then becomes asking how the child recruits information of a certain sort (primary linguistic data, or utterance/situation pairs) and constructs a system of a different sort (sound/meaning, or deep-structure/surface-structure pairs).

3 In detail, they fall out because, apparently, no matter what you say to a young child, it responds by acting if it responds at all. The evidence is from Shatz (1978). She showed that there is a good match between what mothers say (mothers' speech consists largely of *action directives*; whatever the syntactic form, the intent is to get the child to act) and what children are inclined to do. Children "behave" in response to speech acts they even partly understand: They are likely to pick up the blocks if you say, "Pick up your blocks" or, "Could you pick up your blocks?" but they are as likely to act even if your intent was just to get information; for example, if you ask, "Can you jump to the moon?" you are likely to get a little jump from the child. If the mother is implicitly aware that this is the child's bias and her motive is to be obeyed – or, what comes to the same thing, to display for herself and others the child's competence – she will select action directives when she speaks to the child. All descriptive evidence supports that view that action directives occur massively more often (proportionally) in speech to younger children than in speech to older children and adults. Such joint motivations in tutor and learner probabilistically increase the likelihood that the child's interpretation of the meaning of the maternal speech act will be correct.

4 The finding here is that the blind child holds up an object for the sighted listener to perceive at a distance when told to "show," but delivers it to that listener when told to "give." Moreover, the child evidently adapts perceptual–cognitive terms to her own requirements, again in ways hard to explain as effects of maternal modeling. She distinguishes *touch* (contact manually) from *look* (apprehend manually). For example, she touches her back to "Touch behind you" but feels in the space behind for "Look behind you," without turning her head. She taps a cup when told to touch it, but explores it manually when told to look at it. She happily stabs at the air above in response to "Touch up" but is angry (when there's nothing to be found there) when responding to "Look up." She responds by touching when told "Touch

it but don't look at it" but with confusion when told "Look at it but don't touch it." What claims about the natural categorial representations of humans account for the fact that blind and sighted children represent virtually identically despite different exposure to the world? It seems that the developmental literature substitutes semantic categories for syntactic ones successfully only by failing to define the former.

5 The specific acoustic correlates of primary stress in English include longer duration, higher fundamental frequency, and intensity (see Sorensen et al., 1978). For the argument that follows to hold, it would be necessary to show that the same, or definably analogous, acoustic properties are available and exploited to mark phrase boundaries in the nonstress–accent languages, and that these are the properties reproduced in the early child utterances.

6 These phenomena have not been closely studied, to our knowledge, doubtless because their theoretical interest has not been very clear. Hence we can give no quantitative evidence about how often errors of this kind occur, though surely they are not rare. Anecdotal evidence favoring the view that the unstressed items are at first undifferentiated is quite persuasive. For example, the child (of our acquaintance) who said "əportcard" at an early stage of development said "Can we go to grandma's repartment house?" just as she switched to "report card."

7 Some further empirical review is required to stabilize the findings Slobin reports, we acknowledge. That is, there are some methodological complaints one could raise to discount these new results. Owing to the language differences that were under study, and the methods of testing, the Turkish children were exposed to a series of test questions all of which were grammatical in their language (i.e., six possible orders of S, V, and O). The English speakers, just because the materials were constructed in the same way, were exposed to one grammatical sentence along with five ungrammatical ones (again, the six possible orders of S, V, and O). Analysis is on the grammatical sentences only, of course. Nonetheless, there is independent evidence that anomaly is disruptive to the performance of very young listeners (see, e.g., L. Gleitman, H. Gleitman, & Shipley, 1972), and hence there is some question in evaluating Slobin's results as though the stimulus conditions for the various subjects were the same. In general it is harder to evaluate comprehension tasks than spontaneous speech, owing to problems with the cooperativeness and understanding of instructions by youngest populations, as well as the difficulties of constructing appropriate stimulus materials matched across languages. Nonetheless, we interpret the present findings from Slobin on the supposition that they will survive further testing.

8 The same confound (between inflectional items and unstressed items) complicates interpretation of the many studies of related distinctions in adult performance. Hence there is controversy whether the phonological or syntactic properties of the closed class account for their different patterning in various tasks, and with various populations. For example, Kean (1977, 1979) has explained certain speech and comprehension impairments in Broca's aphasics on the phonological hypothesis, while Marin, Saffran, and Schwartz (1976) emphasize the syntactic distinctiveness of the items these aphasics cannot manage. Current evidence, for the various task domains, is insufficient

to give overwhelming support to one or the other hypothesis, though only the phonological hypothesis can serve as part of the explanation (rather than mere description) of language learning. But for the learning hypothesis to do work, it must be that the acoustic facts correlate with the syntactic facts to be learned, and so either or both properties (their acoustic properties or their syntactic properties) could account for distinctive adult performance with open and closed class. As has recently become clear – whatever the correct analysis – this open-class–closed-class distinction has highly reliable effects in a broad range of adult linguistic performances. Speech errors differ for the two classes (Fromkin, 1973; Garrett, 1975); lexical access differs for the two in normals but not in Broca's aphasics (Bradley, Garrett, & Zurif, 1979); forgetting differs in language death (Dorian, 1978); reading acquisition differs for the two classes (Labov, 1970; Rozin & Gleitman, 1977), as does the historical development of writing systems (L. Gleitman & Rozin, 1977); judgmental performance also differs for the two classes (H. Gleitman & L. Gleitman, 1979).

9 Turkish does have some inflectionally functioning morphological items that cliticize, deform the adjacent open-class items, appear in variable (morpheme-order) positions, etc. (Zwicky, 1976). We must predict that, for such items, the Turkish learners will have their own troubles, but, of course, the appropriate studies have not yet been done. In general, we are arguing from the very fragmentary available facts and findings. But in any case, we are not sanguine about the explanatory work that global generalizations from memory and processing can do. After all, one of the most robust findings from developmental psycholinguistics concerns the child's willingness to form a weak verb-ending rule (-*ed*) on variable input data, with simultaneous unwillingness to make a variety of other syntactic and lexical generalizations on data no more or less variable. Hence irregularity or variability of devices in Serbo-Croatian is by itself insufficient to explain the comprehension findings. Most urgently, we assert that the facts Slobin cites about the agglutinative–fusional distinction (our phonological distinction) are sufficient to bear the explanatory burden.

10 All these postulated units make much the same predictions about which NP the child will utter first, which second, in declarative sentences. This is why it is difficult to identify the psychologically functioning unit among these choices.

11 Whatever the theoretical perspective, Slobin's disclaimers about the interest of speech performances are not really persuasive. He argues that children preserve word order in their speech merely "because their brains work that way" and because "the child tends to behave like his or her models." Hence, putatively, the facts about speech are not so important. This argument does not go through, in our opinion, just because the child imposes sequential ordering on his own novel utterances, that he has never heard (this applies emphatically, of course, to Goldin-Meadow's deaf isolates). What is the basis, then, on which the child knows how to behave like his models? It is possible to say that he behaves like his models by uttering the agent first, or the animate entity first, or the subject, or the topic, or the new information; but surely it is not possible to say nothing. If the child honors word-order constraints in

speech simply because this is the way his brain works, then these are just the kinds of behavior we should be most interested in, in explaining language learning.

12 But a good deal of caution is required here. As we discussed in passing, the definitions of the semantic roles are so vague that they never seem quite wrong; but this is scant evidence that they are right. We ourselves have trouble assigning semantic roles to many simple sentences that seem to pose no problem to developmental psycholinguists (see Braine, 1976, for a careful discussion of such difficulties). Moreover, it requires a good deal of temerity to make much of this putative stage in language learning. As Bloom, Lightbown, and Hood (1975) have shown, the period in which the child assigns a unique surface position to each semantic–relational role is brief, if there at all. Moreover, as Wexler and Culicover (1980, p. 403) have pointed out, the lists of children's productions, so analyzed, themselves contain counterexamples. For instance, among the examples Schlesinger (1971) gives of agent + action constructions is the utterance "mail come," and *mail* cannot be an agent, by the usual definitions ("animate instigator . . ."). For a large class of English action verbs of special interest to toddlers, the subject is the agent. If the tots are really biased to use action verbs, for cognitive and motivational reasons, then a coding of the child utterances will pretty well identify subjects and agents. But especially in the light of the occasional counterexamples, it does not follow that the children believe *in principle* that subjects must be agents.

Part II

PRECONDITIONS FOR LANGUAGE ACQUISITION

2. The resilience of recursion: a study of a communication system developed without a conventional language model

Susan Goldin-Meadow

2.1. Constraints on human language learning

The facts of human language learning suggest that we are not free to acquire all types of communication systems at all times during our lifespans. There is evidence that a human must learn a language within some critical developmental *time* period (Lenneberg, 1967). Moreover, there may be constraints on the *type* of language learned as well. All of the languages acquired by humans, although apparently different on the surface, share numerous properties at deeper levels of analysis (Bach & Harms, 1968; Greenberg, 1966). This may suggest that languages with properties differing radically from this set would be difficult, if not impossible, for a human to acquire.

Constraints of a similar nature appear in the communicative behaviors of many species (Mayr, 1974). For example, in order to develop his song, the white-crowned sparrow must receive acoustical experience sometime between one week and two months after hatching (Marler, 1972). Before and after this critical period, the sparrow is not "open" to environmental experience and can make no use of it even if it is available.[1] Further, there are constraints not only on the time during which song may be learned, but also on the type of song that can be acquired during that period. A sparrow exposed only to the song of another species will develop no song rather than an alien song. Thus, even during his critical period, the sparrow is only partially "open" to environmental effects and can incorporate only certain types of information.

The white-crowned sparrow is predisposed to acquire the white-crowned sparrow song. Pushing this phenomenon further, it turns out

This work was supported by National Science Foundation Grant BNS 77-05990 and by the University of Chicago through Spencer Foundation Research Funds, Division of Social Sciences Research Funds, and a Biomedical Sciences Support Grant (PHS 5 507 RR-07029). I am very grateful to both Lila Gleitman and Eric Wanner for helping me consider the broader implications of what I am trying to say, and to Bill Meadow for reading countless earlier drafts of this chapter. I thank Ralph Bloom, Robert Fulton, Jeff Harlig, and Miriam Rabban for help in videotape transcription, and my subjects and their families for their cooperation and friendship.

that the sparrow may be more predisposed to acquire certain properties of this song than others. At less-than-perfect learning times (specifically, at the edges of his critical period), the bird seems to be able to acquire only a subset of the properties of the species song. With exposure to normal song between the fiftieth and one-hundredth day of life, the sparrow can acquire a song with some of the general structural properties of his normal song (i.e., with the expected division into whistle and trill portions), but without the detailed syllabic structure of the normal song (Marler, 1972). Thus certain properties of the sparrow song seem to be *resilient* and can withstand variation in learning conditions, whereas other more *fragile* properties cannot.

Seligman and Hager (1972) have defined the notion of "preparedness" in terms of parameters of this type, that is, in terms of acquisition under variations in learning conditions. A behavior that can be acquired under degraded input conditions is said to be more prepared than a behavior that cannot be acquired (or can be acquired with less ease) under the same degraded conditions. In this sense, the white-crowned sparrow's whistles and trills are prepared song behaviors, whereas his syllabic structure is a less prepared behavior. Prepared behaviors would be expected to appear under widely varying learning conditions, but unprepared behaviors would appear only under more specialized and enriched conditions. Given natural variations in the environment, prepared communication behaviors ought to appear more reliably than unprepared behaviors in each species-member's communication system. As a result, the more prepared a communication system, the more constrained would be the features of that system; but at the same time, the more prepared the system, the *fewer* would be the constraints on the external conditions necessary to develop that system.

Degrading linguistic input. A search for the "prepared" or "closed" properties of human languages can reasonably begin by degrading linguistic input conditions and observing the subsequent course of language development. As in studies of the sparrow, those properties developed under the degraded input conditions (i.e., those more immune to the vagaries of the environment) can be considered the prepared linguistic properties; those not developed under these same conditions are clearly more susceptible to environmental variation and, in that sense, are less prepared.

We can degrade input conditions either by manipulating the time of acquisition (i.e., by observing language learning outside the critical period) or by manipulating the quality of the linguistic input during acquisition (i.e., by observing first-language learning during the critical period but with a degraded linguistic model or with none at all). Ethical considerations prevent us from deliberately creating human situations of either type. However, tragic circumstances and nature itself have fashioned language learners in both types of situations.

At the age of 20 months Genie was confined to a small room and allowed no freedom of movement, no perceptual stimulation, and no human companionship until she was discovered at the age of 13 years, 7 months. This age is generally taken to be outside the critical period for human language learning (Lenneberg, 1967). Under such conditions of extreme deprivation and isolation, it is hardly surprising that Genie did not develop language during the first thirteen years of her life. More relevant to the discussion here is Genie's linguistic progress after her discovery.

When she was discovered, Genie's linguistic skills were minimal. She appeared to be able to comprehend a small number of single words, but gave no evidence of understanding syntax and never spoke. Over the next five years, she made considerable linguistic progress (Curtiss, 1977), an achievement which suggests that human language learning can take place beyond the critical period. However, as was the case with the sparrow, Genie was able to learn certain properties of language (e.g., word-order production rules, constituent structure, recursion) but not others (e.g., pro-forms, movement rules, auxiliary structure; see Section 2.5 for further discussion).[2] Those properties of language which Genie did learn are good candidates for the resilient properties of language, the ones that humans may be prepared to learn; those properties which Genie has not yet learned are good candidates for the fragile language properties, the ones that humans may be less prepared to learn.

The second class of experiments investigating constraints on language learning involves depriving an individual of normal linguistic input during his critical period. Genie herself provides an example of such a study. However, the deprivation Genie experienced was so extreme, involving much more than just linguistic deprivation, that little positive can be said about the human propensity to develop language on the basis of Genie's inadequate language development. Nevertheless, Genie's case does convince us that there are limits on the conditions under which humans can develop language, and that Genie's language-learning conditions, not surprisingly, exceeded those limits.

The population of deaf children of hearing parents that my colleagues and I have been studying for the past several years provides another example of degraded linguistic input, in this case with no other forms of deprivation, during the critical period. These children have hearing losses so severe that they can make no natural use of the oral language that surrounds them; moreover, these particular children have not been exposed to conventional manual languages (e.g., Signed English, American Sign Language) and instead are being trained orally (i.e., trained to lipread and to produce sounds through kinesthetic cues). At the time of our study, the children had made little, if any, significant progress in their oral training. Thus, for all intents and purposes, these children were lacking conventional linguistic input in both oral and manual modalities.[3]

Despite these degraded linguistic input conditions, each of the six children we have studied has developed a gestural system that has many, but obviously not all, of the properties of human natural languages (Feldman, Goldin-Meadow, & Gleitman, 1978; Goldin-Meadow, 1979; Goldin-Meadow, in press; Goldin-Meadow & Feldman, 1977). For example, the children have developed lexical items of two types.[4] First is the nounlike *deictic sign* used to refer to people, places, and things (e.g., a pointing gesture that relies heavily on context for interpretation, analogous to *that* or *there* in the speech of a comparably aged hearing child); semantic case roles, such as patient, actor, and recipient, are conveyed by these deictic signs. Second is the verb/adjectivelike *characterizing sign* used to refer to actions and attributes (e.g., a pantomimed action or trait such as a fist held at the mouth, accompanied by chewing, to signify "eat," or the index finger and thumb forming a circle in the air to mean "round"); predicate functions, both action and attribute, are conveyed by the characterizing signs.

In addition, these lexical items are concatenated into *sign sentences* expressing the typical semantic relations found in normal child speech. These sign sentences conform to syntactic rules of two types. Sign-ordering rules describe where in the surface structure of a sentence a particular case or predicate will tend to be signed (e.g., signs for the patient, or object acted upon, tend to precede signs for the act; for instance, point at bicycle precedes two fists "pedaling" in the air, transcribed as "bicycle-PEDAL"). Production probability rules describe the likelihood of a particular case or predicate's being signed in the surface structure of a sentence (e.g., patients are most likely, actors least likely, to be signed; that is, the patient "curds and whey" would be more likely to be produced in a sentence about eating than would the actor "little Miss Muffett").

Finally, the children produce sign sentences whose surface structures are systematically related to underlying structure. For example, the *actor* is more likely to be signed in the surface of a sentence with a two-term underlying thematic structure, such as a sentence about dancing, "elephant-DANCE," than in a sentence with a three-term underlying structure, such as a sentence about eating, "apple-EAT," and is even less likely to be signed in a sentence with a four-term underlying structure, such as a sentence about transferring objects, "box-GIVE" or "GIVE-me." These language properties, developed without a conventional language model, can reasonably be considered to be resilient properties of language.

In this chapter I suggest that recursion, an important property of all natural languages, may also be a resilient property of language. Recursion provides a language user with the means for expressing more than one proposition in a single sentence. I describe data, primarily from one deaf child of hearing parents (David), on two-proposition sentences developed without a conventional linguistic model. After first describing the types of conjoined sentences David has produced, I look at evidence for underlying structure in these conjoined sentences and explore the nature of this structure. Finally, I summarize the findings on a sign system developed with degraded linguistic input in terms of constraints on language learning in humans.

2.2. Recursion in a language developed under degraded input conditions

The data

The data for this report come, for the most part, from the most prolific subject, David, who over the course of the study produced roughly 350 complex, two-proposition sentences. In contrast, the other five deaf children in our original study as a group produced only 40 such sentences. Whenever numbers permit, the data from the other five children will be cited to supplement David's data, but, in general, this is the story of recursion in David's sign system.

The data were gathered over a period of two years during thirteen sessions, beginning when David was 2 years, 10 months, of age and ending when he was 4 years, 10 months. The five other children ranged in age from 1;5 (years; months) to 4;1 at the time of the first session and from 2;6 to 5;9 at the time of the last; one child was observed for as few as two sessions, one for as many as sixteen. Informal play sessions with a standard set of toys were videotaped roughly every ten to twelve weeks in the child's home. The videotapes were then transcribed and coded according to the system described in detail in Feldman et al. (1978) and Goldin-Meadow (1979); see these reports for information on criteria and reliability for each of the coding categories and also for further details on procedure. Briefly, we reviewed the tapes first to extract those motor acts which appeared to be used symbolically for communicative purposes and then described those acts using the system developed by Stokoe (1960) to describe American Sign Language. We next segmented these gestures into word units and sentence units. Finally, we assigned semantic meanings to each of the sign words and sign sentences, using as guides Bloom's (1970, 1973) method of rich interpretation and Fillmore's (1968a) case descriptions.

In assigning semantic descriptions to sentences, we classified each sentence according to the number of propositions contained within that sentence. Most of David's productions were simple sentences, containing only one proposition. For example,

(1)   drum picture-BEAT (*one beats drums*)   [David VIIIa 5[5]]

However, David did produce a number of more complex sentences, containing more than one proposition. For example,

(2)   knife$_1$-David-knife$_2$-sister (she/mother gave *knife$_1$* to *me/David* and
       she/mother gave *knife$_2$* to *you/sister*)   [David IVa 136]

All the complex sentences containing two propositions that David produced during sessions I through XIII are described in the following sections. I leave aside those complex sentences containing more than two propositions, of which David produced about 150.

Complex sentences

Types of propositions conjoined. My colleagues and I have found previously that the deaf children produced two types of sentences: action and attribute. An action sentence is used to request the execution of an action, or to comment on an action that is being, has been, will be, or can be executed. Sentences (3) and (4) are examples of simple, one-proposition action sentences:

(3)   HIT-mother (*you/mother hit* blocks)   [David IVa 81]
(4)   MARCH-soldier (*he/soldier marches*)   [Chris III 117]

An attribute sentence is one that is used to comment on the perceptual characteristics of an object. Sentences (5), (6), and (7) are examples of simple attribute sentences:

(5)   elephant trunk picture-LONG (*elephant trunk* is *long*) [Tracy I 141]
(6)   black train-black car (*black train* resembles *black car*)
                                                          [David IVa 40]
(7)   picture of soldier-soldier (*picture* resembles *soldier*)
                                                          [Donald IXa 97]

   David conjoined sentences of both types in all possible combinations: action + action, attribute + attribute, and action + attribute sentences. He began to produce action + action sentences earlier than the others (he produced action + action sentences in session I but did not begin to produce attribute + attribute and action + attribute sentences until session II), and he generally produced more action + action sentences (198) then either attribute + attribute (70) or action + attribute (92) sentences. The other five deaf children showed a comparable production pattern (21 vs. 9 and 8, respectively). Sentences (8), (9), and (10) are examples of complex, two-proposition action + action, attribute + attribute, and action + attribute sentences, respectively:

(8)   SIP-cowboy picture-SIP-soldier picture-BEAT (*cowboy* sips *straw*
       and *soldier beats* drum)   [David IXa 105]

(9) BIG-SMALL-BIG-BIG (quarter is *big* and penny is *small*)
                                                        [David Xb 148]
(10) lobster picture-UGLY-DIVE-lobster picture (*lobster* is *ugly* and
      lobster dives into water)   [David VIIIa 177]

Conjoining links between propositions. The two propositions in each of
David's conjoined sentences were linked in one of two ways: temporally
or atemporally. Temporal sentences either described a sequence of events
or requested that a sequence of events take place. The conjunction in
English most appropriate for these sentences is *and then*, or if the child
is suggesting a causal link between the two events, *so that* or *in order to*.
Sentences (11), (12), and (13) are examples of temporally linked two-
proposition sentences:

(11) TAKE OUT-glasses-DON (you/Heidi *take out glasses* and then I/
      David will *don glasses*)   [David VIa 151]
(12) HIGH-FALL-[wait][6] (tower was *high* and then tower *fell* to
      ground)   [David VIa 177]
(13) GO DOWN-EAT[7] (I/David *ate* cookie and then cookie *went down* to
      stomach)   [David Ib 28]

Note that sentence (13) is a causativelike construction in which the actor
acts on a patient which itself then acts (see Bowerman, Chapter 11).
    The second type of link was atemporal; that is, it described events not
ordered in time. Atemporally linked sentences fell into three categories,
the first of which is *coordinate* linkage, that is, sentences that might be
linked by *and* in English. To a certain extent, this is a classification by
default: If the sentence did not describe a situation in which events were
temporally ordered and did not have any of the defining characteristics
of the other two categories of atemporal sentences (discussed next), it
was classified as an *and* sentence. For example, David described the fact
that two Santa toys were strumming two guitars with the following
sentence:

(14) guitar$_1$-STRUM-guitar$_2$-STRUM (Santa$_1$ *strums guitar$_1$* and Santa$_2$
      strums guitar$_2$)   [David VIIIb 4]

    The second atemporal type again is coordinately linked, but with one
of the two propositions (or one element of one proposition) *contrasted*;
such sentences might be linked by *but* or *but not* in English. A sentence
was coded as a *but* sentence if the child described or requested a situation
in which both propositions might have been expected to occur, but in
which only one proposition actually did occur; for example, David produced the sentence "pear-banana [+ss]-ROLL" in a situation in which
either the pear or the banana could be expected to roll toward his leg.
David wanted the pear but not the banana to roll toward him. The [+ss]

in this sentence indicates that a negating side-to-side headshake accompanied the sentence, and we therefore glossed the sentence as "*pear* should *roll* to my leg, but *banana* should not *roll* to my leg." In general, *but* sentences contained either a side-to-side headshake or a two-handed flip out to the sides, both actions conveying negation of some aspect of the sentence.

The third category is *subordinate* linkage, where an element in one proposition is restricted or qualified by the second proposition; sentences in this category are analogous to relativized sentences in English that might be conjoined by *which, who, where,* or a similar word. A sentence was considered subordinately linked if one of the propositions described in the sentence was primary in the situation; for example, David described a picture of a bird pedaling a bicycle with the sentence "bicycle picture-PEDAL-bird picture-WING," and because the primary action in the picture was pedaling, we glossed this sentence as "*bird* who *wings pedals bicycle*." As a second example of subordinate links, David produced:

(15) MOVE-palm-EAT (you/Heidi *move* to my *palm* grape which one
        eats)   [David VIb 34]

to request Heidi to give him a toy grape. In this instance, the giving proposition appeared to be primary because David wanted the giving, but not the eating, to occur in the situation (David was not about to eat the toy grape); the eating act appeared to be signed in order to elaborate on the edibility of grapes in general. In contrast, when David produced sentence (16) to request a hammer so that he could swing it, the giving act did not appear to be primary but was rather one part of a sequence of two actions, both of which were to occur in the situation. Sentence (16):

(16) GIVE-SWING (You/Mother *give* hammer to me/David and then I
        will *swing* it)   [David IVa 82]

is therefore *not* considered to have a subordinate link. Thus a sentence is classified as subordinate if only one of the propositions conveyed in the sentence is the focus of the situation, with the other proposition used to elaborate on an element of the first.

In general, David produced more atemporal sentences (265) than temporal sentences (95), as did the five other children (29 vs. 9). Within the class of atemporal sentences, David produced *and* sentences most often (157), *which* sentences next most often (65), and *but* sentences least often (43); the same pattern is seen in the other five deaf children (12, 12, and 1, respectively). David began producing both temporal and atemporal sentences during session I. However, onset times varied within the class of atemporal sentences: He began producing *and* sentences during session I and *but* and *which* sentences only during session IV.

Shared elements across propositions. In English, when two propositions are conjoined, there is often at least one element of each of the propositions that is redundant or "shared" in both. For example, in the sentence "Mary cut the apples and John ate the apples," *apples* is shared by both propositions. (The second *apples* could of course be replaced by *them*; this overtly marks the property "shared" in surface structure.)

David's complex sentences also had this property of sharedness. Most of his sentences had one shared element (159); however, he did produce sentences with two shared elements (50) or three shared elements (6), as well as some with no shared elements (52).[8] The five other deaf children showed a similar pattern: Most of their sentences had one shared element (19), some had two (6), some none (4); they produced no sentences with three shared elements. Examples (17), (18), (19), and (20) are sentences with no, one, two, and three shared elements, respectively:

(17) key-OPEN-key-PUSH DOWN (you/Heidi *push down key* and then door will *open*) [David VIIa 6]

(18) CLIMB-SLEEP-horse picture (*horse climbed* house and then *horse slept*) [David Va 212]

(19) Lisa [+ ss]-EAT-David-EAT [+ nod]-David (*you/Lisa* will not *eat* lunch but *I/David* will *eat* lunch) [David Vb 73]

(20) [ss]-toy$_1$-village-toy$_2$-village (No. You/Heidi put *toy$_1$* in *village* and you/Heidi put *toy$_2$* in *village*) [David VIIa 51]

An element can be shared across two propositions in one of several ways. It can play the same role in both propositions, as in example (18), in which the horse is the actor of both the climbing and the sleeping propositions. An element can also switch roles, as in the following example:

(21) PUSH-truck picture-CIRCLE-truck picture (I/David *push truck* and then *truck circles*) [David Va 26]

The truck is the patient of the push proposition but the actor of the circle proposition. These two types of element sharing, role-repeated and role-switched, can obviously occur only in action + action sentences, because the shared element either switches from one action role to another action role or maintains the same action role in both propositions. In contrast, action + attribute sentences present a third type of sharing, role-described, in which an element playing a semantic role in the action proposition is described in the second attribute proposition, as in examples (22) and (23):

(22) ROUND-penny-me (you/Heidi give *me* the *penny* which is *round*) [David IXb 21]

Table 2.1 *Actors and patients in sentences with one shared element*

	Shared element	
	Actor	Patient
Then sentences	21	11
And/but sentences	22	12
Which sentences	13	37
Total	56	60

(23)   LAUGH-BEARDED (Santa *laughs* and Santa is *bearded*)

[David VIIIb 6]

In example (22), the penny, which is the patient of one proposition, is described, or modified, by the second proposition. In example (23), Santa is the actor of the first proposition and is described by the second proposition.

David produced more role-repeated sentences than any other type: 112 role-repeated sentences, 20 role-switched sentences, 73 role-described sentences, and 10 sentences with both role repetition and role switching. Comparable numbers for the other five children were 7, 6, 8, and 4, respectively.

Conjoining links and shared elements. Actors and patients, as shared elements, tended to appear in sentences with different conjoining links. The actor was the common element in sentences with one shared element equally as often (56 sentences) as was the patient (60 sentences). However, the actor tended to be the shared element in sentences conjoined by temporal *then* links (e.g., "the HORSE climbed the house and then slept") and in sentences conjoined by the coordinate *and/but* links (e.g., "SANTA laughs and is bearded"), whereas the patient tended to be the shared element in sentences conjoined by subordinate *which* links (e.g., "you/ Heidi give me the PENNY which is round") (see Table 2.1). There is slight corroboration of this pattern from the other five children: The actor was a common element only twice, both times in *and/but* sentences; the patient appeared as a common element nine times, but only in *which* sentences. In sum, David produced two propositions about an actor as often as about a patient. However, the two propositions were structured differently around each case: For the actor, the two propositions tended to be co-ordinately or sequentially conjoined; for the patient, one proposition was embedded within the other.

Underlying structure in complex action sentences

Production probability as a surface measure of underlying structure. In our earlier descriptions of the six deaf children's simple action sentences, my colleagues and I found at least one surface measure, production probability, to reflect the underlying structures of these sentences. Our argument for the relationship between production probability and underlying structure proceeds as follows. We note that a given element, for example, the actor, does not have a constant production probability (the likelihood that an element will be signed when it can be). Rather, we find that, within sentences of the same length, actors who perform (e.g., dancers) are more likely to be signed than actors who alter an object's state (e.g., eaters) and are more likely to be signed than actors who change their own locations (e.g., goers). Moreover, eaters and goers are more likely to be signed than actors who change an object's location (e.g., givers). To explain this variation in surface structure, we have suggested that different structures underlie these different types of sentences; specifically, that two-element (one relational role + predicate) structures underlie sentences about dancing (actor-act), whereas three-element structures underlie sentences about eating (actor-act-patient) and going (actor-act-recipient), and four-element structures underlie sentences about giving (actor-act-patient-recipient).[9] Given the two-sign sentence-length limitation of children in this period, a dancer actor in a two-element underlying structure would be more likely to be signed than would an eater or a goer actor in a three-element underlying structure, simply because the "competition" for one of the two surface slots is increased in a sentence with three elements in underlying structure. By this same hypothesis, a giver actor in a four-element underlying structure would be even less likely to be signed, because competition for the limited number of surface slots is still further increased (i.e., four elements compete in underlying structure). We are, in essence, granting that elements which do not appear in the surface forms of the deaf child's sentences can influence those which do. To sum up the situation for simple sentences, the surface pattern of production probability of the actor (as well as of the patient) appears to reflect the two-, three-, and four-element underlying structures of the deaf child's system: Production probability systematically decreases as the number of elements in underlying structure increases.[10]

Underlying structure in complex sentences: two plausible representations. In considering the deaf child's complex sentences, I will again look to the measure of production probability as a surface indicator of underlying structure. As a first step, I consider some plausible underlying structures for complex sentences. A complex sentence is the conjunction of two propositions. The underlying structure of such a sentence presumably reflects this conjunction. For example, a sentence conjoining one proposition about a soldier beating a drum and a second about a cowboy sipping a straw ought to have an underlying structure of six elements: two actors (soldier and cowboy), two acts (beat and sip), and two patients (drum and straw).

This straightforward heuristic for calculating underlying structure in a complex sentence breaks down, however, when we consider complex sentences with shared elements. For example, consider the conjunction of two requests to Heidi: "You/Heidi open the jar and then you/Heidi blow the wand." In this example, as in the preceding one, there are two actor roles; here, however, one actor (Heidi) is assuming both of these roles. We arrive then at two equally plausible representations of the underlying structure of a complex sentence with shared elements: (1) We could assign the shared element two slots in underlying structure, so that the sentence would have a six-element underlying structure (as in the soldier and cowboy example), or (2) we could assign the shared element only one slot in underlying structure; under this scheme, the sentence would have a five-element underlying structure: One shared actor (Heidi), two acts (open and blow), and two patients (jar and wand).

In terms of the linguistic descriptions proposed to account for conjunction in spoken languages, note that assigning two slots to Heidi in underlying structure is comparable to generating the sentence by sentence conjunction; that is, two complete sentences are generated in underlying structure, and the duplicated element is deleted in a later transformation, "Heidi opens the jar and *Heidi* blows the wand." In contrast, assigning one slot to Heidi is comparable to allowing phrasal conjunction to occur in underlying structure. Phrasal conjunction, as its name suggests, is a coordination of noun phrases, verb phrases, or other nonsentential constituents. When it occurs in underlying structure it allows the conjunction of nonsentential units at an underlying level; consequently, it differs from sentence conjunction, which permits only conjunction of full sentences at this level (see S. Dik, 1968; Dougherty, 1970, 1971; L. Gleitman, 1965; Lakoff & Peters, 1969, for discussions of sentence and phrasal conjunction). Phrasal conjunction in the underlying structure of the example just given would have the two verb phrases (open jar and blow wand) conjoined in underlying structure, so as to create "Heidi opens the jar and blows the wand" at the underlying level. This representation contains no duplicated elements (i.e., Heidi appears only once), and the need for later deletion is therefore alleviated.

In order to determine which of these two hypotheses better describes the representation of underlying structure in the deaf child's complex sentences, we turn again to our surface measure, production probability. As in the deaf child's simple sentences, we expect production probability to decrease systematically as the number of elements in underlying structure increases.

Assigning two slots to shared elements in underlying structure. We first consider the hypothesis that shared elements should be assigned two slots in underlying structure. We calculate production probability, in this instance for the actor, by initially classifying each sentence according to its hypothetical underlying structure. For example, "OPEN-BLOW-wand," glossed as "you/Heidi open the jar and you/Heidi blow the wand," under the two-slot hypothesis has an underlying structure of six elements as already described. We next classify the sentence according to the number of elements explicitly signed in the sentence; this example has three signed elements: OPEN, BLOW, and wand. We then determine the number of times an actor could have been signed (twice in this example) and the number of times the actor actually was signed (none in this example). Actor production probability is calculated for classes of sentences (those having the same number of hypothesized elements in underlying structure and the same number of explicit elements in surface structure; the example being considered is in a class having six hypothesized elements in underlying structure, three explicit elements in surface structure). This probability is derived by dividing the number of times the actor is actually signed by the number of times the actor could be signed in the sentences of a particular class.

Figure 2.1 presents actor production probability for David's complex action sentences, classified according to underlying structure and number of explicit elements. If we assume that production probability reflects underlying structure in complex sentences as it did in simple sentences, and if the two-slot hypothesis is correct, then actor production probability should systematically *decrease* as the number of elements hypothesized in underlying structure *increases*. In addition, as was the situation for simple sentences, actor production probability should increase across the board as the number of explicitly signed elements in the complex sentence increases, but the same pattern with respect to underlying structure should be maintained.

The data in Figure 2.1 do not support these expectations. Actor production probability necessarily increases as the number of explicitly signed elements increases from two to three to four. However, there is no evidence of a systematically decreasing production probability pattern with increasing underlying structures. Thus the hypothesis that assigns two slots to shared elements in the underlying structure of the deaf child's complex sentences is not supported by the data.

Assigning one slot to shared elements in underlying structure. We turn next to our second hypothesis, that shared elements should be assigned

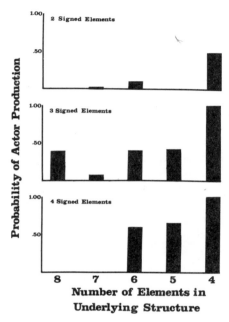

Figure 2.1. Actor production probability in David's complex action sentences as a function of underlying structure assigning two slots to shared elements. Probabilities are based on the total number of actors possible: For 2-signed-element sentences, the number of actors possible in sentences with 8 hypothetical elements was 4; with 7 such elements it was 34; with 6 it was 32; with 5 it was 28; and with 4 it was 8. For 3-signed-element sentences, the numbers of actors possible were 10, 12, 56, 23, and 8, respectively; for 4-signed-element sentences, they were 4, 2, 54, 6, and 4.

only one slot in underlying structure. Actor production probability can be calculated as before, except that now the hypothetical underlying structures are determined by the one-slot hypothesis. For example, the sentence "OPEN-BLOW-wand" would now have a hypothesized underlying structure of five elements: one shared actor, two acts, and two patients (but still would have three explicitly signed elements in surface structure). The number of times an actor could have been signed would now be one (but the number of times the actor actually was signed would again be none).[11]

Figure 2.2 presents actor production probabilities for the data described in Figure 2.1, but this time the sentences are classified according to underlying structures that assign one slot to shared elements. In contrast to our first hypothesis, the one-slot hypothesis results in a pattern that conforms to our predictions: Actor production probability tends to *decrease* as the estimated number of elements in underlying structure tends

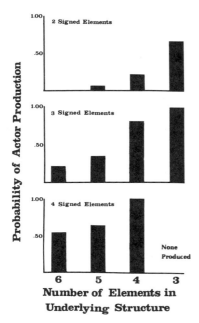

Figure 2.2. Actor production probability in David's complex action sentences as a function of underlying structure assigning one slot to shared elements. Probabilities are based on the total number of actors possible: For 2-signed-element sentences, the number of actors possible in sentences with 6 hypothetical elements was 24; with 5 such elements it was 46; with 4 it was 18; and with 3 it was 6. For 3-signed-element sentences, the numbers of actors possible were 22, 47, 38, and 8, respectively; for 4-signed-element sentences, they were 13, 11, 12, and 0.

to *increase* from three to four to five to six; moreover, this same pattern appears in David's longer sentences with three and four explicitly signed elements, along with the expected across-the-board increase in actor production probability. Thus the generalization that emerged from our studies of the deaf children's simple action sentences (that production probability systematically decreases as underlying structure increases) continues to hold true for complex sentences if one slot is assigned to shared elements in the underlying structures of these sentences.[12]

Patient production probability as a surface measure of underlying structure. A second surface measure, patient production probability, when observed in the six deaf children's simple sentences, was also found to reflect underlying structure. In David's complex sentences, we again find that decreasing patient production probability systematically reflects an increase in underlying structure if underlying structure is formulated by assigning one slot to shared elements. Figure 2.3 presents patient pro-

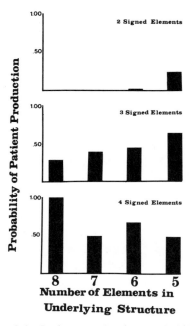

Figure 2.3. Patient production probability in David's complex action sentences as a function of underlying structure assigning two slots to shared elements. Probabilities are based on the total number of patients possible: For 2-signed element-sentences, the number of patients possible in sentences with 8 hypothetical elements was 4; with 7 such elements it was 32; with 6 it was 33; and with 5 it was 8. For 3-signed-element sentences, the numbers of patients possible were 10, 11, 37, and 7, respectively; for 4-signed-element sentences, they were 4, 2, 34, and 2.

duction probabilities for David's two-proposition action sentences classified according to an underlying structure that assigns two slots to shared elements. Figure 2.4 presents the patient production probabilities for the same data classified according to an underlying structure that assigns one slot to shared elements. Although the case is not as strong as for the actor data, postulating an underlying structure with one slot for shared elements better accounts for the patient data (i.e., better upholds the generalizations that production probability decreases systematically as underlying structure increases) than does postulating an underlying structure with two slots for shared elements, particularly for sentences with four explicitly signed elements.

The other five children. When comparable data for the five other deaf children are summed (although the sample is still not large), the hypothesis assigning one slot to shared elements in underlying structure is again

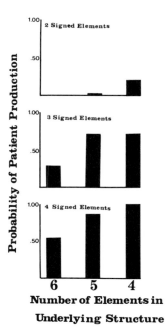

Figure 2.4. Patient production probability in David's complex action sentences as a function of underlying structure assigning one slot to shared elements. Probabilities are based on the total number of patients possible: For 2-signed-element sentences, the number of patients possible in sentences with 6 hypothetical elements was 15; with 5 such elements it was 31; and with 4 it was 9. For 3-signed-element sentences, the numbers of patients possible were 10, 33, and 22, respectively; for 4-signed-element sentences, they were 9, 8, and 6.

supported. If underlying structure is formulated by assigning one slot to shared elements, actor production probability is found to decrease systematically as underlying structure increases from four to six elements (.57 [4/7], .04 [1/25], .00 [0/6] for sentences with two signed elements and .67 [2/3], .50 [5/10], .00 [0/5] for sentences with three signed elements). However, if underlying structure is formulated by assigning two slots to shared elements, this systematic decrease in actor production probability is not found to co-occur consistently with an increase in underlying structure from five to eight elements (.00 [0/4], .21 [5/24], .00 [0/14], .00 [0/2] for sentences with two signed elements and .42 [2.5/6], .38 [3/8], .00 [0/4], .00 [0/4] for sentences with three signed elements). Similar results are found for patient production probability. If underlying structure is formulated by assigning one slot to shared elements, patient production probability tends to decrease systematically as underlying structure increases from four to six elements (.50 [1/2], .56 [5/9], .33 [2/6] for sentences with three signed elements). If underlying structure is formulated by assigning two slots to shared elements, patient production probability does not decrease systematically as underlying structure increases from five to eight elements (.17 [.5/3], .50 [3.5/7], .50 [2/4], .25 [1/4] for sentences with three signed elements).

The units of conjunction. The two-slot hypothesis, which our data do not support, maintains that the underlying structure of every complex sentence contains the conjunction of two full propositions. In contrast, the one-slot hypothesis, which appears to account more satisfactorily for the deaf child's data, allows for the conjunction of parts of propositions as well as full propositions in underlying structure. David did produce a number of sentences conjoining propositions with no shared elements (e.g., "SIP-cowboy-SIP-soldier-BEAT," glossed as "the soldier beats the drum and the cowboy sips the straw"). Sentences of this type must, of course, have underlying structures that conjoin two full propositions. However, David also produced sentences with underlying structures conjoining smaller units, such as two actors ("Heidi-kitchen-David," glossed as "you/Heidi and I/David will go to the kitchen"), two patients ("toy$_1$-village-toy$_2$-village," glossed as "you/Heidi put toy$_1$ and toy$_2$ in the village") and two acts ("[ss]-SWING-CIRCLE AROUND," glossed as "Pinnochio circles around but does not swing"; or "Heidi-STOP-CAPTURE," glossed as "you/Heidi stop and capture the bus"). He also, at times, produced sentences with underlying structure conjoining pairs of elements. For example, he conjoined two acts and patients ("cowboy-RIDE-LASSO," glossed as "the cowboy rides the horse and lassos the steer"), two actors and acts ("TAKE OUT-glasses-DON," glossed as "you/Heidi take out and then I/David will don the glasses"), and two patients and recipients ("knife$_1$-David-knife$_2$-sister," glossed as "she/mother gave knife$_1$ to me/David and knife$_2$ to you/sister").[13] In sum, the production probability data described here suggest that David's system not only allows propositions to be recursive units (that is, units from which we can derive, by the rules of the system, a string which again contains that unit: units that can be derived from themselves) but also allows smaller units, single elements (such as actors) and pairs of elements (such as acts and patients), to be recursive.

Summary

Our results suggest that a deaf child exposed only to a degraded linguistic input can develop a communication system that has the property of recursion, the ability to conjoin two propositions within the boundaries of one sentence. We have found the following properties of recursion to characterize David's communication system.

Conjoining links. Initially, David conjoined propositions that were sequentially linked (*then* sentences) as well as propositions that were atemporally and coordinately linked (*and* sentences). He then began to conjoin propositions that were coordinately but contrastively linked (*but* sentences), as well as propositions that were subordinately linked (*which* sentences).

Shared elements. David's complex sentences contained two propositions that often shared one, and sometimes more than one, element (i.e., sentences in which one element played a role in both propositions). David tended to produce more sentences in which the shared element played the *same* action role in both propositions than sentences in which the shared element *switched* action roles across propositions. Furthermore, in David's sentences, actors tended to be the shared element in temporal *then* sentences and in atemporal coordinate *and/but* sentences; in contrast, patients were shared most often in atemporal, subordinate *which* sentences.

Underlying structure. David's two-proposition sentences appeared to have an underlying structure that took into account shared elements. That is, an element playing two roles, one in each proposition, was assigned only one slot in underlying structure.

   In sum, there appears to be structure in the complex sentences produced by a child with degraded input.

2.3. Comparison to child language developed with normal linguistic input

I have shown that a child with a degraded linguistic input can develop certain properties of recursion in his communication system. I have not yet shown, however, that these particular recursive properties are characteristic of human languages in general. After all, the deaf child's system, although structured, might have very little to do with human language as we know it. In order to assert that recursion as it develops in the deaf child's system is a resilient property of human language, I must show that these particular recursive properties are found not only in the deaf child's system but also in language developed under normal learning conditions. Because my subjects are children and cannot be expected to have developed an adult language, I compare recursion in the deaf child's system to recursion in the language of a child of similar age with normal linguistic input.

Onset. The onset of recursion in the spontaneous utterances of hearing children learning Russian has been set between ages 2;4 and 2;6 (Gvozdev, reported in El'konin, 1973). Brown (1973), observing three children learning English, found two-proposition sentences to appear somewhere between 25 months (Adam) and 42 months (Sarah). When we first observed David at age 2;10, he was already producing a few complex sentences; thus, in terms of onset of conjoined propositions, David's time scale appears to be comparable to that of the hearing child.

Conjoining links. In general, children learning spoken language tend to produce *and* and *then* sentences early in development, as did the deaf child in our study (Bloom, Lahey, Hood, Lifter, & Fiess, 1980; Brown, 1973; E. Clark, 1973c; El'konin, 1973; Menyuk, 1971; W. Miller, 1973). For some speaking children, *but* is a later acquisition (Brown, 1973, p. 30), and for some *which* is acquired still later (El'konin, 1973; C. Smith, 1970).[14] This is, in broad outline, the pattern observed in David. Apparently our deaf child's acquisition pattern of conjoining links is found in some hearing children as well.

Shared elements. Sheldon (1974) has found that hearing children aged 3 to 5 understand English sentences with relative clauses more easily if the shared element is playing the same role in both clauses (e.g., "The dog stands on the *horse* that the giraffe jumps over") than if the shared element switches from one action role to another (e.g., "The pig bumps into the *horse* that jumps over the giraffe"). Goldin and Karmiloff (1970) found a similar result with English-speaking children living in Geneva. Moreover, Goldin (1971) has shown the same preference for role-repeated sharing over role-switched sharing in young children presented with active and passive clauses conjoined by *and*, for example, "The *bear* was licked by the monkey and the *bear* was pushed by the mouse" (role-repeated) as opposed to "The *bear* licked the monkey and the *bear* was pushed by the mouse" (role-switched). I found here that David produced more sentences with role-repeated shared elements. Thus the pattern that we find in David's spontaneous productions is also found in the young hearing child's comprehension of English.

David tended to produce shared actors and shared patients in different types of complex sentences. Specifically, David tended to embed a second proposition around the patient but not around the actor. Children learning English show the same tendency in their spontaneous production (Limber, 1973; Menyuk, 1969). It has been suggested that a clause embedded around an actor in subject position in English is difficult for young children simply because the clause interrupts the flow of the sentence and separates the subject from its verb (e.g., "The man who saw the cat ran away"). However, the fact that David also produced few sentences with propositions embedded around actors suggests that the order of elements in English is not the sole impediment to actor embedding for the young child (see Limber, 1976, for an explanation based on pragmatic factors).

In contrast to his use of the patient case, David tended to produce the shared actor in *and/but* and *then* sentences. There is some evidence that children learning English also focus more on shared actors than shared patients in coordinately linked clauses. In an elicited imitation study of coordinate conjunction, Lust (1977) presented children, ages 2 to 3, with sentences containing different types and different numbers of shared elements (e.g., actor shared, actor and act shared, or in Lust's terms, subject shared, subject and verb shared). The sentence was either a full sentence with the shared element appearing twice in surface structure, or a deleted sentence with the shared element appearing only once. In general, the children were better at imitating full sentences with no deletions; for example, "*Daddy* played baseball and *Daddy* sang a song" was easier to imitate than "*Mommy* cooked the dinner and ate the crackers." However, when imitating the full sentences, the children did occasionally make deletion errors (e.g., they would delete the second *Daddy* in the sentence just given). Deletion or reduction errors of this type were committed in sentences with shared actors but almost never in sentences with shared patients.[15] Thus, in coordinate sentences, the child appears to notice and occasionally to mark (by deletion) the "sharedness" of the actor; in contrast, the child almost never indicates (by deletion) that he might have noticed the sharedness of the patient.

Underlying structure. At present there are no studies designed to investigate the underlying structure of complex sentences spontaneously produced by speaking children. There is, however, some suggestion in the literature that hearing children both imitate (Lust, 1977; Roeper, 1973; Slobin & Welsh, 1973; Thieman, 1975) and spontaneously produce (Limber, 1973; Menyuk, 1969, 1971) sentence conjunction forms earlier than phrase conjunction forms (but see Bloom et al., 1980, whose subjects produced phrasal conjunction forms either at the same time as [three subjects] or before [one subject] sentential forms). That is, as already noted, full forms such as "Daddy played baseball and Daddy sang a song" are produced earlier and imitated with fewer errors than deleted forms such as "Daddy played baseball and sang a song." Slobin (1973) suggests that these facts about complex sentences conform to a universal of child language: "It is easier to understand a complex sentence in which optionally deletable material appears in its full form" (p. 203). Slobin further suggests that this universal, among others, is an outgrowth of one of the operating principles the child brings to bear on the task of organizing and storing language – in this case, the principle that "underlying semantic relations should be marked overtly and clearly" (p. 202).

If this hypothesis is correct, we can infer from the hearing child's preference for the sentential forms over the phrasal forms of sentences having the same meaning that the sentential form is closer to the child's semantic structure than is the phrasal form; that is, that in the hearing child's semantic structure only full propositions are conjoined, so that shared elements must be represented twice. This conclusion appears to be in conflict with my claims about the deaf child's system (that the deaf child's underlying structure is formulated in phrasal, not sentential, form, with shared elements represented only once). The key here is the relation between underlying structure and semantic structure.

2.4. The relation of underlying structure to semantic structure

I have found it necessary to posit two levels of representation in order to describe the deaf child's sign system: a surface level and an underlying level. I have, up until this point, skirted the important question of the relationship between underlying structure and the meaning of the sentence, or what might be called semantic structure. The underlying structures I have posited for the deaf child's simple sentences fit neatly with intuitions about the child's semantic structures for these sentences. There is, in fact, no obvious reason to distinguish underlying structure from semantic structure in the deaf child's simple sentences.

In contrast, there may be good reason to draw such a distinction for the deaf child's complex sentences. For the deaf child's complex sentences, I examined two equally plausible candidates for the underlying representation: (1) structure in which only fully formed propositional units can be conjoined, which thus requires that two slots be assigned to shared elements, and (2) structure in which units smaller than the proposition can be conjoined, which allows one slot to be assigned to shared elements. The second interpretation fits the data better.

It is possible that the underlying structure of the deaf child's complex sentences is isomorphic with their semantic structure. A shared element would then be represented only once in semantic structure, as it is in underlying structure. However, it is equally likely that the underlying structure is an intermediary level of representation between the level of meaning and the level of signs. Under this hypothesis, a shared element would be represented twice in the deaf child's semantic structure. (Note that this description of underlying structure is reminiscent of the description of deep structure in transformational grammar. But it is only reminiscent – there is no claim here that the deaf child's underlying structure has the properties ascribed to deep structure in the adult's grammar.)

One argument in favor of this second possibility is that, when we extrapolate from Slobin's operating principle, shared elements appear to be represented twice in the semantic structure of the hearing child's language. It is not unreasonable to assume that the deaf child's semantic structure is comparable to the hearing child's, and that shared elements are also represented twice in the deaf child's semantic structure. On this assumption, we are led to posit for the deaf child's system an intermediary level of representation (called underlying structure) necessary to generate the surface structure of the child's sentences, in which shared elements are represented only once.

2.5. Resilient and fragile properties of language

We have observed the development of a communication system under degraded learning conditions, and have discovered that certain properties of language can be developed under these less-than-perfect conditions. Specifically, the deaf child can develop a communication system that not only conveys action and attribute propositions, but also conveys relationships among these propositions (e.g., temporal, coordinate, contrastive, and subordinate). Moreover, these semantic notions are expressed through a system with many languagelike properties: (1) lexical items that refer to objects, actions, and attributes; (2) syntactic ordering rules and production probability rules that structure the surface forms of sentences; (3) underlying structures that are systematically related to surface structure; and (4) the property of recursion. None of these properties of language apparently requires a finely tuned linguistic input to develop, and in this sense, all are resilient properties of language.

Further evidence for the resilience of these particular language properties comes from studies of language learning under conditions degraded with respect to time of learning, specifically, the study of Genie's language learning outside the critical period. At this moment in her development, Genie has developed a communication system that conveys both action and attribute propositions, as well as relationships among propositions. Moreover, her system has lexical items, syntactic ordering rules, and the property of recursion (Curtiss, 1977).

In addition, the development of some of these same language properties in normal children has been shown to be relatively unaffected by the normal variations in speech to children. Newport, H. Gleitman, and L. Gleitman (1977) have correlated variation in mother speech to the child at time I with the child's rate of acquisition of certain language properties from time I to time II. They have found that properties such as the number of true verbs in a sentence (in our terminology, the number of characterizing signs in a sentence, a feature that partially determines the number of propositions in a sentence) correlates not at all with variations in mother speech at time I. Thus this property, which roughly corresponds to the concatenation of propositions in the deaf child's system, appears to be relatively insensitive to the small variations in normal linguistic input.

In contrast to these resilient properties of language which, weedlike, appear to grow no matter what the conditions, there are other more fragile properties of language, more like hothouse orchids, which appear to require rather specialized fertilization in order to flourish. Specifically, Genie did not develop properties such as the auxiliary and movement rules in her language, and there is no evidence at the moment for such properties in the deaf child's system. In contrast, the auxiliary is one of the few language properties whose rate of acquisition has been shown by Newport et al. (1977) to be sensitive to variation in mother input. Thus there appear to be certain properties of language (such as the auxiliary) that do not flourish under the degraded learning conditions of either the deaf child or Genie, and that are sensitive to normal variations in linguistic input.

The data from these three studies also suggest that there may be a trade-off between time of learning and the quality of input needed for learning. Newport et al. have shown that the acquisition rate of noun inflections, such as the plural ending, is sensitive to variations in linguistic input and therefore might be taken to be a fragile property of language. Indeed, the deaf children in our study have not yet developed plural endings, and Genie did not spontaneously develop plural markers. However, when given explicit and specific training, Genie did acquire the ability to understand plural endings (Curtiss, 1977). Thus improvements in quality of input might, in certain instances, be able to compensate for difficulties in language learning beyond the critical period.

In sum, my data, in conjunction with other studies on language learning, suggest that the child is predisposed or prepared to abstract a resilient property such as recursion from his linguistic model if one is available or, if a model is not available, to induce recursive properties to describe the world around him. In contrast, the child appears to be less prepared to acquire a fragile property such as the auxiliary structure of English. Without a linguistic model or beyond the critical period he will not develop the auxiliary. Even with a linguistic model, small variations in that model turn out to affect the speed with which the auxiliary is acquired. It therefore appears that different principles of learning are operating in recursion acquisition and in auxiliary acquisition. More generally, I suggest that there may be different principles of learning involved in the acquisition of resilient properties of language and in the acquisition of fragile properties of language. In short, I observe that to learn a resilient property of language, it is best to be prepared – but to learn a fragile property, it is best to prepare the linguistic environment.

Notes

1 Rather than discuss the problem as one of innate vs. learned properties, Mayr has introduced the terms *open* and *closed* genetic programs; a closed program

does not allow appreciable modification during the process of development, whereas an open program does allow for additional input during the life-span of the organism.

2 Genie may, of course, still acquire these properties, because she continues to make linguistic progress; at the very least, however, we can say that these properties are not learned early after the close of the critical period.

3 There is, of course, the possibility that the parents of these deaf children are fashioning a spontaneous gesture system that their children are then imitating; see Goldin-Meadow & Mylander (forthcoming) for comparative data suggesting that this is not the case.

4 The children produced a third type of lexical item that we call *markers*. Markers, such as side-to-side headshakes and nods, are notionally similar to words like *no* and *yes* in English. For the most part, markers are not considered in the analyses presented in this chapter (but see "Complex sentences," in Section 2.2).

5 The following conventions will be used in describing examples:
   1. The example should be read from left to right; the sign that occurs first in the temporal sequence is the first entry on the left.
   2. The referents of deictic signs are in lowercase letters (e.g., drum).
   3. Words in small capitals (e.g., BEATS) are glosses for the referents of characterizing signs.
   4. The sentence in parentheses is an English gloss of the sign sentence. The italicized words stand for those referents which are explicitly signed in the sentence; the remaining words stand for referents that are omitted from the sentence, and that must be inferred from context.
   5. The information in brackets indicates the name of the child who produced the sentence (e.g., David), the session in which he produced the sentence (e.g., VIIIa), and the transcription number of the sentence (e.g., 5).

   Note that any sentence which contains two characterizing signs contains two predicates and therefore is classified as a two-proposition sentence. A characterizing sign identifies an object or action by specifically conveying a relational aspect of that object or action; e.g., THROW (curved palm arcs forward in the air) conveys the "throwability" of an object or the act of throwing. Thus, when two characterizing signs are concatenated, two relational aspects are necessarily conveyed, and the sentence is classified as a complex, multiproposition sentence; e.g., THROW-GIVE, meaning perhaps "you *give* me ball which can be *thrown* by someone," or "you *give* me ball and then I will *throw* it," is a two-proposition sentence and is included in the data base for this study.

   In my report of semantic relation classifications in Goldin-Meadow (1979), I described a class of "static" sentences that were not classified as either action or attribute sentences. A sentence was considered to be static if the sentence could potentially be a comment on the static location or possession of an object. I have classified static sentences along with attribute sentences for my discussion here.

6 *Wait* is a marker in David's system.

7 Note that the order of events conveyed in this sentence does not correspond to the order of events in the real world; i.e., cookies are eaten before they

go down. A sentence was classified as temporal if it described events that followed an ordered sequence in the nonlinguistic situation, even if that real-world order was not mirrored in the sentence.

8 Attribute + attribute sentences are excluded from this description primarily because it was not clear whether to consider the *is* predicate in attribute sentences as a potential shared element. For example, in the structure "Ritchie picture-outside-[flip + ss]-upstairs" (*Ritchie* is not *upstairs* but *Ritchie* is *outside*), *Ritchie* is one element shared in both propositions and *is* is potentially a second. If *is* is considered to be a shared element, all attribute + attribute sentences will necessarily have at least one shared element. Most attribute + attribute sentences did, in fact, have one other shared element in addition to the *is*. Sentences in which we had difficulty determining shared elements are also excluded here.

9 Our earlier reports of the data on underlying structure in simple sentences, (Feldman et al., 1978; Goldin-Meadow, 1979) used "case" terminology rather than "element" terminology. Underlying structure was characterized by the number of cases associated with each predicate. It is, however, a simple matter to convert case to element terminology. Because every simple sentence has one and only one predicate, all we need do is add one unit to our original case assignments. Thus one-case underlying structures become two-element underlying structures, two-case become three-element structures, and three-case become four-element structures.

10 A similar pattern of surface-structure variation is found in the simple sentences of hearing children (see Bloom, Miller, & Hood, 1975) and can also be explained by reference to these underlying structures (Goldin-Meadow, 1979).

11 Repetition was necessarily counted differently for the two hypotheses. Consider the sentence "GO UP-SLEEP-horse," glossed as "the horse goes up to the roof and then the horse sleeps." According to the two-slot hypothesis, the number of actors to be signed is two and the number of actors actually signed is one. For the one-slot hypothesis, the number of actors to be signed is one, the number signed is also one. Now consider what would happen if the horse sign were repeated. For the two-slot hypothesis, the number of actors to be signed would again be two, but the number signed would also be two. In contrast, repetition would not change the calculations for the one-slot hypothesis: The number to be signed and the number signed would remain one. As a general comment on repetition in the deaf child's system, it should be noted that repetition does not appear to distinguish shared elements from unshared elements (those which assume only one role in the two propositions): 12 percent (23/196) of shared elements are repeated, as are 9 percent (55/588) of unshared elements. Thus repetition does not appear to serve as a marking device for shared elements in the deaf child's system.

12 It should be noted that no linguistic description assigns role-switched shared elements (i.e., shared elements that play two different roles in the two propositions of a complex sentence, e.g., patient in one proposition switching to actor in the second) one slot in underlying structure. All generate two full sentences in underlying structure, transform one of the sentences so that the shared element occupies the same position in both sentences, and then delete one of the two role-switched shared elements in a later transformation. The

question of how role-switched shared elements are treated in the deaf child's system is an interesting one, one that bears directly on issues of constituent structure. However, the small number of sentences with role-switched shared elements produced by the deaf children so far does not yet permit us to address this issue.

13 There is disagreement in the literature on which nonsentential units can be conjoined in underlying structure by phrasal conjunction rules. For example, Lakoff and Peters's (1969) rules allow only for the conjunction of noun phrases in underlying structure (comparable to David's conjoining two actors). Dougherty's (1970, 1971) rules allow for conjunction of verb phrases as well (comparable to David's conjoining two acts and patients), but do not permit conjunction across constituent boundaries; e.g., they permit neither the conjunction of noun phrase + verb units (two actors and acts) nor the conjunction of verbs alone (two acts). In contrast, S. Dik's (1968) rules permit conjunction across constituent boundaries on the assertion that sentences like "She greased and I floured the pan" are perfectly grammatical, an intuition not shared by N. Chomsky (1957) or L. Gleitman (1965), in early treatments.

14 But see Brown (1973), who suggest that English-learning children will embed one relation in another (e.g., by means of *which*) before they begin to produce the coordinate conjunctions *and*, *but*, and *then*.

15 Lust argues that actors, or subjects, to use her term, are more likely to be deleted simply because deletion of a shared actor in subject position always involves "forward" deletion (e.g., deletion of *John* in the *second* clause in "John sang and J̶o̶h̶n̶ danced"). In contrast, deletion of a patient in object position involves "backward" deletion (e.g., deletion of *potatoes* in the *first* clause in "John cut t̶h̶e̶ ̶p̶o̶t̶a̶t̶o̶e̶s̶ and Mary ate the potatoes"). The fact that David favors shared actors over shared patients in coordinate sentences suggests that, in addition to "forward" and "backward" deletion, there may be other factors *not* based on the order of elements in English that contribute to Lust's results.

3. Why short subjects are harder to find than long ones

Charles Read and Peter Schreiber

There is every reason to believe that an essential component of language acquisition is learning to recognize the surface phrase structure of sentences. Such a surface "parsing" appears to be necessary in comprehension, for instance; a listener must identify the boundaries of major phrases of a sentence, the type and internal structure of each, and the relations between phrases. H. Clark and E. Clark (1977, pp. 57–72) review the evidence for seven strategies that yield such a parsing, and almost every other recent discussion of comprehension in general has proposed processes with similar outcomes (see J. A. Fodor, Bever, & Garrett, 1974; Kimball, 1973; Massaro, 1975). Accordingly, we assume that a crucial aspect of language acquisition is the building up of tacit knowledge about constituents and their properties, to a level that permits rapid recognition of surface structure.

For this reason we have studied children's implicit parsing of English sentences, using a paradigm in which children demonstrate that they can isolate major surface phrases of various types. This parsing is implicit in the sense that the task requires no conscious formal analysis and no grammatical terminology. The children were 7-year-olds, innocent of any grammatical training. We chose this relatively advanced group of language acquirers because they could perform our task, revealing aspects of their parsing capacity. There are more basic reasons for studying 7-year-olds: Children's knowledge of surface structure takes on special importance when they encounter reading and writing, and evidence is accumulating that acquisition is not complete at this age in significant respects (C. Chomsky, 1969; Roeper, Chapter 9). Our study of parsing has uncovered support for both of these suppositions.

This research was supported by a grant from the National Institute of Education to the Wisconsin Center for Education Research. We wish to thank our research assistants, Jean Walia, Carol Graham, and Theresa Wadden, for their important contributions to the work. We are also grateful to Dr. Clifford Gillman of the Waisman Center on Mental Retardation and Human Development for help in preparing the stimulus recordings, and to the principals, teachers, and students of the Crestwood and Huegel schools in Madison, Wis., and of the McFarland (Wis.) Elementary School for helping us to conduct the experiments. Lists of stimuli and a master table of results for all experiments reported here may be obtained from the authors at the Center for Education Research, 1025 W. Johnson St., Madison, Wis. 53706.

There are several types of cues to surface constituency, including the form-class membership of lexical items (e.g., nouns vs. verbs), the syntactic implications of particular function words and affixes, and prosody. Studies of comprehension have tended to emphasize the lexical and syntactic cues rather than the prosodic. For example, Bever (1970) puts forth some perceptual strategies based on recognizing sequences defined in terms of form classes, such as noun-verb-noun. H. Clark and E. Clark (1977) mention the anticipation of structure appropriate to particular function words, affixes, and verbs among probable comprehension mechanisms. Garrett (1978) suggests that perhaps the "assignment of open-class elements to their appropriate grammatical category is a function of the identification and ordering of closed-class items" (p. 620).

These syntactic cues all depend upon the recognition of particular lexical items or function morphemes. For instance, the English verb *hand* (*Mary handed Bill a dollar*) allows particular syntactic expectations; roughly speaking, it must be followed by two noun phrases or a noun phrase and a prepositional phrase. But to take advantage of this fact, a parser must recognize the item *hand,* must distinguish it from the noun *hand,* and must possess the appropriate lexical information. Prosodic cues are of a somewhat different character. They usually depend not upon the occurrence of particular lexical items, but rather upon the gross syntactic structure of a sentence, its length, and its function (e.g., questions vs. statements).

Separating these correlated properties of surface constituents as they affect performance and acquisition is not easy. Indeed, many of them are interdefined. For example, a speaker of English knows that *the* begins a phrase that must terminate in a noun, but a word is a noun partly because it occurs at the ends of such phrases. Nevertheless, it may well be that the implications of some types of cues are learned earlier than others. One of our goals, then, in studying children's parsing in comparison with that of adults, is to determine the relative salience of various sorts of cues to constituency. If certain cues exert greater influence on children's parsing than others, or if certain cues influence children more than adults, then these are plausible candidates for earlier or more basic roles in acquisition.

In passing, we may note that identifying form-class membership, even with the aid of diagnostic affixes, is a somewhat uncertain matter in English and must be especially so for children. Many high-frequency nouns and verbs in the language are homophones, such as *fly, walk, work, hold,* and *match.* In fact, noun–verb ambiguity is productive in coinages. Creations like *phase out* or *rip off* regularly spread from one class to the other (see Clark, Chapter 13).

Further, inflectional affixes that might indicate form-class membership are themselves often ambiguous. Plural or possessive endings, which help to identify nouns, are homophonic with the third-person singular affix on verbs; thus *matches* is still ambiguous. Likewise, the *-ing* form that signals a main verb in the progressive aspect is homophonic with the affix on present participles and gerunds.

In the case of children especially, one must add to these considerations the effect of encounters with new vocabulary. If 6-year-old children have learned as many as fourteen thousand words, nine new words per day (Carey, 1978, p. 264), then their parsing routines must readily accommodate new words, including familiar-sounding words in a new grammatical role. In short, the fact that pervasive form-class ambiguity is tolerable in comprehension and acquisition shows that, in parsing, form-class identification is supplemented by various other strategies, such as those just mentioned.

3.1. The task

In order to study the salience of particular cues in the recognition of constituent structure, we developed a paradigm in which a person is presented a variety of spoken sentences and is readily trained to isolate and repeat just a particular constituent of each sentence, such as the subject noun phrase. The task is that of repeating selected structures, and therefore it requires the listener to parse the presented sentences, at least partially. In that the listener must manipulate sentences in a novel way, this may be seen as a metalinguistic task, having some properties in common with the interpretation of difficult utterances (L. Gleitman & H. Gleitman, 1970), judgments of syntactic structure (Levelt, 1970), or judgments of well-formedness (deVilliers & deVilliers, 1972; L. Gleitman, H. Gleitman, & Shipley, 1972). Like these other metalinguistic tasks, ours elicits considerable individual variation in performance in some cases. However, our task requires no normative evaluation, no grammatical terminology, and a minimum of explicit awareness of structure.

In fact, isolating and repeating a particular constituent of sentences is not so novel a performance as it might at first appear. Our task has a close analogue in "echo" or confirmation questions where, for instance, speaker A says, "I just saw Professor G—— coming to class on her motorcycle," and speaker B replies, "on her motorcycle?" Likewise, corrections often repeat just the faulty constituent, and answers to *wh* questions generally consist of just the questioned constituent. These everyday performances constitute natural analogues to our experimental task and show that no conscious analysis may be necessary. They also provide one kind of evidence from which constituent structure may be learned.

Our paradigm takes the form of a game called Walrus and Alligator. (We took the name and adapted the procedure from Langendoen, 1970, who suggested a similar technique to demonstrate that speakers follow linguistic rules in forming tag questions.) In our version, the subject (a child, let us suppose) sits down at a table with two adult experimenters, one named Walrus and the other named Alligator. Walrus is to say a sentence of English, and Alligator is to repeat back a special part of that sentence. First the adult Alligator demonstrates, consistently repeating, say, the subject noun phrase of the sentences that Walrus produces. After five such demonstrations, the child is permitted to play the role of Alligator. (From this point on, the adult Alligator functions only as observer.) Besides providing the sentences, Walrus gives consistent feedback, telling Alligator whether Alligator has repeated the right part of the sentence, and if not, repeating the right part. In our experiments using a sequence of, typically, some fifteen sentences, we studied children's learning, their ultimate success in picking out the target constituent, and the nature of their errors. Into this basic scheme we introduced certain variations appropriate to the experiment, as reported in Section 3.3.

3.2. The subjects

The children in our experiments were 7-year-olds from McFarland (Wis.) Elementary School, and (later) 7- and 8-year-olds from Crestwood and Huegel schools in Madison, Wisconsin. Our linguistic adults were paid undergraduate volunteers from the University of Wisconsin-Madison. Clearly, the children and adults differ in respects other than age: The adults represent a population socially and academically selected for university attendance. L. Gleitman and H. Gleitman (1970), among others, have shown that this kind of selection can strongly affect metalinguistic performance. Accordingly, the best we can say is that we have two groups that differ most strikingly in age, but probably in other relevant respects as well.

3.3. The results

Subjects and predicates

First we found that children (and adults) can be trained to repeat the subject noun phrase, even though the children (and some adults) lacked any training in grammatical analysis and had no name in mind for that constituent. For the subject noun phrase as target, our results are displayed in Table 3.1. Overall, the children correctly repeated 57 percent of the subject phrases and 49 percent of the predicate phrases. The adults were tested in a somewhat different way; they repeated subject noun phrases only en route, as it were, to dealing with more difficult cases (described shortly). Nonetheless, 100 percent (26) of our adults reached

Table 3.1. *Percentages of 7-year-olds achieving criterion accuracy in repeating subjects and predicates*

	Subject	Predicate
At least 8 of 15 trials correct	69%	71%
At least 4 trials in a row correct	69%	64%
N	13	14

our criterion of correctly repeating four subject noun phrases in a row. Most (81 percent) did so on their first four tries after the demonstration. Thus most children and all adults reached the criterion and correctly repeated most of the subject noun phrases in the sentences presented. In these instances, the subject noun phrases were deliberately varied in length, complexity, animacy, position of the head noun, and the kind of word that followed the subject noun phrase (e.g., an auxiliary, a main verb, or an adverb). No shortcut strategy that we can think of, other than identifying the subject noun phrase itself, would have led to consistent success. Nor does it appear that the children or adults employed such a strategy, repeating all the words up to the first auxiliary, for instance.

An additional indication that children can learn to identify major constituents is that they succeeded in picking out predicate phrases or verb phrases. (Only three of these fourteen children had participated in the experiment with subject noun phrases three weeks earlier.) Again, we varied the predicate phrases in structure and length: They began with *be* (progressive), *have* (perfect), a modal, or a main verb, and they ranged from three to six words in length. The results, summarized in the second column of Table 3.1, are quite comparable to those for the subject noun phrase. The children repeated 49 percent of the predicates or verb phrases correctly, and 10 children (71 percent) answered more than half of the sentences correctly. The similarity between the subject and the predicate results is not surprising, because in all of our sentences the two were complements: The predicate phrase consisted of everything that followed the subject noun phrase. However, there is some evidence that children may not have simply chosen the complement of the subject noun phrase in order to identify the predicate.

One such bit of evidence is that children tended to repeat the verb phrase, rather than the full predicate phrase, even though Walrus insisted on the latter in giving praise and feedback. That is, the children tended to omit any auxiliary preceding the main verb in the nine sentences that contained surface auxiliaries. The high level of success just reported is true if one accepts either the verb phrase alone or the full predicate phrase

Table 3.2. *Percentages of 7-year-olds achieving criterion accuracy in repeating four-element nonconstituent sentence fragments*

	Four words	Four syllables
At least 8 of 15 trials correct	0%	0%
At least 4 trials in a row correct	0%	0%
N	11	8

as correct. The children actually repeated the full predicate on just 20 percent of the trials overall, and on 39 percent of the trials for the sentences without an auxiliary. These results can be explained by reference either to the integrity of the verb phrase as a psychological constituent or to stress: The main verb was the first stressed word with a full vowel in the predicate phrase. This latter interpretation is not consistent with the hypothesis that children simply chose whatever followed the subject phrase as the predicate unless one is willing to assume that they then forgot the initial unstressed words. An additional respect in which the subject and predicate strategies appeared to differ is reported later on.

Accepting the more generous interpretation of "correct" in this experiment, it is interesting that the results are comparable to those with subject phrases, for the two seem to involve somewhat different requirements. When the target is the subject phrase, one need not listen to the remainder of the sentence at all, once one is certain of having identified the target. When the target is the predicate, however, one must listen to the entire sentence, in order to identify the beginning of the predicate and then to remember it, but the length of time during which one must remember the target is briefer.

Nonconstituents

To place the success with subject noun phrases in perspective, it is important to consider the same task in cases where the target was a nonconstituent of similar length and position in the sentence. We attempted to train children to repeat just the first four words or the first four syllables, for instance. The results are presented in Table 3.2. Though it is difficult to say what constitutes chance performance on this task, it seems unlikely that the children were more successful than one would expect if they were simply repeating a random portion of the beginning of the sentence. Overall, children identified the first four words on only 19 percent of the trials and the first four syllables on only 20 percent; no child succeeded with any consistency. Admittedly, this result is unsurprising, because in

Table 3.3. *Percentages of subjects achieving criterion accuracy in repeating nonconstituent two-word sentence fragments*

	Children	Adults
At least 9 of 18 trials correct	0%	83%
At least 4 trials in a row correct	0%	70%
N	6	23

our attempt to create a nonconstituent, we required the child to count words or syllables, a thoroughly counterintuitive requirement, perhaps.

Next we defined a nonconstituent *in terms of a constituent:* The task was to repeat the last word of the subject noun phrase and the word that followed it, that is, the first word of the predicate. Thus whatever cues the children relied on to identify the subject phrase, along with the ability to identify a single word, would suffice for this task, and yet the target was a nonconstituent. This experiment we carried out identically with both children and adults; Table 3.3 presents the results.

Note that we used very few children (N = 6) in this experiment, as a matter of mercy; they were lost and hated the task. Clearly, neither adults nor children identified the nonconstituent as well as the subject noun phrase, even though the two were closely related. Overall, children responded correctly to 10 percent of the items and adults to 70 percent. The children failed to do better than chance, certainly, whereas the adults varied considerably, from one-third to all correct. Among adults, the individual variation that is typical of difficult metalinguistic performances showed up in this task.

With a different group of children tested subsequently, the nonconstituent target for one subgroup was the head noun of the subject noun phrase and the main verb; for the other subgroup it was the head noun, auxiliary verbs if any, and the main verb. The performance here was even worse than on our previous tasks; of sixty trials, there was exactly one correct response. Again, the number of children (four) was very small because our subjects were clearly frustrated with the task. Overall, it seems fair to conclude that the full subject noun phrase is much more accessible to children than nonconstituents that are comparable in length or related in structure.

This evidence simply supports the widespread conviction that major surface constituents are, in various senses, psychologically real and accessible. It is notable that the subject noun phrase is marked in multiple ways: It is both a syntactic and a semantic unit, ordinarily. In the sentences that we used, the last word of the subject noun phrase was always a noun, either the head noun or the object of a preposition. This noun was sometimes marked by a plural affix. Moreover, a subject noun phrase of more than one word was usually marked off by a characteristic prosodic contour (to be discussed shortly).

Single-word subjects

The experiment resulted in one surprise: Although children succeeded in identifying subject noun phrases of two to six words in length, they utterly failed with single-word subjects. There were two sentences with pronominal subjects in our original list of twenty sentences for the subject-noun-phrase experiment. (In order to discount the effects of these single-word subjects and of possible fatigue, we have reported only the results from the first fifteen sentences in Tables 3.1–3.2.) Of thirteen children, none correctly repeated either of the pronominal subjects. Recognizing this tendency, we substituted one sentence with a single-word lexical-noun subject into our list, namely, *Bees sting people in the garden.* Of the eight children who tried it, none succeeded with this sentence either. This failure with single-word subjects, both pronouns and a noun, suggests that prosody may be a major cue to the identification of subject noun phrases; single-word subjects are typically not marked prosodically, as multiple-word phrases are, but are part of a phonological phrase that includes the main verb.

To evaluate this suggestion, we undertook two further experiments, one to examine the difficulty with single-word subjects more closely and the other to test for an effect of prosody. In both studies, we first presented varied multiple-word subjects of the sort that we had found to be relatively easy for children. When a child had successfully repeated four subject noun phrases in a row, we switched to a new list containing either single-word subjects or misleading prosody (to be described shortly). In that way, we established the concept of repeating the subject noun phrase and then observed the effect of one-word subjects and of misleading prosody. Both of these experiments involved much larger numbers of children, and no child who participated in this second pair of experiments had taken part in the earlier ones.

The single-word subject condition confirmed that 7-year-olds can generally identify multiple-word subject noun phrases in this task. Sixty-four percent (25 out of 39) of the children reached our criterion, correctly repeating four multiple-word subject phrases in a row within the first ten trials. With those who met this criterion, we continued with thirteen additional sentences, nine of them having single-word subjects of various types. The four multiple-word subjects were mixed in to discourage a strategy of simply repeating the first word, and as a check on whether children were in fact adopting such a strategy.

Basically, the single-word subjects indeed proved more difficult, but children could partially overcome this difficulty: They repeated 40 percent of them correctly overall. At the same time, they continued to succeed with the multiple-word subjects (69 percent right); so they were not merely repeating the first word regardless of structure. The presence of an explicit nounlike suffix proved to be irrelevant. With marked plurals (four instances) children got 48 percent correct; with noncount, hence unmarked, nouns (three instances), they got 55 percent correct.

One type of single-word subject continued to pose seemingly insuperable difficulty, however: pronouns. In attempting to identify the two pronouns among our nine single-word subjects, children were right just four times out of fifty tries. Thus the overall 40 percent correct figure is misleading; children correctly identified single-word *nouns* 49 percent of the time, but they identified *pronouns* just 8 percent of the time.

The characteristic error in repeating a single-word subject was to repeat the first few words of the sentence, usually ending at a phrase boundary, rather than to repeat a noun phrase from another position in the sentence. For example, for *He could not answer all my questions,* sixteen out of twenty-two errors (73 percent) consisted of *He could not* or *He could not answer,* whereas only one child said *questions* and one, *all my questions.* Thus both initial position and the notion of a constituent appear to have determined children's responses.

In sum, then, the single-word subjects were indeed somewhat more difficult than the multiple-word ones, but most of the difficulty occurred with the first such subject, understandably, and with the two pronouns, not so understandably. However, when one excludes these three troublesome items, the difference between single- and multiple-word subjects is still statistically significant, $\chi^2(1) = 6.12$, $p < .05$. The difficulty with pronouns cannot be attributed to their lack of nounlike inflections or to their monosyllabic form, because these factors did not influence our results with nouns. The five monosyllabic nouns were correctly identified in 49 percent of the trials and the two polysyllabic ones in 48 percent. In fact, except for the three difficult cases, the success rate with single-word subjects of different types was remarkably uniform (see Table 3.4).

Though pronouns differ from multiword noun phrases in several respects, it is not obvious which property might account for the difficulty in identifying pronouns as constituents. Compare, for example, the following items:

(16) My best friend and I are selling lemonade
(19) We entered the spooky old house through the window

More than half the children identified the five-word subject in the former; none identified the pronoun in the latter. Clearly, the use of *we* in item (19) is not typical of ordinary language use, in that it has no referent in

Table 3.4. *Percentages of 7-year-olds who correctly repeated single-word subjects of sentences (N = 25)*

Subject noun	Percentage correct
Toys	24
Soup	48
We	3
Elephants	52
Soap	56
He	12
People	48
Ghosts	80
Bees	36

the other sentences or in the situation, but of course the same was true for the subjects of all our sentences. Pronouns may in fact need contextual reference more than lexical nouns do, because they appear to lack a meaning of their own. That difference is only a matter of degree, however. *We* has at least the semantic specifications ⟨+ human⟩ and ⟨+ plural⟩, together with the specifications that these redundantly imply, such as ⟨+ concrete⟩, as well as the implication that these humans include the speaker. Thus the pronouns we used were not semantically empty. *My best friend and I* has this same semantic content, plus the specification that the group consists of two people, and the content of *my best friend*. It is not obvious that this difference in degree of semantic specificity should render pronouns inaccessible to parsing.

We are inclined to attribute the difficulty of pronouns not only to their comparative lack of semantic content, but also to the complete absence of suprasegmental marking on pronominal subjects. Supporting the importance of low-level phonetic properties are the results with one particular sentence: *Ghosts come out after dark.* Because of the cluster of consonants ([stsk]) at the subject–predicate boundary, Walrus tended to stress and articulate the word "ghosts" especially carefully. This turned out to be by far the easiest of the single-word subjects (80 percent correct).

We replicated the single-word subject experiment with our linguistic adults (N = 14). One can barely discern a similar pattern, in that *toys*, the first single-word subject, and *we* were the most difficult, but the errors were so greatly reduced that there were no significant differences across subject types. The undergraduates identified 91 percent of our mixed single- and multiple-word subjects correctly.

In the light of the difficulty with pronominal subjects, let us consider again whether there may be a difference between children's strategies for identifying the subject phrase and those for identifying the predicate phrase. Five of our fifteen sentences in the predicate-phrase experiment had pronouns as subjects. Children were no worse in identifying the predicate phrases of these sentences than of the others, which had subject phrases two and three words long. In fact, they were (nonsignificantly) better; the mean number correct was 7.2 versus 6.6. Because entirely comparable groups of children were very poor at identifying pronominal subjects in two other experiments, we conclude that the children probably did not identify the predicate phrase as the complement of the subject, or indeed vice versa.

But does the difficulty of single-word subjects simply reflect a difficulty in identifying a word? On a small scale, we tested whether children of this age have difficulty in identifying a first word regardless of its syntactic function. With five children, 6½ to 7 years old, we played Walrus and Alligator, using simply the first word as target. The sentences were those of our original subject-phrase experiment, with minor changes to eliminate the repetition of certain first words, such as *the;* the children had not participated in any previous experiment.

Every child exceeded our criteria for success; the mean number correct was 14.6 out of 20 trials, with an average of 9.2 in a row correct. Thus a nonconstituent can be identified if it is very short. Interestingly, every child identified the two pronominal subjects correctly, even though these were the same words in the same sentences, and in the same position in the sequence, as in our subject-phrase experiment. Thus first words and pronouns in particular are difficult for children to identify only when the task is to identify a constituent; the difficulty does not inhere in one-word targets per se. This distinction would be predicted if children rely heavily on prosodic cues in identifying the constituent; they could not use such cues to identify single words in general, but would have to rely on lexical recognition. (Also interestingly, the children did not need to be aware of the notion "first word" in order to succeed; four of the five could not name the unit after they had completed the game. Nevertheless, they must have inferred from the demonstration that the target was a single word, for on no trial [total = 100] did any child produce more than one word.)

In an effort to separate the semantic from the prosodic peculiarities of pronouns, we played another version of Walrus and Alligator with a new group of fourteen 7-year-olds. In this version, after the children had learned the game and had reached the criterion with the same ten sentences used to introduce the single-word-subject experiment, Walrus began to produce sentences that formed a connected discourse, a version of the Little Red Riding Hood story. Nine of these fourteen sentences had personal pronouns as subjects. Beginning with the second sentence it was clear that the sentences formed a discourse, and that the pronouns referred to nouns mentioned in previous sentences. Otherwise, the procedure was the same as in other versions: Alligator responded after each sentence, with the subject noun phrase as target.

Giving pronouns an anaphoric referent in this manner dramatically improved their accessibility. Although 7-year-old Alligators had identified the two (nonreferential) pronouns in the single-word-subject experiment only 8 percent of the time, they identified these referential pronouns in 46 percent of the trials. This figure is slightly enhanced by the repetition of particular pronouns, especially *she* referring to Little Red Riding Hood; on the first occurrence of each of the four pronouns, children responded correctly on 41 percent of the trials (excluding the first item with a pronoun, which no child correctly repeated). This proportion is significantly different from the proportion (61 percent) with the five nonpronominal subjects, $t(13) = 2.28, p < .05$; so there remains an effect that we attribute to prosody.

As noted previously, only pronouns appear to require this intersentence reference, and only for children. In the same experiment, with very slightly modified stimulus sentences, adults identified over ninety percent of the subjects, pronominal and otherwise, just as they had in the single-word experiment. Our conclusion is that both relative lack of semantic specificity, requiring anaphoric support, and a lack of phraselike prosody contribute to the inaccessibility of pronouns for children.

As a final test of performance with single words, we examined another group of fourteen children (ages 7 and 8) with the head noun of the subject noun phrase as the target. The internal structure of the noun phrases was again varied. Overall, children responded correctly 43 percent of the time. These children were significantly poorer in identifying the head noun than a comparable group of eleven children was in identifying the full subject noun phrase of the same sentences (65 percent correct: $t(19) = 3.69, p < .002$). Table 3.5 presents additional comparisons.

These results include some sentences with pronoun subjects and some with various kinds of modifiers within the subject. On sentences in which the head noun either was in a determiner-noun structure or was a compound that formed the complete subject, children achieved 63 percent and 82 percent correct answers, respectively. In contrast, on the two sentences with pronoun subjects, children were successful only 11 percent of the time. These results thus further support both the observation that children can identify a word and the claim that prosody plays a major role in the parsing task, because the head noun in the determiner-noun and in the compound-noun subjects bears clear prosodic marking. As one final, intriguing example, we can point to the children's performance on a sentence whose subject was *everyone except me*. Only 14 percent of the children identified *everyone* correctly; of the twelve incorrect responses, eleven (92 percent) were *me*. Although *me* is a pronoun, in this sentence (*Everyone except me hated the story*), it terminates a multiple-word subject and bears major prosodic marking.

Misleading prosody

To test for an effect of prosody more directly, we conducted an experiment using sentences that had misleading prosodic contours near the subject–predicate boundary. Again we introduced our putatively difficult cases after children had identified four consecutive ordinary (multiple-word) subject noun phrases. Again, most 7-year-olds reached this criterion: 71 percent (25 of 35). The misleading sentences were tape-recorded, in order to control prosody; consequently, we presented the demonstration and the initial sentences via recordings as well. As in the single-word condition, there were thirteen test sentences after a child reached the criterion, nine of them having a misleading prosodic contour and the other four having multiple-word subjects and normal prosody.

We constructed the misleading stimuli by tape splicing. For example, we recorded normal pronunciations of the following sentences:

(1)   *Your neighbors shovel* their sidewalk carefully
(2)   *Your neighbor's shovel* got lost in the snow

We then spliced the italicized portion of (2) in place of the italicized portion of (1). The result was a recorded sentence (without extraneous noise from the splice) in which the prosodic contour appropriate to a subject noun phrase fell, misleadingly, on *Your neighbors shovel.* Specifically, the prosodic break appropriate to the last word of the subject noun phrase actually occurred on *shovel,* the main verb. The resulting pattern, though subtle, was noticeably abnormal.

Other stimuli were misleading in the opposite way: The prosodic contour terminated before the end of the real subject noun phrase. Thus we spliced normal recordings of sentences (3) and (4):

(3)   *Our dog's bark* sometimes frightens people
(4)   *Our dogs bark* at the neighborhood cats

replacing the italicized portion of (3) with the italicized portion of (4). Thus the first contour appropriate to a subject noun phrase occurred on *our dog's,* which is not the complete subject phrase.

A third subtype of misleading stimulus also had the prosodic contour terminating before the end of the real subject noun phrase, but here the misleadingly marked pseudo-phrase could not be a subject noun phrase syntactically. For example, we spliced the italicized portion of (6) into the italicized position of (5):

(5)   *When they are* wild, animals are brave
(6)   *Trainers of* wild animals are brave

Thus the pseudo-phrase *Trainers of wild* has a contour (including a noticeable pause) that would normally be appropriate to a syntactic constituent.

With all three types, we were interested in whether the prosody would affect children's (and adults') responses on the Walrus and Alligator task, whether children could overcome any misleading effects, and whether mistakes would tend to follow the prosodic contour. We found a large effect of prosody on children: The 7-year-olds (N = 25) got only 30 percent of the sentences with false contours correct, while continuing to perform at a high level with the four normal sentences (83 percent correct). Moreover, 78 percent of the errors followed the misleading contour; that is, the child's repetition ended where the prosodic phrase ended in the stimulus.

Children were somewhat more likely to repeat incorrectly when the prosodic break came before the head noun (83 percent wrong) than when it came later (56 percent wrong), a finding that suggests an interaction of syntactic and prosodic cues. That is, when children had already encountered a syntactically plausible subject phrase, they were somewhat less likely to be misled by prosody. On the other hand, they were just as likely to make an error when the prosodically marked pseudo-constituent could not have been a noun phrase (e.g., *Trainers of wild*) as they were in the four comparable cases in which it could have been (e.g., *Our dog's*). This observation, however, does not mean that the children were making no use of syntactic or lexical information and were simply following prosody wherever it led. For one thing, *wild* can be used as a noun; it exemplifies another form-class ambiguity in English. Moreover, the children in fact followed prosody less frequently when it marked off a sequence that would not ordinarily be a noun phrase; they made errors just as often, but those errors matched the falsely marked sequence less frequently (55 percent vs. 77 percent). Finally, children did grow somewhat better at ignoring the misleading contour: With the first three sentences, they were right only 26 percent of the time; with the last three, they succeeded 48 percent of the time.

Our adult listeners (N = 12) were far less affected by the misleading contour. They were misled by prosody 18 percent of the time, whereas they were nearly perfect in identifying ordinary multiple-word subjects and single-word subjects after the first item or two. The adults were also more aware of the misleading prosodic contours.

As a further test of prosodic effects, we conducted another experiment in which the stimulus sentences were composed of words that had been recorded separately in random order and spliced together under computer control with 25 msec between words. The resulting sentences thus sounded like lists of words, with a rising intonation on each word. In terms of prosodic cues to syntactic structure, these neutral sentences

Table 3.5. *Percentages of 7-year-olds achieving criterion accuracy in repeating two types of targets under two intonations*

	Head noun only	Full subject phrase	
	Normal intonation	Normal intonation	List intonation
At least 8 of 15 trials correct	29%	91%	37%
At least 4 trials in a row correct	50%	64%	37%
N	14	11	19

were intermediate between the stimuli with misleading prosody and those with normal prosody. As would be predicted if prosody plays a major role in performance on our task, children's success rates were indeed intermediate between those achieved on sentences with normal prosody and those with misleading prosody. The nineteen children who took part in this experiment correctly identified the subject 42 percent of the time. This is better than the success rate on sentences with a misleading prosody, but it is significantly worse than the performance of the children (N = 11) who received prosodically normal versions of the same list of sentences, and who correctly identified the subjects of these 65 percent of the time, *t*(24) = 3.49, *p* < .002 (see also Table 3.5).

It is also interesting here to compare across conditions the results on the sentence *Everyone except me hated the story,* mentioned earlier. In both conditions, correct responses were infrequent, but the response patterns were sharply different. With normal prosody, the responses were nearly always the pronoun *me* when the target was the head noun of the subject, as suggested earlier, but with list intonation, eleven responses (65 percent) were *everyone*, and only four (24 percent) were *me.* This pattern is explicable on prosodic grounds: The pronoun *me* is prominent under normal prosody, as suggested previously, but under list intonation it is equal in prosodic prominence to every other word. Similarly, we can compare across conditions children's performance with *We sometimes go to the zoo on Sunday.* The subject pronoun *we* was correctly identified 32 percent of the time under list intonation, but only 18 percent of the time with normal prosody.

The prosodic cue(s)

In summary, we observed that children have much greater difficulty than adults in learning to pick out single-word noun phrase subjects, even though they are relatively successful in identifying multiple-word phrases. In addition, they have greater difficulty in ignoring the misleading contour created by grafting the prosodic pattern appropriate to one structure onto another. Moreover, their performance on sentences with a list intonation falls between that on sentences with normal prosody and that on sentences with misleading prosody. These observations are consistent with the hypothesis that children rely more heavily on prosodic cues than do adults, even when other cues, such as lexical category membership, are more appropriate.

What might these prosodic cues be, specifically? Of the possibilities – namely, stress, pitch, duration, and pause – one's first candidate must be duration. Investigators such as Martin (1970) and Klatt (1975) have shown that segments tend to be substantially longer when they immediately precede major constituent boundaries. Klatt (1976) reviews syntactic effects on duration, specifically including the subject–predicate boundary. Also, several experiments have shown that speakers use duration at constituent boundaries to distinguish potentially ambiguous utterances (see, e.g., Cooper, Paccia, & Lapointe, 1978; Lehiste, Olive, & Streeter, 1976). In part these findings were anticipated by Martin Joos in a 1957 conference (Joos, 1962). Martin (1972) has shown that rhythm, in the sense of timing between stressed syllables, can play a role in the recognition of hierarchical structure. Nooteboom, Brokx, and de Rooij (1978, pp. 95–8) report a series of experiments on the interpretation of ambiguous Dutch sentences in which syllable lengthening was more effective than pitch change in marking syntactic boundaries. Informally, these investigators also found that pauses alone, without corresponding syllable lengthening, merely resulted in "unacceptable speech."

Phrase-final lengthening appears to be the most salient and reliable of the prosodic cues in our misleading intonation sentences. We measured wide-band spectrograms of the sentences from which our misleading intonation stimuli were spliced. In every instance involving the subject–predicate boundary (fourteen sentences), the last syllabic segment before the boundary was longer than that same segment in the same word when it did not precede the major phrase boundary. For example, the vowel of *dogs* was longer in

(7)   Our dogs bark at all the neighborhood cats

than in

(8)   Our dog's bark sometimes frightens people

Conversely, the /ar/ of *bark* was longer where it preceded the subject–predicate boundary, that is, longer in (8) than in (7). (To achieve reliability, we measured the last syllabic segment together with any sonorant that followed it or glide that preceded it; these are customary units in measurements of durations.) In addition, similar lengthening was apparent in our two remaining pairs of sentences, which involved the boundary between an introductory adverbial clause and the main clause as well as that between the subject and the predicate. Thus nine sentence pairs out of nine showed phrase-final lengthening in eighteen comparisons. Treated as a binomial event with a null probability of .5, this result is highly unlikely to have occurred by chance alone ($p < .001$).

Moreover, these differences in duration were long enough to serve as primary perceptual cues. In the fourteen comparisons of subject versus nonsubject position, the segment at the end of the subject noun was longer by just over 30 msec, on the average, or some 28 percent of the measured duration. These differences exceed those put forth by Klatt (1976, p. 1219) as probable minima for duration to serve as a primary cue, namely, 25 msec, or 20 percent. Also, the observed difference falls high within the range of just-noticeable difference suggested by Lehiste (1970, p. 13) for ordinary (nonoptimal) perceptual conditions, namely, 10–40 msec.

Most importantly, the observed differences in duration appear to have the requisite property of distinguishing between single- and multiple-word subject noun phrases. For example, Goldhor (1976) found that lengthening is greater in the latter type of phrase, even though, as Klatt (1976) notes, this is contrary to speakers' general tendency to produce longer phrases more rapidly. Such a difference appeared in our misleading sample, too, in the pairs (1)–(6) and (9)–(10):

(9) If it's cold, lemonade tastes good
(10) A drink of cold lemonade tastes good

In these sentences, from which a misleading intonation stimulus was spliced, the final vowel of *lemonade* was 25 percent longer in (10) than in (9); that is, it was longer when it was part of a multiple-word subject.

Thus, for the sentences in this experiment, phrase-final lengthening is statistically reliable, is large enough to serve as a perceptual cue, and correctly predicts the distinction between single- and multiple-word subjects. In the same sample of sentences, we observed no such differences in the other prosodic features. As expected, there were no pauses at the subject–predicate boundary that we could detect on the spectrograms. Nor was the stressed vowel of the subject noun usually the greatest in amplitude within the subject noun phrase. In our fourteen comparisons, that vowel was of greater amplitude than any other in the subject noun phrase in only one instance; it was lower in amplitude than some preceding vowel in eight cases and roughly equal to some preceding vowel in the remaining five cases. (We measured relative amplitude from an amplitude section on spectrograms.) Our findings were similar for pitch: On narrowband spectrograms of the actual misleading-intonation sentences, the word marked by the (false) prosodic break typically had a distinct fundamental frequency contour, but these contours were quite varied, including every possible type: fall, rise, fall–rise, rise–fall. Nor was the total amount of frequency change greater than that on other words in the sentence.

We do not suppose that this preliminary evidence, obtained with comparatively crude acoustic measurements of one speaker, settles the issue of what prosodic cues mark off major constituents. It is entirely possible that more thorough studies, using sophisticated measures of speakers under varied conditions, may show that amplitude and fundamental frequency interact with duration. In fact, Streeter (1978) has shown that listeners use both pitch and duration in parsing ambiguous algebraic expressions, such as "(*a* plus *e*) times *o.*" Streeter suggests that the two cues are additive in predicting listener's judgments. We simply report that phrase-final lengthening was a large and reliable contrast in the sentences that we used to create our misleading-intonation stimuli and that no other cue (including form-class membership) was as reliable.

3.4. Alternatives and implications

An alternative interpretation of our results, suggested by Janet Fodor and by Kenneth Wexler, is that the children may have viewed their task as a kind of question–answer session, in which, when the target was the subject, the implicit question was, "Who did it?" or something of the sort. Because *he* by itself is not normally the answer to such a question, this interpretation might account for the difficulty of pronouns. This possibility seems to us unlikely. Because of the variety of sentences that we used, it is difficult to compose a single appropriate question without resorting to a very general "topic" question, such as "Who or what is this about?" In any case, no question that we have thought of accounts for the relative difficulty of single-word subjects in general; *soup* or *elephants* or *people* are perfectly good answers, and yet these were all more difficult for children than multiple-word phrases.

The prosodic account, on the other hand, correctly predicts the increasing difficulty of multiple-word phrases, single-word subjects, and pronouns; pronouns are most likely to form a single phonological phrase with all or part of the predicate; single nouns are less likely to do so, and multiple-word phrases are least likely to do so. It is this gradient, together with the effects of misleading and list intonation, which most directly supports the role of prosody in children's performance.

Notably, the difficulty of pronouns is precisely the opposite of what might have been expected. The word *he* at the beginning of a sentence gives unambiguous structural information; barring *He who . . .* relative clauses, it must be the entire subject noun phrase of a main clause. If children were relying primarily on the syntactic implications of particular lexical items, pronouns should be among the easiest subjects to identify, not the most difficult.

On the other hand, the question-answering strategy may account for our results with the predicate phrase. In these cases, the verb phrase corresponds to the word *do* in a question such as *What was he doing?* With appropriate substitution of subjects and auxiliaries (*What should they do?*), such a question can be constructed for each of the sentences in our predicate-phrase experiment except for one that has *seems* as a main verb. This interpretation would account for children's tendency to repeat just the verb phrase and for the lack of any effect of pronominal subjects. Prosodically, it is predictable that children would use different strategies for the subject and the predicate, for the beginning of the predicate is *not* marked by the kind of prosodic cue that marks the end of the subject. Unless the children assumed that the predicate must be the complement of the subject, they would have to use a nonprosodic strategy to identify it.

The Walrus–Alligator parsing task may involve a degree of metalinguistic judgment; at the least, performance should be facilitated by some syntactic awareness. Nevertheless, our impression is that children and most adults applied little or no explicit analysis of structure. The children, certainly, lacked any grammatical training and could not have named the constituent they were repeating. Surprisingly few of the university undergraduates could do so correctly when asked, saying, for instance, "I never was much good at that sort of thing."

At the opposite extreme from metalinguistic calculation, the task might have elicited too shallow an approach, in which Alligator sought only the first prosodically marked phrase, with no attention to syntax or semantics. But children's and adults' partial success with single-word subjects, misleading and list intonation, and predicate phrases all suggest that they did not adopt this strategy alone. Indeed, their partial success with subject phrases that were quite varied in form and meaning seems to rule out a number of other conceivable ad hoc strategies.

As a more demanding test of how well children can identify subject noun phrases, we played Walrus and Alligator with thirteen more 7-year-olds, using a list of sentences some of which had an introductory adverbial phrase before the subject noun phrase. A sample sentence was

This evening Mom and Dad are going to a party

In such sentences, the subject noun phrase is the second prosodically marked phrase, so Alligator must identify its beginning as well as its end. In this version of the task, children performed well, as usual, on sentences without introductory adverbials: 79 percent correct on six items. Predictably, they did less well on the sentences with adverbials: 47 percent correct on eight items. However, this result shows that they were neither guessing nor repeating just the first prosodically marked phrase.

Not all adverbials proved to be of equal difficulty. With those of more than one word (*Before the movie, After Mary's nap, For her birthday, This evening, Once in a while, Next year*), children were correct on 54 percent of the trials, but with morphologically marked single words (*Luckily, Usually*) they were correct on only 27 percent. Moreover, children did worse with a subject pronoun:

After Mary's nap, she felt better

(31 percent correct) and worst of all on a sentence with both a single-word adverbial and a single-word subject:

Usually spiders don't bite you

(15 percent correct). Nine of eleven errors on this last sentence were *spiders don't bite you;* that is, children tended to identify the prosodically more distinctive boundary. In sum, 7-year-olds can identify medial as well as initial subject noun phrases, though less readily, and the difficulty of single-word phrases is again evident.

Methodologically, these Walrus–Alligator studies illustrate a way of testing the accessibility of various surface (and perhaps nonsurface) constituents without requiring overt grammatical analysis. Thus the technique may be more appropriate for younger children than are judgments of relatedness, the technique used, for instance, in Levelt (1970). We think it constitutes a reasonably natural way of asking children to isolate constituents in order to study the relative salience of various cues to phrase structure. It brings to light the tacit parsing that is an essential part of language acquisition and comprehension.

The Walrus–Alligator paradigm might be applied to a wide variety of constituents and adapted in various ways. Extensions of these initial studies might aim to determine more precisely the sorts of nonconstituents that are accessible, to control more deliberately the prosodic cues and their interaction, and to present more varied predicates, including predicated adjectives, so that *do* is not a possible paraphrase. By extending the technique to embedded clauses, one could contrast such notions as "first subject" with "main clause subject." One might test the suggested development in parsing strategies by working with younger children, but it would evidently be necessary to modify the task, for in a pilot study with fourteen 5-year-olds, only three were able to identify four or more consecutive multiple-word subject noun phrases within ten trials.

Comparison to children's spelling

In previous work, one of us (Read, 1975) analyzed the spelling of children in the preschool years and the primary grades. He found certain frequent patterns of nonstandard spelling; for example, children use the letter *a* to represent the vowel of *bet* as often as 50 percent of the time overall.

In explanation of such patterns, Read hypothesized that children tend to spell alike those speech sounds which they perceive as similar, thus choosing for /ɛ/ the letter that is a standard spelling for /e/ and /æ/. These three vowels are indeed phonetically similar; together they occupy the mid/low front quadrant of the vowel space in English, whether "vowel space" is defined acoustically or articulatorily. In support of this hypothesis, Read put forth several kinds of evidence: Children make other pairings of sounds with spellings (including other vowels) that can be explained by the same principle; even children who do distinguish /ɛ/ from /æ/ in both production and perception nevertheless use the *a* spelling; and nonspelling kindergarten children reveal a perception of these vowel relationships in certain judgmental tasks. Additional evidence of the spelling patterns and their place in a developmental sequence has come from several investigators, working in diverse dialect regions (Beers, 1974/1975; C. Chomsky, 1971a, 1975; Gentry, 1977/1979). The hypothesis that these spellings derive from children's assumption that similar sounds should receive similar spellings has three lines of support: the spellings themselves, the phonetic similarities, and the elicited similarity judgments.

The relationship between this work on spelling and the present research is this: In both cases children appear to have relied on superficial phonetic cues for relatively abstract judgments, namely, for categorizations of speech sounds (in spelling) and segmentation of sentences (in the Walrus–Alligator task). The children involved were of approximately the same age, the age at which they enter school and encounter formal instruction in the written language and other tasks demanding an awareness of language. In addition, the phonetic cues that appear to be salient in each case are outside the awareness of most adults, so that the children's behavior seems obscure. For instance, no literate adult would think of *bat* as a plausible or even explicable spelling for *bent,* though young children create such spellings quite frequently.

Nevertheless, for children of this age to rely on superficial properties of speech sounds when judgments are required seems quite natural. The role of prosody is consistent with the fact that children learn to produce suprasegmental patterns very early, certainly within the first year of life, and before mastering segmental phonology or producing recognizable words. For a brief review of the evidence, see Li and Thompson (1977, pp. 185–6). When children enter school, their primary experience in language has been with its spoken form. They are unaware of the more abstract bases for adult judgments, such as the sound–spelling correspondences and the morphological and historical relationships that underlie English spelling. Similarly, in segmenting sentences into constituents, children may be less inclined to rely on lexical and syntactic cues to phrase structure and more likely to look for phonetic signals. In both kinds of performance, children in the early school years appear to assume that information relevant to segmentation and categorization will be available superficially. We suggest that language development during the school years involves moving toward reliance on more abstract categories and relations.

A relation to reading

The relationship between children's spelling and their identification of constituents is not only that both are tasks in which children use phonetic cues where adults make more abstract judgments. In addition, both may reveal aspects of children's initial approach to reading and writing. We are willing to speculate that children's reliance on prosodic cues in identifying constituents may help explain a particular well-known problem in learning to read.

A significant proportion of beginning readers have difficulty in comprehending what they read, even when they can identify ("decode") the individual words and could comprehend the same sentence if it were spoken or read aloud. Such readers are known as "word callers"; they name the words in the text but fail to comprehend. Interestingly, teachers traditionally use the child's prosodic pattern as a tacit diagnostic tool; when the reading has list intonation, the teacher suspects that the child does not understand and begins to ask comprehension questions.

Comprehension difficulties of this sort are exactly what one would predict, considering that prosodic cues appear to play a major role in children's recognition of constituent structure. That is, if children rely heavily on duration as a cue to structure in comprehending speech, then difficulties ought to arise in beginning reading, for prosodic cues are not systematically preserved in written language. Punctuation represents some such information; periods at the ends of sentences, commas after introductory clauses, and various marks around parenthetical modifiers indirectly correspond to structural information signaled prosodically in speech. But other sentence-internal structure is not represented, including the subject–predicate boundary and embedded clauses, such as complements and restrictive relatives. Indeed, one reason that adults were able to deal with misleading or missing prosodic cues may be that they had learned to read.

Thus, we suggest, one important aspect of learning to read is learning to parse written sentences on the basis of form-class patterns, diagnostic inflections, function words, and punctuation, compensating for the lack of prosodic cues. Because most children do acquire this capacity, albeit some of them with great difficulty, it is worth asking how such learning might take place. Learning to recognize the syntactic structure of the language all over again seems improbable, because many children learn to read in months, not years. Therefore, presumably, a child applies the knowledge of the language that he or she already possesses to the task of parsing without benefit of prosody. Clearly a first grader can bring to bear considerable knowledge of the lexicon and of syntax, though not of punctuation.

Another resource for the beginning reader is experience in organizing speech for production, that is, of planning syntactic constructions and applying appropriate prosodic contours to them. As noted previously, these prosodic signals of syntactic organization are found in children's earliest speech. (Language-acquisition research has relied heavily on such markers in young children's speech in order, e.g., to define an "utterance" at the early stages.) Quite possibly, in learning to read, a child transfers syntactic knowledge previously embedded in production routines to new routines for comprehending written language. For instance, in an analysis-by-synthesis strategy, a child might determine, partly on the basis of context, what a sentence means, then produce the appropriate utterance, and then observe how that utterance is realized in print. One fact in support of such a learning process is that learning to read almost invariably includes a stage of reading aloud, though there are other reasons for this stage as well, such as teachers' need to monitor progress. Also, being read to is a good predictor of children's success in learning to read; this sort of reading, often with very clear or even exaggerated prosodic contours, provides similar opportunities to compare spoken sentences with written ones and to build up strategies for parsing the latter.

A third way for a beginning reader to compare sentences of known constituent structure with their written forms is to produce writing. In writing a sentence and reading it back, a child can gain insight into the indirect ways in which constituent structure is indicated. A child who reads past a phrase boundary in a sentence of his own is likely to notice and correct his mistake. This source of experience supports arguments put forth by Carol Chomsky (1971a, b, 1975) that writing, along with reading, should be part of the primary-school curriculum.

Given some reason to think that performance on the Walrus–Alligator task with misleading or missing prosodic cues might be related to reading comprehension, we looked for such a relation post hoc among our first-graders. Unfortunately, no standardized reading comprehension scores were available for most students. We had to settle for the teachers' subjective global assessment of each student's overall reading ability (high, medium, or low) one year after our Walrus–Alligator experiment. Because only two students were ranked "low," we combined them with the "medium" group. It turns out that the good and the average readers differed significantly in number of correct responses to sentences with misleading intonation, $t(27) = 2.36$, $p < .05$ (see Table 3.6). This result is consistent with our hypothesis, but more specific measures of reading comprehension and other tests of the association with parsing would be

Table 3.6. *Comparison of adults and good and average first-grade readers in number of subject phrases correctly identified despite misleading prosody*

	Adults	Good readers	Average readers
Mean correct responses (of 9)	7.42	3.14	2.07
Standard deviation	1.16	1.41	1.03
N	12	14	15

desirable. Assuming that there is an association, it remains to be learned whether better parsing leads to better reading, or more and better reading leads to better parsing, or some third factor relates to both. We are not aware of more direct evidence linking reading-comprehension difficulty with speech-comprehension strategies, specifically, word calling with reliance on prosodic cues.

At this moment, then, our evidence provides only indirect support for the hypothesis that learning to read involves developing new parsing routines to compensate for the lack of previously relied-upon prosodic cues to constituent structure, but there is ample reason to consider the hypothesis plausible and worth investigating. Studying the relationship between listening–comprehension strategies and reading appears to be one of the directions in which contemporary psycholinguistics may ultimately make a significant practical contribution.

In conclusion, we suggest that of the various cues to surface phrase structure, prosody may have a special bootstrap function. Unlike patterns defined in terms of form classes, or the structural implications of particular function words, affixes, or verbs, phrase-final lengthening is in no sense lexical; it does not require the prior identification of morphemes. In many cases, prosody provides reliable cues to gross surface structure that are accessible with minimal analysis of the acoustic signal and little or no lexical identification. For that reason, these cues may play a special role in the identification of constituent structure and in children's acquisition of that capacity. Perhaps the question of greatest importance is whether some children encounter special difficulty as they attempt to extend that capacity to the comprehension of written language.

4. On mechanisms of language acquisition: Can features of the communicative environment account for development?

Marilyn Shatz

The central puzzle of language acquisition is one of change: How, in a relatively short time, does the young child progress from being a nonlinguistic creature to being a language user, knowing as much about the forms and functions of language as that label implies? Many of the theoretical and empirical efforts made in the field of acquisition research in recent years have been attempts to address this conundrum. The basic approach of such attempts has been to propose constraints limiting possible routes or courses of acquisition, thereby assuring rapid and efficient achievement of the end point. The fact of relatively early and nearly universal acquisition generally supports the argument for a strong set of constraints on the acquisition process.

The proposals can be categorized according to where the primary burden of acquisition is placed, on the child or on the environment. For example, Noam Chomsky (1965) proposed that universal structural principles determine a restricted set of possible variations in language, so that the child's task is only to discover which of these variations apply to the particular language being acquired. In this view, the emphasis is on the child as hypothesis maker and on those inborn characteristics which engender appropriate, restricted linguistic analysis. Another sort of internal constraint that has been suggested involves limitations on the kinds and amount of information about language a learner can utilize. The nature of these limitations has not been completely explicated, but several potential sources have been suggested, involving both perceptual and memorial capacities and strategies for interpreting input (see, e.g., Bever, 1970; Olson, 1973; Shipley, Smith, & Gleitman, 1969; Slobin, 1973). Although this view differs from the Chomskian one in that the proposed

Some of the work on maternal gestures reported herein was done in collaboration with Zoe Graves and was presented at the Boston Child Language Conference, September 1976. The work on maternal repairs was done in collaboration with Rhianon Allen. Mary Hope Lee, Rhianon Allen, and Clare Raizman provided invaluable assistance with transcription and data analysis. I also thank S. Goldin-Meadow, E. T. Higgins, and E. Newport for their comments on an earlier version of the gesture work, and Erika Hoff-Ginsberg, Keith Holyoak, and Lorraine Rocissano for suggestions that improved this paper. The research was supported by NIMH grants R03MH2874 and R01MH30996. Bolt Beranek and Newman assisted in the final preparation of the manuscript.

constraints are derived from considerations of cognitive processing rather than inherent properties of linguistic structure, it again emphasizes the mental processes of the child as a major determinant of the acquisition process.

Other approaches have focused less on the child and more on the role of external elements as important factors in acquisition. For example, Snow (1972) argued that the linguistic input to children constrains the acquisition process by limiting and clarifying the data with which a learner must deal at any given point. However, this view has been criticized on the grounds that the criteria for what constitutes an appropriately simple or facilitative set of input strings for the learner are unclear. By one sort of analysis, at least, the input data do not appear to be linguistically simple (see Newport, H. Gleitman, & L. Gleitman, 1977). More recently, the notion of input has been expanded to include, in addition to the linguistic strings the child hears, other aspects of the communicative setting. In these views external constraints derive from information sources like the nonlinguistic cues found in gesture and joint action as well as the cross-utterance information carried by the sequential relations in discourse (see Bruner, 1975; Ervin-Tripp & Miller, 1977; Macnamara, 1977; Zukow, Reilly, & Greenfield, 1980). Though the basis for constraints has been broadened in these communication- or interaction-based approaches, the emphasis is still on factors primarily external to the child as major determinants of the course of acquisition.

Communication-based approaches typically do not provide explicit characterizations of the mental processes involved in development. Yet the postulation of external determinants does not obviate the need for such characterizations. If the primary question is one of changes in language behavior, then any answer must be expressible in terms of the mechanisms of development – that is, as a description of those mental processes resulting in change. Thus, though it may be implicit, a description of the internal characteristics complementary to an account of external determinants is a necessary component in a theory purporting to explain acquisition.

In this chapter, I consider the description of the child's mental processes implicit in several communication-based approaches to acquisition. I expand on the kinds of environmental support such processes would require in order to account for language acquisition and then present evidence bearing on such an account. The resultant conclusion is that currently formulated communication-based approaches imply too impoverished a view of the child's contribution. In other words, present expansions of the input view to include more than purely linguistic information are still inadequate as attempts to shift the primary explanatory burden of the acquisition process from the internal characteristics of the child to more external factors.

Communication-based approaches to acquisition

Obviously, there are many things that children do learn in the context of communicative interactions, from the specifics of vocabulary items to the general rules governing conversations, such as those for turn taking. However, the issue under consideration is not whether any of the components of communicative competence depend for their acquisition on experience in the communicative setting but whether and how the acquisition of linguistic structure is facilitated by such factors. Thus the claims of particular interest to us are those suggesting how specific conversational devices constrain the way elements of grammatical structure are acquired. In this section, I consider several such suggestions.

There are basically two sorts of dependency relations proposed between the acquisition of grammatical relations and interactional variables. The first involves the laying of grammatical structures onto an already known interactional base. This view is perhaps best exemplified by Bruner's (1975) proposals that case relationships and word-order rules are derivable by analogy from knowledge of joint action patterns on objects. Similarly, other nonlinguistic bases, such as knowledge of the meaning of gestures, have been suggested as systems onto which linguistic structures could be directly mapped (cf. Garnica, 1978; Macnamara, 1972, 1977; Zukow et al., 1980).

The second kind of dependency is one focusing on the sequential structure of conversations. Several kinds of devices have been suggested in this vein. For example, the reformulation sequences frequently found in mothers' conversations with their children have been suggested as candidate facilitating devices, because they seem to highlight the kinds of substitutions, deletions, and movements that can be made on particular segments of sentences (Keenan & Schiefflin, 1976; Snow, 1972).[1] Likewise, Ervin-Trippp and Miller (1977) have suggested that mothers ask questions and then provide answers to clarify the constituent elements of a grammar and hence foster their children's learning. Still other devices like expansions and recasts have been proposed for doing the same kind of work; in these instances, the child's contribution to the dialogue creates the opportunity for the mother to expand and elaborate on an utterance, thus exemplifying allowable structural variations (Brown, Cazden, & Bellugi, 1968; Greenfield & Smith, 1976; Nelson, 1976).

The mapping and dialogic approaches are similar in that the communicative context plays a necessary and important role in both. They are similar, too, in the ways in which the search for evidence to support them has been conducted. In particular, proponents of both approaches have sought examples in the natural environment of the kinds of communicative phenomena their positions require. Because the mapping approach requires that the child have some exposure to and knowledge of nonlinguistic interactional systems, the attempt in this case has been to demonstrate the existence of a rich interactional environment and to give some evidence that the child does indeed attend to and participate in it (see, for example, Bruner & Sherwood, 1976; Ratner & Bruner, 1978, Zukow et al., 1980). Similarly, the dialogic tradition has tried to find examples of the conversational devices that might illustrate syntactic relations and to document their frequency of occurrence in speech to young children. Thus many studies have confirmed that children are exposed to large numbers of question–answer cycles, reformations, expansions, and so on (for reviews of this literature see Newport, 1976; Snow, 1977).

Such research efforts typically result in existence proofs regarding the feasibility of communication-based approaches. That is, they show that the communicative environment does indeed have some characteristics that would be necessary for the approaches to be considered reasonable. The danger in these efforts is that a demonstration of the existence of such phenomena is sometimes taken as evidence that they do in fact bear on the course of language acquisition in an important way. However, this conclusion seems premature for several reasons. For one, a precise description of which aspects of the communicative setting account for which aspects of language has not been forthcoming.[2] Typically, the characteristics of the interactive setting that have been demonstrated have been suggestive only of the way in which the setting might affect acquisition, and only vague connections can be seen between the kinds of facts uncovered and potential benefits for language learning. Secondly, this vagueness has made it very difficult to test whether the discovered phenomena actually do have an influence on learning; there have been relatively few attempts to do so, and those few have produced mixed results (see Hoff-Ginsberg & Shatz, in press; Newport, 1977).

Even more seriously, this vagueness has concealed to a large degree the gaps in the approaches as currently stated. When one begins to examine the kinds of developmental mechanisms derivable from them and then to consider in more detail what the communicative environment would have to look like in order to account for acquisition with just those mechanisms, it becomes clear that further consideration needs to be given to the internal characteristics of the child.

Mechanisms of development

As noted, there are two basic kinds of information postulated to be available to the child in communicative settings. One is the structural facts analogous to interactional or nonlinguistic structures, and the other is whatever relations are revealed by contiguous utterances in dialogue. If these sources of information are implicated in language development, then they must somehow be utilized by the child. However, such information appears to be utilized only via mechanisms that most parallel the kind of relationship postulated. Thus, when analogies between interactive and linguistic structures are proposed, the child is characterized as an analogy maker (Bruner, 1975), because, at a minimum, this description is necessary if the child is to be the sort of organism that can take advantage of the proposed relationship. Researchers in the dialogic tradition have not been as explicit in their characterizations of the child, but presumably the one that is readily inferable in the absence of any other is that of an organism capable of assimilating in rather automatic fashion the exemplified structural relationships. Neither approach, whether recruiting analogy making or automatic assimilation as mechanisms, further constrains the operation of those mechanisms by anything but input data. Apparently, whatever analogies are inherent in the interactional and linguistic data will be made; and whatever structural relationships are exemplified in dialogue will be assimilated. If the mechanisms were meant to operate selectively on the data provided to them, we have not been told how they would do so. The consequence is that the full weight of the course of development rests on the nature of the input.

Taken without qualification, this consequence is clearly not supported by the facts of acquisition already widely known. For example, consider the sort of learning that would be presumed to go on when the child was exposed to sequences like "What does the doggie say? The doggie says what?" The sequence highlights a variety of syntactic phenomena, including *wh* movement, *do* insertion, and morphological rules of number agreement. Yet when children start to use *wh* questions, their productions do not reflect all the relationships revealed in such sequences. It is clear from attempts like "What doggie say?" that not everything available from such input sequences has been assimilated equally. Nelson and his coworkers have suggested that some input sequences may be too complex for children to process because they illustrate too many different relationships at once (Nelson, Denninger, Kaplan, & Bonvillian, forthcoming). They found that simple maternal rephrasings of child utterances, altering just one element, correlated positively with the children's mean length of utterance (MLU) measured several months later, whereas more complex rephrasings did not. However, in the absence of explicit comparisons between the nature of the rephrasings and the actual acquisitions of the child, it is impossible to determine whether a causal interpretation of the correlation is appropriate. Depending on the nature of the knowledge acquired, explanations other than a dialogic one might be feasible as well. For example, the behavior in the "What doggie say?" instance may be more readily ascribable to a bias to attend to the beginnings of utterances than to an ability to assimilate cross-utterance relationships. The data suggest at best, then, that only certain cross-utterance relations can be assimilated, namely, those that are within some unspecified processing capacity of the child.[3] At worst, those cases may be just the ones where other explanations not based on dialogic considerations cannot be readily eliminated. In even the best case, it appears that attention must still be paid to the processing limitations of the child as an additional important constraint on the course of acquisition.

Suppose that we grant that communication-based mechanisms such as cross-utterance assimilation and analogy making do in fact operate in development, if only when the intake system is not overloaded. This fact would still be an insufficient basis on which to conclude that the burden of development is carried by the environment, since such mechanisms in and of themselves are compatible with several different models of development. The difference among the various models is in the nature of the accompanying environment and the additional assumptions that are allowed concerning the internal characteristics of the learner. I consider next two possible models to illustrate this point: the omniscient-mother model, which makes no additional assumptions about the child, and the child-executive model, which does make such assumptions.

Omniscient mothers. If children's capacities consist only of making simple analogies or assimilations automatically, then the environment complementary to those capacities would have the following characteristics. First, the simplest relations and analogies should be presented early on, in order to maximize the amount of input usable by a limited, unskilled learner. As already noted, however, what constitutes simplicity is a difficult problem. For example, it can be defined, as it was earlier, according to the numbers of relations expressed per dialogic unit, without reference to the internal complexity of any of the elements of a particular relation; or the complexity of a given relation may be considered a factor, either because of the degree of formal syntactic complexity inherent in each element of the relation (as in Brown & Hanlon, 1970; or Newport et al., 1977) or because of the number of different relations in which each element can occur in dialogue generally (Shatz, 1979). Whichever notion of simplicity is ultimately found to be the appropriate one, it is commonly agreed that the frequency with which a relation is expressed will affect the probability of learning, if for no other reason than because the more times variably attentive children are exposed to something, the more likely they are to attend to it on at least some of those occasions. Thus some sort of frequency effects on the course of acquisition are commonly expected: Either those relations which occur more frequently are learned first for any given child or those mothers with higher frequencies of a particular relation will produce children who learn that relation before other children do. An ideal early environment, then, would be one in which the frequency of simple relations was extremely high.

Furthermore, in this model, the environment would be expected to change frequently and considerably over time. Because the mechanisms of development operate blindly on available data, the environment must provide fresh input if development is to proceed beyond the learning of simple relations. Moreover, the more finely tuned to the acquisition level of the child the input source is, the more efficiently the mechanisms will operate. The sources of input, then, organize input data on the basis of knowledge about what is simple as well as about what the child already has acquired. With such knowledge, mothers (or to be less sexist, speakers to young children) are virtually the sole mediators of what will get taken up at what point by the developmental mechanisms operating blindly on the data provided to them.

Child executives. In the model just presented, the responsibility for setting and maintaining the rate and order of developmental progress rests on sources external to the child. An alternative to this outside control procedure is to ascribe to the child additional control functions that make the operation of the developmental mechanisms more selective. Suppose, to take an extreme example, that an executive program directs the search for particular kinds of exemplified relations and analogies according to a set schedule. So long as the environment provides examples of the searched-for data, learning will take place according to that schedule. In this model, the environment can be less finely adjusted to the child; it can include both simple and complex relations in roughly equal amounts and it can be relatively stable over time, because the internal program, and not changes in input data, is responsible for maintaining developmental progress. Nevertheless, this model utilizes the same mechanisms of development as does the earlier one. The difference is in the location of the control processes governing the operation of those mechanisms. Because evidence for the mechanisms themselves is not necessarily evidence for any one particular control process, showing their feasibility or even demonstrating their existence is an insufficient basis for claiming that external factors are primary in development. One would additionally have to show that those mechanisms and only those mechanisms operate in a well-ordered, finely tuned environment.

Comparing and testing the models. The question is where to assign the primary burden of development. Although it is likely that both internal and external factors exert some control, the issue still is how and how much each contributes. A more careful examination of just what the external factors provide may reveal the limits of their influence as well as illuminate the role of the internal control processes. In view of this, a series of investigations was undertaken to examine just how closely the communicative environment approaches the ideal presumed in the omniscient-mother model. The data for the studies came from videotaped interactions between seventeen mothers and their children aged 18 to

34 months. I present in Sections 4.1 and 4.2 some of the results of these investigations.

However, before I proceed to the specifics of the work, a word about basic research strategy is in order. Analyzing the environment in ways that bear on the questions raised here is a tedious and time-consuming job. The complexity of contextual and dialogic factors operating in even "low-level" mother–child interactions is apparent to anyone who has spent some time poring over videotapes. To make the task manageable, my collaborators and I examined in detail only selected contextual or dialogic variables that, although not exhaustive of the possible facilitative phenomena that might be found in the communicative setting, were ones that had been suggested in the literature as reasonably likely candidates. In essence, we were looking for an existence proof: If any of the phenomena under investigation proved to function in accord with the description of the environment presumed under the omniscient-mother model, this agreement would constitute evidence that, at least in part, the model was appropriate. If none of these variables so functioned, then, given that they were among the more reasonable ones, it would be less likely that others would be found to support the model. We chose to examine the maternal gestures accompanying speech to children, the form–function relations in maternal questions, and the formal relations exemplified in maternal repair sequences. The gesture study is presented in Section 4.1 in some detail. The studies of questions and repair sequences are included in Section 4.2 as supportive evidence for the conclusion that the communicative environment is considerably less than ideal as a primary determinant of language development.

4.1. The gesture study

As already noted, it has been suggested that the interactional context in which children hear language provides them with a basis on which to map language. One way in which nonlinguistic systems could relate to linguistic ones would be via a commonality of formal properties. Then knowledge of the properties of the more readily accessible system could, by analogy, inform the learning of the structural properties belonging to the more abstract one. However, it has been hard to find evidence for particular structural analogies between interactional systems and languages. For example, the claim that interactive action patterns form the basis for early word-order relations (Bruner, 1975) is not supported by cross-linguistic data (Slobin, Chapter 5; see also Curtiss, Yamada, & Fromkin, 1979, on the general problem of structural analogies between language and action).

A weaker claim on mediational grounds rather than structural ones might be easier to support. Suppose that a child who knew how to assign interpretations to nonlinguistic information observed that language co-occurred with that information. The child might infer that the interpretations based on the nonlinguistic information were appropriate as well to the co-occurring linguistic elements, even when those linguistic elements later occurred alone. Thus linguistic elements could be assigned interpretations, and the ones sharing a history of common co-occurrences with the same nonlinguistic element could be viewed as equivalent. In this way, the interpretable nonlinguistic system could be said to facilitate an understanding of the unknown linguistic one, yet the formal properties of the former need not be parallel to the latter. Of course, it is unclear just how many of the formal properties of the linguistic system could be clarified in this way, but very likely fewer than if structural parallels obtained. Nor is it clear whether this cognitive procedure counts as an instance of analogy making, although it does involve the recognition that elements of one system function as do those of another. Nevertheless, in light of the difficulties with the structural approach, it seems reasonable to examine a speech–context system with the weaker claim in mind.

However, even a weaker view of the speech–context relation requires that several conditions be met before one can conclude that one system facilitates learning of the other. One set of conditions concerns characteristics of the speech–context system: First, the contextual base must relate in a consistent way to some level of language; that is, there must be regular mapping functions between the two domains. Moreover, the mapping functions themselves must be fairly direct and simple ones if they are to be available to the young child. Any more complex systems should be reserved mainly for older, more sophisticated children. The second set of conditions concerns children's understanding and utilization of contextual information. They must somehow understand the contextual system prior to and independent of their linguistic understandings so that the known can potentially be revealing of the unknown. Also, given such a speech–context system, there should be evidence that children do indeed make use of it to enhance their linguistic competence. Currently, no aspect of the speech–context system has been shown to fulfill all of these requirements.

The maternal hand gestures accompanying speech to children are a potential candidate for a component in such a speech–context system because they have been observed to occur frequently in conversations with young children (Garnica, 1978; Shatz, 1978), and children as young as 12 months notice and respond appropriately to at least one gesture, that of offering (Macnamara, 1977). Yet such observations in themselves do not demonstrate that maternal speech–gesture systems generally fulfill the conditions just listed. Therefore, my co-workers and I undertook to examine what gestures mothers use, how gestures relate to maternal speech, and how the system changes with the age and sophistication of the child. We also tried to determine whether children understand gestures, and whether gestures help the children learn something about language. Our results suggest that gestures are not a suitable basis on which to build a linguistic system.

Method

Subjects and procedure. The data presented here are derived from eight of the white, middle-class mother–child dyads mentioned earlier.[4] The children ranged in age from 19 to 34 months and had productive language abilities as measured by their MLUs in words of from one to four words.

All the dyads had been visited in their homes for a get-acquainted play session, during which the child's speech had been audiotaped. These tapes were used to compute an MLU for each child. During a second visit, within a week of the first, the dyads were given a set of toys to play with and told just to act and talk naturally. Videotapes of approximately fifteen-minutes' duration were made of these interactions.

Data analysis. Complete transcriptions of the videotapes included both the speech and the nonverbal behavior of the dyads, along with records indicating the timing of maternal gestures in relation to maternal speech. Two coders independently examined the tapes and transcripts for the occurrence of hand movements that could be intended communicatively (as opposed to incidental movements, e.g., brushing the hair from one's forehead). There was 90 percent agreement between coders on what constituted a gesture and 97 percent agreement on the form of the gestures, to be described shortly.

We then did several analyses to determine the kind of relations that might hold between the gestures and the maternal language. We examined the way gestures mapped onto particular kinds of sentences and their co-occurrence with certain meaning relations expressed in the language. Finding little regularity there, we went on to examine the relation of gestures to the nature of the interactional episodes the mother and child engaged in and the way these relations changed with age. Finally, we examined the way children responded to messages with and without accompanying gestures.

Results

Type and frequency of gestures. Seven basic types of gestures were identified. Two types of gestures served to present objects to the child; these both occurred with the palm perpendicular to the floor and the fingers curled around the object and consisted of either holding an object out in space in front of the child or placing an object near the child, in his or her line of sight. There were two sorts of illustrative gestures: iconic ones, where actions or movements were carried out without touching any objects, and demonstrative gestures, where actions or movements were carried out in part or in full by manipulating or touching objects.[5] There were also points, tapping on objects with an extended finger, and tapping on one object with another object. The most frequent gestures were holding out, demonstrating, and pointing. Over 80 percent of all the gestures occurred during the speaking of a single utterance. Few lasted longer than one utterance, few occurred in combination with other gestures during a single utterance, and few occurred in the absence of an utterance.

Particularly noteworthy is the absence of the fluid, emphatic hand movements normally accompanying flowing speech to adult listeners. Though the mothers were not videotaped talking to an adult, the experimenter did note informally that they used such gestures in their conversations with her. In contrast, the gestures to children were more specific and discrete, confined basically to presenting and pointing at objects and to illustrating actions. On the whole, then, at least one aspect of this speech–context system, the set of physical gestures used with children of this age range, can be described as a simple one, with a small number of discrete gesture types distributed in a one-to-one relation to utterances.

Generally, the proportion of utterances accompanied by gestures decreased with the increasing age and linguistic sophistication of the child, from a high of 43 percent of maternal utterances accompanied by gesture for the youngest child to a low of 23 percent for the oldest. Because age and MLU are highly correlated, partial correlations were used to determine whether the amount of maternal gesturing was more closely related to the age of the children or to their productive linguistic abilities. The partial correlation between the percentage of maternal utterances gestured and the MLU of the child was $-.18$; that with age was $-.59$ and approached significance ($p < .10$).

Mappings between gesture and language. As noted previously, for gestures to be informative in relation to language, there must be a consistent mapping function between types of gestures and some aspect of language. Yet the particular aspect for which gesture might be informative was unknown. Accordingly, we sought to discover the level of linguistic analysis at which particular types of gestures would be found to co-occur consistently with particular linguistic elements. Initially we attempted to discover consistent relations between gesture and grammatical categories. Our first analysis was at the sentence level and showed that gestures tended to occur somewhat more frequently with certain syntactic forms than others. An average of 44 percent of imperatives and 37 percent of interrogatives were accompanied by gesture, whereas only 23 percent of declaratives were so accompanied. However, particular types of gestures or combinations of them were not mapped onto particular sentence types with any degree of consistency. For example, no single gesture type accounted for more than half of all the gesture tokens accompanying a given type of sentence. Thus gestures could not function to differentiate syntactic forms like questions, imperatives, and declaratives from one another.

A second attempt to find a grammar–gesture relation focused on the precise co-occurrence of gestures with the speech expressing semantic relations at the within-utterance level. An average of one-quarter of the gestures occurred as mothers were referring to an object to be named ("What is this?" with the gesture occurring at *this*). About a third of the gestures occurred as the mothers were referring to locations for objects, objects to be located, or both an object and its future location. The remaining gestures occurred with references to objects to be looked at, taken, or acted upon. Though there were no variations among mothers in the distribution of gestures over these various relations, most mothers used gestures at least some of the time with each of them. More important, none consistently mapped particular gestures onto particular relations. For example, a spoken reference to a location for an object (e.g., a car in which to place a doll) could be accompanied by any of several types of gestures, such as pointing to the location, presenting it, or iconically illustrating it by pretending to place something there. Moreover, mothers of younger, less sophisticated children showed no tendency to be more consistent in this regard than did mothers of older children. Because particular gestures did not reliably specify particular semantic relations, the maternal gestural systems could not have functioned to differentiate such relations for the children.

The prior analyses were designed to discover whether the gesture–language mappings were structured in a way that would be useful in determining grammatical categories such as sentence mood or semantic relations. Failing to find sufficient consistency in the mappings at these levels, we turned to a more pragmatic cross-utterance level of analysis. Though analysis at the pragmatic level may seem beyond the scope of my present concern (to investigate the way conversational devices constrain grammar acquisition), it seemed appropriate to pursue a possible relationship at that level for the following reason. Although no direct relation had been found between types of gestures and grammatical phenomena, it was still possible that there was an indirect one. That is, gestures could have been systematically related to some pragmatic phenomena that in turn related to grammatical structures. The first step in uncovering such an indirect system was to determine whether there were indeed gesture–language relations at the pragmatic level and whether those relations fulfilled the conditions described earlier for a useful system. We began with our informal observation that mothers concentrated mainly on two kinds of interactions, one involving object reference and the other activity with objects. Then we used what the mothers were saying as well as what they and their children had been doing to assess the nature of their interactions. The question of interest was whether their gestures could serve to differentiate the kind of interaction (reference or action) in which they were engaging their children.

To address this question we first segmented the transcripts into reference and action sequences or *cycles*, including a catchall category for unclear cases and cases where the mother was doing some third thing (e.g., tickling or hugging the child). *Reference cycles* were segments of interaction involving one or more maternal utterances during which mothers talked about the names of objects or their attributes ("That's a duck"; "That's a smiling face") or tried to elicit such talk from their children ("What is it?" "Is that yellow?"). *Action cycles* were those segments of interaction during which mothers talked about actions on objects as they or their children performed them ("I'll hold it like this") or tried to get their children to perform ("Can you put the blocks in there?"). The basis for isolating a segment of the transcript as a single cycle was that one object or activity was involved. Thus successive unsuccessful attempts to get a child to name two different objects were considered to be two reference cycles. Successive unsuccessful attempts to get a child to name the same object were considered one cycle. A second coder separately segmented two of the tapes and agreed with 75 percent of the original cycle designations with regard to both cycle boundaries and cycle category (action, reference, or other). Table 4.1 presents some examples of cycles.

Action and reference cycles accounted for an average of 80 percent of all the cycles in the transcript. There was no consistent pattern of change with child's age or MLU in the proportion of action to reference cycles, the average ratio being 55 percent to 45 percent. The majority of all the cycles were accompanied by gestures: 67 percent of the reference cycles, 72 percent of the action cycles. Correlations of the age of the child with the proportion of cycle type gestured produced the following results: The proportion of reference cycles accompanied by gesture did not change with age, but there was some tendency for the action cycles addressed to younger children to be accompanied more often by gesture ($r = -.70$, $p < .10$).

In seeking an answer to the question whether gestures are good differentiators of cycle types, we examined the kinds of gestures that occurred over time throughout the two different types of cycles. Even at this cross-utterance level of analysis, we found that the kinds of gestures used did not map in a perfectly consistent fashion to maternal language behavior. This time, however, we found that the mappings between patterns of gesturing and conversational behavior were highly regular, if

Table 4.1 *Examples of conversational cycles*

Reference	
(1) M: What's this?	(holds out block)
C: Man.	
M: Man.	
(2) M: And what's this?	(holds out another block)
C: Umm.	
M: What is it?	(continues to hold out block)
C: Basket?	
M: You know what that is?	" " " "
That is a bag. And it says *malt*	" " " "
on it.	
You know that's something you	· " " " "
find in a barn.	
(3) M: Look, is that a cow?	(holds out block)
	(child takes the block)
M: Is it a moo cow?	(child busy with her activities, ignores mother)
Action	
(4) M: Can you make them slide?	(holds out dolls, demonstrates with toy slide)
	(child watches, takes doll and pushes it down the slide)
M: (They're) sliding!	
(5) M: Can you put the people in the holes?	(pointing at the depression in the merry-go-round)
	(child just looks at hole)
M: Put the people in.	(continues to point)
	(child puts his finger in the hole)
M: Here.	(points to hole)
Put the people in.	(iconic gesture)
	(child again puts finger in the hole)
M: Here.	(mother demonstrates by placing a doll in the hole)
Put this lady in.	
M: Yeah.	(child watches)

somewhat idiosyncratic, for each mother. Thus it was possible in principle for children to make fairly reliable determinations of the topic of conversation using gestural information alone.[6] This conclusion is based on the following analysis.

For each mother, we listed the patterns of co-occurring gestures that accompanied each type of cycle, without regard either to the order in which the gestures occurred or to the repetition of a particular gesture type within any given cycle. For example, pointing in one reference cycle, pointing to and then holding out an object in another, and just holding out an object in still a third cycle were considered three different types of gesture patterns in reference cycles: pointing, pointing–holding out, and holding out. An instance of first holding out an object and then pointing to it later in the cycle was also counted as a token of pointing–holding out; whereas an instance of two points in one cycle was counted as one token of the pointing pattern.

We then found what proportion of each mother's cycles could be differentiated solely on the basis of her accompanying gesture patterns by determining how many of each type of cycle were accompanied by patterns of gesture unique to that cycle type. For each of the mothers of the six youngest children, over 82 percent of their gestured action and reference cycles were accompanied by gesture patterns unique to the particular cycle type. For the mothers of the two oldest children, about 75 percent of their cycles were so accounted for. Thus the data suggest that patterns of gesturing are generally good differentiators of cycle types and that cycles become less differentiable by gesture as children get older.

The first condition on the facilitation of language development by nonlinguistic information appears to have been met: There are consistent, albeit somewhat idiosyncratic, mapping relations between the nonlinguistic and linguistic domains at the conversational level of analysis. The question now is whether the second condition, that the relations be simple enough for a young child to utilize, can also be met.

Are the mapping relations simple? There is no standard metric for determining the complexity of gesture patterns with regard to the ease with which particular patterns are recognized, decoded, or remembered. However, it is reasonable to assume that the complexity of the mapping relations depends to some extent on the variety of gesture types (as described earlier) combining to create gesture patterns for each cycle type, as well as on the number of patterns mapped to each kind of cycle. By both of these criteria, the action cycles were more complex than the reference cycles, with mothers using an average of 4.8 different gesture types in action cycles but only 2.6 in reference cycles, $t(7) = 4.32, p < .01$; mothers used an average of 7 patterns in action cycles and 3 in reference cycles, $t(7) = 3.19, p < .02$. There was no correlation between the number of patterns mothers produced and the age or sophistication of the child. The most patterns produced by any mother were 13 in action cycles and 7 in reference cycles. Thus the numbers of patterns can run distressingly high for some children.

However, the description of the gestural system in terms of the numbers of patterns a mother produces may be misleading in that it ignores possible relationships among patterns. One can write descriptions of each mother's gestural behavior that account for the co-occurrence of gesture types more efficiently than does a list of her patterns. To do this, one considers

Table 4.2 *One mother's gesture-assignment rules and the co-occurrence patterns each generates*

Rules	Patterns
$Ptt\ (Pt) \longrightarrow A$	Ptt
	$Ptt,\ Pt$
$D \begin{pmatrix} B \\ PT\ \ (H) \end{pmatrix} \longrightarrow A$	D
	$D,\ B$
	$D,\ Pt$
	$D,\ Pt,\ H$
$H\ \ \ \ \ (B) \longrightarrow R$	H
	$H,\ B$

Note: Parentheses indicate nonobligatory selection; only one of the items listed vertically therein can be chosen. Pt indicates pointing; Ptt, pointing and tapping; H, holding out an object; B, placing an object; D, demonstrating. A indicates action cycles and R, reference cycles.

which gesture types are obligatory and which optional across various patterns for a given cycle type. The result is one or more *assignment rules* that assign gesture patterns to a cycle type for each mother. The rules are written as generally as possible given the data; that is, they generate all and only those patterns found in that mother's data. Table 4.2 gives an example of the three assignment rules for one mother and the patterns they generate.

Of course, it is not clear that children do take account of co-occurrence relationships across patterns. If they cannot, then assignment rules of the sort proposed would have no reality in the learner's representations. There are few data bearing on how children of this age deal with co-occurrence relations. Hence it seems only reasonable to consider the outcome of organizing the patterns in this way, since we are concerned with the potential viability of all possible representations of the gestural information. Using the assignment rule system, we find that the average number of rules per mother for action cycles is 2.4, higher than the 1.6 found for reference cycles, $t(7) = 3.16$, $p < .02$. A maximum of three rules is needed to describe any mother's behavior in either cycle type. Again, there is no correlation between number of maternal rules and age or linguistic sophistication of the child. Though the assignment rule system requires the capacity to encode cross-pattern relationships, it does involve some advantage for memory. Storing at most three rules per cycle type represents some savings over storing separate patterns, particularly in the action cycles, where the average number of patterns per mother was high. It appears, then, that the mapping relations, although not as simple as possible, are within reasonable range of memory capacity. Moreover, by any measure, the gesture mappings are simpler for reference cycles than for action cycles. However, we obviously cannot claim that the condition on simplicity of mapping relations has been fulfilled. The most that can be claimed is that it has not been clearly violated. Hence it seems appropriate to go on to ask whether children give any evidence of using the relations.

Responses to gestured versus ungestured cycles. We assessed the efficacy of gestures by comparing the children's rates of successful response on gestured and ungestured cycles. To be credited with a successful response, children had to indicate that they knew what kind of response was required even if they did not provide precisely the right one. For instance, examples (1) and (2) in Table 4.1 are both cases of success at recognizing a reference cycle, although the answer in example (2) is not correct. Example (3) is an instance of a failure.

For all eight children, the average success rate for gestured action cycles was 81 percent; for ungestured cycles it was 72 percent. On reference cycles, the success rate was 69 percent for gestured, 61 percent for ungestured. A repeated-measures, two-factor (presence of gesture and cycle type) analysis of variance confirmed that there was no effect of gesture, $F(1, 7) = 1.5$. Action cycles tended to elicit a higher rate of successful response than reference cycles, $F(1, 7) = 4.5$, $p < .1$. As a group, then, the eight children gave no evidence of needing or utilizing gestural cues in order to recognize the kind of interaction they were engaged in and to give some indication of that recognition.

However, the youngest children could be expected to be the ones most dependent on gestural information. We therefore compared rates of response on gestured and ungestured cycles for the three children under 2. Gesturing on action cycles did not facilitate successful responses (62 percent on gestured cycles compared to 56 percent on ungestured); but on reference cycles it appeared to have a considerable effect (53 percent successful responses on gestured cycles compared to 24 percent on ungestured).

Summary. Mothers observed conversing with their children about toys frequently produced tokens of seven types of discrete hand gestures as accompaniments to their speech. However, the patterns of gesturing were found to relate systematically to maternal language only at a cross-utterance level of analysis where the conversational focus on action or reference was determined. Moreover, even at that level, the relations between gesture and language were not especially simple. Nor did younger children appear to receive a generally simpler set of relations than did the older children. Finally, the children revealed little influence of gesture in their response behavior. Only for the three youngest children did gestures seem to be useful, and then only on reference cycles, where the gestural relations were simpler than for action cycles. In light of these findings, we turn now to an evaluation of the role the gesture–language system might play in acquisition.

Discussion

I have argued that for some aspect of the interactional context to be informative for the linguistic system, four conditions must be met: There must be a consistent set of mapping relations between the two systems; the mapping relations must be simple enough for a child to use; children must understand the supposedly facilitating system independent of the to-be-facilitated system; and there must be evidence that children do indeed use the available contextual information in understanding the language addressed to them. In studying the gesture–language relations found during mother–child play sessions, my collaborator and I examined the evidence for all except the third condition.[7] Our results suggest that for children over 1½ years of age the maternal gestural systems directed to them are not likely sources of useful information about grammatical relations. The mapping relations between gestures and the grammatical variables examined are simply not consistent enough to be useful.

At the level of conversational focus, more consistent mapping relations were found. However, an examination of changes in those relations as a function of the developmental level of the child did not indicate much support for the omniscient-mother model. Mapping relations were not simpler or even very different for younger children than for older ones, as would be expected by that model. Further evidence that mothers were not especially sensitive to whether or how their children used maternal gestures comes from considering how frequently gestures accompanied reference and action cycles. Reference-related gesture patterns were somewhat simpler than those for action-related talk, and it was just the gestured reference cycles that showed some response facilitation in the youngest children. Nevertheless, the mothers of younger children were not more likely to accompany reference cycles with gestures than were mothers of older children. Nor did mothers seem sensitive to the fact that gestures were incidental to the likelihood of eliciting an appropriate response on action cycles. All children seemed to be able to respond reasonably well on such cycles, whether or not they were accompanied by gesture,[8] and yet mothers accompanied action cycles with gestures about as often as they did reference cycles. Thus, the frequency of cycles accompanied by gesture was unrelated to the likelihood of the child's responding to such cycles.

Moreover, the apparent maternal insensitivity cannot be explained away on the basis of the gestures' locations within the conversation. If the gestured cycles had required responses more difficult for young children to produce than the ungestured cycles, or if the gestures occurred only late in cycles where children were already evidencing response problems, then one could argue that mothers recruited gestures mainly during cycles unlikely to elicit a ready response from the child. If this were the case, then no correlation would be expected between frequency of gestured cycle and response level. Indeed, the lack of correlation would be compatible with a claim that mothers were very sensitive, providing an additional source of information only when the child needed it. However, gestures were typically spread throughout the utterances in a cycle and were no more likely to occur in the last half of a cycle than in the first half. Moreover, in an earlier study examining responses to directives (Shatz, 1978), gestures did not accompany requests for difficult actions more frequently than for easy ones. Thus there is no evidence that mothers finely paced their production of gestures to the level of the children's understanding. Recall, too, that the frequency of maternal gestures correlated better with children's age than with MLU. This pattern of findings suggests that maternal gestural behavior depends more on a belief that gestures are generally useful to the young child than on a sensitivity to the specific needs and abilities of a child in a given sequence of conversational interaction.[9]

In sum, there is little evidence to support the suggestion that maternal gestures provide a basis on which to map language. The gesture–language relations we found were not especially well suited to displaying important facts about language structure. Nor did the way the gesture–language systems varied with differences in children suggest that the environment was well ordered and finely tuned to a child's progress. It is still possible that gestures do help to focus children's attention and to keep them engaged in an interaction. Just by keeping children in a place where they will attend to the language addressed to them, gestures may have some nonspecific influence on development. That this may indeed be the case is supported by the fact that mothers of blind children appear to have other devices to foster and maintain interaction in lieu of the gestural channel (Urwin, 1979). Nevertheless, while successful attentional devices may be a precondition for language development generally, they have little explanatory value with regard to the question how that development proceeds.

4.2. Further data: questions and repairs in maternal speech

Form–function relations in maternal questions

The gesture study highlights a kind of complexity common to language organization: Elements of different levels of analysis are typically not in one-to-one correspondence to each other. Just as semantic categories do not have unique representations at the syntactic level, so no unique gesture–language relations were found. Although one might argue that the complexity of mappings between one level and another is a crucial language fact to know, it would seem to be an especially difficult one to deal with when first trying to "crack the code." Indeed, the search for language–context relations has been motivated primarily by the desire to make a complex system more accessible. Providing one-to-one pairings between the elements of two systems is one way to do that. Thus, although the two levels may not be so simply related in adult conversation, one might expect the language addressed to young children to utilize more consistent, less complex pairings.

Form–function relations are another instance of the complexity of adult language. It is commonly the case that any one syntactic construction can express more than one sort of communicative function and that a particular function can be encoded by a variety of syntactic forms. For example, interrogatives, besides requesting information, can express requests for action ("Can you shut the door?") or requests for attention ("Do you know what?"). Even mothers use questions for a multiplicity of communicative purposes when addressing their young children (Holzman, 1972). The question of concern here is whether they relate forms and functions in ways that might be helpful to the child. For example, mothers might express relatively few functions to very young children, so that the class of possible functions with which the naive child must deal would be small. They also could simplify the pairing problem by consistently expressing any given function with the most common form found in the language for that function. The usefulness in learning the most common form–function pairings first is obvious: Even a child knowing only a fraction of the possible pairings in the language could assign appropriate interpretations to utterances with a relatively high probability of success. Again, if development is externally controlled, mothers should gradually broaden the range of functions their questions express and the number of forms expressing them as their children indicate an ability to deal with the more characteristic pairings.[10]

To determine whether form–function relations in maternal speech follow this pattern, we examined the questions our seventeen mothers produced and their children's responses to them. The study is reported in detail elsewhere (Shatz, 1979); therefore only pertinent results are summarized here. For these analyses, our subject pairs were divided into two groups: a low one, where the children were two-word speakers or less (N = 9), and a high one, where the children had average utterance lengths of three or four words (N = 8).

For the number of functions expressed by question forms, mothers in the high and low groups did not differ. Most mothers of both groups expressed most of the eleven different functions we observed questions serving. Nor did they differ with regard to the average number of forms used to express those functions. Thus the less sophisticated children had to deal with as large a number of form–function relations as did the more sophisticated children. However, mothers of the younger group used significantly more characteristic form–function pairings than did mothers of the high group. Thirty-eight percent of all their questions formed such pairs, as compared to 25 percent for the high group. Moreover, mothers of low-group children used more of their questions as directives, to elicit action responses from their children, whereas high-group mothers produced relatively more questions requiring informing responses. These results suggest that mothers might have been somewhat sensitive to the response capacities of their children and that they might have tried to provide a reasonable number of opportunities for them to respond successfully. We turn now to the response data to determine whether such maternal sensitivity was well founded.

Low-group children were significantly better at responding to directive questions than to those requiring informing responses, whereas high-group children showed no difference. Indeed, the less advanced children were about as good at responding to directives as were the more advanced children. Thus the greater the extent to which low-group mothers used their questions for directive purposes, the more likely they were to elicit appropriate responses to their questions. However, the children responded well to directives whether or not they were expressed by characteristic pairs, that is, by common forms for such functions. In other words, the children's high rate of appropriate responses to directives does not appear to have depended on the maternal frequency of use of characteristic pairs. Only for one functional category, where mothers used questions to elicit knowledge they knew the children had, did the preference of mothers for characteristic pairs correlate with the children's ability to respond to such pairs. At best, then, it appears that the frequency of form–function pairings is helpful to the children only for certain functions. Again, an unconstrained mechanism of assimilation cannot account for the children's selective use of information.

In sum, the results of the question investigation provide little support for the omniscient-mother model. The form–function relations were not especially simple for unsophisticated children: As many functions and forms per function were addressed to low-group children as to high.

Whereas low-group mothers relied more on characteristic pairs than did high-group mothers, the overall use of characteristic pairs was still less than 50 percent of all questions directed to the low group. Moreover, the usefulness of such pairs for acquiring appropriate response behaviors seems limited to routinized test questions. It is unclear what, if anything, the facilitation of appropriate response behaviors by such routines indexes about the acquisition of linguistic structure. Children may learn rote responses to certain forms that function stereotypically without having to do very much linguistic analysis at all. Though such learning may be very useful for holding one's own in a conversation, it is questionable whether it is a prerequisite to the more complete linguistic analysis necessary for a full understanding of the language. At the very least, a theory relating routine learning to the more abstract level of knowledge is required. It is hard to imagine that such a theory would rely solely on external factors to account for development.

Repairs in maternal speech

As I noted earlier, several researchers have suggested that maternal speech is rich with good examples of the kinds of structural variations allowable in the language. One proposed source of these examples is in the reformulations of prior maternal utterances. Mothers often make such reformulations in the context of repairing an apparent breakdown in communication. Child interlocutors may be slow in responding, respond incorrectly, or not respond at all; in any case, mothers often take such opportunities to foster maintenance of the interaction. One way of doing so is to restructure in some way an earlier utterance. We chose to examine those stretches of conversation which appeared to be *repair sequences* (see Sacks, Schegloff, & Jefferson, 1974) in order to determine more precisely the frequency and nature of structural reformulations within such sequences. Our data base again is the transcripts of the videotaped conversations between seventeen mothers and their children. As in the question study, the data were separated for analysis into two groups of mother–child pairs, a high one and a low one, depending on the linguistic level of the child.

Data analysis. Utterances or sequences of utterances that attempted to reinstate or maintain a message previously ignored or misinterpreted were independently identified in the transcripts by two coders as repair sequences. Of all sequences so identified, 89 percent were selected by both coders. The remaining sequences were discussed and joint decisions concerning their inclusion in the data base were made. The repair sequences were than examined for instances of reformulations, where a reformulation was taken to be any utterance that bore one or more of the following syntactic relationships to the utterance being repaired (i.e., the utterance that generated the repair sequence). A reformulation could involve the deletion of a constituent from the initial utterance, as in "Pick up the ball. The ball"; or the addition of a constituent, as in the temporal reversal of the example sentences. It could also involve within-constituent expansions or reductions, as in "Put the ball in the truck. Put the ball in." Other sorts of reformulations included substitutions of one form for an equivalent one, as in pronominal substitutions, and transformational changes, as in dative movement (e.g., "Give the ball to Mommy. Give Mommy the ball."). Finally, though not strictly syntactic, changes in stress ("What is that? What is *that*?") were also counted as instances of reformulation. Reformulations were categorized according to the kind and number of changes occurring from the initial to the reformulated utterance.

Results. Mothers of more sophisticated children spent about as much time repairing their earlier messages as did mothers of less sophisticated children. An average of 23 percent of all the mothers' utterances occurred in repair sequences, and of those, only an average of 17 percent could be counted as reformulations. Overall, then, only 4 percent of maternal utterances were reformulations. Thus the reformulation device does not provide an especially frequent source of syntactic information for the child. Moreover, mothers of low-group children did not produce significantly more reformulations than did high-group mothers. Nor was there a significant correlation between frequency of reformulation and child's linguistic level.

One might argue that the frequency of reformulation would not be expected to vary with the linguistic level of the child even under the omniscient-mother model, because the reformulation device could be used recursively to present new content. Rather, what would be expected is that the complexity of the reformulations should change in at least one of several possible ways. For one, less sophisticated children should receive more reformulations that are easy to process, that is, utterances in which only one change has occurred from the initial utterance. Second, one might expect that mothers of young children would be inclined to concentrate on only certain kinds of reformulations, rather than providing a wide range of phenomena for their children to have to consider during one short conversation. In fact, neither of these possibilities was realized in the data. Mothers of the two groups did not differ with regard to the number of reformulations that contained more than one change from the initial utterance, with 39 percent of low-group and 36 percent of high-group reformulations being "complex" in this sense. Nor did low-group mothers tend to concentrate on fewer devices than high-group mothers. Almost all made equally frequent use of the kinds of changes just described, with the exceptions of stress changes and movement transformations, which occurred hardly at all for either group.

To summarize, the results of examining repair sequences for syntactical information that could be readily assimilated by the child do not provide a supportive picture for external control of development. For one thing, the information available via reformulations is not especially frequent. Secondly, much of it occurs in potentially difficult-to-process utterances embodying more than a single change from the initial utterance. Finally, there seem to be relatively few changes in the reformulations environment provided for less sophisticated and for more sophisticated children. Without such changes it is unclear how a blindly operating assimilation mechanism could account for continuous growth.[11]

4.3. Conclusion

Currently formulated communication-based approaches to the language acquisition problem imply that only a few unconstrained internal mechanisms are needed to explain language acquisition. Such characterizations of internal mechanisms entail the existence of a complementary rich and highly tailored external environment if they are to account sufficiently for development. I have argued that, even when one expands the learning environment to include nonlinguistic, functional, and dialogical factors, the environment does not seem sufficiently or appropriately structured to control the course of language development as we know it. It appears that additional internal factors must be included in an adequate account of acquisition.

This is not to suggest that broadening our investigation of the input domain results in a futile or uninformative effort. For one thing, knowing what the environment does provide can illuminate the kinds of internal mechanisms that must be assumed. As an example, a close examination of the relationship between linguistic and nonlinguistic factors in the communicative setting raises questions about the general usefulness of analogy as a mechanism, whether such a mechanism operates blindly on an ordered environment or has an internally controlled deployment device. If they exist at all, analogic relationships between linguistic and nonlinguistic systems are hardly transparent or direct; we have little evidence that young children could find and use such obscure analogies.

Second, an examination of the frequency and kind of relationships found in cross-utterance dialogue highlights what we need to know about children's processing abilities. For example, how useful is it for them to observe structurally related utterances occurring closely in time? How many different structural relationships can they work on at once, and what amounts of data about those relationships are optimal (see Wexler, 1978; Chapter 10)? Studying the communicative environment tells us what children have to work with. Studying the children tells us what they do with what they have.

Finally, examining input language in a broader context reminds us how complex communicative behavior is, even that directed to young children. It is perhaps more historical accident than anything else that the relatively early acquisition of complex linguistic structure was taken to be the primary mystery, to be explained in terms of something else that language researchers hoped would be more simple. In fact, how children come to understand others' intentions, nonlinguistic messages, and conversational conventions is a puzzle as well. Surely children's developing understanding of language constrains their growing knowledge of these other systems. Thus it seems reasonable not to try to explain one kind of knowledge in terms of another, but rather to investigate the principles by which children generally acquire various systems of complex knowledge.

Notes

1 Reformulation sequences can illustrate a variety of structural properties of language. For example, (1) illustrates constituent boundaries, pronoun substitution, and noun phrase deletion, whereas (2) exemplifies the dative movement transformation:

   (1)   Put the red ball in the truck. The red ball. Put it in.
   (2)   Give the ball to Mommy. Give Mommy the ball.

2 Newport et al. (1977) have attempted such a description with regard to the grammatical characteristics of maternal speech. However, the domain of information sources of concern to them was primarily the set of sentences spoken to the child. They did not attempt the analysis using a notion of input that included additional sources of information.

3 It is unclear from the preliminary report of the Nelson et al. (1979) data whether children do not profit at all from complex recasts or whether they simply do not profit fully. That is, they may select something from such input to focus on, without being able to process everything. If this is the case, it will be even more difficult to test for direct effects of maternal behavior on acquisition.

4 For two reasons, we analyzed for this study only a portion of the videotapes we had collected. First, the tapes had not been made with the gesture analyses in mind, and on some the mothers' hands were not in view enough of the time for us to draw conclusions. Secondly, the gesture analyses were so time-consuming that we decided to select only a subset of the clear tapes across the broadest age range possible.

5 Some demonstrations were considered co-occurring actions rather than gestures. For example, the action of putting a doll in a truck while saying, "The doll fits in the truck" would not be counted as a gesture unless the doll was immediately removed from the truck.

6 Obviously, the greater the extent to which various adult speakers used gestures in common and consistent ways, the more generally useful a gestural system would be to a young child, because a child with little or no language could "understand" anyone using such gestures. However, attempts to derive general mapping relations across mothers were not successful in accounting for large portions of the data. Hence it appears that any early benefit derived from gesture–language mappings is limited to parental contact. Such a benefit might still serve as an important entree into the linguistic system: Although mothers might use idiosyncratic gestures to signal particular conversational intents, their language co-occurring with those gestures (and consequently coming to be associated with those same intents) seems to be conventional. Children could learn those associations and then be able to generalize their linguistic knowledge to other speakers.

7 Although one might independently want to know whether children understand gestures, that was not our primary interest. Rather, our concern was whether the gestures were used. A positive finding on this issue would entail fulfillment of the third condition. Because the finding was largely negative, we can say nothing about the understanding of gestures in and of themselves.

8 In fact, children of all ages and linguistic abilities responded better on action cycles than on reference cycles, gestured or not. This finding was predictable on the basis of the theory of action response strategies proposed by Shatz (1978). Combined with the finding that reference–gesture relations were generally simpler than action–gesture relations, it casts serious doubt on any position granting a central and general role to gesture systems as essential sources of information in the language acquisition process. If gesture systems were a necessary base on which to map the linguistic aspects of conversational focus, but the action-related gestures had been just too complex for subjects as young as ours to use, then the children should have responded better to reference cycles than to action cycles. Though the action–gesture patterns may indeed have been too complex for the children to use, they do not appear to have needed to use them in any case.

9 More recent analyses of maternal interactions with still younger children than those considered in this study confirm these conclusions. Mothers of 16-month-olds do not produce simpler, more straightforward systems for their children. Indeed, their assignment rules look somewhat more complex than the ones directed to older children (Schnur & Shatz, in press).

10 The characteristics of the form–function pairings were determined from the data on the basis of two criteria: A given form had to be paired with a given function more often than with other functions, and the pair had to occur at least once in the speech of more than half of the mothers in a group. The second criterion assured that any learning based on such consistent pairings would be applicable to a variety of speakers and not just to one's mother.

11 In a dissertation completed since the writing of this chapter, Hoff-Ginsberg (1981) reports that mothers' frequent provision of contiguous sentence pairs with certain kinds of sentence-to-sentence changes is positively associated with the rate of language acquisition, but her work also shows that the usefulness of such input depends on the child's stage of development.

5. Universal and particular in the acquisition of language

Dan I. Slobin

This chapter is the result of cross-linguistic investigation carried out in the United States, Italy, Yugoslavia, and Turkey. Although there are clearly universal processes involved in language development (Slobin, 1973), different types of languages call distinctly different processes into play. It has long been a tenet of our field that all languages should be roughly equal in ease of mastery (e.g., see the exchange between Braine and Bever, Fodor, & Weksel in 1965). I think that, overall, this position is correct. However, there are considerable differences between languages in the relative ease of acquisition of various subsystems. First I examine some predictions of differences in ease of acquisition of various word orders – predictions which do not seem to be supported by cross-linguistic data. Then I explore the general issue of word-order rules and various types of inflectional systems for the expression of underlying grammatical relations, showing that some organizations of linguistic features are more accessible to the child than others. Following this, I show that the acquisition of terminology in a given domain – in this case, that of locative relations – is influenced by language-specific aspects of expression. Finally, after dwelling on ontogenetic linguistic relativism, I return to the search for common features of development.

5.1. The naturalness hypothesis: linguistic categories and word order

The acquisition of language is embedded in contexts of biology, cognition, and social interaction. But linguistic ontogenesis is more than the unfolding of an innate potential, or the mapping of sensorimotor schemata onto speech patterns, or the symbolic crystallization of social interaction. Language reflects the structures of biology, cognition, and discourse in its own ways, and these ways must be discovered by the growing child. The linguistic apriorism of Chomsky has stimulated some psychologists to search for nonlinguistic roots of language development. Although this endeavor is necessary for a full picture, it can lead to an apriorism which attributes the essentials of linguistic structure to the child before he or she has begun to master the grammar of the particular native language.

This new apriorism is based on claims of "naturalness" in the means used by human languages to map underlying'semantic and pragmatic content onto surface utterances. Many of the naturalness arguments are appealing and convincing, and I certainly do not wish to challenge the position that language reflects deep-seated ways of thinking in nonarbitrary fashion. It is indisputable that children are aided in acquisition by the fact that the system was evolved by minds like their own, in adaptation to the human situation. And prelinguistic cognitive and social development obviously prepares children for the acquisition of the native language. But it does not provide the key to the particular categories and structures of that language. Cross-linguistic research cannot help but make one attentive to the diversity of human languages and to the varying acquisition tasks posed by languages of different sorts. My aim is to add to the constellation of nonlinguistic factors the fact that language, in itself, constitutes a complex body of knowledge which must be discovered and structured on its own terms.

The naturalness argument, as presently applied to child language, has two facets: the claim that semantic categories are given in cognition, arising from sensorimotor intelligence and mother–child interaction; and the claim that word order is a natural reflection of the order of thought. The categorization argument has an older history, and was already objected to by Bloom in *One Word at a Time* (1973). Towards the end of that monograph she concerns herself with "rich interpretation" at the one-word stage, and states that "describing relationships within the situation in which the child speaks is different from attributing to the child the linguistic knowledge for talking about such relationships" (p. 137). The issue is whether the categories used in linguistic description are the same as those used in cognizing the world. This position has been taken, with varying degrees of strength, by a number of investigators. For example, Roger Brown, in *A first language* (1973), presents the position in Piagetian terms:

> In sum, I think that the first sentences express the construction of reality which is the terminal achievement of sensori-motor intelligence (the permanence of form and substance of immediate objects) and the structure of immediate space and time does not need to be formed all over again on the plane of representation. Representation starts with just those meanings that are most available to it, propositions about actions, schemas involving agents and objects, assertions of nonexistence, recurrence, location, and so on. [P. 200]

(Brown goes on, however, to clearly distinguish meanings from grammatical relations, leaving open for us the problem of the acquisition of the formal means of grammatical expression.)

Jerome Bruner (1975) seeks to derive Fillmorean case categories from the structure of interaction: "What is universal is the structure of human action in infancy which corresponds to the structure of universal case categories. It is the infant's success in achieving joint action (or the mother's success, for that matter) that virtually leads him into language" (p. 6).

Schlesinger (1977b) has posed thoughtful arguments against strong versions of what he calls "cognitive determinism." He deals primarily with the problem of meaning categories, and points out that, beyond cognitive skills of interpretation, "language learning depends in addition on a categorization of objects and events, which is needed solely for the purpose of speaking and understanding speech" (p. 155).

Shortly I will present my own examples suggesting that language learning involves more than the direct expression of early cognition. First, however, let us consider the other facet of the naturalness argument: the claim that word order reflects the order of thinking. Because so much of our work has dealt with one- and two-word utterances, this argument has not yet received detailed attention (though Braine, 1976, and others have presented evidence of deviations from strict word order at the early stages).

There are at least three major approaches to the word-order argument, coming from spokesmen who, in earlier years, represented quite divergent psycholinguistic positions. All three of them make predictions about both word order in early speech and the relative ease of acquisition of different types of languages – predictions which are not supported by cross-linguistic developmental data.

Bruner (1975) bases his theory of word order on the same grounds as his theory of semantic categories – namely, mother–infant interaction: "The argument has been that the structures of action and attention provide bench-marks for interpreting the order-rules in initial grammar: that a concept of agent–action–object–recipient at the pre-linguistic level aids the child in grasping the linguistic meaning of appropriately ordered utterances involving such case categories as agentive, action, object, indirect object and so forth" (p. 17). The implication seems to be that early speech should follow an order of "agent-action-object-recipient," and that languages which do not adhere to this order in their basic sentence form, or that languages which present the child with a variety of word orders, should be more difficult to acquire. Neither of these implications can be supported by developmental psycholinguistic evidence.

David McNeill (1975) argues from a model of sensorimotor cognition: "When the cognitive schema has an intrinsic sequence, the utterance will tend to be produced in the same sequence" (1975, p. 367). "Intrinsic sequences" are sometimes based on the order of action (e.g., "object" precedes "location" in dynamic contexts, because the object moves to a location; but there is no intrinsic order to "object" and "location" in static contexts, where the two elements are at rest in a single location). Other intrinsic sequences come from mental processes. For example, "actor" precedes "action" or "object" because the speaker experiences his own intention to act before the act is carried out. On this argument, McNeill claims that the actor-action sequence should never be reversed if the child speaker is the actor, because he must be aware of his own intentions; but reversals may occur when he speaks of the actions of other actors, because he may fail to take account of the intentionality of others. Again, a number of specific word-order predictions are made, in this case favoring the acquisition of SVO and SOV languages, and disallowing early word orders which are not consonant with "intrinsic sequences."[1]

Charles Osgood bases his arguments for natural word order on perception: "The natural order of constituents will correspond to that most frequently experienced in pre-linguistic, perception-based comprehending" (Osgood & Bock, 1977). On this argument, actors occur first in sentences because animate, human, and moving beings most readily attract attention. Osgood and Tanz (1977) make very strong (and false) language-specific predictions: "Our intuition about the nature of simple cognitions is . . . that they have an SVO structure" (p. 539). And, in regard to acquisition: "Regardless of dominant-order type, in the process of language development in children there is initially a relatively fixed SVO ordering in 'sentence' productions" (p. 540).

Putting together these various cognitively and perceptually based theories, the task of discovering the grammar of one's language amounts to scanning the input for the terms which express categories such as "agent," "action," "object," "recipient," and the like, and learning the order of expressing these terms in the language. To the extent that the order is "unnatural" or varying, acquisition should be retarded. Add to this the well-established psycholinguistic lore that inflections and function words are difficult to master, and English becomes an ideal language for initial acquisition. When a theory of acquisition fits the local circumstances so well, it is time to look abroad![2]

What's in a sentence?

A sentence is not a verbal snapshot or movie of an event. In framing an utterance, you have to abstract away from everything you know, or can picture, about a situation, and present a schematic version which conveys the essentials. In terms of grammatical marking, there is not enough time in the speech situation for any language to allow for the marking of everything which could possibly be significant to the message. Probably there is not enough interest, either. Language *evokes* ideas; it does not represent them. Linguistic expression is thus *not* a natural map of consciousness or thought. It is a highly selective and conventionally schematic map. At the heart of language use is the tacit assumption that most of the message can be left unsaid, because of mutual understanding (and probably also mutual impatience). The subset of semantic notions which is formally marked in a particular language serves more to guide the listener to the appropriate segments and categories of analysis than to fully represent the underlying notions. The task facing the child learner is to determine which particular subset of notions receives formal marking in his or her language, and to discover the means for projecting these notions onto utterances.

Consider, for example, a child who wishes to report that it is "daddy" (and not someone else) who has just thrown a particular ball. For convenience, let us assume that the schematic core of this communicative intention – the basic features which must be preserved in any description of the situation – can be represented by a proposition about agentively caused object movement, and that the child knows it is necessary to say something about an agent and an object and a directed action relating one to the other. (The issue of the cross-linguistic propositional core is, of course, debatable, but I want to focus on problems of surface grammatical marking here.) A semantic structure of this sort is well available, it has been argued, on the basis of sensorimotor development. The task of language acquisition is learning to map such structures onto utterances.

In English the child might say, "DADDY threw the ball" – one word for each of the basic semantic elements, an extra word, *the*, and stress on the agent. The task seems reasonably straightforward, and well in line with cognitively based models of acquisition. It appears that the child simply has to express these terms in the proper order – which in English may be the "natural" order – ACTOR-ACTION-OBJECT. It also seems natural to focus an element by verbal emphasis. Additionally, in English the child must learn to indicate whether the object was definite (*the*) or indefinite (*a*). Schematically, we can represent the English surface sentence in the following form, in which the putative core semantic elements are given in small capitals and grammatical features are given in square brackets:

DADDY	threw	the	ball
AGENT	ACTION		OBJECT
[focus]	[past]	[definite]	

However, if we look across languages, it is evident that there is more to the task than meets the eye. Why indicate that the object, and only the object, is definite? And why indicate definiteness by a little word that precedes the object name? And why *not* indicate other facts, which are also obvious – the sex of the agent, for example, or that the action just took place, or that the balls are round? These are facts that receive obligatory grammatical coding in some languages. And what of other facts, which probably are not used for grammatical purposes in any language – for example, that the ball was thrown on a sunny afternoon, or that the child was pleased with the way daddy threw the ball, or that the ball was red, or that daddy was squinting at the sun while he threw the ball? It is evident that there are many things that *could* be said about the situation – even things that the child may have attended to and wished to communicate – but that English grammar requires only that basic elements be named, in a given order, with indication that the action was in the past, the object definite, and the agent in focus. Other notions can, of course, be encoded through separate words and phrases, but the issue here is one of *obligatory* encoding, and this is all that English requires for the production of a grammatical and appropriate utterance in this context. What the child must discover is which of the myriad of known aspects of this situation must be mapped onto surface forms in his or her native language. Perhaps the child has some way of limiting this myriad to that smaller myriad of facts which are universally used for linguistic marking, but we have no way of knowing. In any case, the problem is not simple.

Compare English with a closely related language, German:

VATER	warf	den	Ball
AGENT	ACTION		OBJECT
[focus]	[past]	[definite]	
	[3rd person]	[singular]	
	[singular]	[masculine]	
		[object]	

The so-called natural-order rule still holds. And in German, as in English, the child is required to stress the focused element and to mark the object as definite by using a definite article. But German articles also encode gender, number, and case, while the English article, *the*, is neutral in this regard. The German equivalent of *the ball, den Ball*, says, in the single word *den*, that the ball is a definite object which is also singular and considered as masculine. And in German one can also mark the agent by an article (*der Vater*), indicating in this case that it is definite, singular, masculine, and the subject of the sentence. (I return below to the problems of learning this sort of fusional case-inflectional system.) In addition, the German verb indicates not only tense but number. So the mapping problems differ. The nuclear proposition, which may correspond most closely to the child's prelinguistic communicative intention, is elaborated in seemingly arbitrary ways from language to language.

Consider several other examples. In Hebrew the verb encodes more features of the agent than German, indicating sex as well:

ABA	zarak	et	ha	kadur
AGENT	ACTION			OBJECT
[focus]	[past]	[object particle]	[definite]	
	[3rd person]			
	[singular]			
	[masculine]			

But note that this information is not expressed as part of the agent noun phrase, as it is in German, but is part of the verb. (So even if the child is aware that sex is to be coded grammatically, it is not evident where in the sentence such coding should occur.) And whereas the German article, *den,* encodes both object and definiteness in one word, Hebrew uses a separate particle, *et,* to indicate that the following (definite) noun is the direct object. The focused agent still appears in first position, and is stressed.

In these three examples the order of the elements is the same. English, German, and Hebrew differ in how much must be said about number, gender, and definiteness of the participants, and in where and how this information is to be encoded. But – the naturalness hypothesis notwithstanding – there is nothing in the event that gives this order: When father throws a ball, father, throwing, and the ball all occur simultaneously in perception. It is only linguistic expression that requires these elements to be isolated and serialized; and the order of elements is not universal. In Turkish, for example, the basic order is subject-object-verb: *Babam topu attı,* "my-father ball threw." However, in our example, "father" is in focus, and in Turkish the position immediately before the verb encodes focus. So rather than stress the word for "father," the word order is changed:

Top-	u	baba-	m	at-	tı
OBJECT		AGENT		ACTION	
	[definite]		[possessed		[past]
	[object]		by speaker]		[3rd person]
					[singular]
					[witnessed
					by speaker]

(Such pragmatic variations in word order, as discussed below, are easily acquired by Turkish children. The nature of Turkish agglutinating morphology and its acquisition are also discussed later in the chapter.) The Turkish utterance has three words, compressing information encoded by separate words in other languages. Word order does not communicate who did what to whom, but rather what the speaker is foregrounding and backgrounding in the utterance. The semantic relations are encoded by parts of words in Turkish. For example, the word for "ball," *top*, has a case suffix, *-u*, that indicates that it is definite and the direct object. In addition, the Turkish child is required to indicate that it is *"my* father" who acted, and that knowledge of this action comes from direct experience. A different verb ending would be required if the child knew of the action by inference or hearsay. Again, the mapping problem is not at all straightforward or "natural" beyond the basic three elements.

We have encountered variations of order, but the languages we have looked at so far all consider that if someone acts on an object, it is the object that receives special grammatical marking: through a case-marked article, as the German *den*; or an object particle, as the Hebrew *et*; or a direct object suffix, as the Turkish *-u*. Even in English, special marking of objects appears in pronouns: *me, him, her, us,* and *them*. However, just as languages differ in the roles assigned to word order, stress, and grammatical particles, it is not universal that the object be the grammatically marked category. In some languages (called *ergative* languages) it is the agent that receives special grammatical marking. Consider Kaluli, spoken in Papua New Guinea:[3]

Balowɔ	do-	wɛ	sanditabe
OBJECT	AGENT		ACTION
[possessed	[agent		[recent past]
by speaker]	(ergative)]		

Kaluli, like Turkish, is a verb-final language, using the position before the verb for focus. So the order, in both of these languages, is object-agent-verb for this example. But whereas in Turkish a suffix on the word for "ball" indicates that it is the object, in Kaluli it is a suffix on the word for "father" that indicates that he is the agent. Like the Turkish child, the Kaluli child must indicate that it is *"my* father" who acted. And the verb, though unconcerned with issues such as person, number, gender, and source of evidence, notes degree of recency of the event.

One can, of course, go on with such examples, considering languages like Tagalog, that are verb-initial and that indicate focus by an infixed particle in the verb, and so on. The important point is that the grammatical "embroidery" of word order, affixes, and particles is considerably broader and more diverse than envisaged in current Anglocentric psycholinguistics. The reader may object that these examples of forms of adult language do not speak to the point of early acquisition. Although the child must, eventually, go beyond the categories of sensorimotor intelligence (Brown) or the "universal structure of human action" (Bruner), can it not be argued that the child, of necessity, begins on these bases? Recall that our argument has to do with the acquisition of the *grammatical* means of encoding intentions in utterances. As soon as the child goes beyond the use of bare words – as soon as any grammatical morphemes are used consistently – some commitment has been made to the particular set of categories grammaticized in the mother tongue. And, indeed, even on the lexical level, the mold of language-specific categories can be discerned. The English-speaking child, for example, in choosing between *break* and *tear* to refer to a damaged object, must attend to the ways in which our language distinguishes the substance of objects undergoing destruction; the German-speaking child, when speaking of eating, must distinguish between people (*essen*) and animals (*fressen*); and so forth. Such examples have been, of course, the stock-in-trade of Whorfian theorists. But one may cite these facts and remain neutral on the issue of linguistic determinism. American children know that people and animals differ; this is presumably part of prelinguistic knowledge. But the obligatory lexical encoding of this distinction in regard to verbs of eating is language-specific, just as are obligatory grammatical distinctions such as the marking of patient or agency or number. The adult language is not only an eventual end state, but acts as a filter for lexical and grammatical encoding from very early on.

When we consider word order, the issue is even clearer. Naturalness hypotheses rank languages according to ease of acquisition on the basis of word order. Yet languages of different order types do not seem to differ in learnability. Nor are there significant differences between the acquisition of languages with relatively fixed word order and varying degrees of freedom of word order. Striking evidence comes from our Berkeley studies of the acquisition of Turkish (see Section 5.3), and similar evidence is available for other languages with relative freedom of word order (e.g., Finnish: Argoff, 1976; Russian: Gvozdev, 1949; Serbo-Croatian: Radulović, 1975). Turkish, as discussed in Section 5.3, has a regular and reliable case-inflectional system to mark the semantic roles of nouns. Consequently, word order does not play a significant semantic function, and various word orders are freely employed for pragmatic purposes of focus, contrastive emphasis, and the like, as demonstrated above. Children younger than 2 readily and appropriately produce the standard SOV order along with such orders as VO (to focus the verb), OVS (to focus the object), and OSV (to focus the subject). Contrary to McNeill's proposal, frequent OVS and OSV forms involve postposing of the first-person pronoun – intentional ego-as-actor. The naturalness hypothesis overemphasizes the use of speech to convey semantic propositions. Speakers also take different perspectives on the events they communicate, focusing now on one aspect, now on another, of the event. As Bates and MacWhinney (Chapter 6) point out, semantics and pragmatics interact in determining the word order and grammatical shape of particular utterances. Similar to our Turkish findings, they have shown that early verb fronting and subject postposing in Italian and Hungarian can be most readily accounted for in pragmatic terms.

The universal list of word-order types is brief, but the list of features involved in obligatory grammatical markers is much longer – though not indefinitely long. There are obligatory verb particles for shapes of manipulated objects, as in Navajo. There are several gradations of time, such as Kaluli immediate past, recent past, and distant past. Looking across all of the languages of the world, one would find a finite list of those aspects of situations which the grammar requires one to encode – aspects of the temporal nature of the act, physical characteristics of the objects, and various psychological, physical, and social aspects of the human interactants. Some markers will perform primarily syntactic functions, while others will have more obvious semantic or pragmatic components as well. But the particular constellation of features receiving obligatory marking in a particular language must be discovered by the child, along with the particular means (word order, affixes, particles, etc.) of encoding those features. Thus there is a long way between a *communicative intention*, which may be present in basic form even at the one-word stage, and the *semantic structure* containing that particular array of notions which must be mapped onto a grammatical utterance in a specific language.

5.2. Cross-linguistic study of operating principles of acquisition

Opposed to the naturalness hypothesis and to the preformationist version of the innateness hypothesis is the suggestion that children are predisposed to acquire the formal structures of language, and that linguistic universals are the reflection of such universal learning dispositions or strategies. I have used the term *operating principles* to refer to predispositions to perceive speech and construct formal systems in particular ways (Slobin, 1973). Consideration of language-particular acquisitions illuminates the parameters and developmental priorities of such operating principles. Each language poses the child with a different set of problems to solve in discovering the notions to be mapped and the means of mapping. Cross-linguistic examination of the developmental histories of various semantic domains in relation to various forms of linguistic expression is one of the most promising tools for revealing the inner structure of the human language-acquisition device.

In the remainder of the chapter I consider two specific problems in cross-linguistic detail: the mapping of underlying grammatical relations in several different types of word-order and inflectional languages, and the acquisition of locative adpositions. Whether or not there is a strong natural core to language, and a strong prelinguistic determination from cognitive and social development, specific mapping systems of the sort briefly alluded to above must be acquired for each language. By characterizing distinct languages according to the acquisitional problems which they pose, it is possible to arrive at a theory of the initial predispositions of the language learner. Or, put conversely, it is possible to discover which sorts of linguistic structures facilitate or impede the discovery process. In my paper on "cognitive prerequisites for the development of grammar" (1973), I proposed a basic operating principle in acquisition: "Underlying semantic relations should be marked overtly and clearly" (p. 202). Maratsos (1979) has pointed out that children do not always adhere to this principle in their speech production. In the discussion which follows I consider this operating principle as one which guides discovery, rather than production. Surface marking which is "overt" and "clear" is more easily discovered and acquired by the child and the cross-linguistic findings allow a more precise definition of just what constitutes overt and clear grammatical marking for the child. In the earlier work I suggested that postposed markers (suffixes and postpositions) are more salient than preposed markers (prefixes and prepositions). That suggestion has received a great deal of empirical support, and I will not review it here. This time I wish to offer several additional suggestions. I will argue that sentence processing is facilitated by the presence of what I call *local cues*, that is, signals to underlying meaning which occur at localized points in sentences. Consequently, inflectional marking of relations is clearer than the use of word order, and grammatical particles indicating such notions as causation, negation, and aspect may be especially clear grammatical devices. Although Anglocentric theorizing has assigned priority to sensitivity to word-order over other types of grammatical devices (as reflected in early "telegraphic speech"), cross-linguistic data point to early sensitivity to grammatical inflections as well. I also suggest that distinct surface realizations of underlying units in the form of separate clauses are easier to discover than particles which conflate several notions or nominalizations which condense entire clauses. On the lexical level, semantic clarity of forms and a minimum of lexical diversity facilitate acquisition.

5.3. The Berkeley cross-linguistic acquisition project

An extensive study of language development was carried out in 1972–3 in four field settings: Berkeley, Rome, Dubrovnik, and Istanbul.[4] These settings were picked (among other reasons) because of the linguistic contrasts they represent. The three Indo-European languages – English, Italian, and Serbo-Croatian – are all SVO languages, with the collection of features associated with that word-order type (prepositions, postposed relative clauses, etc.). They differ among themselves in degree of flexibility of word order, with English and Serbo-Croatian representing extremes for languages of this type, and with Italian more flexible than English. These three contrast with Turkish, which is an SOV agglutinating language (with postpositions, preposed relative clauses, etc.). Of the two inflectional languages, Turkish and Serbo-Croatian, Turkish represents a pure inflecting system, with maximal freedom of word order, whereas Serbo-Croatian is a fusional language with mixed reliance on both word order and inflections for the expression of grammatical relations. Taken as a group, then, it is possible to compare the acquisition of fusional versus agglutinating inflectional systems, and the acquisition of relatively fixed versus relatively free word-order languages. The study is described in general below, followed by discussion of specific acquisition problems in each of the languages.[5]

Subjects

Our overall research plan was to study matched samples of forty-eight children in each of the four field sites. By and large, we completed this plan, though there are gaps in the data at various points, due to the tribulations of carrying out research in foreign countries within a limited time schedule. We worked with groups of six children – three boys and three girls – at each of eight age levels, spaced at four-month intervals between the ages of 2;0 (years; months) and 4;4. In addition to this cross-sectional design, each child was retested four months later, providing one longitudinal check and giving an overall age range of 2;0 to 4;8. For purposes of this chapter, most of the results are from the first time of testing only, in four age groupings rather than eight: 2;0–2;4, 2;8–3;0, 3;4–3;8, and 4;0–4;4.

Since we were interested in cross-*linguistic*, and not cross-*cultural*, factors, we tried, as much as possible, to equate our samples on socio-cultural grounds. To do so, we limited ourselves to children of urban, professional parents, at least one of whom had a college degree. By and large, we feel that we were working with a fairly homogeneous group of children across the four field sites, at least in terms of early material and intellectual experience. There are no evident cultural explanations for our findings. Nor have we discovered important sex differences. The major variables affecting performance are thus language and child.

Design

Each child was studied extensively, over a period of fifteen to twenty hours, within a ten-day span. The experimenter was always female and always a native speaker. Testing was done in both homes and preschools. At each of the two testing periods, each child was exposed to a battery of sixteen linguistic tests, listed in Table 5.1. Because cross-linguistic

Table 5.1 *Cross-linguistic test battery*

Nonlinguistic Tests	Comprehension Tests
Short-Term Memory	Locatives
Object Order	Static Configurations
Projective Straight Line	Dynamic Scenes
Free Speech	*Wh* Questions
Elicited Speech	Agent–Patient[a]
Locative Elicitation[a]	Causative[a]
Answers to *Wh* Questions	*Before/After*[a]
Imitations	Relative Clause
Locatives	Comparative
Agent–Patient	

[a] Tests summarized in this chapter.

work of this sort had not been done before, our aim was to sample a large collection of abilities across a broad age range. The tasks tapped both comprehension and production; production was both free and elicited. We were especially interested in acquisition of means of expression for locative, temporal, causative, and agentive notions, and these figured heavily in our design of tests. We are currently carrying out semantic and grammatical analysis of free speech protocols and question responses. The present chapter is based on analyses of the four tests footnoted in Table 5.1: comprehension of agent–patient relations, comprehension of causatives of instigation, comprehension of clauses conjoined by *before* and *after,* and elicitation of locative adpositions (pre- or postpositions).

The four tests

Agent–Patient Test. The aim of this test was to assess the child's comprehension of the normal subject-object-verb sentences of his language, and the extension of this comprehension to grammatically deviant sentences. This is the key test in our series for determining attention to word order and inflections, since grammatical relations are expressed by word order in English and Italian, by case inflections in Turkish, and by both means in Serbo-Croatian.

The child was presented with a pair of toy animals or dolls and was asked to demonstrate an action of one object upon the other. Each instruction contained two animate nouns and a "reversible" verb (a verb which could take either noun as agent or patient, e.g., *The squirrel scratches the dog*). In Serbo-Croatian and Turkish all six possible orders of subject, verb, and object are grammatical. In Italian, although SVO is the only standard grammatical form for sentences of this type, the other orders are possible under conditions of contrastive stress on one of the two nouns. (The language also requires SOV order if the object is a pronoun, but we did not include such sentences. Yet it is important to note that they are heard by children.) In English only SVO is possible.

The design is most complex for Serbo-Croatian, where both word order and inflectional rules are at play, because the nominative and accusative cases are not distinctly marked for all genders. We used neuter nouns, for which the nominative and accusative cases are not distinguished morphologically (suffixed *-e* in both cases) and feminine nouns, which have a marked accusative (nominative *-a* versus accusative *-u*). This allowed for (1) fully ambiguous utterances with two neuter nouns, (2) utterances with clear marking of subject only, using feminine nominative and neuter unmarked forms, and (3) utterances with clear marking of object only, using neuter unmarked and feminine accusative forms. Consistent responses to ambiguous utterances would require use of a word-order strategy (e.g., first noun = agent), whereas consistent responses to utterances with inflectional marking could rely on either word-order rules (resulting in errors on sentences with marked object first or subject second) or inflectional rules (resulting in correct performance).

Turkish has a uniformly regular and obligatory definite direct object suffix, and thus allows for six unambiguous and grammatical orders: SOV, OSV, SVO, OVS, VSO, VOS. In order to probe for the application of a word-order strategy in the absence of inflectional cues, some sentences were presented with two uninflected nouns, corresponding to the Serbo-Croatian NNV, NVN, and VNN sentences with two neuter nouns. It should be noted that these sentences are ungrammatical in Turkish (lacking the obligatory case suffix) but grammatical in Serbo-Croatian.

The design was simpler in English and Italian, because there are no case inflections. To parallel the design of the inflected languages, the nouns which received subject or object inflections in Serbo-Croatian received extra stress in English and Italian. Stress plays a role in disambiguating NNV and VNN sentences in Italian, but not in English.[6]

If word-order regularities are basic to initial speech-processing strategies, we would expect good early performance in English and Italian of NVN sequences, with a probable generalization at some point of a first-noun-as-agent strategy to the deviant strings (Bever, 1970). Early correct performance should be limited to SVO sentences in Serbo-Croatian and SOV sentences in Turkish, with overgeneralization of the word-order strategy to sentences in which the first noun is marked as object, and to nonstandard orders. The course of development should be retarded in these languages, due to problems in acquiring the inflectional systems and applying them to sentence interpretation. As we will see shortly, these expectations were not confirmed. But first we must briefly consider the other tests.

Table 5.2 *Causative constructions in the four languages*

English

The horse	makes	the camel	run.
NOUN	VERB	NOUN	VERB
	[causative]		[infinitive]
	[3rd pers.]		

Italian

Il cavallo	fa	correrre	il cammello.
"the horse"	"makes"	"to run"	"the camel"
NOUN	VERB	VERB	NOUN
	[causative]	[infinitive]	
	[3rd pers.]		

Serbo-Croatian

Ždrijebe	tjera	devu	da	trči.
"horse"	"drives"	"camel"		"runs"
NOUN	VERB	NOUN	PARTICLE	VERB
[nominative]	[causative]	[accusative]		[3rd pers.]
	[3rd pers.]			

Turkish

At	deveyi	koşturcun.
"horse"	"camel"	"should make run"
NOUN	NOUN	VERB
[nominative]	[accusative]	[causative]
		[optative]
		[3rd pers.]

Causative Test. This test, following the Agent–Patient Test, assessed children's ability to comprehend structures in which one agent impels another agent to act. Again, two animals were presented, but the instruction followed the pattern *The horse makes the camel run.* A correct response required that the first animal instigate the action (either by direct contact with the second animal, or by verbal instruction uttered by the child for the sake of the first animal) and that the second animal carry out the action. Responses were also counted as correct if, on questioning, the child attributed instigation to the first animal (e.g., *The horse told the camel to run; The camel ran because the horse wanted him to*; etc.). As shown in Table 5.2, the four languages have different means for the production of such expressions. The three Indo-European languages have similar periphrastic constructions, differing in regard to the roles of word order and case inflection. Turkish, by contrast, encodes causation by the insertion of one or more causative particles in the verb. Note that there are word-order differences among the three SVO languages; roughly,

Table 5.3 *Before/After constructions in the four languages*

(1) The camel runs $\left\{\begin{array}{l}\text{before}\\ \text{prima che}\\ \text{prije nego}\end{array}\right\}$ the dog jumps.	

Deve   köpek   atla-ma-dan   önce   koşsun.
"camel" "dog" "jump-negative-ablative" "before" "should run"

(2) $\left\{\begin{array}{l}\text{Before}\\ \text{Prima che}\\ \text{Prije nego}\end{array}\right\}$ the dog jumps the camel runs.

Köpek   atla-ma-dan   önce   deve   koşsun.
"dog"   "jump-negative-ablative" "before" "camel" "should run"

(3) The dog jumps $\left\{\begin{array}{l}\text{after}\\ \text{dopo che}\\ \text{poslije nego}\end{array}\right\}$ the camel runs.

Köpek deve   koş-tuk-tan   sonra   atlasın.
"dog" "camel" "run-nominal-ablative" "after" "should jump"

(4) $\left\{\begin{array}{l}\text{After}\\ \text{Dopo che}\\ \text{Poslije}\end{array}\right\}$ the camel runs the dog jumps.

Deve   koş-tuk-tan   sonra   köpek atlasın.
"camel" "run-nominal-ablative" "after" "dog" "should jump"

Note: The languages are listed in the order English, Italian, Serbo-Croatian, Turkish. Because the constructions are the same in the three Indo-European languages, only the conjunctions are given for Italian and Serbo-Croatian.

these are: English – *The horse makes the camel run*; Italian – *The horse makes run the camel*; Serbo-Croatian – *The horse makes the camel that (it) runs*. In terms of surface marking, Serbo-Croatian provides the clearest cues of these three languages: A particle separates the causative clause from the action clause; the case-inflectional system marks the instigator as subject and the instigated as object; and the causative verb is a specialized one, used to discuss driving animals and impelling action, whereas the English *make* and the Italian *fare* are general verbs performing a large number of functions. The Turkish causative retains standard SOV order, embedding a causative particle within the verb and inflectionally marking subject and object. Again, we can ask whether reliance on such inflectional marking facilitates or retards development.

Before/After Test. This test follows the format familiar in the many English studies of these constructions (e.g., Barrie-Blackley, 1973; E. Clark, 1971; Coker, 1975; Keller-Cohen, 1974; and others). The child was given two animals and instructed to act out temporally sequenced events in which each animal performs a different intransitive action. As shown in Table 5.3, subordination and event ordering with *before* and *after* are identical in the three Indo-European languages, resulting in four sentence types:

(1)   Event 1 *before* Event 2
(2)   *Before* Event 2 Event 1
(3)   Event 2 *after* Event 1
(4)   *After* Event 1 Event 2

Sentences (1) and (3) are syntactically simple, in that the main clause precedes the subordinate clause; sentences (1) and (4) are conceptually simple, in that the order of mention matches the temporal order of occurrence of the events. The Turkish sentences maintain the order-of-mention characteristics, but (1) and (3), rather than being syntactically simple, have embedded clauses. Turkish sentences (2) and (4), like their Indo-European counterparts, have the order subordinate clause–main clause. Thus all of the Turkish sentences are syntactically complex. In addition, the verb of the subordinate clause is always nominalized, with different nominalizations for *before* and *after*. These contrasts make it possible to compare the roles of syntax and the semantics of the two conjunctions. If meaning features of the conjunctions, or order of mention, are the main determinants of complexity, we should expect similar patterns across languages. If syntactic complexity is an important factor, the Turkish pattern should differ from the Indo-European.

Locative Elicitation Test. In this test the child was asked to describe arrays of objects, in an attempt to elicit the prepositions or postpositions for "in," "on," "under," "beside," "between," "in front," and "in back." On grounds of cognitive development, we should expect the same order of emergence of terms across languages. On the other hand, language-specific features could bring about varying orders of acquisition.

Cross-linguistic patterns of results

Figure 5.1 presents four graphs showing change in performance with age on each test for the four languages. The significant fact which emerges from this comparison is that the languages pattern differently according to task. It is crucial to our argument that language and task interact. This is the basis of the claim that subsystems of particular languages pose different kinds of acquisition problems.

The Agent–Patient graph represents average percentage of correct performance on all grammatical sentences in the language – that is, SVO for English and Italian and all six orders for Serbo-Croatian and Turkish (with inflections). The two noninflectional languages, English and Italian, show similar growth curves, with correct performance emerging by the second age group. The two inflectional languages, however, differ dramatically. Turkish shows essentially no development, beginning at a high level from the youngest age group. Serbo-Croatian begins low, dips, and reaches marginal significance only by the third age level. Clearly, there are important differences between the two types of inflectional languages, which we will explore in more detail shortly. This preliminary look at the Turkish data already makes it clear, however, that inflections and free word order do not retard – and can even accelerate – development of comprehension, since the young Turks have already reached a significant level of correct response at the earliest age of testing (see Slobin & Bever, in press, for details and statistical analysis).

The Causative graph divides the languages differently. Here the two inflectional languages, Turkish and Serbo-Croatian, are superior, overall, to the two noninflectional languages, English and Italian. Again, however, we see a dip in Serbo-Croatian performance at the second level, and more precocious achievement of peak performance in Turkish. And again the Turkish inflectional system seems to accelerate, rather than retard development, although low performance in the first age group suggests initial difficulty in acquiring the infixed verbal particle (see Ammon & Slobin, 1979, for details and statistical analysis).

The dip in Serbo-Croatian performance does not appear in the other two graphs – *Before/After* and Locative Elicitation – an indication that we have not simply happened to choose an exceptionally precocious group of Yugoslav children at the first age level. These two tests do not involve case inflections, and as we shall see, the Serbo-Croatian dip on the Agent–Patient and Causative tests can be attributed to problems in reorganizing the inflectional and word-order systems.

On the *Before/After* Test, Turkish again takes the lead, but in this case the three Indo-European languages show more similar patterns of growth. (Detailed analysis is forthcoming from Ammon and Slobin.)

The languages separate in yet another way on the Locative Elicitation graph, where Turkish and Italian form one group, developing more rapidly than English and Serbo-Croatian. These differences are explored later.

All four graphs suggest special advantages to Turkish, either in precocity or in more rapid growth. These advantages require detailed attention. If anything, our studies suggest that Turkish is close to an ideal language for early acquisition.

Figure 5.2 rearranges the same graphs by language. Here we see that the two languages which are most similar structurally – English and Italian – present the most similar pictures. The Agent–Patient Test is consistently superior to the other tests, and the Causative and *Before/After* tests reach only a middling level. In Serbo-Croatian, as suggested above, the two tasks requiring the use of case inflections – Causative and Agent–Patient – show a similar pattern of development, with a dip at the second age but

reaching a high level by the last age. In Turkish, growth between the first
and second ages is rapid, except for the Agent–Patient Test, which is
already at ceiling. By the last age, the Causative and *Before/After* tests
have reached ceiling as well.

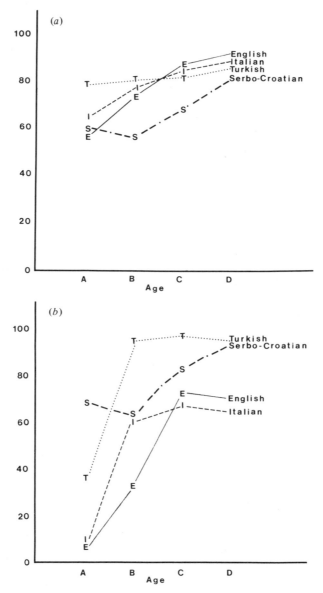

Figure 5.1. Performance on four tests by language and age: (a) Agent–Patient
Test: percentage correct on all grammatical sentences; (b) Causative Test: per-

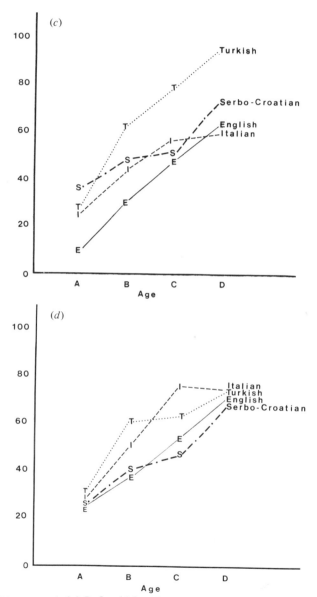

centage correct; (c) *Before/After* Test: percentage correct; (d) Locative Elicitation
Test: percentage of locative terms correctly applied.

In sum, the tests pose different problems to the different languages. That is to say, the child's acquisition of the means of encoding particular relations is influenced by the types of linguistic structures involved. There is something about Turkish which makes these structures especially easy

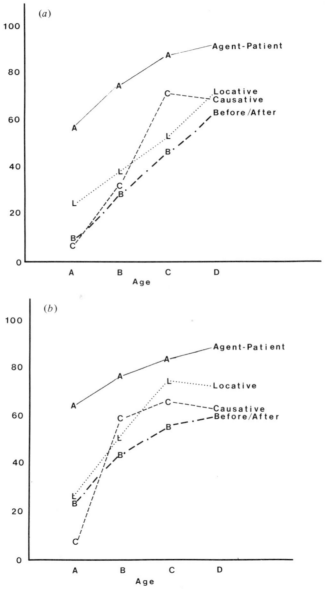

Figure 5.2. Performance in four languages by test and age: (a) English; (b) Italian;

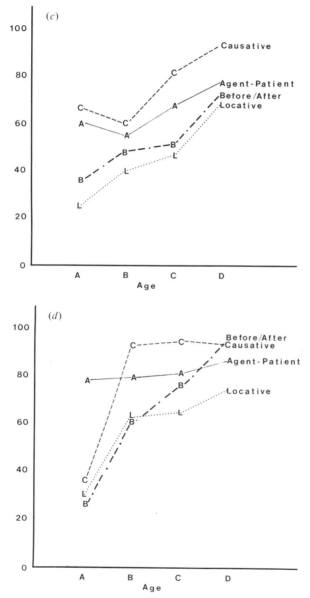

(c) Serbo-Croatian; (d) Turkish.

to discover, and there is something about Serbo–Croatian which both facilitates and impedes linguistic performance at various levels of development. Let us first consider the role of inflections and word order in Turkish, and then turn to comparisons with the other languages.

5.4. The acquisition of inflections and word order

Turkish

Edward Sapir once aptly characterized the Turkish agglutinating system as demonstrating "sober logic." Noun and verb stems, generally monosyllabic, are followed by strings of syllabic grammatical particles agreeing in vowel harmony with the stem. Vowel harmony and the basic stock of particles are easily acquired by age 2 or younger. With a handful of exceptions, all paradigms are almost perfectly regular, and apply to all words in identical fashion, there being no grammatical gender, arbitrary classes of verb conjugations, and the like. The same case-inflectional morphemes apply to nouns, pronouns, demonstratives, question words, and the various nominalized forms of verbs. Thus these morphemes are not only regular but highly frequent. Each morpheme tends to express a single element of meaning, and there are almost no homonyms among functors. Each syllabic morpheme receives equal stress. The system is so finely tuned and balanced – functionally and phonologically – that it has apparently maintained itself intact for two thousand years or more.

Consider, for example, the expression of the accusative, which figures in our Agent–Patient and Causative Tests. The inflectional morpheme is a high vowel which agrees with the stem vowel in fronting and rounding (*-i/-ı/-ü/-u*). For example, compare *ev*, "house," and the corresponding accusative, *evi*. The same morpheme applies to pronouns, as, for example, *ben*, "I"/*beni*, "me"; question words (e.g., *kim*, "who"/*kimi*, "whom"); demonstratives; and any other word functioning as a nominal. The plural is a separate morpheme, *-ler/-lar*, a low vowel agreeing in fronting, and immediately following the stem, as in *ev*, "house"/*evler*, "houses." The accusative plural is formed by simple agglutination: *evleri*. The possessive morpheme can be inserted before the case inflection: for example, *evim*, "my house"/*evimi*, "my house accusative"/*evlerimi*, "my houses accusative." The full set of case inflections includes:

Nominative	Ø	Dative	*-e/-a*
Genitive	*-in/-ın/-ün/-un*	Locative	*-de/-da*
Accusative	*-i/-ı/-ü/-u*	Ablative	*-den/-dan*
Instrumental/comitative	*-le/-la*		

This entire set of morphemes, along with the possessive and plural morphemes and much of the verb morphology, is used productively well before the age of 2 (Ekmekci, 1979; unpublished data of Doğan Cüceloğlu,

Nail Şahin, and the Berkeley Project). The inflectional morphemes are well practiced in question-and-answer routines between parent and child, since the inflection of the question word is required in the answer. For example, a father asks a 2-year-old, *Kimi gördün*? "Whom did you see?" and the reply is *Ahmedi* or *Muradı,* providing a name with an accusative morpheme. One-word requests are often in the form of noun, pronoun, or demonstrative with the accusative.

It is clear that there are many interlocking reasons for the ease of acquisition of Turkish nominal morphology (and similar arguments could be made in regard to the early acquisition of verbal morphology as well). I can think of at least twelve factors which may play a role in facilitating acquisition, and it would take painstaking cross-linguistic research to pull them apart. The morphemes are: (1) postposed, (2) syllabic, (3) stressed. They are (4) obligatory, rather than optional. For example, the optionality of the Japanese object particle delays its acquisition and its use in sentence comprehension, in relation to Turkish (Hakuta, 1977). (5) The inflections are tied to the noun, rather than standing alone as separate particles or being attached to or conflated with other parts of speech. For example, the German case system, which is conflated with articles, is acquired much more slowly than the corresponding Slavic noun suffixes. (6) The postposing of inflections is consistent with the verb-final typology of Turkish. Semantically, the Turkish particles (7) seem to be rationally ordered (plural-possessive-case); and (8) are nonsynthetic in their mapping of function onto form. The fusional quality of Indo-European inflectional morphemes no doubt adds to their complexity (e.g., the typical conflation of number, gender, and case). (9) Functionally, the morphemes express only grammatical roles, while other devices are used for pragmatic functions (e.g., contrastive word orders and focusing particles). Japanese particles which express both pragmatic and syntactic functions seem to be more difficult to acquire. In terms of distribution and diversity, the paradigms are (10) regular (i.e., exceptionless), (11) consistently applied to all pro-forms (pronouns, demonstratives, question words, nominalizations), and (12) distinct (i.e., there are almost no homonymous functors). The absence of such regular and consistent paradigms in Indo-European languages undoubtedly contributes to the prolonged and confused course of inflectional acquisition in those languages (whence the common psycholinguistic assumption that inflectional systems are difficult to master).

Whatever the relative strengths of all of these factors, it is clear that at least some of them greatly facilitate the acquisition of inflections in Turkish. The course of development of case inflections is slower in all of the Indo-European languages that have been studied. In Finno-Ugric languages, which are similar to Turkish in many ways, the course of acquisition is more protracted, due to irregularities and morphophono-

Table 5.4 *Percentage occurrence of utterance types in natural conversation in Turkish*

Sentence type	Children ($N = 14$)[a] (Age 2;2–3;8)	Adult speech to children
SOV	46	48
OSV	7	8
SVO	17	25
OVS	20	13
VSO	10	6
VOS	0	0

[a] Child-by-child analyses show similar word-order preferences.

logical complications (see Argoff, 1976, for Finnish; MacWhinney, 1974, 1978, for Hungarian and other languages). Yet, in all of these languages, inflections are acquired and used productively before the age of 2. There is nothing inaccessible about the notion of marking grammatical relations by noun suffixes. The advantage of Turkish is in the rapid completion of acquisition, and not in the initial discovery.

The ready availability of inflectional morphology allows word order to be used pragmatically. Although SOV is the neutral, or unmarked order, word-order rules are not needed to disambiguate sentences (except in the very rare case of interaction between two indefinite participants, since the accusative is used only for definite nouns, proper nouns, and pronouns). As shown in Table 5.4, Turkish children hear and use almost all possible orders of subject, verb, and object (with the possible exception of VOS, which is very rare). Contrary to the naturalness hypothesis, children use object-subject order even more frequently than adults (27 percent versus 21 percent of the time). In a sample of 500 adult utterances to a child aged 3;2, the first noun in the sentence was the subject only 47 percent of the time. This means that over half the sentences addressed to the child began with a case-inflected noun.

Given these facts, there is no basis in the input for the induction of word-order strategies in sentence processing. If they appear, they must be due to innate or nonlinguistic factors (as has been often proposed). The results of the Agent–Patient Test show clearly that Turkish children orient to case inflections, regardless of word order. The youngest children perform correctly on all six orders, provided the patient is inflectionally marked. At first, performance tends to be random on ungrammatical strings, in which neither noun is inflected. Only older children show some tendency to pick the first noun as agent in these cases, especially in NNV strings, which correspond to the standard word order. This effect is marginal, however, and is a late achievement, rather than being part of Turkish children's early sentence-processing strategies. For normal Turkish sentences, the object inflection, wherever it occurs in the sentence, is a sufficient cue for identification of the patient by the youngest children (2;0) in our sample.

Comparison with word-order languages

In both English and Italian, performance on NVN sentences in the Agent–Patient Test does not reach significance until the second age level. (A similar pattern is revealed if the analysis is done on the basis of mean length of utterance [MLU] [Slobin & Bever, in press].) In Italian, where stress plays a role, performance at the first level is significant only on NVN sentences in which the first noun is stressed. In English, stress has no facilitating effect on early performance. Overall, then, sensitivity to word order is not reliably present in these languages until the second age (or MLU) level, whereas sensitivity to inflections is present at the earliest level among Turkish children.

Furthermore, the nongrammatical NNV and VNN forms do not show a strong effect of word order at any age in English and Italian. Apparently the word-order strategy, when it emerges, applies only to NVN sentences (hence its overextension to the passive in earlier studies of English development). The word-order strategy is thus specific to a certain "sentence Gestalt," or "canonical sentence schema." (This notion is developed at length in Slobin & Bever, in press, and Slobin, 1981.) In order for this strategy to apply, the child must operate on the entire string, identifying it as NVN and choosing the first noun, preceding the verb, as agent, and the second noun, following the verb, as patient. Here we have a possible explanation for the relative advantage of the Turkish inflectional system. The object inflection is a *local cue*. It applies to a particular noun, regardless of its position, and can be processed without taking the entire sentence into account. Word-order languages thus impose a greater burden on short-term processing capacity, with a correspondingly later emergence of word-order strategies in sentence comprehension. (Processing constraints limit the range of possible grammars of human language [E. Clark & H. Clark, 1978; Slobin, 1979, pp. 63–72]. Within such universal limitations, more extreme processing constraints at play in the child may help account for the relative accessibility of various grammatical devices.)

How, then, do American and Italian children appropriately understand everyday sentences before the age of about 2½? Sentences in context are almost never ambiguous. Reversible sentences are rare, and are almost always situationally overdetermined. In addition, English input (based on analysis of the entire input to Roger Brown's Eve) almost always used

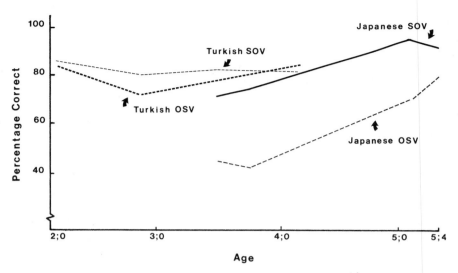

Figure 5.3. Percentage correct performance by age on SOV and OSV sentences in Turkish and Japanese.

pronouns for one or both of the participants in reversible sentences, and pronouns are the one corner of English grammar where case inflections have been preserved. Thus English-speaking children have inflectional cues available for the processing of potentially difficult sentences in context. The Agent–Patient Test assesses the child's *abstraction* of the grammatical devices of his or her language in the absence of normal situational cues. In the comparison of Turkish with English and Italian, the abstraction of inflectional cues to agent–patient relations occurs more readily than the abstraction of word-order cues.

Why, then, do regular orders occur in child speech in these three languages? The fact that regular orders occur does not mean that word order is used as a syntactic device, though word order has traditionally been taken as evidence of grammatical competence. In the case of Turkish, the SOV order is frequent because it is pragmatically neutral, but it is clear from our findings that the order of elements does not communicate grammatical relations. In early English and Italian speech, SVO order may occur simply because it is what the child has heard. Brown and Bellugi suggested long ago that it is possible that the child "preserves word order just because his brain works that way and . . . he has no comprehension of the semantic contrasts involved" (1964, p. 137). I believe that our data support this position. The use of SVO order in these languages may, at first, simply be part of the children's general tendency to behave like their models – on a par with acquiring their parents' pronunciation and intonation, tastes, manner of sitting and walking, and the like. Only later, as more sentence forms are acquired (e.g., passives, cleft and pseudo-cleft sentences, relative clauses), does word order come to play an active grammatical role.

At later stages, the use of order to express underlying relations poses many problems to children learning languages like English – problems which do not occur in languages like Turkish. Each of the more complex sentences requires a different word-order rule. For passives, NVN order expresses OVS. For object relative clauses (e.g., *the man that the dog bit*), NNV expresses OSV. Again, the rules for identifying agent and patient require that the entire structure be kept in mind, and the rules are structure-specific. In Turkish, by contrast, the same inflectional cues identify agent–patient relations in the various pragmatic reorderings. As the Turkish child enters into more complex discourse, calling for distinctions of focus, he or she has less new syntax to learn than the English-speaking child. (However, as we shall see later, the Turkish child has considerably complex new syntax to learn when he or she begins to deal with embeddings and nominalizations.)

Comparison with Japanese

The mere availability of grammatical particles to signal underlying relationships does not guarantee that they will facilitate sentence processing. Japanese, also an agglutinating SOV language, is similar to Turkish in many ways. But there are several important differences: Some of the particles – especially, for our purposes, the object particle *o* – are optional in speech, probably because word order is much less free than in Turkish. In addition, particles serve both focusing and syntactic functions, so that a preposed object is more likely to be marked by a focusing particle, *wa*, than by the object particle. Because the language does not fully exploit its potential for the pragmatic use of word order, Japanese children acquire inflectional strategies at a much later age than Turkish children. Figure 5.3 presents a comparison of our Turkish findings with Japanese data of Hakuta (1977), who had children act out reversible NNV sentences in which either the first or the second noun was marked with the object particle, *o*, or the subject particle, *ga*. The processing of SOV sentences does not seem to be different in the two languages, but whereas the Turkish children correctly interpret OSV sentences at all ages, these sentences pose considerable difficulty to Japanese children well beyond the age range included in our study. In their free speech, even the oldest children used the *o* particle 44 percent of the time in contexts where it is formally required. Thus inflectional strategies present a picture of precocious development only where they are called upon to play a major role in sentence processing. (For a full review of Japanese acquisition, see Clancy, 1983.)

Serbo-Croatian

Serbo-Croatian, like Russian and German and other Indo-European inflectional languages, requires the use of both word-order and inflectional
strategies in determining underlying relations. The Slavic languages originally had special inflectional paradigms for animate nouns, with clear
nominative–accusative distinctions, thus insuring that subject and object
could be uniquely identified in potentially reversible sentences. Neuter
nouns, referring to inanimate objects, did not need these distinctions.
Portions of this system remain, as in the marked nominative–accusative
distinction for singular masculine animate nouns in Serbo-Croatian and
Russian, and for plural feminine animate nouns in Russian. But much of
the system has eroded, and now there are some feminine nouns which
do not distinguish nominative and accusative (e.g., the Russian words for
"mother" and "daughter"), and there are neuter designations of animates, with no marked accusative form available. As a result, if one of
the two nouns in a reversible sentence is of the sort which has a distinctive
accusative inflection, variations in word order are possible, as in Turkish.
However, if an inflectional contrast is not available to distinguish subject
and object, SVO order is adhered to, as in English. The Yugoslav (or
Russian or German) child therefore has to master both kinds of systems.

Furthermore, the inflectional system, being fusional rather than agglutinating, lacks the clarity and transparency of the Turkish system. The
selection of case suffix interacts with gender, number, and animacy, and
there are many irregularities. The paradigms for nouns, adjectives (which
are also case inflected), and the various proforms differ. Stems are sometimes insolable (e.g., *muž*, "man nominative"/*muža*, "man accusative")
and sometimes not (e.g., *žena*, "woman nominative"/*ženu*, "woman accusative," but *žen* does not occur in isolation). This example also reveals
a pervasive problem of homonymity – for example, -*a* is the singular
accusative (and also singular and plural genitive) of masculine animate
nouns, the singular nominative (and plural genitive) of feminine nouns,
and the plural nominative and accusative of neuters. The entire set of
case-inflectional paradigms, with seven cases, three genders, animacy,
and number, is a vast and confused system. Consider simply the nominative–accusative distinction for regular nouns, shown in Table 5.5. Note
that there is no unique marker of number, case, or gender. One can know
the function of a suffix on a particular word only by knowing the class
membership of that word in the overall paradigm.

In spite of the staggering complexity of this system, it is acquired in
the preschool period. An accusative inflection is appropriately used at
the early stages, as in Turkish child speech. However, while the Turkish
child cannot possibly commit an error or an overgeneralization, since
there is only one possible accusative suffix, errors and overgeneralizations

Table 5.5 *The nominative–accusative noun-inflectional paradigm in Serbo-Croatian*

	Singular		Plural	
	Nominative	Accusative	Nominative	Accusative
Masculine				
Animate	Ø	*-a*	*-i*	*-e*
Inanimate	Ø	Ø	*-i*	*-e*
Neuter	*-o/-e*	*-o/-e*	*-a*	*-a*
Feminine				
-a class	*-a*	*-u*	*-e*	*-e*
-o class	*-o*	*-o*	*-i*	*-i*
Consonantal class	Ø	Ø	*-i*	*-i*

abound throughout the course of Serbo-Croatian development (cf. my discussion of Russian acquisition [Slobin, 1966a]). At first the feminine *-u* accusative is overgeneralized in the singular, no doubt because it is the only uniquely accusative inflection in the paradigm. Its use thus ignores gender and animacy, as does the Turkish inflection. Although often an error in formal terms, its use as an accusative is appropriate.

It is a challenge to all of our theories of language development and cognition that such systems are learned in the first few years of life and maintained, with only gradual change, over centuries. Clearly, speech in context provides many more cues to meaning than case inflections. Yet the inflections are needed, because they allow for pragmatic reorderings and because they serve as aids – probably often redundant but necessary aids – to speech processing. As yet we have no model of processing for such languages, but it is certain that the inflectional suffixes must play crucial roles in segmentation and interpretation.

As shown in Table 5.6, both children and adults use varying orders in their speech; but note that the three dominant orders – SVO, SOV, and VSO – preserve subject-object order, varying only position of the verb. Ninety-three percent of child utterances and 87 percent of adult utterances follow this order, as opposed to 73 percent for Turkish children and 79 percent for Turkish adults. What is more, children use the standard SVO order much more frequently than adults (72 percent versus 55 percent). These data suggest that, in the absence of a clear and fully reliable inflectional system, children rely heavily on word order (and that, in this case, the order is the putative "natural" one). This suggestion is also supported by very early developmental data. Radulović (1975) found that Serbo-Croatian child speech begins with ordered sentences, retaining standard order for several months after the acquisition of inflections.

Table 5.6 *Percentage occurrence of utterance types in natural conversation in Serbo-Croatian*

Sentence type	Children (N = 48)[a] (Age 2;0–4;8)	Adult speech to children
SVO	72	55
OVS	1	2
SOV	10	16
OSV	2	8
VSO	11	16
VOS	3	3

[a] Child-by-child analyses show similar word-order preferences.

Varying orders come with fuller mastery of inflections, but at first it seems that the child requires that word order and inflections support each other redundantly.

Results of the Agent–Patient Test also suggest that the youngest Yugoslav children attend to inflections only if they occur in normal sentence positions. Recall that there are three types of noun combination used in the test: (1) subject-marked (feminine subject, neuter object), (2) object-marked (neuter subject, feminine object), and (3) unmarked (two neuter nouns). The earliest performance is correct only in response to object-marked SVO sentences – that is, sentences which follow standard word order *and* mark the object with an inflection. It appears that children require normal marking in both word order and inflection for comprehension, just as they adhere to this redundant marking in production at an earlier developmental level.

The eventual accomplishment of the Yugoslav child is to balance out the two strategies, picking initial object-marked nouns as patients, final subject-marked nouns as agents, and following a subject-object order for unmarked noun pairings. This process requires a reorganization of sentence-processing strategies during the middle period, as reflected in the performance dips on both the Agent–Patient and Causative Tests. The picture is complex, and I will point out only some of its features here. (For a full discussion, see Slobin & Bever, in press.)

Results for the Causative Test are related in an interesting way. Word order and inflection never present contradictory information in that task. Although the same three types of noun pairings are used as in the Agent–Patient Test, in causative sentences like *The horse makes the camel run* the first noun is always subject and instigator, and the second is always object and instigated, regardless of the presence or absence of inflectional marking. But at the second age level, when children begin to be aware that case inflections can countermand basic word-order strategies, confusion is evidenced on this task as well. The performance drop at this age is only in regard to the object-marked sentences. It seems that some children have begun to realize that there is some relation between a marked accusative noun in a sentence and the possibility of reversed interpretation of the order of nouns in that sentence, but they are not yet clear on the interaction of word order and inflection. Thus the mere presence of an object inflection may lead to reversed interpretation in some instances. By the third age level it is the inflectionally marked causative sentences which show the greatest increase in correct performance, with the object-marked sentences reaching 100 percent by the fourth age. This suggests that after the second age level – as shown also in the Agent–Patient Test – Yugoslav children have become more proficient at using inflections to aid sentence processing.

In brief, some languages may require repeated reorganizations of parts of the grammar during the course of development – as in the balancing of word-order and inflectional strategies in Serbo-Croatian, or in the overcoming of word-order strategies in English (allowing for correct interpretation of passives and other reordered strings). As a result, growth curves for such areas of the language show dips or plateaus. In other cases – as in most aspects of Turkish which have been studied so far – growth curves tend to be smoother, differing only in rate of acceleration. In regard to such curves, the problems to be solved may be of varying levels of difficulty, but once solved, they do not have to be reexamined in the light of new acquisitions. One implication of these overall differences between languages is the possibility that the acquisition of later or more complex forms may be retarded because the child is still attempting to resolve problems posed by earlier acquisition. Hopefully, future research will provide clearer explanations of the nature and consequences of such differences in growth patterns.

5.5. The acquisition of locative expressions

Vocabulary development in a given semantic domain should reflect the order of development of the underlying notions. In this regard, we should expect cognitive development to play a more direct role than in the acquisition of syntactic and morphological rules. Yet we should also expect an interaction between general cognitive and language-specific factors. The set of locative adpositions is obviously not acquired at a single phase in development (though there is some evidence that postpositions begin to emerge earlier than prepositions).

Johnston and Slobin (1979) proposed an order of development of locative expressions in terms of cognitive complexity and communicative salience. In the cross-linguistic study we followed the development of seven basic locative relations: IN, ON, UNDER, BESIDE, BETWEEN, BACK, and FRONT (generic locative relations are expressed in small capitals). On conceptual grounds, notions of containment, support, and occlusion predict early acquisition of IN, ON, and UNDER (Piaget & Inhelder, 1967). Earlier developmental linguistic studies support this prediction (e.g., Brown, 1973; E. Clark, 1977; Parisi & Antinucci, 1970). BESIDE, encoding a purely spatial proximity relation, independent of object features or viewpoint of speaker, should follow IN, ON, and UNDER, but should be conceptually simpler than BETWEEN, BACK, and FRONT. BACK and FRONT have two uses: For reference objects with inherent fronts and backs (e.g., people, cars, houses) the terms encode proximity to this inherent feature (referred to here as $BACK_f$ and $FRONT_f$); for objects without inherent orientational features (e.g., trees, blocks, drinking glasses) the terms encode a projective notion with regard to the position of the speaker (referred to as simply BACK and FRONT). The projective notion, requiring attention to the speaker's point of view, as well as a coordination of the relative proximities of speaker, reference object, and located object, is conceptually more difficult than the nonprojective $BACK_f$ and $FRONT_f$, and should be acquired later (Laurendeau & Pinard, 1970; Piaget & Inhelder, 1967). On conceptual grounds, therefore, we predicted a developmental order of $BACK_f/FRONT_f$ < BACK/FRONT. As for the relative conceptual difficulties of $BACK_f/FRONT_f$ and BETWEEN, the former require a specification of object features, and the latter requires a coordination of two proximity relations. Research in object feature specification (Masongkay, McCluskey, McIntyre, Sims-Knight, Vaughn, & Flavell, 1974) and proximity coordination (Braine, 1959; Piaget & Inhelder, 1967) suggests that the latter is developmentally more advanced. If basic cognitive complexity were the sole determinant of acquisition, one would expect locatives to appear in the order:

$$IN/ON/UNDER < BESIDE < BACK_f/FRONT_f < BETWEEN < BACK/FRONT$$

Another aspect of conceptual development concerns the relative *salience* of particular notions. That is, the child is more likely to explore and to communicate about certain aspects of the relational world. The child's focus on disappearing or inaccesible objects, together with the improbability of asking about the location of a visible object, suggest that, all things equal, the relation BACK will have this quality of salience with respect to FRONT. This notion has been developed by Tanz (1980), with empirical support from comprehension studies with children, and statistical evidence on the more frequent use in English of *behind* and *in back of* than *in front of*. Tanz (1980) notes: "When we consider the multiplicity of occasions for using locative expressions, it seems plausible that on

Table 5.7 *Order of acquisition of locative expressions in four languages and percentage of subjects producing each*

English		Italian		Serbo-Croatian		Turkish	
Locative	%	Locative	%	Locative	%	Locative	%
IN	90	IN	91	ON	88	IN	90
ON	83	ON	88	IN	84	ON	80
UNDER	81	UNDER	84	BESIDE	82	UNDER	79
BESIDE	74	BESIDE	77	UNDER	72	BESIDE	79
BETWEEN	49	BETWEEN	57	BACK$_f$	31	BACK$_f$	71
FRONT$_f$	30	BACK$_f$	42	BETWEEN	26	FRONT$_f$	53
BACK$_f$	21	FRONT$_f$	41	FRONT$_f$	19	BETWEEN	50
BACK	14	BACK	23	BACK	16	BACK	7
FRONT	3	FRONT	18	FRONT	12	FRONT	4

balance it is more often when some object is not immediately perceptible to an addressee. This is more likely to be the case when the object is hidden in back of something than in full view in front of it" (p. 41). On salience grounds, therefore, Johnston and Slobin (1979) specified the predicted order of development in more detail:

IN/ON/UNDER < BESIDE < BACK$_f$ < FRONT$_f$ < BETWEEN < BACK < FRONT

In broad terms, Guttman scaling of the order or acquisition of locatives supported this predicted order. For all four languages, IN, ON, UNDER, and BESIDE were mastered prior to BETWEEN and BACK/FRONT with featured objects. These in turn always preceded BACK and FRONT with nonfeatured objects. To this extent, the cross-linguistic study provides support for the primacy of cognitive development in language acquisition, as posed earlier in my own work (Slobin, 1973) and the work of many others.

However, within this broad pattern of developmental similarity, there are language-specific differences in the rate and sequence of development of particular linguistic forms, as shown in Table 5.7. As Johnston and Slobin (1979) have pointed out: "Languages differ – at least for the preschooler – not so much in what *can* be said, but in *how* things are to be said" (p. 530). We identified five major linguistic factors contributing to the language-specific differences of order of acquisition in the middle-level locatives (BETWEEN, BACK$_f$ and FRONT$_f$). As the reader has probably come to expect by now, the least linguistic difficulty is evidenced in the case of Turkish, and the order of development matches that predicted on the basis of conceptual complexity. Overall, the five factors play different roles in each of the languages, resulting in the relative advantage, as shown in Figure 5.1d, of Turkish and Italian over English and Serbo-Croatian.

1. *Placement of adposition.* The three Indo-European languages are prepositional, whereas Turkish is postpositional. Consistent with earlier findings (summarized in Slobin, 1973), part of the Turkish advantage may be due to this factor.

2. *Lexical diversity.* The languages differ in the number of terms available for the expression of a particular notion. For example, English has numerous terms for simple proximity (*beside, by, next to, near, close to*), whereas Turkish has only one (*yanında*). English and Serbo-Croatian always have considerable lexical diversity, whereas Turkish and Italian almost always have a single term for each locative relation. Lexical diversity seems to retard the rate of acquisition of terms. For example, on the Locative Elicitation Test, the languages differ in the frequency of substitutional errors – that is, the use of a locative term of incorrect meaning in describing a scene (e.g., *in the bridge* for *on the bridge*). Substitutions range from 20 percent and 28 percent in Turkish and Italian, to 36 percent in English, to 46 percent in Serbo-Croatian. The two languages which have few or no synonymous adpositions, Turkish and Italian, are low in substitution errors; English is more extreme in both synonymity and substitution errors; Serbo-Croatian is still more extreme on both dimensions. Perhaps lexical diversity encourages a guessing strategy. If there are many overlapping terms, the child cannot be sure of the precise meaning of each, and may be led to search for meaning differences between the terms, resulting in false hypotheses and prolonged patterns of confused acquisition. If, on the other hand, the language presents the child with something closer to a one-to-one mapping between locative notion and adposition – with the concomitant greater frequency of occurrence of each individual term – the child may be more likely to wait until having figured out the appropriate meaning. That is, each term, as it is acquired, may have a more stable meaning, and the probability that it will be substituted for another is therefore decreased.

3. *Clarity of etymology.* Some terms are transparent in the bases of their meaning, such as the English *in back*, which names a body part; while other terms, like *between*, are semantically opaque (at least to a child). In Turkish, all locative postpositions are clear in their etymology, based on nouns that name the relevant locational areas or points of reference (e.g., terms meaning "top," "back," "interior," and the like). Clear etymology should aid acquisition, but it is difficult to isolate this factor from other co-occurring linguistic factors.

4. *Morphological complexity.* Adpositions differ in degree of morphological complexity, ranging from monomorphemic expressions like *in* to multimorphemic forms like *on top of* and *in the middle of.* This factor interacts with other linguistic factors to predict cross-linguistic differences in order of acquisition of terms in the Johnston and Slobin study.

5. *Homonymity.* Some surface terms are homonyms for more than one underlying notion. As pointed out above, the terms for BACK and FRONT are homonyms, in that they encode relations to featured and nonfeatured objects with no difference in surface linguistic form. On the grounds that children prefer one-to-one mappings between semantic concepts and surface morphemes (Slobin, 1977), it was predicted that homonymity should impose a measure of linguistic difficulty on acquisition.

Assigning linguistic complexity scores to the terms for BETWEEN, BACK$_f$, and FRONT$_f$ on the basis of these five factors, we were able to account for the differing orders of acquisition of these three terms across languages. Thus a common order of acquisition predicted on conceptual grounds is realized with language-specific deviations on the basis of relative difficulty of linguistic processing.

5.6. Some general aspects of acquisition

Most of this chapter has dealt with cross-linguistic differences, as a counterbalance to earlier claims of universality. But it is clear that there are general processes at work as well. At some level of abstraction one moves from particulars to universals. The list of five factors of linguistic complexity affecting the acquisition of locative terms is one set of examples of cross-linguistic commonalities. But note that the commonalities are in terms of *factors which influence* ease of acquisition, and not in terms of *common patterns of acquisition.* Form and content may differ more than the procedures employed in the discovery and processing of linguistic structures. In the remainder of the chapter I consider several other cross-linguistic commonalities in processes of linguistic attention and the child's construction of grammar.

The role of "local cues"

In discussing the relative advantage of Turkish over word-order languages on the Agent–Patient Test, I introduced the notion of "local cue." I suggested that the object inflection can be easily processed because it applies to a particular noun and can be interpreted without taking the entire sentence into account. The cue is *local* because it operates on a localized sentence element. There are a number of other phenomena in the data which suggest the importance of this notion for sentence processing and the acquisition of linguistic forms. (The notion is well known in experimental psycholinguistics, where it is phrased in terms of "surface cues to underlying structure" [see, e.g., J. A. Fodor, Bever, & Garrett, 1974, pp. 353–61].)

Ammon and Slobin (1979) introduced this notion to account for the relative superiority of Turkish and Serbo-Croatian on the Causative Test. They noted that these two languages, as opposed to English and Italian, have several morphological particles which may facilitate sentence-processing strategies. The sentence forms are given in Table 5.2. Note that both Turkish and Serbo-Croatian indicate the instigated participant by means of a direct object inflection. The Serbo-Croatian causative verb, *tjerati*, serves a specialized function in the language (as opposed to English *make* and Italian *fare*) and, in this sense, is in some way similar to the Turkish causative morpheme infixed in the verb, which is also specialized in function. The Serbo-Croatian action verb in the causative construction is finite and is separated from the rest of the sentence by a particle, *da*, which may also call special sentence-processing strategies into play for this type of sentence, or may at least serve to block strategies applicable to simple declaratives. Thus, in general terms, Serbo-Croatian and Turkish can be said to provide *local* cues within the sentence, in contrast to English and Italian, where sentence structures require that the listener hold the entire sentence in mind in order to determine the underlying semantic relations.

Turkish performance on other tests also indicates reliance on local cues. *Before* and *after* constructions in Turkish use different nominalizations of the verb in the subordinate clause for the two conjoining terms (postpositions in Turkish). The subordinate clause in *before* conjoining refers to an event which has not occurred at the time of the event of the main clause. Accordingly, the particular nominal form of the verb indicates *potential*, rather than realized action, and is followed by a negative particle (something like "The dog not having jumped first, the camel runs"). In the case of *after*, where the event of the subordinate clause occurs first, the nominal form expresses the *fact* of occurrence and, of course, there is no negative particle. I do not think that children in the age range tested have mastered the distinction between the two nominal forms, but the negative particle in the *before* constructions appears to function as an important local cue. If Turkish children perform only one of the two actions called for in these sentences, they are twice as likely to make a single response in regard to the *before* sentences as the *after* sentences (35 : 17). They apparently interpret the negative particle in these sentences as meaning that one of the actions does not occur.

In the case of correct performance of both actions, the overall course of development for the four sentence types is almost identical (a finding that incidentally poses problems for all semantic and cognitively based explanations of performance on this test in English). The one major exception is an early peak on sentence type (2), corresponding to *Before Event 2 Event 1*. Although this form reverses order of mention, it has the salient local cue of the negative particle; and of the two *before* sentences, it is the one in which the subordinate clause is not embedded. I suggest that the negative particle serves to clarify the temporal order of the two events, once the child comprehends that two events are to be acted out.

Local cues – in this case inflectional once again – play an interesting role in Turkish performance on the Relative Clause Test. In this test (following Amy Sheldon's 1974 design), children were asked to act out relations among three animals, such as *The donkey that the sheep touches rubs the camel*. The four sentence types are shown in Table 5.8. Relative clauses are exceptionally difficult in Turkish, and are acquired much later than in Indo-European languages. None of the Turkish children in our sample (up to age 4;8) correctly performed a single one of these instructions. What is of interest here is the strategy used by Turkish children in determining their partial responses, since they generally carried out a single action involving two animals. As one would expect, they consistently ignored the embedded verb, which is always a nominalized form (perhaps even unrecognizable as a verb) and performed the action of the final verb, which appears in the normal position for Turkish. The patient was always the accusative noun in its normal preverbal position at the end of the sentence. Local cues play their role in the choice of agent. Turkish children do not pick the first noun as agent, as one would expect in the case of a word-order strategy. Rather, they tend to scan the sentence for the first *uninflected* noun – that is, a subject noun (footnoted in Table 5.8). If the initial noun is marked as non-subject (by the accusative or genitive inflection) it is passed over. As in the Agent–Patient Test, an inflectional strategy plays the dominant role. Thus, several years after they have acquired simple sentences, Turkish children employ the same strategies in encountering complex sentences. In the case of sentences with relative clauses, this strategy results in isolation of the main clause. Again, we find a special elegance in the set of strategies for the acquisition of Turkish, since the same basic strategy can be used again, over the course of years, in interpreting more complex sentences.

Late acquisition

There are numerous determinants of structures which are acquired late by children, and I have no space to review them here (see Bowerman, 1979, for a detailed review of the acquisition of complex sentences). Having pointed out so many precocious elements of Turkish acquisition, however, I should make special mention of late acquisition of relative clauses. As is evident in Table 5.8, the clauses do not look much like

Table 5.8 *Schematic descriptions of Turkish relative clause constructions*

===

(1) *subject embedded, object focus*:   The donkey that the sheep touches rubs the camel.
Sheep + genitive touch + object participle + possessive donkey[a] camel + accusative rubs.

(2) *subject embedded, subject focus*:   The donkey that touches the sheep rubs the camel.
Sheep + accusative touch + subject participle donkey[a] camel + accusative rubs.

(3) *object embedded, object focus*:   The donkey touches the sheep that the camel rubs.
Donkey[a] camel + genitive rub + object participle + possessive sheep + accusative rubs.

(4) *object embedded, subject focus*:   The donkey touches the sheep that rubs the camel.
Donkey[a] camel + accusative rub + subject participle sheep + accusative touches.

===

[a] Participant most frequently selected as agent of single action.

surface sentences. The verbs of relative clauses are nominalized, with different participial nominalizations for subject and object focus. The agent of an object relative is marked by the genitive case, since the agent symbolically "possesses" the nominalized form of his action. In short, there is abundant syntactic and morphological complexity, with clauses conflated into nominalizations. By contrast, Indo-European relative clauses do look almost like separate sentences, and are much more amenable to normal sentence-processing strategies, with minimal adaptations to such surface markers as relative pronouns (often case marked) and word-order adjustments. The general moral for acquisition is that surface forms which are considerably different from their underlying representations will be difficult to acquire. The details of this moral, of course, need to be filled in.

In terms of late acquisition in Turkish, one can point to a number of sentence-embedding constructions – relatives, verb complements – and the associated array of verbal nominalizations. Thus languages may not differ considerably, overall, in ease of acquisition. The Turkish advantage in morphology is balanced by a disadvantage in syntax. On the other hand, the ease with which Yugoslav 2-year-olds produce relative clauses suggests that their disadvantage in morphology is compensated for by an advantage in syntax. This formulation, of course, is too simple, but I believe that it is basically correct.

Building consistent expectancies

Having discovered part of their language, children behave as if they expect a certain consistency or generality to their findings. There are several lines of evidence that the interpretation of new forms or deviant forms is based on previously established sets and strategies.

On the Agent–Patient Test, performance was best on those sentence forms corresponding to the standard forms used in the language. The English and Italian children, overall, responded consistently only to NVN sentences. Slobin and Bever (in press) suggest that the failure of any pattern to emerge in response to NNV and VNN sentences may be due to the fact that the child will not apply any systematic analysis to a string which does not correspond to a "canonical sentence form." This notion would also explain early inconsistent interpretation of English passive sentences, since their verb morphology does not fit the canonical form of active sentences.

The notion of canonical sentence form also accounts for some features of the Turkish and Serbo-Croatian data. A small number of Turkish children responded consistently to some of the ungrammatical sequences with two uninflected nouns. The tendency to respond consistently to these forms is related to the frequency of occurrence of the three orders in the language: Thirteen children responded consistently to NNV strings, which parallel the standard SOV; seven were consistent on NVN, which is the next most frequent order in the language; and only four were consistent on VNN, which is the least frequent in Turkish speech. The early Serbo-Croatian tendency to attend to inflections only on SVO sentences is another example of children's notions of what constitutes a possible interpretable utterance in the language. Perhaps children attempt to interpret only structures which fit their notion of the language. As Newport, H. Gleitman, and L. Gleitman (1977) have put it: "The child has means for restricting, as well as organizing, the flow of incoming linguistic data; he filters out some kinds of input and selectively listens for others" (p. 111).

Turkish imitations also reflect a realization that the standard order is NNV. The eighteen sentences of the Agent-Patient Test were offered as stimuli for imitation to thirty of the Turkish children, with an average age of 3;9. Overall, 73 percent of the stimuli were imitated correctly (indicating easy acceptance of all possible orders). Reorderings were rare, but when they occurred, they reflected a sensitivity to the frequency of occurrence of sentence forms in the language: (1) Verb-final strings were almost never reordered; (2) NVN strings were reordered less frequently than VNN, and always into NNV order; (3) VNN strings were reordered most frequently – generally into NNV order, but also into NVN. Younger children reordered most frequently (from 46 percent at 3;0 to 11 percent by 3;8), and younger children made more attempts to move less frequent orders (verb-initial and verb-medial) to verb-final order; these results suggest a greater early role for canonical order on this task, declining sharply by 3;4. Thus, in some circumstances, children may attend to noncanonical forms, but only to assimilate them to the canonical form. (For additional discussion of the notion of canonical form, see Slobin & Bever in press; Slobin, 1981.)

"The waiting room"

As a final suggestion for general aspects of acquisition, I draw upon a metaphor used by Johnston and Slobin (1979). In my earlier work (Slobin, 1973) I had proposed that "new forms first express old functions, and new functions are first expressed by old forms" (p. 184). In the locative study, for example, correct use of a locative term was frequently preceded by substitutions and circumlocutions using known linguistic forms. Such transient old forms expressing new functions can be most clearly seen in children's responses to BETWEEN items on the Locative Elicitation Test. BETWEEN is acquired at a time when the child already has a number of locative terms. Some of these are called upon while the unlexicalized notion is "waiting" for expression. BETWEEN is conceptually complex in that it requires one to take account of two reference objects. For many children, in all four of the languages, there seems to be a stage at which the child realizes the necessary plurality of reference objects, but has not yet acquired the appropriate term. Here several intermediate strategies emerge. A common response is to use some other locative term, generally a term for BESIDE or IN, with a plural noun. For example, an object is placed between two blocks and the child says *beside the blocks* or *in the blocks*, thus indicating his grasp of the plurality of the reference objects. This strategy is often replaced by the use of *in the middle*, which acknowledges the sense of enclosure better than the use of *in*, but does not capture the duality of the reference objects. Often, when *between* emerges, it appears with a singular noun, *between the block,* as if the child has decided that this particular adposition already encodes plurality, without redundant marking on the noun. These examples demonstrate children's ability to make use of linguistic means at their disposal while "waiting" to master the adult forms for particular notions.

The waiting room provides a metaphor for the entire line of cross-linguistic research reviewed here, because it has both a cognitive and a linguistic component. Each linguistic form in this metaphor has its own waiting room. The entry door is opened with the underlying notion as key; the key to the exit door is the appropriate linguistic form. The child receives the entry key when he or she discerns the existence of a given notion – primarily on nonlinguistic grounds, but perhaps at times with some prompting from established linguistic knowledge. The entry is thus determined by conceptual acquisition of the sort generally referred to as *cognitive* development. The problems to be solved in the waiting room are both *semantic* and *morphologico-syntactic*. The child must figure out just what aspects of the particular notion are encoded in the language, and what means are used for the encoding. The solutions take varying amounts of time and effort, depending on linguistic features, but finally the child leaves that particular waiting room with the appropriate "semantactic" key in hand. The important point of the waiting-room metaphor is its two doors: the cognitive entry door and the linguistic exit. I have suggested that we cannot hope to understand language acquisition without understanding the path between these two doors.

Notes

1 This chapter, written in 1978, was based on my interpretation of McNeill's 1975 paper. In his book, *The conceptual basis of language* (1979), McNeill extends his approach and responds specifically to my earlier interpretation of his work (pp. 243–5). Basing himself on the findings of precocious Turkish acquisition of inflectional morphology and flexible word order (described in the present chapter), he concludes, as I do, that "the idea of an 'intrinsic' word order loses credibility" (p. 245). This chapter supports his conclusion that "an iconic method of semiotic extension (involving word order)" does not seem to be easier to learn than "a symbolic method (involving inflectional morphology or other devices)" (p. 245). (McNeill is correct in pointing out that even Turkish-speaking children adhere to subject-first placement in a majority of their utterances (63 percent in our data), thus giving some evidence for "indexical word sequences." But it should also be noted – contrary to McNeill's expectations – that postposing of *first*-person subject is highly frequent in the Turkish speech of both adults and very young children.) This chapter should not be taken as a rejection of McNeill's insights, but more as a collection of caveats based on language-specific characteristics of patterns of acquisition.

2 In support of arguments of natural word order, recourse is often made to the cross-linguistic tabulations prepared by Greenberg (1966) and others of the distribution of various order types among the world's languages. Bruner, for example, quotes Greenberg: "The order of elements in language parallels that in physical experience or the order of knowledge" (Greenberg, 1966, p. 103). However, Greenberg does not make this claim in regard to the ordering of subject and object. Indeed, his claim – and those of following investigators – has been a statistical one of dominant order types (SVO, SOV, and VSO) and co-occurring linguistic features, and not an absolute linguistic or psychological claim. The passage quoted from Greenberg refers to Universals 14 and 15, which have to do with clause orders: "14. In conditional statements, the conditional clause precedes the conclusion as the normal order in all languages . . . 15. In expressions of volition and purpose, a subordinate verbal form always follows the main verb as the normal order except in those languages

in which the nominal object always precedes the verb" (p. 111). I believe that the naturalness position is more tenable in regard to clause orders of these types than in regard to the ordering of constituents of simple sentences. Osgood argues that the relative preponderance of SVO languages supports his position. However, a single counterexample – e.g., a VOS language (and there are some) which can be acquired and maintained in normal fashion – is sufficient to cast grave doubt on his theory. Clearly, to be interesting, the naturalness argument must be reshaped in terms of linguistic universals (see, for example, H. Clark & E. Clark, 1977, pp. 523–51; 1978; Talmy, 1978; in press).

3 My thanks to Bambi Schieffelin for the Kaluli example. She has pointed out to me that *no* SVO orders occur in her extensive corpora of Kaluli child language (for more details, see Schieffelin, 1979a, b).

4 The project was carried out with support from the William T. Grant Foundation to the Institute of Human Learning, and from NIMH to the Language-Behavior Research Laboratory, University of California, Berkeley. Ayhan Aksu, Francesco Antinucci, Thomas G. Bever, Eve V. Clark, Herbert H. Clark, Susan Ervin-Tripp, Judith R. Johnston, and Ljubica Radulović collaborated with me in designing the investigation. I gratefully acknowledge the labors of our testers: Penny Boyes-Braem, Judith R. Johnston, and Gail Loewenstein Holland in the United States; Rosanna Bosi and Wanda Gianelli in Italy; Ljubica Radulović and Emilia Zalović in Yugoslavia; and Alev Alatlı and Ayla Algar in Turkey.

5 The data are selectively summarized in this chapter. Full reports of separate phases of the research can be found in Aksu (1978), Ammon and Slobin (1979), Slobin and Bever (in press), Clancy, Jacobsen, and Silva (1976), Johnston and Slobin (1979), Radulović (1975), and in future papers. Chapters in Slobin (forthcoming) review and compare the acquisition of a wide range of language types, including those considered here: English (de Villiers & de Villiers), Romance languages (E. Clark), Polish and Slavic languages (Smoczyńska), and Turkish (Aksu & Slobin).

6 Because of the need for a standard set of sentences across the four languages, there are some unavoidable differences in the task in terms of grammaticality: All of the stimulus sentences are grammatical in Serbo-Croatian; 67 percent are grammatical in Turkish; and only 33 percent are grammatical in English and Italian.

Part III

THE DEVELOPMENT OF GRAMMAR

6. Functionalist approaches to grammar

Elizabeth Bates and Brian MacWhinney

In his history of linguistics, R. H. Robins (1968) traces the beginning of modern linguistic theory back to Ferdinand de Saussure's famous distinction between *langue*, "language," and *parole*, "speech." *Parole* refers to the speech behavior of individuals. *Langue* is an emergent system that exists *between* individuals. Although the linguist must use the data of speech to discover the properties of language, the language system itself need not exist in the behavior or the mind of any given individual. Indeed, the justification for a separate linguistic science is based upon this distinction. Because linguists are not interested in actual speech behavior (except as a means to an end), they need not concern themselves with states, motives, or underlying processes involved in the production and understanding of speech. Those factors, though interesting, are the domain of psychologists and philosophers of mind.

The development of the relatively new field of psycholinguistics represents a systematic erosion of Saussure's distinction. Psycholinguistics was built in large measure upon Noam Chomsky's (1957) distinction between *competence* and *performance*. *Performance,* as defined by Chomsky, is essentially the same thing as Saussure's *parole*: actual speech behavior by individuals. However, *competence* is different from Saussure's *langue* in one crucial respect: Whereas *langue* is an abstract system that comes to exist between individuals, *competence* is defined as the abstract knowledge about language that is contained in the mind of individual native speakers. Thus, as explicitly stated by Chomsky (1968, p. 1), linguistics once again becomes a part of cognitive science and philosophy of mind.

Given this merger, how can we now distinguish the respective goals of linguistics and psycholinguistics? One possibility is the following division: (1) Linguistics is devoted to the *description* of language as an integrated system (competence); whereas (2) psycholinguistics is devoted to the *explanation* of language in terms of the goals and processes involved in using that system (performance). This approach was implicit in much of the psycholinguistic research of the 1960s. Transformational grammarians handed down descriptions of English as a system; psycholinguists sought to establish the psychological reality of that system within processing and acquisition models. This period in our brief history has been amply reviewed elsewhere. As many of the original proponents of the approach (e.g., J. A. Fodor, Bever, & Garrett, 1974) now readily admit, the abstract descriptions of a transformational grammar do not translate readily into real-time processes. For example, sentences that supposedly involve six rules do not necessarily take longer to produce or verify than sentences with four rules. And although there is a rough correlation between formal complexity in the grammar and order of acquisition by children (see, e.g., Brown & Hanlon, 1970), there are also many exceptions to the acquisition sequences predicted by a model based on addition and reorganization of rules.

In the 1970s, there has been a change in the way that many psycholinguists and students of child language have used linguistic theory. Instead of *accepting* linguistic descriptions and seeking their correlates in psychological processing, many researchers have tried to formulate their descriptions of language behavior directly in processing terms. This approach characterizes much of the recent work on the cognitive and social bases of language, sociolinguistics and discourse factors, prespeech in infant communication, and context effects on language processing in adults. A survey of such research might lead to the following distinction between linguistics and psycholinguistics: (1) Linguistics is devoted to the *description* of the *forms* that are taken by particular languages, and language as a general system; whereas (2) psycholinguistics is devoted to the *description* of the *functions* that are served by particular linguistic forms, and by language in general. Presumably, given this distribution of labor, the joint goal of linguistics and psychology is to describe the relationship between form and function and above all to explain how form and function constrain one another.

As long as linguists and psycholinguists are pursuing their separate descriptive goals, there is little room for controversy beyond minor disagreements concerning method and interpretation. At the level of explanation, however, the matter becomes far more difficult. In exploring how form and function constrain one another, we must also decide just how much the two *fields* can constrain one another. To what extent must the elements, categories, and processes described by psychologists fit the elements, categories, and relationships described by linguists? In describing the mapping between form and function, there is considerable room for disagreement concerning the causal force that each imposes on the other.

In our own research (e.g., MacWhinney & Bates, 1978), we have been interested in the functional system of topicalization or point making in discourse. We have examined the acquisition of that system by children, and its use by adults, in a variety of languages including English, Italian,

Table 6.1. *Grammatical devices associated with topic and comment*

Topicalization devices	Commenting devices
Assignment of sentence subject	Assignment of sentence predicate
Initialization in word order	Initialization in word order
Pronominalization	Specific lexicalization
Ellipsis	Lexicalization
Definite articles and modifiers	Indefinite articles and modifiers
Existential sentences (e.g., *There was this guy. He . . .*)	Connectors to previous discourse (e.g., *yet, now, still, too*)
	Contrastive stress

and Hungarian. More recently we have begun to investigate Serbo-Croatian, Navajo, and American Sign Language. So far, our results suggest that, although the basic communicative function is presumably universal, there is an enormous variation across languages in the particular surface devices or forms used to encode that function. These include variations in the use of word order, verb agreement, ellipsis and pronominalization, definite and indefinite articles, contrastive stress, adverbials, and relative clauses – indeed, almost all of the conceivable kinds of syntactic-morphological devices (see Table 6.1). However, there is a tendency for languages to make particularly frequent use of one subset of devices to encode the topic function. These are the devices typically associated with the hypothetical formal role of "sentence subject," in particular, word order and verb agreement (Li, 1976). We could simply stop with a description of the topic function and a description of associated surface forms. However, if we want to move beyond description to an explanatory account of just how and why particular forms and functions are related in history, used by adults, and acquired by children, then we must face a number of controversial issues. In this chapter, we want to outline those controversies as we see them, separating the possible kinds of functionalist claims and describing the kinds of data relevant to each.

We do not pretend to have resolved very much at this point. However, we do have a bias of sorts, which is best admitted from the outset. That is, we suspect that the point-making function plays a strong causal role in the way particular forms have evolved and in the way those forms are used by adults and acquired by children. Furthermore, we are attracted to linguistic models that offer formal descriptions of the subject system that can be interfaced easily with the functional process of topicalization. In other words, given a variety of possible grammars to describe the same set of surface conventions, we prefer a grammar that maps subject phenomena (e.g., word order and verb agreement) onto the category of "topic" with a minimal number of intervening steps, separate components, and separate categories. This functionalist bias is based on our experience with the above-mentioned languages. It is not, however, a conclusion dictated by existing data. In fact, our goal in this state-of-the-art discussion is to examine the kinds of empirical tests that could decide between "formalist" and functionalist claims about the nature of language. The rest of the chapter is divided into the following sections: (1) a brief look at the history of the functionalist–formalist controversy and a description of four distinct kinds of functionalist claims and the data relevant to each; (2) a description of a "competition model" that is our own best guess about a realistic combination of these four claims; (3) application of the competition model to the internal structure of the topic system; (4) application of the competition model to the relationship between "topic" and "agent" as categories that govern subject phenomena; and (5) some ideas about the kind of grammar that could be written to describe the representational system that mediates between the surface forms of subject and the underlying categories of topic and agent.

6.1. The functionalist–formalist controversy

The issues that separate formalist and functionalist accounts of language can be traced back to the early Greek philosophers, to the classic debate between the Analogists and the Anomalists. As Esper (1973) and Robins (1968) describe this debate, the Greeks were divided on several issues concerning the origin of language – particularly the origin of sound–meaning relationships in lexical items. The Analogists, including Aristotle, proposed that true irregularity in language is rare, that language is governed by reason, and that the bond between sound and meaning is lawful even if it is not obvious. The Anomalists, including the Stoics and the Skeptics, argued instead that language is characterized by irregularity or anomaly, and must have emerged without great reliance on the rational faculties. In short, the Analogists stressed the regularity of patterns as well as their inherent rationality or functional base. The Anomalists stressed the irregularity of patterns, and their arbitrariness with respect to any rational, functional base.

Notice that two claims separate these schools: *regularity* of pattern and *rationality* of pattern. In the modern version of analogy versus anomaly, both functionalists and formalists agree that language is primarily lawful. Indeed, developmental research in the 1960s demonstrated that children not only recognize and seek regularity, but actually impose it in areas where none exists (e.g., turning *feet* to *foots*). The current debate in psycholinguistics centers on the second part of the analogy–anomaly issue: the inherent rationality of patterns, their basis in communicative functions and ongoing processing constraints. Modern-day anomalists, including many transformational grammarians, stress the relative autonomy or independence of form and function. Modern-day analogists, including functionalist grammarians and generative semanticians, stress the contribution of function (e.g., meaning, "perceivability," production constraints, etc.) to the creation and maintenance of linguistic forms.

For the Greeks, the analogy–anomaly debate was in practice related to a second controversy concerning the role of nature versus convention in establishing linguistic forms. The Stoics argued in favor of nature, that is, the "innate" or naturally given basis of language. This approach was compatible with the anomalist view: Arbitrary forms must be studied sui generis, taken as they are, precisely because they are given in nature as absolutes. Aristotle, by contrast, argued for the role of convention in the creation of language. This view was compatible with the analogist position: Language is rational precisely because it is the product of human reason, created by men. It is not *logically* necessary, however, for anomalists and analogists to side respectively with nature and nurture. Indeed, in the modern-day analogy–anomaly debate, we find all possible combinations with respect to the innateness issue. From the "nature" side, Noam Chomsky (1975) has argued that language should be viewed as a "mental organ" that is highly predetermined by genetic factors. Like the Stoics, then, he suggests that an otherwise impenetrable formal system *must* be given in nature; otherwise, it could not be acquired. However, Maratsos and Chalkley (1980; see also Maratsos, Chapter 8) have proposed that human children are extraordinarily good at learning anomalous forms and deriving abstract categories from linguistic input–without innate clues but also without particular functional motivation. In other words, children are excellent pattern analyzers; they learn to do what others do, to manipulate curious linguistic objects because that is how grownups do things.

Similarly, we can find both nativists and empiricists within the functionalist or analogist camp. The term *functionalism* is usually associated with general learning theories, including behaviorist approaches as simple as that proposed by Skinner (1957). However, it is also possible to view the functionalist approach as a particular type of genetic determinism, albeit via an indirect causal route. Let us take one simple example: In all human cultures that have been studied to date, human beings eat with their hands (with or without an intervening tool). It seems perfectly fair to conclude, then, that hand-feeding is an innate human characteristic. But it is also likely that it is innate in a very indirect way, that is, as the most efficient and probable solution to a particular problem. Given the nature of human foodstuffs, the fact that they must pass through the mouth, the availability of hands as excellent all-purpose object manipulators, and the location of the hand vis-à-vis the mouth, it is simply inevitable that human beings will hit upon the solution of hand-feeding even without social reinforcement, imitation, and so on. In the same fashion, a functionalist may view certain universal aspects of grammar as indirectly innate, as inevitable solutions to certain universal constraints of the problem of mapping nonlinear meanings onto a linear speech channel (see Bates, 1979, chap. 1, for a more detailed discussion of functionalism as a nativist position).

In sum, the analogy–anomaly debate is logically independent of the nature–nurture issue. There are, however, several different kinds of claims that can be made within a functionalist or analogist position. We can discern at least four levels of functionalism, ranging from a relatively conservative historical view to some radical proposals about the nature of adult grammatical knowledge. Each level requires qualitatively different kinds of evidence, although the stronger levels presuppose the more conservative ones both logically and empirically. The four respective positions involve (1) claims about diachronic or historical correlations between form and function, (2) synchronic or ongoing correlations between form and function in real-time processing, (3) use of these form–function correlations in the acquisition of language by children, and finally (4) a functionalist approach to the grammar or system of representation that mediates the relationship between form and function.

Level 1: diachronic correlation. The claim of diachronic correlation is that linguistic forms are historically associated with one or more communicative functions, in a manner that suggests a causal relationship. This is the weakest version of the functionalist approach, a purely historical claim that certain forms evolved under pressure from one or more specific constraints. It is a kind of linguistic Darwinism, an argument that languages look the way they do for functional or adaptive reasons. These reasons include a variety of constraints from cognitive, social, perceptual, and production factors. Indeed, the interactions among these factors may be so complex that the relationship between form and function is often opaque.

The appropriate methodology for establishing such claims is of course historical research, demonstrating a series of intermediate forms leading up to the present, in which the constraints that are operating become transparent. For example, Sankoff and Brown (1976) have studied the emergence of relative clause markers during the evolution of a South Pacific pidgin code, Tok Pisin, into a complete creole language. In the creole form, relative clauses begin and end with an *-ia* particle that is now apparently meaningless, for example, "This man-ia he sell me pig-ia he come to my house." However, an examination of the history of this form suggests that it evolved from a tag question, "Hear?" that was used as a discourse marker for topicalizing a referent within two complete main clause sentences, for example, "This man, hear? He sell me pig, hear? He come to my house." Similarly, Givón (1976) has argued that sub-

Table 6.2. *Level 1 evidence for a diachronic relation between syntax and topic–comment functions*

Device	Languages	References
Left dislocation	Several	Givón, 1976
	Italian	Duranti & Ochs, 1979
	Mandarin	Li & Thompson, 1975
Right dislocation	Niger-Congo	Hyman, 1975
	Hungarian, English, etc.	Hetzron, 1975
Agreement	Several	Givón, 1976
	Tok Pisin	Sankoff & Brown, 1976
Relativization	Tok Pisin	Sankoff & Brown, 1976
	Malagasy	Keenan, 1976a
	Hittite	Justus, 1976
	English	Kuno, 1976
Complementation	French	Hyman & Zimmer, 1976
Detopicalization	Indo-European	Lehmann, 1976
	Several	Li & Thompson, 1976
Aspect	French, Malay, Old English, Russian	Hopper, 1977

ject–verb agreement is a device that evolved to meet a discourse constraint for double marking topics when the topic is fronted and the comment postponed to a point much later on in an utterance, for example, "This *guy* I told you about the other day, well *he came* over and . . ." The proform (in this case *he*) that double marks that topic near its predicate gradually erodes phonologically into the verb, to become an inflection marking that verb for person, number, gender, and so on. In a recent volume on the discourse bases of grammar, Givón (1979) gives an impressive list of examples like this in a chapter aptly titled "Where Does Crazy Syntax Come From?" Similar examples are discussed by Slobin (1977) as they relate to child grammar. In short, apparently arbitrary syntactic devices may have their origins in the structure of discourse, evolving in the service of universal communicative functions. Some of the research supporting this type of diachronic correlation is referenced in Table 6.2.

Note, however, that this kind of historical claim does not imply any *ongoing* correlation between forms and the functions that brought them about. For example, a mechanism like subject–verb agreement may have achieved a certain amount of "functional autonomy" (Allport, 1961), existing now as an obligatory device that has little or nothing to do with topic marking in its use by modern-day speakers. A somewhat stronger functionalist position goes beyond the evolutionary analysis of form–function relationships and advances a claim regarding synchronic correlation.

Level 2: synchronic correlation. The claim of synchronic correlation is that, in ongoing processing, linguistic forms are associated with one or more communicative functions, in a manner that suggests a causal relationship. In this view, the functional pressures that operated in language history to create surface forms continue to operate in everyday communication to maintain those surface forms now in use by speakers and hearers. For example, subject–verb agreement may be maintained across languages because it is *still* needed to double mark topics and reduce ambiguity. If that form were not available, something like it would have to be reinvented by speakers. In other words, the claim is that most surface forms never evolve into full functional autonomy.

Several methods have been used to establish synchronic correlations of this type. One is the analysis of "natural text units," preferably informal conversations. Such natural text units provide enough context to allow us to detect the relationships between form and function, such as instances of topic shifting across sentences, cases in which disambiguation of reference is necessary, or instances where topics must be reintroduced because of memory constraints. For example, Duranti and Ochs (1979) have analyzed several Italian texts for the occurrence of left-dislocated (LD) structures. LD structures are active voice utterances in which direct and/or indirect objects occur in initial position, for example, *I spaghetti li voglio,* "The spaghetti I want them." The passive voice supposedly evolved to fill this kind of focusing role. And yet LD structures are preferred overwhelmingly in informal conversation, suggesting that the LD form is somehow easier to plan or produce. By analyzing the contexts in which all instances of LD structures occurred, Duranti and Ochs came to several interesting conclusions. First, LD forms seem to reflect a "middle degree" of givenness along a given–new continuum. They are almost always elements that have already been introduced into the discourse (for example, they are invariably marked with definite articles). However, they also occur at points where two or more potential referents of the same person, number, and gender are available in the discourse space. Because pronominalization or ellipsis would lead to ambiguity, the element must be *reintroduced* before a relevant comment can be made. However, degree of givenness alone is not sufficient to motivate all the LD instances. For example, LDs were several times more frequent in conversations with more than two participants. They often seem to serve as a kind of "pseudo-topicalization" in which a speaker can take or maintain the floor by thrusting relevant material out into initial position – a useful weapon in conversations involving more than two Italians. Hence givenness and problems in turn taking both contribute to the use of LD structures.

Although linguists engaged in this kind of text analysis typically do not use statistical techniques, the approach just illustrated fits conceptually with correlational models using multiple regression analyses. In principle, it should be possible to determine the amount of variance contributed by each factor, in different and perhaps interacting combinations. Such studies would provide evidence that apparently arbitrary syntactic devices are used just because they play a particular communicative role in conversations. It is worth noting, however, that correlational evidence obtained from free speech records can never conclusively establish a causal relationship among variables.

There are, however, additional sources of evidence for synchronic correlation in experiments that manipulate the determinants of the use of linguistic devices in an antecedent–consequent relationship. In most such studies, functional inputs such as givenness–newness of information are treated as independent variables. The dependent variables are the use of one or more grammatical forms, such as initialization or pronominalization. The use of these grammatical forms can be measured in several ways, including production, reaction times and judgments in comprehension and sentence verification, and acceptability ratings. A summary of such studies is presented in Tables 6.3 and 6.4 (for more detailed reviews, see Bates & MacWhinney, 1979; MacWhinney, 1980).

Most of these experiments are designed to assess the relationship between one form and one function. For example, Osgood (1971) has shown that adults are more likely to use definite articles to encode given information than information that is relatively new in discourse. Perhaps justifiably, many linguists regard such demonstrations as trivial demonstrations of facts that are intuitively obvious to any native speaker. However, with a more complex experimental design we can obtain information that is *not* readily available by armchair analysis. One such approach is to manipulate a single function as the independent variable, but leave several options open for the forms that serve as dependent variables. For example, MacWhinney and Bates (1978) manipulated givenness of information in a simple picture-description task, with adults and 3- to 6-year-old children in Hungarian-, Italian-, and English-speaking communities. The given–new dimension was a good predictor of stress and ellipsis and a much weaker predictor of pronominalization; it had almost no effect on the use of sentence-initial position. Furthermore, these relationships interacted with language and with age in complex ways. This approach gives us some idea of the control of a given functional determinant over the use of various potentially available structures. Another approach is

Table 6.3. *Level 2 psycholinguistic evidence for a synchronic correlation between perspective/salience and the device of initialization in adult English*

Technique	Starting point found to:	Reference
Rating	be more "potent"	M. Johnson, 1967
	be drawn larger	Johnson-Laird, 1968a
	be more human, animate, and concrete	H. Clark & Begun, 1971
Elicited production	be good and potent	Boucher & Osgood, 1969
	be animate	H. Clark, 1965
	be animate	Jarvella & Sinnott, 1972
	be large	Johnson-Laird, 1968b
	move first	Osgood, 1971
Problem solving	be more easily moved	Huttenlocher & Strauss, 1968
	be constructed first	H. Clark, 1968
Free recall	be remembered best	B. Anderson, 1963
	be remembered best	H. Clark, 1965
	be remembered best	H. Clark & Card, 1969
	be remembered best	Coleman, 1965
	be remembered best	Kintsch, 1974
Cued recall	be the best cue	Prentice, 1966
	aid recall of passive	Schlesinger, 1968
	aid recall of passive	Turner & Rommetveit, 1968
	work best as a cue when active	Blumenthal & Boakes, 1967

to administer several independent variables and assess their effects on the use of a single surface form. For example, Flores d'Arcais (1975) had demonstrated that animacy, relative size, and direction of movement in picture stimuli all have some effect on the selection of elements to serve as sentence subject in a picture-description task. However, animacy has a much larger effect than either of the two perceptual salience dimensions. Such "one-to-many" or "many-to-one" studies can tell us not only about the presence or absence of synchronic correlations, but also about the relative weights of various functional constraints in determining the use of different surface forms.

Ideally, in the strongest possible statement of a synchronic correlation approach, we should be able to predict *all* uses of surface forms. To do so, we would obviously have to have a great deal of information about the functional constraints that are operating in a given situation, such as

Table 6.4. *Level 2 psycholinguistic evidence for a synchronic correlation between givenness or topicality and five syntactic devices in adult English*

Device	Technique	Finding	Reference
Initialization	Acceptability	Starting points code givenness	Bock, 1977
	Acceptability	Starting points code givenness	Grieve & Wales, 1973
	Acceptability	Starting points code givenness	Hupet & LeBouedec, 1977
	Acceptability	Starting points code givenness	Kleinbort & Anisfeld, 1974
	Acceptability	Starting points code givenness	Wright & Glucksberg, 1976
	Elicited production	Passives code discourse topicality	Carroll, 1958
	Elicited production	Passives code discourse topicality	Tannenbaum & Williams, 1968
	Elicited production	Passives code discourse topicality	Turner & Rommetveit, 1968
	Comprehension	Passive "set" can be induced	Olson & Filby, 1972
	Comprehension	Passive "set" can be induced	Wright, 1969
Ellipsis	Production	Ellipsis codes givenness	Delis & Slater, 1977
Pronominalization	Production	Pronouns code givenness	Delis & Slater, 1977
	Recall	Pronouns serve to bind events	Lesgold, 1972
	Elicited production	Pronouns serve to bind events	Osgood, 1971
Stress	Text analysis	Stress marks contrast	Berman & Szamosi, 1972
	Text analysis	Stress marks contrast	Bolinger, 1972
	Text analysis	Stress marks contrast	Gunter, 1966
Definite article	Elicited production	Definite article codes givenness	Grieve, 1973
	Elicited production	Definite article codes givenness	Osgood, 1973

newness–givenness of information, the type of semantic information that must be mapped, the number of participants in the discourse, and the memory load as a function of both semantic and pragmatic information. Furthermore, we would need to know the relative weights and interactions of these functional constraints in a given context. We are of course a long way from this situation of total predictability. Even if we had the necessary information, the appropriate multivariate statistics for modeling these interactions are still being developed (Rousseau & Sankoff, 1978). Nevertheless, we can at least begin to create conceptual models that take these interacting factors into account.

Suppose that we did eventually achieve the goal of total predictability, capturing all the existing synchronic correlations between form and function. Suppose, for example, that we could invariably predict the semantic element that a speaker will choose to serve as the surface subject of a sentence (e.g., the nominal element that occurs in initial position, agrees with the verb in person and number, and is pronominalized in the nominative case). There is still a great deal that we would not know about the way in which children acquire grammar and about the way in which adults store and access form–function relations. The fact that synchronic correlations are there does not necessarily mean that children use them in acquiring language. They may enter into the linguistic system by a completely different route, guided by abstract and possibly innate clues about the nature of surface conventions in grammar. Furthermore, these correlations could in principle be only peripherally related to adult grammatical competence. They may be epiphenomenal, by-products of an abstract grammatical machinery that manipulates its own autonomous mental symbols.

Level 3: acquisition. The acquisition claim is that the correlation between form and function is sufficiently strong to permit the acquisition or discovery of surface conventions without any other clues about linguistic structure. In other words, children may exploit the correlation between form and function to "crack the code" of their native language. Researchers working from this point of view must adopt a developmental version of the historical method already described. First, they must show that a given function is established in the child's repertoire prior to acquisition of a related form. Second, they must show that the form was acquired in an effort to solve that communicative problem, as the child gropes with a series of alternative surface forms within a particular "function slot." Such studies often involve evidence for creative intermediate stages in form–function mapping in which the child's problem-solving efforts become transparent, and in this respect they are similar to the arguments proposed by Givón (1976) and Sankoff and Brown (1976) at Level 1. Table 6.5 summarizes some of the current evidence for a developmental relation between syntax and pragmatic functions.

Table 6.5. *Level 3 evidence for a developmental relation between syntax and pragmatic functions*

Device	Pragmatic variables	Reference
Lexicalization vs. ellipsis	Informativeness	Greenfield & Zukow, 1978
	Complexity	Bloom, Miller, & Hood, 1975
	Comment	deLaguna, 1963
	Comment	Sechehaye, 1926
	Comment	Vygotsky, 1934/1962
	Newness–givenness	MacWhinney & Bates, 1978
Fronting in two-word utterances	Informativeness	Greenfield & Zukow, 1978
	Importance	Lindner, 1898
	Importance	O'Shea, 1907
	Perspective	MacWhinney, 1975a
	Newness	Dezső, 1970
	Newness	Fava & Tirondola, unpublished
	Newness	Meggyes, 1971
	Newness	Park, unpublished
	Newness	Viktor, 1917
	Focus	Leonard & Schwartz, 1977
Stress	Newness	Wieman, 1976
	Contrast	Hornby, 1971
	Contrast	Hornby & Hass, 1970
	Contrast	MacWhinney & Bates, 1978
Pronominalization	Givenness	MacWhinney & Bates, 1978
Indefinite article	Newness	MacWhinney & Bates, 1978
Definite article	Givenness	Bresson, 1974
	Givenness	Brown, 1973
	Givenness	MacWhinney & Bates, 1978
	Givenness	Maratsos, 1974b, 1976
	Givenness	Warden, 1976

To illustrate how developmental data can provide evidence for the Level 3 version of the functionalist position, let us consider some possible "functional routes" into the discovery of the surface phenomena associated with the sentence subject. For the moment, let us concentrate on three subject phenomena: initialization, noun–verb agreement, and subject pronouns. Applying the developmental criteria just described, Bates and MacWhinney (1979) have reviewed evidence suggesting that the topic–comment function is established in the one-word stage, prior to any use of word order. Similar evidence is available to suggest that the function of "agency" is also available to children before the acquisition of syntax. Hence both topic and agent are functions that precede the onset of word order in child language. In some languages (e.g., Hungarian and Italian), the first word-order hypotheses that children use tend to reflect the topic–comment division (with comments preceding topics). On the other hand, in other languages (notably English), early two- and three-word speech tends to reflect information about agency, with agents or actors preceding action words (Braine, 1976; Brown, 1973). Hence either topic or agent may be expressed in early two-word syntax. What happens to these primitive strategies when other subject phenomena are acquired? Evidence from Fava and Tirondola (unpublished) and Snow (1977) suggests that the set of correlated subject phenomena may be acquired in separate bits, each mapped onto a different aspect of meaning. For example, Fava and Tirondola's Italian children used agreement and pronominalization to map information related to agency, whereas word order was retained for several weeks in the service of topicalization.

Eventually, children have to construct some kind of single "subject" category that can handle the full range of meanings capable of "subjectivalization," and that will govern the full set of correlated surface devices that adults use in subjectivalization. In other words, a heterogeneous set of meaning structures must be mapped onto a heterogeneous set of grammatical devices. There are a variety of views on how this transition takes place. Brown (1973), Sinclair (1975), Maratsos and Chalkley (1980), and Valian (1977) have all argued that the full range of grammatical forms in adult language can only be described with an abstract set of symbols like "+ Subject" – symbols or categories that in some way transcend semantic or pragmatic meanings. Valian adopts Chomsky's nativist anomalist view that such categories are part of the genetic predisposition of our species; they need not be discovered or constructed because they are available to the child from the onset of language acquisition. Maratsos and Chalkley, on the other hand, take a non-nativist anomalist view in which categories like subject are derived from experience with formal regularities. More precisely, the child is said to derive such categories by scanning the set of correlated devices that make up subjectivalization (word order, pronominalization and agreement, the behavior of certain reflexive particles). The child notes that these surface forms behave as a block, and constructs an internal mental symbol "+ Subject" that will be used in all internal manipulations and mappings onto these surface devices. Note that in the Maratsos and Chalkley approach this symbol is entirely independent of meaning structures like "actor" or "topic"; nor are actor and topic in any way involved in the ontogenetic derivation of the subject category. A third approach is a mixture of Level 3 analogy with an anomalist approach to the nature of adult competence. Brown and Sinclair both suggest that children may use natural categories like "actor," "topic," and "action" on the way to discovering abstract categories like "subject" and "predicate," in a sort of "getting hot, getting cold" game of clues about the nature of grammar. However, at some point the child will have to trade in his natural categories for abstract symbols like "+ Subject." In other writings, we have referred to this discontinuous passage as the *developmental shift hypothesis*.

In the final and most radical functionalist view, the categories of adult grammar retain their full functionalist definitions. In other words, a correlated set of surface devices like those that constitute subjectivalization continue to map directly onto a category made up of semantic and pragmatic meanings. After we have outlined that position, we can return to the question of falsifiability, discussing the kinds of evidence that can distinguish Level 4 from the Level 3 developmental shift hypothesis, and from anomalist positions like those of Valian and Maratsos and Chalkley.

Level 4: adult competence. The adult competence claim is that the grammar or system of representation that mediates the interaction between form and function can be fully described in terms of natural functional categories and performance constraints. This is the strongest version of the functionalist hypothesis, in which abstract or purely formal grammars are viewed as epiphenomena of natural processes. In other words, although certain kinds of abstract linguistic models may very well describe sentences, they do not describe tacit knowledge and/or the workings of the mind in processing utterances. A psychologically real description of language can and should be written entirely in terms of cognitive categories and speech processes, without additional symbols.

Note that this view in no way denies the reality of surface rules or conventions, that is, those peculiar facts which make Turkish differ from English, from Chinese, from Navajo. Grammatical conventions cannot ''look like'' the meanings they convey. The mapping from meaning into sound must necessarily be indirect for several reasons. Firstly, except for a few rare onomatopoeic expressions like the word *sneeze*, sounds do not resemble the things they stand for. Secondly, language can provide explicit conventions for only a subset of the possible kinds of meanings or thoughts that we might want to convey. In this regard, Slobin (personal communication, 1979) has noted:

> A sentence is like a conventionalized line drawing. You have to abstract away from everything you know or can picture about a situation, and present a schematic version which conveys the essentials. In terms of grammatical marking, there is not enough time in the speech situation for any language to allow for the formal encoding of everything which could possibly be significant to the message. Probably there is not enough interest either. Language *evokes* ideas; it does not represent them. Linguistic expression is thus *not* a straightforward map of consciousness or thought. It is a highly selective and conventionally schematic map.

Thirdly, it is rarely the case that a single surface convention serves one and only one communicative function. Rather, most aspects of the grammar are governed by several competing aspects of the communicative situation (cognitive structures, social goals, perception, and production constraints). We will return shortly to some ideas about the role of competition in explanatory models of language. For our present purposes, the point is that surface grammatical conventions cannot be isomorphic with functions, even from the point of view of a Level 4 functionalist. However, the relations among arbitrary surface devices should be predictable from processing constraints; and these surface patterns should map onto a set of "natural" and eminently knowable categories without requiring a complex set of intermediary formal objects. Level 4 functionalism is, then, a theory about the nature of *intermediate* structures in the representation of grammatical knowledge.

What kind of research is relevant to Level 4 claims? First of all, a Level 4 model presupposes Levels 1, 2, and 3. Functional categories like "topic" and "agent" can figure preeminently in a psychologically real system of representation only if they have operated for some time – in language history, in the ontogenesis of language in children, and in use by adults. Hence Level 4 requires the full data base that supports correlation and acquisition models. In addition, however, this kind of a functionalist claim will require new methods for manipulating and interrelating those data. The ultimate test is whether a grammar or model of representation can be built out of the elements, categories, and relationships yielded by a functional analysis of a given language.

This brings us to the criteria for selecting among grammars. For a linguist of the Saussurian mode, grammars are selected on purely formal, descriptive grounds. The "best" grammar is that grammar which describes all the possible sentences in a language (and excludes impossible sentences) with the smallest number of rules and elements. However, the Chomskian notion of "competence" introduces another criterion for selection among competing descriptive systems: If a grammar is also a model of psychologically real, tacit knowledge of a language, then the "best" grammar is the one that provides a best fit to the nature of a language-using mind. In principle, a less parsimonious grammar may be preferable as a model of competence if it is more plausible on psychological grounds. But what does "psychological plausibility" mean? Presumably, a complete model of linguistic knowledge should describe and predict a variety of psycholinguistic facts in addition to the set of possible sentences in a language. We might create such a model by describing tacit knowledge of sentence structure in one component, and constructing additional components to handle other "performance" facts (memory, attention, motivation, etc.). Alternatively, it might be possible to construct a unified model in which competence and performance facts are described with the same elements, categories, and relational symbols. Such a unified model might be less elegant in its formal description of sentence relations than a model devoted exclusively to that subset of linguistic knowledge. We assume, however, that an inelegant model will be preferable to a more elegant one if it manages to describe and predict a larger range of facts with a minimal amount of baggage. What is clumsy at one level may be more parsimonious at another.

It seems likely, given our present understanding of form–function relations, that a pure Level 4 functionalist model is *logically* possible but *empirically* implausible. There are certain peculiar subsystems within languages, such as the German gender system, which have defied description in functional terms. There is no conceivable way to map these gender markings onto meaningful "natural" intermediate categories like "sex." This does not mean that the arbitrary German gender system had no function in language history, nor that gender markings are useless baggage within synchronic use of the language. It is possible that such arbitrary systems were used at some point in history to code distinctions such as animacy and inanimacy; but that with time the original distinctions have weakened and the classifications become arbitrary (Bloomfield, 1933/1961, pp. 271–2). However, the category is still needed to mark many of the original distinctions (Grebe, 1973, pp. 161–4). Consider the way that we use numbers and letters in setting up an ad hoc descriptive system, for example, "functionalist Levels 1, 2, 3 and 4." Numerical concepts of ordinality are only marginally related to the concepts being expressed. We could just as well have said "Levels *A, B, C,* and *D*" or "black, white, orange, and blue." However, once such a convention is established in communication, it is difficult to get rid of it, if we are going to continue to understand each other. Readily available metaphorical markings like sex and shape may be used in moments of rapid lexical expansion to differentiate types within a class; once established, they become *perceptually* necessary even if they are *conceptually* opaque. At Levels 1 and 2, then, a functionalist argument could be made regarding systems like gender morphology in German. At Level 3, however, it is extraordinarily unlikely that children could use this function in acquiring the morphological system. Because there are no meanings to serve as mnemonics for recovering a given gender ending, the child must simply memorize the endings by rote, as part of the word (MacWhinney, 1978). A grammar, or model of the set of intermediate categories that constitute knowledge of grammar, will probably have to be written using formal symbols like " + F" and " + M" that correspond to the set of correlated surface forms used to map particular lexical items, within particular semantic relationships.

In short, Level 4 functionalism is useful as a pure analytic position, but is unlikely to work all the time in the analysis of most languages. It may, however, be useful for *parts* of the grammar. For example, we will argue later that a reasonable Level 4 description could be made for the relationship between the surface forms that constitute subjectivalization (e.g., word order, verb agreement) and the underlying categories of "topic" and "agent." We may not need intermediate formal symbols like " + S" to model the way those functions are mapped. Before turning to details of the topic system, however, we think it would be useful to present in more general terms our own position regarding causal relationships between form and function, using the four positions just outlined as analytic tools.

6.2. The competition model of form–function relations

Our arguments in favor of a competition model of grammar revolve around six basic tenets. We believe that a full articulation of the functionalist model will need to build on each of these six tenets. But exactly how these tenets interrelate and how they should be further constrained (N. Chomsky, 1976) must remain a task for future research. At the present stage in the development of this approach, what seems to be most in order is an outline of the principles that should underlie the basic approach.

Tenet 1: channel limitations. The resources of the acoustic–articulatory channel for mapping meanings are limited in two ways: (1) Only four kinds of signals are possible – lexical items, word-order patterns, morphological markings, and intonational contours – and (2) the interactions of these four kinds of signals are further constrained by a variety of perceptual–mnemonic–articulatory factors that converge to create implicational relations among types of surface solutions. To illustrate how these limits operate, let us consider a simple metaphor. Two players are each seated before a Chinese checkerboard. One player has a relatively complex, nonlinear pattern of marbles on his board; the other player has an empty board. The two players cannot see or hear each other. They are connected only by a long tube that permits one marble at a time to be passed between players. Player A must send his marbles down the tube in such a fashion that player B can reconstruct the same nonlinear pattern on his board. These are the only restrictions. The participants will have repeated opportunities to find out if they are successful, and they can work out any solution they like to the problem of mapping nonlinear board patterns onto a linear marble channel. It will soon become clear, however, that the solutions must involve some combination of four types:

1. They can develop rules that particular *colors* or *types* of marbles belong in particular spots on the checkerboard, or in particular pattern configurations;
2. they can develop rules that the *order* of marbles coming down the tube determines their position on the board;

3. they can develop rules connecting particular *markings* on the marbles to positions on the board (with the constraint that these must be small and minimal markings – otherwise one could cheat by writing a picture of the board on each marble!); and
4. they can vary the *speed* or *spin* on the marbles coming down the tube to determine their position in the pattern.

Regardless of which solutions, in what combinations, the participants choose, the nature of the task of mapping nonlinear information onto linear channel with a set of discrete, minimal elements formally constrains the set of possible solutions to the task. The analogies to language are obvious, though overly simple. Mapping by color or type of marble corresponds roughly to choice of lexical items within semantic-pragmatic categories. Order of marbles is analogous to word-order solutions. Mapping through marble markings corresponds to morphological marking of lexical items. The spin, speed, and intensity of marble travel down the chute stands in loose analogy to prosodic phenomena in speech. Nor are these four types of solutions independent of one another. The first and last marble down the chute will probably be the easiest to track; it will be harder to keep track of middle positions. Calculations of speed, spin, and intensity will tend to sum and slide as the marbles come in, so that these solutions will probably interact with order and clarity of marking. As we systematically vary marble color or class with marble markings, it may sometimes be difficult to tell whether we have a new marble per se or a version of marble marking. In other words, there will be interactions between "lexical" and "morphological" solutions. Finally, it is likely that symmetrical patterns across a complex mapping through time will be easier to construct and decode than more irregular patterns (Garner, 1974).

Much of the functionalist literature in diachronic linguistics has involved implicational relations like these within language (e.g., Antinucci, 1977; Bartsch & Vennemann, 1972; Lehmann, 1973). For example, there is a strong statistical tendency for SVO languages to make use of prepositions rather than postpositions, whereas in SOV languages the opposite is the case – as though it were somehow easier to put all the "verby" stuff (e.g., verbs, adjectives, locative phrases) in the same position relative to nouns, either pre- or post-positionally. Vennemann (1974) has suggested that such implicational universals indicate a tendency for languages to make consistent, symmetrical use of either *operator + operand* or *operand + operator* as basic orders. Kuno (1974) has noted how another set of universals reflects the attempt to preserve the "inherent unity" of the verb phrase so that V and O are always close together in a sentence (see also Maratsos & Abramovitch, 1975). Unfortunately, in the absence of a greater amount of psycholinguistic evidence that some combinations are indeed more perceivable or memorable than others, it is difficult to evaluate fully the various functionalistic explanations for such linguistic universals. For present purposes, our point is that the limited stock of channel resources available in mapping nonlinear meanings onto the linear acoustic–articulatory channel can be further depleted by complex interactions among types of surface forms according to their relative "processibility." These varying constraints determine the surface territory or "real estate" that is available for distribution to a larger set of meanings and communicative functions.

Tenet 2: informational pressures on the channel. The set of meanings that any individual might wish to convey is infinite – although there are characteristic classes or types of meanings that seem to be universal (e.g., the relationship among the agent, the action, and the thing acted upon). Furthermore, in a given communicative situation, the same referent may play several communicative roles, just as, in the marble analogy, the same marble may play a role in several cross-hatching patterns on the board. For example, the referent "John" may be an actor in a complex situation, and at the same time be standing in a discourse relation that is relatively independent of his role as an actor. Also, John himself may be present in the communicative situation, demanding an appropriate amount of deference to his status – so we have to be particularly careful how we refer to him, and toward what ends. How can we mark so many patterned relations onto one marble? For purposes of illustration, we will concentrate here on three separable classes of information that can all be assigned to the same referent: semantic-cognitive, pragmatic-attentional, and social-motivational information. However, as we hope to illustrate with regard to one section of the pragmatic component, there are complex competitions and interactions *within* each sector (e.g., factors influencing topic selection), as well as *between* sectors (e.g., topic versus agent).

Tenet 3: two classes of solutions. Given the competitions dictated by Tenets 1 and 2, we suggest that pathways or solutions to the competition for surface forms can be classed into two basic types: "divide the spoils" and "peaceful coexistence." The divide-the-spoils solution refers to a distribution of surface territory in which each sector receives its own set of mappings, that is, a one-function–one-signal approach. For example, a language may reserve word order primarily to mark information about specific case role relations. Pragmatic information will be mapped instead with some combinations of stress and particular lexical items. Alternatively, a language may mark case role information primarily through morphological markings. The word-order signals are then "free" to encode pragmatic information.

The peaceful-coexistence solution is, by contrast, a form of many-to-one mapping. Briefly stated, peaceful coexistence solutions reflect certain statistical regularities in discourse in which two distinct roles are shared by the same element a very large proportion of the time. Given this high-probability overlap, the language may decide not to "waste" two distinct mappings where one will generally suffice. For example, given the statistical fact that human agents tend to be the topic about 80 to 90 percent of the time in informal discourse (see, e.g., Duranti & Ochs, 1979), languages may use particular high-priority surface mappings to encode *both* agent and topic. In short, these two sectors may share a common surface device, in this case the correlated set of surface features involved in subjectivalization. For situations in which the agent is not the topic, alternative routes will have to be found – perhaps low-priority, relatively cumbersome devices that the language can "afford" for low-probability cases (e.g., passives, clefts). In a few cases, the language may allow such low-probability events to remain ambiguous. Thus Lisu has no way of coding agency apart from topicality (Li & Thompson, 1976, p. 473). We will discuss situations like this in more detail later on, when we round out our discussion of Tenet 3 by presenting a prototype model for describing heterogeneous grammatical categories governing peaceful-coexistence solutions.

Tenet 4: conventionalization. Research on human and animal learning is based upon the premise that previously successful solutions tend to be repeated in new instances, even in cases where the solution might be slightly less than optimal. Furthermore, learned behaviors tend to move toward an increasingly stereotyped form as nonessential elements of the original solution drop out (B. Schwartz, 1978). There is, apparently, some kind of trade-off between current fit and the time and effort involved in making new calculations for each new encounter. The phenomenon of stereotypy within individuals is related to the development of conventions between individuals. In encounters between organisms, the cost of new calculations and readjustments to fit the moment may be particularly high, multiplicative rather than additive, because each new adjustment by organism A requires accounting by B, and so forth. Insofar as organisms need to predict one another's behavior, there will be a constant pressure toward conventionalization or stereotyping of signals. This evolutionary process has been noted by many ethologists interested in communicative displays in animals (Bateson, 1973; Eibl-Eibesfeldt, 1977), and by students of communication in human infants (e.g., Bates, Camaioni, & Volterra, 1975; Bruner, 1975). However, in a complex behavioral system, social predictability is only one of several functional pressures on form. If a conventional behavior is in the service of several functions, there will necessarily be a competition between conventionalization and the functional fit of the behavior to a variety of goals.

Applying the principle of conventionalization to the emergence of grammar, we must assume that languages strive toward a "group solution" in meeting the competing constraints of communication. At a given moment in processing, the set of mappings that constitute the group solution may be less than optimal for a particular individual. However, he must adopt the group solution despite some extra costs in efficiency of processing in order to be understood by a fellow human being. The conventional nature of language imposes an inherent conservatism on language change under functional pressures. Any changes that do take place, in response to the functional constraints experienced by individuals, must take place across the group using that language.

Tenet 5: disequilibrium. It is unlikely that any single group solution will preserve the optimal fit between form and function for all members of the group. Thus languages are always undergoing a certain amount of disequilibrium and adjustment. Because changes take place gradually across time (involving mutual adjustments of many individuals to one another), a "repair" or adjustment of the system in one sector may have repercussions throughout the rest of the system that do not become evident until the initial change is well under way. Vennemann (1974) has proposed, for example, that symmetry principles in processing and phonological erosion in production are two competing constraints on language that almost invariably have a contradictory effect on one another. He proposes that this particular competition is responsible for the historical fact that languages move back and forth from SVO and SOV standard orders. Morphological markings may evolve out of individual lexical items that obey a symmetrical "operator-operand" order. However, production pressure may erode these individual words into inflections attached to other words – "attached" in the sense that they are no longer merely adjacent, but are uttered within the intonational contours of a single item. Through further phonological erosion, these inflections may eventually disappear altogether, so that it becomes necessary to "reinvent" separate lexical items that must meet a new group order, and so forth.

Tenet 6: vestigial solutions. The gradual shift from one set of group solutions to another will mean that, at transitional moments, some conventions will have lost their initial motivational base. In the long run, these vestigial conventions or anomalies should be the "weakest" points in the system and should give way to other, better-motivated ways of mapping meaning into sound. A number of linguists and psychologists have provided evidence that functional anomalies are "attacked" by new generations of children who are acquiring the transitional form of the language, so that language change results (e.g., Halle, 1962; Slobin, 1977). Nevertheless, children will also have to have interim strategies or learning mechanisms for picking up vestigial conventions that provide no experiential fit to their own communicative efforts.

These six tenets are implicit in much of the current functionalist research on diachronic linguistics, and might be viewed as an elaboration of Level 1 (see Table 6.1 for references). However, the concepts of *conventionalization* and *vestigiality* are not predicted at the other three functionalist levels. If it is the case that languages temporarily retain vestigial conventions, then it cannot be true all the time that individuals use surface forms for ongoing functional reasons (Level 2). And if there are certain surface forms that have no experiential base whatsoever, then children cannot use functional information to acquire those forms (Level 3). Finally, a model of grammatical knowledge in individuals may need some ad hoc formal symbols or categories to handle those surface facts which have temporarily lost their communicative base (Level 4).

Within the competition model, then, the explanatory principles of conventionalization and vestigiality exist to handle the exceptions to a purely functional system. If they are to have any real explanatory value, these principles must not be applied in a circular fashion; if we simply label as "vestigial" any linguistic phenomenon that we have failed to explain in functional terms, then the notion of vestigiality becomes a fudge factor and nothing more. A complete competition model of form–function relationships must contain a theory of vestigiality that predicts where such events are likely to occur in the language, and how vestigial forms are acquired by children and stored and accessed by adults.

There is no such theory right now, as far as we know. However, a number of ideas that have been proposed by linguists and psycholinguists could be built into a theory of vestigiality. At Level 1, predictions about the nature of vestigial structures are based upon the assumption in a competition model that waste is expensive, and functional anomalies will be tolerated only in sectors where the competition is minimal, and/or only for a relatively brief period in language history. Level 2 functionalism must claim that vestigial solutions would involve additional processing time, anomalist or rote solutions, and inefficiencies in storage and retrieval. Level 3 functionalism must maintain that vestigial solutions would be acquired later, be less productive of overgeneralizations, and not lead to further developmental progressions. Some ideas relevant to a theory of vestigial structures include the following:

1. Vestigial or functionally anomalous structures should be among the first to disappear during language change, as the language reshuffles its precious resources.

2. Temporary exceptions to functional rules should occur primarily in language-specific rather than language-universal aspects of the grammar.

This prediction is based on the assumption that universal aspects of grammar emerge in response to universal and inescapable functional pressures, where "drift" or erosion of a form–function relationship is very unlikely.

3. There may be certain kinds of vestigial devices that do occur in a large set of languages. These devices are likely to be high-probability solutions to a common but temporary moment in language change. For example, when a language is changing from case inflection to word order to encode information about agency, there may be a particularly heavy use of clitic pronouns as a "backup device," to double mark the agent in sentences where word order is ambiguous. To sustain this temporary backup system, certain conventions about agreement between the clitic and the corresponding noun argument may emerge, to make the relationship particularly clear. Once a more reliable word-order system is established, these ancillary conventions may no longer be necessary, and so they drift in different phonological directions within a few generations.

4. Functionally anomalous information is more likely to remain in the language if it involves the form of individual lexical items rather than rules governing constituents from different lexical categories. One consequence should be that meaningless morphological markers would be easier to maintain in the language than meaningless rules of word order. This prediction is based on the assumption that the lexicon is well suited for storing arbitrary phonological information about discrete items, that is, rote information. Hence, although a given vestigial marker is not used to identify the lexical item itself (i.e., it is not part of the word), it may be less expensive to store the leftover marker with other phonological symbols in the lexicon than to create a component to store symbols for syntactic relationships that no longer have a basis in meaning (MacWhinney, 1978).

5. Children will tend to avoid vestigial forms, to delay their acquisition to a relatively late point in development. For example, MacWhinney (1978) has provided evidence that productive (i.e., nonrote) use of gender in German is acquired later than productive use of case marking. Both gender and case marking map onto the same set of devices, but case is functionally motivated whereas gender is not. In the same vein, Moeser and Bregman (1972) have shown in experiments on artificial language learning in adults that meaningless patterns are extremely difficult to acquire compared with patterns that can be assimilated to some semantic base.

6. If a functionally autonomous form is acquired early, its semantic range may be very small indeed, perhaps confined to a few individual lexical items (as in the Hungarian rule of v deletion [MacWhinney, 1978]). In short, the grammatical device may be memorized as part of a particular lexical set or as a nonproductive idiomatic expression.

7. In addition to rote as an acquisition device, children may make relatively greater use of imitation in acquiring vestigial forms. This prediction is based on the assumption that a meaningless item cannot be acquired for its communicative purpose, and hence must be perceived and used at first purely as an interesting vocal event. Newport, L. Gleitman, and H. Gleitman (1977) have provided evidence suggesting that some language-specific aspects of grammar (e.g., auxiliary fronting in English) are "environmentally sensitive," whereas other more universal aspects of grammar are "environmentally insensitive." Environmentally sensitive forms tend to be correlated with aspects of use of those forms by parents, whereas the more universal aspects of grammar apparently require only minimal modeling by the adult. We propose that vestigial structures are more likely to be environmentally sensitive. These are by definition forms that the child is not looking for, because he has no communicative use for them. Hence such functional anomalies will be acquired only if the child is heavily exposed to them by parental modeling.

These ideas are predictions, ideas for future research, and not conclusions based on accumulated evidence. They are presented simply to show that a theory of vestigiality within a competition model could be more than a catalogue of exceptions to functionalist principles. In the next two sections, we will try to be more specific about empirical tests of the competition model, describing some aspects of the topic–comment system and relations between topicalization and case role information.

6.3. Topic–comment relations and grammar: competition within the system

Prague school functionalists (Dezső, 1972; Firbas, 1964; Sgall, Hajičova, & Benešova, 1973) and British functionalists (Firth, 1957; Halliday, 1967) claim that discourse relations like topic and comment are grammatically marked; hence any systematic description of the grammar must take these relations into account. This view is becoming widely accepted in American linguistics (see, e.g., Givón, 1979; Li, 1975, 1976), and there are now a number of proposals describing the relationship among the topic–comment system, the case role system, and various aspects of surface grammar. The semantic-pragmatic meanings that constitute topic and comment have proven elusive and frustrating to linguists who want to incorporate them within a formal grammar. There is very little agreement about the internal structure of this system, and every investigator who studies it feels the need to add new terms and new distinctions. Table 6.6 lists just a few of the terms that linguists and psychologists have used to describe some aspect of the topic–comment system. In some proposals, there is one and only one topic function that is associated with multiple forms (e.g., Givón,

Table 6.6. *Topic–comment terminology*

	Reference
Bipolar terms	
New information/Old information	Bates, 1976; Chafe, 1976; Fava & Tirondola, unpublished
New information/Given information	H. Clark & Haviland, 1977
Comment/Topic	Bates, 1976; deLaguna, 1927/1963; Hornby, 1972; Sechehaye, 1926; Vygotsky, 1934/1962
Figure/Ground	Bates, 1976; MacWhinney, 1974
Bound information/Free information	Rommetveit, 1974
Conversational dynamic element/ Conversational static element	Firbas, 1964
Rheme/Theme	Halliday, 1967
Bifunctional terms	
Information focus/Theme	Halliday, 1967
Secondary topicalization/Primary topicalization	Fillmore, 1968a
Focus/Topic	N. Chomsky, 1971; Jackendoff, 1972; Dezsö, 1970
Emphasis/Theme	Dezsö, 1970
Related logical terms	
Preposition/Presupposition	Bates, 1976
Predicate/Argument	Reichenbach, 1947
Operator/Nucleus	Seuren, 1969

Source: Bates & MacWhinney, 1979.

1979). In other proposals, there are a variety of functional distinctions that are marked onto surface forms (e.g., Chafe, 1976). This diversity of views is discussed in more detail in Bates and MacWhinney (1979). Our point for present purposes is that the topic–comment system, although admittedly an important part of the grammar, turns out to be very difficult to describe.

Why is the topic–comment system so difficult to analyze? Although there is some disagreement concerning details, there is, by way of comparison, much more agreement among investigators concerning the major semantic roles that underlie the case system. However, the case role system corresponds to a world of external objects and events, a referent world that all share and all can use to verify whether an associated linguistic expression has been used properly. The topic–comment system involves elusive internal states, the speaker's ideas about how to structure discourse, "stage" utterances, foreground and background information.

In studying how grammatical forms map onto discourse functions, the linguist is forced to describe psychological structures and mental states that are not well understood even by the psychologists. But we have to begin somewhere.

Our own efforts to describe the topic–comment system revolve around five structural features: one *function,* with *multiple motives,* applied in *layers of points,* in varying *degrees of specification,* resulting in a need for a *diversity of surface options.*

A single function. Topic is defined as *what is being talked about,* and *comment* is defined as *the point being made about that topic.* In other words, the topic–comment system involves a single communicative function of point making, albeit applied in a variety of ways in the service of a variety of motives.

Multiple motives. Some writers have, in contrast with our proposal, defined topic as given information, comment as new information. In our approach, factors like givenness and newness are motives that affect the *selection* of points to be made and things to make points about. But they do not define the function itself. Indeed, a variety of motives compete and converge to determine selection of topics and comments. We will discuss three of these motives here: givenness–newness, perspective, and salience. For a fuller analysis of this system see MacWhinney (1980).

Let us first consider givenness. Givenness is a central motive for topic selection, just as newness is a motive for the selection of comments. These facts are no doubt based on some simple principles of politeness and relevance in discourse (Grice, 1975). Because discourse is a cooperative enterprise we must struggle to provide continuity and to make comments only about information that is already available to both speaker and hearer. Similarly, we add our comments to this shared network of information in an effort to be new, interesting, and at the same time mutually relevant.

However, the topic–comment division is also made in situations in which all the information in the utterance is equally new. In such situations, it is easier to observe how other motives for topic selection operate. One of these has been variously described as "point-of-view" (Friedman, 1955; Owens, Dafoe, & Bower, 1977), "perspective" (S. Dik, 1978; MacWhinney, 1977), "ego-perspective" (Ertel, 1974, 1977), and the "me-first principle" (Cooper & Ross, 1975). Topic selection tends to move along a continuum from elements of discourse closely identified with the speaker to less speakerlike elements of discourse (e.g., agents rather than experiences, instruments rather than locations). Hence, by default, the rest of the relations in a proposition (some or all of which will go into the comment) tend to be relatively more distant from ego. The notion of a case role hierarchy for promotion to subject has been discussed by Dik (1978); Duranti and Ochs (1979); Fillmore (1968a); Givón (1976, p. 152); Kuno (1976, p. 432); and Zubin (1979). According to these writers, the hierarchy for promotion to subject is

agent > experiencer > dative > instrument > patient > location

This hierarchy reflects, in large measure, a preference for animates over inanimates and humans over nonhumans in establishing the point of view for a sentence.

Within case categories, perspective also interacts with the person system to influence promotion to subject (Givón, 1976; Kuno, 1976). Following the "closeness-to-ego" principle, first-person subjects are more probable than second-person, and first- and second-person arguments enjoy certain syntactic privileges over third-person arguments of the same verb. Silverstein (1976) has shown a similar person hierarchy in his description of ergative languages and the process of "ergativization."

In sum, the function of perspective taking influences the selection of topic, and hence the selection of subjectivalization devices associated with topic, via case role hierarchies and person hierarchies within cases. In addition to the relationship between subject and topic, perspective can influence ordering within nominal compounds where no verb is involved. For example, Cooper and Ross (1975) have shown that the me-first principle predicts noun ordering in idiomatic compounds such as "cowboys and Indians" or "man and machine."

There are certainly exceptions to me-first orderings, such as the fact that it is more polite in English to say "you and I" than "I and you" – although some exceptions might in fact "prove the rule" in that they are intentional reversals of a natural tendency in order to be particularly polite or deferential. None of the authors cited so far has argued that the effects of perspective are absolutely determinate across all languages. However, it is possible for the resulting hierarchies to become completely conventionalized in some languages. For example, in Navajo the order of mention of nominal elements in a sentence is fully determined by their relative animacy, with more animate elements coming first. One of the more interesting implications of a functionalist approach involves the historical passage from a probabilistic ordering preference, based on universal tendencies, to the development of a convention that is fully determinate. We will return to this point shortly.

Givenness and perspective still do not account for all instances of topic and comment selection. Both these choices are associated with perceptual and attentional "vividness" or "salience" – a poorly understood dimension, one that requires a great deal of information about specific situations and about the role of attention in information processing. Nevertheless, as Horgan (1978) has shown in delineating the role of idiosyncratic salience effects on child word order, these factors do seem to operate systematically once we have located them. For example, one of Horgan's subjects coded the word *ball* in initial position in describing any picture that had a ball in it – a reliable reflection of his personal preferences, that is, what was important or salient for him. Presumably, once a speaker has decided what is salient, then surface forms that vary with salience can be assigned in turn. The problem for both the psychologist and the linguist is to come up with an operational definition of the highly idiosyncratic notion of salience.

Layers. Consider the following sentence:

> It was *this* beer, not the other one, which was drunk by the man who only *recently* came back from Cincinnati (as opposed to the guy who came back from there a week ago).

Obviously there is more than one topic–comment relationship within this sentence. Moreover, the same element serves as a comment at one level, and as a topic at another:

Topic	*Comment*
the other one	*this* beer
this beer	was drunk by the man
the man	who had only *recently* returned from Cincinnati
had returned from Cincinnati	only *recently*
the guy who came back from there a week ago	the man who had only *recently* returned from Cincinnati

We suggest that the point-making function is recursive, and can be applied within a given utterance an indefinite number of times. Notations could be used to describe such nested point-making relations. These notations would be formally analogous to predicate-argument bracketing in the logical analysis of complex expressions.

Degrees of specification. There is a wide range of variation in the amount of specification necessary to establish topics and make points about them. Here the same point is being made about the same topic, but the circumstances surrounding that point clearly vary:

(1)   Magnificent!
(2)   That was magnificent!
(3)   That violin solo was magnificent!
(4)   That violin solo in the third movement of the Beethoven piece was magnificent!

(5)   I went to the symphony last night and, among other things, heard
       a Beethoven symphony. There was a violin solo in the third move-
       ment that was magnificent!
(6)   In my country we have a form of music in which . . .

The topic for the comment "magnificent" is the same in all six cases.
But these different utterances reflect an increase in the degree of topic
specification necessary for the point to be understood – ranging from zero
specification to a passage that threatens to be infinitely long. The same
continuum also applies to comment specification, which can range from
a small nonverbal gesture (e.g., pointing, shrugging, grinning) to extremely long passages of "commentary."

Devices. Given the complexities of the point-making function, any language must provide many devices to carry out its communicative work.
In our view, some of the confusion in the literature on form–function
relations in discourse results from a failure to separate these psychological
dimensions in explaining the determination of surface forms associated
with the topic system.
     Later on we will describe some Level 2 and Level 3 research that we
are carrying out to test the validity of the competition model within the
topic–comment system. First, however, we must describe further competitions between topicalization and other basic communicative functions.

6.4. Topic–comment relations and grammar: competition with other systems

As noted in the preceding section, perspective or similarity to ego is one
of the motives that operates to determine topic selection. This tendency
provides a reliable point of contact between topicalization and the case
role system, resulting in the high correlation between topic and agent in
the assignment of surface forms, particularly the surface forms associated
with the conventional notion of "subject." Although topic and agent tend
to be assigned to the same element in most sentences, there will inevitably
be instances where these two roles are assigned to different arguments
of the same verb. For example, principles of salience or givenness may
motivate the selection of an inanimate object as the topic, whereas the
animate referent is automatically assigned the agent role. What happens
in these instances of competition?
     The respective contributions of topic and agent are discussed in detail
in a recent volume entitled *Subject and Topic* (Li, 1976). The debate
centers on three kinds of underlying grammatical categories: agent, topic,
and a hypothetical grammatical category called "subject" that is neither
agent nor topic, but is defined exclusively in formal terms. Let us consider

how these categories are apportioned in different languages. The case role hierarchy just described reflects a continuum from more to less speakerlike elements. Although the continuum itself appears to be universal, languages vary in the point at which they draw a conventional boundary separating elements that can be mapped as subjects (Dik, 1978). For example, in English it is possible to assign the subject role to such far-removed arguments on the hierarchy as instrument and location. In Dutch, instruments and locatives cannot be encoded as subjects regardless of what points the Dutchman wants to make about them. There are, however, no known languages in which instruments can be mapped as subjects but agents cannot. In short, there are differences among languages in the "metaphoric range" with which agency dominates subject assignment, but the core or "best" subject is always an agent.

Working from the other side of the competition, there are some languages in which subject phenomena seem to be governed almost exclusively by the category "topic." Some of the debate in the Li volume centers on Philippine languages, particularly Tagalog. In Tagalog, there is an NP that is marked both by the preposition *ang* and by a prefix on the verb. Some Philippinists call this *ang* NP the "focus"; others call it the "topic"; still others choose to treat it as a type of subject in the more traditional sense. The view that the *ang* NP is a "true" subject is difficult to maintain. Keenan (1976b) has provided an extensive list of phenomena that correlate across languages with the role of subject. Applying some of these criteria, Schachter (1976, 1977) has noted that the *ang* NP does not control either reflexivization or co-referential complement subject deletion – properties that Keenan views as central to defining subjects. On the other hand, the *ang* NP does not function entirely as a true topic, that is, a category determined entirely by pragmatic constraints. For example, Schwartz (1976) has argued from data on the closely related Ilocano language that only one focused element can appear in a given sentence. By contrast, in languages like Lisu there can be several topics in a single sentence (layered, as in the beer example cited earlier). Schwartz suggests that this one-per-sentence restriction transforms the *ang* element into a more abstract category that should be defined separately from the topicalization function itself. Similarly, the Philippine focus element cannot be a genitive, whereas topics in other languages can easily be genitives. Finally, the tendency of the Philippine focus to be marked by agreement on the verb convinces some linguists that the *ang* element really is a sentential subject. Hence they would conclude that Tagalog, like all languages, must be described with a universal "subject" category that is neither topic nor agent, although it is associated statistically with both.

Li and Thompson (1976) have proposed a fourfold typology for the languages of the world to describe this kind of distributional evidence.

204   ELIZABETH BATES AND BRIAN MACWHINNEY

The typology is based on a contrast between *subject-prominent* languages like English and *topic-prominent* languages like Lisu. The Philippine languages fall into a third category. Li and Thompson suggest that these languages began with a true topic, which became bound to the case frame of the verb through agreement particles (cf. Givón, 1976). Hence Tagalog and Ilocano have neither clear subjects nor clear topics. The fourth type is exemplified by Japanese, with both subject and topic clearly marked on the surface by separate elements. This type of language supposedly develops out of a subject-prominent language through the increased use of separate topic markers.

The Li and Thompson classification presupposes that subject can exist as an autonomous category. We propose, instead, that the contrast between subject-prominent and topic-prominent languages is really a result of a competition between agent and topic for control of surface phenomena. In the terms that we have introduced here, Japanese and Tagalog can be viewed as two cases of a divide-the-spoils solution. In Tagalog, however, the agent is more clearly marked than the topic, whereas in Japanese the opposite is true. By contrast, English and Lisu represent two different kinds of peaceful-coexistence solutions. English merges agent and topic in most cases, capitalizing on the role of perspective in creating a statistical overlap between these two categories. When the overlap does break down, agency is more likely to dominate in assignment of subjectivalization. Lisu also capitalizes on the overlap between topic and agent, but leans toward topic as a determiner when the two categories diverge.

Our modification of the Li and Thompson typology could be subjected to an experimental test. The various findings noted in Tables 6.3 and 6.4 provide evidence (1) that topics are processed more easily, quickly, and so on as subjects or initial-position elements, and (2) that agents also make "better" subjects in a variety of psycholinguistic tests. Similarly, evidence referenced in Table 6.5 demonstrates that children use both topic and agent information in the acquisition of subject phenomena. None of these lines of evidence, however, tells us what to expect in a situation of competition between topic and agent. We would predict that, in experiments designed to set topic and agent against one another, speakers of Japanese, Lisu, Tagalog, and English would behave quite differently. Suppose we present subjects with picture-description situations (similar to those described in MacWhinney & Bates, 1978), in which one protagonist is set up as topic (using some combination of givenness and salience to achieve that effect) and another protagonist in the same action is more clearly biased as the agent of that particular act. Presumably, an English speaker would be more likely to select the agent as the surface subject of the sentence in his description, whereas the Lisu speaker would assign analogous surface forms to the topic. This would be an excellent example of Level 2 synchronic correlation. It would also support a Level 1 theory about the relationship between form and function across languages. Similarly, if we could demonstrate that Lisu children are drawn more clearly to topic-defined subjects, whereas English children are more likely to use agency in subject assignment, then we might be able to set up Level 3 evidence to test the proposed typology for topic–agent relations.

Although we do not have information of this sort on the more exotic topic-prominent languages discussed in the Li volume, in some of our own ongoing research we are carrying out production experiments contrasting agency and various aspects of topicality in case-marked (Serbo-Croatian, Hungarian) versus word-order (Italian and English) languages. The prediction is that topicalization effects on word order will be greater in the case-inflected languages, where there is an alternative means for marking agency. Part of the problem in carrying out such experiments involves the difficulty of setting up a topic bias. Weak topic manipulations (e.g., two pictures in a row in which one element is given while the others vary) may not be a good analogue to real-life topicalization, where a theme is established along lengthy passages of discourse (see Karmiloff-Smith, 1979b, for evidence on the strength of well-established topic effects across narratives). In MacWhinney and Bates's (1978) experiment on the effects of givenness, a brief givenness manipulation did result in more variations in ordering in Hungarian than in Italian or English, as predicted. However, in current research we are using lengthier topic manipulations, with control over perspective and salience, to determine just how strong the effect of topic is in determining word order in inflected languages.

An alternative type of experiment involves sentence comprehension, when topic information and agent information are set in conflict, in interaction with associated surface forms. We have, for example, used the "enactment" paradigm (Bever, 1970; Dewart, unpublished; Sinclair & Bronckart, 1972; Slobin, Chapter 5) in which adults or children receive a three-element sentence in NVN, NNV, or VNN order and are asked to decide or demonstrate "who did it." The information available for agent selection comes from word order, topicalization (e.g., "This is a cow. Now we're going to talk about this cow. The cow a horse kicks"), contrastive stress (e.g., "THE COW a horse kicks"), and animacy (e.g., reversible sentences like "THE COW a horse kicks" versus nonreversible sentences like "THE PENCIL a horse kicks"). In this kind of many-to-one manipulation, we have set into conflict not only information biasing the speaker toward animacy and topic, but information from surface forms that may vary in the degree to which they exercise absolute as opposed to probabilistic determination of the subject–verb relationship. So far we have results only for the contrast between Italian and English (Bates, McNew, MacWhinney, deVescovi, & Smith, in press). These two languages are both supposedly SVO word-order languages, without case markings for agency (except in the personal pronouns, which are of course eliminated from the experiment). Hence, in principle, the formal conventions of the languages are the same and could map onto underlying categories in much the same fashion. In practice, however, Italians make much more use of alternative word orders than English speakers, at least in informal discourse. Therefore Italians have considerably more experience in using semantic and pragmatic information to interpret various word orders, and this functional difference seems to have an enormous impact on the ways in which Italian and English speakers interpret sentences in this experiment. In English, word order is used heavily. In NVN sentences, the tendency to choose the first noun as agent is almost absolute, even when animacy provides conflicting information (e.g., "The pencil kicks the cow"). In NNV and VNN sentences alike, there is also a strong (though probabilistic) word-order tendency, with significant preference for the *second* noun as agent in both of the noncanonical orders. This second-noun strategy is, in fact, in keeping with permissible alternative orders of left dislocation ("Egg creams I like") and right dislocation ("Really gets on my nerves, that guy") in colloquial English. Italians, by contrast, show a massive preference for animacy, even in NVN sentences. Thus the Italian adult is far more likely to choose the cow as agent than an English speaker in "The pencil kicks the cow." For the NNV and VNN types, when animacy information is not available, the Italians seem to be particularly sensitive to topic and stress to help disambiguate the utterance. There is no word-order strategy analogous to the one adopted by English adults for noncanonical sentences.

These results suggest that the "functional underpinnings" of what is superficially the same kind of formal language can vary enormously. Though both Italian and English are formally word-order languages, the role of word order is more strongly conventionalized in English usage than in Italian. This psycholinguistic fact is consistent with historical facts about the two languages, insofar as Italian is still in transition from its case-marked Latin ancestor to a more fully word-order-based format. Hence we may have captured the functional system that creates formal changes *in vivo* at a transitional moment. In some ongoing research by our group, the same kinds of experiments are being administered in Serbo-Croatian, with particular emphasis on a dialect area between Yugoslavia and Italy where the case system is beginning to erode, but has not gone as far as modern Italian in the transition from case to word order. We expect the "functional map" surrounding performance in this dialect to look much more flexible than, for example, performance by speakers of a less ambiguous, intact case system like Hungarian.

These experiments are in progress, and any results to date are certainly inconclusive. They are presented primarily to illustrate how Level 2 and

3 experiments can be used to map out the "weights" attached to different form–function relations within a competition model. It is our hope that this approach will also be useful for diachronic studies of historical language change (Level 1) and the pathways that children take in the acquisition of form–function mappings (Level 3). It is not enough simply to show that there *is* a relationship between meaning and form (e.g., that definite articles tend to be used to map old information), because such information is available through much more parsimonious armchair techniques. Our goal is not to verify well-known one-to-one mappings, but to examine the *relative* causal control of different forms and functions in a network of relationships, for different kinds of language use (e.g., comprehension versus production), at different points in development, in a carefully selected set of languages that contrast in the kinds of solutions to competition that they provide.

Although research like this could support a Level 4 hypothesis about the nature of the intermediate structures in a form–function mapping, it is in principle possible to explain these findings with functionalist grammars or any of a variety of purely formal systems. However, information like this does make it possible to speculate about just how a Level 4 functionalist description might be built for certain aspects of the grammar. We will conclude with some thoughts about how to construct a grammar for at least parts of a language using only such "natural" functional categories as topic and agent.

6.5. On the internal structure of grammatical categories

First of all, we will define a grammatical category as the set of elements that can be mapped onto a single surface grammatical device, or onto a correlated set of surface grammatical devices. For example, the set of related surface devices that constitute subjectivalization (e.g., initialization, agreement with the verb, nominative case pronouns) are used to map a corresponding class of elements that we will call the category "subject." Similar definitions apply to the categories of verb, noun, and so on. We should note at the outset that this definition is technically at odds with a transformational grammar account of deep-structure subject. Strictly speaking, "subject" is a relation rather than a category in the standard or extended standard theory. It is defined as the noun phrase that is directly dominated by the S-node (Sentence) and that combines with a VP in a hierarchically organized syntactic tree. However, whether it is defined as a relation (as in Chomsky's standard theory) or a category (as in relational grammar of Perlmutter & Postal, 1977), "subject" is treated as an abstract symbol that is the direct input to the transformational component. Such symbols are primary, axiomatic, and unitary. They have no internal structure. Presumably any element marked +S,

+V, +N, and so forth is an equally good candidate for mapping onto corresponding surface forms. The semantic component can act to *interpret* these symbols and to project them onto a variety of semantic categories and/or relations. However, these symbols cannot be defined in terms of their eventual semantic interpretations. In other words, traditional transformational grammars assume an independence of syntactic and semantic categories. Moreover, as Noam Chomsky (1971) has emphasized, it is the syntactic component, and not the semantic or stylistic component, that controls the structural "well-formedness" of the sentence. By contrast, a Level 4 functionalist approach seeks to equate the categories that are mapped onto surface grammar with a set of semantic-pragmatic elements, bypassing an independent, abstract, and unitary set of syntactic categories or symbols.

But what kind of category can contain all of the elements that can be mapped, for example, as surface subjects? Adult English speakers can generate, comprehend, and judge as grammatical a variety of sentences that contain nonagentive subjects (e.g., "The knife cuts" or "The door opened"), nontopicalized agents (e.g., "*John* hit the ball, not Fred" or "In ran the rabbit"), stative as opposed to active verbs (e.g., "John knew Mary very well"), and abstract "entitylike" nouns (e.g., "John's drinking bothers me"). If we are to include this capacity in our description of the native speaker's linguistic knowledge, how do we account for the fact that no single semantic or pragmatic category can contain all the elements that are mapped with a particular surface form? How do we describe the semantic-pragmatic heterogeneity of form-class membership in the grammar?

Criterial attribute models

Traditionally, classes or categories have been defined according to a *criterial attribute model* (see, e.g., Bourne, 1967). Within such models, a category is defined by a set of features shared by all members, which are necessary and sufficient conditions for category membership. If we accept this traditional approach to the internal structure of categories, then we are forced to define categories like subject, noun, and verb so abstractly that we arrive at the equivalent of single-feature definitions like [+S], [+N], and [+V]. To illustrate how the criterial attribute model would work in this case, take the example presented in Figure 6.1. Here we have four individuals or entities (A, B, C, D) that are candidates for category membership. Each of these entities (objects, events, etc.) is comprised of a set of features: A contains features 1 through 7; B contains 3, 4, 5, 6, and 9; C contains 3, 4, 7, and 8; D contains only 1 and 2. Can these four entities be members of the same category? Within a criterial attribute model, they cannot. Thus we cannot form one category con-

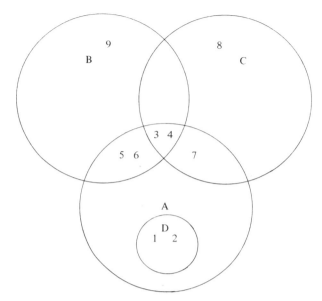

Figure 6.1. An illustration of the category definition problem. Letters A–D label the Euler circles and stand for objects exhibiting the features numbered 1–9.

sisting of entities A through D. The *extension* of this class (i.e., the descriptive list of the members with all their features) includes the *union* of the full set of features 1 through 9. However, the *intension* of the class (i.e., the defining features shared by all members) can include no more than features 3 and 4, the *intersect* of A, B, and C. Because D falls outside that intersect, it cannot be a member, even though its features (1, 2) are contained in the union of A through C. This situation can be summarized as follows:

1. Possession of criterial features 3 and 4 is a necessary and sufficient condition for category membership.
2. Possession of additional features (1, 2, 5–9) is irrelevant to category membership.
3. It is not possible for two individuals to be members of the same class without overlapping in features (at *least* the criterial features).
4. All relevant features are weighted equally, and degrees of possession of features are irrelevant to determining category membership. In other words, there are no grounds by which one member can be a "better" instance of the category than another.
5. Even if a given individual possesses noncriterial features in common with members of the class (D in Figure 6.1), that individual is in no way "closer" to membership in the category.

If we were to assume for a moment that the criterial attribute model could be an appropriate description of the psychological structure of grammatical categories, then it would become obvious why adult competence must be described in terms of abstract syntactic symbols with no internal structure. There would be essentially *no* intersect shared by all the semantic and pragmatic elements that can be mapped as subjects, or as nouns, or as verbs. The "criterial attribute" that unites all the meanings that can be subjectivalized in English would have to be the fact that all of them can be treated as noun phrases. Because English has nominalization mechanisms for turning just about any element into a noun phrase, we would be left with nothing other than / + NP/ and / + S/ to define the grammatical category of subject. Thus, if we accept the criterial attribute model of category structure, we must also accept the system of autonomous syntax as an inevitable corollary.

Prototype models

There is, however, an alternative to the criterial attribute model. This alternative is Rosch's theory of prototypes (see Rosch & Lloyd, 1978). Although this theory has been applied so far primarily to the internal structure of lexical categories (see, e.g., Bowerman, 1976), more recently a few linguists have begun exploring some applications of prototype theory to grammatical categories (Givón, 1979; Lakoff, 1977; Langacker, 1978; Talmy, 1977), and to language learning (Bowerman, 1976; Braine & Wells, 1978; deVilliers, 1980; Schlesinger, 1977b). Rosch's own work deserves more thorough treatment than we can afford here, but fortunately the reader can consult deVilliers (1980) for a brief but thorough review of that research. In this section of the chapter, we will limit ourselves to a condensed set of summary statements about the prototype model for category structure, so that we can demonstrate its applicability to language acquisition as described by the functionalist competition model.

The essential tenets of the prototype approach to category structure can be summarized as follows:

1. *Central tendency.* A category is defined neither by the union nor by the intersect of its members. Rather, a category is defined in terms of a prototypical, or central tendency, member that contains the maximal number of features in common with members of its own set. In a topological system made up of many categories, the prototype stands a *minimum distance* from members of its own set and a *maximum distance* from members of other sets.

2. *Family resemblance.* Category membership is determined on the basis of "family resemblance" to the prototype, that is, on the basis of an overlap in features with the prototypic member.

3. *Goodness of membership.* Just as the prototype is the "best" instance of the category, "goodness" of category membership is defined by the *amount* of overlap in features with the prototype.

4. *Heterogeneous membership.* It is possible for two items to belong to the same category via their overlap with the prototype, but to share no overlap whatsoever with one another (i.e., Cousin John has the family nose and eyes, Uncle Bill has the mouth and hair, whereas Harriet (the prototype) has all four).

5. *Fuzziness.* Although the center of a category may be easy to define, it is more difficult to define peripheral (i.e., minimum-overlap) instances that have more features in common with other sets than with the category of interest. In other words, categories have fuzzy and ill-defined borders that may shift depending on the needs of the category user.

6. *Weighting.* Prototype models can also be used to describe instances in which some *features* of the prototype are more heavily weighted than others. As Tversky (1977) notes, weighting differences may be either *static* (intensive) or *dynamic* (diagnostic). Static weightings focus importance on certain features in all contexts, whereas dynamic weightings change the relative importance of one feature or another in a given context. As certain features increase in their weight or importance in making categorization decisions, a prototype model may come to resemble a criterial attribute model. Hence we can describe prototype structures and criterial attribute structures as two ends of a continuum with feature-weighted models in between. Although not proposed by Rosch herself, the notion of feature weighting is entirely compatible with Rosch's general position. Some recent applications of the feature weighting approach can be found in Tversky's (1977) research on similarity judgments.

If we apply this model to Figure 6.1, the category will be defined in terms of the prototypic member A, because A contains more features in common with the other members of the category than do B, C, or D. This category structure would emerge more clearly if we provided a more complex diagram with several "neighboring" categories. Such a diagram would demonstrate that A has *fewer* features in common with these other classes than do B, C, or D. Although D shares no overlap in features with either B or C, it is entitled to category membership because of its family resemblance to A via features 1 and 2. However, because D shares fewer features with A than any of the other members, it is essentially a "bad" exemplar of the set. Element B, which overlaps with A on four features (3, 4, 5, 6) is the second-best member of the set, and C (which shares only the three features 3, 4, 7) is the third-ranking member. In this model, all the features are weighted equally. However, if the features differed in salience or weighting, then these ranks might change. For example, if 4 and 7 were the most important features of A, then C would be a better exemplar of the set than B.

In an interesting series of experiments, Rosch has demonstrated the psychological reality of prototype structure in a variety of natural categories. She has found that adults have little difficulty rank ordering members of a set. They can easily determine that robins are excellent birds and that ostriches are very poor birds. Prototypic members are easier to comprehend, to produce on demand, and to recall than peripheral members. Moreover, this holds true even when relative frequency in the language is controlled. Information that is learned about a prototypic member is rapidly and easily generalized to peripheral instances, whereas information learned about a peripheral case does not "spread" to the rest of the category so easily. Adults can be shown to derive prototypes in the laboratory, summing across instances in artificial concept learning experiments (Posner & Keele, 1968). In fact, they may even construct a prototype or "best exemplar" that is not administered in the actual stimulus set, an idealization that is judged as "better" than the examples that were actually seen. However, prototypes are not always derived by summing across a large set. Rosch and Mervis (1975) suggest that children build categories around prototypes that are the first exemplars of the set (e.g., the family dog rather than the publicly approved "best" dog). Hence category structure may have to shift across development from first to best instances.

Another point worth mentioning in our brief summary is that the prototype versus criterial attribute dimension in category structure is completely independent of two other dimensions: mode of representation (discrete versus analogue) and abstractness (superordinate versus subordinate class levels). Some confusion in the literature has revolved around the fact that some of Rosch's earlier research investigated domains, such as color, that have analogue structure. Her experiments can also be replicated, however, with stimuli taken from domains that are best described with a discrete feature system. Though prototypes *can* be images or pictures, they are not *defined* as images or pictures. Also, prototypes can exist at any level of superordination in a class hierarchy. The superordinate class "vehicle" can have a prototypic member (in our culture, probably "car"). The class of "cars" can in turn be organized around a prototypic member (perhaps an American sedan, or some composite of small four-door compacts); American compact cars may form a class around a prototypic member (e.g., a Chevette); and so forth. In other work Rosch has also explored this "vertical" dimension, suggesting that it is organized around the so-called basic level or most common level of use. For example, "car" is a basic level in the transportation tree just given; "vehicle" is too superordinate for use in most instances, and "American sedan" is too subordinate and specific for use in all but a handful of cases. In a sense, the basic level is the prototypic level of use in this vertical dimension. However, this abstractness dimension is independent of the "horizontal" dimension of category structure *within* levels.

Finally, we should also note that Rosch does not deny the psychological reality of criterial attribute category structure in some cases, for some purposes. Clearly adults *can* organize categories into the kinds of clear and exhaustive class structures that characterize scientific taxonomies (see, e.g., Bourne, 1967). Rosch's point, however, is that natural categories typically are not organized into criterial attributes for most of the things we do most of the time.

Although prototype theory began as a model of adult categorization, it also provides some striking continuities with what we know about classification abilities in children. Vygotsky (1934/1962) and Bruner (1966) have noted that preschool children tend to group or sort stimuli into "complexive groupings," or family-resemblance structures. For example, a 3-year-old asked to "Put the ones together that are alike" may group a doll, a truck, and a bottle. When probed, he may explain his sorting as follows: "The dolly can ride in the truck, and she can drink the bottle." In other words, the *production* of categories in this age range involves heterogeneous groups, based on featural overlap but not necessarily on intersection of features. Inhelder and Piaget (1959) have reported similar findings for the sorting behaviors of preoperational children. They have argued that the capacity to impose criterial attribute categories on an array is a manifestation of concrete operational logic, and hence is not available until somewhere around 5 to 7 years of age. Bowerman (1976) has suggested that lexical categories in preschool children (particularly very young children) show the same characteristics of complexive groupings. For example, a child might call a nonfurry four-legged animal "kitty," a furry object without legs "kitty," and a nonfurry legless animal with a tail "kitty." However, Thomson and Chapman (1976) have demonstrated that in *comprehension* the child judges some kitties as "better" than others. As E. Clark (1977) has noted, the child seems to be categorizing novel instances according to a logic that can be paraphrased as "This is kind of like a kitty." According to prototype theory, the ways in which children make these extensions are determined by the shape of the prototype and the relative weights of the features it contains.

To summarize, evidence on adult categorization from Rosch and her associates suggests that natural categories are organized around prototypic instances, with membership assigned via family resemblance to the prototype. Evidence on categorization in children suggests that the capacity for criterial attribute classification does not emerge until 5 to 7 years of age. The complexive groupings that characterize preoperational classification can also be used to describe the organization of the lexicon in young children, in both comprehension and production. If we could use similar complexive groupings or prototypes to delineate a model of grammatical categories, we would have made progress toward a more unified theory of natural categories, particularly in very young children.

Prototype theory and grammatical categories

We propose that grammatical categories may also be organized around prototypic members, with assignment of the corresponding surface forms that mark category membership being based upon family resemblance to those prototypes. This solution has been proposed explicitly by Lakoff (1977), Talmy (1977), Langacker (1978), deVilliers (1980), and Schlesinger (1977a), and is implicit in the work of Braine and Wells (1978) and Leonard (1976). Most of the work done by these researchers has concentrated on semantic prototypes, for example, agent as the basis of subject, action as the basis of predicate and/or verb. Furthermore, experimental work from this perspective has been carried out entirely in English, as far as we know. In our view, the prototype model could be expanded to describe peaceful coexistence and competition between semantic *and* pragmatic factors, for example, agent and topic as categories underlying subject phenomena. This approach would provide a good fit not only to facts about English, but to psycholinguistic studies of different language types.

Although Keenan (1976b) has listed more than thirty properties that define "subject" across languages, we will restrict our discussion to three correlated surface conventions: word order, verb agreement, and case markings on pronouns. Hence the category "subject" is defined as the set of elements that are reliably encoded with these three surface forms. Insofar as languages exploit the high probability of overlap between topic and agent by assigning them to the same surface devices, both topic and agent must be built into a Level 4 functionalist description of the grammatical category "subject." A prototype theory permits us to represent this situation directly within a single category structure.

1. *Central tendency.* The category "subject" is defined neither by the union nor by the intersect of its members; rather, that category "subject" is defined in terms of the central tendency member "agent–topic." This prototypic subject shares the largest number of features in common with other subjects; at the same time it has the smallest number of features in common with competing form classes, such as "predicate." In adult English, the central tendency of this subject category lies at the intersect of the agent system and the topic–comment system, with the motive of perspective taking serving as a bridge between agency and topicality (see MacWhinney, 1980). In short, perspective taking is the functional reason why an agent–topic is the prototypic subject.

2. *Family resemblance.* Assignment of the correlated set of surface forms that constitute subjectivalization (i.e., word order, agreement, nominal case) is determined via family resemblance to this agent–topic pro-

totype, that is, to elements that possess some subset of the features of agent–topic. For example, instruments may be mapped as subject via overlap with a subset of agent–topic features (e.g., / + cause/; see the discussion further on in this section). This is the process that Lakoff (1977) refers to as "partial matching." Similar processes of "metaphoric extension" are proposed by deVilliers (1978) and Schlesinger (1979).

3. *Goodness of membership.* Goodness of membership is defined by the *amount* of overlap of potential subjects with agent–topic features. Evidence for the psychological reality of this principle comes from experiments demonstrating that agents and topics are each "good" subjects, insofar as they are far more probable in normal discourse across languages (Duranti & Ochs, 1979); they appear as determinants of the emergence of subjectivalization mechanisms in the histories of particular languages (Li, 1975, 1976); they are easier to comprehend, produce, and verify in laboratory studies with adults (Tables 6.3 and 6.4); and they are acquired earlier by children (Bates & MacWhinney, 1979). Furthermore, there is evidence that topic–agents make better subjects than either agent or topic taken separately (Bates, McNew, MacWhinney, deVescovi, & Smith, in press), a finding which suggests that this particular combination lies at the core of the subject category. This does not mean that peripheral elements *cannot* be mapped as subjects. But they will not become the subject of a sentence when a "better" candidate is available, except under specifiable conditions. (See "Weighting," further along in this list.)

4. *Heterogeneous membership.* It is possible for two items to belong to a category via their overlap with the prototype, and yet share no overlap at all with one another. One element can be exclusively an agent and another exclusively a topic, and both can still be mapped as acceptable subjects. Similarly, one element can be exclusively a comment and another element can be exclusively a process, and both can still qualify for selection as predicates. This is the essence of the peaceful-coexistence solution in the competition model that we have proposed.

5. *Fuzziness.* Although the center of the category "subject" is clearly defined, it is more difficult to make decisions concerning the acceptability of peripheral members. A crucial claim for our version of prototype theory is that there exist difficulties in grammaticality judgments for elements at the semantic-pragmatic periphery of form-class categories. There is evidence for such "fuzzy boundary" phenomena, for example, at the outer boundary between "verb" and "noun" where certain meanings take on mappings appropriate for both classes (Ross, 1973). The advantage of a prototype theory is that both crisp grammaticality judgments and fuzzy or uncertain judgments are predicted with the same unified set of features. In other words, the prototype theory approach can provide a precise theory of imprecise phenomena.

6. *Weighting.* The role of feature weighting in subject selection can be

illustrated by the English passive. In most English sentences the subject is the agent: The *static* weight of the agency feature(s) for English subject selection is fairly high. However, in some cases, dynamic weighting of certain features of topicality can overcome the static weight of agency and lead to the production of a passive. As Horgan (1978) and others have noted, this increased weight on topicality as a feature usually occurs only in the context of formal written discourse. Variations in the occurrence of informal left-dislocated structures (Duranti & Ochs, 1979) may also reflect the operation of dynamic weighting.

The model just outlined can account for most of the existing psycholinguistic data on subject selection. We have concentrated on evidence supporting a prototype model of topic–agent as the defining member of the category governing the surface phenomena of subject. In principle, similar descriptions could be provided for other form-class categories such as nouns and verbs.

With regard to nouns, there is evidence that the central tendency or highest-probability member of the class of nouns is the physical object; for verbs, the "best member" is an intentional action resulting in a change of state in some recipient (Gentner, 1982; see also Slobin, 1979). Adjectives, a third major form class, are typically used to encode qualities or states that have some of the static properties of objects but are at the same time intangible and temporally limited like many actions. These three categories, with their respective "best members," form a "neighborhood of families," a category space in which each category is defined in part through contrast with its neighbors. This means that a given element may have all of the features that are central to a good noun and still be denied "best membership" because it also shares features with the category of verbs. Thus *lightning* is a noun, but also overlaps with certain prototypic features of the verb category; *feature* is a noun, but contains elements that draw it toward the "state" category of adjectives. Ross (1972) has provided syntactic evidence suggesting that there is a continuum between the form classes of "verb" and "adjective." At the center of this continuum are items that take on some of the surface mappings of verbs, though they are treated as adjectives in other grammatical contexts. A similar continuum has been proposed for the transition from "nouniness" to "verbiness." Most of the work on fuzzy boundaries in these form classes has concentrated on a category space made up of semantic features (e.g., +cause, +intention, +static). Applying the same logic used to analyze "subject" as both a semantic and a pragmatic category, we suggest that "verbs" may be best defined in terms of a combination of features including discourse features from the overlapping role of "comment." Indeed, just as agent and topic are joined together via the "bridge function" of perspective taking, verbs and adjectives may have more in common as predicates, in contrast with nouns, via a bridge function of commenting. In support of this suggestion, consider the fact that the verb or predicate in a sentence is more likely to be new information, whereas nouns are frequently used to encode information that is already given in the context (Bates, 1976).

To explore in more detail the overlaps and boundaries among such semantically-pragmatically defined form classes, we will need a more detailed theory of the features that constitute the internal structure of these categories. For example, the two gross categories of "topic" and "agent" presumably contain a set of internal features. "Topic" might be made up of such motivational features as "givenness" and "themacity." "Agent" would contain features like "animacy," "intention," "cause," and "human." Similarly, if the category "*noun*" is indeed best defined in terms of a prototypic physical object, then we will need a psychologically real feature theory to define the internal structure of the object concept (see Gratch, 1975, for a review of "features" or elements of knowledge that constitute the object concept in young infants). And a better definition of "verbs" will require a better theory of "intentional action" as a definitional prototypic member. In short, we are far from a detailed semantic-pragmatic analysis of grammatical categories. But such analyses are in principle possible, and empirically verifiable.

A final advantage of prototype theory in the description of grammatical knowledge is that it provides a plausible route whereby children might pass from poorly organized clusters of information about how to use surface forms to more precise and perhaps criterial definitions of the same grammatical category. Recall the description we provided earlier of the Italian child's acquisition of subject phenomena. Unlike some English children, who begin the two-word period by reliably mapping agent-action and action-object in appropriate orders, the Italian child begins with word-order tendencies that are best described as a comment-topic ordering. At that point in development, the *only* surface phenomenon correlated with subject is initial ordering. When case-marked pronouns and verb agreement are acquired, some children seem to use a divide-the-spoils policy of assigning initial position to the topic system, whereas agreement and case marking are used to mark agency. Eventually, the Italian child learns to coordinate the three surface phenomena into a single system that is mapped by some combination of topic and agent. That "coalition" could be described by merger into a single subject category, organized around a prototypical topic–agent member. Once such a unified category is established, the child may remain there into adulthood. In other words, in the terms described in Section 6.1, there may never be a developmental shift from semantic-pragmatic categories into a more abstract system. Alternatively, through gradual experience with the many kinds of elements that adults can use as sentence subjects, the child may reorganize his unified category around a single abstract formal symbol like " + S," arriving eventually at a formal, autonomous grammar more compatible with those described by transformational grammarians. The point is that, whether or not adults organize their grammatical knowledge in purely functional terms (Level 4), prototype theory provides a way of describing intermediate grammars that children might use as a bridge to a more formal system. As a best guess about when such a change might take place, we suggest the period from 5 to 7 years of age, when children show independent, nonlinguistic evidence of an ability to construct and apply classifications based on criterial attributes.

To summarize, we feel that there is considerable support for functionalist approaches to the acquisition and use of grammar at Levels 1, 2, and 3. Furthermore, there is hope for a precise theory of vestigiality, to predict and explain the existence of anomalous structures that serve no ongoing communicative function. Whether the facts that support Levels 1 to 3 can be built into a Level 4 functionalist grammar remains to be seen. There have, for example, been several proposals in the last few years for nontransformational, generative grammars that map surface forms directly onto a combination of case role information and pragmatic categories (theme, perspective, topic). These include Dik's *Functional Grammar* (1978) and Lakoff and Thompson's double hierarchy theory (1977). Prototype theory provides some possible solutions to the problem of heterogeneous class membership in adult use of the language. Even if prototype theory proves too weak to handle the full range of phenomena in adult language, it may still prove to be a useful system for describing transitional moments between the child's first primitive definitions of grammatical categories and later, more precise knowledge of his language. The analyses we have proposed in this state-of-the-art chapter contain a high ratio of promissory notes, particularly with regard to the many cross-linguistic experiments that remain to be done. Nevertheless, we believe that we have shown that all of the four levels of the functionalist position can be profitably treated as testable hypotheses that lead to interesting predictions.

7. On what case categories there are, why they are, and how they develop: an amalgam of *a priori* considerations, speculation, and evidence from children

Martin D. S. Braine and Judith A. Hardy

At its most basic, a case theory is a system of functional labels that categorize the arguments of a predicate. That is, a label specifies the kind of role played by the argument in the event or state of affairs, for example, Agent of the action, Instrument of the action, Experiencer, and so on. Case theories have had a mixed reception in linguistics in recent years (see, e.g., Mellema, 1974); yet even in theories that reject Fillmore's case grammar, caselike categories often appear somewhere in the system (e.g., in Jackendoff, 1972, under the title "thematic relations"). This fact suggests that although a case grammar formalism (Fillmore, 1968a) may not be required, nevertheless there is some essential role in linguistic theory for which case or caselike categories are needed.

We begin by trying to specify the essential function that makes case categories necessary. Then we elaborate our conception of a case system by proposing five principles that we think should be expected to govern the nature, organization, and development of case categories. We were led to several of these principles as a result of cogitating on the implications of our studies of the case or caselike concepts of preschool children. Therefore, in the third section of the chapter, we report some of our data. Finally, we sketch the kind of case system that the data and principles seem to indicate as having psychological reality.

7.1. Why must there be case categories?

Let us assume that the propositional core of a sentence can be represented by a predicate and one or more arguments. Some predicates have only one essential argument (e.g., Hot_a; Run_a);[1] transitive-verb predicators

The research was partially supported by a grant (HD-08090) from the National Institute of Child Health and Human Development, Martin Braine, Principal Investigator. We are extremely grateful to the children and staff of the following schools for their cooperation: the Wimpfheimer Nursery School and the Poughkeepsie Day School in Poughkeepsie, N.Y., the West Village Nursery School in Manhattan, and the Dutchess Day School in Millbrook, N.Y. We also thank Cynthia DeJesus for running the subjects in one of the experiments.

have two or three (e.g., $Hit_{Bill,John}$; $Give_{a,b,c}$). Now, as speakers, we have to translate such semantic representations into an organized utterance in some consistent way so that the listener can determine, for example, whether John hit Bill or Bill hit John. How can this be done? That is, what apparatus does one need to write rules that linearize $Hit_{Bill,John}$ as *Bill hit John*? Or, more generally, what does one need to realize $F_{x, ...}$ as a linear string for any F and any $x, ...$?

Note that there is nothing explicit in a logical notation like $Hit_{x,y}$ that tells us whether x hit y or y hit x. In a logic text, when such relations are mentioned, one is likely to be told in an aside that it is to be understood that the first-mentioned argument was the hitter. But, obviously, a linguistic theory cannot permit asides of this sort: The information about which argument is doing the hitting must be made explicit in the notation itself. Now note that case labels solve the problem elegantly. Let us label the arguments in the semantic representation so that, for example, the inexplicit $Hit_{x,y}$ is replaced by $Hit_{Actor=x,Patient=y}$, or something of the sort. Now the semantic representation explicitly identifies who did the hitting. Moreover, these labels can be used to identify the arguments in rules that will linearize the representation: For example, in English we preferentially assign Actor to initial sentence position with the result that a listener can know immediately that the subject noun names the one who did the hitting. In sum, a system of case categories provides speakers and listeners with labeled categories in the surface structure that are associated with argument roles in the lexicon.

Thus case categories have exactly two interdigitated functions. First, within the lexicon they have a semantic function: to distinguish the arguments of a predicate by providing each with a distinct label, for example, for $Hit_{x,y}$, to mark which argument is hitter and which gets hit. The labels then provide a way of referring to the arguments in rules. Thus the second function of case categories is syntactic. The rules use the case categories to identify arguments and specify where the arguments are to be found in sentences, so that both speaker and listener know where in the sentence the noun identifying the hitter is going to appear, and where the noun for who or what gets hit will be. We will call the first function the "distinguishing" function and the second the "mapping" function. Note that these functions of case categories must be accomplished somehow: Every language must distinguish between the arguments of a predicate and associate them with positions in sentences that are morphologically or syntactically identified. It would seem to follow, then, that every language must have a case system of some sort.

However, let us ask if one could dispense with case categories and make do with categories like "subject" and "object." If one tried to eliminate case categories in this way, then for every predicate, one would simply mark in the lexicon which argument was grammatical subject and which was object. For *hit,* the child would learn as part of learning the word that the preverbal noun is hitter and the postverbal is what is hit; for *eat,* the child would learn that the subject is the eater and the object the food; and so on for all words in the lexicon. Linguistic systems have been proposed that operate this way. Thus, to illustrate how his system would distinguish the meanings of *x*-verb-*y* and *y*-verb-*x,* J. Katz (1966) provided a model lexical entry for *chase.* The entry records that the deep-structure subject of *chase* is the one who does the chasing and the object is the one that is chased. Nothing in the system would make it unlikely for an action verb to have an entry in which the object was the one that performed the activity. In a more recent system without case categories, Bresnan (1978) proposed some illustrative partial lexical representations for *hit, eat,* and *rely,* as follows:

$$
\begin{array}{lll}
hit\colon & \text{V, } [-\text{ NP}], & \text{NP}_1\text{-HIT-NP}_2 \\
eat\colon & \text{V,}[-\text{ NP}], & \text{NP}_1\text{-EAT-NP}_2 \\
rely\colon & \text{V, } [-[_{\text{PP}}on \text{ NP}]], & \text{NP}_1\text{-RELY-ON-NP}_2
\end{array}
$$

The material in square brackets specifies the syntactic context for each verb, and the formulas on the right indicate what Bresnan calls their "functional structures." NP_1 and NP_2 are called the "logical" subject and "logical" object, distinguished from grammatical subject and object. (Thus, for *rely,* the logical object becomes grammatically a prepositional phrase.) We have no quarrel with the distinction between grammatical and functional structure, and indeed, much of Bresnan's discussion of syntax impresses us as an important step toward psychological reality in linguistic description. However, there is nothing in the concepts of logical subject and object that provides any information about who does what, and there is no mechanism in Bresnan's system, other than the omitted parts of the lexical entries themselves, that could tell us that the logical subjects of *hit* and *eat* are the hitter and eater, and the logical objects whatever gets hit or eaten. Furthermore, there is nothing to lead one to expect that other action verbs will also have the actor in subject rather than object position.

Systems like those of J. Katz (1966) and Bresnan would indeed distinguish the meanings of *x*-verb-*y* and *y*-verb-*x,* but they imply that it is arbitrary which argument is made subject and which object. And it clearly is not arbitrary in English. Consider the transitive verb *kshpizzl* (pronounced [kᵊšpizᵊl]). This is the word for the act that consists in a chair being removed by one party just as a second party is about to sit down on it. You have not heard the word before because it entered the English lexicon only very recently and has not had time to get into the dictionaries. Now we tell you that at dinnertime in some family we know, Mary kshpizzled John. You know immediately, we suspect, that Mary was actor and John was victim. Of course, you would not know if you had to learn, as part of learning the meaning of a verb, which argument was actor and which was acted on. The problem with subject and object is that they have no semantic content. Along the same lines, many years ago now, the first author introduced his 23-month-old daughter to the word *seb* via the one-word utterance, "seb," which accompanied the action of making his fingers walk toward her and tickle her under the arm. Later she held up her teddy bear and said "Daddy seb Teddy" (Braine, 1971b, pp. 55–6). How did she know it had to be *Daddy seb Teddy* and not *Teddy seb Daddy*? Presumably, because, like the rest of us, she had some kind of actor concept that includes sebbers and kshpizzlers, and she knew that Actor has to go first. So some semantic categories, like Actor, are needed, and not just subject and object.

In saying that case categories are needed to permit rules to refer to arguments, we are being deliberately vague about what kinds of rules these will be. That is because the burden of our chapter has to do with what case categories there are, not with their precise locus in a system of rules. Thus we are not concerned here with whether they end up within a set of rules labeled as syntactic rules, or as lexical rules (e.g., perhaps structures consisting of predicates with case-labeled arguments might replace Bresnan's functional structures, and lexical rules might map these onto something like her syntactic contexts), or as rules of the interpretive component. Nevertheless, our bias would be in favor of one of the first two of these possibilities, because there is at least a presystematic sense in which such rules deserve to be called "grammatical." Suppose, for example, that a foreigner who is learning English were to say "Mary hit Jane" when he intended to convey that Jane hit Mary; or suppose he said "The missionary is boiling" when he meant to convey merely that the said individual was boiling some water to make tea. Now in both cases our foreigner has started off with a well-formed semantic representation, but something has gone awry in the mapping of the intended meaning into the sentence uttered. It is an accident that the products happen to have turned out to be well-formed English sentences. It is our intuition that the foreigner's errors are grammatical in nature, and we think this intuition would be shared by most language professionals (e.g., language teachers, literary critics) who are not students of the recent linguistic arguments about generative and interpretive semantics, autonomous syntax, and the like. We do not think this intuition is captured by placing rules that refer to case categories in an interpretive component. However, to discuss usefully where case categories belong in the linguistic system, it would be helpful to have a better idea of what case categories there are.

7.2. Five principles

The conclusion that a case system of some sort is necessary does not, of course, guarantee the validity and psychological reality of the well-known case theories, like those of Fillmore (1968a, 1971) or Chafe (1970). It merely means that some set of distinctive functional labels is needed that permits rules to refer to arguments. Indeed, it is by no means clear that an optimal system for accomplishing the functions for which case categories are needed must be organized along the lines of the systems of Fillmore or Chafe. Without taking these as precedents, let us consider how the functions of case categories might be met, economically and with some intuitive psychological plausibility. We suggest that the following five principles should be expected to govern the nature of case systems.

Principle 1: the naturalness principle. We assume there are cognitive categories that are natural to the perception of events or states of affairs. That is, people see events as having actors or agents, things acted upon, places where the events occur, instruments that are used, and so on. These being basic cognitive categories for apprehending the world, it is natural that the language should draw on them for the purpose of assigning roles to the arguments of predicates. This principle agrees with Fillmore (1968b); we take it to be noncontroversial and will not take time to defend it. However, the operation of this principle is constrained by the next principle.

Principle 2: the economy principle. The economy principle is that cases should perform the argument-identifying function as economically as possible. To see how this might be done, let us perform a thought experiment. Suppose that you were a deity planning a case system for some animal that you could see was about to evolve language, and suppose further that you were a kindly earth-mother type and wanted to make it as easy for them as possible.

We think that you would decide to arrange your case system so that the case categories relevant to a predicate depend upon the number of arguments. This is all that is really necessary for avoiding confusion between the arguments. Consider first the predicates with just one argument. A single argument does not need a differentiating label because there is no other argument to differentiate it from. What the predicate says about the argument will be given in the lexical entry for the predicate. In the case of monadic predicates there is no distinguishing function for the case label to play, only a mapping function. So to keep things simple for your charges, you should have them treat the arguments of monadic predicates as a single category, separate from the cases of polyadic predicates, and realize all such arguments in the same way in the surface structure. Note that it will not matter where you place such arguments in the surface structure. Thus you can let some of your languages be "nominative," and map all arguments of one-place predicates into the same position as Actor arguments of transitive verbs; and you can let other languages be "ergative," and map the arguments of one-place predicates into the same position as Objects of Action. All that matters is that you treat such arguments uniformly in any given language.

To a first approximation we can view intransitive verbs and predicate adjectives as one-place predicates. Then an immediate important prediction from the economy principle is that we should expect to find a single category with psychological reality that includes the subjects of intransitive verbs and adjectives, and that excludes all arguments of transitive verbs. We christen this category in advance the *Subject of Attribution*; it is the focus of the experiments reported later.

What about two-place predicates? It seems that you have two strategies from which to choose. One would be to label just one of the arguments. Provided one of the arguments is labeled, the two are differentiated: In principle, for an *n*-place predicate, the arguments will be differentiated provided $n - 1$ of them are labeled. A second strategy would be to label the arguments in contrasting pairs, such as Actor versus Object of Action for some two-place predicates, Experiencer versus Object of Experience for others, and so on. We think that this was the strategy that our earth goddess adopted for this planet. Note that, for either strategy, there would be no purpose served (so far as the function of distinguishing arguments is concerned) in subclassifying Objects of Action (or non-Actors) into such subcategories as Patient and Factitive.[2] Once we have an Actor–non-Actor distinction, the two arguments are distinguished, and because the precise role of the arguments will have to be specified in the lexical entry anyway, a distinction like Patient–Factitive is bound to be redundant.[3]

For three-place predicates, either of the strategies just described could be extended. However, one simple way of getting extra cases, which we suspect may be common, is by dividing a broad and general case used with two-place verbs into two subcases of more specific content with three-place verbs. Thus cases would be hierarchically organized. For instance, User and Instrument may be subcases of the Actor. (Thus, in *The man broke the window, The branch broke the window, The explosion broke the window*, the man, branch, and explosion are all Actors and the sentences are not committed on whether they are also instruments or users of instruments, but in *The man broke the window with a branch*, the man is User and the branch Instrument.) Some results supporting this suggestion have been reported elsewhere (Braine & Wells, 1978), and are mentioned later. Fillmore (1971) also suggests a hypercase that joins Agent and Instrument. For three-place verbs like *give*, it is possible that

Transferred Object and Recipient are subcases of the Object-of-Action category of two-place verbs, as we suggest elsewhere (Hardy & Braine, 1981). Locatives obviously have an extensive subclassification.[4]

The application of this economy principle to our planet's natural languages would be straightforward if one could view intransitive verbs and predicate adjectives and nouns as one-place predicates, and transitive verbs without indirect objects as two-place predicates. However, the equivalence is not perfect. For example, intransitive verbs and adjectives often have extra optional oblique arguments (e.g., the sea and foredeck in *George fell into the sea from the foredeck,* and George's friend in *George is angry with his friend*). So although it may be true that intransitives have only one main or essential argument, it is not true that they are always pure one-place predicates in a logical sense. Similarly, two-place transitive verbs often have extra oblique arguments. We return later to this problem of the imperfect equivalence of the linguistic and logical categories.

Principle 3: the simplicity-of-identification principle. Other things being equal, it seems to us that a case system should be easier to learn, and sentences should be easier to produce and understand, if the mapping of case categories into sentence positions is simple, that is, many-to-one, the same case being always found in the same position, or with the same case ending or preposition. Thus, on the production side, case determines position or case ending, and on the comprehension side, position or case ending determines a small set of cases to choose among.

Conversely, it should make for complexity, both in learning and in processing, if the same category sometimes appears in preverbal (or nominative) position and sometimes in postverbal (accusative or dative position). Thus, in the systems of Fillmore and Chafe, Experiencer occurs as subject before verbs like *see,* and as indirect object after a verb like *show*; similarly, Patient labels both the subject of *die* and the object of *kill*. Principle 3 says that languages should be biased to avoid such many-to-many mappings between cases and positions.

The systems of Fillmore and Chafe require a many-to-many mapping between cases and positions (or case endings) because they use identity of case labels to serve a cross-referencing function, to mark corresponding arguments of related predicates. Thus, in their systems, giving the subject of *die* and the object of *kill* the same case label, Patient, marks the fact that they are corresponding arguments: It is the object, not the subject, of *kill* that dies. Similarly, the correspondence of the subject of *see* to the indirect object of *show* is marked by labeling both Experiencer.

However, given a predicate-argument notation that is augmented with case labels, assigning corresponding arguments the same case label is not the most perspicuous way of using the notation to indicate correspondence of arguments. One can state the semantic relation between *kill* and *die* perfectly well without giving the subject of *die* and the object of *kill* the same case label. Thus, in the kind of system we have suggested, the relation could be expressed by an entailment rule like the following:

KILL(Actor = x; Object of Action = y) entails CAUSE(Actor = x; Object of Action = [DIE(Subject of Attribution = y)]*)

(The notation "[. . .]*" is to be read as "The event or state of affairs indicated by '[. . .]' "; readers who think that *kill* and *cause to die* are synonymous should read the entailment as two-way.)

We are not sure how Fillmore or Chafe would express the relation between *kill* and *die*, but presumably there would be only two differences from our formula that are relevant to this discussion. Fillmore would have "DIE(Patient = y)" where we have "DIE(Subject of Attribution = y)", and would have y labeled as Patient also in the entry for KILL. Fillmore's formulation would thus give the subject of *die* and the object of *kill* the same case label. Note, however, that this common labeling actually serves no purpose at all: It is the use of the same variable letter (i.e., y) that indicates the identity of the arguments, not the use of the same case label. Moreover, within a predicate-argument notation, the use of the same variable letter is the appropriate and usual method of indicating correspondence of arguments. The only place where the case label "Patient" is needed is in the entry for *kill*, to indicate which argument of *kill* y is (i.e., the Patient, not the Agent); for the entailment rule to work it does not matter how y is labeled in the entry for *die*. (In fact, because there is no oblique argument, it does not need to be labeled at all, either as "Patient" or as "Subject of Attribution.")

Similarly, if one wishes to recover the relation between *see* and *show* by analyzing *show* as "cause to see," the fact that Fillmore's system assigns the same case label (Experiencer) to the subject of *see* and the indirect object of *show* does not actually contribute anything to the statement of the relation. In general, the practice of using identity of case label to mark correspondence of arguments forces complexity into the case system because it requires acceptance of a many-to-many mapping of cases on to positions where a many-to-one mapping might well otherwise suffice. The practice is not needed for the purpose of stating semantic relations between lexical entries.

Principle 4: the principle of tolerance of pragmatic overlap among cases. The boundaries between cases are often hard to draw. Consider the Actor (or Agent) and the Experiencer. The distinction is clear for certain verbs (e.g., *look–see, listen–hear,* and the two *feels: George felt the point against his shoulder* vs. *George felt the point with his hand*), but not so clear for others (e.g., *learn, remember*). For instance, learning and remembering are active processes at least as often as they are passive experiencing ones, and it is easy to see that a child might find it hard to decide whether the subjects of *learn* and *remember* are Actors or Experiencers. But note that as long as the grammar maps Actor and Experiencer into the same sentence positions, it does not matter how the child draws the distinction: Learners and rememberers can be viewed as Actors or as Experiencers, or as both, or as sometimes one and sometimes the other. The boundary need never be clarified. Speakers would be forced to make a sharp (and presumably arbitrary) distinction only if a language mapped Actors and Experiencers differently (say, Actor into preverbal and Experiencer into postverbal position). The tolerance-of-case-overlap principle says that our benevolent deity will be biased against such languages. In general, the principle requires that semantically similar cases that are not in contrast within a sentence be mapped into the same sentence position, or into the same surface case.

Principle 5. The last principle is a strictly developmental one. It states that at early stages of development the naturalness principle takes precedence over the economy principle. The first word combinations of children suggest that the naturalness principle is the overriding one at very early stages of development. The evidence (Braine, 1976) indicates that the early word combinations are generated by formulas of limited scope like Actor + Action, Possessor + Possessed, Located Item + Location, and so on. The categories all seem like natural experiential ones. There is no sign that the economy principle is operating; in particular, there is no evidence for any uniform treatment of subjects of one-place predicates. Assuming that our economy principle is valid, it follows that there must be some reorganization of argument labels during development. First, if one looks at the actions that fall within the children's Actor + Action schema, many of the actions are intransitive verbs in the adult language (e.g., walk, cry, run, sleep). That is, these subjects of intransitive verbs are regarded as Actors, not as Subjects of Attribution, at this stage. (Recall that *Subject of Attribution* is our term for subjects of one-place predicates.) As development proceeds, this proto-Actor case of the first word combinations must become opposed to the Object of Action, so that Actor becomes primarily a case label for subjects of transitive verbs. The other development that must take place is that the Subject of Attribution must emerge. We speculate that the Subject of Attribution first appears as the category of subjects of sentences with predicate adjectives and nouns; however, to become a general category covering intransitive verbs as well as predicate adjectives and nouns, it must absorb the subjects of the intransitive verbs that had been part of the Actor–Action schema. For English-learning children, we do not have to assume that these actor subjects of intransitive verbs lose their Actor status; they could well develop a dual categorization, as Actors and as Subjects of Attribution (cf, the principle of tolerance for case overlap). However, for ergative languages, it is their status as Subjects of Attribution, not their actorness, that determines their sentence position.

7.3. Some evidence

Over the past few years we and our colleague Robin Wells have been gathering empirical evidence on the kinds of caselike concepts that 4- and 5-year-old children possess. We have been using the following method: The children are shown pictures of scenes accompanied by simple descriptive sentences such as *The rabbit is cutting the log with a saw*. During a training phase the children learn to place tokens of different shapes on the objects in the picture according to the role they play in the scene. For instance, they are told, "We're going to put the star on the rabbit because it's the rabbit who is cutting the log. The circle goes on the log because it is the log that he is cutting. We'll put the triangle on the saw because he's cutting the log with the saw." We reasoned that if children actually possess case categories like Actor, Object, and Instrument, then we should be able to lead them to associate the tokens with the roles that they perceive the objects to be playing in the pictured scene. On the other hand, if the posited case categories do not exist, then it should be difficult to train the children. In fact, we have found that children "catch on" very quickly indeed to associating tokens with caselike role categories, often showing errorless learning after a few demonstration trials.

During the generalization trials, the children are presented with new pictures and sentences. There are two ways in which these trials yield information about the definitions and perceived roles of case categories. First, some of the new role exemplars may have attributes that differ from those in the training. For example, the children may be trained on animate actors (e.g., *The elephant is lifting the Indian*). Then they will be presented with inanimate actors during generalization trials (e.g., *The fan is blowing the curtains*). If the child's Actor category includes inanimate actors, then the child should transfer the Actor token to them. But if animacy is an essential criterion for Actors, then the children should become confused when presented with these inanimate "Actors," and their token placement will be either random or based on irrelevant strategies. The second method for querying case definitions is one of forcing the child to choose between tokens. For example, if children have been trained with Actor, Object, and Instrument tokens, which will they choose to put on the knife when presented with *The knife is cutting the cake*?

The initial studies primarily explored the children's Actor concept (Braine & Wells, 1978). The data suggested that the children have an Actor concept based on the notion of "doing something." That is, contrary to the usual notion of Agent (see, e.g., Fillmore, 1968a), the Actor simply "does" the action, rather than wills or instigates it. Thus, although animate actors may be prototypical, the category includes inanimate actors as well. Finally, although the children have Instrument and User (i.e., one who uses an instrument) categories, both seem to be subcategories of the Actor. The distinction between them is made only when both appear in the same sentence. When there is no User, and the instrument is placed in sentence subject position (e.g., *The knife is cutting the cake*), the instrument plays the role of Actor. Actor appears to be a broad and salient category associated with the subjects of many sentences. The economy and simplicity-of-identification principles emerged, in part, from our reflections on these results.

Our recent studies, which we report in more detail here, have continued to explore categories associated with sentence subjects. This time, however, we began with the sentence subjects that are maximally different from Actors, the subjects of predicate-adjective sentences like *The vase is broken* or *The grass is green*. We thought that the children might perceive a similarity in the roles played by such subjects. Such a role might simply be that of the thing having some state or property attributed to it. Thus we tentatively labeled this category the Subject of Attribution. We then wondered about the breadth of this category. If it existed, would it include the subjects of locative predicates as in *The towtruck is in front of the car*? Would it include the somewhat passive subjects of many intransitive verbs like *burning* or *floating* or *falling*? Or would it in fact embrace all subjects of intransitive predicates, including actor subjects of intransitive verbs, as our economy principle would predict? We knew that some influential theories of case grammar make radically different claims about the category to which the subjects of predicate adjectives belong: According to Fillmore (1968a, 1971) and Chafe (1970), these subjects fall into the same category as the objects of many transitive verbs, the Patient case.

We were dubious about the existence of the Patient case for both empirical and theoretical reasons. In the earlier Actor studies, children who were trained with both Actor and Object tokens were confused when they had to choose which of the tokens to place on the subjects of predicate adjectives (Braine & Wells, 1978). If they possess a Patient case, they should obviously have preferred the Object token. Furthermore, the data on Instruments and Actors suggested that children may not associate case categories with more than one deep-structure position (our simplicity-of-identification principle).

The following studies are an attempt to settle the issues raised about the subjects of predicate adjectives. Specifically, is there a Subject-of-Attribution case that embraces all subjects of one-place predicates, and excludes arguments of transitive verbs? Is there, instead, a Patient case that embraces both the subjects of predicate adjectives and the objects of many transitive verbs, while excluding other sentence subjects? Or finally, is the grammatical concept of a sentence subject so potent that the children will respond to the surface-structure or deep-structure subject regardless of its semantic role?

The experiments all had the following general form. The children first learned to put a token on someone or something in a picture that was the subject of a predicate adjective in an accompanying descriptive sentence. (There was always another thing in the picture that was mentioned in the description, and the children had to avoid putting the token on that; thus the token went on the eggs, not the table, for *The eggs are ready on the table*.) After the learning they were given new sentences and pictures of various kinds in generalization trials, in order to define the breadth of the category that had been identified with the token. The training was essentially the same in all three experiments, but the experiments differed somewhat in the generalization trials: After the first experiment some generalization trials were selected to replicate previous results, and some to resolve issues raised by them.

Method

Subjects. The subjects for Experiment 1 were twenty boys and girls from a private day school and from a nursery school in Poughkeepsie, New York. Their mean age was 5;0 (years; months), with a range of 4;2 to 6;4. The subjects for Experiment 2 were twenty boys and girls from a nursery school in Manhattan. Their mean age was 4;5, with a range of 3;11 to 5;8. The subjects for Experiment 3 were twenty-four boys and girls from the nursery and kindergarten classes of a private day school in Millbrook, New York. Their mean age was 4;11, with a range of 3;7 to 6;0.

Training. We used twelve pictures depicting simple scenes that contained at least two salient objects. Each picture was accompanied by a descriptive sentence consisting of a subject, a predicate adjective, and an adjunct phrase (usually a prepositional phrase), such as *The hatchet is stuck in the tree*. To insure that the children could not rely on irrelevant cues, like emphasis or order of mention, we kept vocal emphasis equal, and sometimes put the adjunct phrase before the subject noun (e.g., *Because the ball hit it, the vase is broken*). Because animacy is a salient attribute for children, we varied the animacy of all constituents to discourage the child's use of animacy as a criterion.

There were two parts to the training procedure. For the first eight pictures, the child was told that one thing in each picture should receive a star-shaped token. The experimenter explained that she would demonstrate the correct token placement and the child's task was to learn which object to put the token on so that he or she could perform correctly when it was his or her turn. The experimenter showed the child one picture at a time and described it with the appropriate sentence, such as *The eggs are ready on the table.* She then said, "I'm going to put the star on the eggs because it is the eggs that are ready," and she placed the token accordingly. After presenting all eight pictures, she said it was the child's turn to place the token. The pictures were re-presented along with the accompanying sentence, and the child placed the token. If there was more than one error on the eight pictures, they were presented again until a learning criterion of six consecutive correct token placements was reached.

The experimenter began the second phase of training by showing the child a new picture, and saying, "Sometimes you can say two things about a picture. If we say *The pig is all curled up on the sofa,* then we will put the star on the pig because it is the pig who is all curled up. But suppose we say instead *The sofa is nice and soft for the pig to lie on?* Then we have to put the star on the sofa, because it is the sofa that is nice and soft." The purpose was to reinforce the importance of listening to the description. There were four of these pictures with alternative descriptions. After the placements had been demonstrated, it was the child's turn to place the token. The experimenter reminded the child to listen carefully because she might use either description. During the recall trials, the four pictures were presented with one description, then all four were re-presented with the other description.

Generalization. For the generalization trials, the subjects were divided into two equal groups. Though both saw the same pictures, these were accompanied by a different description for each group. The constituent that was the sentence subject for one group was in the adjunct phrase for the other group. For example, the group hearing *The cat is all dressed up in a hat* should place the token on the cat; those hearing *The hat is too big for the cat* should choose the hat. This design controls for the possibility of response bias owing to factors like perceptual salience in the picture; one can tell whether the picture or the descriptive sentence determines the child's choice. For sentences with transitive verbs, one group heard the sentence in the active and the other in the passive (with half of these sentences in the active and half in the passive in each group).

The various kinds of generalization trials varied between the experiments, but each experiment presented some pictures and sentences with predicate adjectives. The types of generalization sentence, and the actual sentences used, are shown in Table 7.1 for Experiments 1 and 2, and in Table 7.2 for Experiment 3. In all experiments, order of presentation of the various sentence types was balanced. In addition to the generalization sentences listed, three or four of the familiar training sentences (with

Table 7.1. *Frequency of placement of the token on particular constituents in generalization trials using various types of sentences*

Type of sentence	Expt. 1	Expt. 2
Adjectival predicates: placement on subject	88%	77%
The cat is all dressed up in the hat/The hat is too big for the cat		
In the sink the dishes are dirty/With all the dishes in it, the sink is very full		
The man is very tired of pulling the boy/Here's a man, here's a boy, and the boy is happy about riding in the wagon		
Locative predicates: placement on subject	80%	None included
The towtruck is in front of the car/The car is in back of the towtruck		
The apple is on top of the chicken/The chicken is under the apple		
Intransitive verbs with inanimate or passive subjects: placement on subject	75%	80%
The truck is driving around with the cow/The cow is riding around in the back of the truck		
The cloud is floating along beside the airplane/The plane is flying along behind the cloud		
Under the pot the fire is burning/Over the fire the pot is boiling		
Intransitive verbs with Actor subjects: placement on subject	None included	78%
The butterfly is flying around the lion's head/The lion is growling at the butterfly		
Snoopy is running with Woodstock on his head/Woodstock is yoyoing on Snoopy's head		
Over the deer the elephant is standing/Under the elephant the deer is eating		
Transitive verbs:		
Placement on surface-structure subject	49%	50%
Placement on Actor	51%	60%
Placement on Patient	49%	40%
The pig is washing the mirror/The mirror is being washed by the pig		
The ball is being held up by the seal/The seal is holding the ball up		
The turtle is lifting the mouse/The mouse is being lifted by the turtle		
The frog is being kicked by the rabbit/The rabbit is kicking the frog		

pictures) were inserted into the generalization trials at regular intervals to remind the child of the concept he or she had been trained on, and to check that the child's criterion had not shifted or disintegrated.

The experimenter began the generalization trials by telling the child that she had some more pictures. She explained that this time she would not demonstrate the token placement because she wanted the child to decide which object should receive the star. She then presented the new pictures, one at a time, along with a descriptive sentence. After hearing the sentence, the child placed the token. Errors on the training sentences were corrected. On the other sentence types the child's response always met with mild approval.

Results

Training results (all experiments). For the majority of children, training was rapid, a fact which suggests that the category the children grasped during training was one that they brought with them to the task, rather than one that was experimentally induced. There were hardly any errors during the initial phase of training. There were a few errors during the second phase, in which the children were trained with alternative descriptions; there were also a few children who tired of this part of the training. If the performance of these children, who had watched the demonstration but did not complete recall, was errorless until this point, we included them in the generalization trials. In each experiment there were a few children (a maximum of 4 out of 24) who failed to meet the learning criterion. In most instances, failure to learn seemed to correlate with restlessness and lack of attention.

Generalization: Experiment 1. The children's performance on the generalization trials is summarized in Table 7.1. They placed the token on the new subjects of adjectival predicates on an average of 2.6 of the three trials; by t-test, this figure is significantly ($p < .001$) greater than the 1.5 expected by chance. Similarly, the subjects of the locative predicates and of the intransitive verbs also received the token more often than expected by chance ($p < .001$, by analogous t-tests). Thus there was transfer to subjects of all the types of intransitive predicates tested. In contrast, overall performance on the transitive-verb sentences was random; there was no preference for the surface-structure subject, nor for the deep-structure subject (the Actor), nor for the deep-structure object (the Patient). Furthermore, most of the individual children's performances looked random on the transitive-verb sentences; they often hesitated and looked puzzled, the older children occasionally remarking, "That's a hard one."

In general, the results of the generalization trials indicated that it was the descriptive sentence, not the picture, that determined where the child placed the token. Because there were two major constituents in each picture, the probability that the star would be placed on a constituent by chance was 50 percent. When the experimenter said, "In the sink the dishes are dirty," the token went on the dishes 90 percent of the time. On the other hand, the sink received the token 80 percent of the time when she said, "With all the dishes in it, the sink is very full." Similar results were obtained for all sentences with intransitive predicates.

The results from Experiment 1 suggested that the category identified with the token included subjects of predicate adjectives, subjects of locative predications, and subjects of some intransitive verbs; and that it excluded all arguments of transitive-verb predicates. However, the intransitive verbs used all had inanimate or inactive subjects; so after cogitating about the economy principle, we began to wonder what the children would do with animate-actor subjects of intransitive verbs. Consequently, Experiment 2 included intransitive-verb sentences with animate actor subjects. The results from Experiment 1 also suggested a generalization gradient, with transfer greatest to subjects of predicate adjectives, the kind of predicate used in the training, slightly less for locative predicates, and still less for intransitive verbs. So a second purpose of Experiment 2 was to see whether a generalization gradient would be found again. (The locative predicates were omitted in Experiment 2 to keep the length of the experiment within bounds.)

Generalization: Experiment 2. The results of Experiment 2 are shown in Table 7.1. Transfer to the predicate adjectives was again very significantly above chance ($p < .001$, by t-test), although it was not quite as consistent as in the first experiment. The children also placed the token significantly ($p < .001$), and equally, on both the Actor and non-Actor subjects of intransitive verbs. Here there is no sign of a generalization gradient. The Actor subjects of intransitive verbs seemed to be equal members of the Subject-of-Attribution category.

On the transitive-verb sentences, the children again showed no significant biases in placing the token. They showed no tendency to place the token on the surface-structure subject. There was some preference for the Actor, but it was not statistically significant. Again, we found no support for the Patient case. However, some individual performances appeared to be more consistent than before. In the transitive verb sentences, five children always chose the Actor, and three always chose the Patient.

Because the Actor concept is so salient, and because we included seven actors in the generalization trials, we began to wonder if some of the children might not have caught on to this concept during the generalization. Though response to the actors in the transitive verb sentences

Table 7.2. *Placement of token in generalization trials: Experiment 3*

Adjectival predicates: placement on subject	86%

The flowers are pretty on the stems/The stems are long and ugly on
  the flowers
The hat is too big for the cat/The cat is all dressed up in the hat
The man is sunburned from the sun/The sun is angry at the man
On the hill the house is pink/In front of the house the grass is dark
  green

Intransitive verbs with Actor subjects: placement on subject	86%

The cat is jumping towards the boy/The boy is standing waiting for
  the cat
Woodstock is yoyoing on Snoopy's head/Snoopy is running with
  Woodstock on his head
Over the deer the elephant is standing/Under the elephant the deer is
  eating
The father is sitting watching the girl/The girl is dancing for her father

was not significant, it was higher than in Experiment 1. Perhaps the presence of so many actors might have inflated the children's response to the actor subjects of both transitive and intransitive verbs.

The primary purpose for running Experiment 3 was to replicate the Experiment 2 results on the actor subjects of intransitive verbs. We also decided to include some new pictures and descriptive sentences for both the predicate adjectives and the intransitive verbs; if we obtained the same transfer results with them, then our evidence would be drawn from a larger set of sentences and would, therefore, be stronger.

Generalization: Experiment 3. As shown in Table 7.2, the children transferred significantly both to the new subjects of predicate adjectives and to the actor subjects of intransitive verbs ($p < .001$ in both cases). Obviously, there is no statistical difference between the amount of transfer to the two types of sentence subjects. These results, from a substantially new set of generalization pictures and sentences, replicate the transfer obtained in the previous experiments. They also confirm the absence of a generalization gradient, and provide further evidence that the children have a category to which both these types of subject belong.

Discussion

There are several reasons for believing that the children's choices were not based on irrelevant cues. We have demonstrated that it was the sentence, and not the picture, that determined the children's token placement. The children did not utilize other incidental cues, either. We were careful to keep vocal emphasis equal for sentence subjects and for the nouns of the adjunct phrase. We also varied the surface position of sentence subject nouns by placing some of the adjunct phrases in initial sentence position; the placement of the token was not affected by this maneuver. Finally, the children were not placing the marker on the noun that preceded the verb *is* because they did not use this criterion for transitive verb sentences.

Some readers may wonder if the children were able to respond correctly by learning what not to put the token on. Couldn't we have obtained the same results if the children were simply avoiding objects described by prepositional phrases? It seems clear that the children were not using this strategy. For one thing, a few of the adjunct phrases were verbal rather than prepositional (e.g., *The father is sitting watching the girl, The boy is standing waiting for the cat, The man is very tired of pulling the boy*), and the children responded the same way regardless of the type of adjunct phrase. Also, if children were avoiding prepositions, then the subjects of passive sentences should have received the token because the children would have avoided the constituent mentioned in the *by* phrase. Instead, the children's performance was random on these sentences. Because many of the adjunct phrases were locative, one might wonder whether the children were just avoiding locatives. They were not: Overall, 40 percent of the generalization sentences had nonlocative adjuncts, and the tendency to place the token on the subject was high when the adjunct phrase was nonlocative (84 percent, 70 percent, and 83 percent, in the three experiments respectively), as well as when it was locative (79 percent, 86 percent, and 90 percent, respectively). The transfer is statistically significant, for the sentences with nonlocative adjuncts taken alone, in all three experiments.

We conclude that 4- and 5-year-old children possess a caselike category, the Subject of Attribution, that embraces the subjects of adjectival predicates, locative predicates, and intransitive verbs. The Subject of Attribution is not equivalent to the surface-structure subject, or to the deep-structure subject; such strictly syntactic categories may not exist for a child of this age. Furthermore, the children showed no evidence for a Patient case that includes both the subjects of adjectival predicates and the objects of transitive verbs.

In general, we take these results as indications that our economy principle is along the right lines. The principle led us to expect to find a single category with psychological reality, which included subjects of intransitive predicates and excluded arguments of transitive verbs. And the data demonstrate such a category in 5-year-olds.

However, in arriving at this expectation, we set aside the problem that the linguistic category "intransitive predicate" is not identical to the logical category "one-place predicate," because intransitive verbs and adjectives often have oblique arguments in addition to the argument that appears as subject. This means that one cannot define the Subject of Attribution simply as "the single argument of a one-place predicate," but must have recourse to something like "the single essential argument of a predicate with just one essential argument." This more cumbersome formulation requires us to grapple with the term *essential*.

It seems to us that the very process of learning the meaning of an intransitive verb or adjective must involve marking one of the arguments as essential, if there can be more than one argument. Thus one has not learned the meaning of words like *wet* or *messy* unless one knows that they indicate a state of some entity (as well as what kind of state): If one has learned that, then one has marked *grass* and *shirt*, for instance, as the essential arguments in sentences like *The grass is wet from last night's rain* and *The shirt is messy with jam stains*. Similarly, in learning the meaning of an intransitive verb, such as *weep*, one must learn that it is a bodily action or reaction, and the weeper is thereby marked as the main or essential argument, even when there are other arguments, as in *He wept from the frustration of being misunderstood*. Of course, learning the meaning of an intransitive predicate and marking the essential argument is made easy for the child by the fact that on most occasions of usage, the oblique arguments are not present: In practice, intransitive verbs and adjectives are one-place predicates most of the time.

Thus we may suppose that the Subject of Attribution begins as the single argument of one-place predicates, probably of stative adjectives and nouns, as in 2-year-old utterances like *hair wet*, "my hair is wet"; *spoon dirty*, "the spoon is dirty"; *Mommy lady*, "Mommy is a woman"; and so on. The English-learning child learns that the single argument goes in initial position in sentences. When sentences with oblique arguments are encountered, the child finds that the role played by the subject noun is the same as when there is no oblique argument. In effect, the category "single argument" becomes transmuted into "single essential argument," the single essential argument being the argument that is the single argument when the adjective or verb is used as a one-place predicate.[5]

7.4. Overview of the system envisaged

Putting the data and principles together, we arrive at a system organized along the following lines. The cases relevant to a predicate depend on the number of main (or essential) arguments it has. Predicates may have one main argument, or two, or three. There is a single category that labels the main argument of all predicates that have just one main argument (i.e., intransitive verbs, and predicate adjectives, nominals, and locatives); we have called this the Subject of Attribution, and its psychological reality is supported by the data reported here. For predicates with two main arguments (i.e., two-place transitive verbs), the arguments are labeled in contrasting pairs. Actor and Object of Action are the most obvious such pair, and their psychological reality is well supported by data. Experiencer and Object of Experience may well constitute another such pair, but we have not yet investigated their psychological reality. There could be other pairs. For predicates with three main arguments (verbs like *give*), the Actor is one of the arguments. Since this was written we have studied how children draw the distinction between the other two arguments, and elsewhere we report evidence for Transferred Object and Recipient categories that are subcategories of the Object-of-Action category of two-place verbs (Hardy & Braine, in press). Then there is a set of cases of oblique arguments (i.e., arguments that are not "main" arguments): Locative (with its subcategories), Instrument, and so on.

A case system organized along the lines described provides a particularly simple mapping between case labels and positions in sentences. Thus Subject of Attribution, Actor, and Experiencer are associated with subject position (for English); Object of Action and Object of Experience are associated with object position; and the oblique cases, Instrumental and the subcategories of Locative, are each associated with particular prepositions.

In general, the kind of system to which our data and principles point seems simpler and more straightforward than systems like Fillmore's and Chafe's. We think it provides an intuitively sensible and economical way for a language to solve the problem of labeling the arguments of its predicates and locating them in sentences. However, it is still very incomplete because we do not have the data to fill it out.

Notes

1 We ignore time arguments throughout the chapter.
2 The term *factitive* comes from Fillmore (1968a). It refers to an object created by the action of the verb (as opposed to a Patient, which incurs the action). Thus verbs like *draw* and *build* would take Factitive objects, whereas *hit* and *eat* would take Patients.
3 That is, a verb like *draw* is stored in the lexicon with the information that the non-Actor argument is a picture created by making marks on a surface, whereas the verb *hit* is stored with the information that the non-Actor argument is contacted abruptly. In mapping the arguments into sentence positions, the rules can ignore the specific aspects of the roles of the arguments. For both predicates, they simply place the Actor argument in subject position and the non-Actor in object position. But we do not lose the information that the object of *draw* is created by the action, because this information is part of the meaning of the verb *draw*.
4 Diver (1964) makes an argument, for Latin, that is very similar to our economy

principle. We think that Fillmore's (1968a) critique of Diver's proposal entirely missed its logical force. That is, the Latin case organization that Diver argues for (which distinguishes the arguments of intransitive and transitive verbs in much the manner we propose here) is a maximally economic way of providing distinctive functional labels for the noun positions he considers.

5 The data from Experiment 1 indicate that the Subject of Attribution also includes the subjects of locative predications. These require a certain amount of pushing to fit the mold of the one-place predicate. Briefly and roughly, what we think is this. The language has ways of specifying places: They may be specified by single words like *here, there, upstairs,* etc., or by phrases generated by formulas, the most typical formula consisting of a preposition followed by an NP that refers to an object (*on the bed, in the basement,* etc.). (From a logical standpoint, perhaps one might think of the prepositions as operators that map names of objects into names of places.) In sentences with locative predicates (*Daddy is upstairs, The cat is on the bed*), the places function as predicates predicated of the located object.

8. The child's construction of grammatical categories

Michael Maratsos

One of the central tendencies in the study of language development in the past years has been the movement away from purely formal descriptions of children's grammar toward semantically and cognitively based descriptions using categories such as "actor" and "action," or "possessor" and "location" (Bloom, 1970; Bowerman, 1973a; Brown, 1973; Schlesinger, 1971). Such steps have not been arbitrary ones, and they constitute an important contribution to our understanding of the way in which children organize their comprehension of grammar.

These tendencies may be seen to have their culmination in growing attempts to explicate even adult formal categories, which appear to be freer of semantic definition, as having an essentially semantic basis, in works such as Schlesinger (1974) or Bates and MacWhinney (Chapter 6). Thus verbs might be taken to be "basically" actional terms, or nouns to be essentially concrete referent-denoting terms.

The degree to which semantic factors may form central analytic and developmental bases for adult formal classes is an open question. But it seems to me that traditional views that such categories cannot be defined on purely semantic bases, although they require revision, are essentially correct in the basic claim. Nouns and verbs and adjectives, though they have distinct semantic modal tendencies toward denoting objects, actions, and states or properties, cannot be defined by such properties. In this chapter, I would like to outline some ideas that a number of colleagues and I have been pursuing (Maratsos, 1979; Maratsos & Chalkley, 1980; Maratsos, Kuczaj, Fox, & Chalkley, 1979), concerning the problem of how children construct formal grammatical categories such as "verb,"

I am indebted to a number of sources of support for and aid in the completion of this chapter, including the Sloan cognitive sciences visiting scholar program of the University of California at La Jolla, the Center for Advanced Studies in the Behavioral Sciences, the Center for the Study of Human Learning at the University of Minnesota, and the University of Minnesota itself (for sabbatical support). Relevant grant support sources include the Sloan Foundation, the Andrew W. Mellon Foundation, and grants NICHD HD 01136, NSF BNS-75-03816, and NIMH 5-T32-MH14581-05. I also wish to acknowledge the importance of comments and issues raised by a number of colleagues, including L. Gleitman, M. Bowerman, D. Slobin, and E. Wanner, though without any implication that the present study resolves the relevant difficulties.

"noun," and arbitrary noun gender classes in languages such as German. The basic idea, with some revision, bears considerable resemblance to traditional views that, in the end, formal grammatical categories are formed and shaped by the sets of grammatical operations in which their members participate, rather than by their semantic denotations per se. Expositionally, the course taken here will be to stress analogies, both analytical and developmental, between characteristics of classes that are clearly known to be defined in such a way (noun gender classes in German) and the major form classes. It was argued that small-scale operations and markers such as determiner use, tensing, negation, and others are plausible candidates for important organizing properties of formal classes, though the concentration upon these is also partly a matter of space limitations here (for example, central predicate-argument functions such as prenoun head modifications are important defining properties of adjectives). At the same time, however, it is clear that ideas of the kind developed in Maratsos and Chalkley (1980) and here for the explication of these processes are incomplete or problematic in a number of ways, despite their likely utility in an eventually adequate analytic and empirical account. This chapter will thus conclude with a brief exposition of some of these problems, though no attempt will be made to treat them here.

8.1. Formal categories in adult grammar

German noun gender classes

Whether categories such as "noun" and "verb" have an important semantic core remains controversial even among linguists (Lyons, 1968). But it is generally agreed that such a semantic core cannot plausibly be found for most of the systems we call arbitrary noun gender or verb conjugation systems. What I would like to do is outline some properties of such systems, and then show that systems such as verb categories are formal categories because they share highly similar properties. In particular, I will discuss at the outset some properties of the German gender system.

In German, noun gender classes are usually called masculine, feminine, and neuter. Members of the different classes take different determiners, pronouns, and adjective endings in the various case grammatical contexts of nominative, genitive, accusative, and dative. Thus a speaker uses *der* to say "the" for a masculine noun being used in a nominative context, but *die* for a feminine noun in the same context, and *das* for a neuter noun. Similarly, where an English speaker can simply say *it* to refer to an inanimate object, a German speaker has to say *er* (masculine nominative), *sie* (feminine nominative), or *es* (neuter nominative).

Table 8.1. *Definite determiners and pronouns for German singular nouns, by case*

	Masculine		Feminine		Neuter	
Case	Det.	Pron.	Det.	Pron.	Det.	Pron.
Nominative	der	er	die	sie	das	es
Genitive	des	—	der	—	des	—
Accusative	den	ihn	die	sie	das	es
Dative	dem	ihm	der	ihr	dem	ihm

Other case environments also have various determiners and pronouns, depending on the gender of the noun. Table 8.1 gives the paradigm for singular nouns, for the definite determiner (equivalent to *the*) and the definite pronoun (equivalent to *it* or *its* for inanimates).

We can concretize the problem of what we mean by masculine gender, or feminine gender, by asking the question this way: What property or properties of a noun predict that it will take the determiner *der* in a nominative context, or the pronoun *er*, rather than *die* and *sie*, or *das* and *es*? For to give such determining properties is to give an answer to the question of what properties masculine or feminine nouns have distinctively in common, constituting gender-class membership (and so predicting appropriate grammatical uses).

Notoriously, the meaning of the term is not a useful predictor. It is true that terms denoting truly masculine entities, such as the words for "man" and "boy," will reliably be classed as masculine – that is, will take *der* and *er* in the nominative. Terms denoting feminine entities also tend to take the feminine determiners and pronouns (though the word for "maiden" is neuter). But for many terms, meaning offers little if any guidance. The words for "spoon," "fork," and "knife," for example, are masculine, feminine, and neuter, respectively; the word for "utensil" is neuter. The phonological stem of the noun is also usually nonpredictive (a difference from French and Spanish, where the phonological form frequently predicts the relevant gender class). For most nouns, neither the meaning nor the phonological form of the stem predicts which determiners and pronouns can be used.

There are, however, good predictors of whether a noun will take *der* as nominative article, or *er* as nominative pronoun. For if it takes *den* as accusative determiner, we can safely predict that it will take *der* as nominative determiner. Of course, then there is a problem: What predicts whether or not a term will take *den* as accusative determiner (or *ihn* as accusative pronoun)? Among other things, *der* as nominative determiner, or *er* as nominative pronoun, will predict *den* as accusative determiner.

The circularity that clearly results here is what is meant by an arbitrary noun gender class. The combinational possibilities of the masculine noun set, rather than being predicted by some characteristics of the noun itself, predict each other. Nouns that take *der* as nominative determiner take *den* as accusative determiner, and vice versa; similarly, nouns that take *die* as nominative determiner take *die* as accusative determiner, and vice versa.

Such a system, of course, is arbitrary in the sense that the semantic denotations of the nouns do not predict their grammatical combinations (or pronominal replacements). But once it is known, it is orderly. If a knowledgeable speaker hears a single definite determiner use of a noun in a nominative or accusative context, he can predict all of the other determiner, pronominal, and adjectival uses of the class. Because what the members of a noun gender category share in common is the relevant set of grammatical combinations, knowing just one distinctive combination predicts the others. Thus the system, though semantically arbitrary, is highly productive: New uses may be predicted in an orderly fashion from knowledge of the system, and from knowledge of a distinctive grammatical property of a term. Such a system is formal because the categories take their definition from the operation of the system itself.

Arbitrary noun gender categories often seem just that – arbitrary. As such, they may seem like peculiar cases in the study of grammatical categories. But in fact, some analysis shows that highly similar analytic properties lie at the heart of the definition of more central categories such as "verb," "adjective," and "noun," examples of major form-class categories. This proposition will be illustrated briefly with a discussion of properties of the English verb system.

The English verb category

Categories such as "noun" and "verb" have far greater tendencies toward modal semantic clusterings than do categories such as masculine and feminine noun gender in German. Verbs do indeed tend to denote activities, changes, and brief occurrences, whereas nouns tend to denote concrete objects or object classes. Adjectives, somewhat in between, tend to denote relatively stable qualities or states of objects and persons. Furthermore, there is good reason to believe that adults and, at the least, older preschool children have some knowledge of these tendencies (Brown, 1957).

Nevertheless, for adult categories, it is doubtful that properties such as these suffice to characterize the distinctive unifying properties of noun, verb, and adjective grammatical classes. Suppose we concretize the problem by considering what properties of terms predict that they will take a well-known grammatical operation, *-ed* past tensing on verbs. This operation applies to a semantically wide variety of relational terms, including *liked, kicked, pushed, considered, consisted,* and *belonged.* But it does not apply to relational terms such as *active* (*actived*) or *fond* (*fonded*), which instead take a preceding form of *be* to mark past tense, either *was* or *were* depending on the person and number of the subject argument (*was active, were fond*).

The problem, then, is what properties of relational terms predict that they will take -*ed* past tensing rather than tensing with *was* or *were*. A semantic-based account, such as Bates and MacWhinney (Chapter 6), will seek such an answer in analysis of the semantic properties of the terms per se. But it seems clear that the semantic overlap among members of the different categories is too great to allow such an answer to have much application. It is true, for example, that many terms that take -*ed* past tensing denote actions or actional qualities. But many do not, such as *like, consist, belong,* and *comprise.* Furthermore, many of them are very similar in meaning to terms that take *was/were* past tensing. For example, *like* (*He liked it*) is clearly more similar in meaning to the term *fond* (*He was fond of it*) than to the term *kick*. Yet it behaves grammatically far more like *kick* (*He kicked it; He liked it; *He fonded of it*). Conversely, many terms that take *was/were* tensing are quite actional in connotation, including *active, busy, explosive, noisy, snoopy* and adjectives that denote manners of acting, such as *careful, nice,* and *nasty.* The actionlike denotations of such terms are especially clear in uses like the progressive (*He is being noisy; He is being nasty*), or the imperative (*Be noisy! Be nasty to them!*). Fillmore (1968a) and Lakoff (1970) both note that either verbs or adjectives may be process terms or stative terms.

We could say that, for many of the terms, semantic qualities predict the manner of past tensing correctly, and perhaps that for some marginal cases, uses have to be memorized. But in fact, other characteristics of the terms predict fairly reliably, in a general way, what kind of tensing operations they will take. For example, many relational terms also have characteristic ways of taking present tensing. Some take suffixed -*s*, following third-person singular arguments, or nothing at all (*He likes it; I like it; He kicks it; I kick it*). Others take preceding forms of *be* (*He is fond of it; They are fond of it*). The relation between method of past tensing and method of present tensing is highly reliable. A good predictor of whether a relational term will take -*ed* past tensing is whether it can take -*s* tensing, or nothing at all (*He likes it; I like it; We liked it; He kicks it; I kick it; We kicked it*). A good predictor of whether a relational term will take *was/were* simple past tensing is whether it takes preceding *be* forms for present tense (*He is fond of it; He was fond of it*). Other possible predictors include whether a term can take preceding forms of *do*; if it can, it can also take -*ed* past tensing (*He doesn't like it; I don't like it; I didn't like it; I liked it*).

But in turn, of course, whether or not a relational term takes -*ed* past tensing is a good predictor (not perfect, because of irregular verbs) of whether it will take -*s* tensing, ∅ present tensing, or use of *do* forms. All of these predict each other, in application to relational terms. That is, a major part of the adult verb system is comprised of the manner in which grammatical uses predict one another for a set of terms, much as the related forms of nouns predict each other in a noun gender system such as that of German or Russian. This kind of knowledge of how grammatical combinations can predict each other is no doubt at the heart of much of the knowledge tested by the Berko generalization task (Berko, 1958). For example, if we are told that *glin* denotes some kind of emotional state, it might be a verb (*like, hate*), an adjective (*fond, disdainful*), or a noun (*joy, sadness, despisal*), each category taking a characteristic class of grammatical operations. But if we are told it denotes an emotional state, and we hear a single grammatical use such as *John glins dogs*, we can immediately predict other grammatical uses, such as *John glinned dogs*; *Does Mary glin cats? The glinning of turtles by boys is nice; To glin is good*; *Does a turtle glin anything? She will glin this very much*; along with a host of other grammatical uses. Or if we hear a use such as *John was very glin toward dogs*, other uses immediately suggest themselves, such as *To be glin toward dogs is nice*; *He was a glin person*; *Being glin is no fun*; *Mary wasn't as glin toward them as John*; and again, many more.

Thus, in the case of both arbitrary noun gender classes in languages such as German and Russian and form-class categories, core definitional properties of the systems unifying diverse members of the categories include the sets of grammatical uses that are or tend to be common to the members of the categories. As usual, however, aspects of the analytic picture are also more complex, or at least heterogeneous. In particular, semantic denotations of the terms may have some overall tendency known to speakers, or may play a part in the regulation of some grammatical operations (usually not all) characteristic of the category. These problems or concerns are taken up illustratively in the next section.

Semantic factors and grammatical categorial operations

Connotative knowledge. Despite the inability of semantic denotations such as "concrete object" or "action" or "state" to unify and define the grammatical properties of nouns, verbs, and adjectives, it is clear, as mentioned previously, that they tend to do so, and that speakers somehow have access to this probabilistic knowledge (Brown, 1957). Thus a representational and acquisitional system must be able somehow to capture speakers' knowledge of such tendencies.

Coordinations of semantic properties and grammatical use properties. It should be emphasized that for many operations characteristic of a grammatical category such as "verb," the semantic denotation of the members is relatively unimportant. For example, any member of the verb category takes *-s* to mark present tense after third-person singular subjects, whether it is an actional verb such as *hit* or a semantically nondescript term such as *consist* or *belong.* In the case of some rules applicable to a category, however, the formal properties and the semantic denotations of the members interact in complex ways to determine the applicability of the rule. For example, the passive construction, by which the usual second argument of a predicate may be placed in initial position, applies only to verbs. We can say *John was liked by Mary,* but not, despite the similarities in meaning of *fond* to *like,* **John was fonded of by Mary.*[1] Even if an adjective denotes a rather agentive relation, such as *John was nasty to the turtle,* there is no corresponding passive **The turtle was nastied to by John,* or **The turtle was nastied.* So even though both adjectives and verbs can take two arguments, the passive applies only to verbs.

Within the class of verbs, however, the passive seems freely productive only for verbs denoting actional or experiential relations, such as *John was liked by Mary,* or *John was talked about by his friends.* Verbs not having such semantics cannot be reliably predicted to take the passive, but must apparently be marked individually (Maratsos & Chalkley, 1980). Thus, for example, both *own* and *have* denote possession, but *own* can take the passive (*Four houses were owned by those men*) whereas *have* cannot (**Four houses were had by those men*). Other examples of such failures of nonactional and nonexperiencer verbs include **John was fitted by his suit* (compare to *John was fitted by his tailor,* where *fit* is agentive), or **Mary was seemed like by John.* Thus whether or not the passive applies to a relational term depends both on its grammatical category (verb vs. adjective) and on its semantic denotation (actional-experiential vs. other). Other examples where particular grammatical operations are conditioned both by the formal category and by the semantic category of a term are common (see Maratsos & Chalkley, 1980, for more examples).

Cases where semantic properties per se predict or constitute grammatical category membership. Finally, there are some cases where semantic denotation per se predicts the relevant formal category membership. For example, for most German nouns, as already exposited, the semantic denotation of the term is not a good predictor. Instead, various determiner and pronominal uses predict each other, and terms are masculine, neuter, or feminine according to their participation in a given set of uses. But for a few nouns, semantic denotation does predict the set of uses. Truly masculine nouns all take the same set (which is thus called the masculine set), and most truly feminine nouns take the feminine set. Thus, for such terms, both grammatical uses and semantic denotation predict the grammatical uses.

A probably more general and important relationship between meaning and grammatical operations may be found for the class of concrete common nouns as a whole. As noted previously, for terms such as *idea, game, trip,* and *emotion,* semantic denotations do not predict the use of noun grammatical operations. For such terms, the operations instead predict each other. But if a term denotes a concrete object class, it can be safely predicted to take such noun operations. For nouns like *dog* and *table,* grammatical uses both predict each other and are predicted by the semantic denotations of the terms.

These cases are chosen from many (see Maratsos & Chalkley, 1980, for other examples) in which more formal categorization (given by co-predictive uses of terms) and semantic denotations (such as agentivity), or concrete object denotation, interact in complex fashions to determine the applicability of particular grammatical uses. Thus a claim that what makes formal classes formal is definition by appearance in a set of grammatical uses is not a claim that semantic denotations of the terms are necessarily irrelevant. In fact, both kinds of analysis are clearly part of grammatical analysis.

8.2. Acquisitional facts about formal category ontogenesis

In the account given here, the child constructs grammatical categories such as verb, noun, or noun gender class by analyzing the groups of grammatical uses or operations that groups of terms tend to take in common, thereby learning how uses in such operations predict each other. At the same time, however, the child must be capable of taking into account when, and to what degree, semantic properties of the members of the categories are relevant to predicting their appearance in particular operations (e.g., the passive), or in the set of operations characteristic of the category (e.g., the masculine set of noun operations for truly masculine nouns).

What is known empirically about children's ability to construct such complex systems of co-predicting uses of terms? There is actually not very much known, partially because, as Braine (1976) notes, analysts have probably attributed to children much too ready and too early a use of such formal classes as "noun" and "verb." Such descriptions have commonly been presupposed for describing early speech or the early growth of morphological operations (see, e.g., Brown, 1973; Klima & Bellugi, 1966), when it is at least possible that the emergence of such categories, defined by shared grammatical uses of their members, would require time.

This in fact seems to be the case. There is little evidence, as is not surprising, for early use of arbitrary noun subclass systems in early grammar in languages such as Russian or German (MacWhinney, 1978; Slobin, 1973). As Braine (1976) has summarized, there is also no good reason to credit children with having captured formal categories such as "noun" and "verb" in their early speech, even if they use terms such as *dog* and *want*, which are nouns and verbs in the adult system.

Let us put the question this way: What can we mean by asking if categories such as noun or verb should be used to describe children's early constructions? I think what we would mean is something like this: Do any of their grammatical rules make reference to groups of terms that cannot be united by semantic denotations such as "object word" or "action word" or "word denoting a possessor," that is, to groups of terms that are semantically heterogeneous yet seem to approximate, somehow, the boundaries of the adult categories, with a somewhat similar organizational basis?

The evidence concerning this point is summarized in Braine (1976). As he finds, children's early rules seem to consist of a mixture of major semantic-structural patterns, such as "actor-action," "possessor-possessed" (actually a pattern that feels major probably only because of the importance of possession in everyday life), "located object–location," and more specific patterns or word-centered formulas such as "ingestion–ingested object," "*more* + recurring element" (*more car, more hot*), "*nomore* + disappeared element" (*nomore cereal*), "*want* + desired entity" (*want car, want blow*), "*that* + indicated entity," and so on. In all cases, the best description does not seem to require use of anything but specific words to describe a position, or categories defined by the inherent or situational meanings of the words that can appear in the position. Often a child's uses may ignore or cut across potential adult form-class boundaries (for example, *away* can be an action term in the schema "actor + action"), or may fail to unite members of an adult category (*want* and *see* can be part of individual word formulas having nothing to do with the uses of terms such as *get* or *have*, for example). Often when a child's grammatical category seems to include just members of an adult grammatical category, it is because it includes a semantically consistent potential subclass. For example, Andre (Blaine, 1976) used the formula "*other* + *X*" only with nouns (*other bib, other page*), but these were all terms denoting a concrete referent, so that "*other* + concrete object word = 'another member of the concrete object class'" is an adequate characterization.

What sorts of findings are available for periods after this early one? As already noted, there are not very many. What follows is a selective review of some of the findings concerning noun gender-class operations and form-class uses.

Acquisition of noun genders

German-speaking children use determiners relatively late, around the middle or end of the third year (sources summarized in MacWhinney, 1978). When determiners are used, however, gender errors (the use of a determiner of one class for a noun of the other) are surprisingly infrequent. Many such uses, of course, may be individually memorized determiner-noun combinations (memorized according to case context). MacWhinney (1978), however, employed a more severe test of children's productive understanding, a Berko-like task. For example, in one question, the children were shown a nonsense object and told: "Gann. I give you {*ihn, sie,* or *es*}. How do you say, Where is ___ ? [a nominative context for the relevant noun]." In this task, a child must use the form of the accusative pronoun to generate the form of the nominative determiner: *Ihn* implies *der Gann, sie* implies *die Gann, es* implies *das Gann.* Children as young as 3 years of age could sometimes perform the task, and proficiency was good by the end of the preschool years. Thus, though little detailed information is available about developmental patterns, German-speaking children formulate the noun gender system with surprisingly little difficulty (and without instruction) in the preschool years. If anything, observers report more difficulty with *case* errors, such as nominative–accusative confusions in the masculine.

Russian also has a case-gender system, which includes six grammatical cases (nominative, accusative, dative, genitive, prepositional, instrumental) and three noun gender classes (masculine, feminine, and neuter). The Russian case-gender system does not involve determiner endings, but instead consists of sets of markings on the ends of nouns and adjectives. At first glance, the Russian data contradict the German data surprisingly. For although the basic systematic definition is similar (various uses, here noun endings, predict each other), children make errors into the school years, around the age of 7 (sources summarized in Slobin, 1973).

Maratsos and Chalkley (1980), however, have found evidence that makes the Russian and German acquisitional facts more consistent. Briefly, Russian-speaking children begin using noun endings relatively early, near the beginning of the third year sometimes, and do make many gender errors. But evidence from the original sources (e.g., Zakharova, 1973), upon further investigation, shows that Russian-speaking children master the major systematic organizational principles of the gender system by the age of 3 or 4 for all but a few, understandably unclear, cases. The situation has to do with the clarity of the nominative case marker as a predictor of gender uses. Some such markings (the majority) are relatively systematic. For example, should a noun end in stressed /a/ in the nominative, it takes /oy/ endings in the genitive, dative, instrumental, and prepositional cases, and /u/ in the accusative – a pattern of feminine gender uses. If a noun ends in stressed /o/ in the nominative, it takes another corresponding set of endings called the neuter set. A third set, called masculine, takes no endings in the nominative or accusative, and usually the stem ends in hard consonants.

But for other nouns, a minority, the key nominative form does not signal the other uses clearly. For example, nouns that end in palatalized consonants in the nominative are assigned individually and arbitrarily to either masculine or feminine sets of endings. Nouns ending in the unstressed vowel /ə/ in the nominative are arbitrarily assigned as either neuter or feminine. Russian contrasts in this respect with German, in which knowledge of the definite marker or nominative pronoun gives a completely reliable cue to other case uses.

Zakharova (1973) studied 200 Russian children of ages 3 through 7, using both observational and Berko-type experimental methods. She indeed found children observing case distinctions earlier than gender distinctions. But she also found that the productive use of the noun gender ending system is "quickly established" for the clear sets, in which the nominative forms end in stressed /a/ (feminine), stressed /o/ (neuter), or a hard consonant (masculine). It was just the sets in which the nominative form does not reliably cue the other case uses that continued to cause errors for years.

Thus children acquiring German and Russian can apparently formulate the systems of correlated uses of terms that constitute noun gender systems by the ages of 3 or 4. Such findings are important evidence of children's ability to formulate efficiently syntactic classes in which correlated use in sets of grammatical operations, rather than semantic distinctions, is clearly at the heart of providing the differentiations among categories.

Form-class operations

As discussed before, there is little evidence for the presence of grammatical categorical organizations with the properties of the adult system in children's early grammar (this conclusion applies as well, apparently, to grammatical relations such as "subject" and "object," which are not discussed here; see Maratsos & Chalkley, 1980). If we look at the available evidence for positive indications of adult form-class organizations, we see that not very much is presently known. What would constitute such evidence? Essentially, the child would have to show that he could predict new grammatical functions of a term on the basis of knowledge of some of its other functions, when this prediction could not be made on the basis of the semantic nature of the term itself. For example, children's making verb-operation overregularizations such as *breaked* and *runned* is not necessarily strong evidence: Because *break* and *run* are also actional terms, they might be employing the *-ed* past overregularization to apply to actional terms.

The major evidence of this kind so far exposited for English is probably provided by Maratsos et al. (1979) and Maratsos and Kuczaj (1979). These authors studied the frequency and immediacy of past tensing on irregular verbs such as *think, know, see, hear,* and *feel* (*think* and *feel* in their nonactional senses, "to have an opinion" and "to feel (good)"). These terms are highly nonactional for the adult, and there is evidence that they are analyzed reasonably appropriately by children as well. That children understand much of their semantic intension is attested for some terms by studies and interview evidence in L. Gleitman, H. Gleitman, and Shipley (1972), C. Johnson and Maratsos (1977), C. Johnson and Wellman (1980), Shatz and Gelman (1973), and Wellman and C. Johnson (1979). Children also generally fail to use these terms in constructions such as the progressive or the imperative, which are used with actional verbs or adjectives. Nevertheless, as soon as children can encode their meanings in a past context, as shown by the uses of irregulars such as *saw* and *heard*, they generalize *-ed* past tensing to them, producing forms such as *seed, sawed, knowed, thoughted,* and *feeled,* in proportions comparable to those for more actional verbs (Maratsos & Kuczaj, 1979; Maratsos et al., 1979). In the account given here, what such terms that take *-ed* past tensing (such as *kicked, spilled, melted*) are grammatical operations: use of *do* forms (*He didn't kick it; I didn't know*), *-s* tensing (*It spills; He hears it*), appearance after auxiliaries (*He'll kick it; He'll feel good*), and appearance as the only relational term, directly after an argument (*They kick cans; I think he'll come*).

Such overregularizations are in fact not early. They seem to become common around stages IV or V for many children (Maratsos et al., 1979). Thus it seems to me that our earliest positive evidence for the formulation of grammatical categories in which the co-prediction of grammatical operations takes place is actually rather late. On the one hand, this is not surprising if the formation of such categories for productive use requires the accumulation of information about the groups of operations in which terms appear. On the other hand, it may well be that such organizations are taking shape earlier, but the data have not yet been analyzed in a manner to show this clearly. It is also worth emphasizing that we do not really have a very good idea what particular properties of terms such as *think, know, see, hear,* and *feel* may be suggesting to the child the applicability of *-ed* tensing. For example, some grammatical uses might be more critical than others for the child.

Other kinds of evidence about the emergence of the child's analyses of adultlike grammatical categories are more indirect, but still of some importance. One of the major bodies of such facts has to do with the general lack of error in children's form-class operations, that is, their general failure to attach verb inflections to members of other potential adult categories, or to treat members of the adult category of verb in nounlike ways, and so forth. For example, as discussed earlier, many nonverbs do have, either alone or in combination with other terms, highly actionlike semantic qualities. Such terms include adjectives like *noisy, nasty,* and *quick,* or particles such as *up* and *away,* which often form intrinsic parts of an actional denotation. For example, *throw away* carries a sense of "dispose of," which *throw* by itself does not, so it is the two-term expression that means "dispose of." Similarly, *call up* means "phone" in a way that *call* by itself does not, at least not as clearly. If children were formulating verb operations productively on the basis of semantic denotations alone, we could expect many errors such as *He call upped his mother,* or *He is throw awaying the garbage,* or *He is nastying.* In fact, such errors appear to be generally infrequent (Cazden, 1968; W. Miller & Ervin, 1964). Cazden notes that *stand up* seems to be somewhat susceptible to such errors (*It stand ups*), but this could be a segmentation problem, because it rarely takes an intervening term. Errors such as *I call mother upped,* where the intervening term makes clear that the combination is not a single term, seem virtually nonexistent.

At this point, however, this account of the data may seem inconsistent with accounts in other sources, such as those of Clark (Chapter 13) or Bowerman (Chapter 11), who find form-class errors such as treating nouns in verblike fashion to be common. It is certainly true that such uses are anecdotally heard. There is even some source in the language for certain domains of them, because English, for example, has many cases in which what is apparently the same stem can appear in both noun and verb uses (e.g., *Here's a hammer, He hammered the fence; Here's a saw, He sawed the fence; This door is open, He opened the door*).

The whole problem is quite complex, but it seems to me reasonable still to say that form-class errors are generally rare. For example, I have recently looked at a total of seventy-four hours of children's speech, including fifty-six hours from Abe, a subject studied by S. Kuczaj and me, beginning at the age of 2;9 (years; months – Abe was in Brown's Stage V at this time), and approximately eighteen hours of speech from two 2-year-olds, sixteen 3-year-olds, and two 4-year-olds. These last children also had mean lengths of utterance (MLUs) of near or over 4.0. I did not count the number of utterances generally. Abe in two half-hour samples averaged 300 utterances in a half hour, however, and Brown (1973) indicates that a child may easily say about 700 utterances in two hours. Perhaps a reasonable guess is that the sample totaled 15,000–25,000 utterances, or more. In Table 8.2, the total set of form-class errors, from

Table 8.2. *Form-class errors*

Abe K. (2;9–4;0)

(1) Noun used as verb	You were catching, not balling. [= *pitching*]
(2) Adjective used as noun	Where's the dirties at?
	I will be many talls.
(3) Verb used as adjective or noun	Because they call me a grumble boy
	Chew hawks are really strange.
(4) Adjective used as verb (or missing *up*)	I'm getting warmed.[a]
(5) Marking of auxiliary verb	Sometimes her don'ts.
	You say that if somebody don'ts play good.
(6) *Be* used as verb	Because he be's my friend.
	He beed good.
(7) Segmentation, random	We just eat lunched.
	Can you come helps.
	It's getting nighttime.

Other children

(1) Noun used as verb	He necks. That's how he necks. [SS, 3]
(2) Adjective used as noun	That one's got a happy.[b] [JL, 3]
	The squeaky came out.[b] [EA, 3]
(3) Verb used as adjective	See, the go cars.[c] [JM, 4]
(4) Adverb used as noun	I'll be in the downstairs.[d] [ES, 3]
(5) Verb marking on particle	I knock him downs. [JC, 3][e]
(6) Adjective used as adverb	And they went loud[ly]. [BE, 4]
(7) Random (?)	Now they'res all ready. [JC, 3]

---

[a] Could be missing *up*, especially because Abe had not yet used passives with a particle (e.g., *He got knocked over*; *It was stepped on*).
[b] Both adjective-as-noun errors could be missing nouns (*That one's got a happy one*).
[c] Could be word-order error, e.g., *See, the cars go*.
[d] Not clear what the error is.
[e] This child used *knocks down* correctly about fifteen times in the same transcript.

Abe and the other children, is listed. As can be seen, this total set is not large. Furthermore, there is a certain randomness about the set. No particular kind of error stands out, such as use of nouns as verbs, or use of adjectives as verbs. These are, of course, data from mostly rather advanced children. With less advanced children, however, low error rates are also the rule. Cazden's (1968) sample was Brown's well-known three subjects through Stage V. This sample seems to have included about 150 hours of recorded speech. Cazden recorded just four errors involving application of an inflectional morpheme to a member of the wrong major form class. Three of these, made by two of the children, consisted of an adjective being treated like a verb (e.g., *That greens*). The other consisted of a tense marker being applied to a particle (*Look how she stand ups*). M. Smith (1933) finds form-class errors rarer among 2-year-olds than 3-year-olds; so the low rate of errors in less advanced subjects is not unusual.

These data indicate that form-class errors in general are quite rare, and errors of a particular class, such as use of nouns as verbs (Clark, Chapter 13) or adjectives as causative verbs (Bowerman, Chapter 11), are infrequent as well. Why should this be so? One possibility is that of individual differences. Another relevant fact, I think, is that observers making anecdotal observations about their own children may be choosing from very large potential samples. For example, an observer whose effective sample of his or her child was two hours a day, and whose child uttered about 700 utterances in two hours, would have an effective corpus of about 250,000 utterances in a year. It can be seen that a very low error rate would still result in a fair number of interesting errors. The problem is much more complex than this, probably, but I think it is fair for the purposes of general discussion to say that form-class errors are rare. Certain types, such as the use of nonverb actional terms – actional adjectives, for instance – as verbs, are strikingly rare.

What is the significance of the absence of such form-class errors? This seems to depend upon the period studied. When we have positive evidence that the child will actively over-assign some grammatical operation, such as the frequent use of *-ed* past tense on terms that do not take this ending in the adult language, looking at the scope of the child's application gives us an idea of the boundaries for the category to which the child believes the operation can be applied. As we have seen, the child does apply *-ed* past tensing to nonactional terms such as *know, think, see, hear,* and *feel,* which share with terms such as *push, kick,* and *like* employment in a similar set of grammatical operations. At the same time, the child does not apply *-ed* past tensing to potentially actional terms such as *nasty* or *noisy,* or to particles that form part of the essential denotation of an action, such as *up* in *call up* or *away* in *throw away.* The results thus suggest that at this point the child, even if he or she is analyzing that actionality may be more common of terms that take verb operations (as it is), nevertheless is assigning the relevant grammatical operations to a class somehow defined in the adultlike manner, and not assigning the operation to actional terms that do not share in the relevant set of grammatical operations.

What about the early period? For example, it is doubtful that children have a main verb organization approximating the adult's at the end of Stage I, or near the beginning of Stage II, when inflections such as *-ing* begin to appear. They may, however, have categorized terms into classes such as "action" (or into finer classes) for the purposes of representing generalizations about major predicate-argument structure, such as "actor-action." Now -*ing* is heard to apply to terms as *go, move, sing,* and so on – terms that denote actions. Children also seem to include terms like *away, off, bye-bye,* and *out* as action terms in expressions such as *Gia away, car bye-bye,* and so on (Bloom, Lightbown, & Hood, 1975; Bloom, Miller, & Hood, 1975). They do not, however, produce errors such as *Gia awaying,* or *outing car.* Does this provide evidence that categories such as "action" are not grammatical categories for the child after all?

Probably it does not. The most reasonable interpretation is that, despite the availability of such categories for major constituent structure, various individual grammatical operations may be assigned to the relevant terms at least initially in a word-by-word fashion. Even if the child has some early sense that -*ing* goes mostly on terms that denote actions, the child still waits for some time to see for each individual action term whether it takes -*ing.* We do not presently know just when a productive use of -*ing* comes (that is, when it is assigned freely to a process term before the term has been heard to take it) (Brown, 1973; Kuczaj, 1978).

In fact, the acquisition of what will eventually be united as the class of verb operations seems to have a general piecemeal quality about it for some time (Bellugi, 1967; Bloom, Lifter, & Hafitz, 1980). Bellugi found that *don't* and *can't* may initially be assigned to terms individually as negation markers. Her examples furthermore make clear that each may be assigned to semantically heterogeneous sets. *Don't* can be used on terms as semantically different as *sit, want,* and *know.* Bloom et al. found that as late as MLU Stage III, "the morphemes . . . were distributed selectively with different populations of [terms]" (p. 393). The different markers tend to be used on semantically different sets, but their data indicate this to be only a tendency. For example, -*ed* past tense was marked by their subjects about 18 percent of the time on what they analyzed as achievement terms, about 5 percent of the time on simple activity terms, and about 20 percent of the time on a group of frequently used terms. All markings of -*ed* at this point were correct; there were no overregularizations to potentially irregular verbs, or, in fact, to what could be analyzed as achievement or activity terms that should not take the marking at all (being nonverbs in adult grammar).

Thus it seems likely that many future verb operations may have semantic tendencies in their application to groups of terms (the reasons for this may vary), but they also are applied nonproductively; that is, a term must be heard to take the operation for some time before the child will use it this way. Early absence of use of markers such as inflections, or *don't* and *can't,* probably stems from term-by-term assignment, at least in part. This matter will form an important aspect of the theoretical account to be sketched later.

To summarize, it appears that children do not immediately attain formal class organizations such as arbitrary noun gender, or adult verb and noun organizations. Such organizations are, however, attained by the end of the preschool years or earlier, often with surprisingly little error. The available results suggest in a general way that children acquire such systems by making term-by-term assignments of various grammatical operations. Over time, knowledge grows that terms which take some grammatical operations also take others, in a manner not necessarily controlled by the semantic denotations of the terms per se. This last conclusion holds clearly for categories such as arbitrary gender classes, and also holds well for categories such as "verb," as witnessed by the accurate yet semantically heterogeneous range of overregularizations of the *-ed* past-tensing operation.

What I would like to do in the last section of the chapter is to present some ideas on characteristics of likely or possible induction systems for the formation of grammatical categories. The basic idea will be to consider three types of categories in turn, ranging along a continuum of semantic bases. The initial discussion will be of the induction of clearly semantic-based categories such as "agent" and "action"; in this discussion, basic aspects of a general categorical induction model will be introduced. Then categories in which differentiations are clearly formal, noun gender categories, will be discussed. The last part of the section will treat the most problematic case, that of form classes such as "noun" and "verb," where the relative contributions of semantic-based and co-predictive factors in both development and final representation are the most perplexing.

8.3. Induction processes in grammatical category formation

Early semantic-structural categorial growth

As noted in the preceding section, early grammatical rules seem to consist of rules such as "*want* + desired object," "ingestion + ingested object," or "actor + action," along with sets of no doubt memorized individual word combinations. In the account to be given here, larger patterns begin with the analyses of smaller sequences, as sequential loci or slots, each characterized by the kind of term appearing in the slot – that is, characterized by the properties of the term; the rule also includes a specification of the effects of combining the terms.

For example, suppose that a child one day correctly analyzes that *daddy walk* means that daddy moves himself along by movement of the lower limbs. This is entered as a particular small rule something like the following:

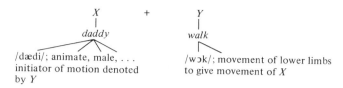

This small rule simply says that if some *X* has the properties characteristic of daddy walking, it can be followed by a term denoting walking.

Suppose the child now hears *mommy walk*. This has an analysis very similar in constituent parts, and in sequential shape, to the already entered pattern for *daddy walk*. Such similarity of parts leads to the assimilation of the new pattern by the old. The result would be something like:

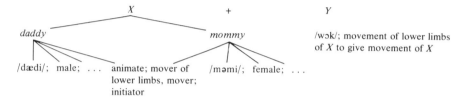

What has happened is that the *X* locus assimilates both *daddy* and *mommy* as examples of what can precede *walk*. The properties they have in common (animacy, movement of lower limbs, initiation) will influence what future examples become assimilated. Properties they do not have in common (maleness, femaleness) will be less influential. Over time, the result should be a representation in which the *X* locus is mostly defined by animacy, initiation, and movement of lower limbs, that is, essentially, "walker + *walk*," an individual word formula much like "*want* + wanted entity."

Of course, such a scheme is capable of assimilatory expansion in the *Y* locus as well. Because the child hears utterances such as *daddy go* and *doggy run,* assimilation by sufficient similarity to the "walker + *walk*" pattern should eventually give something like "mover + movement" (i.e., "self-mover + movement"), a formula for which there is evidence in various analyses (Bloom, Lightbown, & Hood, 1975; Bloom, Miller, & Hood, 1975; Bowerman, 1976; Braine, 1976).

Clearly, children might differ somewhat in their patterns of assimilation. For some children, similarities of major semantic characteristics such as animacy and initiation might be highly salient, so that the relevant rules would form quickly. Other children might require much closer matches of the properties of new examples to old patterns, so that expansion to general patterns would be slower, and so that more specific patterns would be evidenced for some time.

The scheme will not, naturally, assimilate purely on the basis of sequential and phonological similarity. That is, *daddy walk* assimilates *mommy walk* (or, possibly, *daddy go*). It would not, however, be likely to assimilate *daddy chair*, despite the presence of *daddy* in initial position in both. For the function of *daddy* in the two sequences is quite different (daddy as mover/initiator vs. daddy as possessor), and the analysis and functions of *walk* and *chair* are quite dissimilar (an action word denoting an action of some mover vs. an object word denoting a possessed object). The scheme thus builds grammatical categories on the basis of overall sequential similarity, but also on the basis of semantic function and analysis of the parts of the sequence. It is hence not a purely distributional analysis.

It is clear that, potentially, many different sequences have many possible resemblances to one another. Therefore, for any sort of consistency in the product arrived at to obtain across children, certain semantic factors must be inherently more likely than others to be judged similar. Salient characteristics at this early time seem to include actional qualities, animacy, intentionality, location, possession, and other now familiar qualities. In the case of such early categories, it is likely that these properties acquire their salience not because of special characteristics of the linguistic induction system, but because of general cognitive salience (Brown, 1973; Slobin, 1973).

Later categories, however, cannot be formed so clearly on the basis of the semantic-sequential properties of strings. Subsequent parts of this section deal with such categories. It is to be emphasized, however, that in these latter cases, the relevant analyses are also not purely distributional, even if the result is the formation of classes that cannot be distinguished on semantic grounds per se.

The formation of noun gender distinctions

The essence of a noun gender system such as that of German is that different sets of nouns take different sets of determiner endings and pronouns and adjective endings for the encoding of identical functions. The problem is how this variation can come about.

Theorizing about the problem cannot be specific past a certain point, for critical to the induction of such systems are analyses such as nominative case environment, accusative case environment, and so forth. These, however, are no doubt not present early on in their mature form. In fact, they may well depend on the development of the gender system for achievement of final form. It is quite possible that what eventually becomes nominative case, for example, begins as a collection of semantic-structural analyses such as "denotes an agent," or "denotes a described object," whereas what eventually becomes accusative case begins as analyses such as "describes a transferred object," or "denotes a patient." Far smaller beginning categorizations are of course possible. Detailed longitudinal analysis of the patterns of children's marking of such cases would be of enormous general interest.

For the present discussion, however, let us assume that some kinds of early beginnings exist for the differentiation of these case categories. Then the induction of gender systems can be described.

Let us start with definite articles for the nominative. In dealing with the various determiner uses in the singular, the child will encounter three semantic-structural patterns:

$$X_i \qquad\qquad\qquad + Y_i$$
| |
der; + definite + singular + nomi-   + common + argument head
    native of *Y*   (i.e., a noun)

$$X_j \qquad\qquad\qquad + Y_j$$
\   \
die; definite, nominative,   + common, argument head
    singular of *Y*

$$X_k \qquad\qquad\qquad + Y_k$$
\   \
das; definite, nominative,   + common, argument head
    singular of *Y*

By the time different article uses begin to appear, the child may be forming general classes such as determiner and noun. But clearly the child must also memorize which words can be determiners with which nouns, in the various number and case environments. If we refer, for brevity, to the patterns just presented as "*der* + *X* = 'nom sing of *X*'" and so forth, we can symbolize the child's learning of this type by a kind of pattern-lexical linkage:

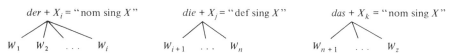

$$der + X_i = \text{"nom sing } X\text{"} \qquad die + X_j = \text{"def sing } X\text{"} \qquad das + X_k = \text{"nom sing } X\text{"}$$

$$W_1 \quad W_2 \quad \ldots \quad W_i \qquad\qquad W_{i+1} \quad \ldots \quad W_n \qquad\qquad W_{n+1} \quad \ldots \quad W_z$$

(W_1, W_2, W_i, . . . are just references to individual words in the lexicon.)

As was discussed previously, by and large the semantic properties of the different groups of nouns cannot be used to distinguish which nouns take *der, die,* or *das* as singular nominative determiners. While nominative determiner uses are being learned, however, it is likely that other operations, such as the use of *er, sie,* and *es* as nominative pronominal replacements for nouns, or the use of *den, die,* and *das* as accusative determiners, are being learned. Referring to the patterns briefly, we can symbolize what begins to happen for just the set of nouns that takes *der* in the nominative as follows:

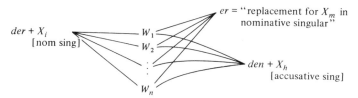

Over time, semantic properties of $W_1 \ldots W_i$ will not generally improve as distinctive predictors of taking *der* in the nominative, *den* in the accusative, and so forth. But the uses will prove to be good predictors of each other. That is, if we ask what the common and distinctive properties of the nouns that take *der* as definite nominative singular might be, a partial answer is that such terms take *er* as nominative pronoun and *den* as accusative determiner. Of course, conversely, taking *der* as nominative definite determiner becomes in turn a property common to, and distinctive of, those terms which take *er* and *den* in the respective environments.

Similarly, for nouns that take *die* in the nominative, use of *die* in the accusative, use of *sie* as nominative pronoun, and other uses that follow the feminine pattern, are mutually predictive. For the neuter group, *das* and *es* nominative and accusative uses come to be similarly co-predictive.

It seems quite impossible to describe the growth of noun gender systems without employing induction processes such as these. For various reasons that I will not discuss here, it is quite clear that these processes cannot be the whole picture. What the analysis and developmental data concerning noun gender systems demonstrate, however, is multifold: First, children are adept at forming systems in which uses come, somehow, to predict each other; second, they are very good at fine-scale analysis of markers such as determiner and pronominal uses as key defining properties for differentiating syntactic categorial classes.

Form classes

Form classes, such as "noun" and "verb," have been presented in this chapter with concentration upon those of their analytic and developmental properties which are similar to those of noun gender classes. I will repeat these briefly here, before considering some other factors that appear different. First, often the most reliable characteristics that might serve to unite the class appear to be fairly small-scale combinations, such as tensing and negation operations for verbs. For example, both verbs and adjectives take initial agentive arguments (Fillmore, 1968a), even if verbs do so more frequently. But only verbs take negation with forms such as *don't* and *doesn't*, or take tense and aspect markers such as present tense

-*s* on the stem or -*ed* past tense. Similarly, for nouns, what appears to unite concrete and nonconcrete nouns like *idea, action, verb, dog,* and *table* are uses such as appearance with articles (*the dog, the idea*), plurals (*dogs, ideas*), and possessives (*John's dog, John's idea*). Thus, analytically, there is evidence that within form-class categories, systems of co-predictive definition might be operating (terms that take *do*-form uses take tense inflections; terms that take article uses take plural and possessive markers). Developmentally, there is some tentative evidence that various form-class operations are initially linked to individual terms in a word-by-word fashion. Over time, it could be expected that information about how uses co-predict each other would grow. Another kind of developmental evidence of some interest is that children observe form-class boundaries very well in assigning grammatical uses such as tense marking, even though central semantic modal tendencies of the classes (e.g., that verbs tend to denote actions) are not perfect. There is also evidence for productive generalization of operations to members not of the appropriate modal semantic class; in particular, children produce overregularizations such as *thinked, knowed, feeled, heared,* and *seed* with reasonable readiness (Maratsos et al., 1979), even though these do not denote actional qualities.

Maratsos and Chalkley (1980) took such analytic and empirical findings to point to a number of probable developmental processes. First, the absence of form-class errors, such as assigning verb operations to nonverb action-denoting terms, suggested that the earlier use of categories such as ''action terms'' in rules like ''actor-action'' did not have much connection to the later formulation of the verb category. Second, Maratsos and Chalkley's account emphasized the child's skill in making small-scale analyses, analyses that are probable in early rules (Braine, 1976) and rules of morphological assignment, and necessary for gender systems. In particular, Maratsos and Chalkley outlined an account in which verb operations such as tensing and negation come to predict each other over time, as they are used of highly overlapping sets of terms – an account quite similar in nature to that given in this chapter for gender classes. They also developed a networklike account in which, in fact, no single categorial node corresponding to ''verb'' or ''noun'' necessarily emerges.

For the sake of expositional concreteness, and also to bring out a few points, I will briefly schematize the kinds of developments Maratsos and Chalkley discuss. In particular, I will schematize operations such as past tensing with descriptions such as ''$X + Y$,'' as in the section on the growth of such early semantic-structural rules as ''mover + movement,'' to see how co-predictive networks can grow from particular analyses. Consider the operation of -*ed* past tensing. Presumably, at some point the child makes his first analysis of an -*ed* past-tense use into its component parts, for example, ''*spilled = spill + ed = '*past of *spill.'''* Following the representational conventions of the initial analytic section, we can describe this as the following analysis:

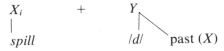

(I will ignore throughout specifications of the grammatical context of operations, though in fact such information must be recorded and analyzed somehow.) What this rule means is that if some term has the properties of *spill*, *-ed* can be added to it to denote the past of the term. *Spill* itself, by now, is a complex coordination of a number of types of descriptions, including phonological and semantic types and links to other semantic-structural patterns, such as "$X + ing$ = 'progressive of X,'" "*don't* + X = 'present negation of X,'" and so forth. It is possibly also linked at this point to major structural-semantic patterns such as "actor + action." Suppose we represent its semantic properties with the notation $S_i \ldots S_n$, and its grammatical properties (that is, its linkages to other semantic-structural patterns) as $G_i \ldots G_n$. Then the early form of the past-tense rule has this form:

Now suppose the child hears and properly analyzes another *-ed* use, such as *moved*. Because of sufficient semantic-structural similarity, this use will be linked to the already present past-tense description. Thus, the X locus in particular will grow; properties common to *spill* and *move* will become more influential in the absorption of new examples, whereas dissimilar properties will become less so. On the other hand, a use such as *blue-eyed*, even if the child should analyze it into two parts *blue eye* and *-ed*, will not be absorbed, for a variety of reasons. In particular, despite an overall possible segmental-phonological similarity ("$X + ed$"), the parts are too dissimilar; *blue eye* is very different in nature from *spill* and *move*, and the *-ed* suffix has little meaning at all, in contrast to the *-ed* past marking.

Over time, the *-ed* past-tense locus will absorb an increasing number of appropriate terms, each linked to a variety of semantic-structural patterns. As the individual terms become linked to a wider variety of verb operations, it will become increasingly true that terms analyzed as taking *-ed* past tensing are those which take *do* forms to mark tense and negation, *-s* tensing, progressive *-ing* tensing (for actional terms of the verb class), and other verb operations. The operations will thus come increasingly to co-predict the applicability of one another. Again referring to the relevant semantic-structural patterns very briefly, this growing network of linkages can be represented as follows, for a hypothetical fragment of the verb system:

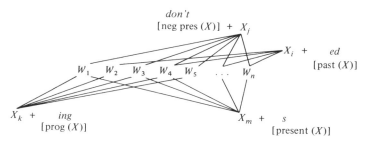

Thus, if we look at what properties tend to be distinctive of, and common to, the terms that can be X in the semantic-structural pattern "$X + ed$ = 'past of X,'" we see that such properties include being able to be X in patterns such as uses of *do* forms, *-ing* tensing, *-s* tensing, and others. Terms like *break, run, think, know,* and *see* happen arbitrarily not to take *-ed* past tensing, but they share many properties in common with those which do; hence the child produces forms such as *breaked, runned, thinked, knowed,* and *seed.* The growth of *-ed* past-tense overregularizations can be seen as symptomatic of the growth of a potentially productive system of organization approximating the adult verb system.

Major constituent structure and form-class categories

Despite what has just been said, it is not clear that the analogies between form-class category membership and gender-class membership can be drawn too sharply. What is interesting about these analogies is the apparent usefulness of looking at various small-marker operations as possible sources of reliable prediction of class membership. This procedure is of course required in the case of noun gender classes, and it is plausible in the case of form classes.

   A problem raised here is that of the relation of form-class properties to major constituent properties of sentences, those which do not in some sense seem to be tied to small-marker properties. These include rules such as the taking of obligatory initial noun phrase arguments by verbs, the use of adjectives as prenominal modifiers when the noun is the head of an argument of a higher predicate, and conjunction and embedding. Another, probably linked, problem is the relation of such analyses to earlier rules such as "actor-action," or to rules such as the placement of locative phrases with respect to subjects or verb phrases denoting transfer activities. Finally, it is apparent that in various cases, small-marker properties of the type discussed here are not sufficient to delineate and differentiate various central form-class properties. For example, prepositions can take the same tense- and negation-marking patterns as adjectives (e.g., *He is happy*; *He is near us*; *He isn't happy*; *He isn't near us*). The differentiation of prepositions and adjectives probably involves major semantic-structural patterns and properties, such as locative as opposed to characteristically nonlocative meanings, prenominal uses, and other properties of this nature.

Another problem of this kind seems to be provided by the noun class, for whereas concrete and nonconcrete common nouns such as *dog* and *idea* are probably united at least partly by their use in common small-marker patterns such as article use (*the dog, the idea*), pluralization (*the dogs, the ideas*), and use with possessives (*John's dog, John's idea*), these patterns will not serve to unite with them pronouns like *I* and *you* or proper nouns like *Mary* and *Paris*, which characteristically do not take such operations. Instead, nouns of this sort seem to share with concrete common nouns the property of being terms that denote concrete referents and serve as argument heads of major predicate-argument configurations (e.g., they can be the heads of arguments of verbs, as in *The dog – likes – bones*; *I – like – bones*, in which *dog* and *I*, respectively, are the central denoters of the liker argument of *like*).[2]

Another problem, especially for form classes such as verbs, arises in the very great variety of grammatical configurations in which they can appear. The schemes discussed in Maratsos and Chalkley (1980) presuppose for various reasons that a good deal of co-predictive validity is required for operations or groups of operations to cue each other effectively. That is, for two or more operations applicable to a term to cue yet another, there must be very high overlap among the operations in the sets of terms to which they apply. Empirically, however, it is simply not known how great this overlap is among terms in the child's experience. If configurations revolving around verbs are taken as units, the co-predictive validity could not be expected to be very high. In Turkish, for example, a verb may have up to seven affixes, chosen from a set of verb affixes. Gleason (1961) estimates the total number of possible configurations for a normal transitive verb to be about two thousand. It is unlikely that all of these configurations would predict each other very well, in the sense of being used on highly overlapping sets of terms. Yet the combinations are highly productive.

A final problem worth mentioning is that, after all, there are quite a few possible combinations of terms for which the child might conceivably attempt to trace the predictive patterns. In effect, the child would do well to let certain marker patterns become influential predictors. But there are far more possible combinations – for example, what properties of relational terms predict that they can be used to predicate things of oneself (practically anything), or to precede *it*, or to take arguments directly afterward – which would not apparently lead to worthwhile categorical organizations. Yet certain types of markers seem to be relatively good ones for these purposes even across languages (e.g., see Pinker, in press). This does not seem entirely coincidental, and it requires some appeal, probably, to innate selective factors in the organism, unless it can be shown that general-purpose heuristic techniques will in fact produce a correct solution. Such factors might be peculiar to linguistic induction, of course, but their prominence could also arise from other sources. For example, it is perhaps not surprising that markers of tense and negation and aspect should play a prominent role in the constitution and differentiation of terms denoting relations and activities. For whether or not something occurred and the place of some event or relation in a temporal framework are at least plausible candidates for cognitively prominent aspects of the human encoding of relations.

These problems indicate that considerable empirical and theoretical analysis is required before we can be said to have any good idea of plausible complete accounts of formal category formation. Furthermore, the problems and solutions are likely to be dissimilar for various major categories. But nevertheless, presently available analyses and empirical data do not leave us without plausible theoretical boundaries for reasonable considerations. First, it is simply not believable that formal categories such as "noun" and "verb" can remain tied to semantic analyses such as "object" and "action." In the end, somehow, such categorical organizations become defined in major degree by the grammatical operations in which terms participate. Furthermore, children's overwhelming absence of expectable form-class errors shows that although actionality and other major semantic factors are clearly important in grammatical categorical organization, they are not as centrally important as entirely semantic-based categorical analyses indicate. That children have considerable skill in making fine-grained grammatical analyses, and often appear to be learning individual word-to-operation links, is clearly demonstrated in work in early grammar (Bellugi, 1967; Bloom, Lightbown, & Hood, 1975; Bloom, Miller, & Hood, 1975; Bloom, Tanouye, & Lifter, 1980; Braine, 1976). Such findings, combined with the fact of children's skill in analyzing gender systems in which such operations form the central basis, also suggest the plausible usefulness of such analyses for investigating the growth of categories such as form-classes. Exactly how the child's diverse analytic abilities and biases combine to result in adult formal categorical organizations remains a central problem. It seems likely, however, that some important aspects of the problem – both empirical and analytical – may presently be discerned.

Notes

1 The problem is not that adjectives such as *fond* take prepositions after them. There are transitive verbs that also do so that nevertheless passivize, such as *speak of* (*John was frequently spoken of by friends*) and *talk about*.

2 It might appear that the central unifying property is being able to provide the head of arguments for predicates. That is, what *he, idea,* and *table* share in common is being able to appear in roles such as the initial argument phrase of predicates like *surprise* and *please* – e.g., *He surprised us*; *The idea pleased us*; *The table surprised them.* Members of other form classes can also be the heads of such phrases, however – e.g., *To sing pleased them,* in which *sing* is clearly the head of the initial argument of *please*.

9. The role of universals in the acquisition of gerunds

Thomas Roeper

Theories of language acquisition come in two distinct brands: "instantaneous" and "interactive." One might regard these theories as incommensurate because they belong to logically different types. I shall argue instead that an adequate model of language acquisition must state an important connection between the two.

The instantaneous model (IM) is a direct reflection of Chomskian linguistic theory in the domain of acquisition. The question addressed by the IM is the traditional question: How does a child acquire an adult grammar? The IM's emphasis lies on the kinds of intricate and abstract principles evident in the complex syntax of the adult grammar. The IM attempts to explain acquisition by means of only two kinds of information: principles of universal grammar (UG), presumably innate, and a representative set of sentences, presumably the input.[1] No information about temporal stages is countenanced. Thus the question becomes: Is it in principle possible to select a particular grammar (say English) from all possible grammars using only these two kinds of information? The instantaneous model assumes that observable interactions between language ability, cognitive ability, and pragmatic factors are all outside the acquisition mechanisms.

The empirical omission in the IM is obvious: Acquisition in fact occurs over time. Moreover, children all follow remarkably similar paths. Is the IM therefore wrong? Or is it an idealization whose claims are not significantly affected by the temporal factor?

The interactive position can itself be divided into two schools. The first school makes the pure claim that language itself is an interaction between

This is a revised version of a paper, *Linguistic Universals and the Acquisition of Gerunds,* that appears in Goodluck and Solan (1978). I would like to thank Tim Austin and Susan Tavakolian for help in the design, execution, and interpretation of the results. In addition, Charles Clifton, Patricia Sorce, and Marianne Phinney helped develop the appropriate statistics. Harold Chipman, Helen Goodluck, Ed Matthei, Larry Solan, Virginia Valian, Edwin Williams, and an anonymous reviewer provided useful comments. I am particularly indebted to N. Chomsky for a number of sympathetic and enlightening comments, and to Eric Wanner for editorial help beyond the call of duty. This research was supported by NIH grant HD09647 to T. Roeper and S. J. Keyser, and NSF grant BNS8014326 to T. Roeper and E. Williams.

a person and the world and among a person's cognitive faculties. It challenges the idea that there is a single coherent language ability. In a word, it argues that there is no grammar. The acquisition process is therefore nothing more than the heaping of one cognitive and pragmatic system upon another in such a fashion that in time they may appear to function as one faculty of mind. This view has been advanced primarily by psychologists with the support of numerous observational and experimental studies that show linguistic abilities to be contingent upon prior cognitive and pragmatic ability.

The second view of the interactive model is one that I will defend and illustrate in the experiment presented here. Under this model, the steps in the acquisition process represent a principled interaction between UG and other faculties of mind. In a word, various cognitive abilities have a biologically specified linguistic function: They *trigger* linguistic abilities. The term *trigger* is used to indicate that the linguistic abilities are not logically entailed in the cognitive capacities. For example, universal grammar permits a small range of specific syntactic structures associated with *causatives* (e.g., *I made John run/*I made John to run*). There are no comparable specific structures associated with cognitive notions like responsibility, enmity, love. For causative structures, I envision an interaction that has two components: First, the causative structure cannot be learned unless a child understands causative cognitively; second, knowledge of causation makes a child look for a small set of special structures associated with causatives but, once again, not entailed by the cognitive notion of causation. The child registers the syntax of causation when he hears a causative sentence, but he does not look for a special syntax for a concept like responsibility because responsibility is not a syntactic trigger.[2]

According to my proposal, language acquisition is largely accomplished by a *hypothesis generator* that has the following properties: (1) It has an *input filter* that allows only those sentences relevant to current hypotheses to be analyzed; (2) it is organized so that it does not attempt to prove or disprove a hypothesis that exceeds maturational limits on performance; and (3) it uses other mental faculties in generating and confirming hypotheses.

The main empirical responsibility of any model of acquisition is to meet what Noam Chomsky (1975) has called "the dual condition of compatibility with the structural principles of universal grammar and with relevant experience" (p. 44). In my model, these responsibilities are met by an operation that can be conceived of as parameter setting. According to this idealization, the child's knowledge of universal grammar provides him with a few parameters that set the formal structure of the language on the basis of a small number of crucial input sentences. These input sentences trigger a row of consequences. For instance, if the child hears an SOV sentence at a crucial moment, then he looks for postpositional markers rather than prepositions. Until the hypothesis is triggered, the acquisition device ignores all prepositional input. Triggers of this type, which relate one aspect of linguistic structure to another, can be called language-*internal*, to distinguish them from language-*external* triggers of the sort just discussed, in which a language-external concept, such as cause, acts as a trigger for certain syntactic hypotheses. In what follows, I will elaborate this view of the triggering function, dealing chiefly with triggers of the language-internal variety.

The second half of this chapter presents some experimental evidence that supports the model. The experiment assesses the claim that children have universal knowledge of a distinction between the abstract categories "noun phrase" and "verb phrase"; in particular, that they understand the difference in meaning between the verb phrase gerund *I enjoyed singing* and the noun phrase gerund *I enjoyed the singing,* where in the verb phrase the one singing is *I* but in the noun phrase anyone can be singing. By hypothesis, acquisition of the article *the* triggers the knowledge that the subject of the noun phrase is unspecified. Other cognitive faculties play a distinct role in the process, but it is the child's innate knowledge of universal grammar that supplies the distinction between NP and VP.

9.1. Four views of interaction

There are four specific kinds of interaction that have been proposed (explicitly or implicitly) in the literature. In their strong form these theories are incompatible, in a weaker form they may each play a role in an acquisition mechanism. The strong versions are (1) the *pragmatic* theory: Context controls the acquisition and comprehension of sentences (see Bates & MacWhinney, Chapter 6); (2) the *cognitive* theory: Linguistic universals are reflections of cognitive universals (see Newport, Chapter 15); (3) the *semantic* theory: The formal character of semantic rules is reflected in syntactic form (see Braine & Hardy, Chapter 7); and (4) the *perceptual* theory: Grammars are reflections of surface-structure strategies derived from perceptual principles (see Bever, 1970). I shall discuss each theory and its relation to hypothesis formation.

Pragmatic theory: inference procedures

Both child and adult must possess a system by which to construct a mental representation of the physical context for any utterance. I shall label that system a set of *inference procedures*. Although basic insights into this procedure are still missing, we can assume that inference procedures include the capacity to recognize *intrinsic connections* between objects. For instance, Eve Clark (1975) has shown that in a situation where there is a bottle and a bottle top a child easily infers where the bottle top goes (on top), though verbal instructions may tell him to put the top underneath the bottle. Inferences also operate between situations and words and between words by themselves (see G. Miller & Johnson-Laird, 1976; Roeper, 1973). Thus if a child hears the words *snow* and *shovel*, he may assume that snow is what is shoveled (L. Gleitman, Shipley, & Smith, 1978; Sachs, 1977). This inference can work even where the two words are discontinuous: *Shovel hay and forget snow* might be understood as *Shovel snow* by a child. Experimental findings by Newport and H. Gleitman (in press) show that very young children do use inferences in this fashion.

There are many possible relations between the analysis of context yielded by inference procedures and the analysis of sentences yielded by the grammar:

1.   The child has a stable analysis of context (C). He selects lexical items from sentences (S) that match C.
2.   The child has a partial analysis of both C and S. He uses either to supplement the other.
3.   ˙ The child has a stable analysis of S. He selects elements from C that match, enhance, or disambiguate S. Here *match* = attach lexical items to things; *enhance* = interpret pronouns and unspecified material; *disambiguate* = choose among alternative structures for S.

The third of these possibilities is equivalent to adult grammar, and the first and second might represent different phases of the acquisition process. Acquisition can be seen as a trade-off process between inference and grammatical analysis; a child relies on inferences to provide meaning until he reaches the point where the grammar can independently provide an analysis.

The acquisition literature contains a great deal of data that points to the use of inference procedures (see Bloom, 1973; Huttenlocher, 1974; Roeper, 1973; and for a summary, Foss & Hakes, 1978.) Slobin (1968) found that preschool children had more difficulty understanding reversible passives like (1) than nonreversible passives like (2):

(1)   The dog was chased by the cat
(2)   The sandwich was eaten by the policeman

Failure on (1) (i.e., *The dog chases the cat*) is a clear indication that the child does not understand passive. We can explain success on (2) by assuming simply that the child uses an inference procedure to connect *sandwich* and *policeman* (see Bever, 1970, for supportive evidence). Policemen eat sandwiches but not vice versa.

The claim that children use pure inference procedures to comprehend (2) does not mean that they must use them to understand (3):

(3)   The sandwich ate the policeman

Children can understand declaratives before they master passives. If they can understand that (3) is nonsense, then inference procedures may be limited to a postsyntactic role. Inferences may be restricted to "unknown" structures like (2) where there is uninterpretable morphological material (*was, is, -ed, by*).

Inferences may also play a specific role in hypothesis formation and grammar revision. The acquisition of the passive may be contingent upon two conditions: a *confident inference* of meaning and a syntactic analysis of object preposing and subject postposing. Sentence (1), being reversible, would never allow a confident inference of who chases whom. A confident inference for (2), however (that the policeman eats the sandwich), could confirm a syntactic analysis that was consistent with that inference (see Wexler, Chapter 10, for a similar assumption about the role of context in determining deep structure). Note that there is no implied connection between the formal structure of the inference (whatever that may be) and the structure of the sentence. The natural connection between an animate policeman and an edible sandwich says nothing about the interpretation of by-agentives and the fronting of objects.

The cognitive theory

Prior to Chomsky, the prevailing assumption about language acquisition was that language must be acquired by means of the same mental principles by which all other knowledge is acquired. Chomsky's claim for an autonomous mental faculty devoted to the acquisition of language directly challenged this view. In recent years there have been any number of attempted rebuttals, all of which, in one way or another, seek to reestablish the idea that general cognitive principles control the acquisition of language. At the risk of some oversimplification, we can distinguish two main variants of this position: (1) maturational, according to which linguistic operations are contingent upon prior cognitive operations; and (2) universal, according to which all linguistic operations are direct reflections of cognitive operations. There can be little doubt that the presence of cognitive powers of various kinds is a prerequisite for the emergence of various linguistic abilities. Nor can one doubt that linguistic operations "correlate" with nonlinguistic abilities. A child cannot use tenses correctly, for example, until he has some concept of time. To this extent the maturational view may be correct. But it is very hard to mount anything approaching a convincing case for the universal view.

Suppose, for discussion, we consider the most extreme version of the correlationist view: Every feature of linguistic ability has an outside correlation in another cognitive faculty. Suppose, for example, that we can establish that hierarchies (trees) and recursion (structures within identical structures) exist both within and beyond language. In addition, suppose that noun and verb correlate with cognitive notions of "thing" and "action" (a claim I dispute later on). We still have not dissolved the need for grammar. Universal grammar stipulates a narrow set of possible *links* between cognitive powers as they involve language. These comprise only a small subset of possible combinations. Thus VPs generate daughter NPs, but NPs do not generate daughter VPs. Some nodes (NP, S, QP) are recursive, whereas others (Det, Aux, Adj, VP) are not. Nothing about the cognitive notions of "thing" or "action" or the structural notions of tree or embedding predicts this array of facts. Furthermore, they differ from language to language: Some languages do not allow recursion on NP nodes, whereas others do. It is hard to see how correlations with cognitive operations could account for these facts.

The semantic theory

There have been many claims that the acquisition of syntax depends upon semantics (for a recent example see M. Miller, 1979). The strongest form of this claim is that semantic relations map directly onto syntactic relations. For instance, *actor-action-object* produces the string NVN and the grammatical relations subject-verb-object. But such claims are demonstrably wrong because they do not account for the existence of SOV languages nor for the fact that some subjects are not actors (e.g., *The chicken weighs two pounds*).

A weaker version of this theory claims that there are formal isomorphisms between some properties of semantics and syntactic representations. Kiparsky (personal communication, based on Fiengo, 1974) has suggested that people possess a particular linear concept of time that predetermines the order of elements in the auxiliary. If the claim is correct, then children might not have to evaluate different possible orders for the auxiliary as suggested by Chomsky (1965). This theory allows a semantic system to constrain syntactic form directly when both share the same linear representation. The theory cannot apply where syntactic terms do not serve distinct semantic functions.

A third version presupposes independent syntactic and semantic representations. But it holds that principles of semantic compositionality (or "logical form") will constrain the set of possible syntactic analyses that a child considers because not all possible syntactic analyses (for given input data) will be semantically well formed. Partee (1979) has made a number of interesting suggestions along these lines, using Montague grammar, which requires that semantic well-formedness exist for subparts of strings through semantic constraints that apply at each stage of a derivation. Some theory of semantic compositionality is assumed by virtually every theory of syntax (suggested to me by N. Chomsky).

None of these theories eliminates the need for an independently defined syntax.

The perceptual theory

Two kinds of strategies have been proposed: (1) probabilistic strategies and (2) parsing strategies.

Under the probabilistic strategy the learner or listener adopts a "word-order strategy" because it is applicable most of the time. The crucial feature is the absence of *structure-dependence*. Bever (1970), for example, has proposed as perceptual strategies "NVN = SVO" and "First N = subject."

In contrast, grammars function as deterministic systems that do not operate in terms of a terminal string but in terms of a tree structure. Thus a grammar can operate both on a noun phrase and on a single noun. Grammatical rules operate on every appropriate input and produce exceptionless outputs.

Suppose one could establish that a probabilistic hypothesis was generated and accepted at some stage in acquisition. Suppose a child believed that the most frequent sentence types were grammatical and the least frequent types were ungrammatical. If this probabilistic hypothesis served as the basis for a subsequent stage in acquisition (a new generalization about grammar was based on it), then it would undermine universal grammar altogether. Universal grammar is a deterministic system in which there is no language to express probabilistic hypotheses; if some of the grammar were probabilistic, then the whole would not be deterministic. Each theory, the probabilistic and deterministic, makes different claims about the kinds of mental operations involved in children's hypotheses.

It is important to note, however, that there could be ancillary functions for a probability analyzer. A performance strategy might employ the principle "First N = subject" until grammatical analysis of the sentence indicates otherwise. However, "firstness" is unstatable in phrase-structure rules and therefore cannot be part of the grammar.

The important point is that if the strategy plays no role in the projection of new hypotheses, then it is not an intrinsic part of the acquisition process. In fact, we believe that "NVN = SVO" is an *adjustment rule* that normalizes to declarative structure sentence types that the child does not know. Beyond that, the rule plays no role in the projection of new hypotheses. Other "overgeneralizations" may also fail to be true hypotheses about grammar.

A parsing mechanism builds a syntactic tree in real time, and it is therefore compatible with grammars. A parsing system operates with certain biases; for instance, it may prefer "flatter structures" (or "minimal attachment"; see Frazier, 1979, for a more technical description). Such parsing biases may affect the learner. For instance, Tavakolian (1977) provides experimental evidence in behalf of a constraint on the grammar of 3- to 4-year-old children that requires all subordinate clauses to be treated as coordinate clauses. In other words, new sentences attach to the S-node and recursion on other nodes is prohibited. This grammatical constraint is consistent with a parsing bias toward flatter structures (see also Matthei, 1979). But any such grammatical constraint introduced by parsing considerations must be short lived. The child eventually learns that recursion on other nodes is permitted whether or not this fact is convenient for the parser. Adult grammars are quite notorious for permitting structures that are difficult to parse (cf. G. Miller & Chomsky, 1963). Therefore parsing considerations cannot permanently constrain the child's acquisition system.

The four interactional theories just discussed, though sometimes collapsed in the literature, constitute separate claims about how language is acquired. Each kind of interaction may affect performance and, in principle, may restrict the hypothesis space available to the child. However, as I have argued, none of these proposals eliminates the need to postulate an innate, autonomous universal grammar, to account for the fact of language acquisition. When we try to stipulate how such a universal grammar is employed during language acquisition, some of the interactional proposals return, albeit in weakened form, as suggestions about how UG interacts with other mental faculties during acquisition.

9.2. A hypothesis generator

I can now sketch a mechanism for acquisition that shows how a hypothesis generator, an inference procedure, and a perceptual strategy might interact. The model is programmatic, but there are many ways in which to make it deterministic so that every input sentence is assigned a unique analysis. I shall provide several examples.

The mechanism has the following components: (1) grammar, (2) a hypothesis generator (HG), (3) an input filter, (4) adjustment rules, and (5) inference procedures. The HG establishes parameters and defines the triggers that set them. There are two kinds of triggers: *universal triggers* and *language-particular triggers*. Universal triggers involve automatic implications: If X, then Y. For instance, if a *noun* is discovered, it must be the head of a *noun phrase*. The hypothesis is confirmed as soon as a noun phrase is received as input.

Language-particular triggers arise when there are several possibilities in universal grammar: If X, then Y, Z, or W. The theory of parameters, which is the focus of Chomsky's current research, says that there are only a few choices (two or three) and that triggers have surface-structure definition. Thus Chomsky and Lasnik (1977) have proposed that, in the unmarked case, infinitives have no surface subjects: *I want to sing*. There is a marked structure in some languages, including English: It involves prepositional *for* (or its equivalent) or an exceptional set of verbs. Thus we find *I hope for Bill to win* and *I want Bill to win* but not **I hope Bill to win*. The exceptional verbs are only locally exceptional: If we insert *very much*, the *for* returns: *I want very much for Bill to win*. The theory says that a child will seek to confirm first the unmarked case and then marked exceptions. (See Phinney, 1981, who shows that children do begin with the unmarked form and learn the marked exceptions at a very young age. Also see Pustejovsky & Burke, 1981, for a general discussion of markedness in language acquisition.)

An input filter

One assumption of the instantaneous model is that adults share the same grammar. This result can be guaranteed only if an acquisition device considers sentences in a fixed order. If grammars were revised following the order in which children literally heard sentences, then different children, hearing sentences in a different order, could arrive at different final grammars.[3]

The input filter can guarantee the construction of a uniform grammar despite variation in input. It is reasonable to assume that a child's environment contains a full range of sentence types on a daily basis. The input filter selects just those which are relevant to current hypotheses. Williams (1981) and Roeper (1981) make a number of specific suggestions about the exact order in which hypotheses are considered and about the data needed to trigger them. In this model there is no "learning" as such, nor does the child project alternative grammars and select the simplest. Instead, the correct grammar is instantiated on the basis of small amounts of crucial data.

Inference rules and adjustment rules

One way a child can understand sentences that his grammar rejects is by means of inference rules. But inference rules fail where meaning does not dictate the probable relations conveyed by the sentence. Take, for instance, the sentence

(4)   Mary was chased by Jane

or

(5)   Who who Bill likes eats cheese

I suggest that there is another way in which a child can respond to sentences that are beyond the scope of his grammar. This alternative is provided by a mechanism I call adjustment rules. These rules apply to sentences rejected by the input filter and adjust them, if possible, to fit the current grammar. One such adjustment is accomplished simply by deleting unknown elements. For example, this rule will adjust sentence (4) to *Mary chase Jane*, an *NP-V-NP* form that will probably be within the scope of even the youngest child's grammar. In (5) it will fail, or if there is the form *NP-V-(to)-V-NP* in the grammar, it will adjust to *Bill likes to eat cheese*.

I have used the term *perceptual strategy* to refer to the claim that NVN = SVO because the claim has had that name in the literature (Bever, 1970). I shift my vocabulary now to the term *adjustment rules*, because the term fits the mechanism I am constructing. The shift is not, however, innocuous. I do not believe that there are "perceptual strategies." Instead, there are mechanisms for language use whose parts must be precisely specified. The term *perceptual strategy* arises because of an intuition about what is easy to process and a failure to envision the mechanism that is necessary to carry out perception. When we make our claims precise, we see that the mechanism involved is dictated by the needs of the early grammar and not by an independently established principle of general perception.

It is important to observe that "adjustment rules" are categorically different from rules of grammar. The adjustment rules delete *unknown* elements of an input sentence. Grammatical rules have *variables* in them, but the variables do not refer to unrecognizable aspects of speech. They refer instead to domains in a rule that do not affect the functioning of a rule. Thus, in a passive, we might find adverbs: *John quickly took the money* → *the money was quickly taken by John*. The adverb does not affect the rule that switches NPs; this switch is allowed for in the passive rule by use of a variable between the noun and verb (NP-*X*-V). In the grammar all variables must be recognizable in order to guarantee that no syntactic constraint is violated. The adjustment rule does not meet this criterion.

Furthermore, if we were to allow "variable unknowns" in the rules of a child's grammar, then we would develop rules so abstract that it would be difficult for an evaluation metric to reject them. The structural description would contain superfluous variables: *X*-*S*-*Y*-*V*-*W*-*O*-*Z*. My proposal not to call such a rule a rule of grammar means that it would never have to be evaluated by an evaluation metric as a possible rule of grammar. I propose in addition that adjustment rules which delete elements meet a much stronger constraint than grammatical rules:

Only function words may be deleted.

Movement rules are excluded, as are deletions of lexical material. Sentences that are converted to known structures are analyzed by the grammar. Sentences that cannot be reduced to known structures are submitted to the inference rules. If inference rules fail, no comprehension is possible.

Inference rules are accessed for two purposes: They construe the meaning of sentences that do not fit into the grammar, and they supplement the grammar by interpreting pronouns and other forms of unspecified material.

Summary

This model is meant to be a programmatic description of how three mental faculties – inferences, adjustment rules, and formal hypotheses – could interact in a systematic fashion. There are many ways to instantiate the particulars so that every sentence will follow a single route. This chapter argues that at one stage children will be sensitive to articles as a trigger for NPs. If the input sentence is *In the evening, eat potatoes*, the adjustment rule will produce *Evening eat potatoes*, which is analyzable (incorrectly) by the grammar, because the grammar has declarative structure. If the input sentence is *Near me he sings*, the deletion mechanism will produce *Me he sings*. This does not reduce to SVO, and therefore it will be sent to inference rules. Inference rules will probably fail to assign a meaning or will incorrectly assume that the meaning is *Me and he sing* (excluding context that could impose a different inference).

Let us consider how a trigger might function. At the first stage it is reasonable to suggest that children identify "noun" with "thing" (= sock, hat, mittens). This is in keeping with evidence from 1- to 2-year-old children. The child then makes a first formal observation: Only nouns take *the* or *a*. This observation triggers a universal: *The* is a specifier or article. This conclusion triggers another shift: Drop the definition of noun as "thing" and define noun as optionally preceded by article. In these circumstances the device hears a phrase of the form *the leap*. It follows that this phrase is a noun. It follows, in addition, as I discuss shortly, that the choice of subject (leaper) is free. Until the child is ready to trigger noun phrases, the input filter will reject *the leap* and send it to adjustment rules. Adjustment rules will delete *the* and return the phrase to the grammar, which will misanalyze *leap* as a verb and possibly consider it an imperative. On the other hand, after the noun phrase has been triggered by recognition of the article, new hypotheses are advanced. For instance, universal grammar allows determiners to contain quantifiers and nouns to have complements: *six of the shots at Bill.* Williams (1981) shows that the microstructure of noun phrases in universal grammar offers rather few options. Therefore, my step-by-step mechanism should be able to recognize it quickly.

In effect, this system claims that, as far as acquisition is concerned, a child ignores 95 percent of the input data and selects just what he needs to advance his grammar. The 95 percent is ignored only for grammar construction, not for real-life comprehension. For everyday comprehension, the sentences that do not fit current hypotheses are either normalized to fit the current grammar or submitted to word-by-word inference. Figure 9.1 presents a flow chart of these components. Information moves through the system as follows:

1. The sentence enters the model. If possible, it is analyzed according to the current grammar. If it is composed of unknown elements or is unanalyzable, it enters the input filter.
2. The input filter examines the sentence to see if it matches the surface characteristics of current projections from universal grammar. If so, it is analyzed by the HG and the analysis is added to the grammar. This triggers the new hypothesis for which specific evidence is needed. If the sentence does not apply to current hypotheses, it is sent to the adjustment component.
3. The HG matches the input to either a universal trigger or a language-particular trigger. If it is a language-particular trigger, a few more varieties of sentences may be needed before a particular hypothesis is confirmed.
4. The adjustment rules take rejected sentences and convert them into a form acceptable to the existing grammar. If the sentence cannot be converted, it is sent to the inference procedure.

This flow chart does not represent two other uses of inference rules. First, a *confident inference* (as discussed in Section 9.1) may facilitate the choice of a new hypothesis. Second, inferences are applied to the output of the syntactic analysis. They help choose which of two ambiguities is appropriate to context, but they may take the perceiver far afield as well. If one hears *John shoves his father* when one should have heard *John loves his father,* one may infer that a Freudian slip has occurred. One might in fact speculate that it is because inference is such a powerful situational influence that the organism develops a separate system for syntactic analysis. The fact that the syntactic system can deliver nonsense readings (*The sandwich ate the policeman*) without being automatically

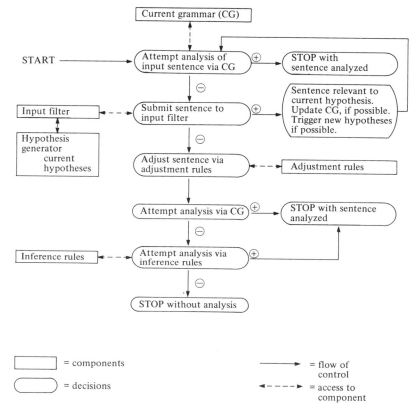

Figure 9.1. A flow chart for the interaction model of language acquisition.

censored by commonsense inference indicates that the syntactic system is independent.

9.3. Experimental evidence

It has seemed self-evident to many investigators that children are born with the notions of "sentence" and "word." I shall argue that they possess a concept of equal importance that falls between word and sentence: "phrase." Each of these concepts serves as a trigger for the projection of other rules.

The structure of noun phrases and verb phrases is largely the same. One feature distinguishes them (see Wasow & Roeper, 1972): Verb phrases require subjects that are specified by some other noun phrase in the sentence; noun phrases can have subjects that are unspecified anywhere in the sentence and must be interpreted from context. If the subject of a noun phrase does appear in the sentence, it must appear within the noun phrase, but its grammatical role must still be determined by context. To illustrate, consider the following sentences:

(6a) John prefers singing songs (verb phrase gerund)
(6b) John prefers the singing of songs (noun phrase gerund)
(6c) John prefers the singing of birds (noun phrase gerund)

In (6a) *John* is the subject of singing, whereas in (6b) the subject is unspecified: Anyone can be doing the singing; in (6c) the subject of the noun phrase is specified by *birds*, but notice that this specification is not fixed by the grammar. The noun following *singing* can be either the subject of the gerund, as in (6c), or the object of the gerund, as in (6b).

The same contrast occurs with negation:

(6d) Verbal gerund: Not singing is good enough for John
(6e) Nominal gerund: No singing is good enough for John

In (6d) it is *John* who does not sing, whereas in (6e) it is *anybody* who is the subject of *sing*.

The grammatical laxity (optionality) of noun phrase subjects contrasts sharply with the rigidity (obligatoriness) of verb phrase subjects, which appear to be governed by a completely general syntactic rule of *control*. A technically simplified way to state the principle of control goes as follows:

> An empty node in a tree must be filled by a noun phrase higher in the tree.

In Figure 9.2a we can see that the NP *John* is closer to S_1 than is the NP delta under S_2. This principle of control works for many other structures in English as well. For instance, *John decided* Δ *to go* assigns the subject to *go* in the same fashion.[4] In the nominal gerund (Figure 9.2b) there is no empty subject position to fill. The perceiver must provide a subject for *singing* simply because we cannot conceive of singing without a singer. Nothing in the structure dictates who that singer should be; therefore it is free in reference.

I cannot prove that the distinction between noun phrases and verb phrases is innate, but the assumption that it is innate has an important implication: If universal grammar is innate, then some grammatical knowledge is not logically inferred from evidence; it is triggered by evidence. In this case, if the distinction between noun phrase and verb phrase is innate, then as soon as a child comes to know that any word marked by a determiner is a noun, he should treat the subject of any resulting noun phrase as uncontrolled. Until the child knows that the affix *the, no,* or adjective marks a noun, we would have no reason to expect him to exhibit (*a*) Verbal gerund:

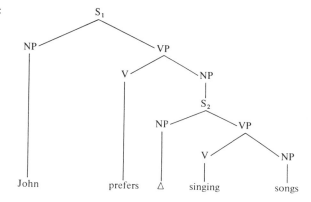

(*b*) Nominal gerund:

Figure 9.2. Simplified phrase structures for nominal and verbal gerunds.

this knowledge. Once the child recognizes determiners, the knowledge about lack of control is immediate; no further hypotheses are necessary.

Hypotheses

I designed an experiment to contrast hypotheses based on adjustment rule strategies with those emanating from universal grammar. The essential contrasts are these (here and in later examples, CYS = Can you show):

Verbal gerunds	*Nominal gerunds*
(7a) CYS John fighting?	(7c) CYS John [the fighting]$_{NP}$?
(7b) CYS John fighting alligators?	(7d) CYS John [the fighting alligators]$_{NP}$?
	(7e) CYS John [the fighting of alligators]$_{NP}$?

Universal grammar predicts:

> Children will recognize the control differences for nominal and verbal gerunds (1) by inventing a subject for nominal gerunds if none appears in the noun phrase, and (2) by taking a noun within the NP as subject for nominal gerunds if one appears.

So if we arrange an experiment to reveal whom children take to be doing the fighting in sentences such as those of (7), UG predicts that they will select *John* in the verbal gerunds and either *alligators* or something or someone unmentioned in the *nominal gerunds*.[5] According to our hypothesis, the predictions of UG will be fulfilled only for those children who know that determiners signal noun phrases. Only those children should show knowledge of the control differences between NPs and VPs. Children who have not mastered the role of determiners should be expected, if this model is correct, to use the adjustment rule to delete function words in the sentences of (7) and to resubmit them to the grammar. Once the determiner is eliminated from the nominal gerunds, they are indistinguishable from the verbal gerunds. Stripped of function words, all gerunds conform to NVN pattern, which should be analyzable as subject-verb-object by even the most immature grammars. Therefore, our model predicts that all children will view *John* as the subject of fighting in the verbal gerunds – either because they appreciate the rule of control (the most mature children) or because they apply the NVN pattern to the adjusted sentence (the less mature children). In contrast, some children (those who have learned about determiners) should appreciate the uncontrolled status of the nominal gerund and select a subject from context or from within the gerund itself.

Experiments

I used a Fisher-Price barnyard set supplemented by a tractor, trees, four people, and a few other animals to create a layout in which children could act out the experimental sentences and so reveal their interpretations of the nominal and verbal gerunds.[6] The layout involved a barn and a corral attached to the barn, which we called the *showplace*. A bench or a large piece of paper was put outside the corral, and this we called the *watching place*. Animals and people were scattered around outside the corral. For each experimental sentence, the child's task was to select the appropriate figures to act out in the showplace the episode conveyed by the gerund. In addition, the child was instructed always to place a figure in the watching place to represent a witness to the gerundive drama. In some sentences, the witness was overtly named, but the children were instructed to keep the watching place occupied whether or not the sentence named the witness.

The first experiment included nineteen 3- to 4-year-olds from two day-care centers. The central contrast involved these eight sentences:

Verbal gerunds
(8a) CYS Mary lying down?
(8b) CYS the cow kicking?
(8c) CYS Mary hitting the dog?
(8d) CYS Bill throwing the bear onto the roof?

Nominal gerunds
(9a) CYS Mary the jumping?
(9b) CYS the kids the kicking?
(9c) CYS the cow the hitting of the horse?
(9d) CYS the sheep the pushing of the dog by the chickens?

The basic results are very simple and very supportive of our model. The verbal gerunds in (8) were given declarative (SVO) interpretation 96.7 percent of the time, and received contextual subjects 3.3 percent of the time. The contextual subjects were not, strictly, incorrect, because it is possible to treat a word like *kicking* as a determinerless noun. The nominal gerunds of (9) were provided a contextual subject 47.7 percent of the time, where, following UG, a sentential reading is ruled out. The remaining 52.3 percent of the nominal gerund trials received SVO answers. One needs no statistics to see that the difference between 48 percent and 97 percent is significant. The only effective difference between (8) and (9) is the article: Therefore it must be the source of the differences in interpretation. The differences in interpretation correlate precisely with the predictions made by universal grammar.

The fact that half of the children's responses deviated from UG in the direction of applying an NVN = SVO strategy is consistent with our view of an adjustment component that normalizes unanalyzable sentences to fit the grammar. If young children detect a conflict between a noun marker, *the,* and a verb, *jumping,* they produce a sentence acceptable to their grammars by deleting *the,* thus leaving an NV or NVN pattern interpretable as subject-verb-(object).

An interesting subsidiary result in this experiment demonstrates the role of inferences as a postsyntactic guide to choices among grammatical alternatives. In addition to the central contrast sentences, we also presented two sentences contrasting the plausibility of the nominal interpretation of the postgerundive noun phrase in the verbal gerund:

(10a) CYS the kicking of the horse?
(10b) CYS the jumping of the fence?

The *horse* was taken as a subject of *kick* by 100 percent of the children although it could have been seen as object. In contrast, only 77 percent of the responses took the *fence* as subject of *jump* in (10b); 22 percent took *fence* as object and chose a pragmatic subject. Some of the children made revealing side remarks: "You mean the fence is alive, too?" or "The fence can't jump." These remarks suggest that the syntactic analysis of the sentence was able to operate without reference to plausibility. Only a conscious postsyntactic review of the sentence led the children to question whether it was sensible or not.

It might be objected that the results of the first experiment are linked only to the article *the*. According to this objection, the differences in interpretation between the sentences of (8) and those of (9) are due not to a knowledge of the distinction between noun phrases and verb phrases but rather to some (unexplained) difference in the interpretive strategies triggered by the presence of *the*. To control for this possibility, we undertook a second experiment that included the article *some* in place of *the* in half of the nominal gerunds. We also used an adjectival form of the verb:

Verbal gerunds
(11a) CYS the dog running fast?
(11b) CYS the father flying the tractor?

Nominal gerunds
(12a) CYS the cow the kissing of the horse?
(12b) CYS the dog some kissing of the chicken?
(12c) CYS the mother the kissing kids?
(12d) CYS the dog some fighting turtles?

We performed the second experiment with the same design, using twenty children from 3 to 5 years of age. The results were essentially the same as in the first experiment: 92.6 percent of the verbal gerunds received the SVO interpretation, whereas only 7.4 percent of the verbal gerunds received contextual interpretation. This finding contrasts significantly with that for the nominal gerunds, which received contextual interpretation 65.5 percent of the time and SVO interpretation 34.5 percent of the time, $t(19) = 3.3.$, $p < .01$.

In order to check the possibility that our results might somehow be task-specific, we ran a third experiment in which we sought to elicit conversational responses that would reveal whether children understood the control distinction in more normal circumstances. We asked a group of ten 4-year-olds the following questions:

(13a) Can you tell me why the mother likes not throwing snowballs?
(13b) Can you tell me why the mother likes no singing?

Four of the ten children made the distinction between the nominal and verbal gerunds in these circumstances. These children showed a sentential interpretation of the verbal gerund by answering something like "Because she doesn't want to" in (13a). For the nominal gerund in (13b), these children showed a contextual interpretation with answers such as, "Because she's got a headache, the kid's noise bothers her." The rest of the children gave indeterminate answers (e.g., "Because it's too loud," for [13b]) so frequently that it was impossible to tell whether they made the control distinction or not. But to the extent that the conversational situation provides usable results, it confirms the claim that a significant proportion of very young children understand the control differences that obtain between noun phrases and verb phrases.

9.4. Conclusion

The results of this study have been, quite literally, surprising. We did not expect when we began that 3-year-old children would be sensitive to the *control* implications of *articles*, nor did we expect that children would master *articles* before other forms that seem more intuitively available. In Roeper (1978) there is evidence that articles are learned before prepositions (*by, for, of*) are mastered. The evidence is compatible with the view that triggers may be immediate not just within the framework of our model, but in fact.

The experiment has also shown that quite different abilities are at work in language acquisition: principles of universal grammar, adjustment strategies for immature grammars, and inferences in cases where grammar is incomplete or open. Language acquisition involves interactions not in a haphazard sense, but in a principled sense that can be expressed through an explicit mechanism. The evidence shows that the grammar is the centerpiece in this interaction.

Adjustment rules, by definition, are defined in terms of a child's grammar. It is true that adjustment rules, like the grammar itself, must be compatible with a child's limited performance capacities. However, it is not clear that performance limitations govern these adjustment strategies in any strong sense. A child's memory is limited, but memory limitations do not explain why a child will reduce a five-word passive to a three-word SVO structure. Children between 2 and 3 can definitely hold a five-word sequence in memory.

Inferences are also directed by the grammatical structure. When a child understands that noun phrases are uncontrolled, he is given license, as it were, to make an inference about the subject of a deverbal noun (*the jumping*). When a verbal gerund is present, license is withheld and the child must determine by a rule of control what noun will function as the subject of the verb. One might now ask where the concept of "inference" fits into current research in language acquisition. I think it covers most of what is commonly referred to as "pragmatics."

Gross aspects of language have, usually, both a linguistic and a non-linguistic aspect. For instance, it has often been noted that, in child language, *subjects* are usually (but significantly not always) *actors*. It is consequently difficult to determine whether the child's notion is limited to "actor" or involves both "actor" and the grammatical notion "subject." My research strategy has therefore been to design experiments aimed at subtle aspects of the grammar for which there is no plausible nonlinguistic correlate.

The experiment described here is not one-of-a-kind. There are a series of experimental results aimed at showing the presence of "invisible" features in children's grammar (Tavakolian, 1981). A related example deserves mention: Solan (1978) has shown that a subtle feature of backward pronominalization is present in the grammar of 4-year-olds. He contrasts *John saw'im in Bill's yard* with *John saw'im after Bill's run*, where careful research has shown that *Bill* can equal *'im* in the latter but not the former case. (The fact that adults' intuitions on these are sometimes hazy makes children's sensitivity to the distinction in performance more impressive.) A pronoun must be lower in the tree than the noun that controls it (the same principle used earlier). Because temporal clauses (*after . . .*) attach to S and locatives attach to VP, the locative is ineligible and the temporal is eligible for control. Solan found significantly more backward control for the temporal sentences than for the locative ones. Goodluck (1978) found corroborative results with infinitival control and prepositional phrases. A number of other experiments have shown subtle effects of tree hierarchy and boundaries (Lust, 1981; Matthei, 1979; Otsu, 1981; Tavakolian 1977).

These results provide significant support for the linguistic theories upon which they are based. It has often seemed that the complexity and abstraction of current work in linguistic theory makes it irrelevant or improbable as a basis for acquisition research. In fact, current work that focuses on a core grammar makes many more precise predictions about language acquisition than were offered by earlier versions of transformational grammar.

Notes

1 The model has many interesting technical consequences. For instance, it requires that all sentences be presented simultaneously, and it requires that no dialect differences be present. Failure to meet either of these requirements could lead to adults' having substantially different grammars under the assumptions of transformational grammar. There are fewer problems under a parametric model of "core" grammar. For discussion see N. Chomsky (1976, 1981), Roeper (1978), S. Peters (1972).

2 This view is not inconsistent with Chomsky's position: "It is a coherent and perhaps correct proposal that the language faculty constructs a grammar only

in conjunction with other faculties of mind. If so, the language faculty itself provides only an abstract framework, an idealization that does not suffice to determine a grammar'' (1975, p. 121).

3 The reason why this claim is true has to do with the large number of ways in which successive grammars can modify first grammars. Here is a simplified example: If a child hears *the truck I like* first he should decide that the grammar is OSV. If he then hears *I like the truck* he should decide to introduce a transformation of object postposing. If he hears them in the opposite order, then he should begin with a different base, and a different transformation should be necessary. This problem can arise in more complex ways, as well, depending on the order in which a child attempts to assimilate new structures.

4 The full theory of control is very complex, with many contributing factors, including lexical exceptions. The fact that the theory is very complex supports the view that it needs to be largely innate, because the surface of the language does not provide enough information to make a systematic induction of the system. Various sorts of exceptions provide interesting challenges to the language learner. See C. S. Chomsky (1969) and Goodluck (1978).

5 This prediction is somewhat complicated by the fact that nouns can occur without determiners (e.g., *Fighting is bad*). Therefore it is possible for children to interpret (7a) either as a sentence (*John fights*) or as two nouns (*John [the] fighting*). I predicted that a significant enough number would choose a sentence interpretation to allow a contrast with (7c, d, e) where the sentential interpretation is ruled out. Primarily in (7c, d, e), therefore, the children should choose an invented subject or *alligators* as subject.

6 For a more extended discussion of the results of these experiments see Roeper (1978).

10. A principle theory for language acquisition

Kenneth Wexler

10.1. Principle theories, common sense, and learnability

For at least two reasons the kinds of notions that I wish to present in this chapter may turn out to be difficult to understand, at least in their intended interpretation. One reason is substantive, the other more methodological. To try to communicate past these difficulties, it will be useful to discuss these issues with the help of some ideas of Albert Einstein concerning theories in science.

It is well understood by now that various theories of language acquisition may be set in the broader context of the empiricist–rationalist controversy. Thus theories that assume that the learner starts out with almost no knowledge of what a language is, but has some simple kinds of information-processing mechanisms, may be called *empiricist*. On the other hand, theories that assume genetically determined specification of forms of language are *rationalist* theories. It is less well understood, I think, that both of these theoretical positions have in common the assumption that the contents of the mind are available to introspection, that is, that we can discover the correct principles of language directly by paying attention to our conscious experience.[1] For example, the principle of "association" is one that is arrived at by the British empiricists on the bases of the direct inspection of subjective experience. One idea leads to another, and so on. Put another way, the explanatory concepts that are introduced must be close to experience. The principle is at least vacuously true even of behaviorists (vacuously if they are strict behaviorists and admit no explanatory concepts at all). It is by definition true of phenomenologists. The (often implicit) view that explanatory concepts must be close to experience dominates psychology, at least those approaches which may be called "cognitive psychology."[2]

Many of the concepts that my colleagues and I have introduced into the study of language acquisition are not concepts that are "close to experience." They depend for their justification on argumentation of a

The research on which this paper is based has been supported by the National Science Foundation under Grant NSF SOC 74-23469.

traditional scientific sort. Yet because such argumentation is not traditional in many areas of psychology, it is sometimes difficult to understand. Correspondingly, the explanatory concepts might be rejected on the wrong grounds. Einstein (1954b) points out that the goal of science is to seek logical, simple, especially *unifying* hypotheses:

> Yet every theory is speculative. When the basic concepts of a theory are comparatively "close to experience" (e.g., the concepts of force, pressure, mass), its speculative character is not so easily discernible. If, however, a theory is such as to require the application of complicated logical processes in order to reach conclusions from the premises that can be confronted with observation, everybody becomes conscious of the speculative nature of the theory. In such a case an almost irresistible feeling of aversion arises in people who are inexperienced in epistemological analysis and who are unaware of the precarious nature of theoretical thinking in those fields with which they are familiar. [Pp. 339–40]

As usual, Einstein tries to present a balanced view of such difficult matters. He adds:

> On the other hand, it must be conceded that a theory has an important advantage if its basic concepts and fundamental hypotheses are "close to experience," and greater confidence in such a theory is certainly justified. There is less danger of going completely astray, particularly since it takes so much less time and effort to disprove such theories by experience. Yet more and more, as the depth of our knowledge increases, we must give up this advantage in our quest for logical simplicity and uniformity in the foundations of physical theory. [P. 340]

Thus we must not reject out of hand theories that contain concepts which are not "close to experience." If the example of the successful sciences is to guide us, in fact, such concepts will be necessary as we move on to more adequate theories.

In addition to conceptual unfamiliarities, the theories that I will discuss will also contain methodological unfamiliarities, even from the standpoint of model construction. Nevertheless, the methodology is not without precedent. Einstein (1954a) distinguished between two kinds of theories. "Constructive" theories start from some relatively simple hypothetical principles and attempt to build up a theory that can predict and tie together phenomena. "Principle" theories, on the other hand, start with some well-grounded and general empirical conditions ("principles"), and attempt to discover mathematically the kinds of conditions on theories that follow from them. Einstein writes:

We can distinguish various kinds of theories in physics. Most of them are constructive. They attempt to build up a picture of the more complex phenomena out of the materials of a relatively simple formal scheme from which they start out. Thus the kinetic theory of gases seeks to reduce mechanical, thermal, and diffusional processes to movements of molecules – i.e., to build them up out of the hypothesis of molecular motion. When we say that we have succeeded in understanding a group of natural processes, we invariably mean that a constructive theory has been found which covers the processes in question.

Along with this most important class of theories there exists a second, which I will call "principle-theories." These employ the analytic, not the synthetic method. The elements which form their basis and starting-point are not hypothetically constructed but empirically discovered ones, general characteristics of natural processes, principles that give rise to mathematically formulated criteria which the separate processes or the theoretical representations of them have to satisfy. Thus the science of thermodynamics seeks by analytical means to deduce necessary conditions, which separate events have to satisfy, from the universally experienced fact that perpetual motion is impossible.

The advantages of the constructive theory are completeness, adaptability, and clearness, those of the principle theory are logical perfection and security of the foundations. [P. 223][3]

Einstein adds that relativity theory is a principle theory. In this sense, the kind of theories that I will be discussing are principle theories, at least in part. Because there are few examples of such theories in psychology or in language acquisition, the methodology is unfamiliar.[4]

We must start with the principles if we are to explain the theory. "In order to grasp its nature, one needs first of all to become acquainted with the principles on which it is based" (p. 223). One must consider first what kinds of claims (with what kinds of justifications) constitute principles, in Einstein's sense. The two principles of (special) relativity theory that Einstein discussed may help. The first (p. 224) is that laws of nature are invariant with respect to uniform translations of the coordinate system. A principle of this sort almost seems to be given as part of our (perhaps implicit) definition or understanding of what an acceptable theory is. In fact, the general theory of relativity, as Einstein points out, extends the principle so that laws are invariant with respect to *any* motions of the coordinate system, on grounds of there not being a special coordinate system in nature – "What has nature to do with our coordinate systems and their state of motion?" (p. 225). Nevertheless, this principle, along with the second one, is "powerfully supported by experience" (p. 224).

The second principle on which relativity theory is based is that "light in vacuo always has a definite velocity of propagation (independent of the state of motion of the observer or of the source of light)" (p. 224). This principle does not strike us as being somehow necessary from the notion of an acceptable theory. In fact, of course, it is quite counterintuitive (to our folk senses of physical interactions) because it says, for example, that light emitted from a very quickly moving body will not be any faster than light emitted from a very slowly moving body (or even from a body moving in the opposite direction). Einstein writes: "The confidence which physicists place in this principle springs from the successes achieved by the electrodynamics of Maxwell and Lorentz" (p. 224). Thus the second principle is given on some kind of combination of empirical and theoretical grounds; it plays a central role in important theoretical successes.[5]

The first principle that we start from is that language *is* learned; that is, every normal child can learn any natural language in a natural way. This principle (of *learnability*) is "firmly grounded in experience." It is a very general characteristic which we say that any theory of language acquisition has to satisfy. We may say that it is one of the "general characteristics of natural processes, principles that give rise to mathematically formulated criteria which the separate processes or the theoretical representations of them have to satisfy."

The second principle (or set of principles) from which we start is that the representation of the final state of the learning process (the adult representation) is to be given by the representation reached by linguistic theory. This representation is reached on the basis of research on adult linguistic abilities. The kind of data that goes into the justification of such theories is not language-acquisition data, but rather judgments of sentences and other forms of "static" data. Nevertheless, the claim of this principle is that such representations must be the final state of the language-learning process. In particular, the representations whose learning we have studied most intensively are syntactic transformations.

Einstein points out that his two principles "are powerfully supported by experience, but appear not to be logically reconcilable" (p. 225). (Reconciliation was achieved by the modification of physical theory.) Likewise, the principle that any child can learn any natural language, together with the complexities of the attained representations that are demanded by the second principle, may appear at first sight not to be logically reconcilable (and indeed, for many assumptions of particular learning processes, they are not). It is our task to reconcile these principles, and in fact, in certain areas learnability theory has succeeded in doing so.

The second principle, by the way, will involve in its realization the specification of linguistic principles (of transformational grammar) that are not obvious in the way that the first principle (of learnability) is obvious. But recall that Einstein's second principle, also, was not obvious (was even counterintuitive), and was justified by its central role in physical theory. Likewise, the assumption that the theory must allow syntactic transformations to be learned is justified by "the successes achieved by" transformational grammar.

From the standpoint of strict logic, principle 2 is not trivially true and has, in fact, been challenged. That is, it is not a tautology to say that the end result of the language-learning process (the final state) will be a representation of language that is the same as the representation achieved by linguistic theory on the basis of adult data.[6] Einstein points out that it was well known in physical theory that inertial and gravitational mass were equivalent, but there was no reason of theory why this should be so. The theory of relativity provided such theoretical reasons. Likewise, we must look for reasons of psychological and linguistic theory that will underpin the equivalence of linguistic representations and the final state of the language-acquisition process. We must also find evidence that confirms the conditions that follow from the posited equivalence.

Principle 1 (learnability) is a kind of clear principle that, although thoroughly grounded in experience, does not depend on extensive development for its statement, at least as it is stated. But notice that the principle requires that language be learnable "in a natural way." Thus the condition not only demands that language-acquisition processes be stated so that in the limit adult language can always be attained, but demands, moreover, that the learning take place in the apparently easy and quick manner in which children do the learning. Not only is convergence demanded, but we must also have quick and simple convergence. We might call this more delineated principle "easy learnability," or "natural learnability."

Although they form part of the basic principles, from which further conditions are to be derived, concepts such as transformational grammar are not obvious *a priori* constructs to be assumed in a language-acquisition theory. But as Einstein points out, the history of physics shows that, ultimately, concepts that are "close to experience" must be given up. Constancy of the velocity of light is a concept that is not close to experience, as is transformational grammar as a representation of adult linguistic abilities. Even further from experience may be the conditions that we derive from the basic principles. In summary, I have tried to point out that the contents of the mind are not necessarily open to introspection, and that this position has the same logical status as the proposition that basic physical constructs are not necessarily close to experience. In addition, the method of deriving conditions on language-acquisition processes from some basic principles is not without scientific precedent in other fields.

It is difficult to think of an alternative coherent framework for the study of language acquisition that has much chance of success. If a language-acquisition theory is not to explain how language comes to be acquired by children, what is it to explain? If the representations that are shown by the theory to be achievable as final states are not representations supported by linguistic evidence about adult language, what means of evidence will support the theories?

Most studies in the field of developmental psycholinguistics are attempts based on various kinds of data to describe the linguistic ability of a child at various stages (or ages). (There are also some other concerns, such as the nature of linguistic input to children, mother–child interaction, etc. I will return to these.) What, then, is to be the goal of such studies? One answer that might be suggested is that the description of linguistic abilities at each stage is the goal in itself. There are a number of problems with this view. In the first place, it ignores the problem of *how* language grows in the child, of the kinds of abilities or mechanisms that allow language growth. One can choose to be interested simply in the description of language at particular ages, but that choice means that traditional questions of explanation in psychology must be given up.

But there are other problems, even if pure description of stages is taken as the goal. The task of describing a child's linguistic abilities purely from data available at a given stage (or age) is exceedingly difficult. In practical terms it may actually be impossible. The data available to developmental psycholinguistics is notoriously weak, as compared, say, to the (adult) data available to the linguist. Adults can judge sentences as grammatical or ungrammatical, synonymous or not, and so on, but children do not have these abilities, at least not in any as yet discovered communicable form. Of course, there are exceptions to this statement on both sides, and students of language acquisition may yet discover more subtle ways of obtaining judgments from children. It would be very surprising, however, if the kind of data available to linguists for adult language were ever to emerge from such techniques.

Even with *adult* data, "pure" description is not a particularly powerful method. This is, the most incisive, compelling results in linguistics (even from the standpoint of *descriptive* adequacy) are found when questions of explanatory adequacy are raised, that is, questions of how a child can ultimately construct an adult grammar.[7] In developmental psycholinguistics, for the most part, this issue (of the ultimate construction of an adult grammar by the child) is not raised. Rather, descriptions of particular stages are carried out in their own terms. Thus, on the one hand, the field of language acquisition has fewer and less trustworthy and relevant data available to it when it is constrained to descriptions of particular stages. On the other hand, the methods of description of particular stages is less powerful than methods that consider the problem of the ultimate construction of a grammar. We should not be surprised if the result of such investigations turns out to be something close to a catalogue of various observable linguistic behaviors, with no particular reason offered to us for believing that these behaviors actually represent the child's abilities.

There is another argument that might be made for the usefulness of trying to describe linguistic abilities at particular stages with no reference to the problem of learnability. One might argue that attaining some empirical knowledge about the different stages of linguistic ability might ultimately be useful to a theory of language acquisition, namely, by the discovery of some empirically true conditions that a language-acquisition theory would have to satisfy. An example might be the order of development of particular linguistic constructions. In principle, it might be possible for such research to play this kind of role. But it must be pointed out that so far it has not done so. One problem is that theories of language acquisition that satisfy the learnability property will not *emerge* from descriptive studies. They have to be actively pursued. Another problem is the one just mentioned: It is difficult without considering learnability and explanatory adequacy to achieve good descriptions. A related problem is the huge array of linguistic behavior, of data that can be collected. Whether "accounting for" a particular observation will give insight is unclear. In short, it is very difficult to build adequate constructive theories. As Einstein says, such theories are "adaptive." The problem, again, is one of a huge array of possible observed data together with the possibility of theories that can adapt to all kinds of data. Can progress be expected? In this regard, principle theories may help to narrow down possibilities, by the derivation of conditions that must hold for a language-acquisition theory.

As a case in point, consider Brown (1973), one of the most intensive studies of early speech. The point of the work is, for the most part, to describe linguistic abilities at two early stages. There is much painstaking discussion of observed data. This is a very difficult job, as I have pointed out, and we should not expect firm or incisive results. Brown is careful to note how tentative any conclusions are, and the conclusions are couched, in general, in vague and tentative terms (with the exception of the discarding of some theories). No precise or articulated theory, *even of the description* of the stages considered, emerges. Moreover, there are of course no proposals for a theory of *how* language is learned, how the child constructs his grammar.[8]

We must remember that observations about a child's linguistic behavior at a given time are just that – observations. They are not a theory of language acquisition, nor are they even necessarily the data that must be explained by such a theory. We must use behavior to guide us in creating a theory. Even for adults, production data would be hardly sufficient to allow creation of an adequate linguistic theory. In short, even if we accept the claim that a theory of language acquisition must predict the "stages" of language growth, there is no reason to think that a theory which ignores learnability can ever attain an adequate description of the stages that a theory would have to predict.

The question how to describe a child's grammar in ways that ultimately meet the criterion of explanatory adequacy has hardly been raised. Presumably, these considerations must have to do with a theory of language acquisition, which includes prediction of the stages of language acquisition (the times course) and a theory of how the child can construct his grammar (over time) under empirically true conditions concerning data (input to the child), memory, and so on. Given the limited kind of data available to developmental psycholinguistics, it is difficult to see how an adequate explanatory theory could be constructed without taking into consideration the final state of the learner.

Actually, linguistic theories often *are* the basis for the consideration of child data. That is, the theories are proposed as models for the description, say, of child speech (or perhaps for the description of child abilities). It is interesting that models of children's speech which have no counterpart in linguistic theory (i.e., which do not correspond to a level of linguistic ability) do not in general find any kind of support even given the limited descriptive goals of many language-acquisition studies. A well-known example is the rejection of the "pivot-open" description by Bloom (1970) and Bowerman (1973a) (see also Brown, 1973, for a detailed summary).

Using adult linguistic theories as hypotheses for the description of child linguistic abilities is not sufficient; it does not mean than an attempt is being made to account for learnability. The essential point is to relate the constructs of such children's grammars to the data (input to the child) on which the construction of such grammars could have been based. It is conceivable that theories might ultimately emerge that explain *how* language is learned – explain, that is, the intrinsic abilities of a child, the kinds of input or data with which he is confronted, the method for creating grammars that the child uses, the ultimate attained state, and so on. A by-product of such a theory might be a principled description of child abilities at particular stages, and the theory might also suggest ways for attaining more adequate tests of the described abilities.

Learnability theory's two principles, of course, are intimately linked. In Einstein's sense, we wish a *unified* theory of linguistic representation and learning. We demand a theory in which linguistic representations are *learnable*.[9]

At least two senses of *learnable* have been used, and I intend only one of them. One sense is that in which *learnable* means learnable by some simple, general learning mechanism, a mechanism sufficient to account for the learning of any kind of human cognitive capacity. In this sense, *learnable* contrasts with *innate*. It is possible that very little that is characteristic and fundamental in human cognition is learnable in this sense, and it is not this sense which I intend.

The second sense, the one I *do* intend, is that *learnable* means "can be learned" (according to some criterion). In other words, an ability (e.g., the ability to speak a natural language) is learnable if there is an (empirically true) way in which the ability can develop. In this sense, if an ability is innate it is learnable (with a perhaps trivial "learning" component). If the ability develops via a learning mechanism based on other innate capacities, the ability is also learnable (with a less trivial learning component). In short, any human capacity is learnable.

One might object that in this second sense of *learnable*, everything is learnable: That is, if there is a problem explaining how an ability is learned on the basis of other mechanisms, we can just build the ability in as innate. This is not the case, however. In the first place, in general, there may be evidence concerning whether an ability is innate, and this evidence must be taken into account. Furthermore, and more convincing in the abstract, it can easily be shown that there are many unlearnable abilities – abilities that, no matter how strong the innate mechanisms, cannot be learned by the mechanisms.[10]

10.2. Learnability theory: a brief sketch

I take a theory of language learning to specify a triple $\langle \mathcal{G}, \mathcal{I}, P \rangle$, where

1. $\mathcal{G}$ is a class of grammars (the possible grammars);
2. $\mathcal{I}$ specifies the kind of information (input or data) I(G) about a grammar G (in $\mathcal{G}$) that is available to the learner who is learning G; and
3. P is a language-learning procedure that constructs a grammar based on inputs.

For the theory to be adequate, it must be the case that

4. Descriptively adequate grammars for every natural language are in $\mathcal{G}$;
5. $\mathcal{I}$ is empirically true; that is, I(G) does not specify more information about G to the learner than is actually available to children; and
6. Every grammar G in $\mathcal{G}$ can be learned by procedure P from information I(G) specified by $\mathcal{I}$.

Naturally, further conditions could be added to the definition of "adequacy"; that is, we could demand that further conditions in the world (order of acquisition, etc.) be true of the theory. I take it, however, that the problem as specified is difficult enough, and that its solution would yield important insights. The goal of learnability theory, then, is to find a specification of a class of grammars $\mathcal{G}$ that includes grammars for all natural languages and to find a language-learning procedure P such that P can learn any of the grammars from the appropriate kind of data. I will define *learn* to mean "learn according to a criterion C," where C will also have to be specified for a complete theory.

The two fundamental principles have been incorporated into this delineation of a theoretical framework. The learnability principle is requirement (6). The second principle, that linguistic representations be the final attained state, is requirement (4). Requirement (5) is (at least part of) the requirement that language be not only "learnable," but "easily" or "naturally" learnable. Some particular processes and definitions will be built into the original specification of an instantiation of this framework. Many other properties, however, will be derived from the principles, as in the notion of "principle theories" already discussed.

Let me very briefly, and with none of the evidence or justification, go over the history of the kind of results my colleagues and I have obtained in this framework.[11] First, let us consider a simple specification of the input I that is presented to the learner. We idealize time as discrete; that is, we have pieces of time t_1, t_2, t_3, ... At each time t_i a piece of information about the language is available to the learner. Suppose he is learning grammar G. Then we will suppose, in this first simple case, that the input I(G) consists only of grammatical sentences generated by G. Thus at each time t_i a sentence generated by G is presented to the learner (every sentence appears at least once in the sequence, so that there is no systematic exclusion of sentences). The criterion C is that there be a procedure P that selects (constructs) a grammar at each time t_i, and that, for any grammar G in $\mathcal{G}$, when information I(G) from G is presented, the procedure ultimately (at some finite time t_i) selects G, and does not change its guess for any later time.[12]

This latter framework is essentially that of Gold's (1967) *text* presentation. The important result for our purposes is that it is relatively straightforward to show (as Gold did) that, given this definition, almost no reasonable class of grammars can be learned. That is, there does not exist *any* procedure P that, from data of the type I(G), can ultimately select G, and not change its guess, and do this for all grammars G in the class. These classes include, for example, the class of context-free languages, the class of regular languages, and classes even more restricted than these.

Thus we have a number of specifications of the triple $\langle \mathcal{G}, \mathcal{I}, P \rangle$, many of which are not learnable. We want to improve these unlearnable theories until they become learnable. Because *unlearnable* means that *no* P exists which can learn $\mathcal{G}$ from input $\mathcal{I}$, we cannot find a stronger P in these cases. (We are holding the criterion C constant for the moment.) Thus we have both $\mathcal{G}$ and $\mathcal{I}$ to reconsider.

Turning first to $\mathcal{G}$, note that the classes of languages that Gold studies are not, in fact, the ones that are natural for linguistic theory. Choosing instead the class of transformational grammars, we might hope to attain learnability. In fact, let us make the definitely too strong assumption that natural languages are transformational languages on a universal context-free base grammar. Although this is too severe a restriction on natural language, we can still prove that, under the same conditions as in the last example, the class of languages is unlearnable (Wexler & Hamburger, 1973).

Our next step is to make a major enrichment of the class of inputs $\mathcal{I}$. If we could assume that the child was corrected for speaking ungrammatically, then we would know from the work of Gold that this was a more powerful method of presentation of information. However, there is little reason to believe that a child is so corrected, except in exceptional cases, and in fact, there is empirical evidence that a child is *not* corrected for speaking ungrammatically (Brown & Hanlon, 1970; see also Newport, H. Gleitman, and L. Gleitman, 1977, for a general consideration of the effect of input on language learning).

However, we can propose the following rationale for data enrichment. The assumptions are once again too strong and general, but they are useful as a start. A child hears sentences whose interpretations relate to situations. In many instances the interpretation of a sentence will be clear from the situation and the words of the sentence, even if the child cannot analyze the sentence. We assume that the child has the cognitive capacity to determine the interpretation from the situation and the spoken words. Furthermore, we assume that interpretations relate directly to syntactic deep structures and that the child has the capacity to map interpretations onto deep structures. (My colleagues and I have also done some quite limited work to show how some of this capacity can be learned.) In short, for purposes of the present investigation, we assume that we have captured the child at a moment when he has certain capabilities. We will later provide empirical justification for this assumption. We now want to study, from these assumptions, the learnability of syntactic transformations, which map base structures onto surface sentences. We assume that the information set contains a sequence of (b, s) pairs, where b is a base phrase marker and s is the surface sentence transformationally derived from b. $\mathcal{G}$ is the class of all possible transformational grammars on a universal base, restricted in a particular way. In this case we obtain a positive result. We define a procedure P that learns any possible such grammar in the limit. (We slightly change the criterion C, adding a probabilistic element, so that the criterion is essentially convergence with probability 1.) The proof is in Hamburger and Wexler (1975).

It is pleasant finally to have a positive result, about a class of grammars that has some empirical validity. But we should be unhappy with the nature of the input that is required. In general, phrase markers of huge depth will have to be part of the input (*b*) data. An algebraic bound is derived in the proof, but it is easy to construct artificial examples (too simple for natural language) that give bounds of, say, 400,000 on the depth of phrase markers that will be needed. (Depth is measured as degree of sentence embedding.)

Thus a study was undertaken to make the information set $\mathscr{I}$ more reasonable. In Wexler (1977b, which also appears in slightly revised form as chapter 4 of Wexler & Culicover, 1980) I proved that, in the framework just presented, transformational grammar is learnable from data of degree less than or equal to 2. That is, nothing more complicated than sentences that contain sentences that contain sentences is needed for convergence.

The learnability theory under discussion is in many ways a principle theory. One example concerns the nature of the input. The learnability principles (i.e., the condition that linguistic representations be learnable) cannot be satisfied if only grammatical sentences are taken as input. Thus the principles lead us to a new theory of the input, namely, (*b, s*) pairs. It would be difficult to obtain direct evidence that this is the form of the input. After all, the actually observable input has a huge array of properties. Focus on the relevant properties is made possible when we start with the basic principle of learnability. (I will return to this property in Section 10.5.)

10.3. Derived principles of mind

Even more direct and explicit examples of the role of principle theory may be found with respect to constraints on the forms of grammar. We start with the principle that we have to show that transformational grammar is "naturally learnable." In order to achieve this result, of course, we must take an explicit formulation of transformational grammar and prove that it is learnable (from [*b, s*] data). In order to prove the result (convergence or learnability theorem), we have to add a number of constraints, conditions, and principles to the standard formulation of transformational grammar. In other words, we are directly led to these conditions by the learnability principle. They must hold if transformational grammar is to be learnable.[13] A further, very interesting property of the principle theory is that it leads to empirical tests of itself. The conditions that follow from the principles can be empirically tested. To the extent that the principles receive support, the entire theory can be taken to be adequate.

The conditions that follow from the learnability principles are numerous, and the arguments are lengthy and complex. Here I can give only one example, to demonstrate how the arguments are made. As I have indicated, the strongest result that we have so far attained is learnability from simple (degree 2) data. This means that the most complex phrase marker that a learner will have to consider as data as he constructs his grammar will be of depth 2 (sentences that contain sentences that contain sentences). We will take this property to be a property of "natural learnability" (our second principle). In order to achieve the goal of proving natural learnability, according to the mathematical methods that we have developed, it is crucial to show that, if a system the learner has attained is not "perfect" – that is, if the learner's system makes an error on some structure (behaves differently than does the adult system on that structure) – then there is a "simple" structure on which the learner's system makes an error. We will call this property K.

To be more precise, recall that a sentence is the terminal string of a surface phrase marker (i.e., one to which transformations have applied). For a given deep structure P we say that the learner makes a *detectable error* on P if the terminal string of the surface structure into which the learner's system maps P is different from the terminal string of the surface structure into which the adult's system maps P. The *degree* of a phrase marker (p.m.) is its depth of embedding of S (Sentence). We now make K more precise by defining the learnability property K in this way: If a grammar makes a detectable error on some p.m., then there is a p.m. P of degree 2 such that the grammar makes a detectable error on P. The importance of *detectable* errors is that they provide information that the learner can use.

It is possible that errors exist that are not detectable. The following artificial example illustrates this possibility. Consider the phrase marker P in (1):

(1)   P   = S_1

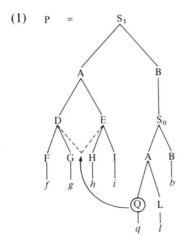

P is dominated by the sentence node S_1. There is one embedded sentence, dominated by the sentence node S_0. Thus P is of degree 1. The words (lexical items) of P are represented by small letters. Now suppose there is one transformation that applies to P in the adult system. This transformation T is a *raising* transformation. That is, it *raises* a node from one embedded sentence to a higher sentence. In particular, T raises Q from S_0 and attaches it as a right daughter of D (right sister of G). The learner, however, has hypothesized a different transformation. This is the transformation T', which also raises Q, but attaches it as a left daughter of E (left sister of H). The dotted line indicates that Q is attached differently by the adult and child (learner) grammars. The surface structures may be seen in (2):

(2a) Surface structure of P for adult

(2b) Surface structure of P for learner

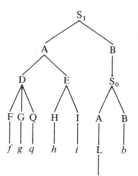 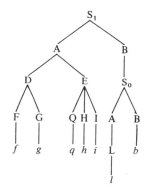

What is important about (2) is that it shows that the learner has *not* made a detectable error on P because the terminal strings of the surface structures are the same for both the adult and the learner, namely, *fgqhilb*. Thus is true despite the differences in the surface structures.

But now suppose that P is part of a larger, degree 3 phrase marker, as shown in (3). I will show that the p.m. in (3) can contain a detectable error, although no smaller p.m. contains a detectable error; the principle K is thus contradicted.

We assume that transformations obey the cyclic principle, that is, transformations apply to S_0, S_1, S_2, and S_3 in that order. At S_1, Q is raised. But, as in the previous example, the child's system attaches the raised node Q to a "wrong" position (that is, to one different from the adult's). Specifically, Q becomes for the adult a daughter of D, and for the child a daughter of E (see [3]). The difference for the adult and child attachments is indicated in (3) by the dotted lines under D and E. But the child does not make a *detectable* error on the phrase marker dominated by S_1, because the terminal strings of the surface structures are the same (*fgqhilb*). But then A is raised from S_1 to S_2, in the same way, by the child and the adult. The attachment is indicated by the dotted line between S_2 and A in (3). When we raise A in (3), no detectable error occurs, because A dominates the same terminal string for both the child and the

(3)

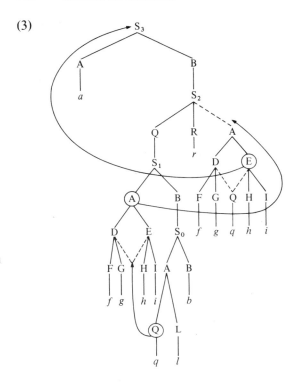

adult (*fgqhi*). However, at S_3, E is raised to the left of the phrase marker, once again identically for the adult and the child. Thus the terminals that start the terminal string of the fully transformed phrase marker are the terminals dominated by E. Thus, for the adult, the terminal string of the fully transformed phrase marker starts with *hi*, whereas for the child the terminal string starts with *qhi*. Thus the child makes a detectable error on the degree 3 phrase marker (3). But there is no detectable error on any phrase marker of degree 2 or less. (The grammar has to be chosen so that this result can be formally demonstrated, as is done in Wexler, 1977b.)

What has happened in this example is that an error made at S_1 was undetectable and remained undetectable even when the error was "raised" to S_2. But a transformation applying at S_3 uncovered the error (made it detectable). We might try to change property K by replacing "degree 2" with "degree 3," that is, by assuming that the learnability property holds that if a detectable error exists then one exists on a phrase marker of degree 3 (instead of degree 2). But this move will not work because the problem is not one of simply adding another level. The error of the mistakenly attached Q can continue to be moved up to higher and higher levels, and the uncovering of the error might take place only after a quite high level is reached. For example, A itself might be raised to S_3, or, in other examples, a node dominating A might be raised to S_3. The error might only be discovered when E is raised to S_4.

This would not be a satisfactory result because the goal is to prove that, if a detectable error is made, then it is made on a phrase marker of quite low degree. If we continued in the manner just outlined, we would not achieve this goal. (There would be a finite bound on the process, but in general the bound would be quite large.) Thus the move to a different learnability property will not work here. Rather, we search for an assumption that will disallow the counterexample. We find such a hypothesis to be the *Raising Principle*: If a node has been raised, then it is *frozen*. That is, further transformations may not apply to nodes below the raised node. The Raising Principle has been assumed just to rule out (3) and similar examples. When A is raised from S_1 to S_2, A becomes frozen by the Raising Principle. Thus none of the nodes that A dominates may be affected by a further transformation. In particular, because A dominates E, E may not be affected by a transformation; and therefore E may not be raised from S_2 to S_3. Therefore no detectable error will be created, and the derivation of P does not contradict learnability property K. In order to preserve the learnability property (needed to prove the learnability principle), we have been led to hypothesize a constraint on the operation of transformations. This constraint can be taken to be a universal principle in the language-learning mechanism and, concomitantly, a universal principle of natural languages. The theory thus leads us to a hypothesis, namely, that the Raising Principle is universal. Linguistic methods can then be used to test the hypothesis for its descriptive adequacy (as is done in Wexler & Culicover, 1980, chap. 5).

Here I will give only a very brief example, with none of the many details and complications. The example is intended merely to show the nature of the kind of linguistic evidence that can be brought to bear on conditions (such as the Raising Principle) to which the learnability principle gives rise. It is well known (see, e.g., Akmajian, 1975) that prepositional phrases that are part of noun phrases can extrapose to the right, via a transformation called NP Extraposition. Thus (4b) is derivable from (4a). The change is shown very schematically in (5).

(4a) A proof of this theorem would be easy to discover
(4b) A proof would be easy to discover of this theorem

(5)

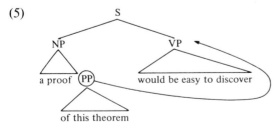

Now suppose we try to question the NP in the PP in (4b), arriving at (6):

(6)   *Which theorem would a proof be easy to discover of Ø?

Ø indicates a site from which something has been moved.) The ungrammaticality of sentences like (6) is well known and has remained a problem for linguistic theory.[14] Note that certain simple explanations are not possible in light of the grammaticality of (7):

(7)   Which theorem did John discover a proof of Ø?

Notice, however, that Extraposition of NP here is a raising transformation. This depends on the assumption that NP is a *cyclic node*, and that moving a constituent outside an NP means that it has been *raised*. (This is a well-known assumption, part of many systems.) Therefore the Raising Principle asserts that the raised PP is *frozen*, which means that no transformation may apply to nodes dominated by PP after it is moved. But then *wh* movement cannot apply, and thus (6) is not derivable.

Therefore we have explained (predicted) the ungrammaticality of (6) on the basis of a condition (the Raising Principle) that was derived from learnability theory. Once again, there are many complications, which, along with further evidence, are presented in Wexler and Culicover (1980, chap. 5).[15]

If sufficient linguistic evidence is found for the hypothesis (the Raising Principle, in this case), then we have evidence for the Raising Principle of two very different kinds. On the one hand, an abstract analysis of conditions under which human learning can take place leads us to the Raising Principle. On the other hand, direct linguistic evidence supports it. Whenever evidence of such radically different kinds is found for a hypothesis in science, it is considered that the argument for the hypothesis is relatively strong.

In no way is the Raising Principle "close to experience." Not only does our commonsense experience with a child learning language not indicate that the Raising Principle is true, but the very categories in which its definition is couched (frozenness of nodes, etc.) are not elements of our intuitive understanding (as humans) of language learning. Although commonsense notions are useful, as Einstein points out, "yet more and more, as the depth of our knowledge increases, we must give up this advantage in our quest for logical simplicity and uniformity in the foundations of [psychological] theory" (p. 340, with *psychological* replacing Einstein's *physical*). It is important to stress that these foundations are not (for Einstein or for us) mere logical niceties. Rather, they are the very stuff of the scientific quest, the only manner in which we can hope to grasp (some elements of) reality.

In summary, we have here an illustration of the way in which our theory is of the type that Einstein called a "principle theory." Basic principles (that language is naturally and easily learnable and that the learned representations of language are those of linguistic theory) "give rise to mathematically formulated criteria which the separate processes or the theoretical representations of them have to satisfy" (Einstein, p. 223). To the extent that we have formulated the theory correctly, we have Einstein's advantages of "logical perfection and security of the foundations" (p. 223). Of course, we must bear in mind that we may have taken incorrect steps; for example, the linguistic representations of principle 2 that we have used may not be absolutely correct, or even if they are, we may not have deduced exactly the conditions that allow the principle to be satisfied. Because we may have erred, learnability theory, like any other in science, is fallible, and stands in need of correction.

The role of the learnability principle (that language is learnable) is very important in all of this development. The example I have given here shows how the attempt to preserve the learnability principle leads to the postulation of certain conditions. In fact, the postulation of conditions (such as the Raising Principle) that solve certain problems (such as that represented by example [3]) is not an end in itself. Ultimately it must be shown that a particular set of conditions (such as the Raising Principle) leads to the learnability principle. In fact, this is what is done in Wexler (1977b), in which it is proven that, for a certain set of conditions (including the Raising Principle), transformational grammar is learnable from data of degree less than or equal to 2 (see also Wexler & Culicover, 1980, chap. 4).

In the one small example that I have given, the reader may perceive some complexity. In fact, the development and proof of the degree 2 result turns out to be rather complex from a mathematical point of view. This is not unexpected in the study of a quite structured system like language. But one should not confuse mathematical complexity with the complexity of the learning theory. Actually, the model of the language-learning *mechanism*, the part of the theory that describes how hypotheses are formed and changed, is quite simple and not particularly structured. More structure is added, of course, by the assumptions of linguistic content. The mechanism, omitting details, creates transformations on the basis of (b, s) data and deletes transformations when a datum is such that a detectable error is made. At any time, the mechanism pays attention to only the latest datum. Thus we do not have to assume that the learner has memory for all past data, which, as Braine (1971a) points out, is quite unlikely. In short, there are certain plausible aspects of psychological or cognitive considerations that are met by the procedure (see Hamburger & Wexler, 1975, for a precise formulation of the procedure, and Wexler & Culicover, 1980, for further discussion and revision based on the degree 2 result of Wexler, 1977b).

I cannot discuss here the large number of properties and results of the theory that my colleagues and I have developed. The degree 2 result demands the postulation of a number of conditions on transformational grammar, some of which are well known to linguistic theory, some of which are implicit but not explicitly stated in linguistic theory, and some of which are new to linguistic theory. We have studied a number of the principles in some detail with respect to linguistic data (see Culicover & Wexler, 1977, and Wexler & Culicover, 1980, chap. 5). Nevertheless, the theory is only a beginning. There are many properties of it that will have to be modified or added, if we are to move in the direction of an adequate theory of language acquisition. Necessary alterations include:

1.   A modification of syntactic properties, to merge further with linguistic theory;
2.   Changes in properties of the learning mechanism, to approach as closely as possible to psychological, cognitive abilities of the learner;
3.   Bringing the theory's conception of the input to the learner into as close a correspondence as possible to the actual nature of the input; and
4.   Extensions of learnability theory to other linguistic abilities, considering properties of language use, semantics, and phonology.

10.4. Derived conditions on input: fine tuning

I have already discussed an example of how, by starting from the learnability principle, we derive conditions on forms of grammar that we can postulate to be part of the language-learning capacity of the child. Furthermore, empirical evidence can be brought to bear on these conditions. Conditions concerning other aspects of the theory of language acquisition can also be derived. I will try to illustrate here how we can derive conditions – two in particular – on the form of input that the language learner uses. The first involves the question whether the mother's speech to a child learning language is "fine tuned" so as to constitute a useful series of "language lessons." The second condition involves the question of (b, s) input, which I have briefly mentioned but have not discussed in detail.

It has often been suggested that the speech behavior of adults who care for children is specially structured so as to provide particular kinds of linguistic information to the child. Moreover, many versions of this argument claim that mothers' speech is graded in syntactic complexity, to correspond in some way to (perhaps, according to some suggestions, to exceed slightly) the child's linguistic abilities at each stage. Furthermore, the claim is often made that this "grading" or presentation of language lessons is important, and even necessary, for the learning of language. This argument is usually taken one step further, to the claim that such fine tuning reduces, or even eliminates, the need for special innate linguistic abilities.

Suppose that we start out with the learnability principle: Language is learned. We then ask, How can fine tuning help in preserving this principle? That is, if we want to prove convergence to an adult grammar, given the appropriate input, how can input that is fine tuned help?

Naturally, the answer depends on the particular definition of fine tuning that is given. Consider one possible aspect, namely, correction of a child by an adult when the child speaks an ungrammatical sentence. Surely this is an activity that a language teacher might perform. And, in fact, correction would provide information to a learner: He or she would know that a corrected sentence was not in the language (assuming a special form of correction that indicated ungrammaticalness, as opposed to ill-formedness for some other reason, such as untruth or oddness). Gold (1967) has shown that such "negative information" is very powerful, as compared to purely "positive" information (examples of grammatical sentences).[16]

Nevertheless, as is well known to students of child language, the best evidence indicates that children are *not* corrected for ungrammatical sentences. By analyzing a mother–child corpus, Brown and Hanlon (1970) showed that mothers did not differentially approve or disapprove grammatical and ungrammatical sentences. Nor did mothers show that they *understood* grammatical utterances of the child any better than ungrammatical utterances. (These results depend, of course, on the extent to which approving and understanding can be measured in behavior.) Brown and Hanlon point out that, in fact, parents correct *semantic* mistakes, not syntactic ones. Qualifications might be necessary, and certainly there are other possibilities based on current evidence. But we cannot assume that children are corrected for speaking ungrammatically.

What other kinds of fine tuning might exist? One suggestion that is often made is that sentences are presented in some special manner, or order, which makes learning easier. It is sometimes suggested that the argument that special restrictions on grammar have to be assumed for the purposes of learnability is misguided because the argument ignores the possibility of "intelligent" text presentation. Presumably, this suggestion claims that, somehow or other, presenting sentences in some kind of special way will provide information that will help learnability. It is often suggested that presenting "simple" examples of language to children will aid them in learning language, thus making less necessary a component of innate linguistic structure. A version of this idea, for example, is presented by Brown (1977), who writes: "But it has turned out that parental speech is well formed and finely tuned to the child's psycholinguistic capacity. The corollary would seem to be that there is less need for an elaborate innate component than there at first seemed to be" (p. 20).

Is this argument correct? Consider the question from the point of view of learnability theory. We start from the learnability principle – language is learnable. Conditions on the processes, constructs, and so on of the theory must allow this result. Does simplified input allow language learning? More formally, does simplified input allow convergence to the hypothesized grammar on the basis of input? We already know that, even with *full* information, many classes of grammars cannot be learned from many types of input; for example, the class of context-free grammars cannot be learned from presentation, one by one, of *all* the sentences in the language. Now we simplify input, according to the suggestion just offered. That is, we present only "simple" sentences. Say that *simple* means "short" (the same argument works if we give some other meaning to *simple*). So we present only short sentences to the learning procedure. Can it now learn any context-free language? Of course not. We are presenting *less* information about the language to the procedure if we choose to present only specially selected sentences (in this case the short ones). Thus the task of language learning will be *more* difficult (or at least *as* difficult) than if we present all the information.

There *are* plausible ways in which presenting only a subset of the possible information (e.g., the short sentences) will help the learner. For example, suppose that presenting very much information to a learner will overload his attentional capacities. That is, the result of presenting too much information might be that the learner will not pay attention to *any* information, and thus language learning will not proceed. Here we have a reason to claim that presenting simple information will help the learner.

Even if the latter claim (concerning attention limitations) is true – that is, even if there is some kind of justification of the role of simplicity of input in language learning – it will not be of such a nature that it can do away with the need for an innate component in language acquisition. The fact that context-free languages are not learnable from text data, for example, is true even for an "ideal" learner, with no memory or attentional limitations at all. Thus the presentation of "simpler" data will have no beneficial effect on the (already perfect) memory or attentional capacities, but *will* have a detrimental effect on the amount of information that is available to the learner, and thus on the learner's powers of inference.

The situation may be seen in the following diagram:

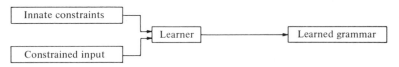

If we fix the attained grammar, then the more we constrain the input (i.e., the less information we provide the learner), the more we will need in the way of innate constraints. Notice also that (as pointed out in Wexler, 1977b), if we constrain the learner (by various kinds of cognitive constraints, such as memory constraints, and computational load limits), then for a fixed attained grammar we will need to postulate stronger innate constraints. (The diagram should not be taken as a flow chart, indicating some kind of real-time order of events. It is intended simply as a representation of the logical problem.)

To summarize, we must distinguish between at least two possible functions of simple and fine-tuned speech to children, with respect to language acquisition. On the one hand, simplified speech might be necessary because of a general limitation in children's cognitive capacities (e.g., inability to deal with a long sentence because of memory limitations) or because special kinds of speech might attract a child's attention. This kind of explanation is sometimes given, and seems plausible. But this function of simplified speech to children will not decrease to a large extent the need for an innate structural component, because that need can be demonstrated by the impossibility of inferring a grammar from data even when we assume an "ideal" learner who does not have any problems of memory or attention. A second possible use of simplified speech for language acquisition would be a use that would somehow help with the logical problem of creating a grammar based on the primary data, given no limitations of attention, memory, and the like. Here arguments are rarely offered, but this is the kind of argument that would be necessary to diminish the force of the argument for innate linguistic structure.

Principle theory thus leads us to the conclusion that simplified speech is not useful for the kind of problems of language learning that have to do with the relation between presented input and attained grammar. Whether it is useful for other reasons cannot be determined strictly from a question of the presented data and the kinds of attained grammars; questions of cognitive capacity must also be taken into account. Because we do have evidence that special attentional and memory limitations exist for the child, it is plausible that simplified input might exist for such reasons. What is interesting, however, is that the characteristics of such input that follow from these considerations might be quite different from the characteristics that would follow from the arbitrarily stated (but unargued) assumption that simplified input aids inference and can reduce the need for an "elaborate innate component" (Brown, 1977).

An example of the unargued assumption that simplified input aids inference is provided by Levelt (1975), who proposes that "intelligent text presentation" will aid the learner and is, in fact, a characteristic of the information presented to the learner. He points out that no formal models are available that make use of these findings (of simplified input), but adds: "It should, however, be obvious that from the purely syntactic point of view the urge for strongly nativist assumptions has been diminished by these findings" (p. 16). Of course, that simplified input will help acquisition in the relevant sense is not "obvious," because, as I have just shown, it is false. Thus there is good reason for the lack of existence of formal models of the kind to which Levelt alludes.

Principle theory (the learnability principle) leads us to the conclusion that simplified input, intelligent text presentation, will not help the child learn language, from the point of view of the learnability problem. Why, then, does fine tuning exist?[17] The simple answer is that the best evidence is that it does *not* exist, in the relevant sense, and that, furthermore, the relevant special characteristics of talk to children do not aid language learning in the way claimed for them.

I do not have the space here to review the relevant literature in any detail. A close perusal of the papers in Snow and Ferguson (1977) convinces one that claims that a "miniature language" is presented (Levelt) or that mother's speech is syntactically simple are false. In most cases, it is important to look at the actual data and results reported in the papers, rather than at the very general conclusions, which often seem to claim that talk to children has the relevant properties, even when the relevant data do not agree. (To some extent, such a discussion is provided in Wexler & Culicover, 1980.)

Here I will only mention briefly the 1977 paper by Newport, H. Gleitman, and L. Gleitman, which (in contrast to many studies on language input) clearly asks the relevant questions and is methodologically sound. The first question is, Is talk to children simple? Of course, such talk is *short*. But is it syntactically simple? Newport et al. try a number of definitions of syntactic simplicity. For most of these, mothers' speech to children does not turn out to be simple. They write: "Overall then, 'syntactic simplicity' is a pretty messy way to characterize Motherese" (p. 122). Another aspect of fine tuning is the claim that mother's speech to children becomes increasingly complex syntactically as the child learns language. Newport et al. find that maternal speech does not "grow syntactically more complex in a fine-tuned correspondence with the child's growing linguistic sophistication" (p. 123). For example, the sentence range (of syntactic types in mothers' speech) narrows as children's linguistic abilities increase. Moreover, Newport et al. show (by partialling out the effects of other variables, a technique widely used for multivariate problems in psychology, but almost never encountered in language-input studies) that many effects of input on language growth that would be expected under the fine-tuning hypothesis do not occur. They write:

> We can hardly agree with such writers as Levelt (1975) who asserts that Motherese has been shown to present the child with a syntactically limited subset of sentences in the language; and that "from the purely syntactic view the urge for strongly nativist assumptions

has been diminished by these findings." On the contrary, nativist assumptions are left intact by a close look at Motherese – they neither gain nor lose plausibility. The point is that demonstrating that speech to children is different from other speech does not show that it is better for the language learner. Most investigators have jumped from the finding of a difference, here replicated, to the conclusion that Motherese is somehow simple for inducing the grammar. But the finding that Motherese has properties of its own does not show that these give acquisitional support. Notice, at any rate, that the view of Motherese as a syntactically simple corpus merely transfers a very strong claim about the child (that, owing to the restrictive and rich hypotheses, he can deduce the grammar from haphazard primary data) to a very strong claim about his mother (that she has some effective notion of what constitutes syntactic simplicity so that in principle she can choose utterances on this basis). [P. 123]

Talk to children *does* have special properties. Newport et al. (1977) argue convincingly that these properties are the result of the exigencies of communication; that is, mothers want their children of limited abilities to understand them. However, such talk cannot be viewed as a set of language lessons except in the sense that it provides examples for the child and that it is very reasonable to expect that, if the child understands sentences, he will learn language more quickly.

In summary, starting from the learnability principle, we see that fine tuning and simplification cannot help language learning in the inference sense. It turns out that the properties of mothers' speech which have been empirically discovered are consistent with this condition, in that they are not examples of fine tuning and simplification in the relevant senses. To the extent that speech to children does have special properties, most of these properties are best understood as contributing toward other functions, not the function of inducing a grammar.

10.5. Derived conditions on input: (b, s) pairs

The example that we have just considered (fine tuning and simplicity) is an example of the inefficacy of a particular input to which we are led by learnability theory. But I have a positive example to present, also. Recall that the impossibility of convergence for presentation of examples of sentences led us to assume that input consisted of (b, s) pairs, where b is a base phrase marker and s is the surface sentence of the phrase marker that results from the application of transformations to b. The effect of postulating such an input is that we do arrive at a theory in which learnability can be proven. Moreover, not only does the learner arrive at the correct language in the sense of "set of strings," but an important aspect of descriptive adequacy is attained: Namely, the grammar that the learner arrives at maps a particular base phrase marker into the same surface sentence (string) as does the adult grammar. Not only is this important for structural reasons, but, given the assumption that at least some aspects of semantic interpretation are done on the deep structure, this competence (correct mapping of base phrase marker to surface string) will be necessary for semantic interpretation.

Thus the learnability principle gives rise to the condition that input consists of (b, s) pairs. Is there any evidence for such an assumption? Note, of course, that in no way is b directly presented. Our assumption, rather, is that the child can construct b from the situation in which the sentence is uttered, given his cognitive capacities (and perhaps some previously developed linguistic abilities). Actually, we do not have to suppose that the child can do this for *every* sentence that he hears, but only that he can do so for a sufficient number of them. It is nevertheless interesting that Slobin (1975) argues that the child can interpret sentences from situations without knowledge of syntax in almost all cases:

> Most studies of child language comprehension put the child into a situation where there are no contextual cues to the meanings of the utterances, but, in real life, there is little reason for the preschool child to rely heavily on syntactic factors to determine the basic propositional and referential meaning of sentences which he hears. Judith Johnston and I have gone through transcripts of adults' speech to children between the ages of two and five, in Turkish and English, looking for sentences which could be open to misinterpretation if the child lacked basic syntactic knowledge, such as the roles of word order and inflections. We found almost no instances of an adult utterance which could possibly be misinterpreted. That is, the overwhelming majority of utterances were clearly interpretable in context, requiring only knowledge of word meanings and the normal relations between actors, actions, and objects in the world. [P. 30]

Newport et al. (1977) provide some suggestive evidence that the extent to which mothers match their utterances to concepts that are at the same time in the child's consciousness correlates with linguistic development. Of course, there is no reason to think that such techniques are *necessary* for language acquisition. We do not know how many utterances must be such that the child can interpret them from the situation (and perhaps from knowledge of the meaning of the words in the utterance). Nevertheless, a number of findings in the papers in Snow and Ferguson (1977) are consistent with the claim that children can interpret utterances in context, even if they are not fully knowledgeable about syntax, and that this ability aids language acquisition. Some of this evidence is discussed in Wexler and Culicover (1980).

Note that, although learnability theory leads to the assumption of a special form of input (*b*, *s* pairs), it nevertheless does not diminish the need for a special innate structural component for language acquisition. Even with this kind of input many conditions (e.g., the Raising Principle) are needed for learnability. As further aspects of descriptive adequacy are added to the criterion of learnability, we might expect that further conditions will be needed.

In summary, I have tried to sketch in outline some aspects of a theory of language learnability. This theory has for the most part been concerned with the learning of syntactic transformations, but this is not a limitation of principle. The theory is a "principle" theory, in Einstein's sense. From a small number of basic principles (with details added by other considerations, such as linguistic theory and results concerning lack of correction for ungrammatical speech in developmental psycholinguistics) learnability theory has been led to a large number of conditions concerning, in particular, innate principles of mind and form of input to the language learner. A virtue of the theory, in my opinion, is that it permits a large number of fascinating and important questions to be asked in a precise and potentially answerable way. Furthermore, I see such a theory as potentially providing a unification between linguistic theory and the theory of language acquisition. There are a great number of unsolved problems, and there is no reason to think that the answers proposed so far are exactly right. We should be satisfied if the results of learnability theory to date are sufficient to encourage further work that will deepen and modify the theory.

Notes

1 This has been pointed out by N. Chomsky (1980, pp. 241 ff.).
2 It is not generally true of more physiological studies or of areas of psychology, such as perception, that have been influenced by and interact with physiological studies. I exclude from consideration here "depth psychology" (e.g., Freud), the position of which with respect to the introspection assumption is somewhat unclear. See N. Chomsky (1980, p. 288, n. 15) for some discussion.
3 Because both Einstein articles (1954a and 1954b) appear in the same book, my references to them will be by page number only.
4 Actually, in the study of language acquisition in developmental psycholinguistics, there really is very little that we should call a theory, even of the "constructive" kind. Most research in the field consists of data collection, with some verbal guiding ideas. There have been some preliminary attempts to provide constructive theories, e.g., Braine (1963), with the constructive principles usually being taken over (perhaps in modified form) from other psychological fields, e.g., the field of "verbal learning." In general, to the

extent that work in language acquisition that might lead toward the creation of constructive theories exists, this work is based on various linguistic theories. See Wexler, Culicover, and Hamburger (1975) for discussion. There have also been some attempts at constructive theories of language acquisition using notions of "network" theory and other concepts of contemporary cognitive psychology, e.g., J. Anderson (1975, 1977). Not much of significance has emerged from such studies (Wexler, 1978).

5 It is often claimed that Einstein came to the principle of the constant velocity of light on strictly empirical grounds, namely, the findings of the Michaelson–Morley experiment. Holton (1973) has gathered extensive evidence and argues effectively against this interpretation. Apparently, at the time of his formulation of the special theory, either Einstein was unaware of the Michaelson–Morley result or it did not play a role in his thinking.

6 The principle was essentially introduced by Chomsky under the term *explanatory adequacy*.

7 This is pointed out by N. Chomsky (1965, p. 36).

8 This is not to say that Brown ignores linguistic theory. Very many of the analyses relate to one or another linguistic theory, generally taken as a representation of a child's linguistic abilities at a particular stage. But no attention is paid to the question how such representations emerge. Any hypothesis concerning linguistic theory is taken, and tested as a representation, strictly in terms of the data available about a child's performance at a given stage. No attention is paid to the question of adequacy of the theories for the description of the attained grammars, or to the question whether and how such description could be learned.

9 I use *learnable* in a systematically ambiguous way, to indicate that an ability (or piece of knowledge) is learnable or that the theoretical representations of these abilities or pieces of knowledge are learnable.

10 Gödel showed that there were no procedures for performing certain functions. The negative results in learnability theory are examples of this kind of demonstration; namely, there are no procedures for performing certain kinds of learning functions.

11 For a general introduction to the framework, see Wexler, Culicover, and Hamburger (1975). The first convergence results are sketched in Hamburger and Wexler (1973), and the mathematical details appear in Hamburger and Wexler (1975). The proof that surface data (grammatical sentences) are not sufficient for learning certain classes of transformational grammar appears in Wexler and Hamburger (1973). The degree 2 convergence results appear in Wexler (1977b) and also in Wexler and Culicover (1980), which contains a detailed study of the results and methodology of learnability theory.

12 It should be clear that this criterion is weaker than one that requires the learning procedure to shut off from processing data at some time and announce its final grammar.

13 Of course, as in the case of any scientific finding, we could be wrong, even with mathematical justification for derivation of the conditions. Our initial assumptions might be wrong; there might be other principles that are more adequate; and so on.

14 If we tried to question the same phrase in the subject of (4), we would still obtain an ungrammatical sentence, namely,

*Which theorem would a proof of Ø be easy to discover?

This can be accounted for, however, by another of the principles that derive from learnability theory, namely, the Binary Principle (which is essentially equivalent to N. Chomsky's [1973] Subjacency Principle). The Binary Principle will not rule out (6).

15 For syntactic evidence concerning two other conditions derived from learnability theory (the Freezing Principle and the Binary Principle), see also Wexler and Culicover (1973) and Culicover and Wexler (1977).

16 But notice that Gold's results deal only with learning a language as a set of strings. Questions of structural correctness, of "descriptive adequacy," are ignored. He considers only what (in Wexler & Culicover, 1980) we call "weak learnability." (This corresponds to the notion of "weak equivalence" in linguistic theory.) The usefulness of negative information (correction, etc.) has thus been demonstrated only for weak learnability, and not for strong learnability (which demands that acquired grammars have appropriate structural characteristics). It is not clear whether negative information can play an important role in questions of learning grammars that are descriptively adequate (strong learnability). To date there are no such results, and I believe that there is reason to be skeptical. The nonexistence of negative information in natural situations of language learning might make this latter question of formal interest only; there may be, however, some reasons of theory that make it interesting. I will argue shortly that other kinds of fine tuning (simplicity, etc.) are not useful for language learning. Therefore, unless there were other reasons for their existence, we would not expect to find such mechanisms.

It would be pleasant to have a kind of converse of this argument. Namely, if mechanisms *are* useful for language learning, they will exist. Of course, this latter claim cannot be absolute, because it is easy to think of useful properties that humans do not have. Nevertheless, because it is so believable that adults have the cognitive capacity to correct ungrammatical sentences, one would expect adults to use negative information if it *were* useful to the language learner. If, in fact, negative information does not help with the problem of attaining *descriptively adequate* grammars, then this might be a reason why it is not used. (Of course, negative information helps the *linguist*, but the child has a different linguistic capacity.) It is important to regard this "functional" argument very tentatively, especially given the lack of precise knowledge of the relation between negative information and descriptive adequacy.

17 It is not a strict implication of learnability theory that such fine tuning does not exist. After all, it *could* exist without being of use for learning. The implication follows only if we add the (functional) assumption that characteristics of the input exist only if there is a function for them. Of course, it is possible that other functions (not learnability) are the "reasons" for the existence of certain characteristics.

Part IV

SEMANTIC AND LEXICAL DEVELOPMENT

11. Reorganizational processes in lexical and syntactic development

Melissa Bowerman

What is the nature of change over time in learning to talk? Most obvious to the casual observer is the expansion of the child's linguistic repertoire: the addition of new content words, new functors (inflections, prepositions, articles, conjunctions, etc.), new patterns for combining words to make sentences, and so on. A second kind of change is more subtle, in that it involves nothing overtly "new." It must be described, rather, in terms of the reorganization of the knowledge underlying elements of the existing repertoire. The term *reorganization* will be used broadly in this chapter to designate both analyses compatible with, but deeper than, the child's initial formulation and more radical "redoings" of existing analyses.

Although certain reorganizational processes have long been recognized by scholars of child language, the phenomenon has until recently attracted only limited interest. The implicit assumption has been that reorganization plays a relatively minor role, one that is perhaps largely confined to certain domains such as inflectional morphology. This attitude is beginning to change, however. The last few years have seen a small but growing number of studies documenting reorganizational changes, and it is becoming clearer that reorganization, far from being an incidental process, flows continually beneath the more overt signs of progress like a subterranean stream.

Covert reorganizational processes seem to be particularly important during the preschool years, after the child has acquired a workable vocabulary and some basic ability at sentence construction. Before reorganization in any particular linguistic domain takes place, children may be able to produce elements from that domain quite fluently. However, the knowledge that enables them to do this may in many cases be relatively

This research was supported in part by Grant HD 00870 from the National Institute of Child Health and Human Development. Some of the writing was carried out during a year's fellowship at the Netherlands Institute for Advanced Study in the Humanities and Social Sciences in Wassenaar, The Netherlands. The support of these institutes is gratefully acknowledged. I also thank Leonard Talmy for stimulating discussions about errors of the type shown in Table 11.3; Mabel Rice and Virginia Gathercole for the errors from Mindy and Rachel, respectively, cited in Table 11.2; and Floris Cohen for helpful comments on an earlier draft.

superficial, consisting of piecemeal rules and unintegrated information for dealing with different kinds of words, sentence patterns, and situations. Only gradually do children begin to discern relationships and regularities among linguistic forms that they have not previously recognized as related, and to integrate these forms into more abstract, patterned systems.

Reorganization in language development has important implications for the way children work out the relationships between linguistic forms (words, inflections, patterns for word combination, etc.) and categories of meaning. In recent years it has been widely assumed that the development of meaning takes place largely prior to and outside the acquisition of linguistic forms. Language acquisition, according to this hypothesis, can be seen as a process of matching forms to preestablished meanings. Studies documenting reorganization indicate that this view is one-sided, however: Much of what goes on in the preschool years seems to involve children's gradual working out of the categories of meaning implicit in the structure of their language on the basis of experience with language itself. One important aspect of this process has been discussed in detail elsewhere: the child's analysis of meanings that are initially understood holistically into semantic components that have organizational significance across a wide range of forms (Bowerman, 1974, 1981b, 1982; Karmiloff-Smith, 1979a). The focus in this chapter will be on a second type of semantic change: the child's abstraction across multiple relatively specific form–meaning correspondences of broader categories of meaning that correlate with regularities in formal linguistic structure.

The chapter is organized as follows. First, the major widely recognized categories of reorganization are summarized to provide a backdrop against which newer phenomena may be evaluated. The next two sections present and discuss some data. The fourth section evaluates these data with an eye toward the developmental relationship between meaning and form, and the fifth continues this theme with a look at how relational syntactic categories are learned. A brief summary concludes the chapter.

The data to be presented come primarily from my two daughters, Christy and Eva, whose language development I followed closely by taping and daily note-taking from the time of first words. I have collected numerous comparable examples of each reorganizational genre from six other children in the same age ranges, however, so we can be reasonably confident that the phenomena to be discussed are of some generality.

11.1. Some existing accounts of reorganization

The major types of widely recognized reorganizational processes include the child's analysis of unanalyzed forms, the successive driving out or replacement of one rule by another, and systematic changes over time in the way children comprehend words or sentence structures. Let us review these briefly.

Analysis of unanalyzed forms

The most familiar cases of "analysis" involve noun and verb inflectional morphology (Ervin, 1964; MacWhinney, 1978; Slobin, 1973). The child appears to start out in these domains by learning both uninflected forms (*shoe, foot; walk, break*) and inflected or irregular forms (*shoes, feet; walked, broke*) on a word-by-word basis. Although the child differentiates the forms semantically at this time (e.g., applies *shoe* to a single shoe and *shoes* to more than one shoe), she apparently does not yet recognize[1] the systematic relationship that holds between the singular and plural forms of nouns, or the present- and past-tense forms of verbs.

At a later point the child begins to "overregularize": apply the regular inflectional endings to forms that should not take them (*foots, breaked*). This is taken as strong evidence that the child has "analyzed" at least some portion of the regular inflected forms in her repertoire into two morphemes, each of which makes a semantic and phonological contribution to the whole. At this time the irregular forms that the child had used earlier fade out in favor of the overregularized forms. When the irregular forms later reassert themselves, they have a new status: They are no longer isolates operating independently from their uninflected counterparts and from regular inflected forms; rather, they are integrated into a system, as exceptions to it.

Many complex linguistic forms in addition to inflected words can initially be acquired as unanalyzed units, or *amalgams*, to use Mac-Whinney's (1978) useful term. These include compound words such as *mailman* and *blackboard* (Berko, 1958; L. Gleitman & H. Gleitman, 1970), contracted forms or phrases such as *don't, can't, it's, it's-a, that's-a, get-it*, and *good girl* (Bellugi & Klima, 1966; Brown, 1973; Nelson, 1973) and complete sentences like *Close the door* and *What's that?* (R. Clark, 1974, 1978; A. Peters, 1977). As in the case of the inflected forms, the child must break down these units and discover the elements of which they are composed, along with the rules according to which these elements are combined. When amalgams are long and relatively complex, as in the case of whole sentences, this breakdown may take place in several steps. In this case the amalgam is first treated as a fixed frame with one or two free slots through which novel words may be rotated (R. Clark, 1974; MacWhinney, in press).

A phenomenon related to the analysis of amalgams is seen in early phonological development. Several studies have noted that at the beginning of vocabulary acquisition children may pronounce certain words more accurately than they do later on. Like the loss of irregular past and plural forms, the temporary "regression" in pronunciation actually marks a step forward: The child has begun to build a phonological *system* on the basis of the existing items in her repertoire, and to assimilate words to the rules of the system rather than dealing with them as isolates (Ferguson & Farwell, 1975; Kiparsky & Menn, 1977; Moskowitz, 1973).

Rule replacement

More spottily documented than the child's analysis of unanalyzed forms has been the process by which the child comes to sort out which of several possible morphological or syntactic rules apply to which members of a group of closely related language forms. This process may be characterized by the child's successive shifting from one rule to another over time. In the realm of inflectional morphology, such shifting has been termed "inflectional imperialism" (Slobin, 1966a). Inflectional imperialism can scarcely be observed in languages with relatively simple inflectional systems, like English. It is rampant, however, in more richly inflected languages like Russian, where there are up to six allomorphs (separate forms) for each case ending, with the choice among them determined by the gender and number of the noun. The child starts out by selecting the allomorph that is least complex on various grounds (see Slobin, 1973) or, all else being equal, most frequently encountered (MacWhinney, 1978), and applying it indiscriminately to all nouns. Later he may shift to a different allomorph of the inflection, dropping the first one completely. This process may be repeated several times. Eventually, however, the child sorts out which allomorphs apply to which nouns, and mistakes subside.

A rule-replacement process similar to inflectional imperialism can also be observed in the pattern over time of children's interpretations of sentences whose syntactic structure must be construed in distinctly different ways as a function of the particular lexical items they contain, for example, *John is eager to see* versus *John is easy to see* (who is doing the seeing?) and *Mary asked Laura to go to the store* versus *Mary promised Laura to go to the store* (who will go to the store?) (C. Chomsky, 1969; Cromer, 1972). The child starts out in these cases by applying a single rule to both members of the pair, thus systematically interpreting half the sentences correctly and half incorrectly. Later he learns a second rule and may either substitute it for the first rule, now reversing his pattern of correct and incorrect interpretations, or use the two rules somewhat indiscriminately until he works out which rule should be triggered by which predicate.

Changing strategies for sentence comprehension

There has been a large number of studies documenting systematic changes over time in the way children respond to various words and sentences (e.g., Bever, 1970; E. Clark, 1975; E. Clark & Garnica, 1974; Maratsos, 1973, 1974a; Tavakolian, 1977). These differ from the "rule-replacement" studies already mentioned in that the shifts do not seem to be closely tied to the child's acquisition of legitimate rules of the adult language. Most of them, rather, appear to be interim strategies for dealing with sentences whose structures are not yet well understood (Cromer, 1976), and so they do not count as true examples of reorganization as the term is used in this chapter. At least one, however – Maratsos's (1973) documentation of a puzzling decline in children's understanding of the word *big* – seems to reflect real changes in the child's semantic system, although for reasons that are as yet unclear (but see Gathercole, 1982).

To summarize, several different kinds of reorganizational processes have been documented. Two points that are particularly fundamental to any further discussion of reorganization should be emphasized. One is that forms that to adults have a complex internal structure – that is, consist of subunits with independent combinatorial potential – can be used correctly by language learners before they are aware of this structure. This insight has been invoked primarily to explain delays in the child's learning of surface morphological structure, but recent studies show that it is also applicable to the child's acquisition of the meaning components of morphologically simple but semantically complex forms (Bowerman, 1974, 1981b, 1982; Karmiloff-Smith, 1979a). The second point – and the one with which this chapter is primarily concerned – is that forms that are initially learned independently of one another can later become integrated into a common rule system. Descriptions of this process have mostly focused on morphological learning, in which the analysis and integration of unanalyzed forms is conceptualized as a dichotomous phenomenon whereby a given form or segment of a form either is "analyzed" or is not. I will argue, however, that this view of analysis is too narrow: We need a broader conception whereby, with respect to any linguistic domain, the child may be described as uncovering successively deeper and more abstract levels of structure and regularity.

11.2. A covert semantic class: verbs prefixed with *un*-

The study of meaning in linguistics and in investigations of language acquisition has been dominated by attention to the semantic categories associated with explicit morphemes such as content words and plural -*s* or past-tense -*ed*, and to the semantic roles noun phrases play with respect to their verbs (e.g., agent, patient). But semantics play a role elsewhere in language as well: in defining what class of items may *co-occur* with given affixes or other words. Whorf (1956) pointed out that these "covert" semantic categories, or "cryptotypes," are easy to overlook partly because they are identifiable only negatively – that is, in terms of restrictions on combinations with a more salient form – and also because their meanings are often elusive and hard to pin down with a verbal label.

One cryptotype in English discussed by Whorf is the category of verbs that can be prefixed with *un-* to designate the reversal of the action specified by the base verb. (This prefix should be carefully distinguished from *un-* attached to adjectives and past participles functioning as adjectives [e.g., *unkind, unbroken*], which means roughly *not* and imposes fewer restrictions on the base form.) Whorf describes verbs that can be *un-*ed as sharing "a covering, enclosing, and surface-attaching meaning . . . Hence we say 'uncover, uncoil, undress, unfasten, unlock, unroll, untangle, untie, unwind,' but not 'unbreak, undry, unhang, unheat, unlift, unmelt, unopen, unpress, unspill' . . . we have no single word in the language which can give us a proper clue to this meaning . . . ; hence the meaning is subtle, intangible, as is typical of cryptotypic meanings" (1956, p. 71).[2]

Whorf goes on to point out that, despite the difficulty of characterizing the class of verbs that can be *un-*ed, speakers have an intuitive feel for it. If a new verb is coined, say, *flimmick*, meaning "to tie a tin can to," speakers would readily say (e.g.), "He *unflimmicked* the dog." But if *flimmick* means "to take apart," "there will be no tendency for anyone to make a form *unflimmick* meaning 'put together'; e.g., 'he *unflimmicked* the set of radio parts'" (1956, p. 71). Notice that the constraint on *un-* verbs has nothing to do with real-word possibilities for reversal. For example, "Will you *unbreak* this?" could be a request to have a broken toy fixed, "How can we *unmelt* this candy bar?" could be said on a hot day, and "The boss felt silly when he slipped on a banana peel but I *unembarrassed* him by pretending not to notice" could be reported to a fellow worker during a coffee break.[3]

How children learn cryptotypes has received almost no attention. In virtually all discussions of the acquisition of inflectional and derivational morphology the emphasis has been on the child's understanding of the affix itself – its meaning and the fact that it has a combinatorial potential independent of the words in connection with which it has been encountered.[4] This exclusive interest in the affix and not what it attaches to is reflected in the format of typical "elicitation" studies (starting with Berko, 1958). In these experiments the child's only task is to supply the affix for a real word or a nonsense word whose meaning, specified by the experimenter, already fits the cryptotype. If she can do this consistently, she is credited with full competence in the use of the form. Investigations of spontaneous speech can extend the picture we get from experimental studies by showing what words the child herself thinks are candidates for affixation. Analyses in some cases reveal an extended learning process that continues long after the child has "analyzed" affixed items into two independent morphemes.

The acquisition by Christy and Eva of the process of deriving novel verbs prefixed with *un-* is instructive. A child learning to use *un-* appropriately is faced with five basic problems: (1) She must identify *un-* as a separate morpheme with a combinatorial potential independent of the particular verbs to which she has heard it attached; (2) she must figure out the basic meaning of *un-* – that it is "reversative" (that it can "undo the result of the verbal action," or "cause the object of the verb to be no longer *-ed*" [Marchand, 1969, p. 205]); (3) she must learn how to order *un-* with respect to the base form (learning to order affixes apparently takes place rapidly and with few mistakes; see Slobin, 1973, p. 197); (4) she must learn the syntactic category of the base forms to which *un-* may be affixed; and (5) she must learn that *un-* cannot be attached to simply any member of this syntactic category to convey a reversative meaning, but is, rather, restricted to the covert semantic class of verbs with a "covering, enclosing, and surface-attaching meaning."

The first *un-* verbs to appear in the records of Christy's and Eva's speech were often-modeled examples like *untangle, unfasten, unbuckle,* and *uncover.* At this stage, the words were generally used in semantically appropriate contexts, although occasionally the *un-* form occurred where the unmarked form was required and vice versa. There was no evidence that *un-* was recognized as an independent morpheme at this stage; words like *unbuckle* were unanalyzed monomorphemic units.

At the next stage (starting at age 3;9 [years; months] for Christy and 3;2 for Eva), *un-* began to generalize to novel verbs, which showed clearly that the original words had been analyzed into their morphemic components. Some examples of novel usages are shown in Table 11.1.

In Christy's case, the reversative meaning of *un-* was learned a good year before the covert semantic class to whose members *un-* can be attached. This is shown by her relatively frequent prefixation of *un-* to verbs that fall outside the covert category of covering/enclosing/surface-attaching meaning (see examples [1]–[3] in Table 11.1). Example (2) (*unstraight,* meaning "bend") is a particularly clear violation, because the meaning of *straighten* is exactly opposite to what is required for prefixation with *un-*.

Christy's eventual recognition of the semantic category associated with *un-* was signaled in two ways. First, most novel verbs prefixed with *un-* were now limited to verbs fitting the category (as in examples [4], [5], [6], and [9]). There were no longer any flagrant violations of the category like example (2), although very occasionally there were still instances of

Table 11.1. *Novel verbs prefixed with* un-

Christy

(1) 3;9:   *This is pooey that's coming out of here.* [in tub, showing cup with water spouting out of the holes]
    *And that's how to make it **uncome**.* [blocking holes with hand]

(2) 4;5:   [C has asked M why pliers are on table]
    M: I've been using them for straightening the wire.
    *C: And **unstraighting** it?* [= bending]

(3) 4;7:   *C: I hate you! And I'll never **unhate** you or nothing!*
    M: You'll never unhate me?
    C: I'll never like you.

(4) 5;1:   [M working on strap of C's backpack]
    M: Seems like one of these has been shortened, somehow.
    *C: Then **unshorten** it.* [= lengthen]

(5) 5;1:   *He tippitoed to the graveyard and **unburied** her.* [telling ghost story]

(6) 5;1:   *I **unbended** this with* [= by] *stepping on it.* [= straightened; after stepping on tiny plastic three-dimensional triangular roadsign, squashing the angles out of it]

(7) 6;0:   *Wait until that **unfuzzes**.* [watching freshly-poured, foamy Coke]

(8) 6;11:   *How do you make it sprinkle?* [C trying to figure out how kitchen faucet works. [after getting it to sprinkle]
    *How do you make it **unsprinkle**?*

(9) 7;11:   *I'm gonna **unhang** it.* [taking stocking down from fireplace]

(10) 4;9:   *You can take it **unapart** and put it back together.* [C manipulating a take-apart toy. Here un- has migrated to the wrong part of speech.]

(11) 4;11:   *Will you **unopen** this?* [wants D to take lid off styrofoam cooler]

(12) 5;6:   *. . . **unpatting** it down.* [as C pats ball of ground meat into hamburger patty]

Eva

(13) 3;2:   [M has taken C's clothes off but done nothing else with her]
    *E: Why did you **unclothes** her?*
    M: Why did I what?
    E: [Repeats]
    M: Why did I what?
    E: Um . . . why did you take her clothes off?

(14) 3;2:   *I can't **untight** –.* [= loosen; E struggling with tight overall strap]

(15) 3;10:   *M: I have to capture you.* [grabbing E in game]
    *E: **Uncapture** me!* [trying to pull loose]

(16) 3;11:   [C coming to M with clip earring hanging from ear]
    *E: How do you **unsqueeze** it?*
    M: What?
    *E: How do you **unget** it . . . undone?*

(17) 4;7   [Holding up chain of glued paper strips]
    *E: I know how you take these apart. **Unsplit** them and put 'em on.*
    M: How do you unsplit them?
    E: Like this [pulling a link apart]

(18) 4;7:   *Will you **unpeel** the banana?* [giving banana to M]

Table 11.1 (*cont.*)

(19) 4;11:	[Showing M how to get playdough out of a mold] E: *. . . and then **unpress** it out.* M: *How do you unpress it out?* E: *You just take it out.*
(20) 4;7:	[Showing M how to work clasp on coin purse] *You slip it across . . . and you **unslip** it like this.* [As E says *slip* she moves the two metal parts past each other so purse closes; as she says *unslip* she opens it]

Note: Notational conventions: C = Christy, E = Eva, M = Mother, D = Daddy.
Ages are given in years;months. Ellipsis dots at the beginning of an utterance
indicate that the first part of the sentence is not included; within an utterance,
they indicate a pause.

un- attached to "neutral" verbs (those lacking either the covering/en-
closing/surface-attaching meaning or its opposite), as in (7) and (8).

Second and even more revealing was that *un-* now began to be used
in a new way: It was occasionally prefixed redundantly to verbs that
already encode actions that reverse acts of covering, enclosing, or surface
attaching, as in (10)–(12). These uses are quite analogous to redundant
past-tense and plural marking (e.g., *camed, jumpeded, feets, footses,
feetses*) and double negatives (*I didn't have no peas*). They show clearly
that the child associates the reversal encoded by *un-* with the particular
subset of reversative acts that involve the uncovering or the separation
or spreading out of parts. Interestingly, such forms also occur occasionally in careless adult speech, for example, *I got them unseparated*, meaning "untangled," said as the speaker worked on a pile of yarn pieces. A
few such forms are in fact by now acceptable or almost acceptable variants
of the unprefixed base: Compare, for example, *loosen* and *unloosen*.

Eva's development differed from Christy's in that she acquired a feel
for the covert semantic category associated with *un-* almost simultaneously with learning its reversative sense. Most of her coinages respected
the cryptotype (e.g., [13]–[15] and the first sentence of [16] in Table 11.1);
she produced no flagrant violations like Christy's *unstraighting*; and, most
important, she began redundant marking with *un-* quite early, as in the
final sentence of (16) and in (17)–(20). Eva's recognition that *un-* designates not only reversal of action but, more specifically, reversal of a
covering/enclosing/surface-attaching action was demonstrated particularly clearly in (20), where she had a completely free choice about whether
un- would be attached to *slip* in connection with a closing action or with
an opening action, and chose the latter.

To summarize, both children initially acquired a number of verbs prefixed with *un-* and used them correctly with no apparent awareness of

their internal structure. Subsequently they analyzed (at least some of) these words into their surface components and figured out the semantic force of *un-*, independent of the particular conceptual packages in which it had been previously encountered. This knowledge is enough to serve as the basis for the generation of new *un-* verbs with a reversative sense. Typical accounts of the "analysis of unanalyzed forms" stop here. However, in order to account for children's eventual avoidance of words like *unhate, uncome,* and *unsprinkle* and the flowering of redundant forms like *unopen, unpeel,* and *untake off,* we must postulate an additional step in their analysis, whereby they recognize that the verbs that are *un*-ed in the speech around them have a subtle semantic characteristic in common. This step apparently can be taken either at the time when *un-* itself is segmented and its meaning worked out, as in Eva's case, or at a later time, as in Christy's. In this latter case, the child's analysis of everyday verbs prefixed with *un-*, like *untie*, takes place in two steps, with an intervening period in which the internal structure of the verbs is only partly understood.

11.3. Partial productivity: early limitations on expressing cause-and-effect relations

In the foregoing section it was argued that even after the child has analyzed amalgams of a given type into separate components, further semantic analysis may be needed to limit the freedom with which the components are combined. In this section, we look at the converse of this process: a situation in which the child has segmented all the morphemes in strings of a certain type and knows something about combining and recombining them, but lacks awareness of the full freedom and flexibility of their combinatorial potential because she has not yet grasped that there is a broad semantic principle involved. In short, the form must be considered "productive" according to usual criteria for establishing productivity, but this productivity turns out to be restricted, relative to what it will later become.

The construction pattern in question is represented by common, everyday sentences like *Daddy chopped the tree down/in half, Mary wiped the table clean/dry, Suzy ate her cereal all gone, Harry pulled his socks up,* and *George pushed/kicked the door closed/open.* These sentences express complex causal events in which a certain action such as chopping on a tree, wiping a table, or pulling on socks is presented as causing or bringing about another event in which an entity (usually but not always the object acted upon) undergoes a change of location (falling down, coming up, etc.) or a change of state (becoming divided in half, clean, closed, etc.).

Certain combinations of causing action and resulting event are so common that many linguists have advocated entering them into the lexicon of a grammar as two-part verbs (*pull up, chop down,* etc.; see, e.g., N. Chomsky, 1962). However, this treatment fails to capture the potential this sentence pattern offers for novel juxtapositions of causing action and resulting event, such as *Don't scream/stamp the house down* (by screaming/stamping cause the house to fall down) or *The locusts ate the prairie brown and bare* (by eating, caused the prairie to become brown and bare [from a Laura Ingalls Wilder book]).

Other linguists, impressed by the flexibility of this pattern, have advocated building productivity into a grammatical description by deriving such sentences from two independent underlying propositions, joined causally: for example, [Harry pulled on his socks] CAUSE [his socks came (went, moved) up] (Fillmore, 1971; Talmy, 1972, 1976b). Such an account handles productivity admirably, but it must be supplemented by various constraints to block sentences that fluent speakers find bizarre (Fillmore, 1971; Green, 1972; McCawley, 1971). For example, past participles and certain adjectives can never serve to specify stative effects (compare, for example, *Mommy combed Mary's hair smooth/*untangled; I cooked the roast to a turn/*burnt; John hammered the metal flat/into a circle/*round/ *circular*). Furthermore, certain verbs, including all those prefixed with *un-*, cannot appear in the role of causing action (or, put differently, cannot be used with the derived meaning "by performing the action usually associated with this verb, cause NP to undergo change") (compare, for instance, *He tied it on* with **He untied it off* and *He pushed/pulled/blew the fence over* with **He leaned the fence over* [caused the fence to fall over by pushing/pulling/blowing/leaning on it]). Still other constraints would be needed to block combinations like *Susan wiped the table dirty* (with a stained rag, for example); neither the verb nor the effect word are in principle barred from participating in such a construction, but their juxtaposition sounds strange to adult ears for reasons that are not entirely clear.

The course of acquisition of these sentences may be described as follows (see Bowerman, 1977, for fuller discussion). Sentences containing common combinations of verb plus effect (e.g., *push* [or *pull*] plus *in* [or *out, up, down, over*]; *eat* plus *all gone*) begin to occur in good number when a child is as young as 2 years. It is conceivable that the child learns each combination on an example-by-example basis; it is more likely, however, that some generalization takes place such that the child can guess, even in the absence of confirming input, that if *push* can take *down/ off/in* and so on and *pull* can take *down* and *off, pull* can probably also take *in*.

For about a year and a half, probably considerably longer for some children, there is no visible change with respect to constructions of this type. Upon casual observation, the child's grasp of the forms seems fully

Table 11.2. *Errors involving the expression of cause and effect*

(1) C	(3;6):	*And the monster would **eat** you **in pieces**.* [telling a story]
(2) C	(3;8):	*I **pulled** it **unstapled**.* [after pulling stapled book apart]
(3) C	(3;10):	***Untie** it **off**.* [wants M to untie piece of yarn and take it off tricycle handle]
(4) C	(4;0):	*I'm **patting** her **wet**.* [patting E's arm after dipping her own hand into glass of water]
(5) C	(6;2):	*It's hard not to knock them down 'cause whenever I breathe I **breathe** them **down**.* [having trouble setting up a paper village]
(6) E	(3;11):	[As M and E go toward Christmas tree with candy canes on it] M: *I'm going to eat a candy cane. Do you want one?* E: *I'm going to **choose** it **off**.*
(7) E	(3;9):	*A gorilla captured my fingers. I'll **capture** his whole head **off**. His hands too.* [playing with rubber band around fingers]
(8) Mindy	(5;10):	*Feels like you're **combing** me **baldheaded**.* [as M combs her hair]
(9) Mindy	(5;6):	*Are you **washing** me **blind**?* [as M wipes corners of her eyes]
(10) Andrea	(4;3):	*When you get to her, you **catch** her **off**.* [She is on a park merry-go-round with doll next to her; wants a friend standing nearby to remove doll when doll comes around to her.]
(11) Rachel	(4;9):	*I'll **jump** that **down**.* [about to jump on bathmat M has just put on top of water in tub]

adultlike. Then, however – rather suddenly in the case of Christy and Eva, the only children for whom detailed longitudinal data are available – there is a flowering of truly novel combinations of causing verb and resulting event. Some of these sound quaint but acceptable (*Don't hug me off my chair*), but others violate the various constraints that operate to limit productivity in adult speech. Some examples are shown in Table 11.2.

These errors, analogous to overregularizations like *breaked* and *foots*, show clearly that the child has discovered an overarching pattern that unites a variety of superficially diverse sentences. To discover such a pattern the child must disregard the specific semantic contributions of the individual lexical items and see what they have in common – that at an abstract level *pull, chop, eat,* and *wipe* (for example) all specify actions that can *cause an entity to undergo a change*, and that *in, out, down, all gone, in half,* and *clean* all specify locative or attributive states into which an entity can enter. Once these abstractions have been made and linked to a certain syntactic pattern (N_1-V-N_2-locative or stative term), the child is in a position to create an infinite number of novel combinations. Before this point, however, productivity is limited to certain previously heard combinations of cause and effect or at best to a collection of independent patterns such as, possibly, *"push/pull/pound . . . + in/out/up/down . . . ," "cut/tear/rip/chop . . . + off/apart/in half . . . ,"* and so on. "Analysis" has taken place, but adultlike ability awaits the child's integration of these patterns into a shared, more abstract system.

11.4. Do meanings always precede forms?

Let us pause briefly here to take stock of the arguments made in the preceding two sections, and to begin to consider the implications of reorganizational errors for the issue of how form and meaning are interrelated in the course of language development.

Forms as a mapping for preestablished meanings

Over the last decade, the emphasis on the role of meaning in language development has grown steadily stronger. From an earlier era in which the child's categorization of reality was held to be largely molded through the semantic structure of the language he was acquiring, we have made a complete about-face to the position that cognitive development precedes, paces, guides, and enables language acquisition.

There is ample evidence for the importance of cognition in language development (see Bowerman, 1976, 1978a; and Johnston, in press, for reviews), and it is not my intention to dispute the "cognition-first" position on general grounds. However, in this and the next section I want to examine the viability of one tenet of this position, first explicitly set out by Slobin (1973) and since adopted by many other investigators: that language, far from instructing the child on how to categorize the objects and events of his world, serves merely to map the meanings that the child has already worked out on a nonlinguistic basis.

This hypothesis has served a valuable function in promoting examination of the relative difficulty for children of various formal linguistic devices for expressing meaning (Slobin, 1973, 1977; Chapter 5). However, it is becoming clearer that it is much too strong. In particular, it errs in its assumption that semantics – that is, meaning in language – is isomorphic with the nonlinguistic way of viewing the world. Among other things, critics have questioned whether children categorize the world on a nonlinguistic basis into just those kinds of concepts needed by language (evidence for language-relevant categorization of concrete objects is strong [Rosch, 1976], but what about actions, attributes, relationships, etc?), and they have pointed to cross-linguistic variation and selectivity among languages in the particular concepts that are obligatorily expressed and in the way even such universally important notions as causation and motion get packaged (Bloom, 1973; Bowerman, 1976, 1980, 1981a,b,c; Dore, 1979; Gentner, in press; Schlesinger, 1977a; Slobin, "The role of language in language acquisition," 1979 manuscript).

Building meanings to fit forms

If meaning in language is not a direct map of thought, then a theory of language acquisition must be capable of explaining how the child formulates categories of meanings to fit the requirements of the particular language she is learning. Clearly, nonlinguistic cognitive abilities feed into this process, but we are still far from understanding how.

The two reorganizational phenomena that have thus far been discussed do not answer this question, but they do strongly implicate the importance of the child's *experience with language itself* in arriving at the meanings required. Consider the category of actions involving covering/enclosing/surface attachment. At least some children develop considerable facility with *un-* prefixation before they evidence awareness that *un-* is restricted to verbs of this category. It is conceivable, of course, that they "have" the category on a nonlinguistic basis all along but simply do not discover that it is relevant to *un-* until relatively late. Why *would* they have this category, however – what would be its nonlinguistic utility? Schlesinger (1977b) has argued that "language learning depends [in part] on a categorization of objects and events which is needed solely for the purpose of speaking and understanding speech" (p. 155). The class of covering/enclosing/surface-attaching actions would appear to be an excellent candidate for such a category.

Identifying the origin of the category "relationship between a causing action and a resulting change of state or location" is more problematic. Clearly humans (and at least the other higher primates) are disposed toward interpreting the world in terms of causal relationships; we would not want to attribute this disposition itself to language. But there may be an important difference between having the nonlinguistic ability to interpret causal events and having the kind of relational category that, as I have posited, underlies errors like *I pulled it unstapled*. In particular, the errors require a detailed mental representation in which a causal sequence is "decomposed" into an actor, an action, an entity that undergoes change, and the nature of the change. Such a finely articulated representation is not required simply for thinking about or interpreting causal events, however (see Bowerman, 1974, 1977, for discussion). Regardless of whether experience with language encourages this representation or it emerges quite autonomously, the relative lateness of the errors indicates that it does not underlie the early sentences with conventional cause-and-effect combinations like *pull up*. Rather, the abstract relational meaning is fitted to the construction pattern only later.

With the possibility in mind that meanings may be constructed to fit forms just as forms may be matched to preestablished meanings, let us now look at a specific issue over which there has been considerable debate: the role of meaning in children's acquisition of relational syntactic categories (or syntactic relations, for short) like "subject of the sentence," "predicate of the sentence," and "direct object of the verb."

11.5. Meaning and the mastery of syntactic relations

According to some researchers, children have a grasp of syntactic relations from the very beginning of word combination or even before (Bloom, 1970; Bloom, Lightbown & Hood, 1975; McNeill, 1966b). Other researchers have argued, however, that evidence for this understanding is lacking, and have proposed instead that children's earliest rules for word combination specify where to position words functioning in various semantic roles such as "agent," "action," and "object acted upon" (Bowerman, 1973b; Braine, 1976; Schlesinger, 1971), or in a combination of semantic and pragmatic roles such as "agent/topic" (Bates & MacWhinney, Chapter 6). A grasp of abstract, meaning-free syntactic relations may eventually be achieved when the child comes to recognize that noun phrases performing a variety of semantic roles may all be treated equivalently with respect to position and transformational possibilities (Bowerman, 1973b). Alternatively, relational semantic categories might serve as core or prototypical meanings to which the properties of various syntactic relations are initially attached. Early exemplars of the syntactic relations in the child's speech would thus be limited to expressions of those core meanings; as the child progressed, however, he would gradually extend the boundaries of the meaning categories to encompass meanings increasingly distant from the core (Bates & MacWhinney, Chapter 6; deVilliers, 1980; Schlesinger, 1977a; Slobin, "The role of language in language acquisition," 1979 manuscript).

There is some evidence that children's early rules for word combination may indeed be based on semantic categories (see, e.g., Braine, 1976), but it is not as strong as would be desirable. In particular, I became somewhat discouraged about the adequacy of an account whereby syntactic learning is mediated by semantic categories after analyzing data collected from Christy and Eva during the early period of word combination (Bowerman, 1976). Although there was a small amount of evidence for rules based on semantic categories like "agent" in Christy's corpus, there was virtually none in Eva's. Rather uncooperatively for the semantic hypothesis I was testing, Eva appeared to make a swift transition

> from an approach based on learning sequentially how to make constructions with particular lexical items to a much more mature system in which words of virtually all semantic subtypes were dealt

with fluently . . . There is no evidence that she achieved this transition with the aid of relational concepts at a level of abstraction between the semantics of particular words and syntactic notions that are independent of any particular semantic content, such as "subject" and "direct object." [P. 58]

Maratsos (1979; Maratsos & Chalkley, 1980), reviewing this and other evidence, concludes that children are capable of arriving at adultlike knowledge of syntactic constructs (including both syntactic relations and part-of-speech categories like "verb" and "noun") without leaning on semantic categories like "agent" and "action." He proposes that this learning takes place through the amassing of detailed information about the syntactic handling of particular lexical items, followed by discovery of how distributional privileges transfer among them. Maratsos does not deny that some children may rely to some extent on semantic categories in the acquisition of syntactic relations and other grammatical forms. His point, however, is that this reliance is less common than many researchers have thought and that the child possesses efficient routes to adult knowledge that do not depend on semantics (see also Karmiloff-Smith, 1979a, for some relevant evidence).

If certain children do not start out basing rules for word combination on semantic categories and are capable of achieving adult fluency without them, does this mean that such categories play no role in their language development? Not necessarily. In keeping with arguments that I advanced in the last section, I will present evidence that the semantic correlates of at least certain configurations of syntactic roles may indeed come to be appreciated by children, but only *after* they have learned a great deal about those syntactic roles on a word-by-word basis. These semantic correlates, once perceived, serve to organize and transform what the child already "knows" on a piecemeal basis into an integrated system.

Coordinating semantic and syntactic roles

Every verb or other predicate of English has one or more noun arguments associated with it. Across verbs, these noun arguments fall into groups that play similar semantic roles ("cases") with respect to their verbs, such as "agent," "location," "patient" (or "object"), and so on (Fillmore, 1968a, 1977; Jackendoff, 1972; Talmy, 1972, 1976b). The cases associated with verbs can be used to classify verbs. At a relatively coarse level, verbs that take the same set of cases can be seen as semantically similar. Finer categorizations can be achieved by taking into account not only which cases are linked to each verb but also whether these cases are optional or obligatory in sentences with that verb and what *syntactic roles* (subject, direct object, etc.) are assigned to them (Fillmore, 1968a).

The assignment of syntactic roles to noun phrases instantiating the semantic roles associated with certain verbs is completely fixed. For example, with *eat*, the one who eats, or agent, must be subject, and that which is eaten, or patient, if specified, must be direct object (thus, *Mary eats pudding*, not *Pudding eats Mary*). For other verbs there is some flexibility. With *blame*, for instance, either the one who is blamed or that for which he is blamed can be direct object: *We blamed John for the accident* versus *We blamed the accident on John*. The resulting meanings are very slightly different (Fillmore, 1968a, p. 48).

The syntax of Figure and Ground in adult English. A particularly large and interesting set of "syntactically flexible" verbs in English includes *load, hit, spray, smear, drain, empty,* and many more. These verbs have three associated noun arguments: an Agent (A), a "moving object" termed Figure (F) by Talmy (Fillmore's [1977] "patient" and Jackendoff's [1972] "Theme"), and an object with respect to which the Figure moves, called Ground (G) by Talmy (Fillmore's and Jackendoff's "Source" or "Goal," depending on the direction of motion).[5]

In sentences with these verbs the Agent is optional. For ease of exposition, however, we will restrict our attention to cases in which A is present, where it obligatorily plays the syntactic role of sentence subject. What shall be direct object? This privilege can go to *either* Figure or Ground. Whichever is *not* chosen becomes oblique object (object of a preposition); in many cases it can be optionally omitted:

F as direct object	G as direct object
(1a) John hit/bumped the stick (F) against the fence (G)	(1b) John hit/bumped the fence (G) (with the stick [F])
(2a) The farmer loaded hay (F) (into the wagon [G])	(2b) The farmer loaded the wagon (G) (with hay [F])
(3a) The doctor drained blood (F) from the patient's veins (G)	(3b) The doctor drained the patient's veins (G) (of [their] blood [F])

As in the case of *blame*, the two treatments are not completely interchangeable; rather, they are associated with slightly different pragmatic and semantic properties. The pragmatic property is that the noun argument in the direct object slot is perceived as being more "in focus" or "in perspective" than the one in the oblique object slot (Fillmore, 1977). Put the other way around, speakers favor the direct object slot for whichever noun argument they want to focus on for reasons of preceding discourse, nonlinguistic salience, and so on. The semantic property is that when G is direct object, it receives a "holistic" reading (S. Anderson, 1971): For example, in (2b), the wagon is perceived as being completely loaded, and in (3b) the veins are taken to be completely drained. If F is direct object, however, no such inference can be made. When G is an animate being or a body part, it is most typically made direct object, perhaps because it is usually perceived as more salient and important than F (Fillmore, 1977) or perhaps because G is then seen as holistically involved.

There are a number of English verbs that are semantically similar to *hit, load*, and the like in that they also have the semantic roles A, F, and G associated with them. However, they lack the syntactic flexibility of the earlier group. For some, which we will term Pattern F verbs, F must be direct object, whereas for others, which we will term Pattern G, G must be direct object:

F as direct object	*G as direct object*
Pattern F	
(4a) John poured/spilled/put water (F) (into a cup/onto the floor[G])	*(4b) John poured/spilled/put the cup/the floor (G) (with water [F])
(5a) Jim stole a watch (F) (from Sam [G])	*(5b) Jim stole Sam (G) (of a watch [F])
Pattern G	
*(6a) Sally touched/felt her hand (F) to the baby (G)	(6b) Sally touched/felt the baby (G) (with her hand [F])
*(7a) Bob filled water (F) into a cup (G)	(7b) Bob filled a cup (G) (with water [F])
*(8a) Jim robbed a watch (F) from Sam (G)	(8b) Jim robbed Sam (G) (of a watch [F])
*(9a) George covered a blanket (F) over the bed (G)	(9b) George covered the bed (G) (with a blanket [F])

Acquiring verbs with Agent, Figure, and Ground

Verbs with the associated semantic roles Agent, Figure, and Ground are among the most common in English, and children start to acquire them as early as the one-word stage. What kinds of order rules do they follow when they begin to combine words with them? The Agent is treated as subject and precedes the verb; this is apparently not problematical. But what about F and G? If children were following a semantically based rule such as "Put the word specifying *the object affected by the action* after the action word," they would run into confusion, because there are really *two* "objects affected" for these verbs – both F, the moving object, *and* G, the object that the moving object leaves or, especially, contacts. And if they used order rules based on narrower semantic categories like "Put the word specifying the moving object, or Figure, after the action word," or "Put the word specifying the reference point object, or Ground, after the action word," they would consistently perform correctly with either Pattern F or Pattern G verbs, and incorrectly with verbs of the opposing pattern.

In fact, however, children show neither confusion nor consistent patterns of correctness and error. Rather, they are strikingly accurate with verbs of all types, correctly choosing as direct object whatever the adult would choose. For example:

> Pattern F: *I put it (F) somewhere (G), I put this (F) mine bed (G) with me* (= I put this into my bed . . .), *pour more milk (F)* (Christy, age 2 or earlier); *I spill water (F), Christy pour water (F) on me (G)* (Eva, age 2 or earlier)

> Pattern G: *Don't touch my B.M. (G)* (*hand* is the implicit F) (Christy, 2;0); *Touch my pussy cat (G), I want touch ceiling (G), cover me (G) up so me go night-night with my piglet* (*blanket* is the implicit F) (Eva, age 2 or earlier)

Syntactically flexible verbs ("Flexible Pattern") are initially represented primarily by *hit* and *bump* with an animate or body-part G; in these cases children make G direct object, as is conventional: *I hit self* (Christy, 2;0); *Don't hit my fanny* (Eva, 2;0).

This initial correctness is strong evidence that the child's choice of direct object for these verbs is *not* at first guided by semantic categories such as those previously proposed. Instead, it indicates that children learn piecemeal for each verb which noun argument associated with it should appear as its direct object. The story might end here – adultlike competence with the syntax of these verbs has apparently already been reached by, let us say, about age 2½. But later developments show us that acquisition is in fact not yet complete. One to 1½ years after Christy and Eva seemed to have mastered these verbs, they began to make striking errors with them. Some representative examples are shown in Table 11.3; comparable errors in my data from other children were produced in the age range 4;3 to 7;2.

By far the most frequent kind of error involves verbs of Pattern G. These require G as direct object, but the child now accords F that privilege, either making G the oblique object (examples [1]–[6] in Table 11.3) or omitting it entirely (examples [7]–[9]). Somewhat less frequently the child "compromises": She omits F but declines to make G the direct object as is required; instead, she "demotes" G to oblique object position (examples [10]–[11]).

Errors of the reverse type with Pattern F verbs are less frequent and do not flourish until somewhat later. These involve making G the direct object and F, if mentioned, the oblique object (examples [12]–[14]).

Table 11.3. *Errors in assigning syntactic role to noun phrases functioning as Figure and Ground*

Pattern G
A. Syntactic roles of F and G reversed:
  (1) E (3;0): *My other hand's not yukky. See? 'Cause I'm going to **touch** it (F) on your pants (G).* [= touch your pants with it]
  (2) C (4;3): [Shows error in comprehension]
      M: *Simon says, "Touch your toes"* (G).
      C: *To what?* [interprets *toes* as F, is looking now for G]
      [A moment later]
      M: *Simon says, "Touch your knees."*
      C: *To what?*
  (3) C (6;10): ***Feel** your hand (F) to that (G).* [= feel that with your hand; wants M to put her hand over one end of hose, then blows through the other end]
  (4) E (5;0): *Can I **fill** some salt (F) into the bear (G)?* [= fill the bear (a bear-shaped salt shaker) with some salt]
  (5) E (4;5): *I'm going to **cover** a screen (F) over me (G).* [= cover myself with a screen]
  (6) C (4;9): *She's gonna **pinch** it (F) on my foot (G).* [= pinch my foot (G) with it (F); protesting as E approaches with a toy. Cf. (11).]

B. G omitted:
  (7) E (4;1): *I didn't **fill** water (F) up to drink it; I **filled** it (F) up for the flowers to drink it.* [= filled the watering can (G) up (with water[F])]
  (8) E (4;11): *And I'll give you these eggs (F) you can **fill** up.* [giving M beads to put into cloth chicken-shaped container (G)]
  (9) E (5;3): *Terri said if this* [= rhinestone on a shirt] *were a diamond then people would be trying to **rob** the shirt (F).* [= trying to rob me (G) (of the shirt)]

C. G "demoted" to oblique object:
  (10) C (3;11): *Eva is just **touching** gently on the plant (G).* [= touching the plant]
  (11) C (4;2): ***Pinch** on the balloon (G).* [= pinch the balloon; giving instructions to M]

Pattern F
  (12) E (2;11): E: *Pour, pour, pour. Mommy, I **poured** you (G).* [waving empty container near M]
      M: *You poured me (G)?*
      E: *Yeah, with water (F).* [= poured water on you]
  (13) E (4;11): [M asks at breakfast if E is going to finish her toast]
      *I don't want it because I **spilled** it (G) of orange juice (F).* [= spilled orange juice on it]
  (14) C (6;5): [Telling of TV episode]
      C: *Once the Partridge Family (G) got **stolen**.*
      M [puzzled]: *The whole family?* [has interpreted Partridge Family as (F), the stolen item, as verb requires]
      C: *No, all their stuff (F).* [Cf. reverse error in (9).]

Table 11.3. (*cont.*)

Flexible pattern with animate or body part G
(15) C (3;4): *I **bumped** this* [= a toy] (F) *to me* (G). [= I bumped myself with this.]
(16) C (3;8): *I **hitted** this* [= a toy] (F) *into my neck* (G). [= I hit my neck with this.]

Unlike errors with Pattern F and G verbs, those with Flexible Pattern verbs like *hit* and *bump* are not ungrammatical, strictly speaking (although the preposition chosen may be incorrect), because these verbs "allow" either treatment. However, after months of assigning the role of direct object to animate beings or body-part Gs, as is conventional, children now occasionally reallocate that role to F (examples [15]–[16]).

Understanding the errors

What causes the errors just outlined? Several possibilities should be considered.

Local confusion between semantically related verbs? A conservative hypothesis would attribute the errors to confusion at the moment of speech between two semantically similar verbs; for example, the child intends to say *rob* and sets up her syntax accordingly, but then accidentally selects *steal*, a verb with an almost identical meaning but opposite syntactic requirements. This explanation must be rejected, however, because it predicts a much narrower range of errors than is actually found: It accounts well for errors with *rob* and *steal* and possibly *fill* and *pour*, but has nothing to say about errors of an identical type involving verbs that lack a semantic partner with opposite syntax, such as *touch, feel,* or *pinch.* A further problem with this hypothesis is that it is not clear how it can account for errors in *comprehension* as opposed to production, for example, (2) in Table 11.3.

A syntactic generalization? A broader hypothesis is needed, then. Most plausible is that the child comes to generalize the syntactic treatment appropriate for verbs of one type to verbs of another type. But along what lines does this generalization take place? Specifically, will it be necessary to invoke semantics in our explanation, or can we manage with an interpretation that does not take meaning into account?

Let us hypothesize that the errors do not involve meaning but stem instead from a relatively superficial syntactic analysis whereby the child notices that strings of the following syntactic descriptions are roughly interchangeable in meaning:

(10a) $\text{NP}_1\text{-VP-NP}_2\text{-}\begin{Bmatrix} against \\ on \\ into, \text{etc.} \end{Bmatrix}\text{-NP}_3$ ↔   (10b) $\text{NP}_1\text{-V-NP}_3\text{-}with\text{-NP}_2$

John hit a stick against the fence.

John hit the fence with a stick.

(11a) $\text{NP}_1\text{-V-NP}_2\text{-}\begin{Bmatrix} from \\ out\,of \end{Bmatrix}\text{-NP}_3$ ↔   (11b) $\text{NP}_1\text{-V-NP}_3\text{-}of\text{-NP}_2$

Jim drained water from the barrel.

Jim drained the barrel of water.

She might then assume that other strings fitting the (10a) description could be converted into (10b) and vice versa, and that those fitting the (11a) description could be converted into (11b) and vice versa. This analysis would indeed lead the child to produce errors like *Feel your hand to that* ([10b] is transformed into [10a]) and *I poured you with water* ([10a] is transformed into [10b]). But it would also lead to many types of errors that do not occur in my data, and that I have never seen reported, such as:

(10a₁) I read a book to Mary   → *(10b₁) *I read Mary with a book*

*(10a₂) *I ate a spoon* $\begin{Bmatrix} against \\ on \\ into \end{Bmatrix}$ *my pudding*   ←(10b₂) I ate my pudding with a spoon

*(10a₃) *I opened my key against (etc.) the door*   ←(10b₃) I opened the door with my key

(11a₁) He read a poem $\begin{Bmatrix} from \\ out\,of \end{Bmatrix}$ the book   → *(11b₁) *He read the book of a poem*

(11a₂) Mother $\begin{Bmatrix} saw \\ called \end{Bmatrix}$ Johnny from the window   → *(11b₂) *Mother* $\begin{Bmatrix} saw \\ called \end{Bmatrix}$ *the window of Johnny*

The absence of these errors means that the child recognizes that the potential for converting (10a) into (10b) and (11a) into (11b), and vice versa, is not general across all sentences meeting these syntactic descriptions. It is, rather, restricted to just those sentences containing verbs whose noun arguments function semantically as Agent, Figure, and Ground. The child's sensitivity to this restriction, then, indicates that she has grasped these relational meanings along with the syntactic flexibility with which they are linked. The reason that errors like *I ate my spoon against the pudding* and *I read Mary with a book* do not occur, according to this interpretation, is that the child does not construe the postverb noun arguments of *eat* and *read* in terms of the semantic functions Figure and Ground, and so does not perceive them as candidates for rearrangement.

Notice that the child cannot arrive at this semantic categorization of verbs on a nonlinguistic basis, purely by observing whether there are "moving objects" and "reference-point objects" in the real-world events specified by the verbs. In "filling" the liquid does move relative to the container, and in "covering" the draping object does move relative to a surface; however, in "eating" the spoon (or other implement) also moves relative to the food source, and in "opening a door" the key moves relative to the door. The meaning distinction that unites *fill* and *cover* (for example) and distinguishes them from *eat* and *open* is therefore more abstract. Like the category "verbs of covering/enclosing/surface attachment," the category of verbs whose noun arguments play the roles of "Figure" and "Ground" appears to be defined not by the nature of the world but by the semantic structure of English. It is consistent with this interpretation that children do not begin to generalize the treatment appropriate to Flexible Pattern verbs to Pattern F and Pattern G verbs until long after verbs of all three kinds are in their vocabularies. That is, to the extent that particular semantic groupings are part of the structure of language and not given directly by the organization of the world or by the child's inherent cognitive biases, we would expect the acquisition of these groupings to require experience with the structural details of the language being learned.

Semantic interpretation: overregularization or manipulation of focus? I have argued that accounting for errors such as those shown in Table 11.3 requires reference to the semantic roles played by the verbs' noun arguments. Still to be discussed, however, is *why* the errors occur, given that the child has already learned the conventional syntactic handling of each verb. There are at least two possibilities: overregularization and attempts to manipulate pragmatic focus.

1. *Overregularization.* Overregularization involves "redoing" the syntax or the morphology of forms that fall outside a particular pattern to make them conform to the pattern. The pattern to which children could be responding in the present case is this: Even though English has many Pattern G verbs (G as direct object), Pattern F verbs (F as direct object) predominate, probably both in sheer numbers and in token frequency. Talmy (1972) therefore proposes that the "F as direct object" pattern should be considered basic or unmarked, and that the "G as direct object" pattern should be considered "inverted" or marked.[6]

According to an overregularization interpretation, children would come to have a general sense that verbs with the configuration of semantic roles A, F, and G have a characteristic syntactic treatment associated with them. Errors like (1)–(11) in Table 11.3, in which Pattern G verbs are given Pattern F treatment, would thus be analogous to morphological overregularizations based on the dominant pattern, such as *foots* and *bringed*. In contrast, errors like (12)–(14) in Table 11.3, in which Pattern F verbs are given Pattern G treatment, would reflect the use of a systematic but statistically subordinate pattern, analogous to *brang*.

The tendency for errors of the first type to predominate early, with a later influx of errors of the second type, is reminiscent of the process of *rule replacement* discussed earlier. One important difference, however, is that at no time did one or the other "rule" completely take over. Most of the time, the various verbs were handled in the conventional way (only one Pattern G verb per child – *touch* for Christy and *fill* for Eva – appears to have been completely reinterpreted as a Pattern F verb for a time). This may be thought inconsistent with more widely recognized cases of overregularization, in which overregularized forms often come to dominate. However, it has become clearer in recent years that overregularization is not the all-or-none phenomenon it was once taken to be: Irregular forms rarely drop out, but rather continue to compete with their overregularized counterparts throughout the period of error making (Maratsos, 1979). The relative strength of the irregular and overregularized forms in this competition reflects a complex interplay of factors, such as how long the irregular forms have been part of the child's repertoire before their role in a broader system is perceived, how frequently they have been said or heard, whether the "irregular" forms are truly mavericks or belong to minor patterns of their own, and whether the child routinely activates a newly grasped systematicity in the course of sentence construction or perceives it only more passively. These factors would work by and large in favor of the children's generally correct treatment of Pattern F and G verbs.

2. *Manipulating focus.* Quite different from the overregularization account is the hypothesis that errors like those in Table 11.3 stem from the child's growing awareness of the differential pragmatic effects associated with the choice of F or G as direct object.

This explanation does not work well for the earlier phase of error making, for two reasons. First, many of the early errors result in pragmatic effects precisely *counter* to what we might expect the child to be trying to achieve if she were actively manipulating focus by putting the noun she wishes to highlight in the direct object slot (e.g., examples [15]–[16] in Table 11.3, where the moving object was incidental and the injury to the body clearly more salient in the child's mind). Second, errors like (10)–(11) in Table 11.3 cannot be accounted for in this way because there is *no* direct object and hence no object "in focus." The overregularization account, in contrast, can handle both of these error types. In the latter case, for example, we simply infer that the child regards the "appropriate" treatment for G to be as oblique object, regardless of whether F is mentioned as well.

Later errors, in contrast, can more often be plausibly interpreted as reflecting attempts to manipulate syntactic assignment to get a desired focusing effect. Such errors seem especially likely to occur when the verb that is clearly optimal on semantic grounds does not allow the syntactic arrangement that is optimal on grounds of (for example) preceding discourse (cf. example [13] in Table 11.3 and discussion of a related example in Bowerman, 1981b). In these situations the adult will typically either give up the optimal syntactic arrangement in order to keep the verb or switch to a slightly less desirable verb to preserve the syntax (see Talmy, 1976a, for relevant discussion). The child, in contrast, may attempt to eat her cake and have it too. Intriguingly, errors that can plausibly be interpreted as motivated by efforts to control focus do not appear in my data until about age 5 to 6; this is precisely the age at which Karmiloff-Smith (1982) found children in a storytelling task beginning to manipulate focus with constructions of a different type as a function of prior discourse.

Summary: finding semantic generalizations that have relevance for syntax

To summarize, this section has sketched a history of acquisition for one set of sentence patterns which indicates that the child comes to link a particular kind of syntactic treatment with an abstract semantic configuration, describable in terms of the meaning relations holding between a verb and the noun arguments associated with it. This semantic–syntactic correspondence is apparently not grasped from the beginning of sentence construction, but instead is established only well after the child is capable of using the verbs in question in a completely adultlike manner. This means that the child's formulation of semantic categories relevant to syntactic relations is not limited to (or even necessarily most characteristic of) the very earliest stages of word combination, as has typically been thought. Quite to the contrary, children's "late" errors suggest that an important component of their grammatical development is their attempt to formulate relational semantic categories – caselike roles – that interact in a regular way with the syntax of the adult language.

11.6. Summary and conclusions

Research of the last few years has increasingly demonstrated the importance of reorganizational processes in the course of language acquisition. In this chapter I have documented and discussed one class of such reorganizations: changes in which the child comes to see relationships between words or construction patterns that were originally learned and used quite independently of one another, and to integrate them as exemplars of a larger pattern of form–meaning correspondences.

The coalescing of fragments of knowledge into larger systems has implications for the question of how form and meaning are interrelated in the course of language development. In particular, it indicates that working out the semantic categories of a particular language may require experience with that language, and may in fact be accomplished only well after the "forms" to which the categories correspond seem at least superficially to have been acquired. In some cases, figuring out a meaning may serve to limit the overly free application of a form. This was illustrated in the present chapter with the example of the covert semantic class associated with verbs prefixable with un-. In other cases, the establishment of a meaning may have the converse effect of introducing real creativity into a domain where productivity has hitherto been somewhat limited. This was seen in the case of linking the causing-action–resulting-event meaning to the form "N_1-V_1-N_2-locative or stative term." And in still other cases, finding a meaning that corresponds with a form may serve no clear-cut purpose: Structure and regularity are induced "because they are there," apparently, not because they increase the child's communicative ability. The child's identification of a certain flexibility in syntactic role assignment with verbs of a particular semantic class illustrates this process (see Bowerman, 1982, on the implications of related changes for hypotheses about the driving force behind progress in language development).

The proposal that meanings may be worked out by the child in response to regularities in the structure of forms that he has already acquired is clearly inconsistent with the prevalent hypothesis that the meanings associated with forms are acquired prior to those forms on a purely non-linguistic basis. However, this proposal in no way should be taken as a return to the linguistic determinism of earlier times. The argument is not that the child is incapable of structuring and interpreting the world without language; it is, rather, that the child's nonlinguistic way of viewing the world cannot serve directly as the semantic basis for language. The semantic system of a language is composed of a highly structured network of interrelated categories of meaning that vary in many nontrivial respects from one language to another. Acquiring these categories is ultimately dependent upon nonlinguistic cognitive abilities, of course, including the child's ability to pick out and combine the perceptual and other cues that define the needed categories, but we are still far from understanding how this transformation takes place. To judge from data of the sort discussed in this chapter, however, the child's early steps in learning the forms of language itself play an important ongoing role in the process.

In closing, one last issue should be mentioned: the extent to which there may be individual differences in reorganizational processes. Studies of adults and older children indicate that there is important variation among speakers both in the *depth* to which particular aspects of language structure have been processed (some speakers recognize structural regularities of which other speakers seem to be unaware; see L. Gleitman & H. Gleitman, 1970) and in details of how particular regularities are mentally represented (Sherzer, 1976). There is also evidence that speakers differ in their willingness to *act on* regularities they have perceived. For example, some people create and accept novel words of a given type more readily than others, even though they may all recognize the regularities in existing lexical items upon which the novel forms are based (Uhlenbeck, 1977).

Presumably preschoolers may also differ in these various respects. Thus some children may do a great deal of in-depth linguistic processing, ferreting out hidden regularities, whereas others do less, getting along indefinitely with relatively unintegrated, superficial rules. In addition, children may differ with respect to the particular domains of language in which they discover regularities. Some patterns are no doubt recognized by virtually all children, whereas others are grasped by fewer. And finally, children, like adults, may differ along the dimension of linguistic caution–innovativeness. This means that if a particular child makes no errors in a certain domain, we cannot necessarily conclude without further evidence that he has not discovered the pattern. An important set of problems for future research must be to determine the extent of these individual differences in development, to identify the domains of language structure they affect, and to discover what factors facilitate or impede the child's search for linguistic regularities.

Notes

1 For lack of more precise terms in English I use the words *recognize, realize, become aware,* etc., to refer to the child's passage from ignorance of a regularity in language structure to knowledge of it, as inferred from changes in her speech. However, I do not intend to imply that the child has any *conscious* awareness of these regularities or could in any way talk about or reflect upon them.

2 There are a few *un-* verbs in English that fall outside this semantic class. Some of these are now obsolete, such as *unsay* and *unthink*; Whorf's editor, Carroll, speculates that this may be because "they had to yield to the pressure of the cryptotype represented by such words as 'uncover, uncoil, undress, etc.'" (Whorf, 1965, p. 71, n. 12).

3 It has been argued that word formation is typically blocked when the language already has a word with the meaning that the new coinage would have (Aronoff, 1976; E. Clark & H. Clark, 1979). This may explain the unacceptability of *unbreak* (= *fix*), but not that of all potential *un-* verbs: E.g., *unmelt* overlaps

in meaning with *resolidify*, but it is not identical with it, and *unembarrass* is deviant even though there is no other verb expressing this meaning.

4 One noteworthy exception is the discussion by Brown (1973) and Kuczaj (1978) of how children learn to restrict progressive *-ing* to "process" verbs (thus *jumping* but not **wanting* or **needing*). Children make almost no mistakes with *-ing*, which might mean either that they recognize the semantic distinction between process and state from the beginning or that they simply learn, verb by verb, which verbs can be *-ing*-ed (Brown, 1973). Kuczaj (1978) presents evidence supporting the latter hypothesis; however, he also shows that the child does eventually discover the semantic basis for the distribution of *-ing* and that he can apply it appropriately to novel verbs. This analysis accords well with the findings presented here for *un-*.

5 The terms *Figure* and *Ground* have wider application in Talmy's analyses, and he chose the terms purposefully for their Gestalt connotations. However, the reader should be forewarned that the noun phrase that functions as Figure may sometimes be backgrounded relative to the one that serves as Ground, as I discuss shortly.

6 If the "F as direct object" pattern is basic, then the prepositions – *with* or *of* – that introduce F when it is oblique object in the inverted pattern can be seen as "demotional" markers: Like *by*, which introduces a "demoted" sentence subject in passive sentences, *with* or *of* introduce Figures that have been demoted from their more "usual" syntactic role. The choice between *with* and *of* is semantically determined: *of* if F moves away from G (except for a subclass of verbs like *explode, spout, erupt,* which take *with*) and *with* elsewhere (see Talmy, 1972, and Fillmore, 1977, for discussion). Intriguingly, children appear sensitive to this semantic basis for the choice between *of* and *with* from the beginning of the period of error making, and rarely confuse the two (see [13] in Table 11.3 for an example of a rare mistake). *From* is frequently used in place of *of*, however.

12. Semantic development: the state of the art

Susan Carey

Young children learn most of their vocabulary from hearing new words in the course of normal conversation and from ostensive definitions. Assuming a representational theory of mind, in both cases the child's mental representation of the linguistic context in which the new word is heard and his mental representation of the nonlinguistic context are his bases for testing hypotheses about the word's meaning.[1] Most psychologists, certainly all cognitive psychologists, would take this characterization of word learning as self-evident; it constitutes the framework within which theories of semantic development are set. This framework is not a theory of semantic development, because (*inter alia*) it lacks constraints on the kinds of hypotheses entertained by the child.

In 1973 Eve Clark published a seminal state-of-the-art paper (1973b) on lexical acquisition that put forward a very strong theory within this general representational framework. She dubbed her theory the "semantic feature hypothesis." I will call the position "component-by-component acquisition" for reasons that will become clear. This theory rests on two tenets: The lexical entries in the adult lexicon consist of definitions in terms of semantic components, and these semantic components constitute the primitive base in terms of which the child's hypothesis about word meanings are formulated. Immature lexical entries differ from mature lexical entries in being incomplete; not all of the components of the adult definition have yet been included in the child's. Clark went on to state even stronger constraints on lexical development, concerning the order of acquisition of the components of the adult's lexical entry.

This view – that semantic development involves building the correct definitions component by component – was presupposed, if not explicitly stated, by most students of language development (see Anglin, 1970; Baron, 1973; Brown, 1956; McNeill, 1970; and many others). Clark's paper was especially important for its clear and focused statement and defense of the position, and her paper has stimulated an immense amount of research.

In this state-of-the-art chapter I argue that, like many strong theories, this one has not stood the test of time. Further, I argue that the adequacy of the component-by-component acquisition hypothesis is important to semantic theory as well as to developmental theory. A detailed diagnosis of what went wrong is therefore needed. I have no account to offer in its place, although I will make several suggestions about fruitful areas for future research.

The plan of the chapter is as follows. Section 12.1 shows that component-by-component acquisition presupposes the classical account of concepts and of word meanings first spelled out by empiricist philosophers such as Locke. In Section 12.2 several criticisms of the classical view are summarized. In Section 12.3 I illustrate the major empirical problems with the evidence that has been offered for component-by-component acquisition of word meanings. In Section 12.4 I describe three major lines of retreat that have been taken in the face of these empirical problems, and point out that they all leave us with no theory of semantic development at all. In Section 12.5 I suggest some goals along the way to finding constraints on a theory of semantic development.

12.1. Concepts and words

Learning a word includes the pairing of a phonological representation of its sound with a representation of its meaning. Almost all accounts of this mapping suppose that meanings are concepts. If we accept this identification, we must regard the characterization of concepts and of conceptual change as at the core of the study of semantic development.

According to the classical view, conceptualization is closely related to categorization. Words have both intensions and extensions. A word's intension is the concept it expresses; its extension is the set of real-world objects, events, actions, and so on that it truly describes. The concepts that constitute the meanings of words may be divided into two types: primitive and complex, with complex concepts in some way built up out of primitives. This characterization of the classical view deliberately leaves open many options for fleshing out a full theory of word meaning. For example, many different proposals have been put forth about the syntax of combinations of primitives in definitions. These range from the empiricists' "concatenation," to Boolean functions (see, e.g., Bruner, Goodnow, & Austin, 1956), to more powerful logics (see, e.g., J. Katz, 1972). Similarly, different proposals have been put forth about the nature of primitives – from sense data through such abstractions as the modal operators (see, e.g., G. Miller & Johnson-Laird, 1976).

The classical view is compelling because it provides a framework for setting and solving a broad range of problems. Its solution to these problems, in turn, serves as a vehicle for seeing the essence of the position:

1. *Reference.* There is a very natural relation between intensions and extensions: The intension of a word provides necessary and sufficient conditions for its application. Intensions determine extensions.

2. *Epistemology.* One concern of the empiricists was the justification of knowledge. (That is, how is it I can *know* that water is H_2O, that vixens are foxes, or that I have two feet?) The empiricists' view of meanings and concepts played at least two important roles in their epistemology. First, it provided a rationale for *a priori* truth. Because the concept of a fox "contains" the concept of a vixen, the statement *Vixens are foxes* is true in virtue of meaning, is analytic. Thus definitions provide a large class of analytic truths that are immune to refutation; the justification for belief in this class of statements need be sought no further. The distinction between analytic and synthetic statements, and the epistemological consequences of this distinction, is part of the essence of the classical view. Second, epistemological considerations were part of the motivation for the empiricists' identification of primitives with sensory concepts. They attempted to reduce the problem of the justification of contingent statements to the problem of the relation between sense data and the world. Of course, most modern adherents of the classical view do not accept the reduction of all concepts to perceptual primitives. Insofar as they do not, the epistemological question of the justification for belief in contingent statements (as well as the mechanism of reference of primitive concepts) is left open (see J. A. Fodor, Garrett, Walker, & Parkes, 1980).

3. *Linguistic semantics.* The classical view provides a framework for the explanation of a wide variety of linguistic phenomena. The program of decompositional semantics is to provide a formal theory of how the meanings of sentences are composed out of the meanings of individual words, along with the syntax of the string. Anomaly, synonymy, paraphrase, entailments, and so on can be explained by selection restrictions and redundancy rules, which are, in turn, stated in terms of the components of definitions (called "semantic markers" in Katz's system; see J. Katz, 1972).

Componential analysis is a related linguistic (especially anthropological linguistic) tradition that draws on the classical conception of meaning. Explained here is similarity of meaning. Many lexical domains (e.g., kinship terms, comparative spatial adjectives, color terms) can be defined by shared definitional components, and the relations among all the words in the domain can be spelled out through contrasts in the features of definitions (see G. Miller & Johnson-Laird, 1976, for a detailed analysis of many different linguistic domains).

4. *Cognitive theory and psycholinguistics.* With a few added assumptions, the classical view of concepts fits well with many current proposals for the representation of knowledge. Concepts, at least primitives, are

elements in the computational formulas that constitute thoughts. There follows a natural account of the lexical contribution to processing models for comprehension and production. In comprehension, a conceptual representation of the sentence is recovered in which individual lexical items are replaced by their definitions. In production, a message is formulated in conceptual primitives and then packaged in words of the language.

5. *Conceptual and semantic development.* Because complex concepts are analyzed as combinations of primitives, it is natural to see concept acquisition as the process of building complex concepts from the primitive base. This view of conceptual development is required to motivate the predictions underlying most current work on semantic development. In particular, the hypothesis that complex concepts are learned later than the primitives by which they are defined is the basis of the prediction that *words* expressing complex concepts will be learned later than the *words* expressing the primitive components of their definitions. And if the process of mapping words onto concepts consists of hypothesis formation and testing in terms of the primitive base, immature lexical entries should differ from the corresponding adult entries in predictable ways. For example, an immature entry might be incomplete, lacking a component of the full definition, or it might have one or more incorrect components in its definition. Many, if not most, disagreements among contemporary students of semantic development have concerned the details of the picture – the relative importance of functional as opposed to perceptual primitives, the order of acquisition of primitives within a domain, and so forth. The basic framework has been widely accepted (see, e.g., Anglin, 1970; Brown, 1956; E. Clark, 1973b; McNeill, 1970; Nelson, 1974).

To see how this theory works, suppose the word that expresses complex concept C is defined as the conjunction of four primitives, $P_1\&P_2\&P_3\&P_4$. The word that expresses C in the adult lexicon might have an incomplete lexical entry in the child's lexicon, for example, $P_1\&P_2\&P_3$, $P_2\&P_3$, or P_4. Examples of lexical entries with incorrect elements might include $P_1\&P_2\&P_3\&P_4\&P_5$ or $P_2\&P_3\&P_7$. (Of course, it is also possible that the two intensions might not overlap at all, as in the case in which the child's definition of C is $P_5\&P_6\&P_7$.) Each of these incomplete or incorrect combinations may in fact be the correct lexical entry for some other word in the lexicon; hence the prediction of apparent synonymies.

What is a primitive?

In my discussion of the classical view, concepts are seen as primitive in three different senses:

> *Definitionally primitive:* If there is a single set of concepts out of which all other concepts expressible in the language can be defined, then the concepts used in the definitions are primitive.

Computationally primitive: If there is a set of concepts that is the final stage of comprehension and/or the first stage of production and/or the elements manipulated in thinking, then this set is primitive.

Developmentally primitive: If there is a set of innate concepts, or at least very early-acquired concepts, out of which all other concepts are built, then this set is primitive.

According to the version of the classical view just sketched, the three sets of primitives – definitional, computational, and developmental – are assumed to be identical. The notion of definitional primitive is the basic one. Because complex concepts can be built out of primitive concepts, it has seemed natural to assume they are so built during on-line processing and in development.

The component-by-component theory of semantic development depends upon the identification of definitional and developmental primitives. Only if the components of the meanings of words in the adult lexicon are the basis for the child's construction of word meanings would it be expected that children's incorrect lexical entries would differ from adult entries in definitional primitives, yielding synonymies with other words in the adult lexicon.

In the early seventies, dozens of papers were published supporting the compositional view of semantic development. In lexical domain after lexical domain, the data confirmed that (1) order of acquisition of words within a domain was predicted by complexity, where complexity is expressed in semantic components, and (2) incomplete semantic representations of some words in the child's lexicon were expressible in definitional components. Immature intensions apparently differed from adult intensions of the same words in one or more definitional component. Often this difference caused the lexical entry for the incompletely represented word to be apparently identical with that of some other word from the same lexical domain. The domains in which apparent support for a compositional process of semantic development has been found include comparative spatial adjectives (*big, little, tall, short*), temporal conjunctions (*before, after*), spatial prepositions (*in, on, under*), kinship terms, pronouns, *front, back*, deictic verbs (*come, go, bring, take*), *more, less*, adverbs of time (*seldom, always, never*), verbs of possession and transfer (*buy, sell, trade*), animal names, color terms, and time-axis verbs (*grow, shrink, raise, lower*).

The component-by-component view of semantic development depends critically upon the central tenet of the classical view of word meaning – namely, that complex concepts can be defined in terms of primitives. The classical view has been vociferously attacked by philosophers, and psychologists have recently joined the chorus.

12.2. Criticisms of the classical view of meaning and concepts

Family-resemblance (cluster) concepts

Wittgenstein (1953) denied the possibility of definitions for many complex concepts. He argued that in many cases there simply are no necessary and sufficient conditions for category membership. His spelled-out example was *game* – the claim being that there are no properties in common to all games that are necessary and sufficient for something to be a game.[2] Wittgenstein likened the structure of such a concept to that of the relations among members of a family, which allows one to see the family resemblance – not all members share particular body structure, facial features, characteristic expressions, and gait, but many distinctive qualities are common to subsets of the family.

In some of his early work on meaning, Putnam (e.g., 1962) developed Wittgenstein's work on family-resemblance concepts, called by him "cluster concepts." For cluster concepts, no single semantic component is necessary for category membership, but there is nonetheless a set of semantic components underlying a cluster concept such that some proportion of them is sufficient for category membership.[3] In a few important respects, Putnam's cluster view of concepts departs radically from the classical view. If there are no definitions in the sense of necessary and sufficient conditions for category membership, then an important class of putative analytic truths does not exist. Thus the cluster view of concepts cannot do the epistemological work that was one of the empiricists' prime concerns. However, in many other respects, a cluster concept differs little from a classical concept. There is still a role for definitional primitives, in terms of which the sufficient conditions for category membership are stated. Further, each concept has an intension, and intensions determine extensions, although in a more complex way.

Rosch's work on family-resemblance concepts extended the philosophical work in two ways. First, she noted that the members of the extension of a cluster concept typically differ from each other in the *number* of the components making up the cluster that apply to them. She defined the "prototypical" member of a category as that member sharing most underlying components with other members and least with members of contrasting categories. Second, she demonstrated the psychological importance of prototypicality structure in many, many different experimental phenomena, ranging from concept acquisition to sentence verification (see Rosch, 1978, for a review).

As just described, the Putnam–Rosch position is not consistent with *all* concepts having a family-resemblance structure, because definitional primitives do not have a structure of this sort. Granting that some complex concepts are cluster concepts, the important question arises whether all complex concepts are cluster concepts, or whether the classical view may apply to some complex concepts (e.g., *vixen* may truly mean *female fox*). Putnam supports a mixed view; Rosch seems to imply that all complex concepts have a family-resemblance structure.

The possibility of a mixed model gives top priority to the project of devising methods for telling, for any particular word, whether its intension is a primitive concept, a cluster concept, or a classical concept. In the absence of widespread agreement on the semantic analysis of any particular word, and the absence of any agreement about the nature of the primitive base, this is no easy matter. Rosch's work raises the possibility that psychological tests might decide the issue. If a concept has a best exemplar, in that subjects agree on a prototypicality ranking and this ranking predicts behavior with respect to linguistic hedges, ease of learning, reaction times in verification tasks, and so forth, then that concept has an internal structure organized around a prototype. It might then safely be concluded that the concept in question is a cluster concept. Unfortunately, Armstrong, Gleitman, and Gleitman (1982) have shown that this program cannot succeed. Armstrong et al. chose several clear examples of concepts that have definitions, that is, that fit the classical mold. One example is the term *odd number*, defined, of course, as an integer not divisible by two.[4] They found that many of Rosch's tests revealed a prototypicality structure for this category. Subjects agreed on *seven* as the best exemplar of odd numberhood, verification times reflected subjects' rankings, and so on. These psychological results do not affect the fact that *odd number* has a definition as in the classical story.

Equally problematic for the program of relying on Rosch's experimental procedures as a test for cluster concepthood is the fact that good candidates for primitive concepts turn out to be diagnosed as cluster concepts. Rosch's own studies reveal a prototypicality structure for primary colors such as red, green, blue, and yellow. G. Miller and Johnson-Laird (1976) provide a review of the literature on color nomenclature, giving an extensive argument for these colors' status as definitional primitives. Thus it seems likely that Rosch's psychological tests incorrectly classify both complex (definable) concepts and primitives as cluster concepts.

The psychological importance of what Rosch calls the internal structure of categories is by now well established, and is not here being denied. Results on concepts such as *odd number* and *red* raise the question what aspects of psychological processing are responsible for the phenomena reflecting this internal structure. Possibly, prototypicality effects may reflect the organization of knowledge about categories, and/or the structure of access routines relevant to the use of this knowledge in certain learning, memory, and problem-solving contexts. Apparently, prototypicality effects do not necessarily determine whether the concept has a definition in the classical mold, is primitive, or is a cluster concept. Thus the prototypicality effects for such concepts as *bird, dog, disease, fur-*

niture, clothes, food, and so forth do not, in themselves, establish these concepts as cluster concepts.

In her most recent review of her work, Rosch (1978) agrees that prototypicality effects may not reflect the nature of concepts. The conclusion to be drawn is simply that other kinds of evidence are required to distinguish primitive concepts, classical concepts, and cluster concepts. Insofar as the lexicon includes words whose intensions are cluster concepts, the classical view must be modified along with the Wittgenstein–Putnam–Rosch lines. What remains to be determined is whether or the degree to which this is so.

Let us grant, for the sake of argument, that the meanings of many words are cluster concepts. If so, Osherson and Smith (1981) point out that major problems regarding a logic of productive conceptual combinations remain to be worked out. What is the consequence for a theory of semantic development, especially for the view that acquisition of a word proceeds component by component? In order to generate consequences for semantic development from the cluster theory of concepts, we shall have to make the same assumption made by the component-by-component theory – that definitional primitives are also developmental primitives. That is, we suppose that the elements that appear in the clusters underlying the adult lexicon are the elements out of which the child builds complex meanings.

As in the classical view, acquisition of cluster concept words would involve hypothesis testing over the primitive base. And the lexical entry for a cluster word could certainly be incomplete (if some components of the adult cluster were not represented) or incorrect (if components were included that in fact were totally irrelevant to category membership). Nonetheless, acquisition would not be expected to proceed component by component. According to the theory of component-by-component acquisition, the child's incorrect lexical entries are expected to differ from adult lexical entries by just one or a few features, and the meanings of words within a domain are expected to differ from each other by just one or a few features. These assumptions are required for the prediction that incorrect lexical entries yield synonymies during childhood, as well as for the general view that meanings are adjusted one component at a time, so that different meanings are yielded with each adjustment. The cluster view of complex concepts denies these assumptions.

That meanings of cluster concepts cannot differ by just a few features is easiest to see in the case of words at the same level within a semantic domain. Remember, no component of a cluster is necessary for category membership; rather, the cluster determines category membership probabilistically. If *orange* and *grapefruit*, for example, differed in meaning only by a few components, the same fruits would often be equally classifiable as either one. Rosch (1978) points out that this potential problem for the cluster view is avoided just because many features distinguish kinds from each other – as she says, many properties are relevant to the classification of objects into categories, and these properties do not vary completely independently; rather, they are often highly correlated.

In most cases, meanings of hyponyms and their supernyms must differ by many components, too, for just the reasons outlined. But for cluster concepts with prototype structure, the story is more complex. The meanings of a supernym, for example, *bird*, and of a prototypical hyponym, for example, *robin*, are hypothesized to be very close indeed (see, e.g., Rosch, 1975). Nonetheless, it seems unlikely that they are even near synonyms, distinguished by only a few components in their meaning cluster. Whereas ROBIN may include all of the cluster specifying BIRD, it presumably also includes many other components as well, sufficient to distinguish robins from other birds, and from BIRD, itself.

As already indicated, that words like *bird, robin, disease, fruit,* and so on actually have cluster meanings has not yet been demonstrated. Here I have argued merely that cluster-concept words, if there are any, would not be expected to yield the patterns of development that support component-by-component acquisition. Therefore, evidence that order of acquisition can be predicted by definitional complexity, and that incorrect lexical entries differ from the adult entries by single components, would provide evidence for the classical view of meaning.

For cluster words with prototype structure, incomplete lexical entries quite different from those envisioned by the classical view might be expected. The prototypical exemplars of any category most closely match the cluster for that category; peripheral members satisfy fewer of the components of the cluster defining the category. Therefore it might be expected that during acquisition, if the cluster is incomplete, it will be incomplete in such a way that it excludes some peripheral members. Thus the child might agree that robins, sparrows, pigeons, and canaries are birds, while denying that penguins, ostriches, ducks, and turkeys are. Evidence for this prediction has been found (Anglin, 1977; Rosch, 1973) and has been taken as developmental support for the cluster-concept view.

Lexical concepts as primitives

Wittgenstein, Putnam, and Rosch questioned the classical characterization of complex concepts. J. A. Fodor and his colleagues, in contrast, raise the possibility that there are virtually *no* nonprimitive words in any natural language. The existence of the complex concepts is not denied, *odd number, televisions built from Heath Kits,* and *running that is faster than a gazelle's* being examples that could be multiplied at will. Fodor's conjecture is that complex concepts are expressed by *phrases* in natural languages, and that almost all lexical concepts are primitives – definitionally, computationally, and developmentally.

Fodor's arguments that all lexical concepts are definitionally primitive rest on the difficulty of finding examples of words that actually can be given classical semantic analyses. But the mere difficulty in finding biconditional decompositional analyses of lexical concepts provides as much evidence for the cluster-concept revision of the classical view as it does for the conjecture that all lexical concepts have primitive intensions. Fodor also argues that if lexical concepts are not definitionally complex, then obviously comprehension cannot be a process of decomposition into definitions. He and his colleagues have offered experimental evidence that lexical concepts are, indeed, computationally primitive. Using two techniques (a reaction-time study [J. D. Fodor, J. A. Fodor, & Garrett, 1975] and a metalinguistic task [J. A. Fodor et al., 1980]), Fodor and his colleagues have failed to find any psychological reflexes of the replacement of complex concepts by definitions during comprehension of sentences (see also Kintsch, 1974). In both sets of studies the techniques were shown to be sensitive to other linguistic expressions of formally identical complexity differences, when these differences did not rest on definitions. For example, negatives marked on the surface (*unmarried* or *not married*) increased processing time in an inference task, whereas these same negatives, when supposedly introduced at the semantic level, as in the definition of *bachelor*, did not (J. D. Fodor et al., 1975). That is, the failure to find a psychological reflex of complexity arose only when the added complexity was supposedly definitional. Fodor and his colleagues conclude that the concepts that replace lexical items in the process of comprehension are of the same grain as the lexical items themselves, not the finer grain required by the classical view.

In these studies, Fodor and his colleagues chose widely accepted semantic analyses, but the correct conclusion may always have been that these particular definitional analyses were wrong, not that there are no definitions. More important, these studies bear directly on only one psychological reflex of the classical view: the issue of computational complexity. From the British empiricists on, a process analogous to the creating of subroutines has been suggested for forming units that, while having internal structure, nevertheless function as single elements for many purposes. Thus it might be maintained that concepts are *definitionally* and *developmentally* compositional and yet not decomposed during comprehension. A revised classical view might hold that complex concepts are constructed from primitives during development, even though the same concepts are computational primitives.

According to Fodor's counterproposal, the concept corresponding to each word is primitive in all three senses – including developmentally. This is a very strong claim, namely, that all lexical concepts are innate.

It entails that the only way a lexical entry might be got wrong during acquisition would be for it to be mapped onto the wrong primitive. Meanings might be incorrect but not incomplete. Results indicating that, during development, meanings are built up feature by feature would provide strong evidence for the classical view and strong counter-evidence for Fodor's position.

One might wonder why Fodor's conjecture should even be taken seriously: Why should we even consider the possibility that all lexical concepts are innate? Fodor sees the three types of putative complexity as intimately intertwined. Clearly, if there are no definitions, then acquisition could not proceed by building definitions component by component, just as comprehension could not involve decomposition into definitions. He also points out that some of the plausibility of the classical view is undermined when the empiricists' requirement that primitives be perceptual concepts is dropped (J. A. Fodor et al., 1980). Take concept acquisition, for example. The classical view explains the acquisition of complex concepts in terms of hypothesis testing over developmental primitives. But how are developmental primitives acquired? If they are innate, what is the mechanism by which they become available to the conceptual system? For perceptual concepts, some process of activation in the presence of the relevant stimuli can be imagined. But for primitives such as CAUSE or POSSIBLE or MALE (take your favorite candidate for a nonperceptual definitional primitive), even the outlines of this process are not clear. Whatever the answer, it could apply to *kill* if it were a developmental primitive as easily as to *cause* and *die*. A similar argument is made with respect to reference. Fodor et al. are attempting to establish that their conjecture that all lexical concepts are primitives (in all three senses) is no more implausible than the conjecture that there are nonperceptual primitives. Although this claim is correct, new implausibilities are introduced. On the face of it, it is certainly unlikely that the concepts corresponding to theoretical terms in advanced sciences (e.g., MESON or ENTROPY), or to recently developed technology (e.g., TELEVISION or LASER), could be innate developmental primitives. What is important to us here is that positive evidence for component-by-component acquisition is positive evidence against Fodor's conjecture. Also, Fodor's discussion raises the important point that we do not have a theory of the mechanism for acquisition of developmental primitives.

The causal theory of reference

According to the classical view, it is necessarily true that *All bachelors are unmarried*, because the relation between being a bachelor and being unmarried is a matter of linguistic convention, therefore immune to reconsideration on any empirical grounds. This analytic truth is unrevisable.[5] The epistemological consequences of the analytic–synthetic distinction have been the focus of concerted philosophical scrutiny. Quine (1951) questioned the possibility of giving identity conditions for meanings and went on to conclude that the idea of truth in virtue of meaning (analyticity) was incoherent. In an elaboration of another Quinean point, Putnam (1962) pointed out that many cases of apparently unrevisable truths (e.g., the definition of kinetic energy for Newtonians, $e = \frac{1}{2}mv^2$, or the statement *All pairs of lines each parallel to a third line never meet* before Einstein) seemed necessary, and therefore analytic, only because of the central role their truth played in an entire conceptual system. The force of these considerations is the denial that there are any truths that are analytic, and therefore unrevisable *on the basis of evidence*, involving theoretical terms of science. A new philosophical development, the causal theory of reference, elaborates this philosophical tradition by challenging the core tenet of the classical view: that intensions determine extensions.

A presentation of the causal theory of reference is well beyond the scope of this chapter (S. Schwartz, 1979, provides an excellent source). Perhaps some feeling for its motivation can be given with the example of proper names. In the classical view, the meaning of a proper name, such as *George Washington*, is a set of descriptions. The unique thing that satisfies the descriptions (or enough of them, according to the cluster view) is the referent of the name. The intension of *George Washington* might include the descriptions WAS A PERSON, WAS MALE, WAS THE FIRST PRESIDENT OF THE UNITED STATES,'' and so on. On the classical view, the referent of *George Washington*, namely George himself, is the person of whom those descriptions are true; the intension of *George Washington* determines the referent.

Kripke (1972) appeals to straightforward and compelling intuitions in his rejection of the classical view of proper names. He points out that almost none of the components of any true description of George Washington are *necessarily* true of George Washington. George Washington, the very same George we have in mind, could have died as a child. If George had died as a child, George would never have become a general and president, would never have married, and so forth. Thus the descriptions of the George that we know are not part of the *meaning* of *George Washington* (if meaning determines reference); the fact that we can imagine that the very child who became president might have gone on to be a plumber, or even might have died in infancy, shows that this is the case. (Try imagining a vixen that is not a fox, a bachelor that is not a male, a case of walking that does not involve moving.)

If descriptions associated with proper names do not fix reference, what does? Kripke gives a two-part answer – a baptism and a causal chain between that baptized person (or place, or other singular object) and a successful act of reference. That I can successfully refer to George Washington is ensured by the right kind of causal chain between George, the man, and elementary-school teachers or my parents (whoever introduced the name to me).

Kripke's theory of proper names is especially important here because of its extension by Kripke and Putnam to other terms – natural kind terms such as *gold, water, tiger, star, electron*, and so on. A large number of the nouns in English refer to entities that figure in natural laws in the domain of one branch of science or another. The Putnam–Kripke extension of Kripke's causal theory of reference to these nouns is based on the idea that a natural kind term denotes the class of entities that bear the relation "member of the same natural kind as . . . " to things that the word has standardly been applied to. Putnam (1975) argues that, for such terms, as for proper names, intensions (in the sense of associated properties) do not determine extensions. That is, no part of any description of a natural kind term is necessarily true of that kind by virtue of the meaning of the term denoting it. This includes even such putative analytic truths as *Cats are animals*, *Gold is a metal*, and so on. Natural kinds do have essences,[6] but the discovery of the essences of natural kinds is a mandate of science, not of linguistics. Essences will not be stipulated as a matter of linguistic convention, and current candidates are always subject to revision in the course of scientific progress.

The causal chain that ensures successful reference in the case of natural kind terms must be more complicated than that envisioned for proper names: There was no single baptism of *gold*. Nonetheless, successful reference is a societal matter, just as in the case of proper names. For natural kind terms scientific experts play a role in the social process of reference, even *my* successful reference to electrons, aluminum, or supernovas (Putnam, 1975).

If the Kripke–Putnam view is correct (see J. Katz, 1977, for counterarguments), the question arises exactly which terms in English, or any other natural language, are natural kind terms. S. Schwartz (1979) suggests that terms for human artifacts (e.g., *pencil*) and human institutions (e.g., *foreigner, bachelor*) may fit the classical or cluster mold. We noted previously that it is not easy to tell of any single word whether its intension is primitive, cluster, or classical. Now we must add a fourth diagnostic possibility – that the word is a natural kind term and has no intension at all, except SAME NATURAL KIND AS THAT, where THAT designates a particular example of the kind in question. Of course, there must be some mental representation of the THAT. Putnam's view requires that there be mental representations for words such as *gold, tiger,* and other natural kind terms, but these representations cannot determine the extension of the terms. Nonetheless, we can ask of these representations whether they are composed out of a smaller set of elements, what their structures are, and what their computational and developmental primitives are.

In sum, even if the causal theory of reference is correct for natural kind terms, an account of the acquisition of meanings of each will include an account of the acquisition of the concept representing a stereotypical member. As far as this aspect of what is acquired is concerned, the causal theory does not affect the controversies previously outlined. I will return in Section 12.5 to some new problems for a theory of semantic development that are raised by the Putnam–Kripke view of natural kind terms.

Semantic development as a compositional process

This section has reviewed three alternatives to the classical view of meaning. A consequence of the first two is that the acquisition of word meanings would not be expected to proceed component by component. However, as already mentioned, evidence supporting a compositional acquisition process has been put forward for many different lexical domains. If this evidence were to stand the test of methodological scrutiny and were to be forthcoming for still further lexical domains, these results would bear on the controversies sketched in this section. They would be one factor in support of the classical view over its competitors.

An important theme has emerged – that the meanings of different words may be of many different types; a single analysis of concepts may well not suffice. Most of the controversy concerning cluster terms, natural kind terms, and classically complex terms concerns nominal terms, yet most of the domains of words for which there are data supporting component-by-component acquisition are not nouns. Gentner (1978) suggested that the decompositional view of meaning, and therefore the compositional process of acquisition, may be correct only for verbs and other restricted lexical domains. If a mixed view of the nature of meanings is correct, then, developmental support for component-by-component acquisition might be one diagnostic tool for deciding, of any particular term, whether it possibly could be definitionally complex in the adult lexicon.

12.3. Status of support for component-by-component acquisition

As indicated in Section 12.1, two kinds of evidence have been adduced in support of compositional processes in semantic development: (1) order of acquisition predicted by relative complexity of definitions, and (2) synonymies resulting from incomplete or incorrect lexical entries at some point during development. It is now commonly recognized that methodological artifacts of many kinds permeate these early studies. In this section I will illustrate these problems and will offer some diagnoses of what went wrong. Those impatient with tedious details may want to skim the first two parts of the section, where I illustrate the ills of the research. Such readers might concentrate on my attempts at diagnosis. I refer those still unconvinced to Richards's excellent and exhaustive review (1979) of research relevant to many of the domains touched on here.

As an organizational device, I will thoroughly review the developmental story for one lexical domain, indicating in notes when the same criticisms apply to developmental research on other lexical domains. The domain chosen – the most studied of the lexical domains that have concerned developmental psychologists – is that of comparative spatial adjectives (*big, little; tall, short; long, short; wide, narrow; thick, thin; deep, shallow; high, low*). Two different complexity orderings have been proposed. One is well motivated linguistically and orders the pairs (e.g., *big* and *little* are less complex than *tall* and *short*, which in turn are less complex than *wide* and *narrow*); the other orders the two adjectives within each pair (the lexical entry for *wide* is less complex than that for *narrow*). In the opening subsections I shall argue that the developmental research supporting component-by-component acquisition with regard to each of these complexity orderings is flawed, as is the linguistic motivation for the within-pair ordering.

Putative complexity differences within each pair of opposites

Each pair of adjectives in this domain picks out a different dimension of comparison, such as width, height, thickness, and so on. One member of each pair can be used to refer to its associated dimension, neutrally, in locutions such as "How tall is he?" or "The bookcase is 16 inches tall." This continuum-naming sense of *tall* is called "unmarked," because it just indicates the dimension and carries no implication of greater than average height. The adjectives in the domain are more commonly used in a contrastive sense, as in "He's tall," or "John is taller than Bill." Here *tall* has a component of meaning indicating height greater than a standard, the standard being the height of an average man in the first case and the height of John in the second. *Short* has only a contrastive use; the negative-pole adjectives can never be used in the unmarked, continuum-naming sense. The difference in complexity between unmarked *tall* and contrastive *short* and *tall* can be represented schematically:

$$\text{(unmarked) } \textit{tall} = \text{[adj] [comparative] [height]}$$
$$\text{(contrastive) } \textit{tall} = \text{[adj] [comparative] [height]}$$
$$\text{[greater than standard } (+\text{pole})]$$
$$\text{(contrastive) } \textit{short} = \text{[adj] [comparative] [height]}$$
$$\text{[less than standard } (-\text{pole})]$$

According to this analysis, the lexical entry for *short* is more complex than the lexical entry for the unmarked, continuum-naming sense of *tall*, as it contains all the same components and the feature indicating negative polarity. This complexity difference has motivated two predictions: that the word *tall* will be learned before the word *short* and that there will be a point in the acquisition of the meaning of the word *short* when it will lack the component of meaning specifying negative polarity.

Many studies of 3- and 4-year-old children yielded more errors on negative spatial adjectives than on their positive counterparts. These studies were taken to support the prediction that words such as *short* were indeed learned later than those such as *tall* (e.g., Bartlett, 1976; Brewer & Stone, 1975; Donaldson & Wales, 1970; Wales & Campbell, 1970). But there is a glaring problem with this inference. In all of these studies the adjectives compared were always used in their contrastive sense (e.g., "Which one is the tall one?" vs. "Which one is the short one?"). But as the schema for *short* and *tall* shows, contrastive *tall* does not differ in complexity from contrastive *short*; both contain one more component in their lexical entries than does unmarked *tall*. That is, no linguistic analysis according to number of components of meaning predicts the result that has so often been found. The relevant prediction would be that the unmarked usages should precede contrastive usages, and this prediction is almost certainly false. My informal observations of 2- and 3-year-olds reveal virtually no productive use of the unmarked form of comparative adjectives. Young children do not measure, and so they are not likely to understand "He's 5 feet tall"; therefore they are not likely to ask, "How tall is he?" In contrast, usages like "He's a tall man," "That's a tiny kitchen," and so on are common in their speech. So, if anything, the order of acquisition truly predicted by the complexity analysis (unmarked before marked) is likely to be exactly the reverse of that actually observed.[7]

How, then, do we explain the findings that negative spatial adjectives *do* seem to be learned later than positive spatial adjectives? Perhaps now is the time to make an obvious point: Order of acquisition is very much weaker evidence for component-by-component development than is evidence for incomplete lexical entries, simply because many factors other than lexical complexity should influence order of acquisition. Positive-pole adjectives are much more frequently heard by the child,[8] and this factor alone could account for their putative earlier acquisition. However, a closer look at the findings shows that the differential error rates observed in the studies just cited do not, in fact, result from the later acquisition of the negative-pole adjectives. We need no explanation of why negative spatial adjectives are learned later than positive spatial adjectives, because they are not learned later.

The tasks that reveal more errors on negative-pole adjectives all involve presenting the child with an array of objects that vary along one or more dimensions and querying, "Which is the shortest one?" "Which is the longest one?" and so on. Work on adults by Herb Clark and others (e.g.,

H. Clark, Carpenter, & Just, 1973) has shown that reaction times to verify "A is taller than B" are faster than those to verify "B is shorter than A," when both are true of the same array. Clark argues that subjects encode the array as A IS TALLER THAN B, and that the longer reaction to verify a sentence indicating which stick is shorter results from a mismatch between the subject's representation of the array and the sentence to be verified. Children also encode such arrays in terms of the positive-pole adjective (see Carey, 1972); perhaps the error-rate differences on the comprehension studies just cited result from the same mismatch. A very reliable generalization is that reaction-time differences in adult responses show up as error-rate differences in young children's responses. If this alternative explanation for error-rate differences is to be established, it must be shown that positive- and negative-pole spatial adjectives do *not* produce differential error rates on tasks that do not require evaluation of such arrays. Two paradigms provide these results. E. Clark (1972) found that when children are required to provide opposites, they do so equally well for negative-pole and positive-pole words.[9] And Carey (1978) presented unambiguously large or small exemplars of familiar objects (e.g., a very short piece of string) and asked yes–no questions (e.g., "Is this a long piece of string?); over the whole range of comparative adjectives, performance ranged from almost no knowledge of the adjective pairs (*deep, shallow*) to almost perfect knowledge (*big, little*), but error rates were not greater for negative-pole adjectives than for positive-pole adjectives in the sample of thirty-two 2- to 4-year-olds. My conclusion is that the differential error rate observed in studies where the child must evaluate a statement against a seriated array is predicted from a processing model that is identical for young children and adults and has nothing to do with order of acquisition of the words.

As mentioned, evidence for predicted order of acquisition, even if forthcoming, is not as good support for component-by-component acquisition as is evidence for incomplete or incorrect lexical entries. No evidence that negative-pole adjectives such as *short* ever receive lexical entries containing the dimension-specifying feature while lacking the polarity feature held up for very long.[10] Assimilated to the spatial adjective case was the claim that, during development, *less* does indeed receive an incomplete lexical entry (marked only for quantity) or an incorrect lexical entry (fully synonymous with *more*). Some evidence for an incomplete or incorrect lexical entry for *less* is provided by the robust finding that many 3- and 4-year-old children consistently point to the larger quantity when asked to indicate the one with *less*, and consistently add when asked to "make it so there is less in here" (Donaldson & Balfour, 1968; Palermo, 1973, 1974). Unfortunately, the upshot of much subsequent research is that the lexical entry for *less* plays no role whatsoever in the generation of these responses, and so they cannot be taken as establishing the status of its completeness or correctness. Strong response biases were demonstrated in these paradigms. If the child is asked only to point to one of the quantities, he often shows a strong preference for the greater one (Trehub & Abramovitch, 1978); if he is asked to adjust water levels, he shows a strong preference to add water rather than subtract (Carey, 1977). But, as Eve Clark has pointed out, such response biases might well contribute to the actual response, given an incomplete lexical entry, or might be a source of an incorrect lexical entry. At any rate, the mere existence of response biases in the absence of instructions containing *more* or *less* does not rule out a contribution from the lexical entry for *more* or *less* in the experimental situation.

An obvious technique for deciding the issue is to replace *more* or *less* with a nonsense syllable (e.g., *tiv*) in some of the instructions. A pattern of responses that would indicate unequivocally that the lexical entry for *less* plays a role would be the child's adding or indicating the greater quantity when the request contained *less* while responding randomly or querying those requests with nonsense syllables. This experiment has now been run four times, and in no case was this pattern observed. In those cases where *less* was treated as *more*, so was the nonsense syllable (Carey, 1977; Ooweneel & Pelgnum, personal communication, 1979; Wilcox & Palermo, 1977). And a recent study succeeded in removing the response bias by introducing arrays that varied in many dimensions other than number and by querying color as well as relative quantity. Here *tiv* was not treated as *more*, but neither was *less* (Gordon, 1978). Thus there is, in fact, no evidence that *less* has an incorrect or incomplete lexical entry during acquisition.

These studies do unambiguously show that *less* is learned later than *more*. Unfortunately, this order of acquisition provides no support for component-by-component acquisition, because it is not predicted by relative complexity of the terms. The *less* in "Which has less?" is no more complex than the *more* in "Which has more?" And *more* does not have an unmarked, continuum-naming sense. Presumably, the child hears *more* in its comparative use much more often than he hears *less*. Further, *more* is already in the child's lexicon, meaning roughly "again," as in "more tickle," or "refill" as in "more milk." There is no comparable early use for *less* for the child to build on.

The within-pair comparative spatial adjective case is one extensive chapter in the component-by-component acquisition saga. I have argued that the predictions were badly motivated, and that both of the major results had different interpretations from those that might have provided support for component-by-component development. I now turn to the next chapter, the between-pair spatial adjective case, which is beset with much more subtle problems.

Complexity difference between pairs of comparative spatial adjectives

Componential semantic analyses (e.g., Bierwisch, 1967) have provided well-motivated complexity orderings among the words *big, long, tall, high, wide, deep,* and *thick*. And that the pair *big/little* is learned before *long/short, tall/short,* and *high/low,* which are in turn learned earlier than *wide/narrow, deep/shallow,* and *thick/thin,* has been very well established in a number of studies with quite different paradigms (e.g., E. Clark, 1972; Wales & Campbell, 1970). This observed order of acquisition, while robust, is not completely comforting to supporters of the compositional view of development, because the Bierwisch analyses have *wide* being less complex than *thick,* and have no way of ordering *deep* and *high*. Indeed, order of acquisition is better predicted by frequency of usage than by semantic complexity, although it is roughly in accord with relative complexity.

To repeat yet again, success at predicting actual order of acquisition supports component acquisition much more weakly than does evidence for incomplete lexical entries. However, this case provides one of the seemingly best examples of incomplete lexical entries during development. It seems that the lexical entries for comparative spatial adjectives, while representing the polarity of each correctly, often incompletely specify the dimension of comparison. That is, it seems as if at some point during the acquisition of each positive adjective (e.g., *tall* or *thick*), its lexical entry is identical to that for *big*. Similarly, *short, thin, low,* and so forth are each hypothesized to be synonymous with *little* at some point in development. Several different paradigms yield data in support of these synonymies. For example, the most common semantically appropriate responses on E. Clark's (1972) opposites task were *big* and *little* (or *small*), as in *tall–little, low–big,* and so forth. For another example, systematic errors on arrays with several dimensions of variation respect the adjective's polarity but not dimension. Asked to indicate the "shortest one," children choose either the shortest one or the thinnest one (Brewer & Stone, 1975).

Not only are data consistent with incomplete lexical entries for these adjectives provided from many different paradigms, but no results from any single comprehension or production study conflict with the existence of these synonymies. However, a stronger test is required. If a child's lexical entry for *tall* is just the same as that for *big,* the child should treat *tall* like *big* across all tasks. But when patterns of judgments across five different tasks were analyzed within individual children, support for stable incomplete lexical entries was strikingly absent (Carey, 1978). That children do not act in accordance with the same incomplete lexical entry across different tasks might have several interpretations. Their lexical entries may be complete and correct, but these tasks may simply exceed the processing capabilities of 2- to 4-year-olds, with occasional errors as the result. Within-child patterns of correct responses on some tasks and incorrect responses on others would then be expected, the actual patterns of incorrect response being determined by task constraints. Alternatively, the lexical entries for comparative adjectives may, indeed, differ from those of adults, but not in the way envisioned by the compositional view of lexical acquisition. This possibility is returned to in Section 12.4.

In sum, in spite of well-motivated componential analysis and many studies with no obvious artifacts, the incomplete lexical entry hypothesis does not pass a final test. Within-child analyses across different tasks have been tried in three other cases that I know of: the productive overergeneralizations of young preschoolers (Huttenlocher, 1974; Thomson & Chapman, 1976), time-axis verbs (Shaker, 1979), and pronouns (Baron & Kaiser, 1975). In the first two of these cases the results are as for comparative spatial adjectives: Within-child consistency that would establish incorrect or incomplete lexical entries was not found.[12] The case of pronouns will be discussed under "Pronouns: the exception that proves the rule," later in this section. The within-child consistency test for incomplete or incorrect lexical entries is required in every case where these have been claimed. So, in some sense, the only conclusion warranted here is that the data are simply not in. However, the magnitude of the failure in the cases of comparative adjectives, time-axis verbs, and overergeneralizations of nominal terms like *doggie* suggests, when we analyze what has gone wrong in these cases, that similar results will be forthcoming for many, if not all, of the other putative incomplete lexical entries now claimed in the literature.

What went wrong – a diagnosis

One conclusion from the failure to find evidence for component-by-component acquisition is that the developmental aspects of the classical view are simply wrong: Learning word meanings does not consist of hypothesis testing over a developmentally primitive base. However, it is more likely that two specific assumptions underlying the research reviewed earlier in this section were wrong. Abandoning these assumptions does not entail abandoning the classical view or its developmental aspects. The first assumption is that definitional primitives are also developmental primitives; the second, perhaps more hidden, is that componential analyses of the lexicon reveal definitional primitives, and hence, by the first assumption, developmental primitives. The problems are twofold – I shall call them the "grain" problem and the "theory-laden" problem. One goal of componential analysis is to find the features needed to individuate all the words in a lexical domain, that is, to capture the contrasts among related words. Such features are likely to be too coarse-grained to be developmental primitives. Also, such features often represent a system-ization of knowledge, the linguistic community's theory building. As such, they depend upon knowledge unavailable to the young child, and they are therefore not likely candidates for developmental primitives. Both types of problem may be illustrated in the domain of spatial adjectives.

The Bierwisch analysis distinguishes *long* and *tall* on the one hand, from *wide* on the second hand, both, in turn, from *thick*, with the components /primary/, /secondary/, and /tertiary/. The idea is that a three-dimensional object's dominant dimension of spatial extent, defined in-trinsically in some cases and deictically in others, is length (or height, if in the vertical); the next dominant is width; and the least dominant is thickness. To see this, consider a door's height, width, and thickness. The extension of this notion of thickness to peels, skin, bark, and so on is principled. The covering may be imagined opened and laid flat; it is now an object whose thickness is indeed the tertiary dimension just as a door's is. Thus componential analyses of the domain of spatial com-parative adjectives reveal an elegant and abstract solution to carving up a conceptual space, but it does not seem overwhelmingly likely that the child will have innate primitives such as the /tertiary/ that distinguishes the systematic uses of *thick* from those of *long*, *tall*, and *wide*. It is much more likely that the child learns, for particular classes of objects, which dimensions of variable extent are labeled in which way (see Carey, 1978). If the child's representations of spatial adjectives are more context-spe-cific than the adult's, then they are finer-grained. *Thick* might pick out bigness of an orange peel as you cut through it and bigness of a slice of bread as it is separated from a loaf. The finer grain of the child's repre-sentations reflects the word's being tied to particular aspects of classes of objects. And if the child does not have an abstract appreciation of space that would enable him to imagine why thickness of an orange peel is the same as the thickness of a board, then he could not appreciate the adult definition of *thick*. Such appreciation must await the child's theory building. Clearer examples of the problem of theory loading will be given shortly.

Pronouns: the exception that proves the rule

One early paper stands immune to the methodological criticisms voiced in this section. Baron and Kaiser (1975) found evidence for incomplete lexical entries for pronouns, evidence that stood the test of within-child consistency across three different tasks. They studied only nominative pronouns, with components specifying person, number, humanness ver-sus inanimacy, and sex. The most common incomplete lexical entry they found involved the failure to mark *he* and *she* for gender.

The domain of pronouns differs profoundly from all the others discussed herein. It is hardly a semantic domain at all; rather, it might be argued that the componential analysis underlying pronouns is part of syntax. Person, number, and gender are marked in the syntax of nearly all languages, often more richly than in English, and in the case of gender often with a semantic arbitrariness. This is a case, then, when a componential analysis does exhaust a lexical domain in terms of primitives of the grain needed for other parts of the child's syntax – pluralization, noun–verb agreement, quantifiers, and so on. Another way of stating the contrast between pronouns and truly semantic domains is that pronouns do not enter into the classification of the world as others do. The controversy over the classical view of concepts simply does not arise for pronouns. The inference from *They ran* to *More than one ran* is analytic (true by virtue of language) if anything is.

Two levels of components are relevant to pronouns – syntactic and semantic. The syntactic level is motivated by distributional evidence within the language. Unlike semantic decompositions, these contrast sets exhaust the features relevant to language use at the level of syntax. Perhaps the English-speaking child makes the masculine–feminine distinction last because the English gender system has disappeared from general syntactic usefulness.

The syntactic features – number, person, gender – must be mapped onto semantic distinctions for the child to use pronouns appropriately. In the case of number, there is good evidence that the distinction between one and many is a developmental primitive (Gelman & Spelke, forthcoming). For person, similarly, the distinction between self and person spoken to, at least, is probably part of the toddler's conceptual system, given evidence for the child's well-developed notion of self by 18 months. Gender is a different matter. Although the child might have an early distinction between male and female based on superficial features such as hair length or clothing, the deep distinction awaits theory building of two kinds – biological and sociological. Until the child has some notion of the life cycle, and of reproduction, a deeper distinction is likely to be unavailable. And until the child has some idea of the world outside, he is likely to fail to appreciate the overwhelming importance in many cultures of being male or female. It is not unreasonable to posit that the child does not consider gender a likely candidate for a semantic distinction to be marked in his syntax until some of the requisite theory building has occurred. If this line of argument is correct, then even in languages where gender is marked syntactically, it might be expected to be mapped late onto the semantic distinction between male and female. Levy (1980) and Karmiloff-Smith (1979a) provide evidence for Hebrew and French, respectively, that the child works out the syntactic reflexes of gender agreement before the corresponding semantic distinction.[13] This finding suggests that the theory-laden problem applies even to those semantic distinctions that are marked by syntax in many languages of the world – a suggestion that runs counter to the reasonable assumption that these sets of concepts, at least, would be developmental primitives.

In sum, the contrast between the developmental results in the pronoun cases and those in clearly semantic domains suggests that component-by-component acquisition may hold only for components motivated syntactically as well as semantically.

The argument so far

At present there simply is no good evidence that a word's meaning is composed, component by component, in the course of its acquisition. The evidence for component-by-component acquisition is flawed even when attention is restricted to those semantic domains which have yielded convincing componential analyses. This state of affairs is important, I maintain, because of the plausibility of a componential theory of meaning acquisition, and because evidence for such a theory would provide support for the classical view of meaning.

Unfortunately, the failure to find evidence for component-by-component acquisition does not provide strong counter-evidence for the classical view. For one thing, success may be just around the corner. For another, I have argued that the failure may be due simply to the assumption that the components revealed in componential analyses, or in definitional analyses, are the primitives over which hypothesis testing about words during development proceeds. Of course, until alternative developmental primitives are proposed and supported, the failure should give pause to those committed both to the classical view of meanings and to component-by-component acquisition.

12.4. Three lines of retreat

Section 12.3 presents many criticisms of the literature that has been judged to support component-by-component acquisition of lexical entries. It is argued that specific predictions were often not well motivated, and that whether or not they were well motivated, results conforming to prediction have often not stood up to further methodological scrutiny. The problems pointed to are, of course, well understood by workers in the field. This section is a description of three different lines of retreat from these problems.

Nonlinguistic strategies

In her paper on *in, on,* and *under,* Eve Clark (1973a) offered what was a radical retreat from the view of lexical development as component-by-component acquisition of adult definitions. Children were asked to place small objects in, on, or under other objects. She found that the order of acquisition was apparently first *in*, then *on*, and then *under*. Further, at certain points in development, *on* and *under* were apparently synonyms of adult *in*, and later *under* was apparently a synonym for *on*. This order of acquisition cannot be predicted by definitional complexity (why is the lexical entry for *in* less complex than that for *on*?), nor are the synonyms predictable because of missing features (the lexical entry for *on* is not identical to that for *in* plus an additional component). Clark's explanation of her results ran as follows: Children have biases toward representing nonlinguistic contexts in certain ways, and therefore interpret requests for actions in certain ways. In the case of requests to place object A with respect to object B, the nonlinguistic bias is to place object A in, if possible, otherwise on, and only as a last resort under object B. Clark provided independent evidence for these response biases by having her subjects mimic the experimenter's actions. Subjects distorted the imitated action in accordance with these biases.

Clark's proposal is that the incorrect lexical entries for *in, on,* and *under* go through two steps. First, *in, on,* and *under* all have radically incomplete entries, something like /preposition/ /spatial relation/. At this point, the child's exact responses are determined by nonlinguistic strategies, and the case is just like that hypothesized for *more*, as discussed in the preceding section.[14] But the important part of Clark's proposal is that these nonlinguistic biases are a source of the child's further hypotheses about these words' meanings. If an adult says, "Put the ball under the table," in a context where the child's representation of the situation leads him to the interpretation that the adult intends the ball to be on the table, then this would be a source of the child's incorrect lexical entry for *under* in which it is actually a synonym for *on*. Thus Clark uses her notion of nonlinguistic strategies in two different ways. These strategies, or biases, partly determine the child's response to any given question or instruction, and moreover, these strategies are a source for incorrect lexical entries.

Clark's general point is almost certain to be right. The problem is that it reduces to the very framework principles with which we began – namely, that the basic word-learning scenario is hearing a new word used in context, and that the child's hypotheses about the new word's meaning are a function of his representation of the linguistic and nonlinguistic contexts in which he heard the word. Clark's position reduces to these framework principles just because nonlinguistic strategies result from the child's conceptual representations of the contexts in which he hears language.

Clearly, many factors other than the child's lexical entry for the word of interest, even factors other than his representation of the whole sentence, contribute to his performance. The term *nonlinguistic strategy* is used to refer to influences on performance other than the language addressed to the child. One consequence of awareness of such factors has been a tendency to focus research on understanding the development of performance on specific tasks, a focus on the nonlinguistic strategies themselves (e.g., Richards, 1979). This is a necessary part of the study of language acquisition, but it must not be seen as the whole. Our interest should remain the lexical entries of particular words and also the child's command of particular syntactic structures. For the most part, we should look at the contribution of nonlinguistic strategies as unavoidable noise in those comprehension studies which tax the child's linguistic knowledge – not as what there is to be said about semantic development. To counteract this noise, the child's representation of the meaning of any particular word must be studied with many different paradigms.

In sum, there certainly are nonlinguistic factors contributing to the child's performance in the experimental paradigms we devise to study language acquisition. Clark's use of the notion "nonlinguistic strategy" goes beyond that fact, and I concur with her: These nonlinguistic factors are a possible source of children's hypotheses about the meanings of words and thus contribute to the explanation of particular orders of acquisition and of incorrect lexical entries (if there ever are stable incorrect lexical entries). The problem is that, as of now, there are no constraints on nonlinguistic strategies. We are left with no theory of lexical acquisition beyond the basic framework principles in terms of which the research problem is set.

Specific exemplars

Many people have proposed that lexical entries of children's words differ from the corresponding adult entries in being narrower (see Anglin, 1977; Rosch, 1973; Saltz, Soller, & Sigel, 1972). In the case of common nouns, the claim is that the extension of the word is smaller than the adult extension. For example, Anglin (1977) showed that children deny that peripheral animals such as praying mantises are animals, that peripheral birds like ducks are birds, and so forth. In the case of other classes of words, the claim is that the contexts in which the word can be used are narrower than for adults. For example, Carey (1977) suggested that the child's early representations of dimensional adjectives were restricted to particular uses. The child might know that *tall* said of men picks out bigness along the axis from head to toe and said of buildings indicates bigness along the axis of street to roof, but he might not yet have abstracted that tallness picks out bigness along the vertical dimension.

Because of the grain problem outlined in the preceding section, I do not doubt that the concepts mapped onto children's words are sometimes narrower in such ways than those mapped onto adults' words. Noting this, however, is telling only a small part of the story. After all, the child does correctly represent what aspect of puddles determines their being deep or not. A theory of language acquisition must spell out how he is able to do so from hearing uses of *deep* in context. Also, insofar as the child is able to generalize at all, the concept underlying his generalization must be described; it may turn out to be a cluster concept, a primitive, or a classical concept, whether or not it is narrower than the adult concept. This last point has often been missed. Evidence for narrower concepts, especially when the members of the adult category that are excluded from the child's category are peripheral as defined by Rosch's scaling techniques, has been taken as evidence for family-resemblance structure of the concepts, both the child's and the adult's. Indeed, such a case is the cluster theorist's version of an "incomplete lexical entry": The lexical entry fails to include some of the components in the adult cluster, so that some peripheral members are not included among the referents of the word.

These developmental phenomena provide further evidence for the psychological importance of prototypicality structure. However, a methodological maxim emphasized in Section 12.3 applies here: Reaction-time differences for adults often appear as differences in error rates for young children. That is, such developmental results cannot be read as automatically indicating that the child does not include peripheral members in his category. More important, as pointed out in Section 12.2, prototypicality structure does not guarantee cluster concepthood. It is perfectly possible for a concept to have a prototypical exemplar, in Rosch's sense, while also being a primitive, or having necessary and sufficient conditions for membership.

There are convincing descriptions of cluster concepts in the acquisition literature. Bowerman's daughter's *kick*, organized around a prototypical kicking episode and generalizing to flapping butterflies and to hitting with a stick, is one case (Bowerman, 1978a). Here several features of prototypical kicking – the flailing of limbs, sharp contact with a limb or a limb extension – seem to be the basis for the extension of *kick* to new instances. The reason this case is convincing, like Wittgenstein's *game* or Putnam's *energy*, is that a semantic analysis of the components of the cluster is given. In the absence of such a semantic analysis, mere evidence for prototypicality structure is not sufficient to indicate the presence of a cluster concept.

In short, children's initial hypotheses about words sometimes consist of concepts that are narrower than the adult concepts. Given that the sources of the child's hypotheses are the particular nonlinguistic contexts in which he hears the word, this is to be expected. Like the appeal to nonlinguistic strategies, the observation that children's concepts are sometimes narrower than adults' does not provide support for any particular view of meaning, for it hardly goes beyond the basic assumptions underlying the study of semantic development.

Components of adult clusters are probably too theory-laden to be candidates for developmental primitives. If so, the evidence that children learn prototypical members first will not be explained by the cluster theorists' version of an incomplete lexical entry. Children's meanings will not differ from the adult's simply by lacking the features of the adult cluster that ensure the inclusion of peripheral members.

The ultimate retreat

A generalization of the conclusion offered in this section is that immature lexical entries differ from the correct entries, when they do so, by being mapped onto the wrong concept, and there is little more of a general nature that can be said. If so, the correct view of semantic development will not constrain a theory of concepts, because all three views under consideration (the classical view, the cluster view, and Fodor's view) allow that children's early lexical entries may differ from an adult's.

The developmental literature contains many examples of putative incorrect lexical entries that are merely different from the corresponding adult entries. For example, Kuczaj and Lederberg (1977) recently showed that the child first interprets *old* as if it meant *big* (or *tall*) and *young* as if it meant *small* (or *short*). Such an incorrect lexical entry does not fit the classical mold – bigness is not part of the definition of age. Although *big* is simply the wrong concept to map onto *old*, the source of this incorrect lexical entry is no mystery. Adults certainly use "when you're older" and "when you're bigger" interchangeably. If the claim that *old* is first mapped onto BIG stands the test of further methodological scrutiny (e.g., within–child consistency), it will occasion speculation about two conditions on one class of stable incorrect lexical entries: (1) A dominant use of the word that a child hears licenses the incorrect hypothesis; and (2) the correct concept is not yet available to the child. The concept of a person's age requires an understanding of birth, an understanding of the continuity of identity, and an understanding of time. These concepts are acquired in the context of theory building about the biological nature of people and about physical reality.

In the course of lexical development, these two conditions are met often. To cite a few examples: Piaget (1928) showed that *brother* is a synonym for *boy* in the lexicons of preschool children. Though he interpreted this finding as reflecting general conceptual limitations on the kinds of concepts representable by children of that age, it can also be seen as analogous to the case of *old*. *Brother* most commonly refers to the child's own brothers and those of his friends, all of whom are children; so the dominant use of the word licenses the putative incorrect lexical entry. And until the child has learned something of the biological context of parenting, he cannot have the concept of *brother* according to which adults and animals have brothers. Similarly, Gentner (1975) found that the paying of money was commonly left out when preschoolers acted out scenes of buying and selling. But the understanding of what money is requires at least a rudimentary conceptualization of matters economical. Thus, if the child's lexical entry for *buy* is stably different from the adult's (meaning, perhaps, something like "get at a store"), this may reflect the dominant usage of the word in his experience as well as a lack of a theoretical context for understanding about monetary exchange.

These examples illustrate the theory-laden nature of definitional primitives (if there are any such things). The components revealed by semantic analyses of the adult lexicon cannot be expected to be the primitives over which the child forms his hypotheses about the meanings of words. Often those components are theoretical terms in theories the child has not yet encountered, and they therefore require theory building on his part before they are available to his conceptual system. Here I wish to draw another lesson from these examples – that often the child maps the wrong concept onto a word in his lexicon, and that this wrong concept is neither broader nor narrower than, nor even necessarily closely related to, the adult's lexical entry for the same word. But with this lesson, we make little progress toward a theory of semantic development: A theory of semantic development will provide constraints on incorrect lexical entries. All we have concluded at this point is that sometimes there are incorrect lexical entries, and no doubt this conclusion is accurate, although it is hard to document (see Section 12.3). Thus, by rejecting evidence for component-by-component acquisition, we have lost support for a very strong set of constraints on immature lexical entries – that they are identical to those of the adult entries for the same words with the exception of some missing components of the correct definitions. We are left with no theory of lexical development to replace the semantic feature hypotheses.

12.5. Where do we go from here?

In this section I outline five research questions, the answers to which would contribute to theory building in the study of semantic development. First, the child's representation of the linguistic context in which he hears a new word is a source of hypotheses about the word's meaning: To what use does the child put this information? Second, evidence for incorrect lexical entries is surprisingly hard to come by; and in the study of frequently encountered words over which the experimenter has no control of input, short-lived incorrect hypotheses might typically be missed: How might this problem be circumvented? Third, several principled distinctions can be made between different kinds of words: Is the course of lexical acquisition the same for all kinds of words? Fourth, are there constraints on all human concepts that rule out large classes of meanings the child might map onto a new word? Fifth, if the young child's concepts were to differ in any systematic way from the adult's, these differences would delimit respects in which the child's meanings of words must differ from those of adults: Are there any differences that would so constrain a theory of semantic development?

The role of syntactic context in lexical acquisition

In the word-learning scenario I have assumed in this chapter, the child picks up his vocabulary from hearing new words in context. Within this framework, it is easy to see why a child's immature lexical entry might often preserve more of particular contexts of use than does the adult's (i.e., the child's concept is often narrower, as in *deep* applied only to depth relevant to wading). Even so, a difficult problem remains – namely, how the child knows which aspect of his representation of the worldly context is relevant to the interpretation of the unknown word (the depth of the puddle, if this is the context in which *deep* is learned). The child's representation of the linguistic context provides two sources of information. First, semantic content of the linguistic context directs the child's attention (e.g., to puddles, to aspects of puddles relevant to the height the water might reach on one's leg, and so forth, depending upon what is said when the word *deep* is used). The second source of information is from syntactic context alone. Compare "Watch out, that puddle is deep," or "That's a deep puddle," with "Watch out, that puddle deeps," or "Watch out, that puddle is a deep." The use of *deep* as an adjective may well suggest a different class of hypotheses than if it had been used as an intransitive verb or a common noun.

Two classic papers show that children can exploit syntactic context in word learning. Shown a picture of a strange action on a strange container filled with strange stuff, preschool children indicated the action when they were asked to show *sebbing*, the container when they were asked to show *a seb*, and the stuff when they were asked to show *some seb* (Brown, 1957). Apparently, by age 4, children distinguish between actions, countables, and stuff, and have learned syntactic cues that classify nouns as referring to one or the other (/a _____ ∅/ vs. /some _____ ∅/ vs. / _____ -ing/). B. Katz, Baker, and Macnamara (1974) studied another contrast in which the determiner plays a role – the distinction between proper and common nouns (*a dax* vs. *Dax*). They showed that 18-month-old girls, introduced to a doll called *Dax*, reserved the name for that doll alone and would not apply it to another similar doll. Introduced to the doll as *a dax*, another group of baby girls applied the noun to both dolls.

Katz et al. also showed that these young children distinguished between at least some kinds of things that are likely to be given proper names (dolls) and some kinds that are not (boxes).

These two elegant studies are demonstrational, and many questions remain to be followed up. When, if ever, do boys behave like girls in being able to use the presence or absence of an article to flag proper or common nouns? What exactly distinguishes the classes of things deemed likely to have proper names from those not? Probably, for very young children, people and animals (including toy versions of both) exhaust the classes whose members are likely to be given individual names. Other proper nouns (*Boston, Venus*) probably presuppose astronomical or geographical concepts not available to very young children. Similarly, when do children acquire the competence to use syntactic clues to pick out stuff, actions, and countables? Brown's subjects were 4 to 5 years old, and their performance was by no means perfect. Here, too, we would want to know exactly what distinctions, for the child, are marked by the syntactic contrasts. For example, would the young child realize that solid material (copper, wood, and so on) is stuff, and that the nouns referring to such stuff are mass nouns ("Buy me some copper"; "Copper is what that's made of")? In other words, when does the child appreciate the stuff–countable distinction as abstractly as adults do? This distinction is roughly captured by the "universal grinder test." Stuff, when put into a hypothetical grinder that cuts it up into arbitrarily small pieces, stays the same – water in, water out; copper in, copper out; sand in, sand out. But countables do not maintain their identity when submitted to the universal grinder – a person in, chemicals out; a shoe in, leather out; a rock in, ore or sand out. Also, there are many different syntactic contexts that distinguish mass from count nouns – can the child exploit all of them?

In sum, the positive results in the Brown study, and in the Katz et al. study, cry out for further research. Specifically, we would like to know exactly what syntactic cues the child knows and exactly what contrasts he thinks they mark. We would also like to know in what word-learning contexts this knowledge can be deployed. In Brown's study, different parts of the picture corresponded to the different entities. Imagine, instead, an unknown entity (e.g., some hardware implement) of an unknown material with a characteristic color (e.g., brass). The child's attention is called to this object and he is told that it is *a plexi*, or that it is *a plexi one*. If asked to find another plexi, or another plexi one, would he choose, appropriately, an identical implement made of some other material in the former case and something else made of brass in the latter? This case is not exactly parallel to that of the Brown study, because the contrast is between a common noun and an adjective, a thing and a property. But my intuition is that the word's applicability to the same object would make the problem more difficult for the child, while also making the syntactic cue more important.

The imagined case of a brass implement parallels the imagined case of the deep puddle, where the adjectival use of *deep* provides at least some constraint on what aspects of the puddle might be relevant to its meaning. Another way in which the studies reviewed here could be extended is in the range of syntactic contexts considered. *Deep* participates in all sorts of comparative frames – for example, "This one is deeper than that one," "Which is deepest?" "How deep is the puddle?" These frames provide the information that *deep* picks out a property of puddles that can vary in quantity, a property similar to bigness in this regard.

The studies undertaken by Brown and Katz et al. were intended to provide empirical support for the semantic basis of syntactic categories. Most would agree that linguistic attempts to reduce syntactic categories to semantic categories have not succeeded (see, e.g., Maratsos & Chalkley, 1980, for a summary). What I am suggesting here is merely that the less than perfectly regular correspondences between syntactic and semantic categories, if known by the child, can be used in word learning. In my view, there is at least one very important reason for finding when and in what contexts children can exploit this kind of information. The semantic categories loosely marked by syntactic cues are very abstract and general. Thus these cues are potentially a source of some semantic overgeneralizations. If it were true, for example, that comparative adjectives sometimes are represented as synonyms for *big* and *little*, the syntactic comparative frames might be one source of the child's incorrect lexical entry.

Studies extending Brown's pioneering work could provide invaluable information about the role of the child's syntactic knowledge in constraining his hypotheses about the lexical entries for words he is in the process of acquiring.

Acquiring a single new word

As we saw in Section 12.3, evidence for stable incorrect lexical entries is very hard to come by. Perhaps this is because of the places in which such evidence has been sought. Cross-sectional studies of groups of children over whose exposure to the words in question one has no control *could* yield evidence for incorrect lexical entries only on unlikely assumptions. First, a substantial number of children would have to agree on particular incorrect lexical entries, in order for the same patterns of errors to emerge from group data. Second, these incorrect lexical entries would have to be stable over relatively long time periods, in order for one-shot studies to pick up a substantial sampling of them. If, for example, all children did indeed represent *less* as a synonym for *more*, but only on the average for three days of their lives, our studies would probably miss that fact.[15]

Surprisingly, the obvious alternative source of data has hardly ever been mined. Except for Bartlett's and my studies on the color lexicon, I know of no experiments in which new words were taught to children and partial lexical entries probed for (see Carey, 1978, for a review of studies in which new words or nonsense syllables have been taught to children). Trying to mimic normal word learning, Bartlett and I (Carey, 1978; Carey & Bartlett, 1978) introduced 2- and 3-year-old children to a new color word, *chromium*, referring to olive green. We then monitored each child's reorganization of his color lexicon as he learned the new word. The children's teacher introduced *chromium* to the children, one by one, in one of several contexts. In all introducing contexts there were two identical objects (e.g., two trays), one olive green and one some other color, such as red. The teacher asked the child to get her "the chromium tray, not the red one, the chromium one." The contrast color was always known by the child, even if the child knew only one or two color words. (Pretest data had established what colors the child knew, and what he called olive green prior to the introducing event.) Several types of tasks, administered at least one week later, by a person different from the teacher who introduced *chromium* to the child, probed for what the child had learned from his one exposure.

These studies were partly motivated by questions particular to the acquisition of the color lexicon, such as the ontogeny-recapitulates-phylogeny hypothesis. (Are basic color terms, as defined by Berlin & Kay, 1969, necessarily the first learned? The answer is no.) Another example also follows earlier work in which Bartlett demonstrated that sometimes a child knows of a color word that it is a color word, but does not know what color it refers to (Bartlett, 1977a). One goal of our second chromium study was to see if such a stage is a universal step in the acquisition of each color word. To find out, we included a hyponym task in our assessment battery: Children were asked such questions as "Is *red* a color?" "Is *square* a color?" "Is chromium a color?" *"Is tearval* a color?" The child was credited with knowing that *chromium* was a color word if he could do the task (was errorless on known color and noncolor words) and if he said yes, *chromium* was a color word, and no, the nonsense-syllable control word was not. The pattern Bartlett had found in her previous work was upheld: Three children showed no knowledge of *chromium* at the first assessment battery (one week after the introducing event) except that it was a color word. But this was not a universal pattern. Other children held for one week information about what color *chromium* named, information gleaned from a single introducing event. Some of these even denied that *chromium* was a color word on the hyponym task.

Thus the universality of the pattern of learning first that a new color word is a color word was not confirmed.

Besides posing such specific questions about the color lexicon, the *chromium* studies were demonstrational explorations of the feasibility of throwing light on lexical acquisition *in general* with such methods. This is why the demands on the word learner were so great (one introducing event, more than a week before assessment) that about half of the subjects appeared to learn nothing, even after two rounds of introducing events and assessments. Several general lessons did emerge. First, it is perhaps surprising that 3-year-old children learned at all under these circumstances, especially those with color lexicons of only one or two words. This initial fast mapping between color concepts and *chromium* was however incomplete. The second lesson was that there were practically as many different patterns of incomplete mappings as there were children. Various systematic subgroups could be identified, such as those children who learned first only that *chromium* was a color word. Another pattern exemplified by several subjects was that of treating *chromium* as a synonym of *green* or *brown* (depending upon what olive green had been called in the pretest). Still other children apparently included olive green among the achromatics, and added *chromium* to the list of more or less interchangeable names for them. A last group of children began at the conceptual end of the mapping, apparently learning from the introducing event that olive takes its own name before they represented anything about the word *chromium*.

Two factors explained part of the idiosyncratic variance among different patterns of incomplete mappings: properties of the child's color lexicon at the time of the introducing event and the name the child gave to olive prior to the introducing event. For example, the false synonym pattern of "*chromium = brown*" was shown only by children who called olive *brown* on the pretest and for whom *brown* was a stable color label. If *brown* was not a stable color label, then a child who called olive *brown* on the pretest might include *chromium* among the other achromatics he confused with one another (*black, gray, brown*, and sometimes *white*).

The third lesson to emerge was that some of the incorrect hypotheses were very long-lived (Carey, 1978). After a remarkably efficient use of information from the introducing event to begin the process of acquiring the new word, months elapsed with some children not completing the lexical entry, in spite of continued introducing events.

The outcome of these demonstrational studies is that the technique does yield the information we want and could be used to trace the acquisition of words in other domains as a function of syntactic context, the status of the child's lexicon, and so forth. Given the poor evidence for stable incorrect lexical entries that emerged upon scrutiny of the studies in Section 12.3, this should be encouraging.

I would like to close this section with a genuine puzzle. In our first study, whose subjects were aware of color words, over three-quarters began a reorganization of the color lexicon as a result of our introducing events and assessment procedures (which also provided information about *chromium*). The subjects in our second study were test-naive, and we made every effort not to focus their attention on color words by including many filler tasks; about one-half began the process under these stringent conditions. But all of our subjects knew at least one color word. Rice (1978) provides a telling contrast. Starting with eleven children who were in the same age range as the subjects of our *chromium* studies but who knew *no* color words, Rice attempted to teach them the words *red* and *green*. As many as 2,000 trials, over a period of several weeks, were required. Our studies showed that knowing one or two color words is as good as knowing nine or more as far as achieving a fast mapping for a new color word is concerned; Rice's results show that knowing at least one is necessary. The puzzle is this: What is the hump a child must surmount to learn that first color word? If we say, as does Rice, that the hump is getting the concept of a color word as a lexical category, we have just restated the puzzle. We know that the infant perceives colors, and so represents them, and that he can remember them (Bornstein, 1975). The concept COLOR is definitionally and developmentally primitive by anybody's account; what is the process of going from COLOR to *color word* and making the latter available as a lexical organizer? No theory of lexical acquisition has even sketched an answer to this question.

Principled distinction among lexical items

In the course of this chapter, several distinctions have been drawn among classes of lexical items. According to both the classical view and the cluster-concept revision, there are at least two kinds of concepts – primitives and complex concepts. Acquisition of the two types must be different: Acquiring a complex concept involves hypothesis testing over a primitive base; acquiring a primitive (J. A. Fodor et al, 1980, call this process "triggering") involves making an innate concept accessible. As already indicated, developmental psychologists have not yet worried about the acquisition of primitives. A second distinction was made between natural kind terms and nonnatural kind nominal terms; I take up next some developmental questions that arise only for natural kind terms.

What other distinctions might have consequences for development? There is abundant evidence that open-class words (so-called content words) have a role in on-line processing different from that of closed-class words (so-called functor words; see Bradley, 1978, for a summary). In development, functor words are learned later than content words, and are available to metaconceptual judgments later. Exactly how is the acquisition of these two classes of words different? Along the same lines, Gentner (1978) has suggested that verbs differ systematically from nouns in a way that has consequences for acquisition, and Huttenlocher and Charney (forthcoming) have distinguished between two classes of verbs, each of which shows a profile of acquisition radically different from the other. Such work is preliminary, but is very important in constraining a theory of lexical acquisition.

Constraints on human concepts

Here I merely point to the work of Osherson and his students (Keil, 1979; Krueger, 1979; Osherson, 1978). Their research program consists in motivating formal constraints on lexical concepts that should rule out, for example, the child's ever judging *table* to mean something like "table and meal," because (in this case) *table* is an object and *meal* an event, and a concept's including just a specific object and a specific event violates certain constraints on conceptual naturalness (see Keil, 1979; Sommers, 1959).

The importance of this research program to constraining a theory of lexical development is obvious.

Conceptual change and meaning change reconsidered

Several prominent students of conceptual development have claimed that the concepts in terms of which the young child represents the world are fundamentally different, in kind, from those of adults (e.g., Bruner, Olver, & Greenfield, 1966; Inhelder & Piaget, 1958; Vygotsky, 1934/1962). As Vygotsky saw clearly, because the meanings of words are concepts, these putative differences place very general constraints on the differences between the lexical entries of adults and those of young children. Such developmental constraints, if they exist, are different from those sought by Osherson, in that Osherson seeks limits on all human concepts.

Vygotsky, Piaget, and Bruner all accepted a version of the classical view of concepts as the characterization of adult concepts. In the version common to the three, adult concepts are Boolean functions of attributes. (The syntax of Boolean algebra is limited to negation, conjunction, and disjunction; a typical concept in the research tradition common to the three is *square red or blue block*.) All three claimed that the conceptual resources of preschool children are limited in a way that prevents them from representing true concepts. Rather, the theory goes, young children are limited to "complexes."[16] No Boolean function of attributes characterizes the extension of a complex; instead, the attributes relevant to complex membership vary from category member to category member. Complexes have family-resemblance structure; they are cluster concepts.

Component-by-component acquisition presupposes the classical characterization of concepts at all points in development. The Vygotsky–Piaget–Bruner claim, in contrast, is that the classical characterization of concepts is correct only for some relatively late stage in development. Thus their position constitutes a line of attack on component-by-component acquisition different from those we have considered.

Several considerations mitigate against the Vygotsky–Piaget–Bruner proposal. First, their characterization of adult concepts is certainly incorrect. Even within the framework of the classical view, a more powerful syntax than Boolean functions is necessary for characterizing lexical entries (cf. J. A. Fodor, 1972; J. Katz, 1972; Kintsch, 1974; G. Miller & Johnson-Laird, 1976; Norman & Rumelhardt, 1975). Indeed, insofar as the cluster-concept revision of the classical view is correct, Vygotsky's "complexes" characterize adult concepts more accurately than do his "concepts." Second, the evidence for this purported shift is practically nonexistent. Vygotsky's block problems, in which the child discovers that *dax* means "large red or blue block," reveal developmental differences, but these differences are relevant to the claim only insofar as this task models normal word learning and insofar as these concepts model real concepts. The task gets low marks on both counts (see J. A. Fodor, 1972; Rosch, 1978). Besides Vygotsky's block studies, the only other source of empirical support for the putative complex–concept shift has come from earlier language production. Diary studies included striking examples of apparent complexes in early speech (e.g., *dog*'s being used to refer to dogs, fur pieces, hourglasses, thermometers, mantel clocks, and so on). However, such striking complexes are found only in earliest speech production, and even then they do not characterize all of the child's lexicon (Bowerman, 1978a). Some children do not produce them at all. Further, some writers have recently questioned the assumption that in such utterances the child is trying to refer. The child might instead be trying to indicate that the fur piece, for example, is "like a dog" (e.g., Winner, 1978). In sum, diary studies do not demonstrate a stage in the acquisition of the lexicon where all words are mapped onto wild complexes rather than onto whatever kinds of concepts adults map those same words.

There is a much more fundamental problem with the hypothesized complex–concept shift. All three authors (Vygotsky, Piaget, and Bruner) saw the shift as a reflection of a general stage change in the child's conceptualization of the world. For example, Piaget saw the preschool child's inability to represent true concepts as part of the preoperational child's general failures at classification. Other manifestations of this putative inability to classify in an adult fashion involved evaluation of arrays of objects (e.g., "Are there more daisies or flowers?" "Are all the red ones square?"; Inhelder & Piaget, 1959). This is not the place for a review of the status of claims about stage changes in conceptual format (see Brainerd, 1978; and continuing commentary in *Brain and Behavioral Sciences*; see also Carey, in press; J. A. Fodor, 1972). Suffice it to say that there is no convincing evidence for across-the-board structural reorganizations in the very format of mental representation (in regard to class inclusion specifically, see P. Harris, 1975; Mansfield, 1977; C. Smith, 1978; Steinberg & Anderson, 1975). Nonetheless, if such reorganizations actually occurred during development, their consequences for a theory of meaning acquisition would be just as Vygotsky claimed.

The causal theory of reference (Section 12.2) raises a version of this fundamental issue for a theory of lexical acquisition. According to the causal view, the lexical entry for a natural kind term contains the information that it is a natural kind term, and also contains some representation of a typical exemplar. The question of semantic development arising from the Putnam–Kripke view, then, is whether natural kind terms in the adult lexicon (e.g., *water, cat, elm, copper, atom*), if they are in the child's lexicon at all, are also natural kind terms for the child.

Whether a term is a natural kind term (in the language, or in an individual's lexicon) does not depend solely upon the nature of its referent. It is necessary that the referent of a natural kind term be a natural kind, of course. *Stack* is extremely unlikely to be a natural kind term in any language, because there is probably no essence of stacks of objects to be discovered, no science of piles to be forthcoming. However, in some languages, or in some individuals, nouns referring to natural kinds in English may in fact function as classical or cluster concepts. *Fish* may actually mean, in some languages, VERTEBRATE THAT LIVES IN THE WATER. That it does not in English, or in my lexicon, is easy to show. I accept that whales are not fish. I could also accept the possibility of a kind of striped bass, evolved in radioactive water over a few years (see *Mundo Cane*), that had adapted to live on the beach, burrowing in the sand to lay its eggs. This animal, as long as it had the right evolutionary history and/or genetic structure, could be a fish – a startling discovery, but a fish nonetheless, a fish that would die if submerged too long in water.

The developmental question under consideration is whether young children's lexicons differ from adults' in containing no natural kind terms. It might be that terms like *tiger* and *gold* begin as nonnatural nominal kind terms (primitives, cluster, or classical) in the child's lexicon, evolving later into natural kind terms. Two kinds of developmental considerations lend credence to this hypothesis. First, the child may need a minimal understanding of the workings of science, in general, before he has the concept of a natural kind term. Second, the child (or adult) may need a minimal knowledge of a particular science before a natural kind term in the theory of that science is recognized as such. For instance, Putnam (1962) suggests that *atom* changed from a classical term meaning SMALL-

EST INDIVISIBLE PARTICLE OF MATTER to its present natural kind status only when enough physics was known for *atom* actually to refer to atoms. Young children are markedly deficient in both reflections of scientific knowledge – the understanding of science in general and of particular theories as well. Piagetians have documented the difficulty preadolescents display in consciously formulating hypotheses and in understanding what is involved in their confirmation and disconfirmation (Inhelder & Piaget, 1958). Grade-school children also do not distinguish natural law from social convention (Lockhart, Abrahams, & Osherson, 1977). Similarly, many studies detail the rudimentary knowledge preadolescent children have of the theoretical underpinnings of particular physical and biological phenomena.

Such considerations are hardly conclusive. The studies regarding children's understanding of science involve their metaconceptual command of the workings of science, and thus do not bear directly on whether their lexicon distinguishes between natural kind terms and nonnatural nominal kind terms. Similarly, although young children's knowledge of particular scientific theory is rudimentary, it is not altogether absent. For example, it is not clear how much biological knowledge is needed before *dog* may be recognized as a natural kind term. The existing literature certainly tells us that young children cannot be probed regarding the intuitions about counterfactuals that can be elicited from adults and that support the Piaget–Kripke view of natural kind terms. Therefore it is not clear at present how the hypothesis that there occurs during development a nominal kind–natural kind shift for some terms might be evaluated.

In an early paper on natural kind terms, Quine (1969) proposed a different developmental shift involving theoretical terms. His proposal was that the categories of a young child depend upon an "innate feature space" in which features are ordered for salience or accessibility. For example, the category DOG may be learned of a specific exemplar and may include other objects sufficiently similar to that exemplar in such salient features as size, type of movement, shape, and so on. The similarity metric could be equivalent either to a cluster concept or to a classical concept; either is consistent with Quine's discussion. Quine's interest is in the need for the construct "similarity" and the need to posit an innate feature space in terms of which similarity is defined. With scientific advances, some terms become natural kind terms that have places in theories. Theoretical terms such as *electron* are precisely specified in terms of other concepts of physical theory, and they meet the world as part of that whole rich theory, not one by one. In Quine's view, there are two consequences of the development of theory: less need for the construct "similarity," and a liberation from the innately given feature space as the basis for conceptualization of the world. Quine's proposal is thus that early concepts are specified according to an innate feature space and later concepts are specified according to their place in theory. He envisioned this shift as occurring within the confines of relatively mature sciences. The developmental question of interest here is whether such a shift occurs, and if so, when?

Quine's claim is related, but not identical, to claims that the definitional primitives for young children are qualitatively different from those for adults. Some have argued that the earliest definitional components are perceptual and later ones are nonperceptual (e.g., Bruner et al., 1966; E. Clark, 1973b; Vygotsky, 1934/1962). Others have tried different characterizations of the earliest definitional components (e.g., Nelson's [1974] *functional*). Quine, in contrast, envisioned a shift from feature-based concepts to concepts that are not feature-based at all. Notice that shifts such as that from perceptual to nonperceptual features require a mechanism for the change. If a nonperceptual component such as CAUSE or ALIVE cannot be built from perceptual features, how does it become available to the child?

In a series of studies on the acquisition of the biological concepts of *animal* and *living thing*, I charted the acquisition of biological knowledge by children between the ages of 4 and 10 (Carey, forthcoming). This age span is characterized by a wide-ranging reorganization of the child's representation of such animal properties as eating, breathing, sleeping, having hearts, having bones, and so forth. For 4- to 7-year-olds, these properties are primarily properties of people and secondarily biological properties of animals. By age 10 this is no longer the case; the biological functions and relations among these animal properties provide the primary organizational framework for the child's knowledge of such properties. My goal was to relate the development of the concepts *animal* and *alive* to the acquisition of biological knowledge, but the studies also bear on the Quinean proposal. The question is to what extent the concept *animal* functions as a natural kind concept in biology even for the youngest children in my study (4-year-olds), children whose biological knowledge is extremely rudimentary. This reduces to the question whether the metric underlying the similarity of animals to one another is determined by a feature space innately given and innately ordered for salience, such that the features underlying the perception of degree of similarity between cars and bicycles, for example, would be the same as the features underlying the perceived degree of similarity between worms and aardvarks. I found that similarity among animals and between animals and other objects varied, systematically, according to context. For example, when subjects were asked simply to rate similarity, a mechanical monkey that banged cymbals together, wore clothes, and screeched was judged more similar to people than was a worm by subjects of all ages, including adults. But when subjects were taught a new property of people ("has a spleen," where a spleen was described as a green thing inside people), spleens

were attributed to worms more than to the mechanical monkey, even by
4-year-olds. That is, with respect to "spleenness," worms are more similar to people than are mechanical monkeys. This reversal requires that
the features used by the child in deciding the probability that a worm has
a spleen, given his knowledge that a person does, are different from an
innately ordered feature space that is neutral for all objects. The point
is that the child's rudimentary biological knowledge influences the structure of his concept *animal* in several ways, even for children as young
as 4. To that extent, *animal* functions as a natural kind concept by Quine's
characterization.

Of course, these data leave open whether concepts such as ALIVE and
ANIMAL, in their theoretical contexts, should be seen as composed from
theory-laden features or should be seen, as Quine would have it, as points
in a theory that meets the world as a whole. All of the positions discussed
in this chapter attempt to characterize concepts one by one. Another
tradition (especially in the philosophy and history of science) views concepts as embedded in structures such as theories, and derives the nature
of concepts from the nature of those structures. I have not explored here
the consequences of this tradition for the classical or cluster views.

The concern of this section has been whether there are wide-reaching
conceptual changes during childhood that constrain a theory of semantic
development. The Vygotsky–Piaget–Bruner proposal of a complex–concept
shift was rejected, but I think the question of such constraints is an
important one and is very much open. One arena in which this general
question might yield specific hypotheses – an arena important to both
Vygotsky and Piaget – is the relation between conceptual change and
theory change. Interdisciplinary research, calling on advances in the philosophy of language, cognitive psychology, and the history and philosophy of science, should allow us to go beyond the early pioneering work
in this area.

Notes

1 I will assume in this chapter that when a person knows the meaning of a word,
 he has a mental representation of the meaning. I will be concerned with these
 representations, and will use *meaning* to refer to them in locutions such as
 "the child's meaning of a word."
2 There are of course some properties common to all games (e.g., being events),
 but no list of these provides necessary and sufficient conditions for being a
 game.
3 In one version of the cluster view, propounded in Putnam's "Brains and
 Behavior" (1980), no set of cluster elements is logically sufficient, not even
 all of them. This view of Putnam's is the forerunner of the causal theory,
 discussed under "The causal theory of reference," later in this section.
4 For the purposes of this example, *integer, divide,* and *two* are taken as prim-

itive. They need not be primitive for Armstrong et al.'s point, as long as each of them is definable in terms of primitives.

5 This is not to say that the meaning of *bachelor* cannot change, or that there could not be empirical evidence that the meaning is changing, or has changed, as a matter of historical fact. But such changes consist of changes of linguistic convention; they do not result from empirical discoveries about bachelors.

6 For example, if current chemical theory is correct, the essence of the natural kind referred to by the term *gold* is something like "element with atomic number 79." Whereas being an element with atomic number 79 is a necessary and sufficient condition for being gold, if current chemical theory is correct, it is not a definition of *gold* because it is conceivably revisable in the light of future scientific advance (Putnam, 1975).

7 Similar considerations bear on the predictions that *before* will be learned earlier than *after* (see, e.g., E. Clark, 1971) and that *in* will be learned earlier than *on* or *under* (see, e.g., E. Clark, 1973a). There may be other bases for these predictions, but they have sometimes been incorrectly assimilated to differential linguistic complexity. Other kinds of problems with linguistic motivation have pervaded the developmental research under review. For example, the early work on *same* and *different* counted as errors responses that were actually allowable interpretations of the words (see Richards, 1979, for a review). Most commonly, although linguistic analyses sometimes correctly motivate complexity differences, they often underdetermine predictions about incomplete or incorrect lexical entries (see Gentner's 1978 work on verbs of possession).

8 The contrastive uses "It's big" or "It's small" would be expected to be about equally frequent, because in any given case equal numbers would be expected to be bigger than average or smaller than average. But in explicit comparisons such as "A is bigger than B," the positive pole adjective is usually chosen. That children are like adults in this respect is shown in Donaldson and Wales (1970) and Carey (1972). Also, word counts such as that of Kucera and Francis (1967) reflect the greater frequency of occurrence of positive-pole adjectives.

9 This is true even when "semantically appropriate" but incorrect (e.g., *tall–little*, or *short–fat*) responses are counted as correct. That is, it is possible to provide a semantically appropriate response to a positive-pole adjective even if the negative-pole adjective is unknown to the child; so the opposite task *could* provide better evidence that positive-pole adjectives are acquired first.

10 In some early studies, arrays varied along only one dimension (e.g., length); so errors on negative-pole adjectives necessarily respected the dimension of variation that adjective picked out. As soon as two-dimensional arrays were introduced, no tendency to confuse *short* with *long, thin* with *thick,* and so on was observed (Brewer & Stone, 1975).

11 This basic nonsense-syllable control is called for whenever the evidence for partial or incorrect lexical entries consists of identical responses to the words under study. The control has been applied for *in, on,* and *under* (Wilcox & Palermo, 1977) and for *seldom* and *never* (Kuczaj, 1975). In both cases, the results were as for *less;* no evidence for incomplete lexical entries survived.

12 The best data to date are from Shaker's elegant study of time-axis verbs. He

hoped to use the incomplete lexical entries during acquisition to decide among alternative decompositions of verbs such as *grow*, and *shrink*. A componential analysis in terms of three partially redundant features specifies the meanings of each verb (/± bigger after time *t*/, /± smaller before time *t*/, /± change size at time *t*/), so that any two of the three is sufficient. Shaker devised several tasks to diagnose the child's lexical entries for such verbs. On each task, many children interpreted *grow* as if it meant CHANGE SIZE and many others as if it meant BE BIG AFTER TIME *T*. These data are consistent with component-by-component acquisition, with two different developmental patterns as far as the order of acquisition is concerned. But because children had been used on several tasks, he was able to analyze within-child consistency. He found that consistency of partial meanings across two tasks was the exception rather than the rule. More common by far was correct response on one of the tasks (requiring a full understanding of the word) and evidence for a partial entry for the same word on another task. Also more common was a pattern indicating one partial entry for a word on one task and a pattern indicating a different partial entry for the same word on another task. Such within-child inconsistency was characteristic of Shaker's results whenever he used more than one task to diagnose incomplete lexical entries.

The other good data concern the overgeneralizations in early production that have been interpreted as reflecting incomplete lexical entries (e.g., E. Clark, 1973b). For example, the child's calling cats, cows, horses, and so on "doggie" was taken as evidence that the lexical entry for *dog* was the same as that for the adult *animal* or *mammal*, lacking features that distinguish dogs from other mammals. However, comprehension studies showed that the very overgeneralizations made in production were denied in comprehension. In light of such results, productive overgeneralizations have been reinterpreted as reflecting the child's stretching of his limited vocabulary (e.g., E. Clark, 1978b), or as a primitive form of metaphor (Winner, 1978). It is no longer widely held that overgeneralizations, in themselves, provide evidence for incomplete lexical entries.

13 It might be argued that this sequence is a result of the semantic irregularity of both the French and the Hebrew gender systems, because in both cases all nouns are marked for gender, including those that are neither male or female. But in Hebrew, there are no exceptions within inanimate nouns; it is remarkable that the child does not recognize this source of regularity until after age 3.

14 It is easy to quibble with this particular example. Clark argues that such nonlinguistic strategies are the explanation for the incorrect lexical entries she observed in her study. But the claim that there actually *are* incorrect lexical entries in this case must be subjected to the same methodological scrutiny as is given to any other case of putative synonymies. Under such scrutiny, the claim is not substantiated. Slightly different paradigms yield conflicting results (see Richard, 1979, for a review), and the nonsense-syllable control militates against there being incorrect or incomplete lexical entries (Wilcox & Palermo, 1977). Also, because adults correct children's semantic misunderstandings, any such false hypotheses would receive correction. And finally, it is unlikely that the situations in Clark's experimental paradigm mimic the actual occasions

upon which the child learns *in, on,* and *under.* Thus it is unlikely that the nonlinguistic strategies in Clark's study contribute in a major way to the acquisition of these three spatial prepositions. However, they do contribute to the child's responses to Clark's task.

15 Indeed, in the studies with nonsense-syllable controls, 1 percent of the subjects gave the pattern consistent with *less*'s truly being a synonym of *more.* We have attributed these patterns to noise, but they might reflect the truth of the incorrect lexical entry hypothesis, *if* that incorrect entry is maintained by each child for such a short period that our experiments miss that period 99 percent of the time.

16 The notion of a complex was first proposed by Vygotsky and then elaborated by Bruner et al. Piaget and Bruner spelled out other ways in which preoperational (Piaget) or presymbolic (Bruner) concepts supposedly differ from those of adults. But a characterization of complexes can be found in all three groups' descriptions of the concepts of preschool children.

13. The young word maker: a case study of innovation in the child's lexicon

Eve V. Clark

Noah: (picking up a toy dog) *This is Woodstock.*
        (He bobs the toy in Adam's face)
Adam: *Hey Woodstock, don't do that.* (Noah persists)
        I'm going home so you won't Woodstock me.

13.1. Introduction

Lexical creativity is widespread in childhood. Children coin new compounds like *plate-egg* and *cup-egg* (for fried and boiled eggs), *tell-wind* (a weathervane), or *fix-man* (a mechanic). They coin agent and instrument nouns like *lessoner* (a teacher), *shorthander* (someone who writes shorthand), *winder* (a machine for making ice-cream), and *driver* (the ignition key of a car). They form adjectives like *toothachey, windy* (used in *a windy parasol*, one being blown by the wind), or *bumpy* (used in *a bumpy door*, for a door that was banging). They ask when cocoons will be *flyable*. They form comparatives and superlatives from nouns, saying that food needs to be *salter* (more salty) or describing a bench as the *sliverest seat*. And they use nouns as verbs, talking about cheese that has to be *scaled* (instead of weighed), about *lawning* (for mowing the lawn), or, as in the dialogue between 3-year-olds cited at the opening of the chapter, about actions connected with a toy called Woodstock.

The questions raised by innovations like these are twofold. First, why do children create new words? And second, how do they do it? The answer to the first question may hinge on the communicative function of language. Children may create new words to fill gaps in their lexicon, to express meanings for which they have no ready-made words. (Of course, children might not be aware in this situation that they are creating new

This research was supported in part by the National Science Foundation (BNS 75-17126). Numerous colleagues have supplied me with examples of child innovations from their own observations, and I am particularly grateful to Melissa Bowerman for letting me cite unpublished data, including an example of her daughter's article use. M. Catherine O'Connor, Lizanne Ball, and Susan Johnson provided invaluable help in collecting and transcribing the tapes from which I have drawn much of the English data; Werner Deutsch and Heinz W. Viethen gave me generous assistance with the German data. I am grateful to Elizabeth Bates, Melissa Bowerman, Robin N. Campbell, Lila R. Gleitman, Ellen M. Markman, and Eric Wanner for their discussions of the ideas put forward here, and to Adam Gallistel, aged 3 years, 7 months, for coining the verb *to Woodstock*. Lastly, I would like to thank Herbert H. Clark, without whom this chapter would not have had its present form.

words.) The answer to how children do this seems to be that they draw on words and morphemes already known to them. By using word stems in new ways or combining them with other stems or affixes, they can express a variety of new meanings. In this chapter I shall argue that children learn very early that the lexicon can be used creatively,[1] and that this knowledge plays an important role in acquisition.

Creativity in the lexicon, though, is not simply a matter of learning which word-formational paradigms are available in a language. This is because the paradigms themselves are open-ended: It is not possible to list all their actual and potential members. For instance, no dictionary lists all the verbs to which the -*er* suffix can be added in English to form an agentive noun, as in *climber, sitter, goer, maker*, and so on. Similarly, there is no *a priori* limit on the possible relations that can hold between the denotata of any two nouns combined to form a new compound on a particular occasion, as in *fire-dog* for a large yellow dog found at the site of a fire (Pelsma, 1910) or the adult *apple-juice-chair* for the place at table with a glass of apple juice nearby (Downing, 1977). They, too, cannot be listed in dictionaries. Lexical innovations, then, are primarily important not because they show mastery of the word-formation paradigms, but because they suggest that children are learning the *process* required in that language for creating new words.

The fact that children are creative and produce numerous lexical innovations raises three major issues for the acquisition process. First, what is the range of productivity among child innovations and why do children use them? Second, what is the relation between child and adult innovations? The latter are governed by conventions that place certain constraints on the process of innovation, and children have presumably to acquire these conventions. Third, what form does the innovative process take? Children could take a particular term already in their repertoire and construct a new one by analogy, say the pair *jump/jumped* as a model for *bump/bumped*, or they could abstract a rule such as "Add -*ed* to all verb stems to express past time" and use that.

In examining these issues and particular hypotheses that arise from them, I will take as my data innovations produced by English-, French-, and German-speaking children and focus on one area of the lexicon only – denominal verbs. And since we already know something about adult usage in this domain, I will begin with a sketch of the categories of denominal verbs in adult speech and the convention that governs their use.

Denominal verbs

In a recent study of denominal verbs (E. Clark & H. Clark, 1979), Herbert Clark and I noted that (1) most denominal verbs can be grouped into a small number of categories; (2) these verbs lie on a continuum, with well-established verbs at one end and innovations at the other; and (3) to use new denominal verbs, speakers of English rely on a convention that places certain constraints on the process of innovation itself. I will take up each of these observations in turn.

Most denominal verbs in English can be grouped very roughly into eight categories, five major and three minor ones, with a few leftovers. Their classification is based on the role played in a situation by the entity denoted by the noun from which the verb is formed – the parent noun. *Locatum verbs* consist of those denominal verbs whose parent nouns denote an object that is placed somewhere. Thus, in *He PLASTERED the ceiling* and *She BLANKETED the bed*, the plaster goes on the ceiling and the blanket on the bed. *Location verbs*, in contrast, have parent nouns that denote the place where some object is put. For instance, in *He STABLED the horses*, we understand that horses are put in a stable. *Agent verbs* have parent nouns that denote the agent of the action, as in *He AUTHORED the books* or *She CAPTAINED the boat*. *Goal verbs* have parent nouns that denote the goal of the activity, as in *They KNOTTED the ropes* (made the ropes into knots) or *He POWDERED the aspirin* (made the aspirin into powder). And *instrument verbs* consist of verbs whose parent nouns denote the instrument used in the activity, as in *She WEDGED the door open* (made the door stay open with a wedge) or *He LAUNDERETTED the clothes* (cleaned the clothes by means of a launderette).[2]

The three minor categories have only a few members. First, *experiencer verbs* have parent nouns that denote the entity experiencing something, as in *They WITNESSED the crime*. *Source verbs* have parent nouns that denote the source from which something is produced, as in *They PIECED the quilt together*. And *duration verbs* have parent nouns that denote a stretch of time, as in *He SUMMERED in Canada* or *They WEEKENDED in the mountains*. Last, there are a few very small clusters of verbs that fall outside the other categories: verbs of consumption with parent nouns that denote meals or food (*to lunch, to snack*), verbs of collection with parent nouns that denote objects that are collected and removed (*to hay, to nut*), and verbs for weather (*to snow, to rain*).

Within these categories, some verbs have a more transparent connection with their parent nouns than others. At the opaque end of this continuum lie verbs whose parent nouns may not even be recognized as such, as in verbs like *lynch* or *boycott*. Next come verbs where the connection between noun and verb is no longer known, as in *to shanghai, to slate*, or *to riddle*. Next come verbs where the connection remains somewhat transparent, as in *to park* or *to land* (but consider *land on water*). And further still towards the transparent end of this continuum lie verbs where the connection seems quite clear, as in *to bicycle, to skate*, or *to hammer*.

Many denominal verbs are well established in the language. The process of forming verbs from nouns has been going on for hundreds of years in

English. This, of course, is one reason why many noun–verb pairs no longer retain a transparent connection in meaning. Well-established verbs belong to the conventional or idiomatic lexicon of a language. In this, they contrast with innovations, newly coined denominal verbs, used with particular meanings on particular occasions.

Innovations are governed by conventions – conventions of language use. The convention on innovative denominal verbs, like other conventions, stems from the fact that many innovative expressions are neither purely denotational (like *dog*) nor indexical (like *he*), but *contextual*. That is, they have the three following characteristics:

1. Contextuals have an indefinitely large number of potential senses. An innovative verb formed from a noun might be used with one sense on one occasion, another on a second occasion, yet another on a third, and so on. There is no limit on the number of senses such a contextual can potentially convey.
2. Contextuals depend for their interpretation on the context in which they are produced. Just as one relies on context to identify the referent of an indexical like *he* or *the dog*, so do facts about the context play an essential role in the interpretation of contextuals.
3. Contextuals demand cooperation between speaker and listener. A speaker must assess what his listener knows or could infer from context, and the listener must use any clues from context plus any other facts he has reason to assume the speaker expects him to use in arriving at the intended interpretation.

In order to interpret contextuals as intended, the speaker and listener rely on a convention that goes roughly as follows. In using an innovative expression to denote some kind of situation, the speaker expects his listener to be able to arrive at a readily computable, unique interpretation by considering both the expression itself (here, an innovative denominal verb) and the speaker's and listener's mutual knowledge. This convention places limits on both the use and the interpretation of innovative expressions.

The convention can be spelled out more formally as follows:

> *The innovative denominal verb convention.* In using an innovative denominal verb, the speaker means to denote (1) the kind of situation (2) he has good reason to believe (3) that on this occasion the listener can readily compute (4) uniquely (5) on the basis of their mutual knowledge (6) such that the parent noun denotes one role in the situation and the remaining surface arguments of the denominal verb denote other roles in the situation. [E. Clark & H. Clark, 1979, p. 787]

This convention places certain constraints on which nouns can be used innovatively as verbs.

One of its consequences is captured by the principle of *pre-emption by synonymy*. Certain innovations are pre-empted, or counted as illegitimate, if there is a common term in the language with just the meaning the innovation would have had. There are three types of pre-emption by synonymy:

1. *Suppletion.* Pre-emption by suppletion occurs when the meaning that would be expressed in context by an innovative verb coincides with the meaning of another verb already in the language. For instance, although most vehicle names can be used as verbs with the meaning "go by *X*" (as in *taxi/taxi, bus/bus,* or *bicycle/bicycle*), the verbs *car* and *aeroplane* are pre-empted by *drive* and *fly*, which have just the meanings the innovative verbs would have.

2. *Entrenchment.* Pre-emption by entrenchment occurs where the existence of one denominal verb with an idiomatic meaning prevents the formation of another, with the same meaning, from the same parent noun. Thus the innovative verb *prison*, meaning "put into prison," is pre-empted by *imprison*, and the innovative *hospital*, meaning "put into hospital," is pre-empted by *hospitalize*.

3. *Ancestry.* Pre-emption by ancestry occurs when the parent noun is itself formed from a verb with the very meaning that the innovative denominal verb would have. For instance, the denominal verb *baker* is pre-empted by *bake*, just as the verb *farmer* is pre-empted by *farm*, and so on.

Of course, if the innovative verbs contrast in meaning with verbs already in the language, they are quite legitimate. The categories of pre-emption just listed operate only where there is no contrast in meaning. All three reflect the fact that speakers have a strong tendency to avoid creating complete synonyms (see Bolinger, 1977).

Another consequence of the innovative denominal verb convention is captured by the principle of *pre-emption by homonymy*. Here, an innovative verb may be pre-empted by reason not of its meaning, but by reason of its form. For instance, the existence of the verb *spring*, meaning "leap, jump," pre-empts the use of *spring* as in *Jeffrey springed in France*, meaning "spend the season of spring." Pre-emption by homonymy prevents the use of innovative verbs that are homonymous with common verbs already well established in the language. It is not clear how strong pre-emption of this type is compared to pre-emptions by meaning.

13.2. Issues and hypotheses

Learning conventions

When children acquire their first language, they learn sounds, morphemes, and words, with their various rules of combination. But this is not all. They also learn the conventions that govern uses of particular forms, and among them, they learn conventions for innovation. When, then, do children learn the innovative denominal verb convention? And what part of the convention do they acquire first?

The first part of the convention that we can be sure children have acquired is the device to be used, the denominal verb. They must give evidence of knowing that nouns can be used as verbs before anything can be said about the remainder of the convention. However, if they only know condition (6) of the convention, there will be no reason for children to observe the consequences of the full convention. Their innovations could as well be illegitimate as legitimate, and could fall into any or all of the pre-empted verb types. Thus use of illegitimate innovations would be evidence for knowledge of condition (6) and against knowledge of the other five conditions of the innovative denominal verb convention. Furthermore, as children acquire the other conditions, they should come to use fewer and fewer illegitimate innovations.

The acquisition of a convention for using innovative verbs must of course go hand-in-hand with the acquisition of well-established verbs and verb meanings. It is the well-established verbs that provide the pre-empting forms, the forms that rule out illegitimate innovations. For example, before children acquire *drive, kick,* or *slap,* there is no reason why they should not use innovative *car, foot,* and *palm,* or *hand,* with just those meanings, to fill these "gaps" in their lexicons. (They might not be understood very easily, however.) But learning the well-established verbs is not enough: Children have also to realize that one of the consequences of the innovative denominal verb convention is pre-emption. In effect, without the convention, there would be nothing to constrain their innovations.

Children's innovative verbs usually allow the listener to arrive at a readily computable unique interpretation. How do the speaker and listener manage this when the speaker is not observing the appropriate convention? One explanation might be that the convention holds by accident for young children. Most or all of their conversation is focused on the here-and-now. This allows their listeners, in most situations, to readily identify a unique activity as the denotation of an innovative verb. In effect, limitation to the here-and-now allows the speaker and listener to operate, by default, with a restricted version of mutual knowledge (see further H. Clark & Marshall, 1981).

As children get older, their earlier accidental observance of the convention no longer holds because they talk more and more about events displaced in place or time from the locus or moment of speech. So for their listeners to grasp their intended meanings, children have to learn to cooperate with their listeners by using the relevant convention. This cooperation is a complex affair. In some situations, children as old as 8 or 9 do not appreciate that what is known to them as speakers is not automatically known to their listeners (e.g., Warden, 1976). Children, then, may well take several years to acquire and be able to use the innovative denominal verb convention in its entirety.

The process of innovation: analogy or rule?

Consider what children must do in order to add a suffix like the past-tense ending in English to a verb. They must first identify the suffix as an element separable from the verb stem, and second work out what meaning it adds. This part of the acquisition process can be represented as follows:

1.   Identify the suffix as an element that can be detached from the particular stem(s) it occurs with (e.g., *jump* + *ed*, *walk* + *ed*).
2.   Identify the meaning of the suffix (-*ed* picks out a time prior to the time of the utterance).

Once these steps are achieved, children can add the suffix to other verb stems:

3.   The suffix -*ed* adds the meaning of completion or past time to verbs.

The general procedure in the first two steps represents the analysis of form and meaning that has to precede extension of that suffix to new verbs. And the statement in the third step represents the modulation of meaning, to borrow Brown's (1973) term, that children can carry out once they have analyzed the meaning of this suffix.[3]

But by what process do children use past-tense forms? Traditionally, there have been two ways of talking about this. The first assumes analogy and would posit that children choose the nearest possible exemplar on each occasion as a model for adding the appropriate past-tense allomorph. For instance, in deciding how to form the past tense of *bump*, children could retrieve a verb with a similarly shaped stem[4] and use it as the model exemplar, for example, *jump/jumped*::*bump/*———. The second way of talking about such a process assumes rule use. Under this view, one would argue that children rely on a rule that represents a generalization (such as that in the third step just listed) drawn from their experience with a number of different exemplars. Because they have abstracted a rule – say, "Express past time by adding -*ed* to the verb stem" – they would have no need to conjure up a particular exemplar but could simply apply their rule in adding the appropriate suffix to any new verb.

Do children rely on analogy or on rules? Early studies constrasted rote memorization with analogy, not analogy with rule use (e.g., Stern & Stern, 1928). Guillaume (1927), for instance, argued that French-speaking children were relying on analogy when they formed incorrect past participles for third-conjugation verbs like *éteindre*, "switch off." Instead of the adult past participle *éteint*, 3- and 4-year-olds produced *éteindé* (from a a first-conjugation model like *donné*)[5] or even *éteindu* (from another third-conjugation model like *descendu*). Such regularizations are incompatible with the view that children learn by memorizing the forms they have heard.

More recent studies have contrasted rote memory with rule use. For example, Berko (1958) showed that children could add appropriate noun and verb endings to new words (nonsense syllables). She argued from this that they could not be relying on rote memorization because (1) they had never heard these new words before, and (2) they consistently chose regular, rather than irregular, forms of the endings added. However, when rule use is contrasted with analogy, it is not clear which position data like Berko's really favor.

MacWhinney (1975b), in his study of Hungarian children's noun plurals, argued that children start out with rote memorization and then progress via analogy to rule use. At the rote memorization stage, words and their endings are unanalyzed wholes. With analogy, children add new plurals to their repertoire by modeling the plural of a new word on the plural of a known word resembling it. Later still, he argued, children progress to using rules. This is shown by their taking into account the complex conditions that govern the choice of the appropriate plural forms for both real and nonsense stems. But it may be hard to distinguish analogy and rule. Indeed, Park (1978) has questioned whether MacWhinney's data provide evidence for rule use rather than analogy.

There may be no single answer. In deciding how to add word endings, children might well begin by comparing new instances to specific exemplars already in their repertoires. But later, after being exposed to a large number of forms in a coherent paradigm, they should have a plethora of exemplars to work from, and their use of an inflection might take on the form of a general rule. Or they might simultaneously use rules in some domains and analogy in others. Overregular use of the English noun plural suffix *-s* would seem to favor a rule interpretation. But construction of a compound like *coffee-churn*, to designate a coffee grinder, by a child who knew *milk-churn* (Pelsma, 1910), would seem to favor analogy.

To summarize, whether children use analogy or rules is not easy to decide from the data available. Some studies appear to support analogy and others rule use, but few have actively contrasted the two in the domain of language acquisition. Moreover, analogy and rule use appear to lie on a continuum, with analogy based on single exemplars at one end, and rules abstracted over multiple exemplars at the other (see further Brooks, 1978; Kossan, 1978; Medin & Schaffer, 1978). In language, this continuum is such that, whereas instances of analogy could actually be instances of rule use, there should be identifiable instances of rule use that could not be accounted for by analogy. I shall consider this issue further for the case of innovative denominal verbs. If children's innovations conform to the model exemplars offered in adult speech, it may not be possible to decide between analogy and rule use. But if they depart from the exemplars offered, this departure would favor rules over analogy in the process of innovation.

Some hypotheses

There are several hypotheses implicit in the preceding discussion that will be tested against the present corpus of children's innovative denominal verbs. First, if children do not know all the parts of a convention about language use – here, the convention for using innovative denominal verbs – they could produce both legitimate and illegitimate innovations. However, the incidence of their illegitimate innovations should decline with age as they learn (1) other terms that would pre-empt particular innovations, (2) that well-established terms do pre-empt, and (3) how to assess mutual knowledge – the special common ground that people need in order to make effective reference and so on (see H. Clark & Marshall, 1981). These predictions, I assume, should hold equally for all three languages under discussion here.[6]

Second, there are several alternative hypotheses about the sources of children's innovations. One source children might use is the set of well-established denominal verbs available in their own vocabularies. To use these, whether by analogy or rule, children will need to have recognized and analyzed the relation that holds for particular noun–verb pairings. Evidence for this source could show up in two ways: First, the innovations children produce should belong to the *same* categories of denominal verbs as their well-established verbs; and second, the frequency of their types should reflect that of their well-established verb categories.

An alternative hypothesis about the source of children's innovations is that, instead, they base them on adult usage. With this source, there are similar predictions: First, the innovations children produce should all fit into the adult categories of denominal verbs; and second, their frequency should reflect the relative frequencies of the adult categories. Of course, if children's well-established verbs happen to fall into the same categories as adult denominal verbs, these two hypotheses will not be distinguishable.

In either case, if there are parallels between the proposed model and children's innovations, one could probably not decide between analogy and rule. Their innovations could be produced by analogy to specific exemplars in their own vocabulary or in adult speech, or by a rule based on their own or adult speech.

A third alternative, in which the potential role of analogy or rule might be easier to assess, is the following: Children could produce innovations because they need a way to express particular meanings on particular occasions. In this case, all they need notice is the general fact that adults use words that denote concrete objects as terms for talking about states, processes, or acts associated with those objects. This would essentially correspond to part (6) of the adult convention, but would involve use of a more general rule, one not governed by the rest of that convention. Under this view, children's innovations – legitimate or illegitimate – would not necessarily parallel either their own well-established verbs or the verb categories used by adults. For example, children might use one or more categories *not* used by adults. This would be strong evidence in favor of rule use.

Data for the case study

The innovations to be analyzed here consist of 224 denominal verbs produced by young children acquiring English (123 verbs), French (35 verbs), and German (66 verbs). The sources for the English data are several. First, there are my own longitudinal records of 2- and 3-year-olds, plus a long-term collection of more casual observations of children's innovations. Examples cited from this source are labeled with the initials D, H, J, K, S, JA, SA, and ME in the tables presented later. A second source of English data is Bowerman (1974, 1978b, and unpublished data), indicated by the initials CB and EB. In addition, I have culled a few instances from other published sources: HO and SO (O'Shea, 1907), EP (Pelsma, 1910), RG (Grant, 1915), DH (Huxley, 1970), HL and JW (Kuczaj, 1977), and AK (Kuczaj, 1978).

My sources for French are sparser. I have relied here on instances appearing in published diary studies and discussions by Decroly (1932a), indicated by WD, YD, and XD; Grégoire (1937, 1947), indicated by CG and EG; and Aimard (1975), indicated by LA, VA, and MA. The German data have also been drawn from published sources. The two main studies I have relied on are Neugebauer (1914), indicated by RN, and Stern and Stern (1928), indicated by HS and GS. In addition, I have drawn on additional examples cited by Stern and Stern from other German studies, indicated as follows: AP (Preyer, 1882), DL (Lindner, 1898), FS and SS (Schneider, 1903), Tö (Tögel, 1905), HF and RF (Friedrich, 1906), and Sc (Scupin & Scupin, 1907). The majority of the innovative verbs for all three languages were produced by children between the ages of 2 and 5.

In addition to the English data on innovative verbs, I have also used a comparison corpus of well-established or idiomatic denominal verbs found in the vocabulary of 3-year-olds. This corpus was compiled from seven vocabulary studies by tallying all those denominal verbs for which children also knew the parent nouns (Bateman, 1915; Bohn, 1914; Boyd, 1914; Brandenburg, 1915; Grant, 1915; Nice, 1915; Pelsma, 1910). A second set of comparison data comes from the adult corpus compiled by E. Clark and H. Clark (1979) of over 1,300 established and innovative denominal verbs in English.

Each of the verbs in the corpus of innovations, from all three languages, as well as each of the well-established verbs from English-speaking 3-year-olds, was classified using the schema in E. Clark and H. Clark (1979). For well-established verbs, the classification was based on the adult meanings; for innovative verbs, the classification was based on contextual information about the occasion of use, together with adult glosses of what the child had intended to convey.

To be sure that children are using a noun as an innovative verb, one has to make sure that they are observing certain syntactic constraints that allow identification of the word class of the stem in question. Utterances from the one- or two-word stage clearly cannot be categorized reliably as nouns or verbs because they cannot meet the adult constraints on uses of different word classes (see Stern & Stern, 1928). The child must therefore be using subject-verb-object sequences in his utterances before he can be credited with any innovative denominal verbs. The problem is an obvious one when one-word utterances are considered. For instance, some children made early verblike uses of *door* (an adult noun) that are exactly paralleled by other children's uses of *open* (an adult verb) (see Griffiths .& Atkinson, 1978). The same problem lingers with two-word utterances that contain a potential denominal verb: In *Daddy brush*, one could have a sequence of noun-plus-noun, in a genitive relation (''Daddy's brush'') or a subject-object relation (''Daddy's doing something to the brush''); noun-plus-verb, in a subject-verb relation (''Daddy's brushing something''); or noun-plus-noun, in a subject–manner adverb relation where *brush* is the instrument used in a particular action (''Daddy's doing something with a brush''). Until children produce subject-verb-object utterances, there is no reliable way to identify the syntactic word class of a particular term.

There are, inevitably, certain problems associated with the use of such data on innovations. Since the sample size for each language is different, the samples may not be truly representative. This problem is compounded by the fact that the data for each language are drawn from several different children, and they in turn may not be representative of children acquiring that language. Despite these problems, the instances of innovations observed in my own data appear very similar to those observed by Bowerman, and they fall into similar categories, as do the data from children acquiring German. Moreover, in the case of German, more recent studies contain observations directly comparable to those noted in earlier diaries (e.g., Augst, Bauer, & Stein, 1977; Panagl, 1977). The French corpus is the smallest and therefore possibly less representative than either the English or German one.

A second source of problems with such data lies in their categorization. As I mentioned earlier, each innovative verb was classified according to the role in the situation of the entity denoted by the parent noun. But how is this decided? Both in my own data and in Bowerman's, detailed contextual notes on what the child was talking about on each occasion and what he intended to convey allow as precise a categorization as for adult innovations. But published sources are not always as detailed either about the context or about the intended interpretation. As a result, some innovations could have been classified in more than one way. (This problem is not unique to child innovations; it also occurs with many adult uses; see E. Clark & H. Clark, 1979.) The adult glosses provided in diaries like Grégoire's (1937, 1947) or Stern and Stern's (1928) vary in the amount of detail provided. Some innovations may be transparent to the observer who knows the child and his routines, while to others the same innovations are opaque. In the relatively few instances that lacked both a context and a gloss, the verb category was determined on the basis of the predominant feature of the entity denoted. If the entity was one normally used as an instrument, for instance, the verb was placed in the instrument category, and so on.

A third problem is related to the sampling issue raised earlier. Comparatively few of the innovative verbs in the corpus are legitimate innovations. In essence, people do not notice when children produce verbs that might as well have been produced by adults, but they do notice when child forms violate adult conventions on innovations. This means that the innovations actually produced by children may be severely underestimated in my data. The criterion of illegitimacy is a very conservative one. And there is a second source of underestimation. In many cases, children may reinvent what for adults are well-established forms. These too should be added to the tally of children's innovations, but there is a detection problem. Reinvention is virtually impossible to distinguish from forms based on observed adult usage. This bias against noticing child innovations, then, will lead to even greater underestimates of innovation in the child's lexicon.

13.3. Innovative denominal verbs

In giving an account of the kinds of innovations typically produced in all three languages, I will go through the verb categories in turn, illustrating them with examples from each language. I will then compare innovative verb categories with well-established ones, and children's denominal verbs with those produced by adults.

Instrument verbs. Typical examples of innovative instrument verbs from children acquiring English, French, and German are given in Tables 13.1,

Table 13.1. *Instrument verbs: some English examples*

(1) S   (2;4, wanting to have some cheese weighed): *You have to scale it first.*

(2) S   (2;4, reaching for the pocket calculator): *I can button it.* [= turn it on]

(3) S   (2;7, having hit his baby sister, explaining what made her cry): *I broomed her.* [= hit her with a (toy) broom]

(4) S   (2;11, not wanting his mother to sweep his room): *Don't broom my mess.*

(5) S   (2;11, telling his father that his mother nursed the baby): *Mommy nippled Anna.*

(6) S   (3;0,21, watching a man opening a door with a key): *He's keying the door.*

(7) S   (3;2, pretending to shoot his mother with a stick): *I'm going to gun you.*

(8) S   (3;2, asking if the pants his mother is mending are ready): *Is it all needled?*

(9) S   (3;2, putting on a cowboy hat with a string-and-bead catch for holding it on under the chin): *String me up, mommy.*

(10) EB (3;10, taking spaghetti out a pan with some tongs): *I'm going to pliers this out.*

(11) EP (4;0, asking for some sticks to be chopped): *Won't you hatchet this?*

(12) CB (4;0, rejecting some paper she'd cut her finger on earlier): *I don't think I'll have it because it papers me.* [= paper cuts me]

(13) CB (4;4, struggling with the lace on her boot): *How was it shoelaced?*

(14) CB (4;6, doing up the seat belt in the car): *I seat-belted myself.*

(15) HL (5;0, complaining about the unfairness of woodchopping assignments): *You axed the wood and I didn't axe it.*

(16) JW (5;7, hitting a ball with a stick): *I'm sticking it and that makes it go really fast.*

Note: Ages are given in years; months, and (sometimes) days.

13.2, and 13.3. The category of instrument verbs comprises those denominal verbs whose parent noun denotes the instrument used in the activity being talked about. Table 13.1 lists instances observed in the speech of several English-speaking children.

Many of the innovations in Table 13.1 are illegitimate for adults, even though they are interpretable in context. Some are illegitimate because they are pre-empted by *suppletion* (the same meaning attached to a different form). The child's *scale* is suppleted by adult *weigh*, *broom* (in [4]) by *sweep*, *nipple* by *nurse*, *gun* by *shoot*, *needle* by *mend*, and both *hatchet* and *axe* by *chop*. Other innovations are illegitimate because they are pre-empted by *homonymy* (a different meaning attached to the same form). Thus the child's *button* (turn on by means of a button) is pre-empted by the adult's "fasten with a button," the child's *key* (open with a key) is pre-empted by the adult's "make a key for," and *needle* (mend

Table 13.2. *Instrument verbs: some French examples*

---

(1) LA   (2;0, no context given): *C'est déconstruit, c'est bulldozé.* [It's unbuilt, it's bulldoze(re)d.]
(2) VA   (3;9, before licking an envelope to seal it): *Je peux la boutonner?* [Can I button (close, fasten) it?]
(3) VA   (3;10, having heard the word Nixon a lot on the radio): *Ce nixon, c'est pour anixonner?* [This nixon, it's for nixoning?]
(4) VA   (4;1, wanting to write with a piece of chalk): *Tu as pas une craie? Je voudrais crai . . . ver.* [Have you got a piece of chalk? I'd like to chalk.]
(5) CG   (4;7,6, talking about raking a path): *On ne rate pas dans les crasses.* [You don't rake in the dirt/filth.]
(6) XD   (no age given), talking about painting with a paintbrush, used the verb *pincer.* [to paintbrush]
(7) YD   (no age given), talking about measuring something, used *mètrer.* [to meter]

---

with a needle) is pre-empted by adult "irritate, annoy." (*Needle* is therefore pre-empted both by meaning and by form.) Other examples of pre-emption by homonymy are *string up* (fasten with a string) beside adult "hang," *paper* (cut with paper) beside "put paper on," and *stick* (hit with a stick) beside "adhere to."

Most of the remaining verbs are legitimate innovations. *Broom* (in [3]) meaning "hit with a broom," *pliers out*, "remove with pliers" (with *pliers* overextended to include tongs), and *seat-belted*, "fasten in with a seat belt," are all legitimate. *Shoelaced*, however, would normally appear in the form *laced* for adults. Since the child was trying to lace her boots, this verb has presumably been formed from an unanalyzed compound, and is pre-empted by the *entrenched* verb *lace* – the same meaning with a different form.

Table 13.2 contains some instrument verbs produced by French-speaking children. As in the English data, a number of these verbs are illegitimate. Several are pre-empted by suppletion, for instance, *Boutonner*, "fasten an envelope" (from *bouton*, "button"), is pre-empted by adult *cacheter*. Similarly, *pincer*, "paint (with a paintbrush)" (from *pinceau*, "paintbrush"), and *mètrer*, "measure" (from *mètre*, "measuring tape"), are pre-empted by adult *peindre* and *mesurer*, respectively. There is also one instance of pre-emption by entrenchment: *Rater*, "use a rake" (from *rateau*, "rake"), is pre-empted by adult *ratisser*, derived from the same noun. (In Old French, however, *rater* did mean "use a rake.") Two verbs are pre-empted by homonymy (the same forms with different adult meanings). *Pincer*, "paint" is pre-empted by *pincer*, "pinch," and *rater*, "use a rake," is pre-empted by *rater*, "fail." These two, then, are pre-empted by both meaning and form.

Table 13.3. *Instrument verbs: some German examples*

---

(1) RN (1;11,21), talking about climbing something by means of a ladder, used *leitern*. [to ladder]

(2) RN (1;11,21), talking about tying a cord, used *schnuren*. [to cord]

(3) RN (2;1,7, talking about a train leaving): *Lekta-sch is forträdelt.* [Electric train has wheeled away.]

(4) RN (2;1,7), talking about using a whip, used *peitschen*. [to whip]

(5) RN (2;2, talking about a buckle): *Wie hannn man das anbroschen?* [Can someone brooch (fasten) this on?]

(6) RN (2;2, using tongs to pick things up): *Mutter, was kann ich noch zangen?* [Mommy, what else can I tong?]

(7) RN (2;9, rubbing stones by running a small stick over them): *Jetz muss ich die noch stöckeln.* [Now I must stick them again.]

(8) Sc (3;6), being sniffed by a dog, used *angeschnauzelt*. [(It) muzzles/snouts.]

(9) HS (3;8, to her mother): *Hast du die Schürze vergürtelt?* [Have you girdled (fastened) your apron?]

(10) HS (3;9), measuring the length of her necklace, used *metern*. [to meter]

(11) HF (3;9,15), talking about sewing with a sewing machine, used *maschinen*. [to machine]

(12) GS (3;11, playing with some glass): *Ich splittre nich. Ich wer mich ja nich splittern.* [I don't splinter. I shan't splinter myself = hurt with splinters.]

(13) HS (4;2), talking about sweeping with a broom, used *best*. [(He/she) brooms.]

(14) AP (no age given), talking about cutting something with a knife, used *messen*. [to knife]

The only legitimate instrument verbs appear to be *bulldozé, anixonner,* and *craiver,* but these forms are not necessarily the ones adults would have created. For example, the parent noun for *bulldozé* is *bulldozer* (borrowed from English). To make this noun into a verb would normally require the addition of the first-conjugation ending in *-er,* resulting in a past participial form *bulldozeré.* *Anixonner* seems to have been created with the child assuming *Nixon* to be the name of a product. Given that, the innovation appears quite legitimate. But *craiver,* "write (with chalk)," ought, strictly speaking, to be *craier* (from the noun *craie,* "chalk"). However, the child may have avoided *craier,* which would be homophonous with *créer,* "create, make." Whether this accounts for the form chosen, though, is not clear. The child may also have been influenced by forms like *écrivez,* from *écrire,* "to write," a semantic neighbor of the meaning being expressed.

Table 13.3 lists innovative instrument verbs from German-speaking children. Again, these verbs can be classified as legitimate or illegitimate. Among the illegitimate ones, there are several instances where the child's verb is pre-empted by suppletion and one instance of pre-emption by entrenchment. Suppletion occurs with *forträdelt*, "leave" (based on the noun *Rad*, "wheel"), pre-empted by adult *fortgefahren*; with *metern*, "measure" (based on *Meter*, "ruler, measuring tape"), pre-empted by *messen*; with *best*, "sweeps" (based on *Besen*, "broom"), pre-empted by *fegen*; and with *messen*, "cut" (based on *Messer*, "knife"), pre-empted by *schneiden*. The latter verb is also pre-empted by homonymy: Adult *messen* means "to measure." Other instances of homonymy are provided by the verb *splittern*, "hurt with splinters" (based on *Splitter*, "splinter, sliver"), which is pre-empted by the adult meaning of "make into splinters," and by *anschnauzen*, "sniff, muzzle at" (based on *Schnauze*, "snout, muzzle"), which is pre-empted by the adult meaning of "talk roughly to."

The remaining innovations all seem to be legitimate. The verb *leitern* (based on *leiter*, "ladder") was intended to mean "climb with a ladder," and although adults normally use *auf eine Leiter steigen* instead, it was transparent in context. The verb *peitschen* (based on *Peitsche*, "whip"), which is actually an established adult verb meaning "whip," was invented spontaneously by RN, who, according to Neugebauer (1914), had never been exposed to it as a verb. *Anbroschen* (based on *Brosche*, "brooch," overextended to include buckles), meaning "fasten (with a buckle)," is legitimate, as are *zangen* (based on *Zange*, "tongs"), *stöckeln* (based on *Stock*, "stick"), *vergürtelt* (based on *Gürtel*, "belt, sash"), and *maschinen* (based on *Maschine*, "machine").

Locatum verbs. After instrument verbs, locatum verbs are the most frequent innovative denominal verbs in children's speech. Representative examples from the three languages are shown in Tables 13.4, 13.5, and 13.6. In locatum verbs, the parent nouns denote the entity that is being placed somewhere.

Table 13.4 presents examples from English-speaking children. Only two of them are illegitimate. The first, where the meaning is expressed with a different form by adults, is pre-empted by *ancestry*: The verb *decoration* is based on a noun derived from a verb with the same meaning, namely, *decorate*. The other illegitimate innovation is pre-empted by homonymy: The verb *cast* for adults means "make a cast from," not "put a cast on." The other locatum verbs in Table 13.4 are legitimate innovations. Notice, however, that some, like *rubber band*, may have an unexpected interpretation. Rubber bands are usually used as instruments for holding things together, not as objects to put somewhere. This clearly makes such verbs difficult to interpret out of context.

Table 13.5 lists some French examples of locatum verbs. As with the English examples in Table 13.4, most of these innovations are legitimate. The two exceptions are both instances of pre-emption by homonymy.

Table 13.4. *Locatum verbs: some English examples*

---

(1) DH (2;3, talking about getting dressed): *Mummy trousers me.*
(2) J   (2;6, asking a teacher to toss a pillow at him during a mock pillow fight): *Pillow me!*
(3) EB (3;4, deciding not to wear her new nightgown outside in the patio): *Mine will dust.*
    Mother: Dust?
    EB: *Mine will get dust on it.*
(4) EB (3;4, talking about her foot that had a Band-Aid put on earlier): *It was Band-Aided.*
(5) CB (3;11, putting crackers in her soup): *I'm crackering my soup.*
(6) JA (4;0, in the role of doctor dealing with a broken arm): *We're gonna cast it.*
(7) CB (4;2, talking about a rag for washing the car): *But I need it watered and soaped.*
(8) CB (4;5, putting first a bead and then a rubber band into the playdough she's kneading): *'I think I'll bead it. I think I'll rubber band it.*
(9) ME (4;11, talking about the Christmas tree): *We already decorationed our tree.*
(10) SA (5;0, to his mother): *Will you chocolate my milk?*
(11) JW (5;7, dressing a doll): *I'm shirting my man.*

Table 13.5. *Locatum verbs: some French examples*

---

(1) VA (4;5, wrapped up in a blanket when asked to put on her slippers): *Je vais me pantoufler dedans.* [I'll slipper myself inside.]
(2) EG (6;8), talking about some bread with egg on it, used *pain enoeuffé.* [egged bread/with egg on]
(3) CG (7;0), talking about bread thickly covered with jam, used *pain enconfituré.* [jammed bread/with jam on]
(4) CG (7;0), talking about putting syrup on things, used the verb *ensiroter.* [to syrup]
(5) CG (7;3,19, talking about his plate): *Mon assiette est entartée.* [My plate is covered with tart.]
(6) CG (13;0, asking for a cup of hot chocolate): *Chocolate-moi.* [Chocolate me.]
(7) CG (16;0, talking about builders who had been repairing the brickwork): *Ils ont bien briqué la maison.* [They've bricked the house well.]

(*En*)*siroter*, meaning "put syrup on" (based on *sirop*, "syrup"), is probably pre-empted by the adult *siroter*, meaning "drink with small sips"; and *briquer*, meaning "put bricks on" (from *brique*, "brick"), is pre-empted by adult "clean vigorously." The remaining verbs all appear to be legitimate.

Table 13.6 contains innovative locatum verbs produced by German-speaking children. Again, there are only a few illegitimate innovations.

Table 13.6. *Locatum verbs: some German examples*

(1) RN	(2;2), poking with a sharp tool into a hole, used *reinspitzen*. [to point-in/put the point in]
(2) HS	(3;0, having drunk enough milk): *Hab genug emilcht*. [(I) have milked enough.]
(3) Sc	(3;2), talking about applying a wet bandage, used *handtucheln*. [to towel]
(4) HS	(3;6, refusing to use a spoon because it had already been used for soup): *Der Löffel ist besuppt*. [The spoon is souped/has soup on it.]
(5) HS	(3;6), putting leaves into paper bags, used *einblättern*. [to leaf-in/put leaves in]
(6) FS	(3;9) talked about something covered in ashes as *vollgeascht*. [well ashed]
(7) GS	(3;11), making a string of beads, used *aufperlen*. [to thread beads]
(8) HS	(4;7, talking about having ribbons on that needed tying, used *zugebändst*. [ribboned]
(9) DL	(5;6, talking about stripes on something): *Hier ist Gold angestreift*. [This is gold-striped/has gold stripes on it.]

One of them is pre-empted by suppletion: *Angestreift*, "striped," is normally expressed by *gestreift* (another form based on *Streife*, "stripe"). There is also one pre-emption by homonymy: The verb *milchen*, meaning "drink milk," is kept by adults for "yield milk" (from *Milch* "milk").

The remaining innovations are all legitimate. In many cases, they are based on the same parent nouns as other adult verbs but contrast with them in meaning. For example, the child's *reinspitzen*, "put the point in," contrasts with adult *spitzen*, "make into a point, sharpen" (both from *Spitze*, "point"); the child's *einblättern*, "put leaves into," contrasts with adult *blättern*, "turn the leaves (of a book)" (both based on *Blatt*, "leaf"); and the child's *aufperlen*, "thread beads on," contrasts with adult *perlen*, "sparkle" (both based on *Perle*, "pearl").

Location, goal, and agent verbs. Innovative location, goal, and agent verbs are comparatively rare in children's speech. Some of the few examples observed for each language are illustrated in Tables 13.7 through 13.9. The parent nouns of these verbs denote the location, the goal, and the agent involved in the activity, respectively. There were no instances of agent verbs observed in the French data; this category was also very rare for English and German.

Table 13.7 gives some innovative location, goal, and agent verbs produced by English-speaking children. These verbs are occasionally hard to classify. For instance, *towel* was used for asking to be wrapped in the towel, not dried with it, hence its classification as a location rather than as an instrument verb. (Location and locatum verbs, in fact, often double as instrument verbs: *Net the fish*, for example, means both "put in a net"

Table 13.7. *Location, goal, and agent verbs: some English examples*

Location
(1) CA (4;6, waving a funnel at her younger sister): *I'm going to funnel you.*
        Ff, ff, ff. You're all in there.
(2) SO (ca. 5;0): *I'm going to basket those apples.*
(3) CB (5;5, asking her mother to stop her sister from putting popcorn
        "beads" on her thread): *Mom, will you keep Eva from threading on*
        mine?
(4) K   (7;0, asking her mother to wrap a towel round her as she got out of the
        bath): *Towel me, mommy.*

Goal
(5) S   (3;1, watching a cement truck with its back revolving): *That truck is*
        cementing. [making cement]
(6) CB (5;6, asking for her hair not to be done in "dogears"): I don't want to
        be dogeared today.

Agent
(7) EB (2;8, after roaring, with "claws" outstretched, at a towel hanging in
        the bathroom): *I monstered that towel.*
(8) AK (5;1, talking about someone dancing in a ballet): *She's ballerining.*
(9) HO (ca. 5;0, after overhearing some remarks about a new governess
        coming): *When is she coming to governess us?*

and "capture by means of a net.") In general, I have assigned such verbs to the instrument class except where the context made clear that they had a location or locatum meaning only (see E. Clark & H. Clark, 1979). Of the verbs in Table 13.7, only one is pre-empted, by homonymy. It is *cement*, meaning "make cement"; for adults, that same form means "put cement on." All the other verbs are legitimate innovations.

Table 13.8 contains innovative location and goal verbs from French-speaking children. Two verbs are illegitimate, both pre-empted by homonymy: *Emboîter*, meaning "put in an envelope" (from *boîte*, "box"), for adults means "nest or encase one box in another." And *bossu*, an adjectival form, means "humpbacked," not "humped," as the child intended. *Bosse* means "hump," but the adult verb has the meaning "fix ornamental humps (bosses) onto." The child's form, then, is illegitimate (quite aside from the auxiliary verb used). The remaining innovations all appear quite legitimate.

Table 13.9 presents location, goal, and agent verbs produced by German-speaking children. All three types were comparatively rare. Three of the verbs here are illegitimate. The one agent verb, *dieben*, meaning "steal" (based on *Dieb*, "thief"), is pre-empted by suppletion: Adult *stehlen* has the same meaning. The other illegitimate verbs are both pre-empted by homonymy: *Wassern*, meaning "place in water" (from *Wasser*, "water"), for adults means "alight on the water"; and *lichten*, mean-

Table 13.8. *Location and goal verbs: some French examples*

Location
(1) MA (3;3), talking about closing an envelope, used *emboîter*. [to box/put in a box]
(2) CG (9;3) described a procession on the water as *une procession eautée*. [a watered procession/on the water]

Goal
(3) EG (3;9,29, talking about some plants): *Elles ne sont pas encore grainées*. [They haven't made seeds yet.]
(4) VA (4;4, talking about an episode at the swimming pool): *J'ai rencontré une vieille dame qui m'avait mis de l'eau quand je m'avais bossu*. [I met an old woman who poured water on me when I made myself into a hump.]
(5) EG (5;8, arming himself with a toy sword and gun): *Je vais m'ensoldater*. [I'm going to make myself into a soldier.]

Table 13.9. *Location, goal, and agent verbs: some German examples*

Location
(1) RN (2;7,15, dipping a stick into a bucket of water): *Der Stock soll bewassert sein*. [The stick is supposed to be in the water.]
(2) Sc (3;11), talking about burying something, used *vererden*. [to earth]

Goal
(3) RN (2;10, talking about making small cakes): *Da wird er glatt und dann wird er ausgeplätzelt*. [Then it's getting smooth and then it's caked/ made into cakes.]
(4) RF (3;6,15), talking about showing one's teeth, used *bezähnen*. [to tooth]
(5) FS (3;11), talking about playing music, used *musiken*. [to music]
(6) HS (3;11), tying something in loops, used *zuschleifen*. [to loop]
(7) HS (5;1,15, talking about lights): *Du brauchst nicht zu lichten*. [You needn't light/shine a light.]
(8) HS (5;4,15, when her brother turned up the lamp): *Günther lichtet mehr*. [Günther lighted more/made more light.]

Agent
(9) GS (4;4), talking about someone stealing something, used *dieben*. [to thief]

ing "produce light" (from *Licht*, "light"), for adults means "make clearings (in a wood)" or "thin trees." *Lichten* is also pre-empted by suppletion since adults express the meaning "produce light" with the verb *belenchten*. Another pre-emption by suppletion occurs with *vererden* (based on *Erde*, "earth"), "bury," where the adult verb is *begraben* or *beerdigen*.

The remaining verbs all appear to be legitimate innovations. The meaning of *ausgepläzelt* (based on *Plätzchen*, "small cakes") is perfectly com-

Table 13.10. *Characteristic activity verbs: some English examples*

Act of
  (1) EB (2;3, when the stove timer went off): *The buzzer is buzzering.*
  (2) RG (3;0, wanting a bell to be rung): *Make it bell.*
  (3) S   (3;0, watching a truck go by): *It's trucking.*
  (4) S   (3;2, looking at a drooping flag that suddenly spread out in a gust of wind): *It flagged.*
  (5) S   (3;2, noticing a picture of trees leaning in the wind): *It winded.*
  (6) CB (3;11, making dots with a crayon over a person she had drawn): *It's snowflaking so hard that you can't see this person.*
  (7) CB (4;0, talking about pictures in a book she's making): *Right now it's storming. Here it's storming too.*
  (8) CB (4;4, describing a storm): *It was winding hard and then it started raining.*

Act done to
  (9) S   (2;4, to mother preparing to brush his hair): *Don't hair me.*
 (10) S   (2;4, eating soup): *I'm souping.*
 (11) J   (2;6, seated in a rocker): *Rocker me, mommy.*
 (12) S   (2;8,15, hearing his father using the vacuum cleaner in the hall): *Daddy's rugging down the hall.* (Later, going out to help): *I'm helping rug.*
 (13) S   (2;9, overheard talking to another child while outside playing with a toy lawn mower): *I'm lawning.*
 (14) EB (3;2, talking about another child): *I saw Julie match up a match.*
 (15) D   (5;0, looking at a picture revealed by moving a puzzle piece): *They're teaing.*
 (16) CB (6;0, bringing her mother two walnuts to crack): *Will you nut these?*
 (17) H   (6;0, during a card game, wanting to cut the deck): *It's my turn to deck the cards.*

---

prehensible. The same goes for *bezähnen* (based on *Zähne*, "teeth"), *musiken* (based on *Musik*, "music"), and *zuschleifen* (based on *Schleife*, "loop").

Characteristic activity verbs. Characteristic activity verbs, together with locatum verbs, form the largest group of children's innovations after instrument verbs. They denote the characteristic activity done *by* or *to* the particular entity denoted by the parent noun of the verb (E. Clark, 1978a). This class of verb is rare or nonexistent in adult speech for talking about the activities of concrete objects; the only potential exemplars in English appear to be the weather verbs like *rain* or *snow* (E. Clark & H. Clark, 1979). Typical examples from English, French, and German children are shown in Tables 13.10, 13.11, and 13.12. Although there are more instances in the corpus for English and German than for French, the French examples appear very similar to those in the other two languages.

The first half of Table 13.10 comprises activities done *by* the entity

Table 13.11. *Characteristic activity verbs: some French examples*

Act of
(1) VA (3;6, talking about the neighbor's cat meowing): *Chez Nan-nan,
j'entends miaou . . . miaouner . . . mianouner le chat de Madame P.*
[At Nan-nan's, I heard Madame P's cat meowing.]
(2) CG (6;3,17, talking about the weather): *I grelonne.* [It's hailing.]

Act done to
(3) CG (4;8,15, to his father): *Pipe un peu.* [Pipe/smoke your pipe a bit.]
(4) EG (11;0, discussing with his brother what to do): *Nous argilerons dans la
chambre.* [We'll clay/play with clay in the bedroom.]
(5) CG (13;0, responding to his brother's utterance, in [4]): *Et nous allons
microscoper.* [And we'll microscope.]
(6) WD (no age given), talking about playing the piano, used the verb *pianer.*
[to piano]

---

named in the verb; the second half comprises activities done *to* the entity
named in the verb, by someone else. Among the illegitimate innovations
in this table, several are pre-empted by suppletion, for example, *bell* or
ring, *match* by *light*, *nut* by *crack*, and *deck* by *cut*. The last verb, *deck*,
is also pre-empted by homonymy, because adult *deck* means either "put
X on a deck," as in *He decked his opponent*, or "put a deck on," as in
They decked and masted the ship. Three other verbs are pre-empted by
ancestry. *Buzzer* and *rocker* are both formed from nouns that are in turn
formed from *buzz* and *rock*, verbs that denote the activities talked about.
And *snowflake* is pre-empted by the simpler adult *snow*.

The legitimate innovations in Table 13.10 tend to fall into various segments of the "Others" category in E. Clark and H. Clark (1979). *Soup*
and *tea* are clearly akin to adult *lunch, breakfast*, and *snack*. *Wind* and
storm fall together with adult *rain* and *snow*. There is no obvious reason
why other weather terms should not occur as verbs in English. (Indeed,
storm is used by some speakers, but not by the parents of these children.)
Truck and *flag* denote the activity of these entities on particular occasions.
The nearest uses of these in adult speech are often figurative, as in *The
market submarined*, but such figurative verbs do not denote an actual
participant in the activity named by the verb. *Hair* represents a use that
was maintained by this particular child over eight months or so without
any encouragement from his parents. It resembles two other verbs used
by the same child, *lawn* and *rug*. Verbs like this do not seem to be
represented at all among adult categories of denominal verbs in English.

Table 13.11 presents a few characteristic activity verbs produced by
French-speaking children. These verbs seem rarer in French than in English or German and in general are produced by older children. Several
are illegitimate. Some are pre-empted by synonymy: *Miaouner* or *mian-*

Table 13.12. *Characteristic activity verbs: some German examples*

Act of
(1) RN (1;10, talking about the cat): *Miezelt.* [(It's) catting/meowing.]
(2) RN (1;10 talking about bees): *Die Biene hummelt.* [The bee is humming.]
(3) Tö (2;3, talking about a dog): *Der Hund waut.* [The dog is woofing.]
(4) RN (2;4,15, screwing in a screw): *Die Schraube tunndelt durch.* [The screw tunnels through.]
(5) RN (2;4,15, shaking out a cloth): *Jetz haben wir aber (ge)flügelt!* [Now we have winged.]
(6) RN (2;6), watching a barrel organ handle turn, used the verb *mühlen.* [to mill]
(7) SS (2;6, listening to bells): *Es glockt.* [It's belling.]
(8) RF (2;6,15, talking about a caterpillar): *Raupt.* [(It)'s caterpillaring.]
(9) RF (2;6,15, talking about a shrew): *Spitzt.* [(It)'s shrewing.]
(10) GS (3;2, talking about a coffee grinder): *Gemühlt.* [(It) mills.]
(11) Sc (4;0, talking about the weather): *Es windet.* [It's winding/the wind is blowing.]
(12) Sc (5;7), talking about waves flowing down, used the verb *runterwellen.* [to wave-down]
(13) HS (6;6, looking at someone blinking): *Du wimperst ja so schnell.* [You're (eye)lashing so quickly.]

Act done to
(14) RN (1;10), turning pages in a picture book, used the verb *bildern.* [to picture/turn pages in picture books]
(15) RN (2;8, when his mother wiped his nose): *Du näselst.* [You nose/wipe noses.]
(16) GS (2;9, after playing on the piano): *Fettig ewiert.* [Done pianoed.]
(17) HS (3;8, when her mother was drumming her fingers on the table): *Warum kawierst du denn dort?* [Why are you pianoing there?]

ouner, based on *miaou*, is pre-empted by adult *miauler*, with the same meaning.[7] Similarly, *grelonner* (based on *grelon*, "hailstone"), meaning "hail," is pre-empted by *grêler*, and *piper* (based on *pipe*, "pipe"), meaning "smoke (a pipe)," is pre-empted by *fumer*. *Piper* is actually pre-empted both by synonymy (the suppletive verb *fumer*) and by homonymy, since the form *piper*, for adults, carries the meaning "deceive." The remaining verbs, *argiler* (from *argile*, "clay"), *microscoper* (from *microscope*, "microscope"), and *pianer* (from *piano*, "piano"), all appear legitimate.

Lastly, Table 13.12 presents some typical examples of characteristic activity verbs from German-speaking children. This table is also divided into two sections, for activities done *by* the entity named in the verb and activities done *to* it. Most of the illegitimate innovations in this table are pre-empted by suppletion. For instance, the three verbs for animal sounds (based on *Mieze*, the name of the cat, *Hummel*, "bumblebee," and *Wau-*

wau, "woof-woof") are pre-empted by adult *miauen, summen*, and *abrinden*. *Tunndelt* (based on *Tunnel*, "tunnel"), meaning "tunnel/screw in," and *flügelt* (based on *Flügel*, "wing"), meaning "shake, flap," are preempted by *einschrauben* and *schütteln*, with those same meanings. And *mühlen* (from *Mühle*, "mill"), used for talking about turning the handle of a barrel organ, is pre-empted by adult *drehen*. Another use of *mühlen*, this time for talking about the action of a coffee grinder, is also preempted, but by the verb *mahlen*, "grind, mill." *Glocken* (from *Glocke*, "bell") occurs in several different records. One child, for instance, commented that people could "bell" every day: *Die könnten jeden Tag glocken* (HS, aged 4; 11, 15). This verb is pre-empted by *läuten*. *Runterwellen* (from *Welle*, "wave"), meaning "flow down (in waves)," and *wimpern* (from *Augenwimper*, "eyelash"), meaning "blink," are preempted by *runterfliessen* and *blinken* or *blinzeln*, respectively. Finally, *naseln*, meaning "wipe one's nose" (from *Nase*, "nose") is pre-empted by homonymy: For adults, this form has the meaning "speak through one's nose."

The remaining verbs in Table 13.12 all appear to be legitimate: They fill gaps in the adult lexicon, either where there is no particular word to express just that meaning or where one would use a phrase rather than a single word. For example, in talking about the typical motion of caterpillars and shrews, the child filled gaps in the adult lexicon by using *raupen* (from *Raupe*, "caterpillar") and *spitzen* (from *Spitzmaus*, "shrew"). *Windet* (from *Wind*, "wind") falls with other weather verbs in German, where the general pattern of use is similar to that in English. All the innovations in the second half of the table appear legitimate: *bildern* (from *Bild*, "picture"), and *ewiert* and *kawierst* (both from *Klavier*, "piano").

Patterns of innovation

The overall patterns of innovation in English-, French-, and German-speaking children are very similar. As the figures in Table 13.13 show, the same categories of denominal verbs were represented in each language, with the largest being instrument, locatum, and characteristic activity. The relative sizes of the six categories used were also similar, with an average rank order correlation between languages for these categories of .87. The one category missing from the French data, agent verbs, was also the smallest for the other two languages (2 percent of the totals). There appears to be considerable unanimity, then, among children in the categories of innovative denominal verbs they produce.

I also compared children's innovative verbs in English to their well-established verbs, and to adult denominal verbs.[8] These comparisons were designed to answer two questions. First, do the categories of well-established denominal verbs represented in 3-year-old speech correspond

Table 13.13. *Categories of innovative denominal verbs used in English, French, and German*

Verb category	English	French	German	% of total
Instrument	42	26	36	37
Locatum	21	34	18	22
Location	5	14	3	6
Goal	11	9	11	11
Agent	2	0	2	2
Experiencer	0	0	0	0
Source	0	0	0	0
Duration	0	0	0	0
Characteristic activity	19	17	30	22

Note: Data are expressed as a percentage of the corpus for each language, for comparison (123 English, 35 French, 66 German).

to the innovative categories children use? And second, do adult denominal verb categories correspond to the innovative categories children use?

For the first question I sorted the denominal verbs taken from seven vocabulary studies of children aged between 2 and 3 into categories, just as I had done with the innovative verbs. Since well-established verbs might provide a model for innovations, I counted only those denominal verbs whose parent nouns were also present in the children's vocabularies, to make sure that in each case there was a noun–verb pairing available. The percentage of well-established verbs in each category is shown in Table 13.14. Instrument verbs made up the largest group, followed at some distance by locatum verbs. The only other well-established verbs were a few instances of location and goal verbs. There were no verbs in any other categories, with the exception of two "weather" verbs, *rain* and *snow*, listed under Others.

A comparison of the first two columns in Table 13.14 reveals both similarities and differences in the categories represented among innovations and well-established verbs. The proportions of verbs for both in the first five categories were similar, although well-established instrument verbs had a larger share of the total (60 percent) than their innovative counterparts (42 percent). Furthermore, there were no instances of well-established agent verbs, as against 2 percent among innovations. From one point of view, this general positive correlation between innovative and well-established verbs could be regarded as surprising: One might expect the child to innovate mainly in categories where he knew fewer well-established verbs. This is clearly not the case. At the same time, the biggest difference between innovative and well-established verbs was in the last category – characteristic activity verbs. Although these made up

Table 13.14. *Child innovations, child well-established, and adult denominal verb categories in English*

Verb category	Child innovations	Child well-established	Adult
Instrument	42	60	32
Locatum	21	25	25
Location	5	3	14
Goal	11	6	12
Agent	2	0	12
Experiencer	0	0	.2
Source	0	0	.2
Duration	0	0	1
Others (combined)	0	6[a]	3[b]
Characteristic activity	19	0	0

Note: Data are expressed as a percentage of the total types for each corpus (123 innovative, 145 well-established, 1,323 adult).
[a] All these verbs were weather verbs.
[b] Weather verbs made up one-tenth of this category, or .3% of the total adult corpus.

one of the three largest categories among innovations (19 percent), they went completely unrepresented among well-established verbs.

For the second question, I examined the categories of denominal verbs represented in adult speech, together with their relative frequency, in a corpus of over 1,300 well-established and innovative verbs compiled by E. Clark and H. Clark (1979). The percentage of verbs in each category is shown in Table 13.14. The first two categories listed, instrument and locatum, between them accounted for 57 percent of the adult corpus, with the next three taking up a further 38 percent (location, goal, and agent verbs). The remaining categories together constituted a mere 5 percent, with no instances of characteristic activity verbs.

When these adult categories were compared to the categories of innovations produced by children, there were again some striking differences. Although adults and children used similar proportions of instrument and locatum verbs, children used fewer location and agent verbs. (This was true for both innovations and well-established forms in the child data.) But the biggest discrepancy was again in the last category: Characteristic activity verbs made up 19 percent of the children's corpus versus 0 percent of the adult one.

Where do characteristic activity verbs come from? There is no obvious model offered either by children's well-established verbs or by adult denominal verbs. The nearest potential candidates that might be considered are weather verbs like *rain* and *snow*, but their claim to the role of models for innovative characteristic activity verbs is at best very tenuous. First, weather verbs cover a very restricted domain of activity compared to the range covered by children's innovations (see Table 13.10). Second, weather verbs are highly restricted syntactically and occur only with subject-position *it*. But children's characteristic activity verbs occurred with animate subjects in the first, second, and third person as well as with *it*. In fact, the *it* used with characteristic activity verbs is rarely the ambient *it* of weather and time expressions (Bolinger, 1977), but is often an *it* co-referential with a non-animate noun phrase. Moreover, in contrast to weather verbs, which are intransitive, there were both intransitive and transitive characteristic activity verbs among the children's innovations.[9] Third, weather verbs made up only a small proportion of children's well-established verbs (6 percent – contributed by only two verbs, *rain* and *snow*) and an even smaller proportion of the adult corpus (0.3 percent). Characteristic activity verbs, then, appear to have no counterpart either in children's well-established denominal verbs or in adult denominal verbs.

13.4. Discussion

Lexical creativity is endemic in children's speech. Children exploit what they already know of their language to create new words. In talking about actions, they appear to draw freely on the stock of nouns they have available to create a wide range of innovative denominal verbs. But why do children create new words with new meanings? And what devices do they rely on in the process of innovation?

Using a rule

The data just considered suggest that in talking about actions, children assume that the noun denoting an entity can be used as a verb for any state, process, or activity associated with that entity. They do this, I argue, because they need the vocabulary to talk about actions with a degree of precision not otherwise available (E. Clark, 1978a). The result of such an assumption is reliance on an extremely general rule for producing new verbs, a rule that is gradually narrowed down in its possible applications as children get older. Let me now spell out the arguments in support of this view of children's innovative denominal verbs.

When young children talk about actions, they appear to face certain difficulties. Their vocabulary for actions typically lags behind that for objects, and they take a relatively long time to work out verb meanings (see, e.g., E. Clark, 1978a; Gentner, 1975, 1978). Naming the entity involved in the action, then, may be a good substitute for finding precisely the right verb. Indeed, many of the denominal verbs children create are pre-empted by specific action verbs already present in the language.

Sweep normally pre-empts *broom, drive* pre-empts *car, fly* pre-empts *airplane*, and *shoot* pre-empts *gun*, to take only a few of the attested English examples. For adults, innovative denominal verbs serve the appropriate purpose only where established verbs are lacking. For children, innovative denominal verbs fill more gaps since they do not yet know many of the established verbs that will later pre-empt some of their innovations. Their rule of using a noun as a verb for talking about a precise action serves them well: They want to express precise meanings and they lack other devices for doing so.

Changing a noun into a verb seems to be a very simple business in English. As many linguists have pointed out (e.g., Adams, 1973; Jespersen, 1942; Marchand, 1969), this process has had a very long history in English. Moreover, the noun-to-verb changeover, with no derivational affix to add to mark the change in form class, has virtually no productive competing patterns in English. This presumably makes the creation of verbs from nouns already known particularly easy for children: They do not have to master any special affixes in coining new verbs.

But where does their rule come from? The comparison made between children's innovative verb categories and their well-established denominal verbs showed that the innovations were not simply modeled on their well-established verbs. Nor were their innovations modeled on adult denominal verb categories (see Table 13.14). Adults produced some categories of denominal verbs that did not appear in children's speech, and children created one large class of innovative verbs that was not represented in adult speech.

Their rule might nonetheless be abstracted from observations of adult usage. There are many instances where the noun–verb pairing is transparent, as in *bicycle/bicycle, brush/brush*, or *dress/dress*. Children could simply make an over-broad generalization from such cases to come up with a rule that might be characterized as follows:

> Any noun denoting a concrete entity can be used as a verb for talking about a state, process, or activity associated with that entity.

Notice that this rule is essentially equivalent to condition (6) of the adult convention governing innovative denominal verbs. The difference is that children apply their rule too generally because, first (unlike the adult rule), it is not constrained by the other parts of the adult denominal verb convention; second, they lack other (pre-empting) vocabulary; and third, they lack the ability to judge mutual knowledge for their interlocuters.

These data, someone might complain, are really just mistaken part-of-speech assignments. Children are using nouns as verbs, not because they are relying on a rule, but because they do not know that those lexical items are really nouns and not verbs. For instance, one possibility might be that children begin by identifying the word *broom*, say, as a verb and at first never use it as a noun. This misassignment would produce just the kind of data we have been considering. Another possibility is that children first identify *broom* as a noun but are confused about whether it is a noun or a verb and so use it in both ways. A third possibility, the one put forward here, is that children know *broom* is a noun but use it as a verb in order to say things they could not say otherwise.

One consequence of the first two possibilities is that children should use verbs as concrete nouns just as often as they use concrete nouns as verbs. However, the data do not fit this prediction: There is a strong asymmetry in children's usage. My records contain only seven verbs used as concrete nouns in English, for example, *the shave* (lather), *the rub* (eraser). In fact, the process of forming concrete nouns from verbs has always been much rarer in English than the formation of verbs from concrete nouns (Marchand, 1969). Moreover, 3-year-old speech is remarkably free of any other part-of-speech confusions. As Brown (1957) demonstrated, children that age are already very sensitive to part-of-speech information provided by the syntactic context of newly introduced words. Using a noun as a verb, then, represents the setting up of a precise means for talking about actions.

Is this rule really a rule for children, or could they instead be using a series of analogies to arrive at the innovations produced? The evidence as a whole favors rule use over analogy. Although children produced a number of innovative verbs that fell into various adult denominal verb categories (see, e.g., Table 13.1, 13.4, and 13.7), they also produced verbs of a type *not* used by adults – namely, characteristic activity verbs (Table 13.10). Had children been using analogy, it should have been possible to identify potential models for each verb type among either children's well-established denominal verbs or adult verb categories. But even if that had been possible, rule use could not have been excluded as an explanation. Either analogy or rule could have been at work. However, since children did produce, as one of their largest categories, a verb type for which there was no model from which to work by analogy, they must have been using a rule.

Although the evidence favors rule use in the case of innovative denominal verbs, this may not necessarily be true of the acquisition process in general. Children may rely on rote, analogy, and rule, in differing degrees at different stages, depending on the aspect of language being acquired. Generalizations about other types of lexical innovation will have to await further case studies like the one undertaken here.

Child rule and adult convention

One consequence of the rule children use is that they produce illegitimate as well as legitimate innovative denominal verbs. But to distinguish illegitimate from legitimate innovations, children need to master the convention that specifies the circumstances under which a denominal verb is legitimate. The rule children rely on is more general than the rule given in condition (6) of the adult convention, largely because the child rule is not yet constrained by the remainder of this convention of use. The convention as a whole has to be acquired. But when does this acquisition take place? Although there are numerous illegitimate innovations in the speech of 3- to 5-year-olds, there are many fewer in the speech of older children. Learning the convention must begin with the rule children abstract, a rule that is virtually equivalent to condition (6). But they may not acquire the rest of the conditions that make up the full convention until many years later.

Although there is little research that bears on the different conditions in such a convention, there are some findings available that seem pertinent to the mutual knowledge condition. As H. Clark and Haviland (1977) pointed out, *the* has among its uses the marking of information as given, or known, to both speaker and addressee. Indefinite *a*, in contrast, is used for the first mention of information new to the addressee. Thus use of *the* assumes mutual knowledge in certain contexts, whereas *a* does not. Studies of *the* and *a* have shown that, although children contrast these articles in some situations as early as age 4 or 5, they overuse the definite *the* in certain first-mention contexts as late as age 8 or 9 (Maratsos, 1976; Warden, 1976). This slowly emerging appreciation of what the addressee knows is illustrated by the following exchange between EB, aged 4; 6, who misused *the*, and her older sister CB, aged 7; 0, who corrected her. The younger child was recounting to her mother a Flintstone episode both children had watched and ended with an allusion to "the island." Her older sister promptly called her to task: "You were saying *the*! She doesn't know!" Appreciation of what is readily and uniquely computable presumably grows slowly too.

Learning the convention, of course, parallels learning a larger and larger vocabulary. And with a larger vocabulary comes the possibility that the meanings of some lexical items will coincide with the meanings of innovations. While true synonyms are hard to find in adult speech, little is known about how much synonymy children may tolerate in their lexicons. The evidence from early language acquisition is that children set up new words in contrast to those already in their repertoire. But no studies have examined what happens with noun and well-established verb pairs like *gun/shoot, needle/mend,* or *broom/sweep.* At what point after adding the verb, say, do children stop using innovative forms based on the parent nouns *gun, needle,* and *broom*? Do pre-empting forms take over as soon as children have worked out their full meaning? Or do both verbs – the illegitimate innovation and the well-established verb – exist side by side for a while until children come to appreciate that pre-emption is one of the consequences of the convention on innovative denominal verbs? The early structuring and restructuring of vocabulary domains like those for animal terms suggest that children *do* treat new lexical items as if they contrast with those already known (E. Clark, 1978a). So, if they are consistent in this, they are acting much as adults do (Bolinger, 1977) and will presumably eliminate illegitimate innovations as soon as they realize that they coincide in meaning with well-established verbs.

The child's overgeneral rule for forming verbs from nouns, therefore, is eventually narrowed down and incorporated into a convention governing such innovations. But the innovative denominal verb convention is only one of many such conventions that operate in English. It is a convention of language use, a convention for creating new verbs. Acquiring such conventions of language use is just as important as acquiring the conventions of a language – the knowledge that particular words or morphemes established as part of the language have particular meanings (Morgan, 1978). Children have to learn both. That they start early on such conventions is attested by their abstraction of the rule for forming new verbs from concrete nouns. That acquisition of the convention itself may take a very long time is attested by the late age at which they seem able to appreciate what is and is not mutually known. In summary, such conventions of language use are an integral part of what there is to learn when one acquires a language.

Parallels across languages

Children acquiring French and German come up with innovative denominal verbs very similar to those produced by children acquiring English. Their verb types parallel those for English (Table 13.13), with the three largest categories being the same – instrument, locatum, and characteristic activity. Their characteristic activity verbs (Tables 13.11 and 13.12) pose the same problem for analogy as they do with English-speaking children: This category is virtually unrepresented in adult speech, yet productive for children. French and German children, then, not only seem to come up with a similar rule for forming new verbs from nouns, but also apply that rule overgenerally in producing innovative denominal verbs. Just like English-speaking children, they too are setting up a precise way for talking about actions.

Innovative denominal verbs in both French and German are added to the largest regular verb paradigm in their respective languages. In French, this is the first conjugation, marked by *-er* for the infinitive and regular inflections to indicate person, number, and tense. Historically, the process of forming verbs from nouns has been fairly productive in French, and it continues to be a productive source of new verbs in various technological domains (Guilbert, 1975). In German, innovative denominal verbs again go into the first conjugation, with an infinitive in *-en* (added to the noun stem) or in *-eln* (with iterative meaning), and with regular inflections for person, number, and tense, just as in French. The formation of new verbs from nouns is very productive in German (Curme, 1922/ 1964; Fleischer, 1969), although, according to Marchand (1969), not quite so pervasive as in English.

Although there has been no analysis of the current productivity of denominal verbs in adult French and German, the data produced by children are striking in their resemblance both to each other and to data from English-speaking children. In all three languages, forming new verbs from concrete nouns is a device available to both adults and children. Children presumably form their rule on the basis of transparent noun–verb pairings in adult speech. But once their rule is formed, they apply it far more widely than adults do, and in the process create a category of denominal verb not found in adult speech. Moreover, the creation of many illegitimate innovative verbs, which are later dropped, is strong evidence for the existence of conventions governing lexical innovation in French and German similar to the convention governing innovative denominal verbs in English.

Further issues

When children coin new words – here, new verbs – they do not do so with a very even hand. Some categories of innovative denominal verbs are much larger than others, and some adult categories are not even represented at all among child innovations. Why this unevenness of productivity? There appear to be several factors that could affect the process of coining new verbs: the size of the child's lexicon, the conceptual salience of particular categories, the child's syntactic knowledge, and economy of expression. I will take up each of these factors in turn.

The size of the lexicon children have at their disposal might be pertinent to productivity in two ways. To begin with, notice that children acquire many more nouns than verbs in the early stages of language. This may be because it is easier to map nouns than verbs onto things they denote in the world (E. Clark, 1978a; Gentner, 1978). As a result, one could propose that the categories of innovative verbs in children's speech represent just those domains in which children have few other verbs available. However, this view does not stand up well to scrutiny. First, since children produce many innovative instrument and locatum verbs, they should have very *few* well-established verbs in these domains. But instrument and locatum turn out to be the *largest* categories among their well-established denominal verbs (see Table 13.13). The only support for this position, then, would be from characteristic activity verbs, because children have no other way of expressing these actions. Second, the wide use children make of general-purpose verbs like *do* and *go* during the early stages of acquisition (E. Clark, 1978a) would seem to remove any imperative to coin particular categories of denominal verbs. Nonetheless, children do do this.

A second way in which the lexicon could affect productivity is in the device used. Because young children dispose of a larger stock of nouns than verbs, their nouns are presumably all the more available for "conversion" into verbs to fill particular gaps of meaning. This asymmetry between children's noun and verb inventories presumably accounts for why innovative denominal verbs are so much commoner in children's speech than deverbal nouns. But the differences observed in the sizes of different innovative verb categories are not explained by this asymmetry per se.

An alternative view is that the larger categories of innovative and well-established verbs reflect instead the conceptual salience of certain types of object. If some types of object are more salient than others, then it could be important for children to look for ways of talking about any actions connected with them. Given the data in Table 13.13, this view would require instruments, locata, and objects with characteristic activities to be the most salient for small children. However, little can be said about this view since there is currently no independent evidence that these categories are conceptually more salient than the others attested among denominal verbs.

As far as syntactic knowledge is concerned, investigators like Bowerman (1974) have linked the appearance of periphrastic causatives with *make* and *get* to the appearance of other causative verb forms, among them innovative denominal verbs. She argued that new causative verbs (e.g., *fall, funnel*) enter the child's repertoire only after the appearance of periphrastic forms (e.g., *make fall, put in the funnel*) to express the same notion. In other words, Bowerman seemed to be suggesting that there is a derivational relation, syntactically, between "unpacked" periphrastic forms of causative (to make the blanket be on the bed) and conflated forms (to blanket the bed). However, my longitudinal data for S show very few instances of periphrastic causative *make, get,* or *be* prior to the appearance of innovative denominal verbs in his speech. This suggests that periphrastic and conflated forms may not be derivationally related. Rather, they could represent alternative ways of expressing causation that may or may not be mastered at the same time by young children. Moreover, notice that the presence of periphrastic verb forms in the child's speech does not seem to explain why children might opt for a denominal coinage rather than a general-purpose verb or a periphrastic expression.

For adult speakers, however, the choice can make a difference. For instance, one can distinguish between manipulative and directive causation in considering the meaning differences between such pairs as *to kill* and *to make die*. Shibatani (1976) argued that in manipulative causation (e.g., kill), the causer or agent plays a more direct role in the action, and the purpose of the act goes beyond the immediate result or outcome. In directive causation (e.g., make die), in contrast, the role of the causer is less direct (and may be secondhand, as in *Bill made John die by having someone else run over him*), but the focus is on the immediate outcome of the act. Lexical (*kill*) and periphrastic (*make die*) causative expressions, then, may contrast in meaning (see also McCawley, 1978).

Although there has been little detailed analysis to date of the possible meaning contrasts between lexical and periphrastic causatives, the distinction is one that is clearly pertinent to uses of denominal verbs. Notice, for instance, that *dress* in *He dressed the child* has the general meaning of "put clothes on," whereas the periphrastic version in *He put a dress on the child* does not. In the latter case, one knows only that the child ended up wearing a dress. The question that requires exploration is whether such contrasts between lexical and periphrastic causatives are at all systematic. In any case, where contrasts do exist, children have eventually to acquire them, and the fact that they exist for such commonly used pairs as *dress* and *put a dress on* may play some role in explaining why children do not rely exclusively on general-purpose verbs but coin denominal verbs as well (see also Ammon, 1980). A further point is that there may be no commonly used periphrastic form even available. This is the case for many characteristic activity verbs (e.g., *It flagged* or *It's trucking*) and indeed could be the reason why children coin characteristic activity verbs in the first place.

Yet another factor behind denominal verb use as opposed to reliance on periphrastic or general-purpose verb constructions may be the placement of information in an utterance. Denominal verbs, unlike periphrastic constructions, allow information about the action and the object involved in that action to be conflated and thus be expressed simultaneously. Otherwise, this information would have to be spread out over the utterance. Moreover, in the case of causative or transitive denominal verbs, the conflated verb precedes the direct object. As a result, denominal verbs allow information to be packaged in a more economical way than periphrastic constructions do. This allows children (and adults) to focus, if needed, on the action as a whole expressed in a single lexical item, instead of in a series of two or more items within the utterance. However, given the meaning contrasts observable between periphrastic and lexical causatives, the search for economy could be only a fragment of the whole story.

In summary, children's denominal verbs are more numerous in some categories than others. Several factors probably contribute to this, among them the size of the early lexicon together with the relative numbers of nouns and verbs available, the conceptual salience of particular categories

of objects, syntactic knowledge of the contrasts between lexical and periphrastic constructions, and finally, economy of expression. The extent
to which these factors play a role in the coining of innovative denominal
verbs cannot be determined at this point. But by drawing attention to
them, I hope to raise further questions about lexical creativity generally
and what it is governed by, over and above the conventions children have
to learn.

13.5. Summary

Lexical creativity is common in children's speech. In the present study
I have focused on just one aspect of that creativity – their coining of
innovative denominal verbs. Children create new verbs for particular
actions from the nouns for the entities involved in the actions they wish
to talk about. They do this, I have suggested, to fill gaps in their current
lexicon.

To form innovative denominal verbs, children use a rule, not analogy.
Their rule can be represented as: "Any noun denoting a concrete entity
can be used as a verb for talking about a state, process, or activity
associated with that entity." The main evidence for this rule is that children produce a large category of innovative denominal verbs – characteristic activity verbs – for which they lack any model in adult speech.

Conventions of language use are an important part of what children
learn when they learn a language. The rule children use coincides with
one condition of the convention that governs adult use of innovative
denominal verbs. But learning the remaining conditions of the adult convention takes time. At first, children simply apply their rule in an overgeneral fashion and produce both legitimate and illegitimate innovative
verbs. Later, they must take into account such factors as mutual knowledge, uniqueness, and ready computability in assessing whether their
listeners will be able to understand innovative verbs as they intended.
Although children begin learning this convention of language use very
early, they take a long time to master it in its entirety. The present case
study has documented some of the first steps in this process of innovation.

Notes

1 Even though lexical creativity pervades everyday adult speech, it has seldom
  been discussed or analyzed in any detail (but see E. Clark & H. Clark, 1979;
  Downing, 1977; L. Gleitman & H. Gleitman, 1970). Most discussion of linguistic
  creativity in children has been limited on the one hand to the combining of
  words to form new utterances, and on the other to the adding of inflections to
  nonsense words.
2 The actual boundaries between these categories are not always clear-cut. For
  example, many locatum verbs can also be instrumental. Contrast *He leashed*

the dog with *He leashed the dog to the post*. In the former, *leash* would be classified as a locatum verb and in the latter as an instrument verb as well (see further E. Clark & H. Clark, 1979, pp. 778–9).

3 The procedures in the first two steps clearly assume that children do not have to learn each present–past pair by rote. If they did, they should never produce incorrect past-tense forms, and they should be unable to use the generalization described in the third step to form past tenses for "new" (nonsense-syllable) verbs. However, even very young children overregularize verb and noun endings (W. Miller & Ervin, 1964) and readily add endings to nonsense forms they can never have heard before (Berko, 1958).

4 Similarity of phonological shape, of course, is only one of many dimensions of similarity that children (or adults) might use in forming analogies. They could equally well rely on conceptual criteria, for instance, where the action to be denoted is similar in some way to some other action for which they already have a word with a present–past contrast. I give phonological shape as the example here simply for illustrative purposes.

  Notice also that although people may appear to favor analogy in very small paradigms like *throw/threw, grow/grew, know/knew, blow/blew*, or *ring/rang, sing/sang*, when presented with nonsense stems of similar shapes, it is quite possible that these, too, involve rule use. The rules here would simply be more restricted than the one for weak verbs taking *-ed*.

5 According to Grevisse (1964), at least 90 percent of all French verbs belong to the first conjugation.

6 Although there has been no research, to my knowledge, on the form of the conventions governing innovative denominal verbs in French and German, I shall assume that they are similar for conditions (1) through (5) to that for English, and have similar consequences.

7 It is possible that verbs denoting animal noises like this ought to be treated as goal rather than characteristic activity verbs (see also Table 13.12). However, these verbs seem to be just as closely linked to other animal verbs where the characteristic activity is the typical motion rather than the noise produced. They are therefore grouped together in the present analysis.

8 These comparisons were confined to English because there are no published data available for the pertinent comparisons in French and German.

9 The range of characteristic activity verbs in English was also typical for the other two languages considered (see Table 13.11 and 13.12). Moreover, the syntactic properties of these innovations are very comparable to the English examples, in contrast to the restricted syntax of weather verbs in both French and German.

Part V

ALTERNATIVE CONCEPTIONS OF ACQUISITION

14. Some implications of the nonspecific bases of language

T. G. Bever

Plato thought nature but a spume that plays
Upon a ghostly paradigm of things;
Solider Aristotle played the taws
Upon the bottom of a king of kings . . .

. . . O chestnut-tree, great-rooted blossomer,
Are you the leaf, the blossom or the bole?
O body swayed to music, O brightening glance,
How can we know the dancer from the dance?

Yeats, "Among School Children"

This essay explores some implications for the study of language acquisition of the view that the essential formal characteristics of language are not human in origin. According to this interpretation they are universal abstract objects whose properties are uncaused. The idea that linguistic universals are uncaused "Platonic" forms, in particular, has been recently suggested by J. Katz (1978, 1979, 1981), who argues that some essential features of language rest on necessary truths. This view attributes the structure of some linguistic universals to factors not uniquely intrinsic to humans. It would remove the explanation of linguistic universals from the strictly human biological or historical domain, by claiming that linguistic universals are purely formal. Accordingly, linguistics would be a nonempirical science, of the same sort as classical geometry or modern logic.

It is impossible to find direct empirical justification for such a Platonic interpretation of language, just as it is impossible by observation to prove that geometries are, or are not, abstract domains. We can, however, pursue the implications of such ideas for the way we study empirically related phenomena. In the case of language, the empirical domain that I shall consider is the psychology of language, with special emphasis on how children learn it.

The nonspecific view of the essence of language could resolve several puzzles in the interpretation of language evolution and psychology of

This speculative essay was stimulated in large part by discussions with Jerry Katz, Terry Langendoen, and my students. The reader interested in Platonic linguistics should consult Katz (1981), which presents the most definitive case to date. I am grateful to V. Valian, R. Gelman, C. Carrithers, P. Postal, and the editors for manuscript advice.

language. From this view, the stultifying conflict between radical nativism and radical empiricism becomes purely an empirical problem for psychologists, with no relation to linguistic investigations. The structure of the essence of language in the child is caused neither by the way it is inherited nor by the way it is learned: It is *discovered* (like atoms, planets, and America, or logic, geometry, and numbers). The origin of the essence of language in the species is no longer necessarily ascribed to purposeful evolutionary causation; rather, it could be the result of the emergence of sufficient complexity (mental or physical) for humans to become susceptible to the relevant forms of language.

This view would also explain why certain linguistically possible languages are unusable; linguistic structures do not overlap completely with cognitive capacities. Certain common cognitive processes never occur in language: Although usable by the human mind, such cognitive processes are not part of the extrinsically determined essence of language. Correspondingly, if the essential features of language are real, independent of humans, then they are not caused by mechanisms of human evolution or learning.

This view has implications for what we should expect to find in language acquisition. There may be special-purpose learning capacities that are adapted to linguistic structure. However, if these capacities do not themselves cause the structures, we may find instances in which children systematically generate false *kinds* of hypotheses about their native language.

14.1. Some puzzles if linguistic structure is caused

We start by distinguishing existing languages from humanly possible languages (Postal, forthcoming). It is clear that the potential varieties of human languages are not exhausted by the languages that happen to have existed. Each language family seems sufficiently distinct to suggest the possibility that an arbitrarily large number of such families could exist. This finding requires that the science of linguistics focus on the form of a possible language, taking existing languages as empirical instances. Such an approach has been the basis for the isolation of a set of universals of language (e.g., N. Chomsky, 1965). Each observed universal has two obvious possible sources: It is accidental, or it is characteristic of what a language in humans must be.

At first consideration, it might seem that all the observed universal characteristics constitute the essence of language, the subject matter of formal linguistic science. However, some of these universal properties are caused by the ways in which human beings learn and use language: Obvious candidates are such universals as the absence of languages with a word made up of ten stop consonants in a row; the absence of languages having neither inflections, function words, nor word-order constraints;

the absence of languages with no way of asking questions. Such linguistic lacunae are reviewed extensively elsewhere (see Bever, 1970; Bever, Katz, & Langendoen, 1976; G. Miller & Chomsky, 1963; Postal, 1980). Their significance for the present discussion is that they force a distinction between two kinds of constraints on humanly possible languages. Certain constraints, such as those just mentioned, are extrinsic to the form of language, and are purely human in origin. No special linguistic account is required of how these constraints are discovered by the child – they emerge as an automatic result of the way language is used.

The child's conformity with certain other universal constraints has no such obvious source: Accordingly, these are interpretable as intrinsic formal constraints. Examples of this may include a distinction between fixed units (e.g., words) and compositional entities that relate the fixed units in specific ways (e.g., sentences); a distinction between inner and outer form; or a semantic interpretation of the compositional entities that is a function of the fixed units and their interrelations.

Such intrinsic constraints are characteristic of the essence of language and provide an account of what is criterially linguistic. A correct account of how these linguistic features emerge in each language is typically interpreted as a psychobiological problem: Namely, what mechanisms allow human children to isolate and integrate these, and only these, features in their linguistic knowledge and behavior? In other words, how does the child extract language from the environment?

There is a startling degree of agreement on this question among the authors of chapters in this volume. Virtually every chapter assumes that the child imposes a rich structure on an impoverished environment and thereby is at least a sufficient cause of the essence of linguistic structures, responding to the varied and sparse linguistically relevant data he or she experiences. Though there are apparent disagreements about how the child proceeds, these are trivial compared with the agreement on the question of nativism. All these writers share the view that the essence of language is caused by humans, and each adheres to at least one of the following three positions (most appear to hold to the first):

1. There is a unique innate faculty of language, which sets criteria on a possible language and thereby determines what the child listens for and accepts in the surrounding language.
2. There is a unique, innate faculty of learning, which forces language to be of a certain form because no other language is learnable (Wexler, Chapter 10).
3. There is an independently emergent faculty of communication, which leads the child to construct language out of different cognitive skills in a specific way (Bates & MacWhinney, Chapter 6).[1]

Each of these somewhat distinct positions maintains implicitly that there is a *genie d'enfant* that constrains a child to create the essence of language out of impoverished linguistic experiences. The difference in the positions lies primarily in how specialized the *genie* is. Willingly (positions [1] and [2]), or unwillingly (position [3]), each claim accepts the following syllogism, outlined in various instantiations by N. Chomsky, and rephrased by many others.

To be proven: Language is innate:

1.   The essence of language has property P_i.
2. P_i cannot be learned by any (known) (conceivable) theory of learning.
3.   Therefore P_i is innate.
4.   Therefore the essence of language is innate (and caused thereby).

The crucial assumption in this proof is the negative statement (2). In most examples of this syllogism, some property P_i of great intricacy is described, rendering implausible any claim that it is extracted by an orderly inductive learning mechanism. Genetically transmitted behaviors such as upright walking or ethologically isolated patterns could be cited as examples of complex behavior patterns that can be transmitted genetically. These behaviors, however, are orders of magnitude less refined and articulate than language appears to be and do not set a convincing precedent.[2]

Therefore, the very intricacy of linguistic property P_i could be the crucial substantive step of a relatively *anti*nativist argument.

To be proven: Language is learned:

1.   The essence of language has property P_i.
2. P_i cannot be transmitted by any (known) (conceivable) genetic mechanism.
3.   Therefore P_i is learned.
4.   Therefore the essence of language is learned (and caused by how it is learned).

There is a dilemma. We must rely either on as yet inconceivably complex genetic mechanisms of behavioral transmission or on an inconceivably delicate and sensitive inductive system of learning. As is often the case with dilemmas, one can blunt its horns by noting that each one presupposes an unnecessary claim, in this case the same claim:

The essence of language has a cause.

Each of the syllogisms offered presupposes that, whether innate or acquired, the essence of language is caused to be the way it is either by genetic or by social factors, by the biology of the human child or by historical accident. To put it contrastively, according to the commonly accepted view, language could have essential features incompatible with those currently proposed if humans were biologically different, or had a different history.

In this sense, the essence of language is claimed to be like color vision in humans. Color vision is a richly structured system, involving complementary colors and focal colors. No abstract property or law of physics forces color vision to operate that way; indeed, many animals are sensitive to different parts of the light-wave spectrum, and many do not differentiate "color" in the same way. Its essential features must be biologically caused by direct genetic transmission, or indirectly caused by interaction of historical accidents and mechanisms of learning. By either interpretation, the essential features of language are empirically, that is, physiologically and/or historically, caused.[3]

Each of the views outlined previously implies that the essence of language, though biologically or culturally caused, is a historical accident. "Language" could have taken an arbitrarily large number of forms: The form taken is explained by evolutionary or social history, in combination with any relevant physical laws governing complex systems such as the human brain. This brings us to the second empirical problem of linguistic nativism: the awesome precision of an accidental evolution of the essence of language. If the essence of language emerged gradually, what enlightened and ever-constant millennial entelechy could have guided it? If it emerged in a single cluster of developments, what mysterious instantaneous entelechy did the dirty deed?

If the essence of language is the way it is by virtue of factors extrinsic to humans, there is no need to explain its structure by reference to historical, social, or evolutionary facts that are true only of humans. If the essence of language is an abstract form, then its particular mastery by humans is not the cause of the form – indeed, the form has no cause. The nature of that linguistic structure would not have to be accounted for by human brains, history, or behavior. This would blunt the poignancy of the evolutionary dilemma. The controversy would no longer concern the explanation of what causes language to be the way it is, since its nature is uncaused.

Of course, how humans discover such basic forms may involve phenomena of a variety of kinds (biological, formal, physical). But the child's discovery procedure would not be an explanation of the structure of what is discovered. Neither evolution nor empiricism would be required to explain why language is the way it is; one has only to explain how language is discovered by individuals. That question is surely a totally empirical one, roughly on a par with such questions as how humans learn about integers or learn to walk. Investigations of this sort are important, especially for the human psychologist and physiologist, but they should not be confused with the view that we cause what we learn.

There is a third problem raised by the theory that language is caused by humans: the mental segregation of linguistic processes within the mind. There are formally possible linguistic rules that do not occur in any known language, and there are cognitively possible processes that do not occur in any known language. That is, the matrix shown here is completely instantiated (notice that this matrix is the universal analogue of the distinction between "grammaticality" and "usability" in individual grammars; see Bever, Carrol, & Hurtig, 1975; Bever & Langendoen, 1973):

	Natural cognitive process	Unnatural cognitive process
Linguistic process	copying (I)	scrambling (II)
Nonlinguistic process	symmetry (III)	hyperbolic function (IV)

It is trivially true that there are types of rules of which we are linguistically and nonlinguistically capable (type I in the matrix), and also rules which are unnatural in behavior, both within and outside language (type IV). I have already noted that there are cases of rules that the essence of language would appear to allow, but that do not occur in any known language (type II). An example might be a total "scrambling" rule that reorders constituents freely (see Bever, 1970, 1975; Bever & Langendoen, 1973, for discussions of such cases). There seems to be no obvious intrinsic constraint against any such rule (within a transformational framework); yet it could lead to an unusable language, because every sentence would be profoundly ambiguous. Hence it may be a linguistically possible process but be nonexistent in humans for nonlinguistic mental reasons.

Such cases are problematic for an interpretation of linguistics as a discipline about actual human knowledge. If there are potential languages allowed by universal linguistic theory that cannot be learned, what is the mental or physiological implication of universal linguistic theory? If some well-formed grammars cannot be learned by humans, linguistic theory is not about the human mind. We must accept the implication of this argument about specific rule processes for the claim that there are linguistically possible languages that are cognitively impossible. That is, a language just like English except for a word-order scrambling rule is a possible "real" language, but not a possible human language (see J. Katz, 1980; Postal, 1980, for further discussion).

The distinction between possible mental process and possible linguistic rule leaves us with a notion of a mentally isolated *Festung Sprache* that is both of the mind and not of it. What could be meant is puzzling even at a physiological or modular level of interpretation. A possible model is that one "part" of the mind can learn language (regardless of usage constraints like those just discussed) while another "part" of the mind imposes usage constraints. By this view, we would have to accept the strange picture of one piece of the mind's inchoately "knowing" something eternally private (all the potential languages) that cannot be used by any other piece of the mind.[4]

Even more telling is the fact that certain mentally natural rules do not appear in any language. The ability to process symmetrical reflections as a special intuitive category of experience is such an example. No language has a rule that allows any arbitrary sequence of constituents to be reversed (e.g., changing *The boy ate the sandwich* into *Sandwich the ate boy the*). Yet general symmetries are frequent in human behavior, ranging from visual sensation to abstract music. Why are there no productive symmetrical rules in language? (cf. N. Chomsky, 1965, for a different discussion of the significance of symmetries). If language is biologically or historically caused by an organism that is thoroughly capable of symmetrical processes, why do they not appear in language? At a formal level, symmetries are extremely easy to describe, with a simple context-free phrase-structure grammar – hence their absence cannot be a result of their formal complexity in languagelike systems (see Bever, Fodor, & Weksel, 1965b). In a transformational grammar framework one can "explain" their absence by noting that symmetrical rules are prohibitively complex to state with transformations over sequences of arbitrary length, and that transformations would have the effect of destroying any symmetries generated by the base structure.

This explanation, however, is parochially formal, and begs the question concerning the causation of the rules. The question is not why transformational grammar, in particular, blocks symmetrical rules, but why language of the symmetry-free form is describable by transformational grammar. If language is an "organ" of a mind that characteristically infects every intellectual adventure with symmetry, why is language itself immune? One cannot argue that a symmetrical rule would serve no communicative purpose. First, there are numerous properties of language that do not serve any obvious communicative purpose. Second, there is ample evidence that other variations in word order serve many linguistic and communicative purposes. One cannot argue that symmetries already exist in language, as exemplified by the canonical CVC form of syllables, or passive syntactic forms: These structures are not symmetries; rather, they converge onto symmetrical form with no systematic basis for it. One cannot argue that the ability to deal with symmetries would break down for long strings, because there are many grammatical constructions that exceed behavioral capacities in complex or long constructions. In short, there are no obvious potential behavioral explanations for the absence of symmetries in language alone. Symmetry simply is not a property of language.

The moral to be drawn from the fact that the matrix presented previously is fully instantiated is that the essence of language is independent from cognition as a whole – the essence of language makes possible certain languages that cannot be used by the mind, and the mind makes possible certain kinds of rules that are not used in any language. It is not a literal contradiction to maintain, despite these facts, that the essence of language is caused by an organ of the mind. But it does present a picture of language as resulting from a capacity that is mentally isolated in sporadic ways. That is, many aspects of cognition as a whole are reflected in language use and structure; why are the specific exclusions the way they are?

None of these puzzles raised by the theory that humans cause language is a logical contradiction, but each is an otherwise unmotivated puzzle. There has been a conflation of the reasonable claim that humans must have some special capacity or history that makes it possible for them to transmit language and the further claim that the mechanisms of learning and transmission cause the structure to be the way it is.

Suppose one stipulated that the essence of language is not caused by humans. This would free psychology of the problems just reviewed. From this perspective, first, the essence of language is caused neither by the way its learnability is transmitted genetically nor by the way that it might be learned by general mechanisms (if such exist). The essential features are instead the result of extrinsic factors. Second, language itself did not evolve with humans; rather, humans evolved to a point of complexity at which learning language became relevant. Finally, the absence in language of an otherwise pervasive cognitive form is explained by its absence from language proper, rather than by its unique absence from a particular part of the mind.

The view that the essence of linguistic structure is nonhuman is consistent with all the facts that have been traditionally taken to indicate the opposite conclusion, that language must be a proper result of evolution (see Lenneberg, 1967). First, the occasion of an extrinsically structured language could still be species-specific, simply by virtue of the fact that only in humans has the required level of complexity been reached for language to be discovered. There might also be a unique, innate mechanism in human infants for the discovery of certain parts of language, both the essential and the peripheral. There could be general patterns in the order of language acquisition, paced either by a language-specific learning mechanism or by nonlinguistic developments. There could be "typical" patterns of brain representation, based on the most natural organization of the behavioral features of language use.[5] Finally, language learning could be largely independent of normal variations in intelligence; a person with a manifest IQ of 60 may already have a brain that is complex enough in relevant ways.

In brief, the view of language as an uncaused structure is entirely consistent with all the usual biopsychological facts pertaining to its human uniqueness. We now turn to the study of how such extrinsic structures might be discovered.

14.2. The discovery of extrinsic structures

It is obvious (to a nonskeptic) that certain structures have a reality outside human knowledge of them: For example, the fact that there are planets revolving around the sun (if this is a fact) is not caused by human cognition or astronomy. I mention such a noncontroversial banality to set the scene for a less obvious claim: The fact that triangles have angles totaling 180 degrees is not the result of human cognition; for example, just as Martians can know about planets, they can know about triangles. Furthermore, planets would exist and the properties of triangles would exist without any knowledge of them. Clearly, the fact that we know that triangles exist is attributable to human cognition; indeed, centuries of (incorrect) acceptance that Euclidean geometry is the only possible natural geometry might be attributed to properties of the human sensorimotor system. But that system does not cause the properties to exist, even if it can provide a partial explanation for the order in which we discover them.

One can argue that geometry does have an initial physical instantiation and that humans learn abstract geometry from that starting point. Whether explanatorily adequate or not, this line of reasoning cannot be extended to other domains of human knowledge, notably logic. Most humans master a degraded version of logic that they use for everyday reasoning. But they usually fail to master certain principles of any formal system without special training, for example, that anything follows from a contradiction or that in certain logics disjunction is best interpreted inclusively. The formal logical principles that human do and do not intuitively master are not physically instantiated in any way – yet the formal properties are necessary and would exist (insofar as they exist at all) with or without any specific knowledge of them by any species. In this sense logic is a necessary abstract form (see Husserl, 1970).

14.3. Implications for the psychology of language

Even if language were uncaused, we still would have to find out how adults use it and how children master it. Does it make any difference to researchers on language behavior like us what the "true" source of the essence of language is?[6]

The first answer to this query is dogmatic: The truth shall set ye free. We sometimes simply do not know how our studies are skewed by mistaken assumptions, until those assumptions are corrected. So if it is, or could be, true that the essence of language is uncaused, then we should consider this possibility and see where it leads. The formal analysis of language structure is a practical and logical prerequisite to a science of language use. If the essence of language is not caused by humans, we must be aware of what its true nonhuman structure is in order to study how humans master it. Consider the following example of what the study of number psychology might be like if it was practiced without an independent theory of the nature of numbers.

Suppose that a psychologist, Dr. P, was studying the nature of discrete quantity terms as used in a primitive culture without explicit mathematics, and suppose that he was himself a member of the culture and unaware of any independent theory of integers (the example under discussion is also typical of children between the ages of 3 and 5: see Decroly, 1932; Descoeudres, 1916; Gelman & Gallistel, 1978). Dr. P might note that there are four quantities for which his subjects have different names, A,B,C,D. By experimenting with manipulations of these quantities (or referring to his own intuitions as a member of the culture), he would find that the combinatorial facts of discretely quantified groups of objects are as outlined here. The following combinations of the quantities always obtain:

$A \pm A,B,C,D = A,B,C,D$
(i.e., adding or removing A changes nothing)
$B + B = C$
$D + A,B,C,D = D$
(i.e., anything added to D results in D)

The following combinations sometimes are true:

$B + C = D$	$C - B = C$	$D - C = C$
$B + C = C$	$C + C = D$	$D - C = B$
$C - B = B$	$D - C = D$	$D - B = C$

The most baffling property of these facts is the presence of inconsistencies. For example, if $C + D = D$, how can $D - C$ ever equal anything other than D? Despite such problems, Dr. P could arrive at some conclusions: A is the smallest quantity; D is the largest. But what more could he conclude? Would he arrive at any internal theory of the quantity relations? Would he not reasonably conclude that relative quantities in humans are innate in origin and nature? That is, the array of partially inconsistent facts above has no extrahuman grounds that Dr. P can see, is learned with little or no instruction, and so on. Of course, we cannot know for sure that Dr. P would come to such a limited conclusion. He might hypothesize an abstract concept, "integer," and discover the true state of affairs underlying his informants' quantity behavior. Suppose he "invented" the positive integers and showed how the mapping functions onto the integers,

$A = 0; \quad B = 1; \quad C = 2\text{--}6; \quad D = 7+$

explain the properties of *A,B,C,D*. He might then claim that integers themselves are "innate." How else, he would ask, can we account for the acquisition of such abstract entities? But he would then be the victim of his culture-specific myopia. Lacking an abstract, or nonhuman, theory of integers, he finds it plausible to assume that they must be human in nature and origin. This claim confuses the manifest capacity of his subjects, which may well have innate components, with the correct structure of what his subjects actually have learned (regardless of the definition of *learned*).

Suppose integers are real. Then Dr. P's subjects are in the position of having discovered a quantity system that reflects certain properties of real entities. But that discovery does not prove that those entities are the way they are because they are innate. Quite the contrary: They are they way they are because they are real.[7]

Of course, Dr. P should be credited with an important discovery – namely, that his subjects' behavior is systematically related to a mapping of his invention "the integers." In fact, his invention would make it possible to study what is innate about discrete quantities. He could now contrast the regularities of the way quantities develop in children with their formal analysis. For example, he could ask what psychological mechanisms give a special status to the differences between 0 and 1, 1 and 2, and 6 and 7, but not to any other one-step difference. In this way, the formal theory of integers would be a critical scientific tool in studying the psychology of quantities in his subjects.

I think we must entertain the possibility that we have all been acting like Dr. P in our studies of language acquisition. We may have confused the fact that language acquisition proves that something is innate with the claim that what is innate must be the underlying theory, or a predisposition which always leads to that theory. Like Dr. P's subjects, the child may master a "language" that is mapped onto a formal theory of language in certain ways. But this mastery does not imply that the formal entities themselves are innate, only that something is innate which allows the child to behave in conformity with some of the laws those formal entities entail. Like Dr. P we need the formal theory, for it gives us an analysis of what the child might learn to contrast with what he or she actually learns. Indeed, a theory can clarify what might be innate to the learning mechanism by giving us a clear picture of what does not have to be innate in the formal structure. Like the structural theory of integers, linguistic theory provides the psychologist with the potential distinctions. It is the psychologist's task to study how and why these distinctions are mastered in some cases and systematically ignored in others.

This view has a number of practical implications for the study of language acquisition. First, it clarifies by contrast that we have not taken seriously enough the implications of the strong nativist position. For example, if language is caused to be the way it is by human biology, we should find radically different kinds of languages appearing as mutants or as the result of organic developmental disorders; we might expect slight structural variations in language structure to run in families; we might expect familially heritable patterns of acquisition; we might expect identical twins to have language structures more similar in detail than fraternal twins; we might expect a correlation between certain linguistic features and otherwise defined racial groups; we might expect highly specific localization in the brain;[8] and so on. Such phenomena are typical of genetically transmitted and caused structures: Why are they not typical of language? The absence of such phenomena might just be a failure of observation. But it might be that they do not exist because the essence of language is not biologically caused.

A second implication for the psychologist is that it clarifies the distinction between *competence* and *performance* (see J. Katz, 1978, in particular). The common use of the term *competence* refers to what the speaker/ hearer "knows" about his or her language. If this competence is also claimed to include an individual embodiment of the complete universal grammar, then we face the conceptual puzzles already reviewed. However, there is no such difficulty if an individual's competence refers only to his or her personal embodiment of the structures inherent in the particular language.

This personal knowledge system combines aspects of the history of the specific language, usage constraints, and uncaused essentials of language. In order to minimize confusion with previous uses of the term *competence*, I use the terms *human language* and *psychogrammar* to refer to an attested language and the individual mental representation of personal linguistic knowledge. I use *real language* and *real grammar* to refer to an uncaused possible language and its correct description.

The distinction between psychogrammars and real grammars raises an intriguing possibility about human languages: Some (or all) of the latter may not be well formed or complete real languages. This possibility would be analogous to the possibility that the human apprehension of space, logic, and numbers may not reflect a complete, or even consistent, formal system. For example, the concepts of the square root of a negative number or of an infinitely small nonzero quantity are not natural concepts in any indigenous number system. With respect to such kinds of knowledge, "there is no particular reason to suppose that . . . the mathematical abilities (of humans) permit them to conceive of theories approximating truth in every (or any) [*sic*] domain" (N. Chomsky, 1980, p. 252). That is, every humanly accessible theory of numbers may be wrong. Just so for language.

A third implication of viewing language as extrinsically determined is the unification of the acquisition of language with the acquisition of other abstract formal skills. It is a startling fact that researchers in language acquisition, as generally represented in this handbook, take for granted that language learning (if it exists at all) is sui generis. It follows principles that are completely unique. So long as we adhered to the empiricist presumption that the human child must either cause linguistic structures or learn them, there was no alternative. However, if we now stipulate the linguistic essentials as uncaused, we can refer to a model of acquisition for other uncaused structures.

One class of models for the acquisition of such structures involves representational conflict resolution. For example, in Piaget's interpretation, formal structures are discovered by the child as resolutions of contradictions produced by emerging everyday habits of behavior. If language is an uncaused structure, then we can interpret its acquisition in the same way as the discovery of the intuitive concepts of number, geometry, or logic. Consider first a simple example of cognitive development as mental conflict resolution.[9]

We can start by investigating how the child categorizes small numbers; that is, we first play the experimental role of Dr. P, with children as our subjects. Various researchers have done this (see Decroly, 1932) and have found that 3-year-old children have roughly the same grouping of numbers as that outlined on p. 438. This gives us some insight into children's categorization of quantities, but it does not bear directly on their concept of number or quantity relations. To study this concept, one must ask children questions about the quantity relationships between one array and another, about how they change under various kinds of transformations. A child can be interpreted as having mastered an intuitive concept of certain properties of numerical quantities when he or she recognizes that it is invariant under all transformations except those that change the actual number of objects in an array. The 3-year-old, for example, may think that a row of dolls has more dolls in it after they are spread out. At the same time, the child will volunteer that a row has less if one of the dolls is taken away from it. Such simple cases illustrate different systems of representation of quantity – one perceptual, the other active. The child has a perceptual rule – "If it looks bigger, it has more" – and an action rule – "If you take some away it has less."

What does the child believe happens to a row if you both remove one element and spread the others out (see Bever, Fodor, & Garrett, 1968; Mehler & Bever, 1967). This tactic places the child in internal conflict: One processing system informs him that the row has more, the other that it has less. It is the ultimate discovery of the conceptual invariance of number that resolves such conflicts in behavioral systems. That is, the motivation for the discovery of number is to resolve these conflicts; the motivational role of the discovery of number is to resolve a conflict in mental representations of quantities. It is important to note that the child does not have to give up one of the behavioral systems he has developed.

For example, even in adults, number estimation can be based on array size under certain circumstances. An important fact about the discovery of intuitive formal systems is that they allow the conflicts in the behavioral systems to continue, but provide an underlying system for reconciling those conflicts when necessary. (The kinds of conflicts are by no means exhausted by these cases; other examples would be the conflict between relying on density and relying on overall area in judging numerosity, and the inconsistencies among the results of combining the four basic "quantities" outlined at the beginning of this section.)

In general, formal intuitive knowledge, such as the intuitive concepts of number, space, and logic, are arrived at as internal solutions to such conflicts in different behavior systems. That is, they are a set of "internal languages" that map one behavioral system onto another, and thereby detoxify the negative force of the superficial conflicts between those systems.

We can use such a model to explain why a child learns a psychogrammar at all. Several common explanations are implicit in most of the literature on language acquisition:

> He or she cannot help it (e.g., it is innate).
> It is a by-product of the urge to communicate.
> It simplifies what must be memorized.

Ordinarily we try not to make ourselves responsible for explaining why language is learned; we suggest only that it lies in the murk of infantile motivation or circular functionalism. Certainly the answers suggested here have these weaknesses. Each states in a somewhat different way that a grammar is learned because infants like to learn it.

The conflict-resolution model just outlined provides a theoretical rationale to explain *why* children learn the concept of number: It resolves representational conflicts among otherwise powerful and useful systems of quantity behavior. I think it is natural to extend the application of such a model to language: The psychogrammar is a level of representation that resolves conflicts between the representational powers of the system of speech perception and production. Of course, a special biological mechanism might be required for the discovery of such a formal system, but it might not necessarily be limited to the discovery of any particular system, such as language (see Bever, 1981, where such a model is presented more fully).

14.4. Implications for the study of language acquisition

The resolution model of language learning needs empirical support. The kind of data required – in particular, systematic comparisons of developments in the production rules, perceptual strategies, and other systems of language use – are almost totally lacking. Cross-psycholinguistic studies of language behavior systems in the adult and child are also of great importance to the verification and expansion of this model (cf. Slobin, Chapter 5). My main point is to show that viewing the essence of language as nonhuman in origin has real consequences for what (I think) we should do in our practical research.

One might object that the conflict-resolution models of the acquisition of intuitive formal structures like number and language are inadequate, because they do not explain why the particular structures are the ones that are discovered. That argument, however, still presupposes that the psychologist must explain why the structures are the way they are. If the structures are nonhuman and real, then the problem of how we discover them is an instance of the problem of how we discover reality. To say that there must be some innate mechanisms that participate in this process is not tendentious. To say that the innate mechanisms themselves cause the structure of reality is to leap into the vat of skepticism.

According to the theory that the essence of language is caused by humans, the specification of the essential universals is exactly a description of what every child is prepared to learn. Accordingly, universal grammar exactly describes the set of possible theories of language acquisition. According to this view, the study of language acquisition and grammar are closely linked. This linkage is frequently reflected in Chomsky's observation that the study of grammar reveals what the learning psychologist must explain.

The complementary line of investigation has been developed by Wexler and his co-workers (see Chapter 10). They explore the extent to which a theory of learning constrains what could be a possible grammar. This is a direct return to the behaviorist dictum that what is known is caused to be that way by how it was learned. Though they are not constrained to operational methodology, nor to traditional empiricism, they embrace the view that the essence of language has a cause and the cause is the language-learning children. (If, however, one examines the constraints they impose on possible grammars, one realizes that they also represent a return to grammars that make deep-structural patterns available in their surface organization – certainly a move compatible with empiricism.)

The linguistic realist is not committed to this position, because to him or her the essence of language has no cause. The child's problem is to apply general intelligence or special capacities to construct a representation of language sufficient to serve human purposes.

It is possible that children never acquire a real language at all, just as they do not acquire a consistent logical system. But just as everyday human reason proceeds well enough with faulty logic, human communication could proceed with a faulty language. It is also likely that the range of learnable languages is smaller than the set of real languages.

Short-term memory limits alone would account for a restriction in the range of many structural processes.

It might seem that the ontological status of the essence of language is not at issue when we are studying how children acquire it. In principle this may be true. But in our practice it makes an enormous difference in what we look for if a property of human language has an uncaused structure. What is at issue is the kinds of hypotheses the child tries out as he or she masters language. If the essence of language is caused by the human brain, it would be very odd if the child ever developed a grammatical hypothesis that contradicted some essential property. The nativist argument that the child acquires the right kind of grammar in the face of rarified data is incompatible with formation of impossible hypotheses; how would the impoverished data ever "correct" such hypotheses, once they were formed? Indeed, if the data were sufficient to correct false kinds of hypotheses, then the case for a language-specific innate acquisition device would be much weaker.

Yet the child does appear to come to the wrong kinds of hypotheses about such uncaused structures as number – for example, that integral operations are not reversible and that relations are not necessarily transitive, as implicit in the patterns in the preceding section. It is not clear how such false kinds of hypotheses would be generated if there were a specifically innate device for the acquisition of number that also caused integers to have the properties that they do. How could this device ever generate hypotheses that contradict essential properties of numbers?

If the essential properties of integers are uncaused, then this at least opens up the opportunity for further experience with numbers to provide crucial information that will lead to correcting the false hypotheses. It is totally mysterious how such correction takes place, just as it is mysterious how we incorporate any aspect of the world. But, at least if numbers are real, we do not have to invoke number-specific learning mechanisms to account for their real properties.

The same might be true of language. We might find that the child develops incorrect kinds of hypotheses about the nature of language. I am referring not to the possibility that the child might generate incorrect rules of a correct form, but rather to the possibility that he or she might generate hypotheses incompatible with an essential property of language. Consider the following example. J. Katz (1981) suggests that one of the uncaused properties of language is "effability," the principle that every sense has (at least) one sentence that corresponds to it. That is, a "language" that could not express some sense would not be a real language. He draws the conclusion from this that languages are recursive, a conclusion that is necessary if every sense is to be represented by a single sentence.

Suppose it is true that for every sense there is a sentence. If this property is intrinsic to the way humans organize languages, then the child should never conclude that some senses are not expressible in sentences. At least some child, for at least some sense, would never experience any data to falsify such a conclusion. Yet it seems possible that children (and perhaps adults) do believe that there are some senses without a sentence. (Remember that I am now pursuing the implications of effability for the study of language acquisition, without commenting on its correctness.) This can be the case only if effability is either false or an uncaused property of language. Surely this makes important the study of effability in children.

There are also false hypotheses that the child might entertain just because they are compatible with uncaused essentials of grammar, even though they are incompatible with any human language. Human beings come to every situation with extreme limits on their serial memory. This factor might exclude them entirely from capitalizing on the recursive character of real languages, because embedding complete sentences in others would quickly multiply the length of sequences. G. Miller and Chomsky (1963) suggest that the functional role of transformations is in fact to compress the information in a complexly embedded structure into a compact and linear form. That is, actual human languages reflect the recursive character of language by utilizing meaning-bearing propositions that are not sentences themselves and that are characteristically shorter (i.e., phrases).

This suggests another false kind of hypothesis that the child might entertain: Every proposition-bearing sequence is a sentence. This is definitely not true of any attested human language, since phrases can often be proposition-bearing sequences. I think that there are certain prima facie indications that children do pass through such a period, as evidenced in their so-called telegraphic utterances. Here too the status of such behavior is unclear, but it would be worth a great deal to know whether the child assigns such sequences a derivational history as a sentence, or goes through a phase of treating a multiphrase sentence as a "discourse."

14.5. Conclusion

I have outlined a number of problems linked to the assumption that the essence of language is caused by human beings. These problems would be resolved if one accepted the view that the essence of language is not caused.

What remains are two empirical questions: What is innate that makes the discovery of language necessary? What is innate that makes it possible? I have suggested that language structure is discovered by the child as a reconciliation of behavioral conflicts that arise among emerging separate systems of communication. By this view, the discovery of language is made necessary by the existence of distinct behavioral systems that manipulate sequences of symbols. Accordingly, the ability to develop those independent systems must be innate. Such abilities are astounding, but not unprecedented in the animal kingdom. There are other species that communicate a variety of messages or rituals, sometimes with complex sequences.

We must also account for what makes the discovery of language possible. The crucial question is whether this capacity is an isolated and psychobiologically unique one, or whether it is an application of a general ability. This part of our investigation will depend crucially on a better understanding of what language is, independent of the subset of languages that humans are able to discover. I pointed out that Dr. P's investigation of the innate basis for the "numbers" *A,B,C,D* would be greatly aided by his discovery of how those numbers map onto real integers. We depend in the same way on understanding how the universal "psychogrammar" maps onto a real essence of grammar. If this research program is correct, we will find that certain features of the real grammar are not part of universal psychogrammar, and that certain features of psychogrammar are not part of the real grammar. These mismatches between the two systems will highlight what the nature of the learning mechanism must be. A theory of that mechanism will then be required to explain why humans fail to acquire real grammar as part of their intuitive formal knowledge, and it will become an empirical question if the mechanism of discovering language structure is like the mechanisms for the discovery of other uncaused structures.

Of course, we know very little about the properties of "real grammar." But we also know very little about universal biological properties that might account for many aspects of human languages. Certain formal constraints that seem unique to language actually may be the linguistic expression of general constraints on rule-governed serial behavior. For example, the "A over A" principle in syntax (and its inheritors) and "the longest environment first" principle in phonology might both be linguistic instances of a behavioral principle: Apply a process at the most general level possible. We do not need to speculate blindly about such a possibility. For example, we can search experimentally for a principle of this sort in the rule-governed serial behavior of nonhuman animals (see Bever, Straub, Terrace, & Townsend, 1980). Such investigations increase our arsenal of possible sources of properties of human languages. We then interpret each linguistic universal as having one of these origins:

1.   It is biologically based in all rule-governed organized behavior.
2.   It is psychologically based in how the human mind goes about discovering and using language.
3.   It is a necessary feature of real grammar.

The hypothesis that the essence of language is uncaused by humans allows for a logically possible world in which we can make relatively modest claims about what evolved in the human species and is inborn to each child:

1. Mechanisms of productive and perceptual use of symbols
2. Mechanisms for processing sequences of symbols (e.g., large short-term memory)
3. Mechanisms for the discovery of real formal structures (e.g., number, logic, language) to resolve representational conflicts within domains like (1) and (2).

According to this interpretation the acquisition of language by a child rests on three presumed mechanisms, none of which is unique to language; there is no special innate language-learning mechanism, though there may well be an innate system that makes possible the discovery of a variety of formal structures.

The corresponding account of the biological basis of language can now be unified with that of the evolution of other capacities. The biological basis for each of the postulated mechanisms must be prodigiously complex, but the first two capacities are not without precedent. Indeed, if we differ at all from certain animals in these capacities, it may be only quantitatively. The ability to discover and intuitively utilize formal structures has less clear biological precedents.[10]

But there is no reason to be categorical about the capacity of our nonlinguistic brethren. Whatever the background for mechanism (3), its presence in humans is *ex hypothesi* a general ability, not one limited to language alone. This does not make its psychobiological basis trivial or uninteresting. But it does mean that the psychobiological basis of the ability to discover language may not involve the evolution of an isolated capacity, focused only on language.

Notes

1 I am giving Bates and MacWhinney the benefit of the doubt: They may wish to claim that a distinguishable faculty of language never emerges – only communication patterns that (benighted) linguists call "language." In that case, they may hold a unique position – that language has no real existence, neither in the child nor in physics nor among the set of universal forms – a curious kind of linguistically localized skepticism.

2 Certain innate body mechanisms appear to exhibit languagelike intricacy and flexibility. The most notable example is the immune system, once often cited by biologists as an exemplar of environment-sensitive "behavior" that is genetically transmitted. Chomsky (1980) discusses this as an example of how biologically transmitted behavior can appear to be creatively "instructive" while actually being "selective." The basic phenomenon is that the immune

system provides a different antibody for all distinguishable pathogens, including those that it has not yet encountered. This would seem to indicate either foreknowledge of all "possible" pathogens, or a kind of "grammar" that constructs each antibody when needed. However, the now commonly accepted view of this process is that the immune system generates a random "library" of antibodies shortly after birth, and periodically during life. If a pathogen happens to enter the system for which there is no antibody already in the library, the organism is not capable of generating specifically the needed antibody. Furthermore, the method by which the library is originally created is by random recombination of genetic material. It is hard to see how such random mechanistic phenomena provide much comfort for the linguistic nativist. The linguistic analogy would be that elementary mental components recombine randomly until an aggregate of them fits the environmental language. But because, by hypothesis, the environment greatly underdetermines the grammar, the recombinations cannot be random in the sense that they are in the formation of antigens. If they are, then the argument that language learning is based on highly constrained mechanisms would not hold.

3 Note that there could, however, be a nonbiological physical basis for the mechanisms that underlie the knowledge of language. If the essence of language is the result of a physical law that becomes relevant only when there are complex living systems like human brains, then the essential nature of language would be literally a law of the universe, not a law of the human brain or human history.

Lest the physical interpretation be sloughed off, consider an example of how a physical law might emerge only in human behavior, but not be caused to have its essential properties by that behavior. Consider upright walking in humans. Suppose there were no other examples (on earth) of self-propelled entities that rely on the mixture of gravity, forward momentum, and balance that walking requires. We could use the study of walking as an empirical territory to explore the interaction of these physical laws and relations. We could stipulate as well that walking in humans is "innate": It is learned with little specific training and involves (already partially known) innate brain mechanisms. But one would not conclude that the physical laws with which the brain mechanisms interact are also caused by those mechanisms. Rather, it would be argued that the physical laws have their particular properties because of the basic nature of matter, not because of the human brain. The human body and brain would be cited as organs of sufficient complexity for the physical laws to become relevant constraints. In this sense, the physical properties are discovered by virtue of their application to human walking.

One could make the parallel argument about the physical basis of language – the human brain may be physiologically adapted to learn language, but if language is the effect of physical laws, then the structure or behavior of the brain cannot explain why language is the way it is. Similar arguments apply to the claim that the essence of language is a nonphysical form. The brain may account for how and why humans discover that form, but the nature of the form itself is not caused by the brain to have the particular form it does.

4 Strange as this view now seems to me, it is exactly the view I once held (see Bever, 1970); it seemed (and seems) to me to be the only way to resolve the

contradictions raised by the combination of the competence–performance "distinction," the claim that "competence" is psychological, and the existence of unlearnable (i.e., unpsychological) well-formed rules. Of course, if "universal competence" (i.e., the essence of language) is not psychobiological in origin, then the contradiction disappears and the strange mental model of *Festung Sprache* is not required.

5 The only evidence of neurological specialization for language involves the claim that it is usually localized in areas of the left hemisphere. However, even the force of this is mitigated by the fact that there is a large variability of that location from individual to individual. It is also not clear that the localization – such as it is – does not result from a general difference in computational power between the hemispheres, rather than a language-specific predisposition of the left hemisphere. See Bever (1980) for a discussion of this.

6 In fact one could maintain that special-purpose causal mechanisms must exist that "harmonize" with the nonhuman linguistic essences, that is, that the essence of language is a synthetic *a priori*. But the view that language is an *a priori* of any kind makes possible nonsynthetic interpretations we can also consider.

7 I am aware that even the structure of integers may be argued by some to be caused by human cognition, in the so-called intuitionist interpretation of mathematical objects and relations. Intuitionism can be interpreted as a claim that mathematical entities and properties all start with those that are intuitively clear to humans. This places the burden on a constructivist mathematics to show that all of mathematics can be demonstrated, starting with just those intuitions. Notice, however, that even if constructivism can succeed as an investigative method in mathematics, its success would not support any particular ontological claim about what mathematical entities in fact are. Intuitionism would remain an unsupported doctrine.

8 See n. 5.

9 The literature on the acquisition of number is very large. My attempt here is to give a programmatic description of how such a phenomenon is interpreted on the mental conflict resolution model. The reader should consult Gelman and Gallistel (1979) for reviews of research paradigms and results in this area. I have also been greatly informed on this topic by the writings of Jonas Langer.

10 Notice that it makes no difference if the evolutionary entelechy is biological, physical, or cultural. That is, any suggestion that the complex brain became capable of creating human language because of the evolutionary operation of an as yet unknown "physical law" simply changes the mystery from one of biology to one of physics. Similarily, discovery by virtue of a "cultural" law presents an anthropological mystery.

15. Task specificity in language learning? Evidence from speech perception and American Sign Language

Elissa L. Newport

The question I would like to consider is what J. A. Fodor, Bever, and Garrett (1974) have called "task specificity": Is there a special language faculty that gives language its organizational character? There are undoubtedly a variety of particular versions of task specificity that one could develop (see Fodor et al., 1974; Osherson & Wasow, 1976; Wasow, 1973, for more general discussions of this issue). However, I will concentrate on one version: that there is a special spoken language faculty, a privileged auditory-vocal language apparatus, that has evolved in humans. Although much of the evidence on this question comes from studies of adult language organization, the consequences for the study of language acquisition are obvious: To the degree that there is a task-specific character to language organization, we must look to task-specific abilities in the learner; and recent moves in the field of language acquisition toward examining sensorimotor development, pragmatics, perception, memory, social interaction, and the like for explanations of early language acquisition will have limited success.

Historically, there have been two major areas of evidence suggesting that spoken language may derive at least in part from a specifically linguistic faculty, and not from more general cognitive abilities: first, the study of speech perception in comparison with the perception of nonlinguistic stimuli; and second, the study of sign languages in comparison with spoken languages. In the study of speech perception, there has of course been the well-known claim that speech sounds are perceived differently from nonspeech sounds – in particular, that speech sounds, unlike nonlinguistic stimuli, are perceived categorically. According to this view, the phonetic categorization of acoustically distinct stimuli is accompanied

This research was supported in part by PHS grant #NS16878 to Newport and Supalla, by grants from the Research Board, University of Illinois, and by NSF grant #BNS-76-12866 to the Salk Institute for Biological Studies. All figures were drafted by Ted Supalla; Figures 15.9, 15.10, and 15.13–15.17 are reproduced, with permission, from Supalla (1978a). I would like to thank Ted Supalla, my collaborator, for his crucial participation in every aspect of this work; Geoff Coulter, who, along with Ted, made important suggestions that started me thinking about "mimetic depiction"; and Lila Gleitman, Jean Mandler, Jay McClelland, Carolyn Mervis, Marilyn Shatz, Len Talmy, Eric Wanner, and Pat Worden for stimulating discussion and helpful comments on earlier drafts of this chapter.

by a highly reduced ability to perform acoustic discriminations within these categories; this is in sharp contrast to the usual fine discriminative ability, relative to categorization, that perceivers have outside the linguistic domain. This view has suggested a special mode of processing (the *speech mode*) that subserves only language stimuli (Liberman, 1970; Liberman, Cooper, Shankweiler, & Studdert-Kennedy, 1967).

Similarly, comparisons between spoken and signed language organization have suggested a special status for spoken language. It has often been argued (Cohen, Namir, & Schlesinger, 1977; Friedman, 1977; Schlesinger, 1970) that sign languages are very different from spoken languages in structure. It has been claimed that sign languages, unlike spoken languages, do not mark grammatical relations, do not distinguish nouns and verbs, do not in general display the syntactic and morphological properties that are characteristic of spoken languages. As Wasow (1973) has pointed out, if this were true, it would be a very powerful argument for a spoken language faculty: Since spoken and signed languages presumably serve the same communicative purposes and use much of the same cognitive mechanisms, deep organizational differences could only be due to the limited availability of a privileged spoken language faculty.

What I intend to argue is that in fact neither of these claims is correct and, more interestingly, that the particular ways in which they are incorrect may require that we make revisions in our thinking about task specificity. In particular, I would like to argue a somewhat different point with regard to these same sets of data: that the resources available in perception and memory seem quite different for the auditory-vocal as opposed to the visual-gestural mode; and yet nevertheless the formal character of languages in these two modes is remarkably similar. Finally, I will try to clarify what I think this says about the task-specificity question.

15.1. Categorical perception and phonetic organization

Although the traditional view of speech perception and its relation to task specificity is well known, I will briefly review it. Liberman (1970), Liberman et al. (1967), and others have argued that speech, unlike nonlinguistic stimuli, is perceived categorically. The phenomenon of categorical perception is defined by the conjunction of two tasks: labeling and discrimination (Studdert-Kennedy, Liberman, Harris, & Cooper, 1970). Figure 15.1 presents an idealized set of results from part one of the task, labeling. Typically, synthetic stimuli are made to vary in small steps along a single acoustic dimension (e.g., voice onset time), between two endpoint stimuli that differ in a single phonetic feature (e.g., [ba] vs. [pa]). Subjects are then presented with these stimuli, one at a time in random order, and are asked to label them with one of the two linguistic labels (e.g., BA or

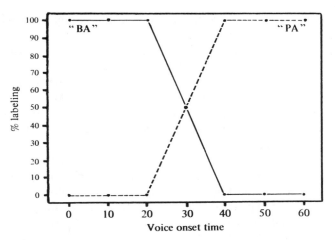

Figure 15.1. Idealized labeling functions for stimuli varying in voice onset time.

PA). In the ideal, labeling of speech stimuli is sharply discontinuous, with stimuli at one end of the continuum uniformly given one label (e.g., BA) and stimuli at the other end of the continuum uniformly given another label (e.g., PA).

However, the crucial part of the phenomenon is the relation between these labeling results and the results on the second part of the task, discrimination. The discrimination task presents subjects with two adjacent stimuli from the acoustic continuum and asks them to discriminate between these two stimuli. It is important to note that this task thus asks subjects, if they can, to ignore the linguistic categorization and to perform a *non*linguistic discrimination between stimuli that are in fact acoustically distinct. Figure 15.2 presents an idealized set of results in this part of the task, along with the results from the labeling task. As the figure shows, although subjects are perfectly capable of discriminating between stimuli that fall in different phonetic categories, they are at chance in discriminating between stimuli that differ by the same amount acoustically but that fall within the same phonetic category. Until recently, this reduced ability to discriminate between stimuli within a category appeared to be true only of speech stimuli; control acoustic stimuli that are nonlinguistic are discriminable across the continuum. Similarly, until recently, selective adaptation of the categorical perception functions has been found with exposure to linguistic stimuli, but not with exposure to nonlinguistic control stimuli (Cooper, 1974; Eimas, Cooper, & Corbit, 1973; Eimas & Corbit, 1973).

These early findings were taken to show that there is a special mechanism, specific to spoken language, for processing linguistic stimuli. Moreover, it has been argued that this categorical perceptual mechanism

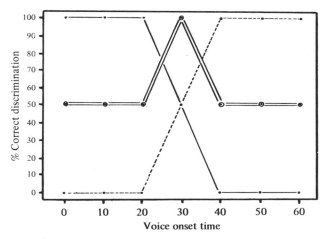

Figure 15.2. Idealized discrimination function in relation to the idealized labeling functions for stimuli varying in voice onset time.

is intimately connected with, perhaps in part responsible for, the discrete and categorical nature of phonetic organization (Liberman, 1972).

More recently, however, investigators have found a wide variety of acoustic nonlinguistic stimuli that show the whole set of findings associated with categorical perception. Cutting and Rosner (1974) and Cutting, Rosner, and Foard (1976) have demonstrated categorical perception and selective adaptation for musical stimuli, namely, plucked and bowed tones varying in amplitude rise time. Pisoni (1977) has found categorical perception of the relative onset time of two pure tones. Moreover, Arty Samuel and I (Samuel & Newport, 1979) have recently demonstrated that selective adaptation effects can be obtained across nonlinguistic–linguistic stimuli that are matched in specifiable acoustic ways. Figure 15.3 presents our findings diagrammatically. Our stimuli in this experiment were two sets of nonlinguistic adaptors: the plucked and bowed tones of Cutting

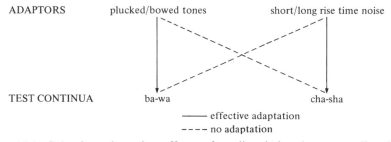

Figure 15.3. Selective adaptation effects of nonlinguistic adaptors on linguistic test continua. Based on data from Samuel & Newport, 1979.

and Rosner (1974), both periodic stimuli differing in rise time, and two noise stimuli, both aperiodic and shaped to match the musical tones in rise time; and two speech continua: a [ba]–[wa] continuum, periodic stimuli varying in rise time, and a [cha]–[sha] continuum, aperiodic stimuli varying in rise time. In short, all stimuli varied in rise time but differed in periodicity. Our results showed that while musical tones adapted only the perception of [ba]–[wa], noise adapted only the perception of [cha] –[sha]. In other words, whatever mechanisms subserve categorical perception in speech are sensitive to certain *acoustic* properties of stimuli (for example, periodicity); whether the stimuli are linguistic or nonlinguistic appears to be irrelevant.

This body of recent findings thus argues that categorical perception and associated phenomena are in fact not special to speech; rather, they appear to arise for certain types of auditory stimuli more generally. The current view of speech perception is that these experiments tap the auditory bases on which speech perception is built (Cutting & Rosner, 1974; Pisoni, 1977). This view suggests that the phonetic categories used in language are actually recruited from nonlinguistic auditory perception, and that limitations on our abilities to perform discriminations in the auditory domain may give us the categories we use for phonetics in language. In fact, this view of the literature on speech perception fits in rather nicely with the view of the psycholinguistics literature more generally, that much of language organization may derive from constraints on perception and memory (see Bever, 1970; Slobin, 1973, 1977).

However, I believe that the picture changes somewhat more radically if we begin to look at American Sign Language (ASL). To begin, it is important to note that ASL, like spoken languages, has "phonetic" categories: physically nonidentical stimuli that are treated within the language as identical (Bellugi & Klima, 1975; Klima, Bellugi, et al., 1979; Stokoe, 1960; Stokoe, Casterline, & Croneberg, 1965).[1] The question I will address first is whether we can similarly say for ASL that the phonetic categories of the language arise from the lack of perceptual and memorial ability to discriminate within these categories; in short, is there categorical perception in ASL?

The experiments I will discuss were all done in collaboration with Ted Supalla, a deaf native signer as well as a psycholinguist. In the first set of experiments (Supalla & Newport, 1975), we concentrated on the phonetic parameters of location (or place of articulation) and handshape, each of which distinguish minimal pairs in the language. The experiments were likewise the closest analogy to categorical perception experiments with speech that we could achieve. We thus needed sign continua in which one feature of the sign, either location or handshape, was varied along its continuum, while the other features of that sign remained the same. Given the lack of a synthesizer for signs, we produced sign continua by

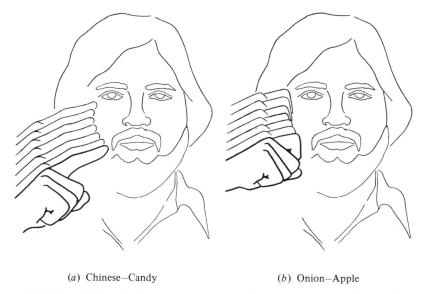

(*a*) Chinese–Candy   (*b*) Onion–Apple

Figure 15.4. Two ASL stimulus continua varying in location: (a) continuum from the sign CHINESE to the sign CANDY; (b) continuum from the sign ONION to the sign APPLE.

filming large numbers of carefully staged and timed productions by a real signer (Ted Supalla), performed in as robot-like a way as possible, and then chose from those the particular filmed productions that were distributed in equal steps over the dimensions of interest[2] and that were as identical as possible in all other ways (e.g., in facial expression, posture of the head, etc.). Figure 15.4 presents pictorial representations of the final continua for the location parameter: one continuum varying in location from the sign CHINESE to the sign CANDY and one continuum varying in location from the sign ONION to the sign APPLE. Figure 15.5 presents pictorial representations of the final continua for the handshape parameter: one continuum varying in handshape from the sign CHINESE to the sign ONION and one continuum varying in handshape from the sign CANDY to the sign APPLE. To reiterate, the actual stimuli for these first experiments were not static pictures, but were movies. Each of the signs consisted of a brief transition to the location of the sign, the sign itself (which always included a movement and lasted .5 sec), and a brief transition back to rest. Each sign was followed by a 1-sec visual mask consisting of moving random lines, made by sandpapering the film strip.

The experimental tasks for each of these four sets of stimuli were the usual ones: a labeling task, and an ABX discrimination task. Figure 15.6 presents the results of the labeling task, averaged over four deaf subjects fluent in ASL. In all cases, labeling is quite comparable to that obtained

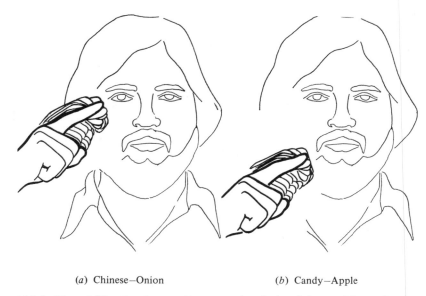

(a) Chinese—Onion   (b) Candy—Apple

Figure 15.5. Two ASL stimulus continua varying in handshape: (a) continuum from the sign CHINESE to the sign ONION; (b) continuum from the sign CANDY to the sign APPLE.

in speech studies, with several steps along each continuum labeled roughly identically and with sharp crossovers in labeling between categories. However, these results merely indicate what we knew from our linguistic analyses: There are in fact nonidentical stimuli that are equivalent within the language. The critical test for categorical perception (as distinct from mere categorization) is in the relationship of labeling to discrimination. Figure 15.7 presents the discrimination functions obtained from an ABX task, along with the discrimination functions that would be predicted from labeling if perception were indeed categorical. As is clear from this figure, discrimination between adjacent stimuli is excellent within categories as well as across categories, and therefore is radically different from the function predicted by assuming categorical perception. In short, there is no categorical perception of these stimuli.

Given that one finds categorical perception for nonlanguage as well as language stimuli in the auditory domain, we became curious about what one needed to get categorical perception of language stimuli in vision. In our first set of ASL experiments, it was possible that we failed to find categorical perception because the stimuli were too long (a total of 1 sec each, including transitions) or too rich (with many visual landmarks on the face that could be used to help discriminate positions of the hand on that face); or because the visual masks were too simple to wipe out visual aftereffects successfully. (All of these factors are known to influence

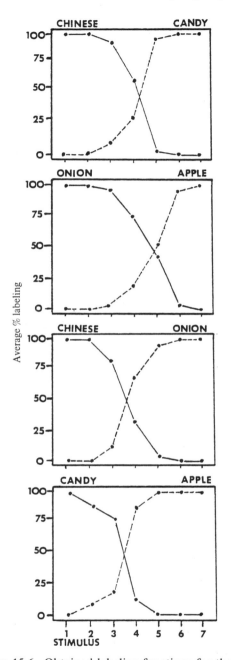

Figure 15.6. Obtained labeling functions for the four ASL stimulus continua.

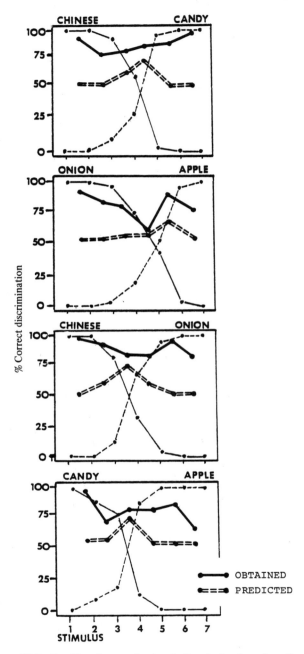

Figure 15.7. Predicted vs. obtained discrimination functions for the four ASL stimulus continua.

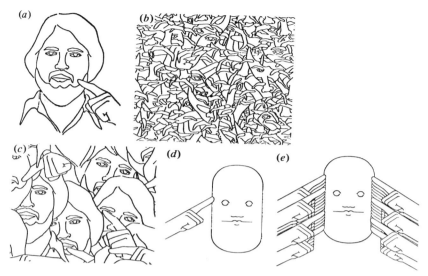

Figure 15.8. Stimuli and masks used in pilot versions of follow-up studies: (a) an example stimulus; (b) mask used with stimulus in (a); (c) another mask used with stimulus (a); (d) an example stimulus: one more try; (e) mask used with stimulus in (d).

categorical perception of speech; see Pisoni, 1971, 1973, 1975.) We therefore undertook a series of pilot studies, in collaboration with Jay McClelland, presenting pared-down stimuli tachistoscopically, with richer masks that would eliminate visual aftereffects of somewhat higher-level configurational features.

Our next set of stimuli were line drawings varying in the location of the finger along the face, from the sign CHINESE to the sign CANDY. An example stimulus is shown in Figure 15.8a. The stimuli were presented tachistoscopically, with an exposure duration of 50–100 msec,[3] and were followed by the mask presented in Figure 15.8b. In addition, we tried the mask presented in Figure 15.8c. Finally, we simplified the stimuli even further, and included yet higher-level configurational features in the mask, as shown in Figures 15.8d and e. The data I will report are fragmentary, since they are only pilot data collected on two subjects for one stimulus set and one subject for the other; unfortunately, these pilot results did not justify undertaking a full-blown experiment. To summarize the results, we found that we could lower the exposure duration to the point where discrimination ability dropped to chance, but it dropped to chance everywhere along the continuum; with very short exposures, there was no peak in the discrimination function at the category boundary. On the other hand, when we increased the exposure duration to the point where discrimination was above chance, it was above chance everywhere along the continuum. We were unable to find any intermediate point where there was discrimination ability across categories but not within categories. In short, we could not obtain categorical perception for these stimuli.[4]

To summarize, there is categorical perception for certain classes of auditory stimuli, whether they are linguistic or nonlinguistic; but not for these visual stimuli, even though they are linguistic. In other words, categorical perception is not task-specific: It is not unique to speech, and it is not characteristic of all language perception. No matter what you wish to call language, categorical perception appears orthogonally to the language–nonlanguage distinction.

Perhaps more important, the presence or absence of categorical perception appears to be irrelevant to the nature of linguistic organization: Both spoken and signed languages are organized phonetically in terms of categories – physically distinct stimuli are treated within the linguistic system as identical – regardless of whether these stimuli are categorically perceived as defined by the experimental tasks.

Understanding this latter point requires considering the nature of the categorical perception tasks. The critical portion of the categorical perception task does not ask whether subjects process stimuli in categories linguistically, but rather whether they are *able* to process stimuli *non*categorically, *non*linguistically; categorical perception involves the inability to access low-level nonlinguistic information when the task requires it. In spoken language, these lower-level nonlinguistic distinctions seem not to be accessible after a few seconds (although they are reflected in very immediate processing, as revealed by reaction-time studies, for a matter of milliseconds; see Pisoni & Tash, 1974). For at least certain types of stimuli within the auditory mode, the lower-level acoustic distinctions are highly transient; subjects asked to perform a nonlinguistic task cannot get access to the information that would support discrimination. In contrast, in the visual mode, fine distinctions are accessible if the task requires it; subjects seem to have a great deal more flexibility in deciding what level they will attend to and encode in memory: Subjects appear to be able to look at sign stimuli pictorially and focus on where the finger is and what it is doing, or on other occasions to attend to the stimuli as linguistic. However, even though, in these respects, processing appears to be different in the two modalities, the linguistic organization is much the same: In both cases, language is categorial.

Much the same kind of point can be made at higher levels of language organization: Despite fairly radical differences in the processing resources made available in the auditory-vocal versus the visual-gestural modes, the formal organizational character is the same for spoken and signed languages. In the following section I will concentrate on morphology, the structure of the word, in spoken language and in ASL.

15.2. Analog representation and morphological organization

To what extent is the formal organization of ASL like that of spoken languages? Previous literature has often argued that the grammatical structure of signed languages is very different from that of spoken languages. For example, although spoken languages universally use word order or case marking to express grammatical relations (e.g., subject vs. object), there is some question about the existence of such formal devices in sign languages (Fischer, 1974; Schlesinger, 1970). Moreover, it has been suggested that sign languages do not distinguish between nouns and verbs (Cohen et al., 1977; Stokoe et al., 1965), whereas in spoken languages such a form-class distinction is universal (Hockett, 1963; Slobin, 1977). Wasow (1973) and Osherson and Wasow (1976) have used such evidence to argue for the task specificity of at least some linguistic universals.

On the other hand, more recent studies of sign language have often uncovered formal devices overlooked by early investigations, which have turned out to be quite analogous to those in spoken language. For example, in ASL, word order and spatial arrangement, along with grammatically functioning facial expressions, operate quite systematically to mark subject versus object (Fischer & Gough, 1978; Liddell, 1977). Similarly, Supalla and Newport (1978) have found a consistent distinction in ASL between related nouns and verbs in manner and frequency of movement.

This question is not merely a point of interest for those who study sign languages. As noted earlier, if in fact sign languages are quite different in organization from spoken languages, the notion of a special spoken language faculty would receive strong support; at minimum, such a finding would suggest important contributions of the auditory-vocal modalities to language structure. If, however, sign languages are very similar to spoken languages, there is little reason to hypothesize a special faculty restricted to spoken language, and little reason to suggest that modality is a significant contributor to language structure.

Morphology in spoken language

Spoken languages tend to be what I will call analytic in character. I use this term not as it is used in linguistics (as equivalent to "isolating"); rather, I use it to mean that sentences, and words within sentences, are made up of (i.e., are analyzable into) a number of discrete morphological parts, components of form that have a consistent meaning.[5] Across languages, there is a relatively small number of morphological parameters, and on each of these parameters a small number of discrete morphological distinctions. For example, in English one morphologically distinguishes number into singular versus plural (e.g., *boy* vs. *boys*); there is no continuum on which a short -*s* means just a few boys and longer and longer -*s* means more and more of them. (Note that there are not always just two distinctions; my point is that there are always discrete alternatives.)

Moreover, there are consistent ways in which these morphemes are organized within the word (Aronoff, 1976; Nida, 1949): Derivational morphemes must be encompassed within inflectional morphemes.[6] The central morpheme of a word is known as the root; this root is immediately preceded (in prefixing languages) or followed (in suffixing languages) by derivational morphemes, which add components of meaning to the root or change its grammatical category (e.g., from verb to noun); and the derivational morphemes are then preceded or followed by inflectional morphemes, which apply paradigmatically to the word to signal such things as number, tense, or aspect. For example, in English the root *estimate* may take derivational morphemes immediately surrounding it, like *over-* or *-ion* ($\rightarrow$ *overestimation*). Inflectional morphemes, like the plural -*s*, must then appear outside these derivational morphemes ($\rightarrow$ *overestimations*, but not **overestimates-ion*). Inflectional morphemes cannot appear inside derivational morphemes (e.g., one cannot say *drover* to indicate a person who was a driver in the past; -*er* is a derivational morpheme, while the past-tense morpheme is inflectional).[7] In short, the characteristic pattern is

$$[\text{INFL} + [\text{DERIV} + [\text{ROOT}] + \text{DERIV}] + \text{INFL}],$$

a shell-like or layered arrangement of discrete units.

In fact, in spoken languages these constraints are strong enough that, as elements change from being separate words to being morphemes within the same word, the placement of inflections shifts. For example, *teaspoons full* $\rightarrow$ *teaspoonsful* $\rightarrow$ *teaspoonfuls*; the loss of a word boundary between *teaspoons* and *full* is currently resulting in a rearrangement of morphemes to observe the patterning constraint.[8]

Morphology in American Sign Language

I argued in the previous section that the visual modality seems to make accessible a great deal more richness than the auditory mode (at least in that portion of the auditory mode which spoken language uses). In theory, then, signed languages could be quite different in organization from spoken languages. What is, in fact, the morphological character of American Sign Language?

Table 15.1. *English translations of ASL*
"mimetic depiction" in Figure 15.9

(a) A car wanders uphill.
(b) The car skids on the road.
(c) The car goes across the road.
(d) The car crashes through a fence.
(e) The car turns to avoid hitting a tree.
(f) The car hits a telephone pole.
(g) A person falls out of the car.
(h) The telephone pole falls down.

To answer this question, one must consider two domains in ASL. First, there is what I will call the *frozen lexicon*. These are the single-morpheme signs well standardized among signers, typically listed in standard dictionaries of ASL, learned early by adults and children acquiring ASL, and borrowed for use in Signed English. Most of the current literature on ASL has concentrated on these signs. (For further discussion, see Supalla, 1978a.) Second, there is another portion of the language which has been called "mimetic," "nonstandardized," "analogue," or "nonlinguistic;" by deaf people, it is called "sign mime." These signs seem to reflect aspects of the real world in form: Handshapes often refer to shapes of objects, and movement of these handshapes through space in front of the signer is used to represent the motion of objects through real-world space. As an example, Figure 15.9 presents a sign sequence of this type of "mimetic depiction." Table 15.1 presents an English translation.

In the ASL literature there have been two rather different points of view on the character of mimetic depiction. According to one view, only the frozen lexicon is the lexicon of the language; "mimetic depiction" is considered a nonlinguistic extension of the mode, analogous to "vroom-vroom" for the sound of a motorcycle in the auditory mode (Klima, Bellugi, et al., 1979, pp. 13–15). On this view, ASL becomes like spoken languages by excluding from the bounds of the language proper much of the communicative use of the modality. However, several investigators have recently suggested a second, radically different position: that "mimetic depiction" is part of ASL proper, that it is built on an analogue use of movement and space, and therefore that ASL is dramatically different in organizational character from spoken languages. For example, De-Matteo (1977) has proposed that these signs vary continuously in form and meaning, in an analogue way, to match the visual images they represent. This is in sharp contrast to the discrete distinctions of spoken language. Moreover, DeMatteo has suggested that the grammar of ASL, in contrast to that of spoken languages, must include mechanisms for mapping continuously varying forms onto visual images. Similarly, Cohen

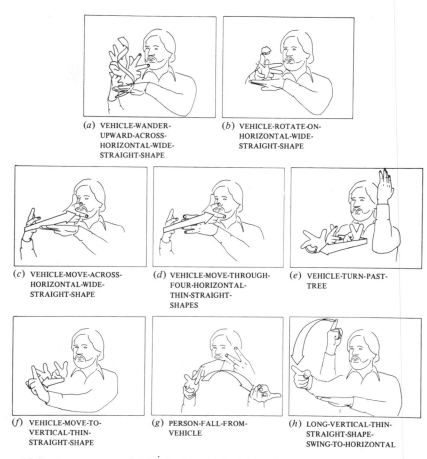

Figure 15.9. A sequence of ASL "mimetic depiction."

et al. (1977) have claimed that many signs in Israeli Sign Language covary continuously and indefinitely with their meanings, a property that they attribute to the iconic potential of the visual-gestural mode. This view, then, argues that the organizational character of a language is highly determined by the modality in which that language is transmitted.

It is quite true that the modalities used by a signed language have the *potential* for an analogue, rather than a discrete, system. In preceding sections I presented evidence that perception and immediate memory for signlike items are continuous rather than categorical. Moreover, with a system of gestures that uses handshape to represent shape, and hand movement to represent movement, there is clearly the possibility for analogue flexibility. In fact, Carol Schwartz, Ted Supalla, and I (C. Schwartz, Newport, & Supalla, in preparation) have demonstrated experimentally that hearing subjects, using sign-like gestures nonlinguistically, vary their mimetic gestures continuously in correspondence with continuous variations in real-world stimuli. However, what I will argue, once again, is that the language does not take advantage of this potential: Despite the additional and somewhat different resources offered by the visual-gestural modality, the language looks in many ways the same as spoken languages. In particular, our analyses suggest that "mimetic depiction" in ASL is strikingly like morphology in spoken languages: "Mimetic" forms within American Sign Language are not at all analogue in nature; rather, like morphologically complex forms in spoken language, they are constructed from a relatively small number of discrete components, which mark familiar distinctions of meaning and are combined in familiar ways. Unlike spoken language, these morphemes are largely simultaneous rather than sequential; moreover, the form of each morpheme has some clear relation to its meaning (i.e., the morphemes are iconic). However, the organization of these components is like that of other languages of the world.

The evidence for these claims comes from a linguistic analysis of "mimetic depiction" in American Sign Language conducted by Ted Supalla and me (Newport, 1981; Newport & Supalla, in preparation; Supalla, 1978a, 1982), as well as from suggestions in prior work of Coulter (1975, 1977) and Newport and Bellugi (1978). Supalla and I have initially focused our attention on ASL depictions of motion and location, using standard linguistic methodologies to elicit from native speakers judgments of what forms are possible in the language and what forms are contrastive in meaning, and then determining the internal structure of these forms from the range of possibilities and contrasts within the set. The results of this analysis are presented, in overview, in this chapter; for further detail, see Supalla (1982) and Newport and Supalla (in preparation).

Handshape as a classifier. There is a limited number of discretely different handshapes that can be used in "mimetic depiction," each with its own consistent meaning. The handshape of a sign within "mimetic depiction," then, is itself a morpheme. (This is not generally the case within the frozen lexicon; for frozen signs, handshape is a phonological parameter with no associated meaning.) In the mimetic depiction sequence rendered in Table 15.1, handshapes are roughly translated into English nouns (e.g., the horizontally extended index and second finger and the vertically extended thumb, a handshape known within the ASL literature as a 3-hand, is translated as "car"). However, a more precise translation is given in Figure 15.9 (i.e., "vehicle" for the example just given; for other signs of Figure 15.9, "person," "long-vertical-thin-straight shape," etc.). The handshapes of these signs mark the semantic category or the size and shape of the associated noun. In actual discourse, these forms are preceded by full nouns from the frozen lexicon: for example, CAR$_{frozen}$ VEHICLE-WANDER-UPWARD.[9]

As noted by Frishberg (1975), Kegl and Wilbur (1976), and Supalla (1978b), these handshapes function similarly to morphemes known in spoken languages as *classifiers*, which commonly appear in verbs of motion and location. For example, in Navajo the final morpheme of the verb of motion or location varies according to the shape of the object involved in the action (from Allan, 1977):

béésò sì-ʔá	= money lie-of round entity	"A coin is lying (there)."
béésò sì-ltsòòz	= money lie-of flat flexible entity	"A bill is lying (there)."
béésò sì-nìl	= money lie-of collection	"A pile of change is lying (there)."

The corresponding sentences of ASL are formally analogous, with the classifier morpheme occurring simultaneously with the movement or location morpheme:

MONEY	⌈ FLAT-ROUND-SHAPE (F-handshape) ⌉ ⌊ BE-LOCATED (contact movement) ⌋	"A coin is lying there."
MONEY	⌈ FLAT-WIDE-SHAPE (B-handshape) ⌉ ⌊ BE-LOCATED (contact movement) ⌋	"A bill is lying there."
MONEY	⌈ DOME-SHAPE (5-handshape) ⌉ ⌊ BE-LOCATED (contact movement) ⌋	"A pile of change is lying there."

The ASL verbs from these three sentences are illustrated in Figure 15.10.

ASL has several different handshapes that function as classifiers in "mimetic depiction"; on the basis of characteristics of form as well as meaning, these fall into two main groups.[10] One group includes size-and-shape specifiers (SASSes), which classify objects on the basis of their size and shape. The other group are abstract classifiers, which classify objects on the basis of semantic characteristics. All of these classifiers fall within the types Allan (1977) has found in spoken classifier languages of the world.

The SASS handshapes actually consist not of a single handshape morpheme, but of a group of simultaneous hand-part morphemes: Each finger, as well as the thumb and forearm, is a possible morpheme that can combine in specifiable ways to form a handshape (Supalla, 1978b). Figure 15.11 presents examples of two morphologically related groups of SASSes. The SASSes on the left all share the morpheme STRAIGHT; those on the right all share the morpheme ROUND. The rows differ formationally in whether the index finger (and, for the round shapes, the thumb) occur alone (row 1); or whether the middle finger (row 2)[11] or the full hand (row 3) are involved as well; the meanings of these forms differ correspond-

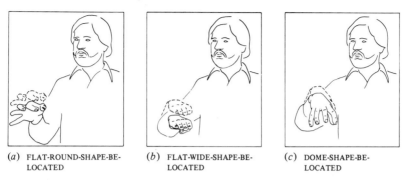

(*a*) FLAT-ROUND-SHAPE-BE-
      LOCATED

(*b*) FLAT-WIDE-SHAPE-BE-
      LOCATED

(*c*) DOME-SHAPE-BE-
      LOCATED

Figure 15.10. Three ASL verbs of location.

ingly, as indicated in the figure. In addition, there are discrete morphological values of size that must be marked on the SASSes as well; for further details, see Supalla (1978a, b). In sum, for the SASSes there are a limited number of discrete values along several dimensions of handshape; hand parts form a morphophonological system that relates the phonology of the hand to the visual-geometric features of the referent object.

The second group of classifier handshapes, although they may have originated as SASSes (see Supalla, 1978a), are currently composed of a single morpheme (rather than a group of morphemes), and represent the semantic category of the associated object (rather than its visual-geometric properties). Figure 15.12 presents several examples of these semantic classifiers. The first, a V-handshape oriented downward (in its unmarked orientation),[12] is used with animate human nouns, as illustrated in Figure 15.9g for a person. The second example, a bent V oriented downward (in its unmarked orientation), is used with animate nonhuman nouns, for example, a dog, a bird, or a bug. The 3-handshape, used for vehicles (e.g., a car, a boat, or a motorcycle), was illustrated in Figure 15.9a–g. In contrast, the airplane classifier is used only for airplanes (but

THIN & STRAIGHT

NARROW & STRAIGHT

WIDE & STRAIGHT

FLAT & ROUND (circle)

SHALLOW & ROUND (shallow cylindrical)

DEEP & ROUND (cylindrical)

Figure 15.11. Morphologically related size-and-shape specifiers.

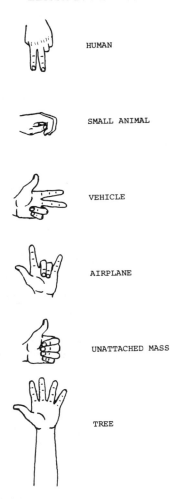

HUMAN

SMALL ANIMAL

VEHICLE

AIRPLANE

UNATTACHED MASS

TREE

Figure 15.12. Some examples of semantic classifiers.

not helicopters). The fifth example, a fist with the thumb extended upward, is used for three-dimensional objects that are separable from their
ground: a flowerpot, a house, a bottle, a potted tree. In contrast, a rooted
tree must be classified by the last example, a classifier for trees that is
used for palm trees or evergreens as well as for more prototypically
shaped trees. In short, although there is some clear iconic relationship
between the form of the classifier and its meaning (e.g., and "tree
category"), these forms within contemporary ASL are used in semantic
and grammatical ways extended systematically beyond their iconic
properties.

As one may notice from the descriptions of the domains of these classifiers, for any given noun more than one classifier might be appropriate. In ASL, as in spoken classifier languages (see Allan, 1977), different classifiers may be used with the same noun to focus on different characteristics of the referent. For example, to talk about a person moving, one could use the index finger oriented upward (VERTICAL-THIN-STRAIGHT-SHAPE) or the V-handshape; the former classifies the noun in terms of its visual-geometric properties (classifier languages commonly include people in the category of long thin things), whereas the latter classifies the noun as two-legged human and requires further morphemes to specify manner of movement (e.g., walk vs. slide).

These classifier handshapes, then, are a set of discrete morphemes that occur within "mimetic depiction." These handshape morphemes occur in combination with movements which are described in the next section.

Movement as a root morpheme. Movement within "mimetic depiction" appears on first inspection to vary continuously with movement in the real world; prior linguistic investigations, as well as more superficial observation, have suggested that classifier handshapes can be manipulated through the signing space to mirror the paths and manners of movement taken by the referent object. However, our own analyses (Newport, 1981; Newport & Supalla, in preparation; Supalla, 1978a, 1982) have suggested that movement, like handshape, does not vary continuously or indefinitely in either form or meaning. Rather, as in spoken classifier languages, the classifier is combined with a limited number of discretely different morphemes representing categories of movement to form a verb of motion or location.

Not all conceivable paths of movement are acceptable or contrastive in ASL "mimetic depiction." Those paths of movement which are acceptable in the language are constructed from only seven basic movement patterns, or *movement roots*; each root is a morpheme within verbs of motion or location. (As with handshape, the same movements may occur within the frozen lexicon, but within the frozen lexicon these movements are phonological entities with no associated meaning by themselves.) These roots may each occur alone (in combination with morphemes from the other morphological parameters) to represent simple events, or may combine with each other (and with morphemes from the other morphological parameters) to represent complex events. The seven roots are listed in Figure 15.13.

The first is the *hold root*, in which there is no movement and the hand remains in one place. This root has the meaning "be stationary." For example, a bent-V handshape combined with the hold root (that is, held stationary in neutral space in front of the signer) means "small animal

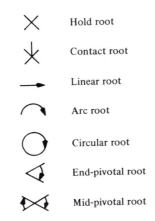

Figure 15.13. Movement roots.

[e.g., a bird] is stationary''; a 3-handshape with the same movement means ''vehicle is stationary''; the airplane-handshape with the same movement means ''airplane is stationary.''

The next is the *contact root*, in which there is a brief movement before the hand stops at a specified location. This root has the meaning ''be located'' and is found in all verbs of location. (It is therefore the movement occurring in all three ASL equivalents of the Navajo verbs discussed under ''Handshape as a classifier'' and illustrated in Figure 15.10.) This root in combination with a bent-V handshape means ''small animal [e.g., a bird] is located (there)'' and forms a minimal morphological pair with the first example in the previous paragraph; the same movement in combination with the 3-handshape means ''vehicle is located (there)'' and forms a minimal pair with the second example of the previous paragraph; the same movement in combination with the airplane-handshape means ''airplane is located (there)'' and forms a minimal pair with the third example in the previous paragraph.

The contact root can also be extended to use for more abstract grammatical purposes. In this case, classifiers are combined with the contact root to establish arguments whose spatial locations will later be used in marking case relations. For example, to sign ''The dog bites the cat,'' one can sign the following sequence: the frozen noun DOG, followed by the animal classifier with the contact root performed on one side of the signing space; then the frozen noun CAT, followed by the animal classifier with the contact root performed on the other side of the signing space; and finally the sign BITE, performed directionally from the location of the dog classifier to the location of the cat classifier.[13] In contrast, to sign ''The cat bites the dog,'' the sequence is identical except that BITE is performed from the location of the cat classifier to the location of the dog classifier. In this type of usage, the contact root does not necessarily indicate an actual physical location for the referent objects, but rather a grammatical location to be used in a later verb.

The remaining five roots in Figure 15.13 are used in verbs of motion. In all these roots the hand starts at an initial point in the signing space and moves to an end point; they differ from one another in the form of the movement path. In the *linear root* the hand moves in a straight path from the initial point to the end point. For example, this root in combination with the bent-V handshape means "small animal [e.g., bird] moves from one place to another"; the root in combination with a 3-handshape means "vehicle moves from one place to another"; and the root in combination with the airplane-handshape means "airplane moves from one place to another." Again, these examples form minimal pairs with the examples given for the hold root and the contact root.

In the *arc root* the hand moves in an arc from the initial point to the end point. This root has a concrete meaning, "to move through an arc"; but it also has a more abstract meaning, "to move from one point to another (with the path unspecified)." For example, in combination with the bent-V handshape, the more likely reading would be "small animal jumps from one point to another." In contrast, for the same root in combination with the 3-handshape, the more likely reading (given the abilities of vehicles) is "vehicle moves (in an unspecified path) from one location to another"; the vehicle could have moved in a straight line or in a zigzag, it could have been lifted from one place to another, or it could have vanished at the point of origin and reappeared at the final point. For the same root in combination with the airplane-classifier, either reading is likely.

In the *circular root*, the hand moves through a circular movement path, with the meaning "move in a circle." In combination with the bent-V handshape it means "small animal [e.g., bird] moves in a circle"; in combination with the 3-handshape it means "vehicle moves in a circle"; in combination with the airplane-handshape it means "airplane moves in a circle."

In the three previous roots the whole hand moves across space. In contrast, for the last two movement roots, one part of the hand is fixed in space while other parts of the hand move across space; both of these roots signal changes of orientation. In the *end-pivotal root*, one end of the hand is fixed while the other end moves, with the meaning "swing." For example, Figure 15.9h shows this root in combination with the LONG-VERTICAL-THIN-STRAIGHT-SHAPE SASS, with the meaning "long vertical thin straight shape swings to the ground." The same movement performed horizontally[14] in combination with the WIDE-STRAIGHT-SHAPE SASS means "wide straight shape [e.g., gate] swings." In the *mid-pivotal root*, the hand changes orientation with the middle of the hand fixed. For example,

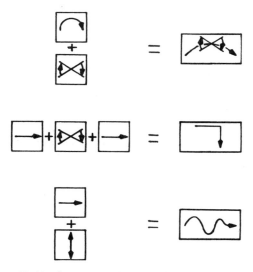

Figure 15.14. Some combinations of movement roots.

this root in combination with the bent-V handshape means "small animal [e.g., bird] turns upsidedown"; in combination with the 3-handshape it means "vehicle turns upsidedown" (pivoting vertically) or "vehicle rotates [e.g., slips on the ground]" (pivoting horizontally). The latter example is illustrated in Figure 15.9b.

All of the above examples involve one movement root per sign. However, certain movement roots may also combine within a verb of motion to represent more complex events. Figure 15.14 shows several permissible combinations.

Certain movement roots may combine simultaneously, as in the first example in Figure 15.14. In this case, the arc root is combined simultaneously with the mid-pivotal root with the meaning "fall" (= "move" + "change of orientation"). This complex movement contrasts in meaning and in form with the simple arc movement meaning "jump"; the latter involves the arc root alone and signifies only movement to a new location (without a change of orientation).

In other combinations, the roots are combined in sequence, as in the second example of Figure 15.14. In this case, a linear root is combined with a mid-pivotal root and another linear root, with the three sequential roots well merged and performed with smooth transitions. This movement combination has the meaning "turn," as in the example VEHICLE-TURN in Figure 15.9e. Like the other movement forms already described, this form is not limited to an analogue usage: The referent movement need not be precisely 90 degrees, and the form is unchanged for a wide range of referent movements. Rather, like the English word *turn*, the form refers to a category of real-world events.

The last example of Figure 15.14 is a movement pattern in which sideways linear movement is combined simultaneously with forward linear movement, with the meaning "move randomly," or "wander." Again, this form is used not for one particular path, but for a variety of random paths. For example, this complex movement in combination with the 3-handshape (VEHICLE-WANDER) is shown in Figure 15.9a.

In sum, movement in "mimetic depiction" does not vary continuously as an analogue to real-world movement. Rather, there is a small number of movement categories that are marked in ASL; complex paths of movement are marked by combinations of these forms. The analyses described thus far, then, suggest that these signs are *not* mimetic depictions, but multimorphemic verbs of motion and location.[15] Additional sets of morphemes within these verbs are described below.

Base point as a morpheme. Thus far I have described the handshape and movement of the active, or dominant, hand (for right-handed signers, this is typically the right hand). In verbs of motion and location, this hand marks the action of the central or moving object and is, of course, an obligatory part of the sign. The nondominant hand, known as the base hand, is optionally part of the verb as well, remaining in one place while the active hand moves. We have found that this base hand and its placement in verbs of motion and location involve several independent morphemes, all of which mark aspects of a secondary object (for example, the source or goal) related to the action of the central object. (As with handshape and movement, the base hand within the frozen lexicon is a phonological entity with no associated meaning by itself.)

First, the handshape of the base hand is a classifier for the secondary object, just as the handshape of the active hand is a classifier for the central object. For example, the base hand with the index finger oriented upward (VERTICAL-THIN-STRAIGHT-SHAPE) can be combined with an active hand with a 3-handshape (VEHICLE) and a linear movement to mean "vehicle moves to a vertical thin straight shape" (e.g., "The car hits the telephone pole"). This verb is shown in Figure 15.9f. In contrast, the base hand with a bent-V handshape (ANIMAL) can be combined with the same active handshape and movement to mean "vehicle moves to a small animal" (e.g., "The car hits the bird"). Since the base hand classifiers are identical to those of the active hand,[16] I will not discuss them further; see the subsection entitled "Handshape as a classifier."

Second, the placement of the base hand with respect to the path of the active hand is another morpheme, marking the semantic relationship of the secondary object to the central object. There is a limited number of

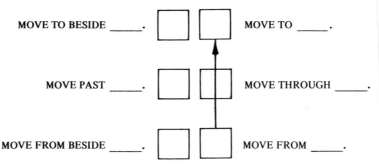

MOVE TO BESIDE _____.   MOVE TO _____.

MOVE PAST _____.   MOVE THROUGH _____.

MOVE FROM BESIDE _____.   MOVE FROM _____.

Figure 15.15. Base points of the linear movement root.

possible locations around the movement path that can be marked with a base hand. We have called these locations *base points*. The set of all base points for a given movement root is called the *base grid system*.

Figure 15.15 illustrates the base-point morpheme possibilities by showing the possible locations of a base hand along or adjacent to the linear movement root. As shown in this figure, there are only three possible locations for a base hand on the movement path of the linear root: the initial point, the midpoint, and the end point. For example, a base hand with the index finger oriented upward (VERTICAL-THIN-STRAIGHT-SHAPE) is placed at the initial point, marking the source of the movement, with a 3-handshape of the active hand, to mean "vehicle moves from a vertical thin straight shape" (e.g., "The car leaves the telephone pole"). The same handshapes and movements with the base hand placed at the midpoint mean "vehicle moves through a vertical thin straight shape" (e.g., "The car goes through the telephone pole"). The same handshapes and movements with the base hand placed at the end point, marking the goal, mean "vehicle moves to a vertical thin straight shape" (e.g., "The car hits the telephone pole"). The last example is illustrated in Figure 15.9f. Figures 15.9a, c, d, and g illustrate other base handshapes at the mid- and end points of the movement path.

Figure 15.15 also shows three locations adjacent to the linear movement path at which a base hand may be placed: adjacent to the initial point, midpoint, and end point. For example, the handshapes and movements just described, with the base hand placed beside the initial point, would mean "vehicle moves from next to a vertical thin straight shape"; with the base hand placed beside the midpoint, the meaning is "vehicle moves past a vertical thin straight shape"; and with the base hand placed beside the end point, the meaning is "vehicle moves (to) next to a vertical thin straight shape."

Finally, there are several more base points not illustrated in Figure 15.15: ahead of or behind the movement path, or along the movement path. (In the last, the entire movement path is marked with a base hand, with the meaning "moves along on." An example with the mid-pivotal movement root is shown in Figure 15.9b.)

Other internal morphemes. By this time it should begin to be clear that there is a large number of morphological dimensions in ASL verbs of motion and location. Although this degree of morphological complexity is unlike English, it is not uncommon in languages of the world: Some languages, known as *polysynthetic* languages, may have as many as ten or fifteen possible morphemes within a single word.

Thus far I have described only some of the ASL morphological dimensions. There are several others: for example, a set of morphemes that mark the orientation of the central and secondary objects with respect to the movement path and to the external world; a set of morphemes that mark the orientation and spatial plane (e.g., above the ground vs. below the ground) of the movement path and the base grid; and a set of morphemes that mark the manner of movement of the central object (e.g., rolling vs. sliding). For further details, see Supalla (1978a) and Newport and Supalla (in preparation). Like the morphological dimensions already described, each of these consists of a discrete set of alternatives; although each of the morphemes is iconic (i.e., there is a clear relationship between the form of the morpheme and its meaning), none varies continuously or indefinitely.

Noun derivation and inflectional processes. The movement root, hand-shape, orientation, (optionally) manner, and (depending on the syntactic context) basehand morphemes together form the *stem* of the verb of motion or location. There are in addition several *process morphemes*[17] that can be added to this stem, to form a noun rather than a verb, and to inflect either the noun or verb for number or temporal aspect. Formal rules for these processes are presented in Supalla and Newport (1978).[18]

When semantically appropriate, certain verb stems can undergo a change in the manner of movement to become *noun stems*. While the movement of verb stems is either a continuous or a hold movement, that of noun stems is restrained in manner: The movement is quick and stiff (rather than smooth), and the hand bounces back to its initial position. In addition, when the noun is not inflected, repetition is also added to the stem to form the surface noun. This morphological process is a highly regular and systematic way of forming concrete nouns in ASL (Supalla & Newport, 1978). Figures 15.16a and 15.17a illustrate this distinction for the verb FLY (airplane-classifier + linear movement) and the noun AIRPLANE: The hand moves steadily forward for the verb, whereas it moves in a restrained fashion for the noun.

Inflectional processes can then be applied to the verb stem to form an

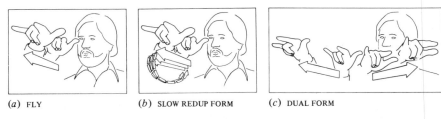

(a) FLY   (b) SLOW REDUP FORM   (c) DUAL FORM

Figure 15.16. FLY: base form and two inflected forms.

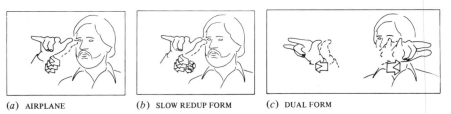

(a) AIRPLANE   (b) SLOW REDUP FORM   (c) DUAL FORM

Figure 15.17. AIRPLANE: base form and two inflected forms.

inflected verb, or to the noun stem (including restrained manner of movement) to form an inflected noun. For example, a slow reduplication process can be applied to either stem, as illustrated in Figure 15.16b for the verb and in Figure 15.17b for the noun. Notice that, although the inflection itself has the same form for the two stems (a reduplication with a slow, arc-shaped transition back to the initial point between reduplicated units), the resulting inflected stems are distinct: The inflected verb is continuous in manner of movement, whereas the inflected noun is restrained in manner of movement. In short, the inflection operates on the stem, reduplicating its constituent morphemes. In a related way, the inflection has a somewhat different interpretation for the two types of stems: When applied to the verb, it has the interpretation of *continuous aspect*, marking the verb for iteration or elongation of the action (e.g., "flying and flying and flying") (Fischer, 1973; Fischer & Gough, 1978). When applied to the noun, it has the interpretation of *serial pluralization* (e.g., "airplane after airplane after airplane") (Supalla & Newport, 1978). Both are common inflections in spoken languages of the world.

There are many other inflections that can be applied to verbs or nouns in ASL; see Fischer and Gough (1978) and Klima, Bellugi, et al. (1979) for a more exhaustive description of inflectional processes. I will describe only one more example: Like many spoken languages, ASL inflects verbs and nouns for *dual*, as well as multiple, plural. In the dual inflection, the stem is performed once in each of two locations in space. This inflection is shown in Figure 15.16c applied to the verb stem FLY, and in Figure

15.17c applied to the noun stem AIRPLANE. Again, the inflection has the same form in both cases, but the resulting inflected verb is continuous in manner, whereas the inflected noun is restrained in manner. When applied to the verb stem, the inflection has the meaning of performing the action twice (e.g., "fly to two places or at two times"); when applied to the noun stem, it means two objects (e.g., "two airplanes").

These inflectional processes can also both be applied to the same stem, with the order of application corresponding to the semantic scope of the inflections. For example, the verb stem FLY can be inflected for continuous aspect, and that stem can then be inflected for dual: $[[FLY_{cont}]_{dual}]$. This complex inflected form has the meaning "flying and flying on two different occasions." The noun AIRPLANE with the same sequence of inflections, $[[AIRPLANE_{serial}]_{dual}]$, has the meaning "two rows of airplane after airplane." In contrast, the same inflections can be applied in the reverse order, with the dual inflection applying before, or inside, the inflection for continuous aspect. The verb form $[[FLY_{dual}]_{cont}]$ has the meaning "flying twice over and over again"; the noun form $[[AIRPLANE_{dual}]_{cont}]$ has the meaning "pairs of airplanes, pair after pair." Finally, the same inflection may be applied recursively to the stem, for example, $[[FLY_{cont}]_{cont}]$, "flying continuously over and over again." In short, like certain inflectional processes in spoken languages (Chapin, 1967, 1970), the inflections of ASL operate hierarchically and recursively (Klima, Bellugi et al., 1979; Supalla & Newport, 1978).

Summary: structure of the "word" in American Sign Language

As we have seen, what appeared to be continuously varying "mimetic depiction" in ASL turns out to be complex morphology much like that in spoken languages. In ASL, the morphemes are often highly iconic, and they are most often combined simultaneously rather than sequentially. However, as in spoken languages, complex forms are made up of a limited number of discrete components. Moreover, these discrete units are combined with a *shell-like structure* like that in spoken languages. Figure 15.18 summarizes the internal structure of the "word" in American Sign Language. Significantly, the inner layer of this shell consists of the root and derivational morphology, those components which add basic meanings to the root; operating outside these is the derivational morphology that changes the grammatical category of the stem from verb to noun; and outside these is inflectional morphology.[19] In short, American Sign Language has the same kind of analytic character, with discrete units inside discrete units, that is displayed by spoken languages. It therefore appears that language demands this type of organization, even when the modality would permit other quite different organizational possibilities.

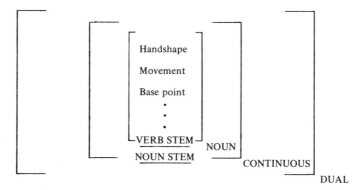

Figure 15.18. Structure of the "word" in American Sign Language.

15.3. Conclusions

Task specificity and modality constraints on language

In preceding sections I have reviewed our work on ASL in comparison with the literature on spoken language in two domains: categorical perception and its relation to phonetic organization, and morphology as an instance of higher levels of language structure. Historically, the findings in these two domains have provided strong support for a task-specific view of language structure and processing, and therefore of language acquisition.

As we have seen, it does not appear that categorical perception is special to speech or even to language more generally. Rather, categorical perception is orthogonal to the language–nonlanguage distinction: It occurs for certain spoken language features and for certain auditory nonlanguage features, but not for the visual language features we have investigated. Moreover, it does not appear that categorical perception is responsible for phonetic organization: Language is categorial at the phonetic level even when there is not categorical perception. As I have argued, categorical perception fundamentally involves *non*linguistic abilities (i.e., the ability to perform discriminations that language does not use) and therefore is not relevant to questions of language organization.

Similarly, it does not appear that the higher-level aspects of language organization investigated here are special to speech: A variety of syntactic and morphological characteristics of spoken languages are found in ASL as well. Moreover, this is the case even though processing and production in the visual-gestural modalities would permit other, quite different organizational possibilities. In sum, then, although the processing resources of the auditory-vocal and visual-gestural modalities seem quite different, the organization of languages in these modalities is at a variety of levels very much the same.

These findings thus rule out the version of task specificity with which we began, and which has heretofore been the predominant one. At least for the language characteristics discussed here, there apparently is not a privileged spoken language faculty.

In addition, these findings are at odds with the view that language is shaped by perception and memory. Although this view is undoubtedly correct for certain aspects of language organization (see Bever, 1970; Slobin, 1973, 1977), it will not account for those aspects of language organization discussed here: As I have argued, there is richness available in the visual, if not the auditory, mode that would permit a type of organizational system rather different from what one finds in ASL. Therefore there must be, within the bounds of what perception and memory permit, still other, more severe constraints that underlie much of language structure.

What possibilities remain as explanations for the characteristics of language we have considered? One possibility is a task-specific language faculty that underlies not just spoken language, but language more generally. According to this view there is not a privileged auditory-vocal apparatus that shapes language, but rather a more modality-independent apparatus that expresses itself through the hands (or other peripheral output devices) if expression through the mouth is blocked. This alternative will not account for categorical perception, since categorical perception does not characterize all language processing; however, it will account for those aspects of phonetics and morphology which I have described. As Osherson and Wasow (1976) have pointed out, answers to the task-specificity question need not in principle turn out the same for different levels of language analysis: Descriptions of real-time processing may look quite different with respect to task-specificity than formal linguistic descriptions. Determining whether this is the correct account at the formal linguistic level of analysis requires the study of nonlinguistic systems in the formal terms, and with the formal methodologies, of a linguistic analysis. Only if the results of such analyses for nonlinguistic systems are systematically different from those for linguistic ones would such a view receive support.

Finally, there is the possibility of abandoning task specificity altogether, and instead searching for ways in which modality-independent nonlinguistic systems through which language operates might constrain language severely enough to account for linguistic universals. Because ASL differs from most spoken languages in its circumstances of acquisition as well as in modality, its study has given us the opportunity to examine this additional factor in the structuring of a language. Therefore, as an example of the approach I am suggesting, I describe next our current work in progress, and our initial speculations, on the role of learning in language design.

The influence of learning on language

According to our linguistic analyses, signed languages (at least American Sign Language) have the same kind of analytic character as spoken languages. First, ASL marks the same kinds of semantic distinctions marked by many spoken languages. More important, ASL has the same kind of formal apparatus for marking these distinctions: a limited number of parameters along which a limited number of discrete values are signaled, and a shell-like, hierarchically organized combinatorial system governing the permissible ways in which these discrete units may co-occur. Moreover, this analytic kind of organization appears in ASL despite the very clear iconic base for these forms, and despite the resulting potentially different options the visual-gestural modality makes available.

Why are languages organized in this way? I would like to suggest that the property of having highly analytic forms, with units inside units organized in constrained ways, arises from the learning process through which such systems are passed.

What is the evidence for this claim? In fact, not all communication systems are organized in this fashion; early, newly evolved communication systems display this analytic character to a lesser degree than older, more successively learned communication systems. One example of this contrast can be found in the history of writing systems (Gelb, 1952; L. Gleitman & Rozin, 1977). The earliest writing systems were first pictographic, representing a complex idea through a global picture, and then logographic, representing the spoken language at the level of the whole word. As these writing systems were picked up by new cultures, they apparently were reanalyzed in more and more analytic ways, resulting in a systematic progression from logography to syllabary, with representation of the internal syllables of the spoken word, to alphabet, with representation of the morphemic and phonemic structure of the word. Significantly, these evolutionary changes generally occur not within a single culture, where the use of the system tends to become frozen, but rather when the system is adopted and reanalyzed by a new culture for use with its language.

A similar phenomenon occurs within the invention and evolution of new spoken languages. *Pidgins* are communication systems invented by adults for communication with other adults with whom they do not share a language (typically in trade situations). Pidgin languages are universally isolating, with little or no morphology internal to the word and with grammatical functions performed through separate words and word order; this is true even when the creators of the pidgin are both native speakers of languages with rich morphologies (Broch, 1927; Kay & Sankoff, 1974; Slobin, 1977). When children are born to pidgin speakers and acquire the pidgin in infancy, as a native language, the communication system is known as a *creole*. In contrast to pidgins, creole languages universally include morphology internal to the word; this internal morphological structure is apparently added to the system through reanalysis of the input language by the second-generation learner (Sankoff & Laberge, 1973; and see Slobin, 1977, for an important discussion of the significance of these facts to language acquisition).

Finally, the deaf community presents an exceptionally striking example of the same phenomenon. Ninety percent of the deaf population in the United States are first-generation deaf, deaf children born to hearing parents. The earliest communication for these children is often a "home sign" system invented for use within the family in the absence of any exposure to other gestural communication systems. Recent studies of "home sign" (Feldman, Goldin-Meadow, & L. Gleitman, 1978; Goldin-Meadow, 1979) have revealed that it is composed of signlike gestures without internal morphology and with fairly consistent gesture ordering. Our own work in progress suggests that these first-generation deaf individuals go on later in life to acquire predominantly the frozen lexicon of American Sign Language, those signs lacking much of the internal morphology discussed in this chapter. The highly analyzed morphology I have described is largely a property of the sign competence of only second-generation deaf, those who learn ASL as a native language in infancy. This suggestion is in line with the findings of Woodward (1973), who has shown that the use of certain rules of ASL inflectional morphology is related to having deaf parents and to acquiring ASL before age 6, and with those of Fischer (1978), who has presented evidence that ASL has arisen under creolizing circumstances.

These findings suggest that complex internal morphological analysis is performed by second-generation deaf on an input that does not itself contain this morphology. This is not to say that such analysis occurs entirely in the absence of environmental support; in fact, Newport, H. Gleitman, and L. Gleitman (1977), Feldman et al. (1978), and Goldin-Meadow (Chapter 2) have presented evidence that grammatical morphemes are acquired with dependence on a linguistic environment. The frozen lexicon of ASL, which is the predominant linguistic input for most second-generation signers, includes the handshapes, movements, and so on of complex verbs of motion and location as phonological entities inconsistently associated with particular components of meaning. The second-generation learner, then, regularizes these associations, ending up with productive form–meaning components that were not characteristic of the language of his or her parents.

All of these examples, taken together, suggest that the learning process itself may contribute certain types of organizational characteristics to languages. This is not an entirely new claim: N. Chomsky (1965), McNeill (1966b), Wexler and Culicover (1980), and others have argued that there must be strong constraints on the learning process for any language to be learned from only a sample of input strings. I am suggesting even more strongly that learning may go well beyond what is justified by the input, that the output of such a process may be more highly structured than the input (see also Kiparsky, 1971). Moreover, I suggest that these contributions to structure may be made by a general learning process, not necessarily specific to language.

To examine this claim in more detail, we must consider the nature of the acquisition process. In the more familiar language-acquisition situation, that of the infant acquiring the language from his native user parents, children learning ASL proceed through a series of stages quite similar to those of children learning spoken languages. During the first years the child seems to organize his language primarily in terms of individual lexical items, each related to its meaning but unrelated, or loosely related, to others across the system. During this time the child acquiring ASL produces sentences composed predominantly of single-morpheme forms, many of which are frozen signs (that is, phonologically complex forms whose internal parts are not analyzed by the child); the latter are like what MacWhinney (1978) has called *amalgams* in the early stages of acquiring spoken languages with complex morphology.

With increasing age, the child begins to analyze internal morphemes, producing a large number of errors in which some individual morphemes are produced correctly while others are omitted; in fact on occasion the child produces all of the correct morphemes, but in sequence rather than simultaneously. Finally, of course, the child produces complex forms, with multiple morphemes combined simultaneously as is appropriate for ASL. (See Newport, 1981, and Supalla, 1982, for the details of this acquisition pattern.)

The significant point for present purposes is that, while the early stage of acquisition involves organizing the lexicon in terms of individual lexical items, each related to its meaning, the subsequent stage requires that the child perform a distributional analysis across (some portion of) the lexicon, deriving morphological components by analyzing the form–meaning relations shared by numerous lexical items across the system; morphological analysis cannot be performed on individual form–meaning pairs, but only across a set of such pairs. Moreover, it requires building paradigms into which the individual items fit.

In fact, the creolization and the ASL data suggest that the young learner is driven to move from a set of individual items to a set of items related across the system. He or she seems at some point in acquisition to require that items contrast minimally and paradigmatically with one another; even when items are not so structured as to have such relations, the child modifies individual items in form, and generalizes local regularities, so that they are. Internal morphological components are the result of this reorganization.

Certainly there must be constraints on the ways in which such paradigmatic relations can be constructed by humans (see, for example, Talmy, 1972, for proposed constraints on semantic and morphological configurations in verbs of motion). Whether such constraints include any task-specific restrictions is currently unknown. But in any case the strong tendency of learners to organize and perform such an analysis appears *not* to be task-specific. Within language, such a tendency is known to be widespread: Children have been described as organizing their early language around individual, internally unanalyzed units and subsequently reorganizing in a paradigmatic fashion by performing contrastive analyses across the set within the domains of syntax (Maratsos & Chalkley, 1980), closed-class morphology (Karmiloff-Smith, 1979), lexical semantics (Bowerman, 1982; Chapter 11; Carey, 1978; Chapter 12), and phonology (Jusczyk, in press) (see also Bowerman, Chapter 11; L. Gleitman, 1981; L. Gleitman & Wanner, Chapter 1, for general discussions of reorganization within language). It also occurs, however, in possibly quite similar fashion outside language. For example, L. B. Smith and Kemler (1977, 1978) describe the organization of a similarity space within which a set of colored objects is perceived as changing developmentally from wholistic to dimensional; within the latter kind of organization, but not the former, objects are compared with one another along independent dimensions of size and color. See also Sugarman (in press) for a relevant description of the development of early classification; Karmiloff-Smith (1979b) on micro-developmental changes in abstract notation systems; and all of these authors as well as Bowerman (1982) for theoretical accounts of the nature of these phenomena. Moreover, ongoing work on the acquisition of miniature languages in the laboratory (Morgan & Newport, 1981; Newport & Morgan, forthcoming) suggests that at least some of the principles by which such an analysis is performed on linguistic material are related to those which operate in nonlinguistic cognition.

In short, my claim (see also Karmiloff-Smith, 1979b,c) is that young learners tend to move from organizing units independently of one another to organizing them in paradigmatic systems; that they do this outside language as well as within language; and that they do this even when the data they are organizing in fact do not quite fit into neat paradigms. In the case of the second-generation deaf child, whose parents do not control all of the highly analyzed morphology of verbs of motion and location, the child himself appears to overregularize form–meaning relations which occur only probabilistically in his input; he thereby creates an analytic, paradigmatic organization in his language that was not present in the language of his parents. In contrast, the first-generation learner who is exposed to ASL late in life does not appear to organize his language in this fashion. Rather, the late learner appears to be capable of continuing indefinitely to organize his language in the fashion of the early child learner: as a large lexicon organized primarily in terms of individual lexical items, each related to its meaning but unrelated, or loosely related, to others across the system.

This argument is at present clearly speculative. It is quite possible that indeed language is shaped by the learning process, but that this learning process itself is task-specific and unrelated to the learning that operates in nonlinguistic cognition; moreover, it is possible that adults do not show this kind of learning because they have matured beyond the time when this task-specific learning device operates. On the other hand, there is accumulating evidence that certain phenomena of reorganization may be occurring across a variety of domains, outside language as well as in; and it is possible that an account of the processes involved in such reorganization will explain why it is at least sometimes the case that adults need not reorganize their knowledge in the same way. In any case, our findings on ASL, along with others in the literature on language evolution and acquisition, suggest that the explanation of certain structural regularities in language may lie in such an understanding of the learning process itself.

Notes

1 Signs, unlike words, are not organized into simultaneous phonetic features (phones) that are then sequentially organized. Rather, the sign itself is made up of simultaneous phonetic features (at least under current analyses). See Klima, Bellugi, et al. (1979) for further discussion.
2 Stimuli differing by equal step sizes were chosen by projecting a single still frame from each production onto a piece of paper, tracing the outline of the hand and face, and physically measuring with a ruler the distances (in location of the finger or in bend of the finger) between stimuli.
3 As is common in visual information processing studies, exposure duration was determined by presenting a randomized set of stimuli, including all steps along the continuum, and adjusting the exposure duration until a target level of accuracy was achieved. In this case, the target was 67 percent correct discrimination, which is the average level of discrimination when perception is categorical.
4 It is nevertheless possible that one can obtain categorical perception of ASL stimuli varying along phonetic parameters other than those we investigated. For example, although our stimuli in the first set of studies included a movement component, what was varied to form a continuum was handshape or location, relatively static parameters of a sign; one might get categorical perception for stimuli varying in any of a number of aspects of movement rather than in handshape or location. In this case, the results would be somewhat analogous to obtaining categorical perception for speech stimuli that undergo

rapid change (e.g., stop consonants) but not for relatively more static stimuli (e.g., vowels). We have not investigated these parameters because of the lack of a synthesizer for stimuli varying in movement; thanks to recent innovations in sign language technology, such studies are under way (Bellugi & Poizner, in progress). In any case, the conclusions that follow remain unchanged, since it would still be true that there are phonetic categories in the language for stimuli that are *not* categorically perceived. The same point is true for speech stimuli as well, in that vowels and consonants are both phonological entities handled linguistically in similar ways, although one set of entities is perceived categorically and one is not.

5 A few spoken languages (e.g., Vietnamese, Chinese) are isolating; that is, they uniformly consist of words that are unanalyzable single morphemes. However, most spoken languages have fairly complex morphologies, i.e., words that are analyzable into a number of regular parts.

6 As has been pointed out by many investigators, "The distinction [between derivational and inflectional morphemes] is delicate, and sometimes elusive, but nonetheless important" (Aronoff, 1976, p. 2). Nida (1949) and Matthews (1974) suggest the following: If a simple form can be substituted for a complex form in a sentence, then the complex form is derivational (that is, a property of the lexical item but not the construction). If a simple form cannot be substituted for a complex form in a sentence, but instead every lexical item that can go in the slot must be likewise complex, the complex form is inflectional (that is, a property of the grammatical construction). This criterion must be supplemented by other facts, e.g., the paradigmatic nature of inflections, to deal with special problems like suppletion. See Matthews (1974) and Aronoff (1976) for more extensive discussion.

7 Technically, the correct generalization concerns rule ordering: Derivational changes must apply before inflectional changes. For most languages, these two ways of stating the generalization are equivalent. However, for languages in which inflections are infixed to the root, only the latter statement is accurate. I am grateful to Mark Aronoff (1976 and personal communication) for a discussion of this issue.

8 I would like to thank Lila Gleitman for suggesting this example to me.

9 Following the notational conventions of the ASL literature, I use an English gloss in capitals to represent a sign, and an English gloss or translation in lower case, enclosed in quotation marks, to represent the meaning. Wherever possible, multimorphemic signs are represented by multiple words, in capitals, with one word glossing each morpheme and hyphens between the words.

10 The discussion here focuses on intransitive verbs of motion. There are also transitive verbs of motion (e.g., *bring, carry*), which have other sets of classifiers. The latter classify the instrument (e.g., "by hand" vs. "by forklift") as well as the object or patient of the action.

11 The SASS for shallow cylindrical shape (i.e., both the index finger and the middle finger bending along with the thumb into a circle) does not occur in many signers' dialects. In this case, the handshape with only the index finger and thumb is used for both the flat round shape and the shallow cylindrical shape.

12 Each semantic classifier has an unmarked orientation; changes of orientation are additional morphological parameters. For further discussion see the subsection entitled "Other internal morphemes" and Supalla (1982).

13 It is not yet clear whether this ASL sequence is one sentence with three clauses, or three separate sentences. This question awaits further analyses of ASL syntax.

14 For all movement roots, the plane in which the movement is performed is an additional morphological parameter; see the subsection entitled "Other internal morphemes."

15 On very rare occasions signers may attempt to outline the precise path of a moving object or the precise shape of an object. However, this continuous type of movement differs in a number of ways from the discrete movement forms already described. First, it is produced very slowly, with the eyes oriented toward the hands rather than toward the listener's face. Second, its use is restricted to the special purpose of specifying precise outlines; it is considered unacceptable for ordinary conversation. This type of signing is thus like the "drawing in air" that a hearing person might produce for similar functions, and it is marked by speed and eye gaze as being outside the normal use of the language. This is not what previous investigators have called "mimetic depiction," "sign mime," or "analogue signing." For a further discussion of these distinctions, see Coulter (1977).

16 Within the frozen lexicon, the phonological possibilities for the base hand are more restricted than those of the active hand; see Battison (1974) for a description of these phonological constraints. However, in complex verbs of motion and location, where the base handshape is itself a morpheme, these constraints do not apply.

17 In spoken languages, some morphemes are *segmental* (that is, have as their surface form an isolable component of the stem), whereas others are *process* morphemes (that is, have as their form processes applied to the stem). For example, in many languages the marking for a derived noun or for continuous aspect is a reduplication of the unmarked verb stem. Similarly, in ASL, derived nouns, number, and aspect are marked by various types of reduplication processes.

18 Our earlier description treated noun derivation and inflections as applying to a single-morpheme underlying form, or root. Our current analysis, as presented in this chapter, differs in one significant respect: What was previously treated as the underlying form, or root, of the sign we are now claiming is, at least for verbs of motion and location, a complex stem composed of several independent morphemes.

19 The evidence for the distinction between derivational and inflectional morphology in ASL comes not only from the meanings of the morphemes in question, but also from the substitutability criterion presented in n. 6.

References

Adams, V. *An introduction to modern English word-formation*. London: Longman, 1973.

Aimard, P. *Les Jeux de mots de l'enfant*. Villeurbanne: Simép-Editions, 1975.

Akmajian, A. More evidence for the NP cycle. *Linguistic Inquiry, 6*, 1975, 115–29.

Aksu, A. The acquisition of causal connectives in Turkish. *Papers and Reports on Child Language Development* (Department of Linguistics, Stanford University), No. 15, 1978, pp. 129–39.

Allan, K. Classifiers. *Language, 53*, 1977, 285–311.

Allport, G. *Pattern and growth in personality*. New York: Holt, Rinehart and Winston, 1961.

Ammon, M. S. H. Development in the linguistic expression of causal relations: Comprehension of features of lexical and periphrastic causatives. Unpublished doctoral dissertation, University of California, Berkeley, 1980.

Ammon, M. S. H., and Slobin, D. I. A cross-linguistic study of the processing of causative sentences. *Cognition 7*, 1979, 1–17.

Anderson, B. The short-term retention of active and passive sentences. Unpublished doctoral dissertation, Johns Hopkins University, 1963.

Anderson, J. R. Computer simulation of language acquisition system: A first report. In R. Solso (ed.), *Information processing and cognition: The Loyola symposium*. Hillsdale, N.J.: Erlbaum, 1975.

Anderson, J. R. Induction of augmented transition networks. *Cognitive Science, 1*, 1977, 125–57.

Anderson, S. On the role of deep structure in semantic interpretation. *Foundations of Language, 6*, 1971, 197–219.

Anglin, J. M. *The growth of word meaning*. Cambridge, Mass.: MIT Press, 1970.

Anglin, J. M. *Word, object, and conceptual development*. New York: Norton, 1977.

Antinucci, F. *Verso una tipologia linguistica*. Rome: Il Múlino, 1977.

Argoff, H. D. The acquisition of Finnish inflectional morphology. Unpublished doctoral dissertaton, University of California, Berkeley, 1976.

Armstrong, S. L., Gleitman, L. R., and Gleitman, H. What some concepts might not be. *Cognition*, 1982 (in press).

Aronoff, M. *Word formation in generative grammar*. Cambridge, Mass.: MIT Press, 1976.

Aronoff, M. Contextuals. *Language, 56*(4), 1980, 744–58.

Augst, G., Bauer, A., and Stein, A. *Grundwortschatz und Ideolekt*. Tübingen: Max Niemeyer Verlag, 1977.

Bach, E., and Harms, R. T. (eds.). *Universals in linguistic theory.* New York: Holt, Rinehart and Winston, 1968.

Baron, J. Semantic components and conceptual development. *Cognition, 2,* 1973, 299–318.

Baron, J., and Kaiser, A. Semantic components in children's errors with pronouns. *Journal of Psycholinguistic Research, 4,* 1975, 303–17.

Barrie-Blackley, S. Six-year-old children's understanding of sentences adjoined with time adverbs. *Journal of Psycholinguistic Research, 2,* 1973, 153–65.

Bartlett, E. J. Sizing things up: The acquisition of meaning of dimensional adjectives. *Journal of Child Language, 3,* 1976, 205–19.

Bartlett, E. J. Semantic organization and reference: Acquisition of two aspects of the meaning of color terms. Paper presented at the biennial meeting of the Society for Research in Child Development, New Orleans, 1977a.

Bartlett, E. J. The acquisition of the meaning of color terms: A study of lexical development. In P. Smith and R. Campbell (eds.), *Proceedings of the Stirling Conference on the Psychology of Language.* New York: Plenum, 1977b.

Bartsch, R., and Vennemann, T. *Semantic structures: A study in the relation between semantics and syntax.* Frankfurt: Athenaum Verlag, 1972.

Bateman, W. G. Two children's progress in speech. *Journal of Educational Psychology, 6,* 1915, 475–93.

Bates, E. *Language and context: Studies in the acquisition of pragmatics.* New York: Academic Press, 1976.

Bates, E. *The emergence of symbols: Cognition and communication in infancy.* New York: Academic Press, 1979.

Bates, E., Camaioni, L., and Volterra, V. The acquisition of performatives prior to speech. *Merrill-Palmer Quarterly, 21,* 1975, 205–26.

Bates, E., and MacWhinney, B. The functionalist approach to the acquisition of grammar. In E. Ochs and B. Schieffelin (eds.), *Developmental pragmatics.* New York: Academic Press, 1979.

Bates, E., McNew, S., MacWhinney, B., deVescovi, A., and Smith, S. Functional constraints on sentence processing: A cross-linguistic study. *Cognition,* 11, 1982, 245–99.

Bateson, G. Redundancy and coding. In T. A. Sebeòk (ed.), *Animal communication.* Bloomington: Indiana University Press, 1973.

Battison, R. Phonological deletion in American Sign Language. *Sign Language Studies, 5,* 1974, 1–19.

Beers, J. W. First and second-grade children's developing orthographic concepts of tense and lax vowels (Doctoral dissertation, University of Virginia, 1974). *Dissertation Abstracts International, 35,* 1975, 4972-A. (University Microfilms No. 75-4694.)

Bellugi, U. The acquisition of negation. Unpublished doctoral dissertation, Harvard University, 1967.

Bellugi, U., and Klima, E. Syntactic regularities in the speech of children. In J. Lyons and R. Wales (eds.), *Psycholinguistics papers.* Edinburgh: Edinburgh University Press, 1966.

Bellugi, U., and Klima, E. Aspects of sign language and its structure. In J. F. Kavanagh and J. E. Cutting (eds.), *The role of speech in language.* Cambridge, Mass.: MIT Press, 1975.

Berko, J. The child's learning of English morphology. *Word, 14,* 1958, 150–77.

Berlin, B., and Kay, P. *Basic color terms: Their universality and evolution.* Berkeley and Los Angeles: University of California Press, 1969.

Berman, A., and Szamosi, M. Observations on sentential stress. *Language, 48*(2), 1972, 304–25.

Bever, T. The cognitive basis for linguistic structures. In J. Hayes (ed.), *Cognition and the development of language.* New York: Wiley, 1970.

Bever, T. Functionalist models of linguistic structures presuppose independent models of language behavior. In R. Grossman, J. San, and T. Vance (eds.), *Papers from the parasession on functionalism, Chicago Linguistic Society.* Chicago: University of Chicago, 1975.

Bever, T. Broca and Lashley were right: Cerebral dominance is an accident of growth. In D. Kaplan and N. Chomsky (eds.), *Biology and language.* Cambridge, Mass.: MIT Press, 1980.

Bever, T. Normal acquisition processes explain the critical period for language learning. In V. Diller (ed.), *Individual differences and universals in language learning aptitude.* London: Newbury House, 1981.

Bever, T., Carroll, J. M., and Hurtig, R. Speech production, perception and the formalization of linguistic analogy. In T. Bever, J. J. Katz, and D. T. Langendoen (eds.), *An integrated theory of linguistic ability.* New York: T. Y. Gerwell (Harper and Row), 1976.

Bever, T., Fodor, J. A., and Garrett, M. A formal limitation of associationism. In T. R. Dixon and D. L. Herton (eds.), *Verbal behavior and general behavior theory.* Englewood Cliffs, N.J.: Prentice-Hall, 1968.

Bever, T., Fodor, J. A., and Weksel, W. Is linguistics empirical? *Psychological Review, 72,* 1965a, 493–500.

Bever, T., Fodor, J. A., and Weksel, W. On the acquisition of syntax: A critique of "contextual generalization." *Psychological Review, 72,* 1965b, 467–82.

Bever, T., Katz, J. J., and Langendoen, D. T. *An integrated theory of linguistic ability.* New York: T. Y. Gerwell (Harper and Row), 1976.

Bever, T., and Langendoen, T. Can a not unhappy man be called a not sad one? In S. R. Anderson and P. Kiparsky (eds.), *Festschrift for Morris Halle.* New York: Holt, Rinehart, and Winston, 1973.

Bever, T., Mehler, J., and Epstein, J. What children do in spite of what they know. *Science, 162,* 1968, 921–24.

Bever, T., Straub, R. O., Terrace, H. S., and Townsend, D. J. The comparative study of serially integrated behavior in humans and animals. In P. W. Jusczyk and R. M. Klein (eds.), *The nature of thought: Essays in honor of D. O. Hebb.* Hillsdale, N.J.: Erlbaum, 1980.

Bierwisch, M. Some semantic universals of German adjectivals. *Foundations of Language, 3,* 1967, 1–36.

Bloom, Lois. *Language development: Form and function in emerging grammars.* Cambridge, Mass.: MIT Press, 1970.

Bloom, Lois. *One word at a time.* The Hague: Mouton, 1973.

Bloom, L., Lahey, M., Hood, L., Lifter, K., and Fiess, K. Complex sentences: Acquisition of syntactic connectives and the semantic relations they encode. *Journal of Child Language, 7*(2), 1980, 235–61.

Bloom, L., Lifter, K., and Hafitz, J. Semantics of verbs and the development of verb inflections in child language. *Language, 56,* 1980, 386–412.

Bloom, L., Lightbown, P., and Hood, L. Structure and variation in child language. *Monographs of the Society for Research in Child Development, 40* (Serial No. 160), 1975.

Bloom, L., Miller, P., and Hood, L. Variation and reduction as aspects of competence in language development. In A. Pick (ed.), *Minnesota Symposia on Child Psychology*, Vol. 9. Minneapolis: University of Minnesota Press, 1975.

Bloom, L., Tanouye, E., and Lifter, K. Semantic organization of verbs in child language and the acquisition of grammatical morphemes. *Language, 56,* 1980, 386–412.

Bloomfield, L. *Language*. New York: Henry Holt, 1933. (Reprinted 1961.)

Blount, B. The pre-linguistic system of Luo children. *Anthropological Linguistics, 12,* 1970, 326–42.

Blumenthal, A. R., and Boakes, R. Prompted recall of sentences: A further study. *Journal of Verbal Learning and Verbal Behavior, 6,* 1968, 674–76.

Bock, K. The effect of a pragmatic presupposition on syntactic structure in question answering. *Journal of Verbal Learning and Verbal Behavior, 16,* 1977, 723–34.

Bohn, W. E. First steps in verbal expression. *Pedagogical Seminary, 21,* 1914, 578–95.

Bolinger, D. Accent is predictable (if you're a mind-reader). *Language, 48,* 1972, 633–44.

Bolinger, D. *Meaning and form*. London: Longman, 1977.

Bornstein, M. H. Qualities of color vision in infancy. *Journal of Experimental Child Psychology, 19,* 1975.

Boucher, J., and Osgood, C. The pollyanna hypothesis. *Journal of Verbal Learning and Verbal Behavior, 8,* 1971, 1–8.

Bourne, L. Learning and utilization of conceptual rules. In B. Kleinmuntz (ed.), *Concepts and the structure of memory*. New York: Wiley, 1967.

Bowerman, M. *Early syntactic development: A cross-linguistic study with special reference to Finnish*. Cambridge: Cambridge University Press, 1973a.

Bowerman, M. Structural relationships in children's utterances: Syntactic or semantic? In T. Moore (ed.), *Cognitive development and the acquisition of language*. New York: Academic Press, 1973b.

Bowerman, M. Learning the structure of causative verbs: A study in the relationship of cognitive, semantic and syntactic development. *Papers and Reports on Child Language Development* (Department of Linguistics, Stanford University), No. 8, 1974, pp. 142–78.

Bowerman, M. Semantic factors in the acquisition of rules for word use and sentence construction. In D. M. Morehead and A. E. Morehead (eds.), *Normal and deficient child language*. Baltimore: University Park Press, 1976.

Bowerman, M. The acquisition of rules governing "possible lexical items": Evidence from spontaneous speech errors. *Papers and Reports on Child Language Development* (Department of Linguistics, Stanford University), No. 13, 1977, pp. 148–56.

Bowerman, M. The acquisition of word meaning: An investigation into some current conflicts. In N. Waterson and C. Snow (eds.), *The development of communication*. New York: Wiley, 1978a.

Bowerman, M. Semantic and syntactic development: A review of what, when, and how in language acquisition. In R. Schiefelbusch (ed.), *Bases of language intervention*. Baltimore: University Park Press, 1978b.

Bowerman, M. Systematizing semantic knowledge: Changes over time in the child's organization of meaning. *Child Development, 49,* 1978c, 977–87.

Bowerman, M. The acquisition of complex sentences. In P. Fletcher and M. Garman (eds.), *Language acquisition: Studies in first language development.* Cambridge: Cambridge University Press, 1979.

Bowerman, M. The structure and origin of semantic categories in the language-learning child. In M. Foster and S. Brandes (eds.), *Symbol as sense: New approaches to the analysis of meaning.* New York: Academic Press, 1980.

Bowerman, M. Beyond communicative adequacy: From piecemeal knowledge to an integrated system in the child's acquisition of language. *Papers and Reports on Child Language Development.* (Department of Linguistics, Stanford University), No. 20, 1981a, pp. 1–24.

Bowerman, M. The child's expression of meaning: Expanding relationships among lexicon, syntax, and morphology. In H. Wintz (ed.), *Proceedings of the New York Academy of Sciences Conference on Native Language and Foreign Language Acquisition.* New York: New York Academy of Sciences, 1981b.

Bowerman, M. Language Development. In H. Triandis and A. Heron (eds.), *Handbook of crosscultural psychology.* Vol. 4: *Developmental psychology.* Boston: Allyn and Bacon, 1981c.

Bowerman, M. Starting to talk worse: Clues to language acquisition from children's late speech errors. In S. Strauss (ed.), *U-shaped behavioral growth.* New York: Academic Press, 1982.

Boyd, W. The development of a child's vocabulary. *Pedagogical Seminary, 21,* 1914, 95–124.

Bradley, D. C. Computational distinctions of vocabulary type. Unpublished doctoral dissertation, MIT, 1978.

Bradley, D. C., Garett, M. F., and Zurif, E. G. Syntactic deficits in Broca's aphasia. In D. Caplan (ed.), *Biological studies of mental processes.* Cambridge, Mass.: MIT Press, 1979.

Braine, M. D. S. The ontogeny of certain logical operations: Piaget's formulation examined by nonverbal methods. *Psychological Monographs, 73,* 1959, 1–43.

Braine, M. D. S. On learning the grammatical order of words. *Psychological Review, 70,* 1963, 323–48.

Braine, M. D. S. On the basis of phrase structure: A reply to Bever, Fodor, and Weksel. *Psychological Review, 72,* 1965, 483–92.

Braine, M. D. S. On two types of models of the internalization of grammars. In D. I. Slobin (ed.), *The ontogenesis of grammar: A theoretical symposium.* New York: Academic Press, 1971a.

Braine, M. D. S. The acquisition of language in infant and child. In C. E. Reed (ed.), *The learning of language.* New York: Appleton-Century-Crofts, 1971b.

Braine, M. D. S. Children's first word combinations. *Monographs of the Society of Research in Child Development, 41* (Serial No. 164), 1976.

Braine, M. D. S., and Wells, R. S. Case-like categories in children: The Actor and more related categories. *Cognitive Psychology, 10,* 1978, 100–22.

Brainerd, C. J. The stage question in cognitive-developmental theory. *Behavioral and Brain Sciences, 1,* 1978, 173–213.

Brandenburg, G. C. The language of a three-year-old child. *Pedagogical Seminary, 22,* 1915, 89–120.

Bresnan, J. A realistic transformational grammar. In M. Halle, J. Bresnan, and G. A. Miller (eds.), *Linguistic theory and psychological reality.* Cambridge, Mass.: MIT Press, 1978.

Bresnan, J. (ed.). *The mental representation of grammatical relations.* Cambridge, Mass.: MIT Press, 1982.

Bresson, F. Remarks on genetic psycholinguistics: The acquisition of the article system in French. In *Current problems in psycholinguistics.* Paris: Editions de CNRS, 1974.

Brewer, W., and Stone, J. B. Acquisition of spatial antonym pairs. *Journal of Experimental Child Psychology, 19,* 1975, 299–307.

Broch, O. Russenorsk. *Archiv für slavische Philologie, 41,* 1927, 209–62.

Broen, P. A. The verbal environment of the language-learning child. *American Speech and Hearing Association Monograph,* No. 17, 1972.

Brooks, L. Non-analytic concept formation and memory for instances. In E. Rosch and B. B. Lloyd (eds.), *Cognition and categorization.* Hillsdale, N.J.: Erlbaum, 1978.

Brown, R. Language and categories. Appendix in J. S. Bruner, J. J. Goodnow, and G. A. Austin, *A study of thinking.* New York: Wiley, 1956.

Brown, R. Linguistic determinism and the part of speech. *Journal of Abnormal and Social Psychology, 55,* 1957, 1–5.

Brown, R. *A first language: The early stages.* Cambridge, Mass.: Harvard University Press, 1973.

Brown, R. Introduction. In C. E. Snow and C. A. Ferguson (eds.), *Talking to children: Language input and acquisition.* Cambridge: Cambridge University Press, 1977.

Brown, R., and Bellugi, U. Three processes in the child's acquisition of syntax. *Harvard Educational Review, 34,* 1964, 133–51.

Brown, R., Cazden, C., and Bellugi, U. The child's grammar from I to III. In J. Hill (ed.), *Minnesota Symposia on Child Psychology,* Vol. 2. Minneapolis: University of Minnesota Press, 1968.

Brown, R., and Hanlon, C. Derivational complexity and order of acquisition in child speech. In J. R. Hayes (ed.), *Cognition and the development of language.* New York: Wiley, 1970.

Bruner, J. S. On cognitive growth: II. In J. S. Bruner, R. Olver, and P. M. Greenfield (eds.), *Studies in cognitive growth.* New York: Wiley, 1966.

Bruner, J. S. From communication to language: A psychological perspective. *Cognition, 3,* 1974/75, 255–87.

Bruner, J. S. The ontogenesis of speech acts. *Journal of Child Language, 2,* 1975, 1–19.

Bruner, J. S., Goodnow, J. J., Austin, G. A. *A study of thinking.* New York: Wiley, 1956.

Bruner, J. S., Olver, R., and Greenfield, P. M. (eds.) *Studies in cognitive growth.* New York: Wiley, 1966.

Bruner, J. S., and Sherwood, V. Early rule structure: The case of peekaboo. In J. S. Bruner, A. Jolly, and K. Sylva (eds.), *Play: Its role in evolution and development.* New York: Basic Books, 1976.

Carey, S. Are children little scientists with false theories of the world? Unpublished doctoral dissertation, Harvard University, 1972.

Carey, S. Less may never mean more. In R. Campbell and P. Smith (eds.), *Recent advances in the psychology of language*. New York: Plenum, 1977.

Carey, S. The child as word learner. In M. Halle, J. Bresnan, and G. A. Miller (eds.), *Linguistic theory and psychological reality*. Cambridge, Mass.: MIT Press, 1978.

Carey, S. Do children think differently from adults? In S. Chipman, J. Segal, and R. Glazer (eds.), *Thinking and learning skills: Current research and open questions*. Hillsdale, N.J.: Erlbaum (in press).

Carey, S., and Bartlett, E. Acquiring a single new word. *Papers and Reports on Child Language Development* (Department of Linguistics, Stanford University), No. 15, 1978, pp. 17–29.

Carroll, J. Process and content in psycholinguistics. In R. Patton (ed.), *Current trends in the description and analysis of behavior*. Pittsburgh: University of Pittsburgh Press, 1958.

Cazden, C. B. The acquisition of noun and verb inflections. *Child Development, 39*, 1968, 433–48.

Chafe, W. L. *Meaning and the structure of language*. Chicago: University of Chicago Press, 1970.

Chafe, W. L. Givenness, contrastiveness, definiteness, subjects, topics, and point of view. In C. Li (ed.), *Subject and topic*. New York: Academic Press, 1976.

Chao, Y-R, The non-uniqueness of phonemic solutions of phonetic systems. In M. Joos (ed.), *Readings in linguistics* (2nd ed.). New York: American Council of Learned Societies, 1958. (Originally published in *Bulletin of the Institute of History and Philology, Academica Sinica, 4*, 1934, 363–97.)

Chapin, P. *On the syntax of word derivation in English*. Information Systems Language Studies No. 16. Bedford, Mass.: MITRE Corp., 1967.

Chapin, P. On affixation in English. In M. Bierwisch and K. Heidolph (eds.), *Progress in linguistics*. The Hague: Mouton, 1970.

Chomsky, C. S. *The acquisition of syntax in children from 5 to 10*. Cambridge, Mass.: MIT Press, 1969.

Chomsky, C. S. Invented spelling in the open classroom. *Word, 27,* 1971a, 499–518.

Chomsky, C. S. Write first, read later. *Childhood Education, 47,* 1971b, 296–9.

Chomsky, C. S. How sister got into the grog. *Early Years, 6,* 1975, 36–9; 78–9.

Chomsky, N. *Syntactic structures*. The Hague: Mouton, 1957.

Chomsky, N. A transformational approach to syntax. In A. Hill (ed.), *Proceedings of the Third Texas Conference on Problems in English*. Austin: University of Texas Press, 1962. (Reprinted in J. Fodor and J. Katz (eds.), *The structure of language*. Englewood Cliffs, N.J.: Prentice-Hall, 1964.)

Chomsky, N. *Aspects of the theory of syntax*. Cambridge, Mass.: MIT Press, 1965.

Chomsky, N. *Language and mind*. New York: Harcourt Brace Jovanovich, 1968.

Chomsky, N. Deep structure, surface structure, and semantic interpretation. In D. Steinberg and L. Jakobovits (eds.), *Semantics*. Cambridge: Cambridge University Press, 1971.

Chomsky, N. Some empirical issues in the theory of transformational grammar. In S. Peters (ed.), *Goals of linguistic theory*. Englewood Cliffs, N.J.: Prentice-Hall, 1972.

Chomsky, N. Conditions on transformations. In S. Anderson and P. Kiparsky (eds.), *Festshrift for Morris Halle*. New York: Holt, Rinehart and Winston, 1973.

Chomsky, N. *Reflections on language*. New York: Random House, 1975.

Chomsky, N. Conditions on rules of grammar. *Linguistic Analysis, 2,* 1976, 303–51.

Chomsky, N. *Rules and representations*. New York: Columbia University Press, 1980.

Chomsky, N. *Lectures on government and binding: The Pisa lectures*. Dordrecht: Foris, 1981.

Chomsky, N., and Lasnik, H. Filters and control. *Linguistic Inquiry, 8,* 1977, 425–504.

Clancy, P., Jacobsen, T., and Silva, M. The acquisition of conjunction: A cross-linguistic study. *Papers and Reports on Child Language Development* (Department of Linguistics, Stanford University), No. 12, 1976, pp. 71–80.

Clark, E. V. On the acquisition of the meaning of "before" and "after." *Journal of Verbal Learning and Verbal Behavior, 10,* 1971, 266–75.

Clark, E. V. On the child's acquisition of antonyms in two semantic fields. *Journal of Verbal Learning and Verbal Behavior, 11,* 1972, 750–8.

Clark, E. V. Non-linguistic strategies and the acquisition of word meaning. *Cognition, 2,* 1973a, 161–82.

Clark, E. V. What's in a word? On the child's acquisition of semantics in his first language. In T. Moore (ed.), *Cognitive development and the acquisition of language*. New York: Academic Press, 1973b.

Clark, E. V. How children describe time and order. In C. A. Ferguson and D. I. Slobin (eds.), *Studies in child language development*. New York: Holt, Rinehart and Winston, 1973c.

Clark, E. V. Knowledge, context, and strategy in the acquisition of meaning. In D. Dato (ed.), *Georgetown University Round Table on Languages and Linguistics*. Washington, D.C.: Georgetown University Press, 1975.

Clark, E. V. Strategies and the mapping problem in first language acquisition. In J. Macnamara (ed.), *Language learning and thought*. New York: Academic Press, 1977.

Clark, E. V. Discovering what words can do. In *Papers from the parasession on the lexicon*. Chicago: Chicago Linguistic Society, 1978a.

Clark, E. V. Strategies for communicating. *Child Development, 49,* 1978b, 953–9.

Clark, E. V., and Clark, H. H. Universals, relativity, and language processing. In J. H. Greenberg (ed.), *Universals of human language*. Vol. 1: *Method and theory*. Stanford, Calif.: Stanford University Press, 1978.

Clark, E. V., and Clark, H. H. When nouns surface as verbs. *Language, 55,* 1979, 767–811.

Clark, E. V., and Garnica, O. Is he coming or going? On the acquisition of deictic verbs. *Journal of Verbal Learning and Verbal Behavior, 13,* 1974, 559–72.

Clark, H. Some structural properties of simple active and passive sentences. *Journal of Verbal Learning and Verbal Behavior, 4,* 1965, 365–70.

Clark, H. Linguistic processes in deductive reasoning. *Psychological Review, 76,* 1968, 387–404.

Clark, H., and Begun, J. S. The semantics of sentence subjects. *Language and Speech, 14,* 1971, 34–46.

Clark, H., and Card, S. Role of semantics in remembering comparative sentences. *Journal of Experimental Psychology, 83,* 1969, 545–53.

Clark, H., Carpenter, P. A., and Just, M. A. Semantics and perception. In W. G. Chase (ed.), *Visual information processing.* New York: Academic Press, 1973.

Clark, H., and Clark, E. V. *Psychology and language.* New York: Harcourt Brace Jovanovich, 1977.

Clark, H., and Haviland, S. E. Comprehension and the given–new contract. In R. O. Freedle (ed.), *Discourse production and comprehension.* Norwood, N.J.: Ablex, 1977.

Clark, H., and Marshall, C. Definite reference and mutual knowledge. In A. K. Joshi, B. Webber, and I. Sag (eds.), *Linguistic structure and discourse setting.* Cambridge: Cambridge University Press, 1981.

Clark, R. Performing without competence. *Journal of Child Language, 1,* 1974, 1–10.

Clark, R. Some even simpler ways to learn to talk. In N. Waterson and C. Snow (eds.), *The development of communication.* New York: Wiley, 1978.

Cohen, E., Namir, L., and Schlesinger, I. M. *A new dictionary of sign language.* The Hague: Mouton, 1977.

Coker, P. L. On the acquisition of temporal terms: Before and after. *Papers and Reports on Child Language Development* (Department of Linguistics, Stanford University), No. 10, 1975, pp. 166–77.

Coleman, E. Learning of prose written in four grammatical transformations. *Journal of Applied Psychology, 49,* 1965, 332–41.

Collins, A. M., and Quillian, M. R. Retrieval time from semantic memory. *Journal of Verbal Learning and Verbal Behavior, 8,* 1969, 240–7.

Cooper, W. E. Adaptation of phonetic feature analyzers for place of articulation. *Journal of the Acoustical Society of America, 56,* 1974, 617–27.

Cooper, W. E., Paccia, J. M., and Lapointe, S. G. Hierarchical coding in speech timing. *Cognitive Psychology, 10,* 1978, 154–77.

Cooper, W. E., and Paccia-Cooper, J. *Syntax and speech.* Cambridge, Mass.: Harvard University Press, 1980.

Cooper, W. E., and Ross, J. Word order. In R. Grossman, L. San, and T. Vance (eds.), *Papers from the parasession on functionalism.* Chicago: Chicago Linguistic Society, 1975.

Coulter, G. American Sign Language pantomime. Salk Institute Working Paper, La Jolla, Calif., 1975.

Coulter, G. Continuous representations in American Sign Language. In W. Stokoe (ed.), *National symposium on sign language research and teaching.* Washington, D.C.: National Association of the Deaf, 1977.

Cromer, R. The learning of surface structure clues to deep structure by a puppet show technique. *Quarterly Journal of Experimental Psychology, 24,* 1972, 66–76.

Cromer, R. Developmental strategies for language. In V. Hamilton and M. Vernon (eds.), *The development of cognitive processes.* London: Academic Press, 1976.

Cross, T. G. Mothers' speech adjustments: The contribution of selected child listener variables. In C. E. Snow and C. A. Ferguson (eds.), *Talking to children: Language input and acquisition.* Cambridge: Cambridge University Press, 1977.

Culicover, P. W., and Wexler, K. Some syntactic implications of a theory of language learnability. In P. W. Culicover, T. Wasow, and A. Akmajian (eds.), *Formal syntax,* New York: Academic Press, 1977.

Curme, G. O. *A grammar of the German language.* Pt. III: *Word-formation.* New York: Ungar, 1964. (2nd rev. ed., 1922.)

Curtiss, S. *Genie: A psycholinguistic study of a modern-day "Wild Child."* New York: Academic Press, 1977.

Curtiss, S., Yamada, J., and Fromkin, V. How independent is language? On the question of formal parallels between grammar and action. *UCLA Working Papers in Cognitive Linguistics, 1,* 1979, 131–57.

Cutting, J., and Rosner, B. Categories and boundaries in speech and music. *Perception and Psychophysics, 16,* 1974, 564–70.

Cutting, J., Rosner, B., and Foard, C. Perceptual categories for musiclike sounds: Implications for theories of speech perception. *Quarterly Journal of Experimental Psychology, 28,* 1976, 361–78.

Decroly, O. *Comment l'enfant arrive à parler,* Vol. 2. Brussels: Cahiers de la Centrale, 1932a.

Decroly, O. Etudes de psychogenèse: observations expériences at enguêtes sur le développement des aptitudes de l'enfant. Brussels: Mauvaise Lamiritin, 1932b.

deLaguna, G. A. *Speech: Its function and development.* Bloomington: Indiana University Press, 1963. (First published 1927).

Delis, D., and Slater, A. Toward a functional theory of reduction transformations. *Cognition, 5,* 1977, 119–32.

DeMatteo, A. Visual imagery and visual analogues in American Sign Language. In L. Friedman (ed.), *On the other hand.* New York: Academic Press, 1977.

Descoeudres, A. *Le développement de l'enfant de deux à sept ans.* Paris: Delachaus and Niestlé, 1921

deVilliers, J. G. The process of rule learning: A new look. In K. E. Nelson (ed.), *Children's language,* Vol. 2. New York: Gardner Press, 1980.

deVilliers, J. G., and deVilliers, P. A. Early judgments of semantic and syntactic acceptability by children. *Journal of Psycholinguistic Research, 1,* 1972, 299–310.

Dezsö, Laszló. A gyermeknyelv mondattanának elvi-modszertani kerdesei. *Altalános nyelvészeti tanulmányok, 7,* 1970, 77–99.

Dezsö, Laszló. *Bevezetés a mondattani tipológiába.* Budapest: TIT Központja, 1972.

Dik, S. C. *Coordination.* Amsterdam: North-Holland, 1968.

Dik, S. *Functional grammar.* New York: North-Holland, 1978.

Diver, W. The system of agency in the Latin noun. *Word, 20,* 1964, 178–96.

Donaldson, M., and Balfour, G. Less is more: A study of language comprehension in children. *British Journal of Psychology, 59,* 1968, 461–71.

Donaldson, M., and Wales, P. J. On the acquisition of some relational terms. In J. R. Hayes (ed.), *Cognition and the development of language.* New York: Wiley, 1970.

Dore, J. What's so conceptual about the acquisition of linguistic structures? *Journal of Child Language, 6,* 1979, 129–37.

Dorian, N. D. The fate of morphological complexity in language death. *Language, 54*(3), 1978, 590–609.

Dougherty, R. C. A grammar of coordinate conjoined structures: I. *Language, 46,* 1970, 850–98.

Dougherty, R. C. A grammar of coordinate conjoined structures: II. *Language, 47,* 1971, 298–339.

Downing, P. On the creation and use of English compound nouns. *Language, 53,* 1977, 810–42.

Duranti, A., and Ochs, E. Left-dislocation in Italian conversation. In T. Givon (ed.), *Syntax and semantics,* Vol. 12. New York: Academic Press, 1979.

Eibl-Eibesfeldt, I. *Ethology: The biology of behavior.* New York: Holt, Rinehart and Winston, 1977.

Eimas, P., Cooper, W., and Corbit, J. Some properties of linguistic feature detectors. *Perception and Psychophysics, 13,* 1973, 247–52.

Eimas, P., and Corbit, J. Selective adaptation of linguistic feature detectors. *Cognitive Psychology, 4,* 1973, 99–109.

Eimas, P., Siqueland, E. R., Jusczyk, P., and Vigorito, J. Speech perception in infants. *Science, 171,* 1971, 303–6.

Einstein, A. What is the theory of relativity? In A. Einstein, *Ideas and opinions.* New York: Crown, 1954a.

Einstein, A. On the generalized theory of gravitation. In A. Einstein, *Ideas and opinions.* New York: Crown, 1954b.

Ekmekci, Ö. F. Acquisition of Turkish: A longitudinal study on the early language development of a Turkish child. Unpublished doctoral dissertation, University of Texas, Austin, 1979.

El'konin, D. B. General course of development in the child of the grammatical structure of the Russian language (according to A. N. Gvozdev). In C. A. Ferguson and D. I. Slobin (eds.), *Studies in child language development.* New York: Holt, Rinehart and Winston, 1973.

Ertel, S. Satzsubjekt und Ich-Perspektive. In *Bericht über den 28. Kongress der deutschen Gesellschaft für Psychologie.* Vol. 1: *Wissenschafts Theorie und Psycholinguistik.* Gottingen: Hogrefe, 1974.

Ertel, S. Where do the subjects of sentences come from? In S. Rosenberg (ed.), *Sentence production: Developments in research and theory.* Hillside, N.J.: Erlbaum, 1977.

Ervin, S. Imitation and structural change in children's language. In E. Lenneberg (ed.), *New directions in the study of language.* Cambridge, Mass.: MIT Press, 1964.

Ervin-Tripp, S., and Miller, W. Early discourse: Some questions about questions. In M. Lewis and L. A. Rosenblum (eds.), *Interaction, conversation, and the development of language.* New York: Wiley, 1977.

Esper, E. *Analogy and association in linguistics and psychology.* Athens: University of Georgia Press, 1973.

Feldman, H., Goldin-Meadow, S., and Gleitman, L. Beyond Herodotus: The creation of language by linguistically deprived deaf children. In A. Lock (ed.), *Action, symbol, and gesture: The emergence of language.* New York: Academic Press, 1978.

Ferguson, C., and Farwell, C. Words and sounds in early language acquisition. *Language, 51,* 1975, 419–39.

Fiengo, R. Semantic conditions on surface structure. Unpublished doctoral dissertation, MIT, 1974.

Fiengo, R. *Surface structure: The interface of autonomous components.* Cambridge, Mass.: Harvard University Press, 1980.

Fillmore, C. J. The case for case. In E. Bach and R. J. Harms (eds.), *Universals in linguistic theory.* New York: Holt, Rinehart and Winston, 1968a.

Fillmore, C. J. Lexical entries for verbs. *Foundations of Language, 4,* 1968b, 373–93.

Fillmore, C. J. Some problems for case grammar. In R. J. O'Brien (ed.), *Georgetown University Round Table on languages and linguistics.* Washington, D.C.: Georgetown University Press, 1971.

Fillmore, C. J. The case for case reopened. In P. Cole and J. Saddock (eds.), *Syntax and semantics.* Vol. 8: *Grammatical relations.* New York: Academic Press, 1977.

Firbas, J. On defining the theme in functional sentence analysis. *Travaux Linguistique de Prague, 1,* 1964, 267–80.

Firth, R. *Papers in linguistics, 1934–1951.* London: Oxford University Press, 1957.

Fischer, S. Two processes of reduplication in the American Sign Language. *Foundations of Language, 9,* 1973, 469–80.

Fischer, S. Sign language and linguistic universals. In C. Rohrer and N. Ruwet (eds.), *Actes du colloque Franco-Allemand de grammaire transformationelle. Band II: Etudes de semantique et autres.* Tübingen: Max Niemeyer Verlag, 1974.

Fischer, S. Sign language and creoles. In P. Siple (ed.), *Understanding language through sign language research.* New York: Academic Press, 1978.

Fischer, S., and Gough, B. Verbs in American Sign Language. *Sign Language Studies, 18,* 1978, 17–48.

Flavell, J. H. Structures, stages and sequences in cognitive development. In A. Collins (ed.), *Minnesota Symposia on Child Psychology,* Vol. 15. Hillsdale, N.J.: Erlbaum, in press.

Fleischer, W. *Wortbildung der deutschen Gegenwartssprache.* Leipzig: VEB Bibliographisches Institut, 1969.

Flores d'Arcais, G. B. Some perceptual determinants of sentence construction. In G. B. Flores d'Arcais (ed.), *Studies in perception.* Milan: Martello-Guinti, 1975.

Fodor, J. A. Some reflections on L. S. Vygotsky's *Thought and language. Cognition, 1,* 1972, 83–95.

Fodor, J. A. *The language of thought.* New York: Crowell, 1975.

Fodor, J. A., Bever, T. G., and Garrett, M. F. *The psychology of language: An introduction to psycholinguistics and generative grammar.* New York: McGraw-Hill, 1974.

Fodor, J. A., Garrett, M. F., Walker, E. C., and Parkes, C. H. Against definitions. *Cognition, 8,* 1980, 263–367.

Fodor, J. D., Fodor, J. A., and Garrett, M. F. The psychological unreality of semantic representations. *Linguistic Inquiry, 6,* 1975, 515–31.

Foss, D. J., and Hakes, D. T. *Psycholinguistics: An introduction to the psychology of language*. Englewood Cliffs, N.J.: Prentice-Hall, 1978.

Frazier, L. *On comprehending sentences: Syntactic parsing strategies*. Bloomington: Indiana University Linguistics Club, 1979.

Freyd, P., and Baron, J., Individual differences in the acquisition of derivational morphology. *Journal of Verbal Learning and Verbal Behavior*, in press.

Friedman, L. (ed.). *On the other hand*. New York: Academic Press, 1977.

Friedman, N. Point of view in fiction: The development of a critical concept. *PMLA, 70,* 1955, 1160–84.

Friedrich, G. Psychologische Beobachtungen an zwei Knaben. *Beiträge zur Kinderforschung und Heilerziehung, 17,* 1906.

Frishberg, N. Arbitrariness and iconicity in American Sign Language. *Language, 51,* 1975, 696–719.

Fromkin, V. A. *Speech errors as linguistic evidence*. The Hague: Mouton, 1973.

Furrow, D., Nelson, K., and Benedict, H. Mothers' speech to children and syntactic development: Some simple relationships. *Journal of Child Language, 6,* 1979, 423–42.

Garner, W. R. *The processing of information and structure*. New York: Wiley, 1974.

Garnica, O. Non-verbal concomitants of language input to children. In N. Waterson and C. Snow (eds.), *The development of communication*. New York: Wiley, 1978.

Garrett, M. F. The analysis of sentence production. In G. H. Bower (ed.), *The psychology of learning and motivation,* Vol. 9. New York: Academic Press, 1975.

Garrett, M. F. Word and sentence perception. In R. Held, H. W. Leibowitz, and H. L. Teuber (eds.), *Handbook of sensory physiology,* Vol. 8. Berlin: Springer Verlag, 1978.

Gathercole, V. C. Decrements in children's responses to *big* and *tall*: A reconsideration of the potential cognitive and semantic causes. *Journal of Experimental Child Psychology, 34,* 1982, 156–73.

Gelb, I. *A study of writing: The foundations of grammatology*. Chicago: University of Chicago Press, 1952.

Gelman, R., and Gallistel, C. *The young child's understanding of numbers: A window on early cognitive development*. Cambridge, Mass.: Harvard University Press, 1979.

Gentner, D. Evidence for the psychological reality of semantic components: The verbs of possession. In D. A. Norman, D. E. Rumelhart, and the LNR Research Group, *Explorations in cognition*. San Francisco: Freeman, 1975.

Gentner, D. On relational meaning: The acquisition of verb meaning. *Child Development, 49,* 1978, 988–98.

Gentner, D. Why nouns are learned before verbs: Linguistic relativity vs. natural partitioning. In S. Kuczaj (ed.), *Language development: Language, culture, and cognition*. Hillsdale, N.J.: Erlbaum, 1982.

Gentry, J. R. A study of the orthographic strategies of beginning readers. Unpublished doctoral dissertation, University of Virginia, 1977. (University Microfilms, 1979, No. 7901152.)

Givón, T. Topic, pronoun, and grammatical agreement. In C. Li (ed.), *Subject and topic*. New York: Academic Press, 1976.

Givón, T. *On understanding grammar*. New York: Academic Press, 1979.

Gleason, H. A. *An introduction to descriptive linguistics* (Rev. ed.). New York: Holt, Rinehart and Winston, 1961.

Gleitman, H., and Gleitman, L. R. Language use and language judgment. In C. J. Fillmore, D. Kempler, and W. S. Wang (eds.), *Individual differences in language ability and language behavior*. New York: Academic Press, 1979.

Gleitman, L. R. Coordinating conjunctions in English. *Language, 41,* 1965, 260–93.

Gleitman, L. R. Maturational determinants of language growth. *Cognition, 10,* 1981, 103–14.

Gleitman, L. R., and Gleitman, H. *Phrase and paraphrase: Some innovative uses of language*. New York: Norton, 1970.

Gleitman, L. R., Gleitman, H., and Shipley, E. F. The emergence of the child as grammarian. *Cognition, 1,* 1972, 137–64.

Gleitman, L. R., and Rozin, P. The structure and acquisition of reading: I. Relations between orthographies and the structure of language. In A. S. Reber and D. Scarborough (eds.), *Toward a psychology of reading*. Hillsdale, N.J.: Erlbaum, 1977.

Gleitman, L. R., Shipley, E. F., and Smith, C. S. Old and new ways not to study comprehension, *Journal of Child Language, 5,* 1978, pp. 501–19.

Gold, E. M. Language identification in the limit. *Information and Control, 10,* 1967, 447–74.

Goldhor, R. Sentential determinants of duration in speech. Unpublished master's thesis, MIT, 1976.

Goldin, S. The development of relative clauses in children. Unpublished honors thesis, Smith College, 1971.

Goldin, S., and Karmiloff, A. The relative pronoun. *Psycholinguistics Research Series,* University of Geneva, 1970.

Goldin-Meadow, S. Structure in a manual communication system developed without a conventional language model: Language without a helping hand. In H. Whitaker and H. A. Whitaker (eds.), *Studies in neurolinguistics*, Vol. 4. New York: Academic Press, 1979.

Goldin-Meadow, S. Language development under atypical learning conditions. In K. E. Nelson (ed.), *Children's Language*, Vol. 5. New York: Gardner Press, in press.

Goldin-Meadow, S., and Feldman, H. The development of language-like communication without a language model. *Science, 197,* 1977, 401–3.

Goodluck, H. Linguistic principles in children's grammar of complement subject deletion. Unpublished doctoral dissertation, University of Massachusetts, 1978.

Goodluck, H., and Solan, L. *Papers in the Structure and Development of Child Language*. University of Massachusetts Occasional Papers in Linguistics, Vol. 4, 1978.

Grant, J. R. A child's vocabulary and its growth. *Pedagogical Seminary, 22,* 1915, 183–203.

Gratch, G. Recent studies based on Piaget's view of object concept development. In L. Cohen and P. Salapatek (eds.), *Infant perception: From sensation to cognition,* Vol. 2. New York: Academic Press, 1975.

Grebe, P. *Duden Grammatik der deutschen Gegenwartssprache*. Mannheim: Dudenverlag, 1973.

Green, G. Some observations on the syntax and semantics of instrumental verbs. *Papers of the Chicago Linguistic Society, 8*, 1972.

Greenberg, J. H. (ed.). *Universals of language* (2nd ed.). Cambridge, Mass.: MIT Press, 1966.

Greenfield, P., and Smith, J. *The structure of communication in early language development*. New York: Academic Press, 1976.

Greenfield, P., and Zukow, P. Why do children say what they say when they say it? An experimental approach to the psychogenesis of presupposition. In K. Nelson (ed.), *Children's language*, Vol. 1. New York: Gardner Press, 1978.

Grégoire, A. L'Apprentissage du langage (2 vols.). Paris: Droz, 1937, 1947.

Grevisse, M. *Le Bon usage: Grammaire française avec des remarques sur la langue française d'aujourd'hui* (8th ed.). Gembloux: Editions J. Duculot, 1964.

Grice, H. Logic and conversation. In P. Cole and J. L. Morgan (eds.), *Syntax and semantics*. New York: Academic Press, 1975.

Grieve, R. Definiteness in discourse. *Language and Speech, 16*, 1973, 365–72.

Grieve, R., and Wales, R. Passives and topicalization. *British Journal of Psychology, 64*, 1973, 173–82.

Griffiths, P., and Atkinson, M. A "door" to verbs. In N. Waterson and C. Snow (eds.), *The development of communication*. New York: Wiley, 1978.

Guilbert, L. *La Créativité lexicale*. Paris: Libraire Larousse, 1975.

Guillaume, P. Le Développement des éléments formels dans le langage de l'enfant. *Journal de Psychologie, 24*, 1927, 203–29.

Gunter, R. On the placement of accent in dialogue: A feature of context grammar. *Journal of Linguistics, 2*, 1966, 159–79.

Gvozdev, A. N. *Formirovaniye u rebenka grammaticheskogo stroya russkogo yazyka*. Moscow: Izd-vo Akademii Pedagogicheskikh Nauk RSFSR, 1949.

Hakuta, K. Word order and particles in the acquisition of Japanese. *Papers and Reports on Child Language Development* (Department of Linguistics, Stanford University), No. 13, 1977, pp. 110–17.

Halle, M. Phonology in generative grammar. *Word, 18*, 1962, 54–72.

Halliday, M. Notes on transitivity and theme in English: Part 2. *Journal of Linguistics, 3*, 1967, 177–274.

Hamburger, H., and Wexler, K. Identifiability of a class of transformational grammars. In K. Hintikka, J. Moravcsik, and P. Suppes (eds.), *Approaches to natural language*. Dordrecht: Reidel Press, 1973.

Hamburger, H., and Wexler, K. A mathematical theory of learning transformational grammar. *Journal of Mathematical Psychology, 12*, 1975, 137–77.

Hardy, J. A., and Braine, M. D. S. Categories that bridge between meaning and syntax in four-year-olds. In W. Deutsch (ed.), *The child's construction of language*. London: Academic Press, 1981.

Harris, P. Inferences and semantic development. *Journal of Child Language, 2*, 1975, 143–52.

Harris, Zelig S. *Methods in structural linguistics*. Chicago: University of Chicago Press, 1951.

Hetzron, R. The presentative movement or why the ideal word order is V.S.O.P. In C. Li (ed.), *Word order and word order change*. Austin: University of Texas Press, 1975.

Hockett, C. F. The problem of universals in language. In J. H. Greenberg (ed.), *Universals of language*. Cambridge, Mass.: MIT Press, 1963.

Hoff-Ginsberg, E. The role of linguistic experience in the child's acquisition of syntax. Unpublished Ph.D. dissertation, University of Michigan, 1981.

Hoff-Ginsberg, E., and Shatz, M. Linguistic input and the child's acquisition of language. *Psychological Bulletin,* in press.

Holton, G. *Thematic origins of scientific thought: Kepler to Einstein*. Cambridge, Mass.: Harvard University Press, 1973.

Holzman, M. The use of interrogative forms in the verbal interactions of three mothers and their children. *Journal of Psycholinguistic Research, 1,* 1972, 311–36.

Hopper, P. Some observations on the typology of focus and aspect in narrative language. *Linguistic Studies in Indonesian and Languages in Indonesia, 4,* 1977, 14–25.

Horgan, D. The development of the full passive. *Journal of Child Language, 5,* 1978, 65–80.

Hornby, P. Surface structure and the topic–comment distinction: A developmental study. *Child Development, 42,* 1971, 1975–8.

Hornby, P. The psychological subject and predicate. *Cognitive Psychology, 3,* 1972, 632–42.

Hornby, P., and Hass, W. Use of contrastive stress by preschool children. *Journal of Speech and Hearing Research, 13,* 1970, 395–9.

Hupet, M., and LeBouedec, B. Definiteness and voice in the interpretation of active and passive sentences. *Quarterly Journal of Experimental Psychology, 27,* 1975, 323–30.

Hupet, M., and LeBouedec, B. The given–new contract and the constructive aspect of memory for ideas. *Journal of Verbal Learning and Verbal Behavior, 16,* 1977, 69–75.

Husserl, E. *Logical investigations,* Vol. 1. New York: Humanities Press, 1970.

Huttenlocher, K. The origins of language comprehension. In R. L. Solso (ed.), *Theories in cognitive psychology: The Loyola symposium*. Hillsdale, N.J.: Erlbaum, 1974.

Huttenlocher, J., and Strauss, S. Comprehension and a statement's relation to the situation it describes. *Journal of Verbal Learning and Verbal Behavior, 7,* 1968, 300–4.

Huxley, R. The development of the correct use of subject personal pronouns in two children. In G. B. Flores d'Arcais and W. J. M. Levelt (eds.), *Advances in psycholinguistics*. Amsterdam: North-Holland, 1970.

Hyman, L. On the change from SOV to SVO: Evidence from Niger-Congo. In C. Li (ed.), *Word order and word order change*. Austin: University of Texas Press, 1975.

Hyman, L., and Zimmer, K. Imbedded topic in French. In C. Li (ed.), *Subject and topic*. New York: Academic Press, 1976.

Inhelder, B., and Piaget, J. *The growth of logical thinking from childhood to adolescence*. New York: Basic Books, 1958.

Inhelder, B., and Piaget, J. *The early growth of logic in the child.* New York: Harper and Row, 1959.

Jackendoff, R. S. *Semantic interpretation in generative grammar.* Cambridge, Mass: MIT Press, 1972.

Jakobson, R. *Kindersprache, Aphasie, und allgemeine Lautgesetze.* Stockholm: Almqvist and Wiksell, 1941.

Jakobson, R. *Child language, aphasia, and phonological universals.* (Janua Linguarum, Series Minor, 72.) The Hague: Mouton, 1968.

Jarvella, R., and Sinnott, J. Contextual constraints on noun distribution to some English verbs by children and adults. *Journal of Verbal Learning and Verbal Behavior, 11,* 1970, 47–53.

Jespersen, O. *A modern English grammar on historical principles.* Part VI: *Morphology.* Copenhagen: Munksgaard, 1942.

Johnson, C. N., and Maratsos, M. P. Early comprehension of mental verbs: Think and know. *Child Development, 48,* 1977, 1747–51.

Johnson, C. N., and Wellman, H. M. Children's developing understanding of mental verbs: "Remember," "know," and "guess." *Child Development, 51,* 1980, 327–38.

Johnson, D. E., and Postal, P. *Arc-pair grammar.* Princeton, N.J.: Princeton University Press, 1980.

Johnson, M. Syntactic position and rated meaning. *Journal of Verbal Learning and Verbal Behavior, 6,* 1967, 240–6.

Johnson-Laird, P. The interpretation of the passive voice. *Quarterly Journal of Experimental Psychology, 20,* 1968a, 69–73.

Johnson-Laird, P. The choice of the passive voice in a communicative task. *British Journal of Psychology, 59,* 1968b, 7–15.

Johnston, J. R. Cognitive prerequisites: The evidence from children learning English. In D. I. Slobin (ed.), *Cross-linguistic studies of language acquisition.* In press.

Johnston, J. R., and Slobin, D. I. The development of locative expressions in English, Italian, Serbo-Croatian, and Turkish. *Journal of Child Language, 16,* 1979, 531–47.

Joos, M. The definition of juncture and terminals. In *Second Texas conference on problems of linguistic analysis in English.* Austin: University of Texas, 1962.

Jusczyk, P. W. Auditory versus phonetic coding of speech signals during infancy. *Proceedings of the CNRS Conference, 1980,* in press.

Justus, C. Relativization and topicalization in Hittite. In C. Li (ed.), *Subject and topic.* New York: Academic Press, 1976.

Karmiloff-Smith, A. The interplay between syntax, semantics, and phonology in language acquisition processes. In R. Campbell and P. Smith (eds.), *Recent advances in the psychology of language.* New York: Plenum, 1978.

Karmiloff-Smith, A. *A functional approach to child language.* Cambridge: Cambridge University Press, 1979a.

Karmiloff-Smith, A. Micro- and macrodevelopmental changes in language acquisition and other representational systems. *Cognitive Science, 3,* 1979b, 91–118.

Karmiloff-Smith, A. Language as a formal problem-space for children. Paper presented at *Beyond description in child language,* Max Planck Gesellschaft, Nijmegen, The Netherlands, 1979c.

Karmiloff-Smith, A. The grammatical marking of thematic structure in the development of language production. In Deutsch, W. (ed.), *The child's construction of language.* London: Academic Press, 1982.

Katz, B., Baker, G., and Macnamara, J. What's in a name? On the child's acquisition of proper and common nouns. *Child Development, 45,* 1974, 269–73.

Katz, J. J. *The philosophy of language.* New York: Harper and Row, 1966.

Katz, J. J. *Semantic theory.* New York: Harper and Row, 1972.

Katz, J. J. A proper theory of names. *Philosophical Studies, 31,* 1977, 1–80.

Katz, J. J. Effability and translation. In F. Guenlhins and M. Guenlhins-Rueler (eds.), *Meaning and translation: Philosophical and linguistic approaches.* Cambridge, Mass.: MIT Press, 1978.

Katz, J. J. The neoclassical theory of reference. In P. A. French, T. F. Vehlers, and H. K. Wellstein (eds.), *Contemporary perspectives in the philosophy of language.* Minneapolis: University of Minnesota Press, 1979.

Katz, J. J. *Language and other abstract objects.* Totowa, N.J.: Rowman and Littlefield, 1981.

Kay, P., and Sankoff, G. A language-universals approach to pidgins and creoles. In D. DeCamp and I. Hancock (eds.), *Pidgins and creoles: Current trends and prospects.* Washington, D.C.: Georgetown University Press, 1974.

Kean, M. L. The linguistic interpretation of aphasic syndromes: Agrammatism in Broca's aphasia, an example. *Cognition, 5,* 1977, 9–46.

Kean, M. L. Agrammatism: A phonological deficit? *Cognition, 7*(1), 1979, 69–84.

Keenan, E. O. Remarkable subjects in Malagasy. In C. Li (ed.), *Subject and topic.* New York: Academic Press, 1976a.

Keenan, E. O. Towards a universal definition of "subject." In C. Li (ed.), *Subject and topic.* New York: Academic Press, 1976b.

Keenan, E. O., and Schiefflin, B. Topic as a discourse notion. In C. Li (ed.), *Subject and topic.* New York: Academic Press, 1976.

Kegl, J., and Wilbur, R. Where does structure stop and style begin? Syntax, morphology and phonology vs. stylistic variation in American Sign Language. *Chicago Linguistic Society, 12,* 1976, 376–96.

Keil, F. C. *Semantic and conceptual development: An ontological perspective.* Cambridge Mass.: Harvard University Press, 1979.

Keil, F. C., and Carroll, J. J. The child's conception of "tall": Implications for an alternative view of semantic development. *Papers and Reports on Child Language* (Department of Linguistics, Stanford University), No. 19, 1980, pp. 21–8.

Keller-Cohen, D. The acquisition of temporal reference in preschool children. Unpublished doctoral dissertation, State University of New York, Buffalo, 1974.

Kimball, J. P. Seven principles of surface structure parsing. *Cognition, 2,* 1973, 15–47.

Kintsch, W. *The representation of meaning in memory.* New York: Wiley, 1974.

Kiparsky, P. Historical linguistics. In W. O. Dingwall (ed.), *A survey of linguistic science.* College Park: University of Maryland Press, 1971.

Kiparsky, P., and Menn, L. On the acquisition of phonology. In J. Macnamara (ed.), *Language learning and thought*. New York: Academic Press, 1977.

Klatt, D. H. Vowel lengthening is syntactically determined in a connected discourse. *Journal of Phonetics, 3,* 1975, 129–40.

Klatt, D. H. Linguistic uses of segmental duration in English: Acoustic and perceptual evidence. *Journal of the Acoustical Society of America, 59.* 1976, 1208–21.

Kleinbort, I., and Anisfeld, M. Markedness and perspective in the interpretation of the active and passive voice. *Quarterly Journal of Experimental Psychology, 26,* 1974, 189–95.

Klima, E., and Bellugi, U. Syntactic regularities in the speech of children. In J. Lyons and R. Wales (eds.), *Psycholinguistics papers*. Edinburgh: Edinburgh University Press, 1966.

Klima, E., and Bellugi, U., with Battison, R., Boyes-Braem, P., Fischer, S., Frishberg, N., Lane, H., Lentz, E., Newkirk, D., Newport, E., Pedersen, C., and Siple, P. *The signs of language*. Cambridge, Mass.: Harvard University Press, 1979.

Kossan, N. E. Structure and strategy in concept acquisition. Unpublished doctoral dissertation, Stanford University, 1978.

Kripke, S. A. Naming and necessity. In D. Davidson and G. Harman (eds.), *Semantics of natural language*. Dordrecht: Reidel, 1972.

Krueger, J. T. A theory of structural simplicity and its relevance to aspects of memory, perception, and conceptual naturalness. Unpublished doctoral dissertation, University of Pennsylvania, 1979.

Kucera, H., and Francis, W. N. *Computational analysis of present day American English*. Providence, R.I.: Brown University Press, 1967.

Kuczaj, S. A. II. On the acquisition of a semantic system. *Journal of Verbal Learning and Verbal Behavior, 14,* 1975, 340–58.

Kuczaj, S. A. II. The acquisition of regular and irregular past tense forms. *Journal of Verbal Learning and Verbal Behavior, 16,* 1977, 589–600.

Kuczaj, S. A. II. Why do children fail to overgeneralize the progressive inflection? *Journal of Child Language, 5,* 1978, 167–71.

Kuczaj, S. A. II, and Lederberg, A. R. Height, age, and function: Differing influences on children's comprehension of "younger" and "older." *Journal of Child Language, 4,* 1977, 395–416.

Kuhl, P. K., and Miller, J. D. Speech perception by the chinchilla: Voiced–voiceless distinction in alveolar plosive consonants. *Science, 190,* 1975, 69–72.

Kuno, S. The position of relative clauses and conjunctions. *Linguistic Inquiry, 1,* 1974, 117–36.

Kuno, S. Subject, theme, and the speaker's empathy: A reexamination of relativization phenomena. In C. Li (ed.), *Subject and topic*. New York: Academic Press, 1976.

Labov, W. The reading of the -ed suffix. In H. Levin and J. P. Williams (eds.), *Basic studies on reading*. New York: Basic Books, 1970.

Lakoff, G. *Irregularity in syntax*. New York: Holt, Rinehart and Winston, 1970.

Lakoff, G. Linguistic Gestalts. In *Papers from the 13th Regional Meeting of the Chicago Linguistic Society*. Chicago: University of Chicago Linguistics Department, 1977.

Lakoff, G., and Peters, S. Phrasal conjunction and symmetric predicates. In D. A. Reibel and S. A. Schane (eds.), *Modern studies in English*. Englewood Cliffs, N.J.: Prentice-Hall, 1969.

Lakoff, G., and Thompson, H. Introducing cognitive grammar. *Papers of the Berkeley Linguistic Society, 3*, 1977.

Landau, B. Will the real grandmother please stand up? *Journal of Psycholinguistic Research*, in press.

Langacker, R. The form and meaning of the English auxiliary. *Language, 54*, 1978, 853–82.

Langendoen, D. T. *Essentials of English grammar*. New York: Holt, Rinehart and Winston, 1970.

Laurendeau, M., and Pinard, A. *The development of the concept of space in the child*. New York: International Universities Press, 1970.

Lehiste, I. *Suprasegmentals*. Cambridge, Mass.: MIT Press, 1970.

Lehiste, I., Olive, J. P., and Streeter, L. A. Role of duration in disambiguating syntactically ambiguous sentences. *Journal of the Acoustic Society of America, 60*, 1976, 1199–1202.

Lehmann, W. A structural principle of language and its implications. *Language, 49*, 1973, 47–66.

Lehmann, W. From topic to subject in Indo-European. In C. Li (ed.), *Subject and topic*. New York: Academic Press, 1976.

Lenneberg, E. H. *Biological foundations of language*. New York: Wiley, 1967.

Leonard, L. *Meaning in child language*. New York: Grune and Stratton, 1976.

Leonard, L., and Schwartz, R. Focus characteristics of single-word utterances after syntax. *Journal of Child Language, 5*, 1978, 151–8.

Lesgold, A. Pronominalization: A device for unifying sentences in memory. *Journal of Verbal Learning and Verbal Behavior, 11*, 1972, 316–23.

Levelt, W. J. A scaling approach to the study of syntactic relations. In G. B. Flores d'Arcais and W. J. Levelt (eds.), *Advances in psycholinguistics*. Amsterdam: North-Holland, 1970.

Levelt, W. J. What became of LAD? *Peter de Ridder Publications in Cognition*, No. I. Lisse, Netherlands: Peter de Ridder Press, 1975.

Levy, Y. Gender in children's language: A study of first language acquisition. Unpublished doctoral dissertation, Hebrew University, 1980.

Li, C. (ed.). *Word order and word order change*. Austin: University of Texas Press, 1975.

Li, C. (ed.). *Subject and topic*. New York: Academic Press, 1976.

Li, C., and Thompson, S. A. The semantic function of word order: A case study in Mandarin. In C. Li (ed.), *Word order and word order change*. Austin: University of Texas Press, 1975.

Li, C., and Thompson, S. A. Subject and topic: A new typology of language. In C. Li (ed.), *Subject and topic*. New York: Academic Press, 1976.

Li, C., and Thompson, S. A. The acquisition of tone in Mandarin-speaking children. *Journal of Child Language, 4*, 1977, 185–99.

Liberman, A. M. The grammars of speech and language. *Cognitive Psychology, 1*, 1970, 301–23.

Liberman, A. M. The specialization of the language hemisphere. In *Status report on speech research* (SR-31/32). New Haven, Conn.: Haskins Laboratories, 1972.

Liberman, A. M., Cooper, F. S., Shankweiler, D. P., and Studdert-Kennedy, M. Perception of the speech code. *Psychological Review, 74,* 1967, 431–61.

Liberman, A. M., and Pisoni, D. B. Evidence for a special speech-perceiving subsystem in the human. In T. H. Bullock (ed.), *Recognition of complex acoustic signals.* Berlin: Dahlem Konferenzen, 1977.

Liddell, S. An investigation into the syntactic structure of American Sign Language. Unpublished doctoral dissertation, University of California, San Diego, 1977.

Limber, J. The genesis of complex sentences. In T. E. Moore (ed.), *Cognitive development and the acquisition of language.* New York: Academic Press, 1973.

Limber, J. Unravelling competence, performance and pragmatics in the speech of young children. *Journal of Child Language, 3,* 1976, 309–18.

Lindner, G. *Aus dem Naturgarten der Kindersprache.* Leipzig: Grieben, 1898.

Locke, J. An essay concerning human understanding. New York: Macmillan, 1965. (Originally published, 1706.)

Lockhart, K., Abrahams, B., and Osherson, D. N. Children's understanding of uniformity in the environment. *Child Development, 48,* 1977, 1521–31.

Lust, B. Conjunction reduction in the language of young children. Unpublished doctoral dissertation, City University of New York, 1974.

Lust, B. Conjunction reduction in child language. *Journal of Child Language, 4,* 1977, 257–88.

Lust, B. Constraints on anaphora in child language: Predictions for a universal. In S. Tavakolian (ed.), *Language acquisition and linguistic theory.* Cambridge, Mass.: MIT Press, 1981.

Lyons, H. *Introduction to theoretical linguistics.* Cambridge: Cambridge University Press, 1968.

McCawley, J. D. Prelexical syntax. In R. O'Brien (ed.), *Georgetown University Round Table on Languages and Linguistics.* Washington, D.C.: Georgetown University Press, 1971.

McCawley, J. D. Conversational implicature and the lexicon. In P. Cole (ed.), *Syntax and semantics.* Vol. 9: *Pragmatics.* New York: Academic Press, 1978.

Macnamara, J. Cognitive basis of language learning in infants. *Psychological Review, 79,* 1972, 1–14.

Macnamara, J. From sign to language. In J. Macnamara (ed.), *Language learning and thought.* New York: Academic Press, 1977.

McNeill, D. Developmental psycholinguistics. In F. Smith and G. Miller (eds.), *The genesis of language: a psycholinguistic approach.* Cambridge, Mass.: MIT Press, 1966a.

McNeill, D. The creation of language by children. In J. Lyons and R. Wales (eds.), *Psycholinguistics papers.* Edinburgh: Edinburgh University Press, 1966b.

McNeill, D. *The acquisition of language: The study of developmental psycholinguistics.* New York: Harper and Row, 1970.

McNeill, D. Semiotic extension. In R. L. Solso (ed.), *Information processing and cognition: The Loyola symposium,* pp. 351–80. Hillsdale, N.J.: Erlbaum, 1975.

McNeill, D. *The conceptual basis of language.* Hillsdale, N.J.: Erlbaum, 1979.

MacWhinney, B. How Hungarian children learn to speak. Unpublished doctoral dissertation, University of California, Berkeley, 1974.

MacWhinney, B. Pragmatic patterns in child syntax. *Papers and Reports on Child Language Development* (Department of Linguistics, Stanford University), No. 10, 1975a, pp. 153–65.

MacWhinney, B. Rules, rote and analogy in morphological formations by Hungarian children. *Journal of Child Language, 2,* 1975b, 65–77.

MacWhinney, B. Starting points. *Language, 53,* 1977, 152–68.

MacWhinney, B. Processing a first language: The acquisition of morphophonology. *Monographs of the Society for Research in Child Development, 43*(1–2) (Serial No. 174), 1978.

MacWhinney, B. A framework for sharing points. In R. Schiefelbusch (ed.), *Communicative competence: Acquisition and intervention.* Baltimore: University Park Press, 1980.

MacWhinney, B. Levels of syntactic acquisition. In S. Kuczaj (ed.), *Language development: Syntax and semantics.* Hillsdale, N.J.: Erlbaum, 1982.

MacWhinney, B., and Bates, E. Sentential devices for conveying givenness and newness: A cross-cultural developmental study. *Journal of Verbal Learning and Verbal Behavior, 17,* 1978, 539–58.

Mansfield, A. F. Semantic organization in the young child: Evidence for the development of semantic feature systems. *Journal of Experimental Child Psychology, 23,* 1977, 57–77.

Maratsos, M. Decrease in the understanding of the word "big" in pre-school children. *Child Development, 44,* 1973, 747–52.

Maratsos, M. Children who get worse at understanding the passive: A replication of Bever. *Journal of Psycholinguistic Research, 3,* 1974a, 65–74.

Maratsos, M. Preschool children's use of definite and indefinite articles. *Child Development, 45,* 1974b, 446–55.

Maratsos, M. *The use of definite and indefinite reference in young children: An experimental study of semantic acquisition.* Cambridge: Cambridge University Press, 1976.

Maratsos, M. How to get from words to sentences. In D. Aaronson and R. Reiber (eds.), *Perspectives in psycholinguistics.* Hillsdale, N.J.: Erlbaum, 1979.

Maratsos, M., and Abramovitch, R. How children understand full, truncated, and anomalous passives. *Journal of Verbal Learning and Verbal Behavior, 14,* 1974, 145–57.

Maratsos, M., and Chalkley, M. A. The internal language of children's syntax: The ontogenesis and representation of syntactic categories. In K. Nelson (ed.), *Children's language,* Vol. 2. New York: Gardner Press, 1980.

Maratsos, M., and Kuczaj, S. A. II. The child's formulation of grammatical categories and rules: The nature of syntactic categories. Paper presented to the biennial meeting of the Society for Research in Child Development, San Francisco, March 16, 1979.

Maratsos, M., Kuczaj, S. A., Fox, D. E., and Chalkley, M. A. Some empirical findings in the acquisition of transformational relations. In W. A. Collins (ed.), *Minnesota Symposia on Child Psychology,* Vol. 12. Hillsdale, N.J.: Erlbaum, 1979.

Marchand, H. *The categories and types of present-day English word-formation* (2nd rev. ed.). Munich: Verlag C. H. Beck, 1969.

Marin, O., Saffran, E., and Schwartz, M. Dissociations of language in aphasia: Implications for normal function. *Annals of the New York Academy of Sciences, 280,* 1976, 868–84.

Marler, P. A comparative approach to vocal-learning: Song development in white-crowned sparrows. In M. E. P. Seligman and J. L. Hager (eds.), *Biological boundaries of learning.* New York: Appleton-Century-Crofts, 1972.

Martin, J. G. On judging pauses in spontaneous speech. *Journal of Verbal Learning and Verbal Behavior, 9,* 1970, 75–8.

Martin, J. G. Rhythmic (hierarchical) versus serial structure in speech and other behavior. *Psychological Review, 79,* 1972, 487–509.

Masongkay, Z., McCluskey, K., McIntyre, C., Sims-Knight, J., Vaughn, B., and Flavell, J. The early development of inferences about the visual percepts of others. *Child Development, 45,* 1974, 357–66.

Massaro, D. W. *Understanding language: An information-processing analysis of speech perception, reading, and psycholinguistics.* New York: Academic Press, 1975.

Matthei, E. Stalking the second green ball. Unpublished doctoral dissertation, University of Massachusetts, 1979.

Matthews, P. H. *Morphology: An introduction to the theory of word structure.* Cambridge: Cambridge University Press, 1974.

Mayr, E. Behavior programs and evolutionary strategies. *American Scientist, 62*(6), 1974, 650–9.

Medin, D. L., and Schaffer, M. M. Context theory of classification. *Psychological Review, 85,* 1978, 207–38.

Meggyes, K. Egy keteves gyermek nyelvi rendszere. *Nyelvtudomanyi Ertekezesek* (Whole No. 73), 1971.

Mehler, J., and Bever, T. G. A cognitive capacity of young children. *Science,* October 6, 1967.

Mellema, P. A brief against case grammar. *Foundations of Language, 11,* 1974, 39–76.

Menyuk, P. *Sentences children use.* Cambridge, Mass.: MIT Press, 1969.

Menyuk, P. *The acquisition and development of language.* New Jersey: Prentice-Hall, 1971.

Miller, G., and Chomsky, N. Finitary models of language users. In R. Bush, D. Luce, and E. Galanter (eds.), *Readings in mathematical psychology,* New York: Wiley, 1963.

Miller, G., and Johnson-Laird, P. *Language and perception.* Cambridge, Mass.: Harvard University Press, 1976.

Miller, M. *The logic of language development in early childhood.* Berlin: Springer-Verlag, 1979.

Miller, W. R. The acquisition of grammatical rules by children. In C. A. Ferguson and D. I. Slobin (eds.), *Studies of child language development.* New York: Holt, Rinehart and Winston, 1973.

Miller, W. R. and Ervin, S. The development of grammar in child language. In U. Bellugi and R. Brown (eds.), The acquisition of language. *Monographs of the Society for Research in Child Development, 29* (Serial No. 92), 1964, 9–34.

Moeser, S., and Bregman, A. The role of reference in the acquisition of a miniature artificial language. *Journal of Verbal Learning and Verbal Behavior, 11,* 1972, 759–69.

Morgan, J. L. Two types of convention in indirect speech acts. In P. Cole (ed.), *Syntax and semantics.* Vol. 9: Pragmatics. New York: Academic Press, 1978.

Morgan, J., and Newport, E. L. The role of constituent structure in the induction of an artificial language. *Journal of Verbal Learning and Verbal Behavior, 20,* 1981, 67–85.

Moskowitz, A. Acquisition of phonology and syntax: A preliminary study. In K. Hintikka et al. (eds.), *Approaches to natural language.* Dordrecht: Reidel, 1973.

Nelson, K. Structure and strategy in learning to talk. *Monographs of the Society for Research in Child Development, 38*(1–2, Serial No. 149), 1973.

Nelson, K. Concept, word, and sentence: Interrelations in acquisition and development. *Psychological Review, 81,* 1974, 267–85.

Nelson, K. E. Facilitating children's syntax. *Developmental Psychology, 13,* 1976, 101–7.

Neugebauer, H. Sprachliche Eigenbildungen meines Sohnes. *Zeitschrift für Kinderforschung, 19,* 1914, 174–81, 242–6, 362–70.

Newport, E. L. Motherese: The speech of mothers to young children. In N. Castellan, D. Pisoni, and G. Potts (eds.), *Cognitive theory,* Vol. 2. Hillsdale, N.J.: Erlbaum, 1977.

Newport, E. L. Constraints on structure: Evidence from American Sign Language and language learning. In W. A. Collins (ed.), *Aspects of the development of competence: Minnesota Symposia on Child Psychology,* Vol. 14. Hillsdale, N.J.: Erlbaum, 1981.

Newport, E. L., and Ashbrook, E. F. The emergence of semantic relations in American Sign Language. *Papers and Reports in Child Language Development* (Department of Linguistics, Stanford University), No. 13, 1977, pp. 16–21.

Newport, E. L., and Bellugi, U. Linguistic expression of category levels in a visual-gestural language: A flower is a flower is a flower. In E. Rosch and B. B. Lloyd (eds.), *Cognition and categorization.* Hillsdale, N.J.: Erlbaum, 1978.

Newport, E. L., Gleitman, H., and Gleitman, L. R. Mother I'd rather do it myself: Some effects and non-effects of maternal speech style. In C. E. Snow and C. A. Ferguson (eds.), *Talking to children: Language input and acquisition.* Cambridge: Cambridge University Press, 1977.

Newport, E. L., Gleitman, L. R., and Gleitman, H. A study of mothers' speech and child language acquisition. *Papers and Reports on Child Language Development* (Department of Linguistics, Stanford University), No. 10, 1975, pp. 111–16.

Newport, E. L. and Supalla, T. The structuring of language: Clues from the acquisition of signed and spoken language. In U. Bellugi and M. Studdert-

Kennedy (eds.), *Signed and spoken language: Biological constraints on linguistic form.* Dahlem Konferenzen. Weinheim/Deerfield Beach, Fla./Basil: Verlag Chemie, 1980.

Nice, M. M. The development of a child's vocabulary in relation to environment. *Pedagogical Seminary, 22,* 1915, 35–64.

Nida, E. *Morphology: The descriptive analysis of words* (2nd ed.). Publication in Linguistics II. Ann Arbor: University of Michigan, 1949.

Nooteboom, S. G., Brokx, J. P. L., and de Rooij, J. J. Contribution of prosody to speech perception. In W. J. M. Levelt and G. B. Flores d'Arcais (eds.), *Studies in the perception of language.* Chichester: Wiley, 1978.

Norman, D. A., Rumelhart, D. E., and the LNR Research Group. *Explorations in cognition.* San Francisco: Freeman, 1975.

Olson, D., and Filby, N. On the comprehension of active and passive sentences. *Cognitive Psychology, 3,* 1972, 361–381.

Olson, G. Developmental changes in memory and the acquisition of language. In T. E. Moore (ed.), *Cognitive development and the acquisition of language.* New York: Academic Press, 1973.

Osgood, C. E. Where do sentences come from? In D. D. Steinberg and L. A. Jakobovits (eds.), *Semantics.* Cambridge: Cambridge University Press, 1971.

Osgood, C. E., and Bock, J. K. Salience and sentencing: Some production principles. In S. Rosenberg (ed.), *Sentence production: Development in research and theory.* Hillsdale, N.J.: Erlbaum, 1977.

Osgood, C. E., and Tanz, C. Will the real direct object in bitransitive sentences please stand up? In A. Juilland (ed.), *Linguistic studies offered to Joseph Greenberg on the occasion of his sixtieth birthday.* Saratoga, Calif.: Anma Libri, 1977.

O'Shea, M. V. *Linguistic development and education.* New York: Macmillan, 1907.

Osherson, D. N. Three conditions on conceptual naturalness. *Cognition, 6,* 1978, 263–89.

Osherson, D. N., and Smith, E. E. On the adequacy of prototype theory as a theory of concepts. *Cognition, 9,* 1981, 35–58.

Osherson, D. N., and Wasow, T. Task-specificity and species-specificity in the study of language: A methodological note. *Cognition, 4,* 1976, 203–14.

Otsu, Y. Universal grammar and syntactic development in children. Unpublished doctoral dissertation, MIT, 1981.

Owens, J., Dafoe, J., and Bower, G. Taking a point of view: Character identification and attributional processes in story comprehension and memory. Paper presented to the meeting of the American Psychology Association, San Francisco, August 1977.

Palermo, D. S. More about less: A study of language comprehension. *Journal of Verbal Learning and Verbal Behavior, 12,* 1973, 211–21.

Palermo, D. S. Still more about the comprehension of "less." *Developmental Psychology, 10,* 1974, 827–9.

Panagl, O. Aspekte der kindersprachlichen Wortbildung. University of Trier, Linguistic Agency, Paper No. 24 (Series B), 1977.

Parisi, D., and Antinucci, F. Lexical competence. In G. B. Flores d'Arcais and

W. J. M. Levelt (eds.), *Advances in psycholinguistics*. Amsterdam: North Holland, 1970.

Park, T. Z. Plurals in child speech. *Journal of Child Language, 5,* 1978, 237–50.

Partee, B. Montague grammar and the well-formedness constraint. In F. Heny and H. Schmelle, *Syntax and Semantics*. Vol. 10: *Selections from the third Groningen round table*. New York: Academic Press, 1979.

Pelsma, J. R. A child's vocabulary and its development. *Pedagogical Seminary, 17,* 1910, 328–69.

Perlmutter, D. M. Relational grammar. In E. Moravcsik and J. Wirth (eds.), *Syntax and semantics*. Vol. 13: *Current approaches to syntax*. New York: Academic Press, 1980.

Perlmutter, D., and Postal, P. Towards a universal characterization of passive. In *Papers from the 3rd Annual Meeting of the Berkeley Linguistics Society*. Berkeley, Calif.: University of California Department of Linguistics, 1977.

Peters, A. Language learning strategies. *Language, 53,* 1977, 560–73.

Peters, S. The projection problem: How is a grammar to be selected? In S. Peters (ed.), *Goals in linguistic theory*. Englewood Cliffs, N.J.: Prentice-Hall, 1972.

Phillips, J. Formal characteristics of speech which mothers address to their young children. Unpublished doctoral dissertation, Johns Hopkins University, 1970.

Phinney, M. The acquisition of embedded sentential complements. Unpublished doctoral dissertation, University of Massachusetts, 1981.

Piaget, J. *Judgment and reasoning in the child*. New York: Harcourt and Brace, 1928.

Piaget, J., and Inhelder, B. *The child's conception of space*. New York: Norton, 1967.

Pinker, S. Formal models of language learning. *Cognition, 7,* 1979, 217–83.

Pinker, S. A theory of the acquisition of lexical-interpretive grammars. In J. Bresnan (ed.), *The mental representation of grammatical relations*. Cambridge, Mass.: MIT Press, in press.

Pisoni, D. B. On the nature of categorical perception of speech sounds. *Status Report on Speech Research* (SR-27). New Haven, Conn.: Haskins Laboratories, 1971.

Pisoni, D. B. Auditory and phonetic memory codes in the discrimination of vowels and consonants. *Perception and Psychophysics, 13,* 1973, 253–60.

Pisoni, D. B. Auditory short-term memory and vowel perception. *Memory and Cognition, 3,* 1975, 7–18.

Pisoni, D. B. Identification and discrimination of the relative onset time of two-component tones: Implications for voicing perception in stops. *Journal of the Acoustical Society of America, 61,* 1977, 1352–61.

Pisoni, D. B., and Tash, J. Reaction times to comparisons within and across phonetic categories. *Perception and Psychophysics, 15,* 1974, 285–90.

Posner, M., and Keele, S. On the genesis of abstract ideas. *Journal of Experimental Psychology, 77,* 1968, 353–63.

Prentice, J. Response strength of single words as an influence in sentence behavior. *Journal of Verbal Learning and Verbal Behavior, 5,* 1966, 429–33.

Preyer, W. *Die Seele des Kindes*. Leipzig: Schaeffer, 1882.

Pustejovsky, J., and Burke, V. (eds.). *Markedness and learnability*. University of Massachusetts Occasional Papers in Linguistics. Vol. 6, 1981.

Putnam, H. The analytic and the synthetic. In H. Feigh and G. Maxwell (eds.), *Minnesota Studies in the Philosophy of Science,* Vol. 3. Minneapolis: University of Minnesota Press, 1962.

Putnam, H. The meaning of meaning. In K. Gunderson (ed.), *Minnesota Studies in the Philosophy of Sciences,* Vol. 7. Minneapolis: University of Minnesota Press, 1975.

Putnam, H. Brains and behavior. In N. Block (ed.), *Readings in Philosophy of Psychology,* Vol. 1. Cambridge, Mass.: Harvard University Press, 1980.

Quine, W. V. Two dogmas of empiricism. *Philosophical Review, 60,* 1951, 20–43.

Quine, W. V. *Word and object.* Cambridge, Mass.: MIT Press, 1960.

Quine, W. V. Natural kinds. In W. V. Quine, *Ontological relativity and other essays.* New York: Columbia University Press, 1969.

Radulović, L. Acquisition of language: Studies of Dubrovnik children. Unpublished doctoral dissertation, University of California, Berkeley, 1975.

Ratner, N., and Bruner, J. S. Games, social exchange and the acquisition of language. *Journal of Child Language, 5,* 1978, 391–401.

Read, C. *Children's categorization of speech sounds in English.* Urbana, Ill.: National Council of Teachers of English, 1975.

Reichenbach, H. *Elements of symbolic logic.* New York: Macmillan, 1947.

Remick, H. The maternal environment of linguistic development. Unpublished doctoral dissertation, University of California, Davis, 1971.

Rice, M. The effect of children's prior nonverbal color concepts on the learning of color words. Unpublished doctoral dissertation, University of Kansas, 1978.

Richards, M. M. Sorting out what's in a word from what's not: Evaluating Clark's semantic features acquisition theory. *Journal of Experimental Child Psychology, 27,* 1979, 1–47.

Robins, R. H. *Short history of linguistics.* Bloomington: Indiana University Press, 1968.

Roeper, T. Theoretical implications of word order, topicalization, and inflections in German language acquisition. In C. A. Ferguson and D. I. Slobin (eds.), *Studies of child language development.* New York: Holt, Rinehart and Winston, 1973.

Roeper, T. Linguistic universals and the acquisition of gerunds. In H. Goodluck, and L. Solan (eds.), *Papers in the structure and development of child language.* University of Massachusetts Occasional Papers in Linguistics, Vol. 4, 1978.

Roeper, T. In pursuit of a deductive model of language acquisition. In C. L. Baker and J. Macarthy (eds.), *The logical problem of language acquisition.* Cambridge, Mass.: MIT Press, 1981.

Rommetveit, R. *On message structure: A framework for the study of language and communication.* New York: Wiley, 1974.

Rosch, E. On the internal structure of perceptual and semantic categories. In T. E. Moore (ed.), *Cognitive development and the acquisition of language.* New York: Academic Press, 1973.

Rosch, E. Cognitive representation of semantic categories. *Journal of Experimental Psychology: General, 104,* 1975, 192–233.

Rosch, E. Classifications of real-world objects: Origins and representations in cognition. In S. Erlich and E. Tulving (eds.), *Bulletin de Psychologie* (Special issue on semantic memory), 1976.

Rosch, E. Principles of categorization. In E. Rosch and B. Lloyd (eds.), *Cognition and categorization*. Hillsdale, N.J.: Erlbaum, 1978.

Rosch, E., and Lloyd, B. (eds.). *Cognition and categorization*. Hillsdale, N.J.: Erlbaum, 1978.

Rosch, E., and Mervis, C. B. Family resemblances: Studies in the internal structure of categories. *Cognitive Psychology, 7*, 1975, 573–605.

Ross, J. A fake NP squish. In C. N. Bailey and R. W. Shuy (eds.), *New ways of analyzing variation in English*. Washington, D.C.: Georgetown University School of Languages and Linguistics, 1973.

Rousseau, P., and Sankoff, D. Advances in variable rule methodology. In D. Sankoff (ed.), *Linguistic variation: Models and methods*. New York: Academic Press, 1978.

Rozin, P., and Gleitman, L. R. The structure and acquisition of reading: II. The reading process and the acquisition of the alphabetic principle. In A. S. Reber and D. Scarborough (eds.), *Toward a psychology of reading*. Hillsdale, N.J.: Erlbaum, 1977.

Russell, B. *Our knowledge of the external world*. New York: Humanities, 1961.

Sachs, J., and Devin, J. Young children's use of appropriate speech styles in social interaction and role-playing. *Journal of Child Language, 3*, 1976, 81–98.

Sachs, J. and Truswell, L. Comprehension of two word instructions by children in the one word stage. *Journal of Child Language, 5*, 1978, 17–24.

Sacks, H., Schegloff, E., and Jefferson, G. A simplest systematics for the organization of turn-taking for conversation. *Language, 50*, 1974, 697–735.

Saffron, E. M., Schwartz, M. F., and Marin, O. S. The word order problem in agrammatism: II. Production. *Brain and Language, 10*, 1980, 263–80.

Saltz, E., Soller, E., and Sigel, I. E. The development of natural language concepts. *Child Development, 43*, 1972, 1191–1202.

Samuel, A. G., and Newport, E. L. Adaptation of speech by nonspeech: Evidence for complex acoustic cue detectors. *Journal of Experimental Psychology: Human Perception and Performance, 5*, 1979, 563–78.

Sankoff, G., and Brown, P. The origins of syntax in discourse. *Language, 52*, 1976, 631–66.

Sankoff, G., and Laberge, S. On the acquisition of native speakers by a language. *Kivung, 6*, 1973, 32–47.

Schachter, P. The subject in Philippine languages: Topic, actor, actor–topic, or none of the above. In C. Li (ed.), *Subject and topic*. New York: Academic Press, 1976.

Schachter, P. Reference-related and role-related properties of subjects. In P. Cole and J. Sadock (eds.), *Syntax and semantics*, Vol. 8. New York: Academic Press, 1977.

Schank, R. C. Identification of conceptualizations underlying natural language. In R. C. Schank and K. M. Colby (eds.), *Computer models of thought and language*. San Francisco: Freeman, 1973.

Schieffelin, B. B. A developmental study of word order and casemarking in an ergative language. *Papers and Reports on Child Language Development* (Department of Linguistics, Stanford University), No. 17, 1979a, pp. 30–40.

Schieffelin, B. B. Getting it together: An ethnographic approach to the study of the development of communicative competence. In E. Ochs and B. Schieffelin (eds.), *Developmental pragmatics*. New York: Academic Press, 1979b.

Schieffelin, B. B. *How Kaluli children learn what to say, what to do, and how to feel: An ethnographic study of the development of communicative competence*. Cambridge: Cambridge University Press, 1982.

Schlesinger, I. M. *Sentence structure and the reading process*. The Hague: Mouton, 1968.

Schlesinger, I. M. The grammar of sign language and the problems of language universals. In J. Morton (ed.), *Biological and social factors in psycholinguistics*. Urbana: University of Illinois Press, 1970.

Schlesinger, I. M. The production of utterances and language acquisition. In D. I. Slobin (ed.), *The ontogenesis of grammar: A theoretical symposium*. New York: Academic Press, 1971.

Schlesinger, I. M. Relational concepts underlying language. In R. L. Schiefelbusch and L. Lloyd (eds.), *Language perspectives: Acquisition, retardation, and intervention*. Baltimore: University Park Press, 1974.

Schlesinger, I. M. *Production and comprehension of utterances*. Hillsdale, N.J.: Erlbaum, 1977a.

Schlesinger, I. M. The role of cognitive development and linguistic input in language development. *Journal of Child Language, 4*, 1977b, 153–69.

Schneider, O. Die schöpferische Kraft des Kindes in der Gestaltung seiner Bewusstseinszustände bis zum Beginn des Schulunterrichts. *Zeitschrift für Philosophie und philosophische Kritik, 121*, 1907, 153–75.

Schnur, E. and Shatz, M. The form and function of maternal gestures in conversations with young children. In H. Sypher and J. Applegate (eds.), *Social cognition and communication*. In press.

Schwartz, A. On the universality of subjects: The Ilocano case. In C. Li (ed.), *Subject and topic*. New York: Academic Press, 1976.

Schwartz, B. *Psychology of learning and behavior*. New York: Norton, 1978.

Schwartz, S. Natural kind terms. *Cognition, 7*, 1979, 301–15.

Scupin, E., and Scupin, G. *Bubis erste Kindheit*. Leipzig: Grieben, 1907.

Sechehaye, M. A. *Essai sur la structure logique de la phrase*. Paris: Champion, 1926.

Seligman, M. E., and Hager, J. L. (eds.). *Biological boundaries of learning*. New York: Appleton-Century-Crofts, 1972.

Seuren, P. *Operators and nucleus: A contribution to the theory of grammar*. Cambridge: Cambridge University Press, 1969.

Sgall, P., Hajičova, E., and Benešova, E. *Topic, focus and generative semantics*. Kronberg, Germany: Scriptor Verlag, 1973.

Shaker, D. C. On the acquisition of the meaning of time-axis verbs. Unpublished doctoral dissertation, University of California, Irvine, 1979.

Shatz, M. Children's comprehension of question-directives. *Journal of Child Language, 5*, 1978, 39–46.

Shatz, M. How to do things by asking: Form–function pairings in mothers' questions and their relation to children's response. *Child Development, 50,* 1979, 1093–9.

Shatz, M., and Gelman, R. The development of communication skills: Modifications in the speech of young children as a function of listener. *Monographs of the Society for Research in Child Development No. 152, 38*(5), 1973.

Sheldon, A. The role of parallel function in the acquisition of relative clauses in English. *Journal of Verbal Learning and Verbal Behavior, 13,* 1974, 272–81.

Sherzer, J. Linguistic games: Implications for (socio)linguistics. In B. Kirshenblatt-Gimblett (ed.), *Speech play on display.* Philadelphia: University of Pennsylvania Press, 1976.

Shibatani, M. The grammar of causative constructions: A conspectus. In M. Shibatani (ed.), *Syntax and semantics.* Vol. 6: *The grammar of causative constructions.* New York: Academic Press, 1976.

Shipley, E. F., Smith, C. S., and Gleitman, L. R. A study in the acquisition of language: Free responses to commands. *Language, 45,* 1969, 322–42.

Silverstein, M. Hierarchy of features and ergativity. In R. Dixon (ed.), *Grammatical categories in Australian languages.* Canberra: Australian Institute of Aboriginal Studies, 1976.

Sinclair, H. J. The role of cognitive structures in language acquisition. In E. H. Lenneberg and E. Lenneberg (eds.), *Foundations of language development: A multidisciplinary approach,* Vol. 1. New York: Academic Press, 1975.

Sinclair, H. J., and Bronckart, J. S. V. O.: A linguistic universal? A study of developmental psycholinguistics. *Journal of Experimental Child Psychology, 14,* 1972, 329–48.

Skinner, B. F. *Verbal behavior.* New York: Appleton-Century-Crofts, 1957.

Slobin, D. I. The acquisition of Russian as a native language. In F. Smith and C. A. Miller (eds.), *The genesis of language: A psycholinguistic approach.* Cambridge, Mass.: MIT Press, 1966a.

Slobin, D. I. Comments on McNeill's "Developmental psycholinguistics." In F. Smith and C. A. Miller (eds.), *The genesis of language: A psycholinguistic approach.* Cambridge, Mass.: MIT Press, 1966b.

Slobin, D. I. Recall of full and truncated passive sentences in connected discourse. *Journal of Verbal Learning and Verbal Behavior, 7,* 1968, 876–81.

Slobin, D. I. Cognitive prerequisites for the development of grammar. In C. A. Ferguson and D. I. Slobin (eds.), *Studies of child language development.* New York: Holt, Rinehart and Winston, 1973.

Slobin, D. I. Language change in childhood and in history. In J. Macnamara (ed.), *Language learning and thought.* New York: Academic Press, 1977.

Slobin, D. I. *Psycholinguistics* (2nd ed.). Glenview, Ill.: Scott, Foresman, 1979.

Slobin, D. I. The origins of grammatical encoding of events. In W. Deutsch (ed.), *The child's construction of language.* London: Academic Press, 1981.

Slobin, D. I., and Bever, T. Children develop canonical sentence schemata. *Cognition,* in press.

Slobin, D. I., and Welsh, C. A. Elicited imitation as a research tool in developmental psycholinguistics. In C. A. Ferguson and D. I. Slobin (eds.), *Studies of child language development.* New York: Holt, Rinehart and Winston, 1973.

Smith, C. S. An experimental approach to children's linguistic competence. In J. R. Hayes (ed.), *Cognition and the development of language*. New York: Wiley, 1970.

Smith, C. Children's understanding of natural language hierarchies. *Journal of Experimental Child Psychology, 27,* 1978, 437–59.

Smith, L. B., and Kemler, D. G. Developmental trends in free classification: Evidence for a new conceptualization of perceptual development. *Journal of Experimental Child Psychology, 24,* 1977, 279–98.

Smith, L. B., and Kemler, D. G. Levels of experienced dimensionality in children and adults. *Cognitive Psychology, 10,* 1978, 502–32.

Smith, M. E. Grammatical errors in the speech of preschool children. *Child Development, 4,* 1933, 183–90.

Smith, W. J. *The behavior of communicating.* Cambridge, Mass.: Harvard University Press, 1977.

Snow, C. E. Mothers' speech to children learning language. *Child Development, 43,* 1972, 549–65.

Snow, C. E. Mothers' speech research: From input to interaction. In C. E. Snow and C. A. Ferguson (eds.), *Talking to children: Language input and acquisition.* Cambridge: Cambridge University Press, 1977.

Snow, C. E. The role of social interaction in language acquisition. In W. A. Collins (ed.), *Minnesota Symposia on Child Psychology,* Vol. 12. Hillsdale, N.J.: Erlbaum, 1979.

Snow, C. E., Arlman-Rupp, A., Hassing, Y., Jobse, J., Joosten, J., and Vorster, J. Mothers' speech in three social classes. *Journal of Psycholinguistic Research, 5,* 1976, 1–20.

Snow, C. E., and Ferguson, C. A. *Talking to children: Language input and acquisition.* Cambridge: Cambridge University Press, 1977.

Solan, L. Anaphora in child language. Unpublished doctoral dissertation, University of Massachusetts, 1978.

Sommers, F. The ordinary language tree. *Mind, 68,* 1959, 160–85.

Sorensen, J. M., Cooper, W. E., and Paccia, J. M. Speech timing of grammatical categories. *Cognition, 6*(2), 1978, 135–54.

Spelke, E. S., Perceptual knowledge of objects in infancy. In J. Mehler, M. F. Garrett, and E. C. Walker (eds.), *Perspectives in mental representation.* Hillsdale, N.J.: Erlbaum, 1982.

Starky, P., Spelke, E., and Gelman, R. Detection of intermodal numerical correspondences by human infants. Manuscript, University of Pennsylvania, 1981.

Steinberg, E., and Anderson, R. Hierarchical semantic organization in 6-year-olds. *Journal of Experimental Child Psychology, 19,* 1975, 544–53.

Stern, C., and Stern, W. *Die Kindersprache: Eine psychologische und sprachtheoretische Untersuchung* (Rev. 4th ed.). Leipzig: Barth, 1928.

Stokoe, W. C., Jr. Sign language structure: An outline of the visual communications system of the American deaf. *Studies in Linguistics, Occasional Papers,* No. 8, 1960.

Stokoe, W. C., Jr., Casterline, D., and Croneberg, C. G. *A dictionary of American Sign Language on linguistic principles.* Washington, D.C.: Gallaudet College Press, 1965.

Streeter, L. A. Acoustic determinants of phrase boundary perception. *Journal of the Acoustical Society of America, 64,* 1978, 1582–92.

Studdert-Kennedy, M., Liberman, A. M., Harris, D. S., and Cooper, F. S. Motor theory of speech perception: A reply to Lane's critical review. *Psychological Review, 77,* 1970, 234–49.

Sugarman, S. Transitions in early representational intelligence: Changes over time in children's production of simple block structures. In G. Forman (ed.), *Action and thought: From sensorimotor schemes to symbolic operations.* New York: Academic Press, in press.

Supalla, T. Morphology of verbs of motion and location in American Sign Language. In F. Caccamise and D. Hicks (eds.), *National Symposium on Sign Language Research and Teaching.* Washington, D.C.: National Association of the Deaf, 1978a.

Supalla, T. Morphophonology of hand classifiers in American Sign Language. University of California, San Diego, Working Paper, 1978b.

Supalla, T. Acquisition of morphology of American Sign Language verbs of motion and location. Unpublished doctoral dissertation, University of California, San Diego, 1982.

Supalla, T., and Newport, E. L. In search of categorical perception in sign. University of California, San Diego, Working Paper, 1975.

Supalla, T., and Newport, E. L. How many seats in a chair? The derivation of nouns and verbs in American Sign Language. In P. Siple (ed.), *Understanding language through sign language research.* New York: Academic Press, 1978.

Talmy, L. Semantic structures in English and Atsugewi. Unpublished doctoral dissertation, University of California, Berkeley, 1972.

Talmy, L. Communicative aims and means – a synopsis. *Working papers on Language Universals* (Department of Linguistics, Stanford University), No. 20, 1976a, pp. 153–85.

Talmy, L. Semantic causative types. In M. Shibatani (ed.), *Syntax and semantics.* Vol. 6: *The grammar of causative constructions.* New York: Academic Press, 1976b.

Talmy, L. Rubber-sheet cognition in language. In W. Beach, S. Fox, and S. Philosoph (eds.), *Papers from the thirteenth regional meeting.* Chicago: Chicago Linguistic Society, 1977.

Talmy, L. The relation of grammar to cognition – a synopsis. In D. Waltz (ed.), *Proceedings of TINLAP – 2* (Theoretical Issues in Natural Language Processing). Urbana: University of Illinois, 1978.

Talmy, L. Lexicalization patterns: Semantic structure in lexical forms. In T. Shopen (ed.), *Language typology and syntactic description.* Vol. 3: *Grammatical categories and the lexicon.* Cambridge: Cambridge University Press, in press.

Tannenbaum, P., and Williams, F. Generation of active and passive sentences as a function of subject or object focus. *Journal of Verbal Learning and Verbal Behavior, 7,* 1968, 246–50.

Tanz, C. *Studies in the acquisition of deictic terms.* Cambridge: Cambridge University Press, 1980.

Tavakolian, S. Structural principles in the acquisition of complex sentences. Unpublished doctoral dissertation, University of Massachusetts, 1977.

Tavakolian, S (ed.), *Linguistic theory and language acquisition*. Cambridge, Mass.: MIT Press, 1981.

Thieman, T. J. Imitation and recall of optionally deletable sentences by young children. *Journal of Child Language, 2*(2), 1975, 261–70.

Thomson, J., and Chapman, R. Who is "Daddy" revisited: The status of two-year-olds' over-extended words in use and comprehension. *Journal of Child Language, 4*, 1976, 359–75.

Tögel, H. 16 Monate Kindersprache. *Zeitschrift für Kinderforschung, 10*, 1905, 156–65.

Trehub, S. E., and Abramovitch, R. Less is not more: Further observations on non-linguistic strategies. *Journal of Experimental Child Psychology, 25*, 1978, 160–7.

Turner, E., and Rommetveit, R. Focus of attention in recall of active and passive sentences. *Journal of Verbal Learning and Verbal Behavior, 7*, 1968, 543–8.

Tversky, A. Features of similarity. *Psychological Review, 84*, 1977, 328–52.

Uhlenbeck, E. The concepts of productivity and potentiality in morphological description and their psycholinguistic reality. In G. Drachman (ed.), *Salzburger Beiträge zur Linguistik: Akten der 3. Salzburger Jahresstagung für Linguistik*. Salzburg: Verlag Wolfgang Neugebauer, 1977.

Urwin, C. Preverbal communication and early language development in blind children. *Papers and Reports on Child Language Development, 17*, 1979, 119–27.

Valian, V. Talk, talk, talk: A selective critical review of theories of speech and production. In R. Freedle (ed.), *Discourse production and comprehension*. Norwood, N.J.: Ablex, 1977.

Vennemann, T. Topics, subjects and word order: From SXV to SVX via TVX. In J. M. Anderson and C. Jones (eds.), *Historical linguistics*. Vol. 1: *Syntax, morphology, internal and comparative reconstruction*. Amsterdam: North-Holland, 1974.

Viktor, G. *A gyermek nyelve: A gyermeknyelv irodolmának ismertetése főként nyelvészeti szempontból*. Nagyvarad, 1917.

Vygotsky, L. *Thought and language*. Cambridge, Mass.: MIT Press, 1962. (Originally published, 1934.)

Wales, R. J., and Campbell, R. On the development of comparison and the comparison of development. In G. B. Flores d'Arcais and W. J. M. Levelt (eds.), *Advances in psycholinguistics*. Amsterdam: North Holland, 1970.

Warden, D. A. The influence of context on children's use of identifying expressions and references. *British Journal of Psychology, 67*, 1976, 101–12.

Wasow, T. The innateness hypothesis and grammatical relations. *Synthese, 26*, 1973, 38–56.

Wasow, T., and Roeper, T. On the subject of gerunds, *Foundations of Language, 8*, 1972, 44–61.

Wellman, H. M., and Johnson, C. N. Understanding of mental processes: A developmental study of "remember" and "forget." *Child Development, 50*, 1979, 79–88.

Wexler, K. Empirical questions about developmental psycholinguistics raised by a theory of language acquisition. In R. N. Campbell and P. T. Smith (eds.), *Recent advances in the psychology of language*. New York: Plenum, 1977a.

Wexler, K. Transformational grammars are learnable from data of degree 2. *Social Sciences Working Papers*, No. 129, School of Social Sciences, University of California, Irvine, 1977b.

Wexler, K. A review of John R. Anderson's *Language, memory and thought. Cognition, 6,* 1978, 327–51.

Wexler, K., and Culicover, P. Two applications of the freezing principle in English. *Social Sciences Working Papers*, No. 38, School of Social Sciences, University of California, Irvine, 1973.

Wexler, K., and Culicover, P. *Formal principles of language acquisition.* Cambridge, Mass.: MIT Press, 1980.

Wexler, K., Culicover, P. W., and Hamburger, H. Learning-theoretic foundations of linguistic universals. *Theoretical Linguistics, 2,* 1975, 213–53.

Wexler, K., and Hamburger, H. On the insufficiency of surface data for the learning of transformational languages. In K. Hintikka, J. Moravcsik, and P. Suppes (eds.), *Approaches to natural languages.* Dordrecht: Reidel, 1973.

Whorf, B. *Language, thought, and reality* (J. Carroll, ed.). Cambridge, Mass.: MIT Press; New York: Wiley, 1956.

Wieman, L. Stress patterns of early child language. *Journal of Child Language, 3,* 1976, 283–6.

Wilcox, S., and Palermo, D. *In, on, under; more, less;* some artifacts revealed. Paper presented at the Eastern Psychological Association meetings, Boston, 1977.

Williams, E. Language acquisition, markedness and phase structure. In, S. Tavakolian (ed.), *Language acquisition and linguistic theory.* Cambridge, Mass.: MIT Press, 1981.

Williamson, S. Tamil baby talk: A cross-cultural study. Unpublished doctoral dissertation, University of Pennsylvania, 1979.

Winner, E. New names for old things: The emergence of metaphoric language. *Papers and Reports on Child Language Development* (Department of Linguistics, Stanford University), No. 15, 1978, pp. 7–16.

Wittgenstein, L. *Philosophical investigations.* New York: Macmillan, 1953.

Woodward, J. C. Inter-rule implication in American Sign Language. *Sign Language Studies, 3,* 1973, 47–56.

Wright, P. Transformations and the understanding of sentences. *Language and Speech, 12,* 1969, 156–66.

Wright, P., and Glucksberg, S. Choice of definite versus indefinite article as a function of sentence voice and reversibility. *Quarterly Journal of Experimental Psychology, 28,* 1976, 561–70.

Zakharova, A. V. Acquisition of forms of grammatical case by preschool children. In C. A. Ferguson and D. I. Slobin (eds.), *Studies of child language development.* New York: Holt, Rinehart and Winston, 1973.

Zubin, D. Discourse function of morphology. In T. Givón (ed.), *Syntax and semantics,* Vol. 12. New York: Academic Press, 1979.

Zukow, P. G., Reilly, J., and Greenfield, P. M. Making the absent present: facilitating the transition from sensorimotor to linguistic communication. In K. Nelson (ed.), *Children's language,* Vol. 2. New York: Gardner Press, 1980.

Zwicky, A. M. On clitics. Paper read at the Third International Phonologie-Tagung at the University of Vienna, September 2, 1976.

Index